Citizen Airmen

A History of the Air Force Reserve

1946–1994

Gerald T. Cantwell

AIR
FORCE
History
and
Museums
PROGRAM
1997

Library of Congress Cataloging-in-Publication Data

Cantwell, Gerald T., d. 1994.
    Citizen airmen : a history of the Air Force Reserve, 1946–1994 /
Gerald T. Cantwell.
       p. cm.
    Includes bibliographical references and index.
    1. United States. Air Force Reserve—History. I. Title.
UG853.C36 1997   95–44624
359.4′137′0973—DC20   CIP

The Air Force Reserve received its first F–16s (shown being refueled, front cover) in January 1984. The C–5 (top image, back cover) came into the Reserve's strategic airlift force in December 1984; C–141s (middle image, back cover) came in July 1986. Tactical airlift groups obtained C–130s (lower left, back cover) in this same Total Force period of the 1980s. All aircraft images are from the photograph collection maintained by the 11th Communications Squadron, Andrews AFB, Maryland.

For sale by the U.S. Government Printing Office
Superintendent of Documents, Mail Stop: SSOP, Washington, DC 20402-9328
ISBN 0-16-049269-6

…to the "Eighty-five Percenters"

The Reservists: "pure, downtown, off-base"

FOREWORD

For nearly fifty years, citizen airmen have served in the nation's defense as members of the Air Force Reserve. *Citizen Airmen: A History of the Air Force Reserve, 1946–1994* begins with the fledgling air reserve program initiated in 1916, traces its progress through World War II, and then concentrates on the period 1946 through 1994. The study skillfully describes the process by which a loosely organized program evolved into today's impressive force. The Air Force Reserve story is told within the context of national political and military policy and stresses that over the decades, as national needs have increased, reservists have met the challenges.

Initially, the Air Force treated its reserve units as supplemental forces and equipped them with surplus equipment. Shortly after the Air Force Reserve was established in 1948, its members mobilized for Korean War duty and they served throughout the conflict. The Reserve program subsequently fell into disarray and required patient rebuilding. The passage of a series of key federal laws related to personnel issues and the introduction of the air reserve technician program greatly assisted in this rejuvenation process. In the 1960s, the Air Force Reserve demonstrated its mettle as it participated in numerous mobilizations reflecting the Cold War tensions of the era. Reservists were involved in operations ranging from the Berlin Crisis of 1961–1962 to the Southeast Asia mobilizations in 1968.

In the 1970s, the Air Force Reserve program assumed heightened importance when the Department of Defense adopted the Total Force Policy. This concept treated the active forces, the National Guard, and all reserve forces as an integrated force. Reservists were now expected to meet the same readiness standards as their active duty counterparts. Since then, the Air Force Reserve has demonstrated its ability to perform a wide variety of missions. Air Reservists participated in American military operations in Grenada and Panama. During DESERT SHIELD and STORM, some 23,500 reservists were mobilized for service. They performed in combat in the Persian Gulf and provided vital support services at overseas locations. Stateside, they served at home stations or other locations in place of deployed active duty personnel.

Today, the Air Force Reserve performs major portions of the Air Force mission. Reservists are equipped with front-line weapons systems and have supported United Nations operations in Somalia, Bosnia, Rwanda, and Iraq.

The Air Force Reserve

They have exclusive responsibility for aerial spray operations and weather reconnaissance and they contribute large portions of the airlift and rescue missions. Reservists may also be found performing humanitarian medical missions and varied nation-building projects.

The book's author, Gerald T. Cantwell, passed away in 1994, before he could see the work through final publication. He brought to the study a wealth of knowledge—he served as the Air Force Reserve Command Historian for nearly twenty years—and a continuing desire to bring the Reserve story to a wider public. The account stands as but one example of his dedication to this purpose. His former colleagues, Dr. Charles F. O'Connell, Jr., Dr. Kenneth C. Kan, Ms. Margaret L. MacMackin, and Mr. Christiaan J. Husing, dedicate their contributions to Mr. Cantwell's volume in his memory.

RICHARD P. HALLION
Air Force Historian

PREFACE

Lt. Col. William R. Berkeley, an Air Force information officer with whom I enjoyed consecutive tours at two headquarters when Air Force historians were assigned to the information function as the 1950s turned into the 1960s, used to talk about the Air Force Reserve's many "publics" and our obligation to explain the component to them.

These publics included the reservist's neighbors, his church, his employer, his co-workers, members of the active Air Force, his family, and, above all, the reservists themselves. Each public was in some way puzzled, and often irritated, by a reservist's behavior, because it often set him apart from normal community activities. Neighbors and congregations wondered about this person among them who came and went in military uniform; employers denied, or only grudgingly approved, absences required by annual military encampments; members of the active force derided the reservist as an occasional and amateur soldier; his family resented the lost vacations, late hours, and weekends that took their family member away from them; and the reservist himself had his own questions, not the least of which was why the active force treated the Air Force Reserve program and its members as country cousins while giving the Air National Guard the best equipment and missions.

Fifteen years later, those publics that Bill talked about were still out there with the same unanswered questions. This was especially so as the nation recovered from the trauma of its Southeast Asia experience. My intent in writing this book is to answer those questions for the reservist and all his publics. The book's concept is to discuss these problems in terms of changing national policy.

Planning for employment of the post–World War II Air Force Reserve was seldom precise or prescient, and funding was often limited. Nevertheless, as one of the two civilian components of the Air Force (the other being the Air National Guard), the component was active in the nation's defense through thirty-five years and seven presidential administrations.

In the early 1950s, when President Harry S. Truman committed the nation to war in Korea to support the United Nations in its first major challenge, the Air Force Reserve provided the necessary augmentation while the skimpy active force rebuilt itself under wartime conditions. During the presidency of Dwight D. Eisenhower (1953–1961), the component became a training force

The Air Force Reserve

for reservists with no prior military service. The experienced troop carrier force meanwhile provided actual peacetime airlift missions for the Air Force.

In the fall of 1961, the Soviets threatened to deny the United States access to Berlin. President John F. Kennedy mobilized reserve units of all the services including five Air Force Reserve transport groups as he bought time to rebuild and restructure the active forces. A year later, when Soviet offensive missiles appeared in Cuba, the Air Force Reserve helped deploy an invasion force to the southeast corner of the United States. Then, as the crisis deepened, the President mobilized eight reserve troop carrier wings and supporting aerial port units to participate in the apparently inevitable invasion of Cuba. Assembly of the invasion force, including the recall of citizen airmen to participate, demonstrated U.S. resolve and contributed to a resolution of the crisis short of war.

During the administration of President Lyndon B. Johnson (1963–1969), the Air Force Reserve continued its inactive duty contribution to the nation's airlift operations and again experienced partial mobilization as the war in Southeast Asia ground on. Volunteer air reservists participated in U.S. airlift operations into the Dominican Republic during the revolution there in 1965, and at about the same time that Air Force Reserve troop carrier units took over Atlantic coast airlift operations from the active force, the heavier air transport units began flights into Southeast Asia that continued until war's end. Reservists on inactive duty participated in all of the war's major airlifts, including the repatriation of U.S. prisoners of war and the evacuation of refugees and U.S. personnel from Vietnam. On the other side of the world, in 1973 volunteer reserve aircrews flew hundreds of missions into the Middle East during the Arab-Israeli conflict.

As an aftermath of the Southeast Asia experience, President Richard M. Nixon (1969–1974) did away with the draft and established the reserve forces as the primary source of augmentation in future military contingencies. His administration also began the process of integrating the reserve forces more completely into defense plans.

Becoming President in 1977, Jimmy Carter continued the process of defining the role of the reserve forces more precisely and of integrating them into war and mobilization plans. Consequently, the Air Force Reserve, units and individuals, began to participate in deployments to overseas locations where plans called for them to fight upon mobilization.

Along the way, the Air Force took three significant steps which stimulated the development of the Air Force Reserve as an active part of the total operational Air Force. In 1957 it authorized implementation of the Air Reserve technician program which provided the reserve units management and training continuity. In 1968, far more than the other services, the Air Force conscientiously applied Public Law 90–168 which called for the creation of the Office of the Chief of Air Force Reserve, among other provisions to strengthen management and advocacy of the Air Force Reserve. Finally, long before the

Preface

Defense Department adopted the concept as national policy, the Air Force embarked on its own Total Force, under which, fully integrated with the active force in matters of programming, planning, equipping, and training, the air reserve components made a proportionate contribution to peacetime operations as they prepared for mobilization. Air Force Chief of Staff General David C. Jones could assert unequivocally that the Air Force Reserve was simply "part" of the Air Force.

This is a story about the Air Force Reserve, not the Air Force's civilian components and auxiliaries generally. It touches upon the Air National Guard and the Air Force Reserve Officers Training Corps at isolated points only insofar as the commentary would be awkward if their contributions were to be omitted. Since the record presented here deals solely with a national force, it includes no mention of individual state militia nor national guard policies. Also, as an account that focuses on the component itself, management agencies, the Continental Air Command, and Headquarters Air Force Reserve are mentioned only when such a discussion is essential to the flow of the narrative.

All history is to some extent revisionist and presented from the peculiar perspective of the author. Honesty to my readers requires some indication of my stance on some of the issues the book discusses. I agree with the late, very popular historian, Barbara W. Tuchman when she declared that there is no such thing as a neutral or purely objective historian. "Without an opinion, a historian would be simply a ticking clock, and unreadable besides," she said. Elsewhere she wrote that it was better that her bias stuck out than be hidden; it could then be taken into account. "To take no sides in history," she wrote, "would be as false as to take no sides in life."

I could not spend a quarter of a century as a contemporary historian in management headquarters of the Air Force Reserve without having acquired certain biases. The most pervasive of these is my belief that many failures in managing and administering Air Force Reserve programs resulted from the failure of the active Air Force, which is to say the Air Staff and the major gaining commands, to fully ascertain the nature of the reservist as an immobile citizen for whom reserve participation is a patriotic avocation. That is why the establishment of the Office of Air Force Reserve under a reservist was so important. I hasten to add, however, that this has not led me to share the paranoiac belief held by some Air Force Reserve officials as an article of faith that the active force is out to persecute the reserves.

Foremost among the unknowing on the Air Staff is the manpower community. Blinded by an addiction to numbers that surpasses even that of the accountants in the budget world, the Air Force's manpower officials have created some disharmony in forcing structures that mirror the active force upon reserve organizations which really did not have the same peacetime role as the active force units.

Almost equally dominant in my view of things is my belief that the staff of the Office of the Air Force Reserve is permitted to take a too active role in the day-to-day management of the field force. This is the province of Headquarters Air Force Reserve, and the program would be better served if the Washington staff confines itself to serving the Chief of Air Force Reserve in the programming and planning roles envisioned for it. Nevertheless, I would not abolish the institution of the Dual Hat. Far from it! It is essential that the leadership of the entire component, structure and forces, be unified in the person of a single official. There may be room for adjusting the mechanics, but the essential features should be retained.

Finally, the Air Reserve Personnel Center came into being as a separate entity by an accident of history. I believe that the average reservist has been ill served by the failure of the Air Force Reserve leaders to subordinate the center to Headquarters Air Force Reserve when sundry management studies gave them the opportunity to do so. In this one instance, one easily sympathizes with manpower officials in their despair over the fragmentation of Air Force Reserve personnel administration into three parts.

It has been suggested that this book should not be a substitute for the historical archives at Headquarters Air Force Reserve with its trove of massive detail on the evolution of the component. The admonition is noted, but the average Air Force Reservist does not have access to that archive. Consequently, since the reservist is the primary audience and "public" for which this book is intended, by design it includes some details on the programs, operations, and especially the mobilizations in which the reservists participated.

GERALD T. CANTWELL

ACKNOWLEDGMENTS

My earliest obligation in preparing this book rests with the late Francis A. Arlinghaus, University of Detroit. Within the Air Force, they go back to Lt. Cols. Donald M. Bell, Raymond L. Towne, and Alfred J. Lynn, and Bill Berkeley.

Within the history program, my earliest debts are to the late Joseph W. Angell, Jr. Also guiding me were J. J. Lichman, Director of Historical Services in Headquarters Continental Air Command, and John T. Bohn, Strategic Air Command historian.

Within Headquarters Air Force Reserve, I am indebted to Maj. Gen. Sloan R. Gill, Maj. Gen. James E. McAdoo, Col. William H. Holland, Clyde O. Bloodworth, Wilbur H. Keck, and Winton P. Cain.

Easing the research process for me were Mrs. Grace Rowe, Documentation Management Branch, Headquarters USAF; Alfred Goldberg, Brian V. Kinney, and Sandra Meagher, Office of the Secretary of Defense; John Machado, Helen Embleton, and Patricia Butler, Washington National Records Center; William Cunliffe, John Taylor, and Edward J. Reese, Modern Military Branch, National Archives; and Horace Hilb, Manuscript Division, Library of Congress.

Presidential Library staffs helped me as did James E. O'Neill, Assistant Archivist of the United States. Of special note were Warren Ohrvall, Harry Clark, and Irwin Mueller, Harry S. Truman Library; Gary Gallagher, David Humphrey, and Linda Hanson, Lyndon B. Johnson Library; Karen Rohrer, Dwight D. Eisenhower Library; Suzanne K. Forbes, Barbara Anderson, and Michael Desmond, John F. Kennedy Library; William McNitt and Dennis Dallenback, Gerald R. Ford Library; and Bonnie Baldwin, Nixon Presidential Materials Project.

Sharing their memories of the evolution of the Air Force Reserve program were Mary Flanagan and Charles F. Bock from the Office of Air Force Reserve in the Pentagon.

Among other Air Force historians who helped me were John T. Greenwood, William Heimdahl, Warren A. Trest, Col. John F. Shiner, Marcelle Knaack, Walton Moody, Bernard C. Nalty, Charles J. Gross, Richard H. Kohn, Herman S. Wolk, Diane T. Putney, Albert E. Misenko, and Roma K. Simons.

Discussions with Maj. Gen. Richard Bodycombe and Brig. Gen. Billy M. Knowles helped shape the book. Brig. Gen. James L. Colwell and J. J. Lichman

The Air Force Reserve

read every line of the penultimate draft.

I am also indebted to Gen. Robert C. Mathis, Lt. Gen. Howard W. Leaf, and Maj. Gen. William R. Usher for taking the time to help me resolve some vexing questions concerning the constitution of the Management Assistance Group in 1982.

Mrs. Levina E. Owens provided administrative and clerical services. Patsy R. Stone read the entire manuscript. Suzaneva Wade established early editorial and style practices, and Suzette G. Staples typed drafts of many of the early chapters and produced a working bibliography.

CONTENTS

FOREWORD v
PREFACE vii
ACKNOWLEDGMENTS xi

1. *THE NATIONAL DEFENSE ACT TO PEARL HARBOR, 1916–1941* .. 1
   Origins of the Air Reserve 5
   The Air Reserve Between the Wars 7

2. *THE FIRST POSTWAR AIR RESERVE PROGRAM, 1946–1947* 23
   Administration and War Department Policies 23
   Army Air Forces Reserve Policies and Plans 28
   The Initial Air Reserve Management Structure 37
   Early Problems in Conducting the Air Reserve Program 39
      The Impact of Budget Reductions 41
      The State of Reservists' Records 43
   Major Command Cooperation with the Air Defense Command 43
   Activation of Units 45
   The Formation of Composite Units 46
   Training Mobilization Assignees 47
   Active Duty Training for Air Reservists 48
   The Air Reserve's Disgruntled Publics 48
   The Role of the Associations 51
   Evaluating the First Effort 53

3. *DEVELOPMENT OF A NEW PROGRAM, 1948–1949* 57
   The Selective Service Act of 1948 and the Reserve 58
   The Gray Committee Reviews the Civilian Components 59
   Development of U.S. Air Force Reserve Policies 61
   The President Demands a Revitalization of the Reserve Program ... 64
   Phasing the 1950 Program into Being 72

The Air Force Reserve

    Miscellaneous Lasting Developments of the First Program 80
        Resolution of the Inactive Duty Training Pay Issue 80
        Provision of Retirement Benefits for Reservists 82
        Provision for Blacks and Women in the Air Reserve 82
    The Air Reserve and Service Unification 84
    General Whitehead Evaluates the Program 85

4. *MOBILIZATION FOR KOREA AND EXPANSION* 87
    Background of the Korean Mobilization 88
    The 1950 Unit Mobilizations 92
    Mobilization of the 375th and 433d Troop Carrier Wings 94
    National Emergency and the 1951 Unit Mobilizations 95
    The Air Force Reserve Units on Active Service 98
        452d Light Bombardment Wing 98
        731st Bombardment Squadron 103
        437th Troop Carrier Wing 104
        437th Command Succession 106
        403d Troop Carrier Wing in the Far East 106
        Employment of the Eighteenth Air Force Units 108
    Some Reserve Personnel Problems in the Far East Air Forces 108
    The Recall of Individual Air Force Reservists 109
    The "Fear of Flying" Incident 113
    Assessing the Mobilization 115

5. *DEVELOPMENT OF POST–KOREAN WAR POLICIES FOR*
      RESERVE FORCES 121
    Universal Military Training and Service Act of 1951 122
    The Armed Forces Reserve Act of 1952 124
    The Eisenhower Administration and National Reserve Policy 126
    Establishing the Mobilization Requirement 128
    Development of the National Reserve Plan 130
    Passage of the Reserve Forces Act of 1955 132
    The Reserve Officers Personnel Act 133
    Changes in the Reserve Policy and Management Structure 135
    The Air Force Long-Range Plan for the Reserve Forces 139
    The Reserve Program Review Board 140
    The Twining Memo, January 1955 141

6. *IMPLEMENTING THE REVISED CONCEPTS AND PROGRAMS* .. 145
    Implementing the Long-Range Plan: A Divided Responsibility 146
    Manning the Air Force Reserve Wings 151
        The Detached Squadron Concept 156
        The Selective Assignment Program 156
        The Option Letters 157

Contents

Establishment of the Air Reserve Records Center 158
The Air Reserve Technician Program 159
The Reserve Facilities Problem 165
Changing Operational and Mobilization Considerations 167

7. *A RETURN ON THE INVESTMENT, 1961–1965* 171
Revisions to Air Reserve Forces Management 172
The Berlin Crisis of 1961 and Mobilization 177
The Cuban Missile Crisis, October–November 1962 184
Military Air Transport Service Use of Reserve C–124s 192
POWER PACK and the C–119s' Offshore Mission 195

8. *THE AIR FORCE RESERVE IN THE VIETNAM ERA, 1965–1975* .. 197
The Question of Mobilization for Southeast Asia 198
    The Southeast Asia Contribution of Reservists on Inactive Duty 209
    The Associate Unit Contribution 210
The Air Force Reserve Intelligence Specialists 211
Operations NEW LIFE and BABY LIFT 212
Other Air Force Reserve Support 213
The 1968 Mobilizations 214
    C–124 Units on Active Duty 216
    305th Aerospace Rescue and Recovery Squadron 216
    Utilization of Mobilized Personnel 217
Circumstances of the May 1968 Mobilizations 220
The Air Force Reserve Units on Active Duty 221
Release of Mobilized Reservists 222
Evaluation of the 1968 Mobilizations 223

9. *A BILL OF RIGHTS, THE DUAL HAT, AND TOTAL FORCE* 227
General LeMay Reopens the Merger Issue 227
Public Law 90–168 and a "Bill of Rights" 238
Some Growing Pains and the Dual Hat 241
The Total Force Concept and Policy 249
The Air Force Concept Becomes Defense Policy 251
Revision of AFR 45–1 in the Name of Total Force 254

10. *ADMINISTERING AND TRAINING INDIVIDUALS, 1953–1981* ... 259
The Unassigned Air Force Reservists 260
The Air Reserve Center Program 260
Mobilization Requirements and the Match-Merge 262
Revision in 1960 and the Air Force Reserve Recovery Program ... 265
Reserve Element Training 271
Evolution of the Mobilization Augmentee Program 273

xv

The Air Force Reserve

11. *MANNING CONSIDERATIONS IN THE VOLUNTEER FORCE* ... 287
    An End to the Draft and the Advent of the Volunteer Force 287
        Manning the Air Force Reserve in the All-Volunteer Era 289
    The Air Reserve Technician System Under Attack 298
        The Excepted Service Controversy 298
        The Militarization Test 302

12. *THE AIR FORCE RESERVE MATURES IN THE TOTAL FORCE* .. 309
    Modernization and Expansion of the Reserve Role 310
        The Air Force Reserve Airlift Associate Program 310
        Revision of the Tactical Airlift Force 312
        The Jet Fighter Returns to the Air Force Reserve 312
        The Airborne Early Warning and Control Group 314
        Acquisition of Other Missions 315
    General Lyon's Perception of Modernization 317
    Training By-product Becomes Directed Missions 322
        Extension of the Airborne Surveillance Mission 322
        The Weather Surveillance Mission 323
        The Air Refueling Mission 323
    Rescue Operations in the Later Period 326
    Support of Israel in the Yom Kippur War 327
    The Postal Mobilization of March 1970 328
    Air Force Reserve Exercises/Deployments 329
        The REDOUBT Series of Mobilization Exercises 329
        Exercising the Rescue Force 332
    Assessing the Air Force Reserve Within the Total Force 333
    The Air Force Reserve Mobilization Capabilities 335
    Presidential Recall Authority 337
    The Management Assistance Group and Its Implications 339

13. *FROM FLYING CLUB TO TOTAL FORCE* 345
    Evolution of the Structure 345
    Emergency Relief and Contingency Operations 357
    The Mobilized Reserves 360
    Operation JUST CAUSE 362
    The Air Force Reserve and the Persian Gulf War 364
    The Air Force Reserve in the 1990s 375
    In Summation 385

Contents

APPENDICES
1. Air Force Reserve Officials, 1946–1994 388
2. USAF Reserve Personnel Statistics, Fiscal Years 1947–1994 ... 392
3. Department of the Air Force, Air Force Reserve Direct Obligations 394
4. Air Force Reserve Aircraft, Fiscal Years 1947–1994 396
5. 452d Light Bomb Wing Operations, Korea: October 1950–May 1952 398
6. Operations of 437th Troop Carrier Wing on Active Military Service, August 1950–June 1952 399
7. Air Force Reserve Flying Units, 1958–1967 400
8. Harris Ellsworth Letter, June 21, 1957 403
9. Public Law 90–168 404
10. Melvin R. Laird Letter, August 21, 1970 412
11. James R. Schlesinger Letter, August 23, 1973 414
12. Air Force Reserve Regulation 45–1 417

NOTES 427
BIBLIOGRAPHIC NOTE 495
INDEX 527

PHOTOGRAPHS

Lt. Col. Raynal C. Bolling 3
President Woodrow Wilson 4
Maj. Gen. Mason M. Patrick 11
Maj. Earle E. Partridge 24
President Harry S. Truman 25
General George C. Marshall 25
General Henry H. Arnold 30
Maj. Gen. Lauris Norstad 30
Lt. Gen. Hoyt S. Vandenberg 31
Lt. Gen. Ira C. Eaker 31
General Carl A. Spaatz 32
Lt. Gen. George E. Stratemeyer 34
Maj. Gen. St. Clair Streett 35
Brig. Gen. John P. McConnell 54
Secretary of Defense James V. Forrestal 60
Lt. Gen. Elwood R. Quesada 71
Lt. Gen. Ennis C. Whitehead 77
Secretary of the Air Force Thomas K. Finletter 88
Chief of Staff General Hoyt S. Vandenberg with Generals White and Twining and Secretary Talbott 91

xvii

The Air Force Reserve

Brig. Gen. Luther W. Sweetser, Jr.	100
Brig. Gen. Chester E. McCarty	107
Brig. Gen. Herbert B. Thatcher	116
Secretary of the Air Force Harold E. Talbott and Chief of Staff General Nathan F. Twining	122
President Dwight D. Eisenhower	127
Maj. Gen. Earl S. Hoag	137
Lt. Gen. Leon W. Johnson	141
C–46	148
Maj. Gen. William E. Hall	155
Assistant Secretary of the Air Force for Manpower David S. Smith	155
L. C. Lingelbach	161
Lt. Gen. Charles B. Stone III	165
President John F. Kennedy, General Walter C. Sweeney, Jr., and Brig. Gen. John S. Bagby	172
General Curtis E. LeMay	174
Secretary of Defense Robert S. McNamara	176
C–124	181
SA–16 crew	183
Cuban mobilization	188
Cuban demobilization	191
Lt. Gen. Joe W. Kelly	193
C–119s	195
President Lyndon B. Johnson	199
General William C. Westmoreland	202
C–124	215
Southeast Asia mobiliztion	218–219
Return of mobilized squadron	224
General Curtis E. LeMay with Lt. Gen. Bryan M. Shotts and Col. Ronald R. Blalack	229
Secretary of the Air Force Eugene M. Zuckert	230
Lt. Gen. Edward J. Timberlake	231
Maj. Gen. Curtis R. Low	234
General John P. McConnell with Lt. Gen. Henry Viccellio and Brig. Gen. Rollin B. Moore, Jr.	241
Maj. Gens. Tom E. Marchbanks, Jr., and Rollin B. Moore, Jr.	243
Brig. Gen. Alfred Verhulst	247
President Richard M. Nixon and Secretary of Defense Melvin R. Laird	252
Maj. Gen. Robert E. L. Eaton	264
Maj. Gen. Sory Smith	266
Air Force Reserve Recovery Squadron team	268
Maj. Gen. Homer I. Lewis leaves Headquarters AFRES	277
Maj. Gen. Homer I. Lewis	280
General David C. Jones	280

Contents

Maj. Gen. Earl O. Anderson 295
Air Force Reserve Commanders' Conference, August 1974 295–297
Col. Benjamin S. Catlin III 304
General Lew Allen, Jr. 305
Air Force Reserve Recovery Squadron members 313
Air Force Reserve Special Operations Squadron drill 316
AC–130 gunship 316
Maj. Gen. William Lyon 318
Maj. Gen. Sidney S. Novaresi with Cols. James C. Wahleithner and
   Charles B. Coleman 319
Maj. Gen. John W. Hoff 320
Maj. Gen. Earl O. Anderson with Maj. John J. Closner 320
Maj. Gen. Roy M. Marshall 321
Maj. Gen. Richard Bodycombe 322
Brig. Gen. James L. Wade 324
Air Refueling Wing reservists 325
Special Operations Group training session 332
Maj. Gen. Richard Bodycombe and Generals Lew Allen, Jr., and
   David C. Jones 337
Maj. Gen. Edward Dillon 340
Maj. Gen. Sloan R. Gill 343
Airplanes in the associate's program 349–353
Maj. Gen. Roger P. Scheer 354
Gulf War AC–130 gunship 367
A–10 368
Maj. Gen. John J. Closner 382
Maj. Gen. Robert A. McIntosh 383

TABLES

Programs Available in Original and Revised 1948 Budgets 41
Air Force Reserve Units Table of Organization and Equipment, Fiscal
   Year 1950 75
Mobilization and Inactivation of Filler Units, 1951 97
437th Troop Carrier Wing Members, September 1950 104
Air Force Reserve Flying Wing Program, September 1955 147
Air Force Reserve Units Mobilized During the Cuban Missile Crisis ... 189
Mission Forces Furnished by the Air Force Reserve, Fiscal Year 1981 .. 335

1

The National Defense Act to Pearl Harbor, 1916–1941

> That the Army of the United States shall consist of the Regular Army, the National Guard of the United States, the National Guard while in the service of the United States, the Officers' Reserve Corps, the Organized Reserves, and the Enlisted Reserve Corps
>
> —The National Defense Act of 1916, June 3, 1916

On February 5, 1982, Maj. Gen. Richard Bodycombe, Chief of the Air Force Reserve and Commander of Headquarters Air Force Reserve (AFRES), closed a commanders' conference in Washington, D.C., by asserting that the reserve component had attained a historic peak of strength and readiness in the recently ended fiscal year 1981. General Bodycombe then recited a litany of indices of perfection: full unit membership, 100 percent flying-hour use, perfect inspection pass rates, timely and successful aircraft conversions, and historically low aircraft accident rates. By every traditional criterion of military readiness, the United States Air Force Reserve as of September 1981 had attained a peak of efficiency.[1] A decade later, this readiness and availability would be confirmed in its response to the crisis in the Persian Gulf when Air Force Reservists actively participated in Operation DESERT SHIELD/STORM between August 1990 and February 1991.

The Air Force Reserve of 1981 had not emerged full grown like Athene from the brow of Zeus; it had endured a long, painful evolution from the early uncertain days of military aviation. As one of the two civilian components of the United States Air Force (the other being the Air National Guard of the

The Air Force Reserve

United States), the Air Force Reserve traced its formal origins to the National Defense Act of 1916.

The National Defense Act represented the confluence of several tributary developments into the mainstream of U.S. military history. These were the development of the airplane, the acceptance of military aviation by the War Department, and increasing military preparedness by the United States as World War I developed in Europe.

Two events in the first decade of the twentieth century had a lasting effect upon the nation's military establishment, including its reserve components. On December 17, 1903, Orville Wright conducted the first sustained, controlled powered airplane flight at Kitty Hawk, North Carolina. Not quite four years later, on August 1, 1907, the U.S. Army established the Aeronautical Division in the Office of the Chief Signal Officer as the focal point of all matters pertaining to military ballooning, air machines, and kindred subjects.[2]

The Air Service acquired more definite status with the passage of legislation on July 18, 1914, which directed the creation of the Aviation Section of the Signal Corps consisting of 60 officers and 260 enlisted men as an addition to the authorized strength of the Signal Corps. The act created the grades of Junior Military Aviator and Military Aviator and authorized flying pay equal to 25 percent of the normal pay for grade and service.[3]

Anticipating the need for more trained personnel than the law allowed, in 1914 the Chief Signal Officer, Brig. Gen. George P. Scriven, recommended legislation providing for a reserve aviation service.[4] The requested legislation did not immediately move out of committees, but support for an aviation reserve developed outside the government and led to the formation of aerial units in the National Guard. In 1915, with army and navy aviation units possessing few airplanes and Congress appropriating insufficient funds, the federated Aero Clubs of America inaugurated a subscription drive to raise funds for airplanes and to develop aviators. The Aero Clubs were soon overwhelmed with requests from National Guard organizations for information, and the War Department furnished approved organization tables. On November 1, 1915, the Aviation Detachment, 1st Battalion, Signal Corps, of the New York National Guard was organized under Raynal C. Bolling at Mineola, New York.[5]

The Dick Act of 1903 confirmed the National Guard as the nation's organized militia, a role evolving shortly after the Civil War. Designated as the nation's militia, the National Guard and, later, the Air National Guard acquired a preeminence that the Air Force Reserve found difficult to overcome even after legislation in 1947 and 1949 established the two as equal components of the Air Force. Nevertheless, in 1912 Maj. Gen. Leonard Wood, U.S. Army Chief of Staff (1910–1914), sought to circumvent the National Guard in reorganizing the Army. General Wood's proposals were endorsed by Secretary of War Henry L. Stimson, but President William H. Taft ignored them, not

Lt. Col. Raynal C. Bolling commanded the First Reserve Aero Squadron at Mineola, New York, after its activation in May 1917.

foreseeing any likelihood of the United States' going to war. When war erupted in Europe in 1914, a national movement for military preparedness demanded that the nation's military forces be enlarged. Woodrow Wilson, who had become President in 1913, opposed the movement. Like Taft before him, he observed that the United States had no issue with any belligerent nation and initially rejected military expansion.[6]

Although emitting great sound and fury, the Preparedness Movement had made little progress by May 1915. It received an infusion of life that month when Germany, which had declared the waters around the British Isles a war zone, sank the British steamer *Lusitania* off the coast of Ireland with the loss of 1,198 lives, including those of 128 Americans. This action turned American public opinion predominantly against Germany, and the Preparedness Movement became a crusade. The Navy League called upon the President to summon Congress into special session, and editors and journalists took up the cry for action. Still not convinced of the need for overt action, President Wilson, nevertheless, asked the War and Navy Departments to develop national defense plans.[7]

In response, Secretary of War Lindley M. Garrison proposed a program and legislation to establish a Regular Army at a strength of 142,000, a Continental Army of 400,000 part-time reserve trainees, and increased recognition and support of the National Guard. The Democrats in Congress opposed a

The Air Force Reserve

Enacted as a compromise endorsed by President Woodrow Wilson, the National Defense Act of 1916 strengthened the National Guard's position as the primary reserve force of the country but also established the beginnings of a federal reserve.

Continental Army and anything like federal control over the guard. After the Attorney General affirmed that there was no constitutional barrier to federal control of the National Guard, Wilson cooperated with James Hay, Chairman of the House Military Affairs Committee, to develop effective defense legislation which included the guard. Representative Hay reported H.R. 12766 out of committee as "the President's Bill." Motivated by the press of international events involving both Germany and Mexico and presidential mediation, Congress produced the National Defense Act which the President signed on June 3, 1916. Compromise that it was, the National Defense Act of 1916 was nevertheless the most comprehensive military legislation yet enacted by Congress.[8]

The new law authorized the Regular Army a strength of 206,169 men, expandable to 254,000 under the threat of war; federalized the National Guard at a strength of 425,000; and authorized the President to draft men into service to bring the Regular Army up to authorized strength during wartime. The act directed creation of an Officers' Reserve Corps and an Enlisted Reserve Corps and defined the militia of the United States as consisting of all able-bodied male citizens between 18 and 45 years of age. The militia would consist of three classes: the National Guard, the Naval Militia, and the Unorganized Militia. The act also expanded the Aviation Section of the Signal Corps by allowing the appointment of aviators from civilian life.[9]

In federalizing the expanded National Guard, the government would provide pay for forty-eight training periods a year. Although the National

Guard would clearly be the principal trained reserve, as James Hay had wanted all along, in authorizing a Regular Army enlisted reserve, the act provided for an enlisted reserve of veterans which the Army hoped to recruit by a series of bonuses. Businessmen and student military training camps, sponsored earlier in an informal endorsement of the Preparedness Movement, were placed on a firmer legal basis as the Officers' Reserve Corps and the Reserve Officers Training Corps. An Enlisted Reserve Corps would enlist specialists for the engineer, signal, quartermaster, ordinance, and medical services. The Officers' and Enlisted Reserve Corps and their members were clearly federal reserve, not militia.[10]

Origins of the Air Reserve

In addition to its general provisions for an Organized Reserve Corps, the National Defense Act of 1916 strengthened the Aviation Section of the Signal Corps. Originating the nation's air reserve program, it authorized creation of a Signal Officers' Reserve Corps of 297 officers and a Signal Enlisted Reserve Corps of 2,000 enlisted men. Congress soon reinforced the national defense legislation by including $13,281,666 for the Aviation Section in the Army's appropriations act. This included $900,000 to train and pay officers and men of the Organized Reserve Corps when called to active duty for training.[11]

The Officers' Reserve Corps was established to provide a reserve of officers available for military service when needed. Normally appointed for five years, in wartime their service could be extended six months beyond the end of the war. When authorized by the Secretary of War, the Aviation Section could order reserve officers to active duty for training for fifteen days a year, during which they would get the same pay and allowances as officers of the same rank in the Regular Army. Provisions were also available for the Secretary of War to place reserve officers on active duty for extended periods. The Aviation Section's Enlisted Reserve Corps was to consist of three-year volunteer specialists with technical backgrounds.[12]

The creation of the Organized Reserve Corps added 296 officers and 2,715 men to the Aviation Section of the Signal Corps. In July 1917, the Judge Advocate General interpreted the National Defense Act of 1916 to mean that officers of the Organized Reserve Corps were entitled to the rating of Junior Military Aviator when qualified. The practice the air service actually followed, however, was to rate most civilian candidates as Reserve Military Aviators and give the Junior Military Aviator examination to qualified Regular Army candidates and a few arbitrarily chosen reserve officers.[13]

The opportunity to enlist in the Signal Enlisted Reserve Corps of the Aviation Section proved popular. More than a hundred civilians enlisted as sergeants by the end of 1916 and were ordered to active duty for flying training

The Air Force Reserve

at the Curtiss schools at Miami, Florida, and Newport News, Virginia, and later to the Signal Corps schools at Mineola; Chicago, Illinois; and Memphis, Tennessee. These flying students of the Signal Enlisted Reserve Corps were enlisted with the understanding that if they completed the required training, they would be commissioned as members of the Signal Officers' Reserve Corps.[14]

Upon passage of the National Defense Act of 1916, the Aviation Section was faced with the problem of expanding its aviation training program. Replacing what had been a purely military operation, as of October 1916 the new program called for separate categories of schools to be operated by the Army and by airplane manufacturers or private individuals. The plan called for sending all aviation personnel, except Regular Army, to civilian schools for their preliminary instruction, after which they were to finish their training at the army schools where they would receive their Military Aviator ratings. The government was to pay the schools $500 for each student who passed the preliminary flying test and an additional $300 if he went on to earn his Military Aviator rating. Upon completion of his training, the aviator was to be commissioned in the Aviation Section of the Signal Corps if he met all other qualifications.[15]

War Department officials were pleased by the provisions and results of the National Defense Act of 1916 insofar as they pertained to the Organized Reserve Corps of the Aviation Section. The provision of the Enlisted Reserve Corps seemed particularly efficacious and provident to Secretary of War Newton D. Baker. The purpose of this corps was to furnish enlisted men skilled for technical staff positions in engineer, signal, and quartermaster services. It was impracticable to maintain sufficient numbers of such technicians in the peacetime Army, and the Enlisted Reserve Corps overcame for that deficiency.[16]

Chief Signal Officer Brig. Gen. George O. Squier proclaimed the inclusion of the Organized Reserve Corps as being among the most important sections of the National Defense Act, and he aimed to develop it to its full potential. He sought to acquire a body of experienced technical men whom he could organize and train in peacetime for availability when needed. Since the use of aviation seemed to be increasing in the European war and comparatively few men in the United States had aeronautical skills, Squier thought it all the more important in late 1916 that a large air reserve be trained. He intended to organize reserve aero squadrons gradually from the commissioned and enlisted reserve personnel acquired under the law.[17] During the war, the Signal Enlisted Reserve Corps also served as an administrative vehicle for enlisting candidates for flying training who were tested at ground schools organized at a number of large universities. The Aviation Section developed a perpetual waiting list of candidates for aviation training, and it never lacked applicants for enlistment.[18]

Pursuant to General Squier's wishes, the War Department authorized two air reserve units near New York City and Philadelphia, Pennsylvania, in the early weeks of the war. The 1st Reserve Aero Squadron was organized at Mineola on May 26, 1917. Veterans of the disbanded National Guard 1st Aero Company, including Raynal Bolling, formed the nucleus of the squadron there. Bolling became its first commander, but he went to Europe on a special mission early in June, and Capt. Philip A. Carroll took command. The squadron trained at Mineola until August 23, 1917, when it went to France as the nucleus of the Third Aviation Instruction Center at Issoudun. On October 1, 1917, it was redesignated the 26th Aero Squadron and became part of the Regular Army. The 2d Reserve Aero Squadron was organized about July 12th at Chandler Field, Pennsylvania. Redesignated the 45th Aero Squadron on August 8, it moved to Gerstner Field, Louisiana, where it spent the rest of the war.[19] The advent of war having overtaken the requirement for a peacetime reserve, no further reserve aero squadrons were organized.

That first air reserve unit at Mineola had no recruiting difficulties. This resulted in large measure from the activities of the Aero Clubs which actively supported the Preparedness Movement and furnished money to train National Guardsmen. By June 20, 1916, the club had sent twenty-six officers and twelve enlisted men to aviation schools so they could volunteer for the punitive campaign being conducted by the United States against Pancho Villa in Mexico.[20]

The United States went to war within a year of the passage of the National Defense Act, and the War Department used the aviation cadets from the Organized Reserve Corps. The number of Reserve Military Aviators that had completed military and civilian flying school programs before the United States entered the war was negligible. In April 1917, the Army's air component consisted of 131 officers, mostly pilots, student pilots, and 1,187 enlisted men. After the United States' entry into the war, however, flying schools sprang up overnight. By November 1918, nearly 9,000 Reserve Military Aviators had graduated from schools in the United States. Counting the other 2,300 or so had received their ratings overseas, about 11,300 of the Air Service's pilots in World War I were reserve officers.[21]

The Air Reserve Between the Wars

For almost twenty years after the fighting stopped in World War I, the U.S. Army and its reserve components endured a period of benign neglect. During this time, the nation drifted into a policy of international isolationism and subsequently suffered economic depression.

Pending the outcome of President Wilson's campaign to lead the United States into the League of Nations after the war, the nation did not immediately define a military policy. Lacking definition of its active forces, the War

The Air Force Reserve

Department could not devise an appropriate reserve program. One thing was certain however; if there was to be any kind of a post–World War I air reserve, its members had to fly to maintain the skills they had acquired during the war. In December 1918, the War Department's Division of Military Aeronautics permitted former Reserve Military Aviators to fly simply by presenting their flying credentials at active airfields.[22]

Establishment of postwar reserve policy became hostage to an eighteen-month dispute between the War Department and Congress over the size and structure of the Army. Ultimately, President Wilson approved the Army Reorganization Act of 1920 on June 4, 1920, as an amendment to the National Defense Act of 1916. Also known as the National Defense Act of 1920, the measure confirmed the forces constituting the Army of the United States as the Regular Army, the National Guard while in the service of the United States, and the Organized Reserve, still comprising the Officers' Reserve Corps and the Enlisted Reserve Corps. It authorized the Army an average strength of 297,000 men organized into nine geographic corps areas, according to population. The law specified that each corps area was to contain at least one division of the National Guard or Organized Reserves. It also authorized the President to give five-year reserve commissions.[23]

In May 1920 the Air Service designated seven of its active fields as places where reservists could fly under a more formal arrangement with active duty instructors and mechanics assigned to assist them.[24] Arrangements at the seven fields were not always satisfactory because equipment or supervisory personnel were often lacking. Then too, the Air Service was already encountering two characteristics of the reservist with which the Air Force of the 1980s still had to cope. He was first a civilian member of the community of his choice. He did not always live near a military airfield and, thus, was basically immobile. Moreover, as a civilian, his daily pursuits were typically geared to the operating rhythm of his community, a Monday through Friday daylight work schedule. He did his reserve flying during his free time, which for the most part was on weekends when the Air Service fields were closed or, at best, operating at a reduced level.[25]

In 1922 the government subsidized the opening of twenty commercial fields for reserve flying, as Congress authorized the War Department to provide a system of airdromes for the Air Service and its reserve components. The department began establishing airdromes at large population centers for the training of reservists and opening of the airways thought essential to national defense and the development of commercial aviation. By June 1924, reserve flying was under way at four fields, and eleven others were in some degree of construction. As part of its support, the Air Service transported excess hangars to each of these airdromes, where they were erected with funds raised by popular subscription.[26]

Beyond directing that reserve and National Guard units would be established in each of the nine corps areas, the 1920 legislation specified no details of the national defense organization. Primarily because of the incapacitation of President Wilson during the latter part of his administration, the War Department received no guidance for implementing the law until June 1921 when President Warren G. Harding transmitted his interpretation. He observed that the act of June 1920 maintained the national tradition of providing a small peacetime Regular Army to be augmented by great citizen forces in the event of war. Whereas in the past these larger war forces had been extemporized after the occurrence of an emergency, the new law provided that the framework for the organization of citizen forces should be developed in time of peace through the voluntary service of citizens of military age. The President emphasized that the keynote of the new law was its insistence upon the establishment of this framework during peacetime. Within it, the Regular Army, the National Guard, and the Organized Reserve were to be mutual counterparts, differentiated only by the extent of their commitment.[27]

Lacking any precise direction before June 1921, the Air Service had done little about organizing its reserve effort other than by tentatively allotting some reserve units to the corps area air service units. There was another reason that the Air Service could only tentatively allot units. It had very little control over the National Guard and Organized Reserve units. The chief of the Militia Bureau was responsible for the National Guard, and the commanders of department and corps areas were responsible for the Organized Reserve. Having no authority, the Air Service chief acted only upon invitation of those officials. Late in fiscal year 1921, Maj. Gen. G. T. Menoher, Chief of the Air Service (1919–1921), recommended a tentative allotment of reserve units for War Department consideration to induce coordination among the agencies. The War Department allotted more than 500 aviation units to corps areas as the Air Service elements of the divisions, groups, and armies of the Organized Reserve.[28]

In some parts of the country, the organization of Air Service reserve units was encouraged by the civilian communities. The introduction of reserve and civil air activity in the vicinity of Cincinnati, Ohio, was typical. On April 18, 1922, the Aero Club of Cincinnati, consisting mostly of reservists, held a dinner to promote interest in the Air Service units of the Organized Reserves in that area and to secure a municipal field for Cincinnati. The hundred or so guests included the presidents of the chamber of commerce, of the businessmen's club, and of the automobile club. Civic leaders were receptive, the Air Service cooperated, and a lease was consummated between the federal government and the city within the year.[29]

At some places the activity was entirely military. In 1922, at the Presidio of San Francisco in California, Crissy Field became an active site of air reserve training on the West Coast. The reserve program there included the 91st Division, Organized Reserve, and the 316th Observation Squadron, Organized

The Air Force Reserve

Reserve, generally under the instruction and guidance of the active Air Service's 91st Observation Squadron. In time, reserve units were also organized at San Jose, California, thirty miles south on San Francisco Bay. Assisted by 1st Lts. Benjamin S. Catlin, Jr., and W. A. Maxwell, 1st Lt. Robert E. Selff was in charge of instruction of the reserve squadrons in the triangle formed by Crissy, San Jose, and Mather Field, near Sacramento, California. On February 4 and 5, the squadron mustered for its formal sign-up session, and the Air Service officers accepted twenty-three reserve officers into the squadron as members of the Air Service Reserve Officers Corps.[30]

With the assignment of Capt. Armin F. Herold to the 91st Division as Air Officer and the acquisition of two Wright-Hispano–powered aircraft, the actual business of flying training began. The division also acquired an old DeHaviland for the instruction of enlisted mechanics and it detailed a staff sergeant and four specialists to duty with the reserve squadron for this purpose. By April 25, the squadron had thirty-three officers assigned, just two short of its authorized strength, and twenty-five enlisted men under instruction.[31]

The reserve unit at Crissy Field progressed, and on the weekend of February 20–21, 1925, it sent fourteen aircraft on a cross-country flight to Mather Field and back. Departing Crissy in the rain, the planes flew in and out of a 500-foot ceiling all the way across the San Francisco and San Pablo Bays. But, from Benicia, about the midpoint to the Sacramento destination, the ceiling varied, sometimes rising to 1,500 feet. In spite of the clouds and intermittent rain, the formation arrived at Mather on schedule. The return flight next day was uneventful except for a 400-foot ceiling in the Sacramento Valley.[32]

Clover Field at Santa Monica, California, was among the first of the commercial fields to become operational as a reserve training base. Its experience typified the enthusiasm and cooperation which reservists throughout the country exercised in getting the first postwar reserve programs under way. Because of the limited funds appropriated for the program, the War Department could provide only the actual equipment for training at the commercial fields, that is, two hangars and aircraft—in the case of Clover, two steel hangars, nine Curtiss JN-4Hs, and a DeHaviland DH-4B. No allowance was made for a headquarters building or a hospital in which the flight surgeon could conduct physical examinations or provide medical treatment. Except for a limited number of mechanics and one night watchman, no support personnel were authorized.

Encouraged by 1st Lt. C. C. Mosely, Clover Field Commander, the reservists obtained scrap lumber from Ross Field at Acadia, California, and built a headquarters and medical building. Then, after the operation had struggled for some time and was becoming inundated by the paperwork associated with the field's dual mission, they found a former Army clerk willing to care for the records in return for lodging on the premises. By January

National Defense Act to Pearl Harbor

Upon becoming Chief of the Air Service (1921–1927), Maj. Gen. Mason M. Patrick acquired authority to place 500 reservists on the active duty at all times.

1924, about 380 Air Service Reserve officers were attached to Clover for flying.[33]

While the army corps area commanders supervised the organization of units and provided reservists some opportunities to sustain their flying skills, the chief of the Air Service coped with broader challenges. General Menoher and his successor, Maj. Gen. Mason Patrick (1921–1927) sought to utilize the reservists to solve contemporary force problems. One of the Air Service's major problems was that of maintaining a proper balance of commissioned grades. The Air Service's active flying mission required that fully 75 percent of its officers be young men, twenty-one to thirty-five years of age, normally lieutenants and captains. Thus, in any comparison with the Army as a whole, the Air Service's conspicuous feature was a preponderance of commissioned officers in the lower grades.

Moreover, the Air Service operated under severe regular officer personnel ceilings. It was impossible to retain all officers of the Air Service as permanent commissioned officers in the Regular Army. Even if the ages of all Air Service officers were distributed evenly between 21 and 64 years and if each grade had the correct proportionate strength, the number of captains and lieutenants each year who could no longer fly would more than double the number of vacancies arising in field officer grades. Moreover, with 85 percent of the commissioned personnel of the Air Service composed of captains and lieutenants all the same

11

age, practically all would end their flying days simultaneously. The Air Service would then have on its hands about 800 officers who, owing to their places on the promotion list, would still be in junior grades and for all practical purposes would be out of jobs.

Therefore, the Air Service needed a different personnel system. General Menoher thought the reserve could furnish the junior officers in excess of that number whose coming and going could be accommodated by normal promotion processes and attrition. He recommended that reservists be retained on active duty during their maximum efficiency as flyers, then thought to be about five years, and then be returned to reserve status to be available for active service in case of emergency. To induce reservists to serve such tours of active duty, he suggested legislation to provide increased compensation while they were on active duty or a substantial bonus upon their separation. He further urged that flying pay be provided for reserve and National Guard pilots who flew, and that they be authorized government insurance, hospital treatment, disability retirement, and care of dependents and burial in the event of death.[34]

No remedial action was taken, however, and inheriting these same problems in 1921, General Patrick asked for immediate legislative relief. Therefore, he included in the 1922 Air Service's appropriations request funds to retain 500 reserve pilots on active service at all times. He also suggested offering temporary reserve commissions and, like Menoher, asked for authority to recall temporarily to active duty a number of young reserve officers at the peak of their flying abilities. He also suggested that more reservists might be attracted by arranging some sort of continuing pay when these men left active duty. Some money was allocated in the fiscal 1922 budget for reserve officers to take fifteen-day tours of active duty for training in the summer months. General Menoher thought that fifteen days were insufficient to be of any appreciable value to either the Air Service or the reservist, and he sought more money to place reservists on active duty for extended periods with Air Service tactical units.[35]

General Menoher's views on the efficacy of the fifteen-day tours notwithstanding, they were ideal training vehicles from the standpoint of the many reservists who worked them into their summer vacations. Each officer was given a physical examination, and those who reported for flying training were tested by a flying instructor and then turned loose. Behaving precisely as a later generation of air reservists would, they started their day early, trained vigorously for about eight hours, and then recreated equally vigorously during the evening hours.[36]

In 1925 General Patrick was able to place sixteen reserve officers on extended active duty for concentrated training at Langley Field, Virginia, and Selfridge Field, Michigan. Agreeing with Menoher's views, Patrick recommended that the incidence of such tours be increased, with a concomitant reduction in funds for fifteen-day tours.[37]

National Defense Act to Pearl Harbor

During 1923, 341 reservists attended the summer camps conducted at fifteen Air Service sites. The most active sites were Chanute Field, Illinois, attended by 63 reservists, and Mather Field, where 60 reservists turned out. The Air Service programs of instruction for 1923 were prepared to arouse interest in new developments, both tactical and technical. Arrangements were made to provide as much flying in service aircraft, that is, mission aircraft, as was possible under the limiting conditions of time, with frequent demonstrations and tactical operations also conducted.[38]

A number of developments in 1926 directly affected the Air Reserve. The organization got a new name on July 2, 1926, when Congress passed legislation creating the Air Corps and the Air Corps Reserve. The law authorized a five-year program of expansion in personnel and equipment. Under its terms, by 1932 the peacetime Air Corps was authorized 4,000 officers, 2,500 flying cadets, 25,000 enlisted men, and 550 reservists on active duty. The act also authorized the President to recall voluntarily up to 550 reserve officers in increments of 110 annually. Finally, it specified that Air Corps airplane authorization include a sufficient number of aircraft to equip and train the National Guard and the Organized Reserve, but it left the determination of the actual number up to the Secretary of War's judgment.[39]

The Air Corps kept putting reservists on active duty, but it never quite got the numbers it wanted. At first, it had many applicants but too few airplanes and quarters. Then, a new factor evidenced itself, not for the last time in Air Reserve history. Many recalled reservists requested relief from active duty before their terms expired, either to accept Regular Army commissions or positions in commercial aviation.[40] Aside from the problems in getting reservists onto active duty and keeping them there, the Air Corps could not make enough flying hours available to reservists on inactive duty. The situation became so bad in November 1926 that flying was practically eliminated that month.[41]

The flying-hour squeeze, a scramble to provide airplanes for reserve flying as the World War I aircraft became unsafe, and an emerging emphasis on unit training led the War Department to reexamine the whole subject of reserve flying. In October 1926, it classified each Air Corps Reserve flying officer into one of three categories in terms of experience: those capable of flying service airplanes without additional instruction, those capable of flying service and training airplanes with a little instruction, and all others. Of the approximately 6,000 rated reservists classified, about one-tenth (631) were put into Class 1 and another 1,000 or so into Class 2. Henceforth, only these two classes of flyers were authorized flying training.[42]

The problem of providing a modicum of flying training to the pilots in Classes 1 and 2 was severe enough without the 4,400 or so individuals in Class 3. The 16,500 flying hours appropriated by Congress for reserve flying offered just a little more than ten hours per year to each of the 1,600 pilots in Classes

The Air Force Reserve

1 and 2, which the War Department and the Air Corps considered inadequate. The two agencies believed 48 hours annually were necessary to keep a reserve pilot in Class 1, which would require more than 30,000 hours annually just to support the 631 pilots in that class. Assistant Secretary of War for Air F. Trubee Davison fruitlessly importuned the Bureau of the Budget to approve 22,500 hours, about 36 hours per man, as the minimum the Air Corps needed for reserve training in 1929.[43] The problem intensified as economic depression struck the nation in 1929, and many reserve officers lost civilian jobs and tried to spend more time flying. The shortage of flying hours for reservist veterans of World War I intensified as the Air Corps gave priority for flying to graduates of the Air Corps Training Center at Kelly Field, Texas, and to Army-trained personnel who had acquired some tactical flying training.[44]

Even Selfridge Field, traditionally beneficent with reserve flying opportunities, could not always offer the reservist much flying time. The 96 reserve flyers from V Corps who participated in one summer camp at Selfridge in 1927 flew an average of 5.1 hours each, while 67 from the VI Corps later that summer averaged 4.9 hours each.[45] Selfridge Field provided inactive duty flying training for about 20 reservists on a regular basis after the classification went into effect. The matter of making the annual 48 hours available to them was of some concern in 1930. When the hours were available, however, Selfridge offered the reservists a good fleet of modern service airplanes to fly. At the peak of the 1931 summer training season, these included two PT–3As, three P–12Cs, four P–6As, four O–19s, and an O–33.[46]

The flyers at the reserve airdrome on the Boston airport seldom got as much time in the air as their Michigan counterparts did. On one particular Saturday in April 1928, fourteen reserve pilots, six observers, and four enlisted pilots shared three airplanes. Consequently, each pilot and observer got about forty minutes' flying time. The Boston reservists' fortunes improved three months later when they were able to check out in a VE–9 and a DH, a welcome relief from flying the primary trainers.[47]

By 1931, the reservists in Boston also had available several O–1Es, an O1–B, two BT–1Bs, and two PT–3s. But, as elsewhere, the allotment of flying hours for them was seriously curtailed. Moreover, an increase in the number of reservists flying from the station compounded the problem. Reserve officers at the field believed the limitation had reached the point where it was impairing their efficiency and that the little flying time they acquired in service airplanes was below the minimum for safety. Their situation had not improved by February 1932 when the best a reservist could anticipate was about an hour a month.[48]

The Air Corps received nothing more than a small percentage of the trained reserve active or inactive duty pilots required by the mobilization plans. This situation was peculiar to the Air Corps. Other branches of the service had no difficulty in acquiring the numbers of combat reserve officers specified in their mobilization plans. The Air Corps, however, needed trained pilots in its reserve. It could not depend upon many of the airline pilots although more than 15,000 of them were licensed. Only about 6,000 were highly qualified transport pilots; the rest could not be considered in any emergency national defense calculation because they would require almost as much training in the event of war as would personnel who had had no flying experience. For that matter, even the transport pilots, except for those few in Class 1 in the Air Corps Reserve, would require some military training before they could go into combat. Moreover, the Air Corps estimated that very few of the transport pilots outside the military service would be available as combat personnel. Demands of the aeronautical industry and the air transportation system would be very great in case of war, and the possibility of drawing aviation personnel from these sources would be remote.[49]

The potential of one source of reserve officers always eluded the Army Air Corps. The Morrill Act of 1862 granted land to enable states to establish agricultural and mechanical colleges offering military studies, and the National Defense Act of 1916 authorized a formal Reserve Officers Training Corps (ROTC) at all accredited four-year institutions. Beginning in 1920 the Air Service established Air ROTC units at six major universities with strong engineering departments. They were the Massachusetts Institute of Technology; Georgia Tech; the University of Illinois; Texas A&M; the University of California; and the University of Washington. These ROTC graduates were the only source of reserve officers that the Air Service/Air Corps had other than the graduates of the service flying schools. The number of flying cadets was limited until the late 1930s by law and appropriation to a fluctuating annual figure of about 200. The chief of the Air Corps estimated that the service required an annual replacement of about 2,000 cadets, with 500 from the ROTC units.[50]

For a number of years, therefore, successive chiefs of the Air Corps recommended that the number of Air ROTC units be at least doubled. Their appeal availed nothing, and in 1935, in the midst of a particularly brutal budget reduction, the War Department eliminated all six units. It was questionable that the Air ROTC units would have met the Army Air Corps' requirement for pilots even if the program had been continued. Against an objective of 2,131 officers in 1924, the Air Service ROTC units produced a mere 49, not all of whom had had any flying training.[51]

In 1932, Brig. Gen. Oscar Westover, then Acting Chief of the Air Corps, evaluated the effectiveness of the five-year expansion program that had been authorized by the Air Corps Act in 1926. He noted that the program required the Air Corps to increase progressively the numbers of qualified reservists on active duty to fill vacancies in newly created tactical units. However, in part because of limited funding, the Air Corps had not developed a reserve pilot training program to keep pace with the need. General Westover also observed

The Air Force Reserve

that the five-year program had made very little provision for a commensurate expansion of Air Reserve active and inactive duty training: It provided neither additional Regular Air Corps personnel necessary to support the reserve activity nor an adequate amount of tactical equipment. Improved training policies implemented late in the five-year period were developing a sufficient number of qualified reserve pilots to satisfy any reasonable expansion of the Air Corps, but the minimum number required for full mobilization had yet to be trained. In his annual report later in the year, Chief of the Air Corps Maj. Gen. Benjamin D. Foulois recommended that any future Air Corps expansion program recognize the importance of the reserve in national defense and provide accordingly for personnel and proper equipment for concomitant development of the Air Reserve.[52]

The reservists themselves viewed the five-year expansion program as a mixed blessing. Operational aircraft replaced the old trainers, and eventually there were enough airplanes. There were still too few flying hours, however, and the competition to fly them intensified throughout the period. Two phenomena compounded the problem for the actively participating reservist. First, after 1928, he was forced by classification to fly tactical airplanes. Second, the Air Corps could not accommodate on active duty all flyers graduating from the Advanced Flying School. Accepting commissions in the Air Corps Reserve, these men entered into the competition for airframes and flying.

Despite the periodic shortages of airplanes or flying hours, or both, the Air Corps Reserve program progressed in patches around the country. Early in 1932, Capt. Joseph A. Wilson, the commanding officer of the Boston Airport detachment, arranged a schedule of night flying. He and other regular officers first demonstrated landings by the light of flares they had dropped from varying altitudes. Then after a discussion of night flying problems and a training flight as a passenger, each reserve officer took off, flew around Boston, and returned to land by flarelight. Since none of the participating reservists had flown at night since the war, they received the training with great enthusiasm.[53]

The 430th Pursuit Squadron, formed from Kansas City reservists, deployed from its base at Richards Field, and flew to Marshall Field at Fort Riley, Kansas, in August 1932 for its two-week active duty training. There, for the first time in its history, the squadron had available fourteen service planes—three P-6s, three O-25s and eight O1-Es. In addition, a BT-2C and a PT-3 were available to flyers who needed dual work. This was also the first year the 430th could count a large number of its men who were experienced in all types of service planes. Many of its younger officers, graduates of the Air Corps Advanced Flying School, had served on active duty for a year or two with a tactical unit. Many others were commercial pilots who flew the military service planes on inactive duty at Richards Field. Fortified by this caliber of flying personnel, the squadron launched a tactical training program immediately upon reaching Fort Riley. In other years, more than half the time at camp had been consumed by dual instruction for officers who had not flown since their last active duty periods. Consequently, in 1932 the 430th put in much time on gunnery and bombing ranges as well as on formation flying and combat routine. In addition, typifying the training all across the country that year, the airmen completed a map problem, working with the ground units of the Kansas National Guard.[54]

By 1932 reservists were getting most of their flying in service airplanes. However, one drawback existed. The service planes identified for reserve flying were observation planes, not completely suitable to the many units designated to perform pursuit, attack, and bombardment functions. To properly round out the equipment of reserve units, the proper type of airplanes would have to be furnished.[55]

In 1934 the reserve training program was set back by three factors: a severe government economy program, the establishment of priorities for reserve flying, and the Air Corps mail operation. The necessity to use a large portion of the airplanes assigned to Air Reserve training for the air mail program greatly curtailed the flying training for approximately four months.[*56]

Reserve activity at Crissy Field slipped into history when the Air Corps evacuated the Presidio in June 1936 and moved across the bay to Oakland. There the pace of the reserve detachment's life quickened. First, in March 1937, the detachment checked out fifteen reservists in the BT–9. At midmonth, the commanding general of IX Corps area made his annual inspection. Four days later, the instructor led seventeen reserve pilots on a cross-country flight to Long Beach, California, in nine airplanes—five PT–3s, two BT–9s, one BT–2B, and an O–46. On the return leg the next day, a Sunday, the formation encountered driving rain and a low ceiling. One PT–3, along with the new BT–9 and the O–46, made it back to Oakland. Four others put in at Modesto, and the other two recovered at Livermore. There then occurred one of the early manifestations of a common reserve phenomenon which made active force officials frantic. Having some sort of civilian pursuits to attend to on Monday morning, all the reservists secured their planes and bussed or hitchhiked back to the Bay area. Monday morning, other reservists, who were always around with plenty of time to devote to the program, went out and ferried the airplanes home. By 2:00 in the afternoon, all nine airplanes were secured at Oakland.[57]

By the mid-1930s, the United States could no longer ignore the din of war penetrating its isolationism. In the Far East, Japan had invaded China's

---

[*]In February 1934, when he learned that government mail contracts with commercial airlines had been fraudulently negotiated, President Franklin D. Roosevelt asked the Army Air Corps to take over domestic airmail delivery pending renegotiation of contracts. For the resultant Air Corps airmail fiasco, see John F. Shiner, *Foulois and the U.S. Army Air Corps* (Washington, 1983), pp 125–149.

17

The Air Force Reserve

Manchurian province in 1931. In Europe, Germany rearmed in 1935 in violation of the disarmament provisions of the Treaty of Versailles and reoccupied the Rhineland in 1936. Civil war erupted in Spain, and Italy conquered Ethiopia in a conflict that demonstrated the ineptitude of the League of Nations to deter or stop war.[58]

Against this background, the War Department and Congress acted to bring the Air Corps up to the strength authorized by the Air Corps Act. As the only resource at hand, reservists were soon offered dramatically increased opportunities for active duty. The War Department authorized reserve officers who had already served active duty tours to return to active duty in the grade of second lieutenant for up to three years. All Air Corps Reserve officers were to be promoted to first lieutenant upon completion of three years' cumulative active duty service. Along with other Army reservists, members of the Air Corps Reserve were given the opportunity under the provisions of the Thomason Act of August 1935 to be examined for appointment as second lieutenants in the Air Corps, Regular Army. The act authorized the Secretary of War for a period of ten years beginning in July 1936 to select annually, in addition to the graduates of the United States Military Academy, fifty reserve officers to be commissioned in the Regular Army.[59]

During fiscal year 1935 the number of Air Corps Reserve officers on extended active duty with tactical units averaged 192. As the growing requirement moved the War Department to waive restrictions on maximum age and additional tours, participation increased yearly. The number on active duty averaged 250 in fiscal year 1937, 506 in 1938, and 650 in 1939. In the four years following 1935, 313 Air Corps Reserve officers accepted commissions in the Regular Army.[60]

Although funding to support the action would lag, in June 1936 Congress passed legislation expanding to 1,350 the number of Air Corps reservists the President might recall voluntarily to extended active duty for five years of training. This authority was necessary to provide the pilots who would be required to man new aircraft already authorized for procurement. Accordingly, within the limits of appropriations, the War Department began to place newly appointed Army Air Corps Reserve second lieutenants on active duty with the Regular Army Air Corps voluntarily for three years. Following their initial tours, some reservists were then offered the opportunity to serve two additional years as first lieutenants. All who completed the three-year tour became entitled to a lump sum payment of $500 upon return to inactive status.[61]

In January 1938 the Air Corps offered qualified reserve pilots who had not graduated from the Air Corps Training Center the opportunity to take refresher flying training and serve active duty tours. The first group of eighteen reserve pilots began the course at Randolph Field, Texas, on October 10, 1938. The first among them completed the second phase at Kelly Field, Texas, on December 23; the last completed refresher training at Kelly on April 14, 1939.

National Defense Act to Pearl Harbor

A total of seventy-five reservists completed the training.[62]

Between 1935 and 1939, many reservists left active duty to join the commercial airlines as pilots. In 1937, for example, 63 percent of all American Airline pilots had trained in the military, 56 percent from the Army Air Corps alone. The reason was threefold. First, Army-trained pilots proved ideal material for airline work. Disciplined and thoroughly versed in the fundamentals of flying, these individuals were usually quick to get into step with airline requirements. Second, the airlines provided the ideal opportunity for the Army pilot whose term of service had ended but who wanted to continue flying. Finally, there was the prohibitive cost of private pilot training. No pilot could qualify for a second pilot's position at American until he had amassed a minimum of 1,000 hours actual flying time, and the cost of buying this was conservatively estimated at $10,000. So, unless the candidate was wealthy or had a private flying job, the logical place to accumulate time was in the Air Corps.[63]

In 1938, with war developing worldwide, Congress gave President Franklin D. Roosevelt the largest peacetime military appropriations in U.S. history, but by 1939 the Army Air Corps was handicapped by dual personnel problems. Its force was undermanned and its experience level was dangerously low for accepting rapid modernization of equipment. The Roosevelt administration had begun to procure aircraft, but personnel procurement, especially the commissioning of regular officers, lagged. The War Department planned to overcome the shortage of regular officers in the Air Corps by augmenting the Corps over a ten-year period. Pending completion of this augmentation, the deficiency would be rectified by placing more reserve officers on extended active duty. One Air Corps planner estimated that during the ten-year program an average of 2,100 reserve officers would be on extended active duty. This solution to the War Department's problem was not completely attractive to the reservists. They had little incentive to remain on active duty because no more than a hundred regular commissions a year were available to them. Thus, their chance for active duty was about 1 in 21.[64]

In 1939, however, greater opportunities were offered to the career-minded reservist. Besides continuing to bring reservists who had not graduated from the Training Center onto active duty for refresher training and assignment, Congress authorized the President to call to duty annually for a year's service sufficient reservists to maintain a roster of 3,000 reservists on active duty. The law also authorized the War Department to commission 300 second lieutenants from the Air Corps Reserve as regular officers and approved a commissioned Air Corps strength of 3,202.[65]

The War Department immediately implemented this authority, rescinding all earlier policies on the subject of extended active duty for Air Corps reservists. Thereafter, to the extent permitted by appropriations, newly appointed Air Corps Reserve officers were voluntarily called to extended active

The Air Force Reserve

duty with the Army Air Corps as second lieutenants for one year. Their appointments could be extended annually, not to exceed a total of seven years. The War Department also authorized the retention of those reserve officers then on active duty, again with the seven-year limitation, and the return to active duty of officers who had previously served but were currently in inactive status. All categories were eligible for promotion to first lieutenant after three years' cumulative service and a lump-sum benefit of $500, payable upon return to inactive status.[66]

Many career-minded reservists had still another problem, however. By the end of 1939, the War Department was exercising congressional authority to appoint about seventy-five reserve officers to the Regular Air Corps annually. These men had to be second lieutenant graduates of the Training Center who were under thirty years of age. This opened the door for some of the younger pilots, but the prospects for the older men remained poor. Moreover, many of the younger men would become thirty years old before they completed their seven-year tours and, consequently, would become ineligible for regular commissions. Many reservists therefore declined the call to active duty, and many of those on active duty requested relief after one year to take advantage of good paying jobs in the flying schools, civilian airlines, aircraft manufacturing plants, or elsewhere in the aircraft industry. On August 5, 1939, a new law waived the thirty-year age limit for the appointment of second lieutenants in the Regular Army. This applied to Air Corps reservists on extended active duty with two years of such service and to warrant officers and enlisted men who were qualified pilots.[67]

Until August 1940 it had been War Department policy to grant all requests for relief from active duty upon completion of the initial tour. By that time, however, the Air Corps' need for trained officers had become critical, and on August 8 the department began tightening the screw. Thereafter, all graduates of the Air Corps Training Center were required to accept extended active duty upon being appointed second lieutenants in the Air Corps Reserve. Moreover, applications for relief upon completion of their initial one-year tours were routinely denied.[68]

In September 1940, Congress authorized the President to recall involuntarily all reservists for a year's service. The Judge Advocate General ruled that under the terms of this legislation voluntarily recalled reservists were subject to having their tours extended annually until they had served seven years, just as were those recalled under the April 1939 law. Only those ordered to active duty involuntarily would be eligible to apply for relief at the expiration of a twelve-month tour. Even this avenue of relief was closed to them when the President proclaimed an unlimited national emergency on May 27, 1941.[69]

Beginning in November 1939, the War Department authorized the Air Corps to recruit reservists from other arms and services who did not hold aeronautical ratings. The Air Corps first sought to fill a large number of vacancies in its procurement activities. In August 1940, however, it put out a call for practically any nonflying reservist. In July 1941, having called all its own reserves who voluntarily accepted active duty, it began to call the rest involuntarily.[70]

By September 1940, 4,022 were reservists on extended active duty with the Army Air Corps. Among them were 3,001 rated officers, of whom 1,453 were graduates of the Training Center. Demonstrating the importance of the reserve contribution to the overall force at this time, only 2,270 regular officers were on duty with the Air Corps. Nine months later, the reservists' number had risen to 8,346, and on December 31, 1941, three weeks after the Japanese strike at Pearl Harbor brought the United States into World War II, the number became 19,427, including 9,257 pilots and 6,039 from other branches and services.[71]

The Organized Reserve contemplated by the National Defense Act of 1920 was unlike any of its predecessor reserve programs. With the past offering no guidelines, the War Department was plowing new ground in developing the component. Although the Organized Reserve annually increased its numbers, it did not enjoy stability between the wars. This was especially true of the Organized Reserve's Air Service/Air Corps units. Although a 1935 Organized Reserve Air Corps station list reflected 328 units—4 divisions, 8 wings, 48 groups, and 268 squadrons—this nucleus of expansible units envisioned by the National Defense Act of 1920 was a paper tiger. Aside from some formation flying, the reservists did well to fly some basic observation exercises in cooperation with the ground forces. Only about 1,600 truly qualified military aviators were among the reservists in the early 1930s, but the War Department budget simply could not provide the Army Air Corps sufficient funds to furnish enough instructors to form reservists into tactical units and provide the flying hours necessary for even that small number to attain individual proficiency. Moreover, the Bureau of the Budget often withheld the little money approved.[72]

The Air Corps Reserve did not meet the specific objectives of the National Defense Act of 1920. The 12,000 reservists on extended active duty at the end of 1941 had gotten there as individuals, not as members of the units foreseen by the law. It is difficult to overemphasize the contribution its members made to the expanding air arm after 1937. Not only did the aviators among them supplement the flying personnel available for training and tactical assignments, nonflyers made it increasingly possible for the Army Air Corps to relieve experienced pilots from purely administrative nonflying duties.[73] Even before expansion and war, the reservists were used to help relieve various personnel problems as the Army Air Corps sought to resolve such issues as grade spread and promotions, to say nothing of its very strength which was rigidly limited by legislative and budgetary restrictions.

The Organized Reserve Corps made another great contribution between the wars in spawning the service associations. These pressure groups and lobbies influenced the passage of legislation which not only redressed reserve problems

The Air Force Reserve

but also strengthened the active establishment as well. Chief among the organizations pertinent to the air arm were the Reserve Officers Association formed in 1922 and its offspring, the Air Reserve Association, founded a decade later. The legislation they promoted pertained to such issues as separate promotion lists for regulars and reservists, flying pay, insurance for reservists, flying hours, and active duty training tours.[74]

Finally, the evolution of an air reserve between the wars revealed certain principles essential to the retention of a reserve force. Fundamentally, the reservist was a citizen who lived in a particular community by choice and normally did not have the mobility to get to a reserve training site hundreds of miles away. Reserve training opportunities had to be located near the major population centers of the country. As a citizen, the reservist's activities usually fit the operating rhythm of the civilian community, such as having an occupation performed on a five-day-a-week schedule during daylight hours. Training had to match the reservist's availability on the weekends and in the evenings. Occasionally, in the years to follow, the active force would forget, or ignore, these principles to the detriment of itself and its reserve components.

2

The First Postwar Air Reserve Program, 1946–1947

> ... The Air Reserve is a stew-pot, composed of leftovers not included in either the Regulars or Air National Guard.
>
> —Maj. Gen. Earle E. Partridge

Following World War II, officials of the Army Air Forces were convinced that the service required some kind of a reserve force in peacetime, although they had no clear concept of what the size and scope of such an effort should be. They were also troubled by the War Department's insistence that the Army Air Forces fit its reserve programs under the umbrella of a national universal military training and service program desired by the President. Planning for reserve forces took second place, in any event, to the officials' efforts to win the separation of the air forces from the Army. Their single firm conviction about the nature of the reserve program was that it must provide opportunites for pilots to fly. The Army Air Forces Air Reserve program approved by the War Department in July 1946 provided these opportunities. Otherwise, it offered a broad program of individual participation which unrealistically attempted to include every air reservist across the country who wanted to participate. It was a costly and inefficient effort, and when it fell victim to the budget restrictions of 1947, reservists complained bitterly.

Administration and War Department Policies

The United States emerged from World War II victorious and accepted as a

The Air Force Reserve

As Assistant Chief of the Air Staff for Training, Maj. Gen. Earle E. Partridge devised many innovative policies to facilitate the Air Defense Command's efforts to train a reserve force.

world leader. Its new President, Harry S. Truman, having succeeded the fallen Franklin D. Roosevelt on April 12, 1945, believed that the country had an obligation to assert this leadership to secure world peace. Shortly after the war ended, President Truman proclaimed that U.S. policy would be to foster and support the newly organized United Nations in its stated purpose of promoting international peace. The President asserted that the United States could not escape the responsibility thrust upon it by the power it had acquired during the war. It had to remain strong to assure peace in the world.

While hoping that the United Nations would eventually attain its goal of world peace, the President was not so sanguine as to expect that it would happen soon or easily. Therefore, the United States had to remain militarily strong both in the transition between war and peace in the long term. "The stabilizing force of American military strength must not be weakened until our hopes are fully realized," he said. Until a system of collective security was established under the United Nations, the United States could not allow itself to become weak; it had to remain strong.[1]

To sustain its military strength, the President thought that the nation had to unify its armed forces, temporarily extend the draft, and establish a program of universal training, a concept the President had supported ever since World War I.[2] General George C. Marshall, the Chief of Staff of the U.S. Army, shared the President's desire for universal training. General Marshall's

First Postwar Air Reserve Program

As President, Harry S. Truman (1945–1951) directed the military services to vitalize their reserve programs in 1948 and throughout urged Congress to authorize some form of universal military training or service.

Army Chief of Staff General George C. Marshall strongly supported the need for universal military training and, as the price for gaining its support, reconfirmed the primacy of the National Guard among the reserve components.

The Air Force Reserve

endorsement rested on two considerations. Recalling its behavior after World War I, he believed the nation, speaking through Congress, would reject a large peacetime military establishment. He was equally certain that the advanced state of technology would deny the United States much time to prepare for a major war. His solution required well-trained National Guard and reserve components fed by a system of universal military training. Using every forum available to him as Chief of Staff, he pressed these points upon the U.S. public, Congress, his Washington staff, and the U.S. Army.[3]

General Marshall actually began to prepare for the postwar period before the United States had even entered the war. On November 13, 1941, he recalled to active duty as his personal adviser on postwar Army organization Brig. Gen. John M. Palmer who had advised Congress during the development of the National Defense Acts of 1916 and 1920. General Palmer was the quintessential advocate of the true citizen army. His concept of the peacetime force required a small Regular Army core of professionals along with a trained citizen army formed into reserve units. The units were necessary to forestall the reserve's simply becoming a pool of cannon fodder and to enable reservists to advance through the ranks to leadership. By World War II, Palmer, who spent a lifetime thinking about these things, advocated a dual reserve system which accommodated both a national reserve army raised under the "Army" clause of the Constitution, and the National Guard raised under the "Militia" clause. General Marshall accepted General Palmer's tenets and recommendations during his tour as Chief of Staff.[4]

In July 1943, after some preliminary work was done by the Postwar Planning Board appointed a year earlier, General Marshall established the Planning Division of the War Department Special Staff to develop plans for demobilization, universal military training, a unified defense agency, and postwar organization of the Army, with General Palmer as adviser.[5] General Palmer soon learned that not every War Department or Army official automatically endorsed the notion of a citizen army just because it had the backing of the Chief of Staff. Many officials clung to old concepts of a large standing army of regulars to be expanded in wartime by individual reservists and conscripts. Palmer had fought this concept in 1919 with General John J. Pershing as his ally; now he contended against the issue with George C. Marshall at his side. Palmer and the Special Planning Division spent most of the spring and summer of 1944 developing a policy statement on the citizen army for Marshall's approval.[6]

General Marshall approved the paper, and the War Department published it as policy in Circular 347 on August 25, 1944. The statement dealt with the structure that would become the United States' permanent military establishment after the foundation of peaceful world order had been laid. It assumed that the Congress would enact legislation requiring every able-bodied young American male to be given military training and serve in the regular or reserve

First Postwar Air Reserve Program

forces. The circular ruled out large standing armies and called for the development of a military institution through a national citizen force. It prescribed a small professional peacetime establishment to be reinforced in time of emergency by organized units, not by individual riflemen and litter bearers, drawn from an organized and trained citizen army reserve. The members of such a reserve army would be given practical experience through temporary active service and the opportunity to rise, not by political appointment but by successive steps, to any rank and position for which they could definitely qualify.

Palmer saw three great advantages to such a military establishment. The efficiency of the institution would naturally depend upon expert professional control, but it would also encourage citizen soldiers to develop their capacities of leadership. And since most leaders of wartime armies were civilians in peacetime, they could be expected to provide an informed contribution to public opinion about military affairs. Finally, since a properly organized citizen army reserve did not require personnel to perform specific duties in the Regular Army that reservists could perform satisfactorily, the size and cost of the permanent establishment could be reduced prudently.[7]

At General Palmer's urging, meanwhile, the War Department reinstated the General Staff Committees on National Guard and Reserve Policy, the National Guard Committee in August 1944, and the overall and reserve committees in October 1944.[*] In the year following, the reinstated Section 5 committees and the Special Plans Division developed a series of statements establishing the mission of the reserve components and a training policy for them. These culminated in separate, definitive policy statements governing the postwar reserve components which were approved by General Marshall on October 4, 1945, and by Secretary Stimson nine days later. Their approval committed the War Department to the creation of a dual component reserve system for both the Army Ground Forces and the Army Air Forces and established the official basis for Army Air Forces planning of its postwar reserve programs.[8]

The official War Department policies relating to the Organized Reserve

---

[*]Primarily at the insistence of the National Guard, Section 5 of the National Defense Act of 1920 mandated the establishment of these committees, a parent committee representing all three components with one each for the National Guard and Organized Reserve to promulgate Reserve/National Guard policy and regulations. As adviser to the Senate Military Affairs Committee, Palmer had inserted the provision into the initial draft of the National Defense Act of 1916. He recalled that it was the intent of Congress that officers of the citizen components have an equal part with the regulars on the policymaking level in all matters affecting either or both civilian components (Memo, Palmer for Committee on Civilian Components, subj: Inter-relations between Professional and Non-professional Personnel in the Armed Forces of a Democratic State, Jan 9, 1948—AFRES IXC).

The Air Force Reserve

Corps assumed the postwar military establishment would consist of the Regular Army, National Guard of the United States, and the Organized Reserve Corps in a balanced force of 4.5 millon men. The Army would consist of the Army Air Forces, the Army Ground Forces, and the Army Service Forces. Each, able-bodied American male would be subject to one year of universal military training. After completing this phase, he would have the option of volunteering for service in the regular establishment or a reserve component. If he selected the reserve, he could be called to active service only during a national emergency declared by Congress.

The Organized Reserve Corps, consisting of officers, enlisted men, and units, would consolidate the Organized Reserves, Officers' Reserve Corps, and Enlisted Reserve Corps as a federally controlled reserve component of the Army of the United States subject to mobilization and field service. The Organized Reserve was to be capable of furnishing expandable trained units and individual officers for rapid mobilization and deployment. In addition to preparing units for mobilization, the reserve training program would seek out and develop officers with the potential for technical, staff, command, and instructor duties and foster their advancement to the highest possible ranks and authority. To the degree possible, reserve active and inactive duty training was to be conducted as unit training with modern arms and equipment. All training was to conform to War Department's doctrine and be conducted under the supervision of the appropriate major command or agency. The Organized Reserve Corps was to consist of an Active Reserve and an Inactive Reserve. The former was to comprise units organized and trained in peacetime for rapid mobilization, expansion, and deployment, and trained individuals as replacements and for expansion of the Army of the United States. The Inactive Reserve would simply be a reservoir of officers with various specialties who were available for assignment as needed. The Active Reserve would comprise those units and individuals in sufficient numbers and types which would, together with the Regular Army and the National Guard, constitute a balanced Army of the United States of 4.5 million persons.[9]

Army Air Forces Reserve Policies and Plans

Planning for a postwar air reserve by Headquarters Army Air Forces generally paralleled that of the War Department. Organized efforts began in the spring of 1943 when General Henry H. Arnold, Commanding General of the Army Air Forces, appointed Col. F. Trubee Davison to lead the Special Projects Office and directed him to develop plans for the organization, composition, and disposition of the postwar air forces. When he was also named as the Army Air Forces representative in the War Department's Special Planning Division, Colonel Davison kept the Air Staff apprised of the division's plans for a

First Postwar Air Reserve Program

postwar reserve as well as the plans of the committees for National Guard and reserve policy.[10]

General Arnold had anticipated that Colonel Davison's Special Projects Office would be the focal point for postwar planning, but Air Staff consideration of a postwar air reserve became fragmented. Between February and July 1945, Assistant Chief of the Air Staff for Personnel Maj. Gen. Frederick L. Anderson established a Reserve and National Guard Division; Maj. Gen. Lauris Norstad, Assistant Chief of the Air Staff for Plans, prepared a long-range reserve policy paper; and Lt. Gen. Hoyt S. Vandenberg, Assistant Chief of the Air Staff for Operations, recommended that the Army Air Forces resume reserve flying training and initiate a college ROTC program as soon as the necessary manpower could be spared from the war against the Japanese.[11]

On September 22, 1945, General Arnold asked Lt. Gen. Ira C. Eaker to bring him up to date on the status of the postwar reserve plans. Subsequently, on November 1, 1945, General Eaker assigned Air Staff responsibility for Air Reserve, Air National Guard, and Air Force ROTC affairs to the Assistant Chief of the Air Staff for Operations, Commitments, and Requirements, and he transferred Col. Luther W. Sweetser, Chief of the Reserve and National Guard Division, to fill that position.[12] General Eaker concurrently directed General Vandenberg, Chief of the Operations, Commitments, and Requirements agency, to submit an Army Air Forces plan for the postwar Air Reserve, Air National Guard, and ROTC that would provide for 27 Air National Guard and 34 Air Reserve flying groups. This reserve forces composition reflected the provisions of the forthcoming Army Air Forces definitive plan for its peacetime forces. Approved on December 26, the plan assumed that a system of universal military training and the resulting million-man reserve in the peacetime Air Force would enable the air forces to mobilize 1.5 million men organized into 131 groups—70 Regular Army, 27 Air National Guard, and 34 Air Reserve.[13]

General Vandenberg submitted the same basic plan Colonel Sweetser had prepared for General Arnold in September, and on November 26, General Eaker presented it to the Chief of Staff of the Army for approval. Basically, the plan provided for an Air National Guard with about 2,700 aircraft distributed to 84 bases; an Air Reserve with approximately 3,000 aircraft at 100 detachments; and the Air ROTC program designed to meet an annual requirement of 15,250 graduates from a minimum of 100 colleges. The War Department–approved troop basis for the Army Air Forces was 1.5 million, with 400,000 to the active air forces, 43,914 to the Air National Guard, and 1,056,086 to the Air Reserve.[14]

The seeds of reservist discontent and the potential for political protest were planted by this very first formal Army Air Forces reserve forces plan. Responsible for more than a million reservists, the Army Air Forces placed a mere 87,500 in its Active Reserve. These included 17,500 combat pilots, 5,000 staff pilots, 20,000 other rated officers, and 45,000 enlisted personnel.

The Air Force Reserve

As Commanding General of the Army Air Forces after World War II, General Henry H. Arnold initially supported his friend General Marshall on universal training, but before retiring he decided that the Army Air Forces required a force in being rather than one in reserve.

In May 1945, when a major general, Lauris Norstad, Assistant Chief of Air Staff, Plans, developed the first Army Air Forces long-range policy paper for reserve forces.

First Postwar Air Reserve Program

As the first Chief of the Air Staff for Operations, Commitments, and Requirements, on November 1, 1945, Lt. Gen. Hoyt S. Vandenberg (above) acquired the responsibility for Air Reserve, Air National Guard, and Air ROTC affairs. Lt. Gen. Ira C. Eaker (right) solicited the War Department and obtained its approval to initiate Air Reserve training at 40 of the proposed 130 bases.

The Air Force Reserve

Presumably, the remaining 970,000 or so would be relegated to the Inactive Air Reserve for which no training was envisioned.[15]

Because of many unsettled organization factors, especially the uncertainty regarding whether the Army Air Forces would remain an integral part of the Army, General Thomas T. Handy, the Deputy Chief of Staff of the Army, returned the Army Air Forces plans to General Arnold on December 4, 1945, without action.[16] By April 8, 1946, universal military training and unification legislation were stalled in Congress, and Army Air Forces veterans were clamoring for information about reserve training opportunities. General Eaker, therefore, solicited War Department approval to initiate Air Reserve training at 40 of the proposed 130 bases immediately and to phase in training into the remaining 90 during the following fiscal year. Air Staff officials believed that a sufficient geographical spread of units to get the basic administrative structure established for organizing the major pockets of reservists around the country required about 40 bases, and that sufficient aircraft were available. Two days later, War Department training officials authorized the Army Air Forces to proceed with the requested interim program.[17]

Nevertheless, the War Department also asked the Army Air Forces to revise its proposed training categories. This was done, and General Carl A.

Carl A. Spaatz, as Commanding General, Army Air Forces, and subsequently Chief of Staff, United States Air Force (February 9, 1946–April 30, 1948), tried to support the Air Defense Command's reserve programs, but he was restricted by War Department budget policies.

First Postwar Air Reserve Program

Spaatz, who had succeeded General Arnold as Commanding General of the Army Air Forces on February 9, submitted the third revision of the Army Air Forces Plan for the Air Reserve for approval. On July 12, 1946, more than nine months after the Assistant Chief of Staff, Personnel had presented General Eaker with the first version of the plan, the War Department formally approved the third revision. As finally published, the document incorporated all the recommendations of the General Staff Director of Operations and Training and faithfully reflected the War Department's policies of October 1945.[18]

However sugarcoated, the approved plan left no doubt of the preeminence of the Air National Guard over the Air Force Reserve. The mission of the Air Reserve simply would be to provide the 1,033,000 persons required to bring the Regular Army Air Forces and the Air National Guard to a mobilized strength of 1.5 million.

The National Guard's post–World War II reinstatement as the Army's first-line reserve component was the quid pro quo promised by General Marshall for the guard's endorsement of universal military training. Maj. Gen. Ellard A. Walsh, president of the National Guard Association, gave his public assent to universal training during the Woodrum Committee hearings in June 1945. General Marshall reciprocated by advocating the guard as the second line of defense in his final report on World War II in August, and in October the official War Department postwar policies relating to the National Guard and Organized Reserve confirmed the National Guard as the first-line reserve component of the postwar military establishment.[19]

Comparisons of the positions of the two reserve components as perceived by the official policies are illustrative.

Definitions

The National Guard. The National Guard of the United States will be an integral part and a first line reserve component of the postwar military establishment. The National Guard of the United States and Territories will continue to exist in the postwar military establishment.

The Organized Reserve Corps. The Organized Reserve Corps, consisting of officers, enlisted men, and units, will be a federally controlled reserve component of the Army of the United States capable of mobilization and field service at times, places, and in numbers according to the needs of National Security.

Mission

Air National Guard of the United States. To provide a reserve component of the Army of the United States, capable of immediate expansion to war strength, able to furnish units fit for service anywhere in the world, trained and equipped:

The Air Force Reserve

>   a. To defend critical areas of the United States against land, seaborne, or airborne invasion.
>   b. To assist in covering the mobilization and concentration of the remainder of the reserve forces.
>   c. To participate by units in all types of operations, including the offensive, either in the United States or overseas.
>
> *Active Reserve.* To be capable of furnishing in the event of emergency:
>   a. Units effectively organized and trained in time of peace for rapid mobilization, expansion, and deployment. Along with the Regular Army and the National Guard, these reserve units will constitute in type and number the balanced forces of the Army of the United States.
>   b. Additional trained commissioned and enlisted personnel for necessary replacements and expansion of the United States.[20]

In other words, serving as organized and equipped units, the Air National Guard would participate in the Army Air Forces defensive and offensive missions. The Air Force Reserve, on the other hand, was relegated to a replacement and augmentation role.

Since it had no overall mobilization plan, the Air Force could not even devise a troop basis for the Air Force Reserve, that is, a firm calculation and definition of the numbers and kinds of reservists needed upon mobilization. Lacking such a concrete plan, the Army Air Forces and the Air Force proceeded on the vague notion that the highest priority should be given to individual reservists with specific assignments to the major air commands. Even so, aside from a subsequent unilateral effort by Lt. Gen. George E.

Lt. Gen. George E. Stratemeyer. The first commander of both the Air Defense Command (March 1946–November 1948) and Continental Air Command (December 1948–April 1949), he strove mightily with inadequate resources to forge a representative air reserve program.

First Postwar Air Reserve Program

Maj. Gen. St. Clair Streett, Deputy Commanding General of the Strategic Air Command, advocated his support for the air reserve program by providing resources via his command.

Stratemeyer as commander of the Air Defense Command, the Army Air Forces never organized a mobilization assignment program. Lacking a true basis and justification for its existence, the Air Reserve program was susceptible to budget reductions because Army Air Forces officials could not defend its importance, and a paranoid generation of reservists was left to complain about its second-class citizenry.

Quite aside from the political clout it derived from a Constitutional tradition and sponsorship by forty-eight governors, the Air National Guard had a mission that defined it as the first line of the reserve. Consequently the guard got the facilities, the equipment, and the aircraft; the reserve got what was left over. As assessed by General Partridge in November 1946, "The Air Reserve is a stew-pot, composed of leftovers not included in either the Regulars or the Air National Guard."[21] That was the way it was.

Aside from the disparity in status between the two components, their joint existence was clouded at times by some ambivalence on the part of the active force as to the necessity for two air reserve components, and if there was to be one, which should it be. Friction had been present from the beginning in the staff of the Assistant Chief of Air Staff for Training as some officials favored the Guard and others, the Reserve.[22]

In July 1946 Maj. Gen. St. Clair Streett, Strategic Air Command Deputy Commander, suggested that the problems could be greatly simplified by eliminating the distinctions between the Air Reserve and the Air National Guard and administering all reservists under laws governing the Air Reserve. Such a consolidation would simplify legal issues, administration, and supply, and would reduce costs. It would, he said, forestall allegations that most of the Air Force Reserve was being discriminated against in favor of the minority Air National Guard. General Streett recalled the interwar difference in treatment between guard and reserve officers as a source of controversy and bitterness.

The Air Force Reserve

He saw the dual postwar system as perpetuating the controversy in addition to making it more cumbersome for the Army Air Forces to administer its reserve components.[23]

General Streett's suggestion of unifying the two reserve components ignored a number of realities, as would many Air Force and Defense Department officials in the next thirty-five years. The National Guard is the designated state militia by the Constitution of the United States. Woven into the very fabric of the nation, the National Guard *is!* Since it *is*, the national government makes what use of it it can. Although the National Guard fulfills state and some federal needs, it fails to satisfy others. In the first place, not every person in the United States with an obligation or desire for mlitary service wants to serve in a state militia. Second, the legally prescribed nature and organization of the National Guard does not provide for service as individuals; the guard consists of units only. Finally, the military services have a quite natural desire to have some reserve forces fully under their control; hence federal reserve forces. Along with formidable political barriers, these among other reasons militate against merging the Air Force Reserve into the Air National Guard or the converse action, both of which have been proposed a number of times. Both components are necessary and inevitable.

Consisting of duly appointed officers, enlisted personnel, and designated units, the Air Reserve was to be a federally controlled reserve component of the Air Forces, ready for mobilization and active duty at the time, places, and in the numbers indicated by the needs of national security. The Air Reserve would comprise two categories: the Active Air Reserve and the Inactive Air Reserve. In event of an emergency, the Active Air Reserve was to be capable of furnishing units effectively organized and trained in time of peace for rapid mobilization, expansion, and deployment, and of furnishing additional trained commissioned and enlisted personnel to augment units of the Regular Army Air Forces, air units of the National Guard, and the Air Reserve. The Inactive Ait Reserve was to provide a reservoir of officers for low-priority assignments.

The Active Air Reserve was to include three basic classes of Air Reserve units. Class A units were to be organized at full strength of officers and enlisted men, fully equipped, and trained during peacetime. Most would be nonflying service units, affiliated with civilian industry and available on mobilization day (M-Day).* Other Class A units would be combat units organized at full strength of officers and enlisted men, fully equipped, and trained so far as practicable during peacetime. Requiring additional training, they would not be expected to be ready until 90 to 150 days after mobilization.

Class B combat and service units would be organized with a full strength

---

*D-Day is the unnamed day on which hostilities start; M-Day is the day on which mobilization of forces occurs or is projected to occur. M-Day may precede, follow, or coincide with D-Day (*United States Air Force Dictionary* [Maxwell AFB, 1956]).

of officers and at least a cadre of enlisted men. Essential individual and training equipment would be provided to these units. After mobilization, the units would be filled to full strength and their members given additional training and be expected to be ready within three to six months. Class C combat and service units would be organized with officers only and would be given the same peacetime training as Class B units. They would not be available for at least six months after mobilization.

The objective of the training of the Active Air Reserve was to attain individual and unit proficiency based on the standards applicable to the Regular Air Forces. The training would include classroom instruction and supervised aerial flight. Aircraft would be distributed according to population density to air bases throughout the United States to afford a means of maintaining the flying proficiency of Active Air Reserve personnel.

Regular Air Forces base units would be established at each air base to supervise and support Air Reserve training. Active Air Reserve officers would be authorized to fly not more than ten hours a month, except when on active duty. Qualified transient reserve officers would be permitted to fly at any Air Reserve location. Active duty with Regular Army Air Forces units might be offered members of the Active Air Reserve, and additional tactical training might be given by assigning individual officers to Army Air Forces units for extended periods of active duty. Within the availability of funds, fifteen-day annual summer camps would be offered to all Active Air Reserve personnel. To the greatest extent possible, such training was to be conducted as unit training. The Air Reserve plan contemplated proficiency flight training for approximately 22,500 pilots.[24]

The Initial Air Reserve Management Structure

Initially, the postwar Air Reserve was to have been administered by the Continental Air Forces, created December 15, 1944. A reorganization on March 21, 1946, eliminated the Continental Air Forces, however, as the Army Air Forces grouped its U.S.-based combat forces under three new functional commands: Air Defense Command, Tactical Air Command, and Strategic Air Command.[25]

Oriented to a concept of global air power based on intercontinental bombing capabilities, the postwar Army Air Forces relegated air defense to a low priority. Since the United States had nuclear hegemony, air or sea attack upon the country would probably be the final act of hostility in a developing war. Consequently, continental air defense would not become operative until just about the time the United States would be mobilizing its reserve forces. Therefore, the Air Staff looked upon air defense as a mobilization mission to be conducted by the Air Reserve and the Air National Guard in the historic

The Air Force Reserve

militia, home defense role. When he was named Commanding General of the Air Defense Command, General Stratemeyer was instructed to give most of his attention to establishing an aircraft control and warning system and to managing the Air National Guard and the Air Reserve.[26]

Headquarters Air Defense Command was activated at Mitchel Field, New York, on March 27, 1946, and, matching the alignment of the U.S. Naval districts and the U.S. Army areas, was soon assigned six numbered air forces to discharge its field responsibilities on a regional basis. Thus, in March 1946, the field responsibilities for the Army Air Forces reserve program devolved upon the Air Defense Command, a new organization created only in part for that purpose.[27]

The Air Defense Command anticipated establishing ten of the interim Air Reserve training bases units about June 1 and the remaining thirty by July 2. Its plan stipulated that the training at these units would initially take the form of a flying club with the primary objective of providing pilot proficiency. This reflected the widely held belief among Army Air Forces officials that the reserve aviators, most of whom had not flown for more than a year by this time, had to resume flying as soon as possible if they were to regain flying proficiency. The Air Defense Command anticipated that 4,480 rated personnel would initially participate. At first, training would be confined to flying technique and standards of pilot proficiency, with each pilot being permitted to fly four hours per month. The command projected a peak requirement of 1,350 aircraft—982 AT–6s, 184 AT–11s, and 184 P–51s—for the initial program.[28]

The basic complex for the conduct of local air reserve activities was the Air Reserve training detachment supported by an Army Air Forces base unit (reserve training) organized by the Air Defense Command at each training location. Commanded by the same officer, both the reserve and the base units were regular units. The base unit furnished the personnel to operate the detachment and provided essential base services.[*]

The burden of the success of the local reserve program rested squarely upon the shoulders of the detachment commander. He ran a shoestring operation, and its effectiveness depended in large measure upon his own initiative. The equipment, supplies, and facilities furnished to him by the Army Air Forces were not always adequate for the task, and he often had to rely on the largesse of local civilian authorities and airport officials for additional support. He had to exercise great ingenuity to make his training program attractive to Air Reserve personnel, often combining social events with training activities.

---

[*]The base unit was one which the commanding general of an Army Air Forces command designated and organized with permanent party personnel to operate a base or establish another activity. The base units were not constituted or activated but were like contemporary major command or separate operating agency controlled units (WD Cir 473, Dec 16, 1944; AFP 210–2, *Guide to Lineage and Unit History*, June 2, 1957).

First Postwar Air Reserve Program

Early Problems in Conducting the Air Reserve Program

After adjusting its plan to accommodate the changing availability of some facilities, the Air Defense Command intended to activate forty base units by July 1, 1946. In getting the reserve base program underway, Stratemeyer and his headquarters staff encountered severe problems from the very beginning. They included delays in the assignment of bases, facilities, and aircraft; insufficient permanent party personnel; and severe budget limitations. The first of many obstacles arose when it became evident on May 22 that, because of War Department delays in approving the Army Air Forces plan, permanent party personnel for the base unit cadres could not meet their reporting dates. The Air Defense Command therefore delayed activating each base for fifteen days, and the Air Staff postponed delivery of aircraft until after July 1.[29]

The Air Defense Command organized the first four reserve training base units on June 15 and another twenty-one by the end of the month.[30] Among the latter was the 468th Army Air Forces Base Unit (Reserve Training) at Memphis Municipal Airport (MAP), Tennessee, where on July 1 reservists conducted the first postwar Air Reserve training flight in an airplane, probably a C–47, borrowed from the 4th Ferry Group—twelve days before the War Department formally approved the Army Air Forces Air Reserve plan.[31] By the end of 1946, the command had organized Air Reserve training detachments at seventy bases and airfields.

Another early difficulty involved the identification and acquisition of bases and training facilities for the base units which were to train the air reservists. The problem was threefold: the War Department and the Army Air Forces did not immediately identify installations that would be retained for long-range postwar use; the Air National Guard had first choice; and municipal authorities sought to attract civil aviation in preference to government activity.* Various Air Staff agencies began coordinating the location of guard and reserve units in September 1945, but a year would passed before the fields for the first forty Air Reserve units were firmly identified. This was but one of the fruits of the long delay in planning an Air Reserve program.

The War Department approved implementation of training by the Army Air Forces at the first forty bases. Still, the Reserve and National Guard Division

---

*The flying fields on which the War Department and the Army Air Forces planned Air Reserve activities included Army Air Forces bases intended as permanent installations, Army Air Forces bases intended only for interim use, former National Guard training sites, and municipal fields expanded by the Army Air Forces for military use during World War II. Among other related issues, the states were authorized by law to base National Guard units wherever they chose, the municipalities wanted their fields returned complete with improvements, and the Army Air Forces did not want to spend money on temporary fields.

The Air Force Reserve

of the Air Staff was negotiating selection of airfields with the Air Installation Division through June 1946. On June 19, Col. Monro MacCloskey, Colonel Sweetser's successor as Chief of the Reserve and National Guard Division, rejected some of the Air Defense Command's May 15th suggested locations. They conflicted with some cities identified by the states for their Air National Guard units.[32]

A week later, MacCloskey met in General Eaker's office with representatives of the War Department General Staff, the National Guard Bureau, the Assistant Chief of the Air Staff for Materiel, and the Air Defense Command. This meeting was to confirm policy on Air Reserve and Air National Guard use of facilities. The group agreed that the Air Reserve would relinquish facilities used by National Guard units before World War II which the Air National Guard now sought. Units commanders of the Air Reserve bases had to evacuate their facilities immediately. Among others, they had occupied Lambert Field in St. Louis and Buckley Field in Denver.[33]

Agreement on a policy for the National Guard's use of facilities did not resolve the problems on commercial fields or interim bases. In July, for example, the Air Reserve had to abandon plans to establish itself on the municipal airport at Oakland, California, because of strenuous objection from city officials who wanted to expand commercial operations there. The First Air Force's experience at Syracuse, New York, typified the difficulty of facilities acquisition in the area. The War Department declared the airfield surplus in January 1946, but it had identified the facilities for use by the Air Reserve. Unfortunately, the installation drawing was never updated to reflect this fact. Just after the declaration of surplus was made, the state housing authority was granted access to the field.[34] When the commander of the reserve detachment attempted to take possession of his buildings in June, he found the housing authority had appropriated his facilites. Despite comparable difficulties throughout the country, by mid-August 1946, the Air Defense Command had activated thirty-six base units and their reserve training detachments, and reserve flying was actually under way at twenty-five of them.[35]

Training aircraft for the Air Reserve program were delivered to the units late. In May 1946, the Air Materiel Command agreed to turn over the first 90 of a projected 1,420 aircraft to the Air Reserve program on June 15, with delivery to be completed by September 1. The aircraft were delivered 30 to 45 days late, and most reserve flying during the first month was done in borrowed aircraft.[36]

In mid-July, Colonel MacCloskey advised the Assistant Chief of the Air Staff for Operations, Commitments, and Requirements Operations Division of the Air Reserve program's initial requirements for tactical aircraft. In the fall of 1946 Headquarters Air Materiel Command allocated 400 P–51s, 52 B–25s, 42 C–47s, and 50 B–29s.[37] The Materiel Command began to deliver the P–51s and held the other tactical aircraft in storage pending the availability of reserve

First Postwar Air Reserve Program

funds. In December 1946, however, in the wake of the Air Reserve budget reductions, the Air Staff directed the Air Defense Command to transfer all P-51s to the Air National Guard to conserve Air Reserve funds. The C-47s and the B-29s were soon dropped from the reserve program as well.[38]

The P-51 was a prime sacrificial candidate. It cost more to operate than a trainer and carried only one crew member. By withdrawing the P-51 and using only two-seat trainers in the Air Reserve program, the Air Defense Command not only economized on the cost per hour of aircraft operations, but a single flight provided flying time for two people. Moreover, less supply and other support were required.[39] When Army Air Forces officials failed to explain the reason for transferring the P-51s, air reservists were embittered.

The Impact of Budget Reductions

From the beginning, the Air Reserve program was hobbled by financial restraints. President Truman sought to reduce defense spending, and the reserve components shared in the austerity. In May 1946 the Bureau of the Budget reduced the War Department's proposal for the 1947 Organized Reserve Corps program from $94.4 to $56 million, a figure that Congress ultimately appropriated. The Air Reserve share was $33 million.[40] The Air Reserve program fared no better in fiscal year 1948. The Army Air Forces submitted a 1948 budget for the Air Reserve of $139,167,721.[41] The Bureau of the Budget reduced it to $33 million again, but Congress intervened and appropriated slightly more than $40 million for the 1948 Air Reserve program. The contrast between the program planned under the original budget estimate of $139,167,721 and the one possible under $40 million is illustrated in the following table:[42]

Programs Available in Original and Revised 1948 Budgets

Program	Original (Budgeted)	Revised (Budgeted)
Program Expenditures		
Budget	$139,167,721	$40,000,000
Reserve Bases	117	41
Aircraft	2,456	1,320
Flying Hours	2,039,520	700,000

Programs Available in 1948—*Cont'd*

	Budgeted	
Program	Original	Revised

Personnel Receiving Maximum Inactive Duty Training

Pilot Officers	22,500	9,600
Other Rated Officers	11,056	2,211
Nonrated Officers	16,444	3,289
Enlisted Men	120,000	10,000
Total Personnel	170,000	25,100

Personnel Receiving Active Duty Training

Pilot Officers	22,500	8,700
Other Rated Officers	11,056	2,200
Nonrated Officers	16,444	3,200
Enlisted Men	120,000	10,000
Total Personnel	170,000	25,100

In view of the approved 1948 program, on February 21, 1947, Headquarters Army Air Forces directed the Air Defense Command to eliminate twenty-nine reserve training detachments as quickly as possible. After these bases were eliminated, the Air Reserve program operated on forty-one bases.[43]

Despite the base eliminations, Headquarters Army Air Forces and the Air Defense Command tried to make flying training available to reservists in the vicinities of the lost bases. The planners were motivated by a desire to extend some kind of reserve activity to as many veterans as possible and by pressure brought upon the Army Air Forces by congressmen and local chapters of the service associations. The Air Defense Command thereupon spread its scant resources even thinner. It established satellite bases on civilian airports (to which training aircraft were ferried for local use) and pickup stations (from which, conversely, rated personnel were transported to a reserve training detachment for flying). By the end of fiscal year 1948, the Air Defense Command was operating a network of sixty-seven satellite locations and eighty-four pickup stations.[44]

First Postwar Air Reserve Program

The State of Reservists' Records

Probably the most frustrating aspect of Air Reserve program administration was the condition of the service records of individual reservists. By February 20, 1946, the Army Air Forces had released 734,715 servicemen in a process that was difficult to characterize as a demobilization. Brig. Gen. Leon W. Johnson, Chief of the Air Staff's Personnel Services Division, later noted that "we merely fell apart . . . we lost many records of all the groups and units that operated during the war because there was no one to take care of them."[45] In June 1946, the Army Air Forces acquired from the Army Service Forces the responsibility for administering all Air Reserve members of the Organized Reserve, including maintaining their individual records. The Air Staff delegated this responsibility to the Air Defense Command which placed an Army Air Corps liaison officer on duty with each of the Army areas.[46]

Serious problems immediately became apparent. In the first place, the Army areas did not have all the records. The Adjutant General maintained in Washington, D.C., a basic file on each veteran to retain records that might be necessary to integrate personnel into the Regular Army and to adjudicate various claims involving Veterans Administration programs. Because the information in these files was to duplicate that contained in copies held by the Army areas, the offices of the Adjutant General would not release their files to the Army Air Forces. Unfortunately, the area copies were often incomplete and imperfect, and it was often impossible to determine the number of reserve officers in an area by branch and service. Approximately 20 percent of all records bore no occupational skill number; they simply identified the member as affiliated with the Air Corps. In many instances the record folders of enlisted men lacked their individual service records. When service records did exist, the date of appointment in the Enlisted Reserve Corps was missing or obviously wrong. About two months after the Army Air Forces began to acquire its records, Assistant Secretary of War for Air W. Stuart Symington admitted that the service had no record of the officers who had just served with it in the war, although it hoped soon to account for all those who had accepted reserve commissions.[47] The new Air Corps liaison officers and Air Defense Command officials at the bases tediously reconstructed the records of active individual reservists to impart to them some degree of accuracy.

Major Command Cooperation with the Air Defense Command

Although the Air Defense Command was primarily responsible for administering reserve training, Generals Stratemeyer and Spaatz soon agreed that every major air command had to participate. Reserve training would have to be conducted on the bases of the major commands as well as by the training detachments specifically established for that purpose. It was not sufficient that

The Air Force Reserve

Partridge, as Assistant Chief of the Air Staff for Training, be charged with planning reserve programs and General Stratemeyer be charged with their execution. The reserve program was a national endeavor and required all major commands to conduct some form of training on their bases. On July 31, 1946, General Spaatz directed the other major commanders to cooperate fully with the Air Defense Command in carrying out this program.[48]

General Stratemeyer identified specific assistance the commands could render in the functions of operations and training, public relations, budget, medical services, maintenance, and supply. The major commands tried to comply with General Spaatz's guidance. General Streett, Deputy Commander of the Strategic Air Command, was particularly aggressive in directing his subordinate unit commanders to cooperate.[49] As the Air Defense Command began to discontinue some training detachments in January 1947, Maj. Gen. Elwood R. Quesada, Commanding General of the Tactical Air Command, offered the reserve program extensive support, directing his commanders to accommodate the training of as many disfranchised reservists as possible.[50]

The program's contractions caused by the fiscal year 1947 budget reductions made it even more evident that there would never be enough units to accommodate all Air Force Reservists who wished to be trained. In March 1947 General Spaatz reemphasized his desire that the major commands do everything possible to retain the interests of air reservists. He wanted them to understand that even though the Army Air Forces did not have the money to conduct all the reserve training it thought necessary, it wanted their support and interest. Spaatz wanted the major commands to arrange for reservists to participate when possible in the regular flying activities of the active force units. He thought that such an approach might bring up the manpower of fighter units from peacetime to wartime strength quickly.[51]

General Spaatz's instructions caused some confusion and exposed an issue that lay at the basis of planning and programming for reserve training. The commanding general's guidance implied that air reservists might be given unlimited opportunities to fly at the active force bases. This was not his intention, however. General Partridge explained that the theory behind and the basis of the training of reservists with Regular Air Force units was to negate the difference between peacetime and wartime strengths of such units; it was out of the question to absorb all the reservists available, regardless of their number.[52]

The use of the mobilization requirement as the guide to determine how many air reservists should be trained was sensible, and was really the only justifiable approach to the question. Nevertheless, the Army Air Forces, and the Air Force after it, refused to embrace the mobilization requirement as the only rule for reserve affiliation in an active program. Whether this was the prudent course or not, selecting it created great problems for reservists for the next quarter century, the career span of an entire generation of air reservists.

The problem derived from the Air Force's desire to hold the loyalty and support of reservists who, for a variety of reasons, could not be fitted into active programs. As Air Defense Command Commander, General Stratemeyer frequently came into contact with such reservists and, empathizing with them, championed their desire to participate. He noted that the interest, enthusiasm, and loyalty of the senior reserve officers did not rest solely on active participation. They had supported Air Corps and Air Reserve activities at great personal effort and sacrifice during the long years preceding World War II. He was convinced that they would continue to give generously of their time and energy in the training and administration of a new generation of reservists. Stratemeyer thought the Army Air Forces had to reach out to accommodate and encourage these men.[53] He insisted that the service could derive real value from the influential positions the senior reservists held in their communities and from their contacts with their congressional delegations. He noted that friendly support of air power at the local level might become especially valuable for the Air Forces in the quest for independence and conformation of the strategic bombing mission.[54]

Activation of Units

War Department and Army Air Forces policies and plans required the Air Defense Command to form various kinds of air reserve units at different times during the program's initial two years. As distinguished from the regular force air base units and training detachments that administered and supported them, the air reserve units were reserve units commanded and manned by air reservists. They included combat, composite, and service units. A combat unit was a table of organization and equipment unit designated to perform a specific mission and equipped with the necessary aircraft, for example, a troop carrier group equipped with C–47s. Composite units consisted of individuals of the Active Air Reserve who for sundry reasons could not be fitted into the combat units. Service units had administrative or technical functions and supported combat organizations with services or supplies.

The provision in the Army Air Forces plan for the Air Reserve that the Air Reserve would ultimately include combat units was illusory and misleading. Colonel Kenneth P. Bergquist, the Deputy Assistant Chief of the Air Staff, told General Stratemeyer in May 1946 that the allocation of combat units to the Air Reserve had been made simply for tentative planning purposes to effect a distribution of reservists consistent with the allocation of aircraft and the reserve population density in the areas of the proposed reserve bases.[55]

An Air Defense Command mobilization plan of January 1947, supplementing the War Department and Army Air Forces plans of October and December 1946, included the bald assumption, "All members of the Organized Reserve

The Air Force Reserve

Corps will be mobilized as individuals." National Guard units on the other hand would "be mobilized by calling the units into Federal service on M-Day in their then existing state of training, equipment, and service strength."[56]

The Army Air Forces mobilization plan was hastily devised and based upon the War Department's mobilization plan which, in the opinion of the Air Staff officials, contained many unwarranted and unrealistic assumptions. Nevertheless, the 1946 plans were then operative, and their assumption that Air Reserve units would not be mobilized had the potential for great mischief. Recognizing this, Maj. Gen. Charles B. Stone III, the Air Defense Command Deputy Commander, urged secrecy upon the command's numbered air force commanders. He foresaw that if the reservists realized that the concept of organizing combat units was a false front and the real intention was to use them as individual fillers, even as a temporary concept, they would lose all enthusiasm for the program.[57]

This fundamental condition of the Air Reserve program remained constant during the first decade of the postwar program. The War Department, the Army Air Forces, and the U.S. Air Force never developed concrete war and mobilization plans. There was no intention to mobilize reserve units as units.[58]

Legitimate or not, combat units were required by the Army Air Forces plan, and the Air Defense Command set out to develop them. The command activated the first of these as Class C units on January 10, 1947. By June 30, 1948, although periodic funds shortages occasionally forced a slowdown of the effort, it had formed 246 combat units, 15 of which had actually attained Class A status, meaning they had their full complements of personnel and some kind of airplanes. Included were light bombardment, troop carrier, and fighter units equipped with minimum numbers of B–25s, C–47s, and T–6s.[59] These combat units were very popular with reservists who enthusiastically set out to develop them into first-class organizations. General Stratemeyer's temporary order that the numbered air forces not create additional combat units during the budget crisis of 1947 became a second source of bitter disillusionment for reservists.

The Formation of Composite Units

It was never envisioned that enough combat or service units could be formed to accommodate all the reservists who would wish to become active, and the War Department policies of October 1945 provided for the formation of composite units. In mid-1947, the Air Defense Command organized Air Reserve composite units to accommodate reservists who either lived in areas where no combat units were located or were surplus to the needs of such units.[60]

Assisted by the Air Reserve training detachment, the reservist commander of each composite unit trained all assigned staff personnel in the conduct of the squadron's administration and functions. Additionally, he administered some kind of training to all assigned personnel who held common military occupational skills. He also conducted any other practicable training, including instruction in broad principles of military and Army Air Forces operations and in Army Air Forces doctrine, tactics, and techniques. The composite units were not authorized active duty training, but their members were eligible for active duty tours for training, subject to the availability of funds.

This was a feckless program which reservists perceived as a holding pool, and from the beginning, Air Defense Command officials urged Headquarters Army Air Forces to strengthen its content. They believed the training programs should be developed by the training of technicians, that it be taught by Regular Army officers to the extent possible, and that it stress advanced knowledge rather than the dry, obsolete material presented to the reservists by their peers.[61]

The Air Reserve composite unit program was flexible enough to accommodate specialized flights, and in April 1948 the Air Defense Command established composite units for supply and logistics personnel at each reserve training detachment. The Air Materiel Command identified reservists qualified for its programs and furnished the Air Defense Command lists of desirable occupational skills to guide the assignment of personnel to the units. All training in these units was the responsibility of the Air Materiel Command. The Air Defense Command soon organized similar units for the Air Transport Command. These specialized flights offered the only effective training produced by the composite unit program[62]

Training Mobilization Assignees

In April 1947 General Stratemeyer tried to establish the example for the rest of the Army Air Forces by training air reservists who could not be assimilated into any of the unit programs. It was his policy that his command use whatever facilities it had available for the inactive duty training of reservists. He charged the numbered air forces and each headquarters staff division to expand themselves with reservists by 50 percent to permit continuous, reduced operations twenty-four hours a day. Reservists volunteering for this duty were to be given inactive duty training credit once the War Department announced procedures for allowing such credits.[63]

Several of the major commands, especially the Tactical Air Command, followed Stratemeyer's lead and offered a modicum of training to individual reservists. Yet, as another six months passed, Stratemeyer remained dissatisfied with major command participation in the reserve program. To give the commands their due, however, full attention to their primary missions generally restricted their capability to support the reserve program. At a conference in December 1947 major air command representatives agreed that an effective Air

The Air Force Reserve

Force Reserve could be created only if every element of the Air Force participated in its training. Nevertheless, they would not accept these responsibilities until the Chief of Staff directed them to do so.[64]

Upon learning of this from Stratemeyer, General Spaatz quickly initiated a number of actions within the Air Staff and amended the major air commands' mission directives to incorporate specific reserve training responsibilities. The new directives gave the commands administrative as well as training responsibilities.[65]

By this time also, the Air Staff had coordinated the long-awaited directive on the assignment, administration, and training of individual air reservists at Air Force bases where no reserve units were located. The guidance authorized Air Force unit and base commanders to assign qualified air reservists to mobilization positions. The commander was to determine the number of reservists he could accommodate; he was not constrained to consider area of residence as a prerequisite if training could be accomplished other than by frequent base training attendance.[66]

Active Duty Training for Air Reservists

In addition to the inactive duty training offered by the Air Defense Command training detachments and Regular Air Force units, a limited number of two-week active duty tours for training were available for reservists from time to time during 1947 and 1948. Great uncertainty marked the administration of the tours in 1947. In May it suddenly appeared that money was available to finance several thousand tours in the remaining two months of the fiscal year. Reacting quickly, the Air Defense Command and other major air commands tried to call as many reservists as possible to active duty for training. The War Department then discovered it had made a bookkeeping error, and the Army Air Forces had to limit the fiscal 1947 active duty training to that which the Air Defense Command numbered air forces budgets could already afford.[67]

Despite the attendant administrative confusion, about 10,000 air reservists served active duty tours for training in 1947, primarily in the last quarter of the year. These included about 5,000 pilots, 1,000 other rated personnel, 2,000 nonrated officers, and 2,000 enlisted men.[68]

The Air Reserve's Disgruntled Publics

As the Air Reserve program got under way in the summer of 1946, the Army Air Forces and the Air Defense Command initiated a belated publicity campaign to inform the American public in general and the Air Force Reservists in particular about the program. Both headquarters urged reserve

First Postwar Air Reserve Program

training detachment commanders to engage maximum local publicity when conducting formal reserve training-unit opening ceremonies. The commanders were to invite local air reservists, civilian and military officials, and the general public to participate in the festivities and to inspect the aircraft and facilities.[69]

But it was too late. Officials in Washington and at Mitchel Field soon discovered that reserve programs were conducted in the view of many publics: each public had to be satisfied that the portion of the program affecting it promised some ultimate good. These publics included the reservist's family, his employer, his neighbor, his church, his community, and, above all, the reservist himself.

By July 1946, reservists and their advocates were disgruntled over the Army Air Forces' failure to reestablish an Air Reserve program since the end of the war. Reservists complained to the Secretary of War and the Secretary of the Navy, the commanding generals of the Army Air Forces and the Air Defense Command, the service associations, and their congressmen. They criticized the lack of general information and the absence of an Air Reserve program, especially as it contrasted to the Navy's organized activity for which Naval reservists received training pay.[70] Stung by the criticisms, Symington sought some explanations from the Air Staff for the apparent slow progress and asked General Spaatz to prepare a weekly report on National Guard and Air Reserve programs.[71]

Much of the criticism directed at Stratemeyer involved complaints that officers on his staff who were assigned Air Reserve duties were undermining the program by intemperate remarks or ill-advised actions. In July 1947, fully a year after the reserve program got under way, for example, Stratemeyer learned that a major on his staff, possibly reflecting an ill-concealed sentiment among regular officers, had stated, "Only Reserve personnel belonging to a T/O&E [table of organization and equipment] unit should receive active duty training.... Reserves not continuously active while on inactive status would be worthless during an emergency." Agreeing that the first priorities for flying training had been given to members of the combat units and reservists with individual mobilization assignments, Stratemeyer nevertheless counseled the officer on the general inadvisability of his remarks. He reminded him that it was also Air Defense Command policy to keep every air reservist actively interested in the Air Reserve program whether he was able to train immediately or not.[72] About the same time, Stratemeyer was told of an instance in which a reservist was told by a training detachment commander that "they didn't know what they were supposed to do with anyone who wasn't a pilot!"[73]

General Stratemeyer was exceptionally distressed to learn of a disheartening occurrence in New York City in September 1948 which involved officials of Headquarters First Air Force. The training center at Mitchel Field had convened a meeting in a high school auditorium in the city at the beginning of the fall session, after the summer slump, to arouse more interest among

The Air Force Reserve

reservists in the composite units. This initiative dissolved to dust when, with 1,800 reservists crowded into a hall that might comfortably have accommodated 1,500, no one told the attendees anything. The meeting should never have been held. The colonel who had arranged it spent twenty minutes inviting the reservists to come to his office to get information. Three other speakers, including Maj. Gen. Robert E. Webster, Commander of First Air Force, did no better, although the meeting had been scheduled since July. To put it mildly, Stratemeyer was astonished that First Air Force had treated the meeting so cavalierly, and he personally reprehended General Webster.[74]

The attitudes that surfaced in his command to distress General Stratemeyer permeated the active force and disturbed General Dwight D. Eisenhower, who had succeeded General Marshall as Chief of Staff of the Army in November 1945. Eisenhower wrote to all major commands in April 1947 urging their leaders to take the initiative in securing cooperation and coordination of effort from their staffs. Asserting that nothing was more important than coordination and cooperation during the critical period of establishing the civilian components, he urged "a sympathetic approach to National Guard and Organized Reserve problems of organization, training, supply, and administration." He directed the commanders to indoctrinate all regular personnel with the importance and magnitude of their reserve administration and training responsibilities and to solve the problems of the civilian components through cooperation.[75]

Many senior reservists were displeased when the Army Air Forces had to cut back the Air Reserve program in the spring of 1947. Colonel T. G. Graff, then acting Public Relations Officer of the Air Defense Command, attended a meeting of Air Reserve Association officials at Eglin Air Force Base (AFB), Florida, in April 1947. He reported to General Stratemeyer that the reservists were especially disappointed about the suspension of the activation of combat units, discontinuation of the twenty-nine reserve training detachments, and the transfer of Air Reserve P–51s to the Air National Guard. It was the halt in activating combat units which they thought the most serious error, and about which some of the Air Defense Command's staunchest supporters at the meeting were very bitter. Colonel Graff himself thought that this blow to reservist morale had been unnecessary.[76]

Graff was persuasive, and Stratemeyer attempted to repair some of the damage. On April 15 he directed the air forces to resume organizing the units and he also urged his commanders to launch an aggressive publicity campaign to disseminate this news to the greatest possible number of Army Air Forces veterans. The air force commanders were to send their public relations officers and other qualified personnel to the locations where units were proposed for activation and conduct the same kind of campaign Stratemeyer had called for in connection with the original opening of the reserve training detachments. In this instance, however, the speakers were to explain the economic reasons for

First Postwar Air Reserve Program

closing the twenty-nine detachments and transferring the P-51s to the Air National Guard.[77]

The Role of the Associations

As a movement, the various service associations comprised a strong voice on Air Reserve matters which the Army Air Forces, and later the U.S. Air Force, could not ignore. They were well-organized lobbies and offered effective channels of complaint for individual reservists. By the end of 1947, the Air Force Association and the Air Power League had joined the Reserve Officers Association and the Air Reserve Association as civilian air power groups.

Although often critical of official inactivity or incompetence, the service associations fostered the ends of the postwar air power movement. Soon after the war, each of these three associations issued major policy statements supporting air power. In October 1946, the Air Force committee of the Reserve Officers Association urged upon Army Air Forces' officials twenty-two measures for improving the "manifestly inadequate" Air Reserve program. Along with a number of administrative measures, the committee's suggestions included establishment of a Class A unit program with a minimum of 75 tactical groups and support units; establishment of at least 200 Air Reserve bases with adequate equipment, maintenance, and personnel; provision of funds for flight and ground training; active duty training for all Air Reserve personnel; inclusion of funds in the fiscal 1948 budget and thereafter for inactive duty training pay of all flying and nonflying Air Reserve personnel; and lowering the priority of the affiliation units, which it saw as inefficient.[78]

In November 1946, Col. Theron B. Herndon, president of the Air Reserve Association, urged General Spaatz to act on inactive duty training pay, the participation in reserve flying activities of noncommissioned officers of the Regular Army who held reserve commissions in the Air Corps Reserve, and the expediting of reserve flying physicals.[*79]

Speaking at the Air Reserve Association's convention at Memphis later that month, General Partridge responded to Colonel Herndon's criticism and tried to explain the program's difficulties. He thought that much of the difficulty had been caused by the Army Air Forces' inability to reach reservists with program information because of the chaotic condition of their personnel records. He also noted that no administrative machinery existed to handle a

---

[*]Some measure of the influence of the Air Reserve Association in the early postwar years may be derived from the fact that 17 of 19 Air Force Reserve colonels promoted to brigadier general in January 1948 were leaders of the association, including the national president (Release, HQ ADC [promotion of Air Force Reserve colonels], 1 Apr 48–AFRES IX C).

The Air Force Reserve

national reserve program until the Air Defense Command's six numbered air forces were created.

General Partridge refuted characterization of the initial $40 million appropriation as inadequate. He maintained that although it was less than the headquarters had requested, the amount was sufficient for the progressive implementation of the program planned for fiscal year 1947. He declared that the limited size of that initial appropriation was due largely to the fact that all aircraft and most other equipment were being obtained from surplus stocks and that instructor personnel were being paid from Regular Army funds. Moreover, where Regular Army Air Forces installations were used, no cost was associated with the use of the facilities. Finally, he said, the program started from scratch in July 1946 and would not reach full operation until mid-1947.

General Partridge also disagreed with Colonel Herndon's recommendation that Headquarters Army Air Forces establish an Air Staff section comparable to the War Department's Executive for National Guard and Reserve Affairs. He argued that if all matters pertaining to the Air Reserve were concentrated in a single office, it would be necessary to set up a small-scale Air Staff within that office. This would require a large number of people, many of whom would be duplicating work being conducted elsewhere in the headquarters. The Air Staff had concluded that Air Reserve activities were so broad in scope and so important in character that they required the attention of the heads of Air Staff sections, and accordingly, it established the Reserve and National Guard Division as a small monitoring office. Any decisions affecting the Air Reserve received consideration through the heads of the Air Staff sections concerned, and when necessary, they were approved by the Chief of the Air Staff in the same manner as those that affected Regular Army Air Forces activities.[80]

Partridge's argument was eminently sound from the point of view of the Air Staff, but then as later, this group made no effort to understand the reservist's perspective. Blithely ignoring the nature of the reservist grounded in his part-time, immobile availability, Regular Air Force officials took the same approach to managing the Air Reserve as they did to managing the active force, and it simply would not work.

Coming late to the scene, the Air Force Association formed in New York in 1945 to foster fellowship among Army Air Forces veterans and members, to promote recognition of airpower, and to disseminate information on new developments in the field of aviation. Among the resolutions it passed at its first national convention in Columbus, Ohio, in September 1947 were many demanding a better organized and financed Air Reserve program.[81]

First Postwar Air Reserve Program

Evaluating the First Effort

By the end of fiscal 1948, the Army Air Forces and the U.S. Air Force had been conducting the post–World War II Air Reserve program for two years. Restricted by budget reductions, the program had not achieved the training objectives envisioned for either 1947 or 1948. The original 1947 plan called for 170,000 reservists, including 22,500 pilots, to be enrolled in inactive duty training. Following the budget cuts of January 1947, a reduced plan called for 30,600 reservists overall and 9,500 pilots. In the end, 10,058 reservists, comprising 9,061 pilots, 656 other rated officers, 138 nonrated officers, and 203 enlisted men, participated. Of them, 1,160 officers and 200 enlisted men underwent active duty tours for training. The 1947 plan called for the organization of 312 combat units and 656 service units, but only 75 Class C combat units and 5 service units below division level were organized. As occurred in the 1947 program, reductions in the 1948 effort were announced at midyear. The original program again called for 170,000 reservists to participate in inactive duty training, with all to receive active duty training tours. A revised plan reduced the overall figure to 37,712, with about half programmed for active duty tours. Actual participants numbered 25,112, of whom 21,460 performed active duty tours. Suffering from stop-and-go programming, the Air Defense Command managed to have 289 units in existence by June 1948; 264 were combat and 25 were service.[82]

Aside from budget restrictions, other factors generally beyond the command's control limited the Air Force Reserve program's progress. Two were paramount: relegation of the Air Reserve as an augmentation force, in contrast to the Air National Guard's lofty status as a mobilization force, and consequent lower support priorities; and the absence of firm Army Air Forces/Air Force mobilization plans. All else—delays in acquiring personnel, bases, facilities, equipment, and aircraft, and budqet reductions—flowed from these two.

By the end of fiscal 1948, Brig. Gen. John P. McConnell had concluded that most problems in administering and training the Air Reserve Forces would disappear if the two components were combined into a single federally controlled reserve force.[83] Evaluating the Air Reserve program in September 1948, McConnell enumerated five major factors for the Army Air Forces' failure to develop a realistic, phased, Air Reserve program. The first was that Headquarters Army Air Forces and all its agencies had been too absorbed in the quest for air autonomy to spare much thought to the reserve programs. Second, the programming necessary for the realistic buildup of the seventy-group active force precluded detailed programming for the Air Reserve. Third, the rehabilitation of the Army Air Forces following its collapse upon demobilization also consumed the Air Staff's energies. Then there was the fact that nothing existed of comparable nature before the war to serve as a guide for

The Air Force Reserve

As Chief of the Civilian Components Group, in September 1948 Brig. Gen. John P. McConnell conducted the first comprehensive evaluation of the postwar Army Air Forces reserve program.

devising the new program. Finally, General McConnell asserted that there had been a general apathy on the part of World War II veterans for active association in any part of the military establishment, including the Reserves, with the exception of the flying program. This last was not universally true. Possibly a majority of World War II veterans shunned reserve participation, but a great many would have accepted it if the Army Air Forces had managed to bring a program to them, as witness the hundreds of letters from veterans complaining about the lack of such a program and the 25,000 who actually participated in a manifestly inadequate program.

Aside from these major causes of the failure of the initial Air Reserve program, McConnell also identified some lesser, contributory factors. The Army Air Forces, for example, was hindered in conceiving and conducting its reserve programs by its subordination to the Office of the Executive for Reserve and ROTC Affairs in the War Department, which had little understanding of and less care for the nature of an air reserve. The dilution of the Air Defense Command's reserve training efforts and resources in a network of satellite bases and pickup stations in an attempt to satisfy reservists and congressmen was an flagrant error, McConnell thought. Finally, greatly restricting all its efforts was the Army Air Forces' absolute inability to arrive at anything like a firm estimate of the amount of funds that would be available to it for reserve training from year to year.

First Postwar Air Reserve Program

General McConnell observed that the Air Reserve program had been permitted, with minor modifications dictated by expediency, to continue for lack of anything better. Each succeeding year the goal of achieving the entire program was reestablished unrealistically as a requirement for the following year. Funds, materiel, and personnel were not available, and probably would not become available, but each year the leadership went back to the first step, and no progressive phase or plan had been possible to implement.

The tendency was to judge the first postwar Air Reserve program a failure. Nevertheless, by the terms of the approved plan under which the Air Defense Command had conducted the program, it did not perform so badly. The plan had stipulated that Air Reserve training would initially take the form of a flying club with the primary objective of providing pilot proficiency.[84] Although budget cuts reduced the number of places at which the command could offer flying training (compared with the Air Force Reserve program of the 1980s), that flying club was pretty active. With an average of 1,100 aircraft on hand monthly and about 9,500 pilots participating, the Air Reserve program generated a total of 1,070,828 flying hours in fiscal years 1947 and 1948.[85] In fiscal year 1982 (when by all standard measures the Air Force Reserve performed exceedingly well), with an average of 420 aircraft on hand monthly, 2,751 pilots flew 209,517 hours.[86]

By August 1948, when McConnell developed his assessment, the Air Staff was completing a comprehensive review of the Air Force Reserve program with the goal of revising it extensively. However, many other government agencies, including the Office of the President, had also interested themselves in the problem and were conducting their own evaluations. In fiscal 1949 the Air Force would not be the sole arbiter of the destiny of the Air Force Reserve.

3

Development of a New Program 1948–1949

> The Secretary of Defense, and the head of each department in the National Military Establishment shall proceed without delay... to organize all reserve component units, and to train such individuals now or hereafter members of the active reserve, as may be required for the national security; and to establish vigorous and progressive programs of appropriate instruction and training for all elements of the reserve components, including the National Guard.
>
> —Harry S. Truman, Executive Order 10007, October 15, 1948

The Air Force Reserve and its role in national defense were under review throughout 1948 as the White House, Congress, the Office of the Secretary of Defense, and the Air Force itself sought to define the place of the component. This examination was conducted in a Cold War environment that led to the reinstatement of the draft as a major source of manpower for the military services. As approved in June 1948, moreover, the new Selective Service Act was intended to strengthen the reserve as well as the active forces.

Under constant criticism for the inadequacy of its Air Force Reserve program, the Air Force began to revise it in 1948. Before the Air Staff could complete this task, however, the President himself intervened to direct the military establishment to vitalize its reserve programs. Thus stimulated, the Air Force moved expeditiously to implement the new reserve program it had been devising.

The Air Force Reserve

The Selective Service Act of 1948 and the Reserve

On March 17, 1948, after consulting with the National Security Council, President Truman went before Congress and asked for three measures to reinforce the security of the nation in the face of mounting evidence that the Cold War would intensify. He asked Congress to fund the European Recovery Program fully in the belief that strengthened economies would enable European nations to resist Soviet pressure. With respect to the armed forces, the President asked Congress to reinstate the draft and to authorize and fund a universal training program.[1]

The President and Congress had let the wartime Selective Service and Training Act expire on March 31, 1947, at a time when the service recruiting programs seemed to be meeting reduced postwar authorizations for manpower. A year later, however, enlistments were not keeping pace with need, and citing the nation's depleted military strength and the fact that the threat to peace and security worldwide seemed as serious as it had at any time in the past, the President asked that the draft be reinstated.[2]

The Senate Armed Services Committee was already conducting hearings on defense manpower needs in peacetime, and a selective service bill progressed rapidly through both houses. Approved as Public Law 80–759 on June 24, the Selective Service Act of 1948 required every male citizen and resident of the United States between the ages of 18 and 26 years to register for the draft. Each man inducted was to serve on active duty for 21 months and then be reassigned to a reserve component for 5 years. While in reserve status, no one was required to render active duty service or attend drills or classes. A man could reduce his obligation by 2 years if he enlisted in an organized reserve unit, or he could discharge it entirely by remaining on active duty for an additional year. The law also provided that up to 161,000 18-year-olds could enlist for one year, acquiring a reserve obligation of 6 years. Two provisions of the law would significantly affect the Air Force Reserve soon thereafter. By providing that enlistment in an active unit of a reserve component meant deferment from active duty, the law encouraged voluntary enlistment with the intention of strengthening the reserve components, and many young men availed themselves of the opportunity. The law also gave the President easier access to the reserve forces by authorizing him to mobilize voluntarily members of the reserve components for no more than 21 months without declaring a national emergency or asking Congress to declare war. The Selective Service Act of 1948 was to remain effective for 2 years, that is, to June 24, 1950.[3]

In addition to giving the President the Selective Service Act, Congress enacted the European Recovery Program he had sought, but once again it withheld authorization of a universal training program. The Senate Armed Services Committee concluded that the passage of a bill providing for both

Development of a New Program

selective service and universal training was inexpedient both from fiscal and political standpoints. The committee did not believe that the military service could develop the required active force strength in 1948 while simultaneously initiating a universal training program. The Senate also noted a changing signal from the White House on universal training. Supplemental appropriations for fiscal year 1948 would be required to finance the actions the President requested of Congress on March 17. In a compromise with the Joint Chiefs of Staff on the amount of the supplemental appropriation, Secretary of Defense James V. Forrestal dropped recommendations for universal training. When the President accepted the revised proposal and authorized Secretary Forrestal to present it to Congress, the legislators were quick to note the omission.[4]

Passage of the Selective Service Act of 1948 without adoption of universal military training meant that if the United States engaged in another war, its reserve forces would consist of veterans, either from World War II or those created by the Selective Service Act. That force would be the only source of expansion for the active forces.

The Gray Committee Reviews the Civilian Components

On November 20, 1947, Secretary Forrestal appointed the Committee on Civilian Components under Assistant Secretary of the Army Gordon Gray to review the civilian components. Forrestal charged Secretary Gray to consider seven issues: appropriate missions and functions for the civilian components; their size, composition, and organization; uniformity and standardization of policies, procedures, and practices among the several reserve components; joint use of facilities, equipment, and training personnel; training and ROTC programs; relationships of the several civilian components to the regular forces; and procurement and retention of the best quality of personnel for the civilian components.[5]

Along with Secretary Gray as chairman, the Committee on Civilian Components included an assistant secretary and one other member from each of the services. The Air Force members of the committee were Assistant Secretary Cornelius V. Whitney and General McConnell, then the Chief of the Reserve and National Guard Division of the Directorate of Training and Requirements. Welcoming the establishment of the committee, Secretary Whitney represented an Air Force point of view that sought greater equity and uniformity in reserve matters—standardization of personnel and promotion policies; uniformity of pay and emoluments; equity in retirement, insurance, and ROTC policies; and standardization of procurement of personnel.[6]

Reporting to Secretary Forrestal on June 30, 1948, the committee offered ninety conclusions and recommendations. As the centerpiece of its report, the committee asserted that national security required that each service have one

The Air Force Reserve

As Secretary of Defense, in October 1948 James V. Forrestal strongly resisted President Truman's desire to publish an executive order directing the military services to vitalize their reserve forces.

federal reserve force and it called for the individual services to merge their civilian components. Air Force implementation of the recommendation would require that the Air National Guard be merged into the Air Force Reserve.

The body concluded that of the six civilian components, only the Naval Reserve was then capable of discharging its major combat missions upon mobilization. While conceding that part of the Air Force Reserve's problem was the lingering influence of War Department and Organized Reserve Corps policies, the committee blamed the Air Force itself for others. It noted that the Air Force had given reserve pilots the opportunity to maintain flight proficiency but then largely negated the effort by failing to give them modern aircraft to fly. Moreover, it had done little to maintain the efficiency of its nonrated reserve personnel. The commission regarded the Air Force Reserve composite units as ineffective because they lacked a comprehensive training plan to cover disparate specialties in a single unit, and it criticized the Air Force for its decision to give a little training to many people rather than concentrating its efforts on an essential hard core.

Contrary to the tendency of the Air Defense Command to orient the Air Force Reserve program as an individual augmentation force, the Gray committee stated that the Air Force's mobilization requirements called for organized units, both for training and combat. It recommended that all Air Force Reservists be organized into tactical or training units to facilitate administration and training. It also suggested a number of means to increase the time allotted to training as well as improve its caliber and uniformity. It asserted the flow of trained personnel into the Air Force Reserve should be continuous, which would not only eliminate the need for basic training in the units but also enable all members to progress more rapidly. It recommended that full-time personnel, preferably reservists on extended active duty, be assigned as members of Air Reserve units in administrative positions.[7]

The opposition of the Reserve Officers Association, the National Guard Association of the United States, and the Adjutant Generals Association blocked implementation of the Gray committee's recommendation that the guard and reserve components be merged. President Truman judged the committee's report as "political dynamite . . . during a Presidential campaign," but he promised to discuss some of its general ideas and specific recommendations later with the Secretary of Defense.[8]

Reflecting later upon his report's sudden loss of popularity, Secretary Gray recalled that Secretary Forrestal accepted it and distributed advance copies to the press. Then, suddenly, people began backing away from it, especially Gray's politically attuned superiors who anticipated the storm the report's merger recommendations would raise with the state governors. Bending before the political winds, Forrestal withdrew the report before its official release date, thereby generating more publicity.[9] Although the Gray committee's major recommendation for merger was rejected, many others were at least partially implemented, and the principles the committee proclaimed became a baseline for many subsequent reserve forces studies.

Development of U.S. Air Force Reserve Policies

While the Gray committee delved and reported, the Air Force itself was attempting to impart more realism into its reserve programs. The Air Reserve program had never satisfied its participants, and, abetted by the Air Reserve Association and the Reserve Officers Association, the reservists complained bitterly to the White House, Congress, the National Military Establishment, and the Air Force about perceived inadequacies.

In January 1948, Maj. Gen. Junius W. Jones, the Air Force Inspector General, recommended sweeping changes in the reserve program to General Spaatz. General Jones believed that the primary domestic mission of the Air Force should be to train the reserves. This led him to recommend that the Air Force eliminate the Air Defense Command; assign Air National Guard units, along with the continental air defense mission, to the Tactical Air Command; develop the fifty-five group program authorized in the President's 1949 budget, augmented by Air Force Reservists as necessary; activate the fifteen additional groups to round out the seventy-group force, supplementing cadres of regulars

The Air Force Reserve

with reservists; make Saturdays and Sundays Air Force workdays to accommodate reservist availability, with Tuesdays and Wednesdays off; and utilize all available Air Force facilities to train reservists on Saturdays and Sundays. Although conceding that some of General Jones' suggestions had merit, the Air Staff generally rejected his proposals as too radical.[10]

Nevertheless, General Jones' proposals led the Air Staff to examine the management of the reserve program. Among the questions considered was whether the Reserve and National Guard Division, which had been headed by General McConnell for several months, should continue under a Regular Air Force general officer or whether it should be relegated to a lower place on the staff under a National Guard or a reserve officer called to active duty. General Stratemeyer offered the unsolicited advice that placing a guard or reserve officer at the head of the division would be a mistake. He told General Spaatz that since McConnell had headed the division, Headquarters Air Defense Command had been kept better informed, papers had been acted upon more expeditiously, and the command's whole job with the reserve forces had been facilitated by the superior work performed by General McConnell and his staff. Stratemeyer believed that the Air National Guard would resent a reservist's being placed in charge of the division, and that the reverse would be true if a guardsman were given the post. He recommended that the function be elevated on the Air Staff under a Regular Air Force major general with an Air National Guard brigadier general and an Air Force Reserve brigadier general on extended active duty to assist him with their respective programs.[11] McConnell's conscientious performance of his job did indeed serve the Air Reserve components well, but there was no inherent guarantee that his successors in the position would be equally dedicated and possess the same understanding of the reserve programs.

While the placement of the reserve oversight function in the Air Staff was being determined, McConnell and Headquarters Air Defense Command intensified their efforts to develop new policies upon which to revise the Air Force Reserve program. In developing the Air Defense Command proposals, General Stratemeyer appointed a board of reserve officers under Brig. Gen. Joseph L. Whitney to evaluate the old program. Although emphasizing the standard reserve complaints about inequities in pay, privileges, training opportunities, and equipment, General Whitney's report now had the advantage of registering these complaints in the official report of a review board established at least in part for that purpose. Entered into formal Air Defense Command reporting channels, the grumbling was dignified beyond the status of association meeting discussions and bar talk. Now Air Force officialdom had to acknowledge it. On the policy level, General Whitney recommended that the priority of the Air Force Reserve program be invested in training the individuals necessary to bring active force units up to their wartime strengths. He also suggested that full-time personnel, preferably reservists, be assigned to newly established reserve units to give them some continuity in training and administration.[12]

On February 27, 1948, General Stratemeyer submitted a set of new principles to McConnell on which to develop an Air Force Reserve program. They asserted the absolute necessity for identifying Air Force mobilization requirements, ascertaining the status of currently assigned reservists, identifying firm training standards for both reserve units and individuals, and assuring a flow of trained personnel into the Air Force Reserve, either from active duty or appropriate civilian occupations. Reflecting the views of General Whitney's board, Stratemeyer's staff thought that the Air Force Reserve program's first priority should be to provide individual reservists to enable active force units to attain their wartime strengths. As a second priority, the Air Defense Command recommended that the Air Force identify new valid wartime requirements for individuals and units which the Air Force Reserve could satisfy. Only as a third priority should the Air Force create reserve combat and service units to be located primarily at bases where Regular Air Force or Air National Guard units with identical missions were also housed. McConnell incorporated the Air Defense Command thinking into a position paper which he later circulated through the Air Staff for comment.[13]

On March 3, meanwhile, Lt. Gen. Lauris Norstad, Deputy Chief of Staff for Operations, solicited McConnell's views on strengthening the Air Force Reserve. McConnell urged upon General Norstad the need for greater participation of all commands in reserve training, higher priority in procuring reserve training aids and equipment, definition of specific reserve mobilization requirements, selective assignment of reservists as permanent party personnel in training centers, and greater efforts in securing an adequate reserve budget.[14]

Then, on March 22, 1948, General Spaatz removed the Reserve and National Guard Division from the Directorate of Training and Operations and established it as the Civilian Components Group under General McConnell, reporting directly to General Norstad. The move was undertaken to elevate the visibility of the reserve components in the Air Staff.[15]

Thus, reacting to universal criticism, throughout fiscal year 1948 the Air Staff and the Air Defense Command strove to strengthen the Air Force Reserve program. Closer to the problem than any other official, General Stratemeyer had established General Whitney's board to help analyze the program and identify its weaknesses. At the instigation of McConnell, the Air Staff had studied the problem and was moving toward establishing firm Air Force policy for the administration and training of the Air Force Reserve. On October 6, General McConnell announced new policies for governing the Air Force Reserve program for the remainder of fiscal 1949 and beyond.[16] The hour was late, however, and by that time the Air Force had already lost its initiative to the President of the United States.

The Air Force Reserve

The President Demands a Revitalization of the Reserve Program

On June 25, 1948, Maj. Gen. Harry H. Vaughan, U.S. Army, President Truman's military aide, and William H. Neblett, who had just relinquished the presidency of the Reserve Officers Association, discussed an action with the twofold objective of strengthening the reserve components and reelecting the President. They sought a presidential directive to expand the nation's reserve programs into every corner of the land to give all reservists the opportunity to participate. The next day, Neblett furnished Vaughan a draft presidential memorandum which would direct the Secretary of Defense to act.

Neblett urged that the memo be sent and publicized at once. He observed that if it appeared that very week, it would have a salutary effect on the Democratic National Convention's resolutions committee. Moreover, it would impress the large number of the convention delegates who were veterans and reservists. The directive would garner to the President the immediate support of the majority of the nation's twelve million veterans of World War II as well as the parents of the young men then subject to the draft or about to come of military age. It would, he thought, "probably collapse the Eisenhower boom in the south." He also outlined several other advantages the directive would offer. Among them Neblett thought that such a presidential directive would support the Selective Service Act's purpose of building an adequate reserve, revive in the public's mind the need for universal military training, and weaken the Republican Party's plank on national defense. He maintained that the directive's most important effect was the probability that in the upcoming election it would generate support for the President from veterans and patriotic organizations.[17]

The President did not immediately issue the proposed order, but on July 22, he asked the Secretary of Defense some penetrating questions about the reserve forces in the context of the recently passed Selective Service Act. Basically, he wanted to know how many Organized Reserve units were capable of conducting unit drills, how many men were assigned to them, how many men were being held in reserve pools, and what arrangements were being made to provide facilities and equipment to execute the training programs contemplated.[18]

The President wanted this information by August 2, but Secretary Forrestal put him off pending an analysis of the Gray committee's report, of which he furnished the President a synopsis. Reflecting General Vaughan's prompting, Truman rejected most of the proposals enumerated in the summary on the basis of their resting on a false premise. They were based, he said, "upon the assumption we have an organized reserve," and he protested that if the reserves were really organized, the substantial amendments proposed by the Gray committee to the National Defense Act of 1916 were unnecessary.

To take advantage of the availability of almost two million veterans of all

Development of a New Program

services who had accepted some kind of reserve affiliation, but whose terms would soon expire, President Truman wanted the Secretary of Defense and the military departments to organize all into actual units located as near their homes as practicable. This would establish the nucleus which the Gray committee report implied already existed. He wanted this organization of the reserves completed by October.[19]

Not getting satisfactory responses from the Secretary of Defense, on October 5 President Truman had General Vaughan and John R. Steelman, a presidential assistant, draft an executive order directing what steps he wanted taken. The proposed order proclaimed it necessary for national defense that strong volunteer citizen military forces be organized throughout the United States. It directed the Secretary of Defense to organize by January 1, 1949, reserve units of one or more components in every state and to assign all reservists to units of their own component established near their homes. The draft explained that the purpose of the directed actions was to augment those units of the Organized Reserve which already existed and to make the skills of veterans whose training had already been financed available on a unit basis at a relatively small cost.[20]

From this action and remarks the President made from time to time, it seemed he wanted a far-flung network of reserve units so extensive that every veteran in the country could be assigned to some organization and have a sense of belonging, the very thing for which the Gray committee had criticized the Air Force. The President was conditioned by his long membership in the National Guard and Army Reserve artillery and infantry units, where the basic requirement had been for riflemen, ammunition loaders, and stretcher bearers—soldiers with mundane skills requiring little practice in peacetime to maintain efficiency. Comradeship and serving with one's friends and neighbors had counted for much when the future President and Harry Vaughan had served during and after World War I. This approach was impractical for the Air Force because the required number of skilled ground or air technicians was not available at every crossroads of the nation.

Secretary Forrestal received the draft executive order on October 6 while he was at lunch with the three service secretaries and their military chiefs. Truman had sought their counsel on its wording, but they rejected its very concept. Forrestal sent word back, "I have just read the Order, and I want to urge you as strongly as I can against signing any order of this type."

The secretary thought the order would have great political repercussions because it omitted the National Guard. He objected that his office had been making strenuous efforts to strengthen the reserve components, an effort complicated by the fact that the Air Force and the Army each included reserve and National Guard components. Defense officials were developing plans to implement many of the Gray committee's recommendations. Aside from the question of merger, he said, many highly constructive steps could be taken.

The Air Force Reserve

Some would require legislation, but most could be implemented by administrative action.

Forrestal protested that the President's proposed executive order would jeopardize the orderly progress then being made. Moreover, he warned that the proposed organization of reserve units in all communities of the United States by January 1, 1949, would seriously disrupt the military establishment's plans for augmenting the strength of the regular forces themselves. He simply could not believe the President was willing to divert the money and effort that would be required to execute this directive. Forrestal thought the costs in new armories alone would be more than $1 billion, and other material and pay requirements would undoubtedly require major readjustments in the entire federal budget in the coming year.

Forrestal so strongly opposed the proposed order that he refused to do anything about it until discussing it with the President. As a candidate for reelection, President Truman was then traveling on a campaign train, and Secretary Forrestal could not sit down with him to discuss the matter. So the initial communications between them on the subject were transmitted by official pouch, with attendant delays.[21]

Consistent with the Truman White House procedures, Mr. Steelman turned over the draft executive order and supporting notes to Frank Pace, Jr., the acting Director of the Budget, for completion. Mr. Pace revised the draft to avoid some of the problems identified by Forrestal while still satisfying the objectives of President Truman. He included the National Guard in the directive's purview. Pace also agreed with Forrestal's belief that it would be impracticable to establish reserve units in every community in the United States, certainly not by January 1, 1949. The armed forces were not organized to do this, and many communities were not capable of supporting any kind of a reserve unit. In the absence of adequate plans and personnel to carry them out, an order establishing such a deadline could not be executed. The failure would arouse severe criticism and might defeat the entire purpose of the order. Pace's revised draft contemplated immediate action to establish vigorous reserve and guard programs without setting a deadline. However, it required a report of progress within sixty days.

Like Forrestal, Pace saw that the program would be extremely expensive both initially and for the foreseeable future. He estimated it would cost more than $1 billion to start the program, and at peak operation, continuing pay and training costs would require billions annually. Mr. Pace was also concerned by the implied requirement to expand the reserve without regard to other current activities of the armed forces which heretofore had been given some priority. Diversion of the personnel and material resources of the regular armed forces establishment to a very large-scale reserve program would impair other activities, including the manning of the regular forces in the combat units.[22]

Nevertheless, Pace envisioned several actions which could be taken by the

Development of a New Program

Departments of the Army and the Air Force to apply the President's wishes without impairing other programs of equal or higher priority. He outlined these specific actions to remedy some of the serious problems in the reserve programs in a proposed letter of instruction to the Secretary of Defense that would accompany the executive order.[23] Returning to Washington for the weekend, the President reviewed the two drafts on Saturday, October 9. Basically satisfied with them, he made a few editorial comments before handing them to Secretary Forrestal during a meeting the next day.[24]

Forrestal remained distressed by the proposed order and urged the President not to issue it. He still insisted that, far from being neglected, the reserve programs had been of primary importance to the service staffs. The major difficulties to date, he said, had stemmed from the lack of funds, equipment, and facilities, with consequent effects on individual participation. Another major problem was a shortage of instructors, particularly in the Army Reserve and Air Reserve Forces programs. He now submitted the statistical data the President had initially requested, earlier submission of which might have forestalled the whole business. He also asserted that the "Unit training programs are flexible, comprehensive, and adequate to meet requirements," to which, passing the letter on to the President, General Vaughan added the marginal notation, "This is not true."[25]

The secretary summed up his argument by saying he was convinced that the reserve programs of the three services were reasonably sound because they were based upon mobilization requirements—which was certainly not true of the Air Force program—however, its implementation was handicapped by a lack of funds. He also stated that the major effort should be directed toward full implementation of existing programs. Augmentation beyond the requirements of these programs would exceed mobilization requirements and adversely affect the establishment's major objectives through diversion of the limited means available. On October 15, he again recommended the proposed executive order be withheld. Against the probability that the President would insist, however, Forrestal submitted an alternative executive order which the military services would find more palatable than the original had been. Mr. Steelman incorporated Forrestal's ideas into the final version of the order.[26]

President Truman was not dissuaded and released the executive order during a press conference aboard his campaign train at Clarksburg, West Virginia, on October 16. Dated a day earlier, the order directed the Secretary of Defense and the service secretaries to invigorate their reserve programs.

> The Secretary of Defense, and head of each department in the National Military Establishment, shall proceed without delay, utilizing every practicable resource of the regular components of the armed forces, to organize all reserve component units, and to train such additional individuals now or hereafter members of the active reserve, as may be required for the national security; and to establish vigorous and progressive programs of

The Air Force Reserve

appropriate instruction and training for all elements of the reserve components, including the National Guard.[27]

In an accompanying letter, the President further directed the secretary to report within sixty days on the action taken and to propose any legislation deemed necessary.

Although he generally disagreed with the Gray committee's report, President Truman accepted its view that Naval Reserve programs were superior to those of the other services and he gave Secretary Forrestal additional guidance for strengthening the Army and Air Force Reserve programs. He requested the assignment of an active, capable, high-ranking officer to head the reserve program in each department; the assignment of adequate numbers of young and vigorous officers as instructors and administrative officers to reserve training programs; increased attention on the part of all General Staff and Air Staff divisions to planning and directing reserve activities and reviewing reserve program progress; development and institution of training programs which would hold the interest of reservists at all levels and would maintain and improve their military skills; and the provision of more adequate training facilities and equipment, including active cooperation among all reserve components in the effective use of existing facilities.[28]

In a public statement the President appealed to all citizens to do their part in aiding the development of effective reserve components and he appealed to those qualified to take an active part in building up the strong and highly trained reserve forces which he considered so vital to the defense of the United States to do so. He confirmed his dissatisfaction with the Army and Air Force Reserve programs while complimenting the "progress which has been made by the Navy Department and the members of the Naval and Marine Corps Reserve in building up their post-war Reserve organizations" and the recent successes of the National Guard. For many reasons, though, he lamented, "the Organized Reserve Corps of the Army and the Air Force have not made as rapid progress." He went on to assure Army and Air Force Reservists that "the full force of the Government will be exerted toward creating appropriate and effective reserve establishments as rapidly as possible."[29]

The Reserve Officers Association hailed President Truman as something of a reserve folk hero for issuing the executive order and counted this action among its own "historic victories."[30] Nevertheless, President Truman had always had the power to do more for the reserve forces. If cool toward universal training, Congress was otherwise cooperative on defense matters, even to the point of appropriating more money than the President wanted.*

---

*A coalition of congressmen from the Midwest and South blocked a succession of universal training bills in the House. Midwesterners opposed the concept of the legislation for its high cost, similarity to peacetime conscription, and encouragement

Development of a New Program

Consummate politician that he was, it is unlikely that President Truman would have overlooked the potential vote that would accrue to him by taking an action that would appeal to veterans. He was involved in a presidential election many experts said he could not win. The idea for the executive order originated with Mr. Neblett's conversations with General Vaughan, and at least part of the President's public statement was addressed to veterans. There were about twelve million of them among the electorate when he assured members of the Army and Air Force Reserves that the government was about to exert its full force in creating, as soon as possible, effective reserve establishments, and he could expect some support at the polls.

Having been directed by their Commander in Chief to act, Secretary Forrestal and the Air Force did so. In addition to establishing the Office of Special Assistant to the Chief of Staff for Reserve Forces in Headquarters U.S. Air Force (USAF), the Air Force quickly published regulations governing inactive duty pay for reservists and allotted funds to the field for that purpose. It also allotted mobilization assignment quotas and training funds to the major commands and surveyed the Air Force Reserve training centers with a view to relocating reserve units to provide better coverage of the reserve population and more realistic training activity. The major commanders were directed to emphasize reserve forces training, and newly revised directives specified each Air Staff agency's responsibilities to the reserve forces.

Secretary of the Air Force W. Stuart Symington advised Secretary Forrestal that the Air Force was developing a corollary unit training program to make the resources of active force units available for reserve training. Corollary units consisting of Air Force Reservists, formed in the vicinity of Regular Air Force bases, were trained and administered by Regular Air Force units of the same type, and used Regular Air Force equipment. The service was also developing a plan to use reservists on extended active duty to serve as instructors for reserve units and to staff the training centers.[31]

Evaluating the adequacy of the Air Force's proposed and actual steps to implement the executive order, Brig. Gen. Robert B. Landry, President Truman's Air Force aide, assured the President that if the Air Force carried the reported actions through to their logical conclusion, "the Air Force Reserve, as a whole, can assume its proper place as a component of our Armed Forces." As he led the President point-by-point through the Air Force report, General Landry defended some of his service's actions. He noted the importance the Air Force attached to the proposed merger of its two reserve components and

---

of militarism; Southerners' opposed it on the grounds that it encouraged racial desegregation ("Universal Military Training," in Sundry Legislation Affecting the Naval and Military Establishments 1952, Hearings before Committee on Armed Services, 82d Cong., 2d sess., GPO 1952, pp 2293–2301 passim; *Congressional Record*, vol 98, Pts 1 & 2, pp 1421–25).

The Air Force Reserve

speculated that the resultant consolidation of sites would alleviate the facilities problem. General Landry went out of his way to discuss the implications of one of the personnel proposals that would run counter to the President's announced wishes. He recounted how funds shortages had forced the Army Air Forces to reduce its initial 131-base program and how the Air Defense Command had devised a system of satellite bases and pickup stations to sustain the widespread training effort. The Air Force's current planning, on the basis of expected funds for fiscal year 1950 and a new policy of training only the number of reservists who could be adequately prepared, would result in a further reduction to about twenty-seven training bases.

General Landry conceded that such an action would undoubtedly have national repercussions and reduce the likelihood of a nationwide reserve presence that the President sought. Nevertheless, he expressed his "strong feeling" that a small, well-organized and well-trained reserve establishment was more desirable than a larger and inadequately trained force.[32] In November 1948, General Hoyt S. Vandenberg, who had become Chief of Staff of the Air Force on April 30, 1948, appointed Lt. Gen. Elwood R. Quesada, Commander of Tactical Air Command, as the first Special Assistant to the Chief of Staff for Reserve Forces. His staff was drawn from the former Civilian Components Group headed by McConnell, who became General Quesada's deputy. In his new role, General Quesada was to act as the principal adviser to the Chief of Staff and assist him on all matters concerning the Air Force Reserve, the Air National Guard, the Air Force ROTC, the Civil Air Patrol, and the Air Scouts, and he was to coordinate the overall policy and implementation of the Air Reserve Forces programs. Vandenberg told Quesada that the success of the Air Force's efforts to vitalize the reserve forces programs would depend to a great extent upon the complete assumption by all Air Staff agencies and the major commands of their responsibilities to the reserve forces. He therefore suggested that Quesada assure himself that each Air Staff agency vigorously discharge equally the services for the reserve forces that they were providing for the active forces.[33]

General Quesada has been described as "an organizer, with a broad background and a facility for knowing how to get things done."[34] These talents failed him in his new job as Special Assistant to the Chief of Staff for Reserve Forces, for, by his own admission, he was unable to complete what he perceived to be his primary job. As he saw it, he was brought to Washington to preside over the demise of the Air National Guard. He said it was his job to prepare the legislation to merge the Air National Guard into the Air Force Reserve as recommended by the Gray committee. It was a fruitless task, "the political forces were such that there was no hope of getting it done."[35]

Oversight of the proposed merger was hardly the only thing Quesada was to do in his new job, but it was certainly a major one. Secretary Forrestal recommended to the President that the Gray committee's recommendations to

Development of a New Program

Lt. Gen. Elwood R. Quesada, Commanding General of the Tactical Air Command, responded actively and enthusiastically to support the air reserve program with the resources of his command.

merge the components be undertaken promptly, and Secretary Symington was anxious to get on with it.[36] On December 15, the Secretary of Defense designated the Air Force as the responsible agency to prepare appropriate legislation. Preliminary to drafting such a bill, General Vandenberg appointed General Quesada as chairman of an ad hoc committee established to study the problems the Air Force could anticipate when implementing such a merger. Briefing the Air Force's position to the Secretary of Defense late in January, General Quesada said the service felt so strongly about the need for the merger that if the Gray committee's recommendations were not accepted, the Air Force itself would frame the legislation to provide for a single, federal reserve component.[37]

General Quesada was right. The opposition of the Reserve Officers Association and the National Guard to a merger of the components was so vocal that Congress not only rejected the merger idea, it also established the Air National Guard as a legal component of the Air Force of the United States along with the U.S. Air Force and the Air Force Reserve. The battle was fought in February 1949 during hearings conducted by the House Committee on Armed Services on a bill to authorize the composition of the Army and the Air Force. In view of the proposed language of the bill and recommendations of the Gray committee (both supported by the Air Force), National Guard witnesses protested that interpretation of the proposed legislation would permit the Air Force to destroy the Air National Guard. Committee chairman Carl Vinson forced a compromise language that confirmed the existence of the Air National

The Air Force Reserve

Guard in law when the Army and Air Force Authorization Act of 1949 was eventually approved in 1950.[38] Celebrating their apparent victory, National Guard officials overlooked the significance that the law established the Air Force Reserve as an equal component of the Air Force.

The Air Force established the Office of the Special Assistant to the Chief of Staff for Reserve Forces in Headquarters USAF. It also reorganized its field structure for reserve matters, establishing the Continental Air Command on December 1, 1948, with headquarters at Mitchel AFB, New York. At the same time, the Air Defense Command and the Tactical Air Command were subordinated as operational air commands of the new organization. The six numbered air forces and the tactical units formerly assigned and attached to the two demoted commands were reassigned to Headquarters Continental Air Command. The numbered air forces were assigned area responsibilities, and their boundaries were made coterminous with those of the six U.S. Army areas. In addition to their roles as operational commands, Headquarters Air Defense Command and Headquarters Tactical Air Command were to act in their respective functions as staff for the Commanding General of the Continental Air Command.[39]

The purpose of these arrangements was to relieve the new Headquarters Continental Air Command of the burden of tactical air and defense planning, thus permitting it and its area air forces to devote the greater part of their energies to the administration and supervision of the training of the reserve forces. The reduction of the Air Defense and Tactical Air Commands to the status of operational commands also helped achieve the reductions in the budgets of the military services demanded by the new Defense Secretary, Louis Johnson.[40]

Phasing the 1950 Program into Being

Although there was a promise of a new deal for the Air Force Reserve, the program which the Continental Air Command inherited in December 1948 was essentially the same as the one in place in July 1947. Frozen in December 1947 by Headquarters USAF to allow a period of financial stocktaking, the program became static pending the results of a careful cost survey until late in the fiscal year.[41]

On March 8, 1949, the Air Force submitted a new program for the Air Force Reserve to the Bureau of the Budget for fiscal year 1950, with the hope that early approval would permit the service to initiate at least some of its elements immediately. After some Air Force prodding, on April 20, 1949, Frank Pace, Jr., then Director of the Bureau of the Budget, approved for presentation to Congress a revised fiscal year 1950 program for the Air Force Reserve at an estimated cost of $82 million.[42] As finally promulgated on May 9, 1949,

Development of a New Program

the Air Force Reserve program for fiscal year 1950 consisted of four distinct parts: the Air Force Reserve training centers supporting reserve combat wings, individual mobilization assignments, a new program of corollary units integrated with active force units, and a Volunteer Air Reserve training program to accommodate all reservists not fitted into one of the other three programs. In addition, all Air Force Reservists were encouraged to participate in an expanded Air Force correspondence course program. Headquarters USAF and the major commands were to conduct the corollary unit and mobilization assignment programs while the Continental Air Command would handle the rest.[43]

General McConnell's staff anticipated that paid training would be available to 12,523 mobilization assignees, 28,630 in the corollaries, and 36,113 in the reserve units assigned to the training centers. In addition, his staff expected that about 60,000 reservists would be attracted to participate in the Volunteer Air Reserve training program without pay but with credit toward promotion and retirement. Mobilization assignees were to be trained at active force facilities as were the corollary units which would operate at 107 locations. The Continental Air Command was to operate 23 centers to train 25 combat wings. The command would also conduct the extensive Volunteer Air Reserve training program which had no ceiling on its strength. By training and funding priority, the mobilization assignees ranked first; they were followed by the corollary units, the equipped wings, and the Volunteer Air Reserve training program. The mobilization assignee program was a continuation of the program the Air Force had started earlier in 1948 under which individual reservists were given M-Day assignments with an active force unit, organization, or agency.[44]

A superficial logic to the corollary unit concept appealed to government officials responsible for designing reserve programs. It just seemed so obvious that the best and simplest way to train a reservist was to mix him in with an existing regular force unit and let him go at it. This was the basic concept of the reserve corollary unit program as an integral part of the Air Force Reserve fiscal year 1950 program. It was an idea that appealed to President Truman, congressmen, and other civilian authorities. About a month before any of the other program elements had been approved in the spring of 1949, General Quesada told Secretary Symington that the corollary program had been accepted by the Budget Bureau and that the President had declared it was the best reserve program to date.[45]

The objective of the corollary unit was to develop sufficient individual and unit proficiency to permit employment of the corollary unit personnel immediately upon mobilization as individual replacements or augmentees or as an integral unit.[46] The Air Force Reserve training center program was also a continuation of the old center program, but the number of centers was reduced from 41 to 23, and they would provide the personnel, equipment, facilities, and manpower to administer and train 25 attached Air Force Reserve combat wings.[47]

Perhaps the principal difference between the Volunteer Air Reserve

The Air Force Reserve

training units and the composite units they replaced was that the new program was set in an organizational framework of wings, groups, squadrons, and flights. Although not conforming to any formal table of organization, the structure did provide a chain of administrative control. The avowed purpose of the program (really no different from that of its predecessor) was to keep assigned personnel abreast of new policies, procedures, weapons, and techniques of the Air Force and to maintain their military proficiency.[48]

By this time, the Air Staff Committee on Reserve Policy consisting of six reservists and six regular officers had come into being. The committee drew its authority from the National Security Act of 1947 which, in creating the Air Force, applied to it the provisions of the National Defense Act of 1916 for a reserve advisory body in the headquarters. The directive establishing the committee named McConnell as the chairman, but at the first meeting in June 1948 he invited the members to choose their own chairman, whereupon they unanimously selected reservist Brig. Gen. Robert J. Smith.[49]

The Air Staff Committee on Reserve Policy cautiously approved the program planned for 1950. Acknowledging that the plan was a substantial improvement, General Smith, nevertheless, cautioned that its favorable reception in the field would be determined by the speed with which the plan was executed and by carefully managed widespread publicity. General Smith further warned, "It is imperative that the revised program be given continuing emphasis and close scrutiny at all times to impress the Reservist that he is an important member of the National Defense Team."[50]

The fiscal year 1950 Air Force Reserve Program was designed for a three-year period, but it had barely thirteen months to operate before it would be tested by extensive mobilization of its members. In that short period, the Continental Air Command succeeded relatively well in building the combat wing and the Volunteer Air Reserve training programs for which it was responsible. It activated and equipped the twenty-five reserve combat wings at its flying centers in short order, and by the end of fiscal year 1950 the units were progressing acceptably toward operational readiness. The command even managed to enroll many thousands in the far-flung Volunteer Air Reserve program, despite its skimpy attractions. The rest of the Air Force did not succeed nearly so well with the higher priority programs. The corollary units were beset with sundry problems, and the Air Force never really defined the objective of the mobilization assignee program during fiscal year 1950.

The entire, new Air Force Reserve program was to become effective on July 1, but on May 6, 1949, General McConnell directed Headquarters Continental Air Command to implement immediately that phase of the new program pertaining to the training of Air Force Reserve wings at the twenty-three Air Force Reserve training centers. The reserve units included twenty troop carrier wings equipped with C–47s or C–46s and five light bombardment wings flying B–26s. These missions were selected for the Air Force Reserve

Development of a New Program

because the Air National Guard was already primarily a fighter force, and the Air Force did not have the installations, materiel, nor technical personnel to support medium and heavy bomber units in the Air Force Reserve. The reserve wings would differ from active force wings in that air installation, food services, air police, and motor vehicle squadrons were omitted from their organizations, and all units were limited to 25 percent of the normally required personnel and equipment. On the other hand, four tactical squadrons were allotted per wing instead of the usual three, thus providing a total of sixteen aircraft.[51] With the allocation of the last unit on August 4, 1949, the Air Force Reserve combat wings under the flying centers were aligned as depicted in the following table.[52]

Air Force Reserve Units
Table of Organization and Equipment
Fiscal Year 1950

Location	Wing*	Squadron	Aircraft
Marietta AFB, Ga.	94 LBW	331, 332, 333, 410	B–26
Philadelphia International Airport (IAP), Pa.	319 LBW	46, 50, 51, 59	B–26
Tinker AFB, Okla.	323 LBW	453, 454, 455, 456	B–26
Long Beach MAP, Calif.	448 LBW	711, 712, 713, 714	B–26
Long Beach MAP, Calif.	452 LBW	728, 729, 730, 731	B–26
Floyd Bennet Naval Air Station (NAS), N.Y.	63 TCW	3, 9, 52, 60	C–47
Hanscom Airport, Bedford, Mass.	89 TCW	24, 25, 26, 30	C–46
Hamilton AFB, Calif.	349 TCW	311, 312, 313, 314	C–46
Greater Pittsburgh Airport, Pa.	375 TCW	55, 56, 57, 58	C–46
Portland MAP, Ore.	403 TCW	63, 64, 65, 66	C–46
Scott AFB, Ill.	419 TCW	339, 340, 341, 342	C–46
Cleveland MAP, Ohio	433 TCW	67, 68, 69, 70	C–46
Atterbury AFB, Ind.	434 TCW	71, 72, 73, 74	C–47
Miami IAP, Fla.	435 TCW	76, 77, 78, 79	C–46
Godman AFB, Ky.	436 TCW	79, 80, 81, 82	C–47
Chicago Orchard Airport, Ill.	437 TCW	83, 84, 85, 86	C–46
Offutt AFB, Neb.	438 TCW	87, 88, 89, 90	C–46

Air Force Reserve Units, 1950—*Cont'd*

Location	Wing*	Squadron	Aircraft
Selfridge AFB, Mich.	439 TCW	91, 92, 93, 94	C–46
Wold-Chamberlain MAP, Minn.	440 TCW	95, 96, 97, 98	C–46
Chicago Orchard Airport, Ill.	441 TCW	99, 100, 301, 302	C–46
Fairfax Field, Kansas City, Kans.	442 TCW	303, 304, 305, 306	C–46
Hensley Field, Dallas, Tex.	443 TCW	309, 310, 343, 344	C–46
Reading MAP, Pa.	512 TCW	326, 327, 328, 329	C–46
Birmingham MAP, Ala.	514 TCW	335, 336, 337, 338	C–46
Memphis MAP, Tenn.	516 TCW	345, 346, 347, 348	C–46

*LBW=Light Bombardment Wing; TCW=Tactical Control Wing.

The Volunteer Air Reserve constituted the numerical bulk of the Air Force Reserve. Designed to provide a reservoir of trained personnel rather than functional units for mobilization, it was a refinement of the composite unit program that it replaced. The Volunteer Reserve offered no training pay and few opportunities for active duty training, but its members could earn points for promotion and retirement. Suffering the lowest priority for funds in the Air Force Reserve, in turn the lowest in the Air Force, the Volunteer Air Reserve training program received little financial support.[53]

Thus, the Air Force encouraged the Continental Air Command to conduct a virtually cost-free program, suggesting it make every effort to obtain the cooperation of local educational institutions and other agencies in making facilities and equipment available without cost. Reflecting the caliber of local reserve commanders and instructors, the quality of the Volunteer Air Reserve training program varied from location to location. In some areas, the leaders overcame the challenges and conducted attractive, vital training programs. Elsewhere, other reserve officials permitted the training to deteriorate into a lifeless program of lectures on dull subjects, usually conducted by a reservist. Although the Air Staff announcement of the Volunteer Air Reserve program promised that the 1950 program included the funds and personnel to man 185 Volunteer Air Reserve training units, Continental Air Command officials soon saw that this was not so. Convinced the program would amount to nothing unless the Air Force gave the units some help in the form of liaison personnel, Lt. Gen. Ennis C. Whitehead, who became Commander of Continental Air

Development of a New Program

Lt. Gen. Ennis C. Whitehead, Commander of Continental Air Command. On the eve of his transfer to the Far East, General Whitehead advised the Chief of Staff of the Air Force that the basic problem faced by the Air Force Reserve was the Air Force's failure to define a role for it in war and mobilization plans.

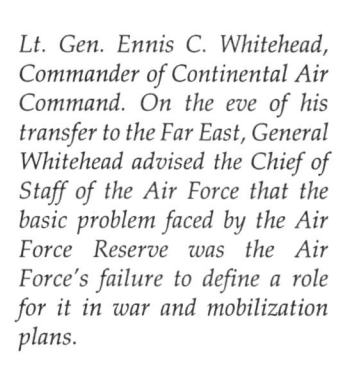

Command on April 15, 1949, asked for authority to implement a liaison program. When the Air Staff made only 164 airmen and officers available, Whitehead reassigned 79 officers from the flying centers to duty with the Volunteer Air Reserve training program. Ninety-seven enlisted men also became available for liaison duty when one of the flying centers became a tenant rather than a base operator as originally programmed.[54]

Headquarters Continental Air Command also struggled to obtain the necessary supplies and equipment to support the volunteer units on a uniform basis. Supply officials in Headquarters Air Materiel Command rejected the Continental Air Command's request for a special issue of supplies and equipment and resisted publishing a requested table of allowance for the program's units. With all the obduracy of World War II supply sergeants, they simply cited the Volunteer Air Reserve program's own constituting directive—denying it equipment—in justifying their refusal. In June 1950, however, the Air Staff overruled the Materiel Command and established an appropriate equipping policy for the program, authorizing sufficient equipment for it to operate.[55]

The Volunteer Air Reserve training program soon occasioned as many complaints among its members as its predecessor had. Many questioned the caliber of liaison personnel, claiming indeed that some instructors did not even attend meetings. Unit commanders protested that not only did they have to pay

77

The Air Force Reserve

the postage to obtain training films, they could not obtain official rosters of their units nor could adequate distribution of official publications pertaining to the Volunteer Air Reserve training program. Some noted they still had difficulty in establishing firm meeting places a year after the program's start-up, and many complained that they had never been visited by a numbered air force representative.[56] Nevertheless, after a year's operation, the volunteer program claimed more than 67,000 adherents, reservists who hung on hoping for better programs and opportunities and, if nothing else, accruing promotions and retirement credits.

As the Continental Air Command got its two Air Force Reserve programs under way, the Air Staff and the other major commands were having difficulties managing the two higher priority programs for the mobilization assignees and the corollary units. The Air Staff made its first attempt to create a program for mobilization assignees in July 1948, establishing procedures by which M-Day assignments could be given to Air Force Reserve personnel not assigned to the combat or corollary units. The major commands received quotas of assignees by grade and became responsible to administer those assigned to them.[57]

The Air Staff also tried to apply logic to support the program's budget by surveying the commands for a statement of the total number of officers by grade and specialty who had received mobilization assignments and the average number of training periods they would require in fiscal year 1950. Air Force headquarters seemed interested in only two factors when compiling these numbers: the number of reservists available for assignment and the capability of a headquarters to train them. No consideration was given to war mobilization requirements.[58]

General Quesada's staff recognized the lack of attention to requirements as a deficiency of the program. Late in 1949, staff members attempted to correct the imbalance of priority and began with an appeal to the operations and planning communities of the Air Staff to define wartime requirements for individual reservists. Nothing came of this initiative, however; the Air Staff became mired in such considerations as whether a separate category should exist for mobilization augmentees whose experience and civilian occupations seemed to obviate the need for routine training.[59]

Rejecting the Air Staff approach as unsound, in January 1950 General Whitehead insisted that requirements must be established on the basis of confirmed Air Force war and mobilization plans. Until requirements were established for each command on a firm, meaningful basis, he said, estimates of command training capability and availability were useless. He insisted that positive and prompt actions had to be taken to establish a proper war plan, troop basis, and mobilization plan. General Whitehead's eloquence failed him, however, and he was unable to persuade the Office of the Special Assistant for

Development of a New Program

Reserve Forces, then headed by Maj. Gen. Earl S. Hoag, to reconsider its basic tenets.[60]

Late in June 1949 the Continental Air Command activated 152 corollary units for itself and the other major commands. These included light and medium bombardment, all-weather fighter, troop carrier, reconnaissance, vehicle repair, communications, pilot training, technical training, bombardment training, air weather, air transport, airways, and air communications and air rescue units. The corollary training program progressed slowly. No specific training directive was prepared until 1950. Although the 1950 Air Force Reserve Program assigned a higher training priority to the corollary units, in practice the equipped reserve wings assigned to the centers fared better. The training centers existed primarily to train members of reserve units, but the Regular Air Force units supporting corollary units had operational missions that came first. Each corollary unit was to train one weekend per month and have a two-week tour of active duty each year. This sacrificed the regular unit's effectiveness, which the Chief of Staff had accepted, but it was a fine point as to how much its combat efficiency could safely be dissipated in training duties.[61]

In November 1949, after five months' experience with the program, the Headquarters Continental Air Command staff concluded that the tactical squadrons of combat wings should not be burdened with reserve corollary training responsibilities. General Whitehead suggested to General Muir S. Fairchild, Air Force Vice Chief of Staff, that the tactical squadrons of all corollary units be replaced by aircraft control and warning units. He believed these geographically stable units were capable of training reservists without materially detracting from their primary missions. After some initial resistance, the Air Staff yielded as General Whitehead's views began to acquire support from other major commands.[62]

The active force's tactical flying units were not well suited to conduct corollary unit training from the standpoint of the reserve. Units of such commands as the Air Training Command and the Military Air Transport Service had relatively stable locations, but tactical combat units were mobile by nature. The tactical forces frequently deployed from one station to another as strategic or tactical considerations dictated. They often participated in exercises and maneuvers, with a resultant interruption in reserve training. Reservists, bound to their communities as citizens, could not accompany the deploying units for indeterminate or long training periods. This instability in corollary unit training was conducive neither to the development of proficiency nor to the maintenance of reservist good will. Nevertheless, at the end of the first year of the new program, the Air Force Reserve corollary program included about 15,000 members who comprised an individual resource that the Air Force ultimately used.[63]

The Air Force Reserve

Miscellaneous Lasting Developments of the First Program

By June 1949, as the Air Force began to implement the 1950 Air Force Reserve Program, a number of developments had occurred which became permanent features of the Air Force Reserve program. These included provisions for inactive duty training pay and additional retirement benefits, the admission of Blacks and women into the program, and the redesignation of the component as the Air Force Reserve.

Resolution of the Inactive Duty Training Pay Issue

Air reservists in training status were entitled to certain disability and death benefits, but, as one of the major irritants in the conduct of the early program, no Army reservist was paid for his inactive duty training, although his peers in the National Guard and the Naval Reserve could be. The National Defense Act of 1916 authorized inactive duty training pay for guardsmen, and the Naval Reserve Act of 1938 authorized it for Naval reservists. Authorization for payment to members of the Organized Reserve required congressional action, and as early as April 17, 1946, the War Department sought legislation permitting Army reservists to be paid for inactive duty training.[64]

After one such bill had failed in 1946, President Truman signed Public Law 80–460 on March 25, 1948, establishing uniform standards for inactive duty training pay for all reserve components of the armed forces. The law also consolidated the Officers' Reserve Corps, the Organized Reserve, and the Enlisted Reserve Corps as the Organized Reserve Corps, and it incorporated the provision for the Class A, B, and C Organized Reserve Corps units that the War Department had adopted.[65]

The Air Force's first implementing instructions typified its penchant for creating difficulties for itself and its reservists. On October 11, 1948, Headquarters USAF authorized pay for some reservists who participated in inactive duty training periods on or after October 1st. The Air Force initially limited pay to reservists whose training it deemed most valuable to its mobilization needs, that is, mobilization assignees and members of combat units. The mobilization assignees, then regarded as filling the most valuable M-Day function, were permitted the maximum forty-eight paid training periods per year authorized by law. Only reserve units specifically designated by Headquarters USAF for "prompt mobilization" were authorized a similar number of pay periods; others were limited to twenty-four.[66]

Reservists at a unit training assembly might qualify for pay if 60 percent of the officers and 60 percent of the airmen were in attendance. At first, pay for attending unit training assemblies was available only for assigned members of units. Since only officers were authorized in Class C units, airmen who had been brought in to participate in unit activities to provide the cadre necessary to expand the units were not eligible for pay. Similarly, airmen exceeding the

Development of a New Program

authorized cadre strength of a Class B unit were ineligible. Moreover, since upgrading of units had been frozen while the Air Force was working out the details of the fiscal 1949 and 1950 programs, even units that had recruited all the airmen necessary to advance to the next higher classification had to remain in their existing status. It was a classical standoff. Commanders could not compensate airmen for whom there was no authorized position, and units could not advance to a higher classification until they had sufficient airmen awaiting assignment.[67]

Thus, instead of immediately becoming the long-awaited panacea for all the Air Force Reserve program's ills, the authorization for inactive duty pay actually compounded problems for the unit commander. It became even more difficult for him to attract airmen to the reserve program and retain them thereafter. These pay provisions tried the patience of airmen who had been participating in the training activities of units not fully manned. In January 1949, Headquarters USAF partially extricated unit commanders from this dilemma when it allowed them to pay airmen who before January 1, 1949, had been assigned as overages.[68] This did not, however, solve the problem with respect to airmen who joined after January 1st or who might in the future be recruited to bring the units up to strength. Moreover, it was questionable if lost interest might be rekindled. As the commander of one reserve unit put it, "These men have come out to a makeshift training program, have been pushed from one Squadron to another, have listened to new promises of pay every time they turn up, until they are now at a point where it will take something of an unusual nature to bring their interest back."[69]

The Air Staff published its second version of the inactive duty pay directive on March 22, 1949. The new regulation permitted pay for two training assemblies on one calendar day, with the proviso that the aggregate duration of training was at least eight hours, and it encouraged the use of two successive calendar days of the weekend to achieve continuity of training. Authorized reservists attending such a weekend of training would thus receive pay for four training periods, up to a maximum of six or twelve such weekends a year, depending on the status of the reservist.

The new regulation still stipulated that only mobilization assignees and members of Class A units designated for prompt mobilization would be eligible for forty-eight periods per year while it authorized all other units twenty-four. It did change attendance requirements for pay, however. Officers were not to receive pay unless 60 percent of the entire unit strength was present, but airmen could be compensated for attending a training period regardless of total attendance. Even when all assigned officers attended a session, if they did not constitute 60 percent of the assigned unit strength by themselves, they could not receive pay unless the requisite airmen also attended. Thus, the pay of officers was dependent on the attendance of airmen, and this stipulation stimulated greater officer interest in airman recruiting and participation.[70]

The Air Force Reserve

Provision of Retirement Benefits for Reservists

Congress also acted to provide retirement benefits for Army and Air Force Reservists in 1948. Under the existing laws, officers of the Regular Army and Air Force could request voluntary retirement after fifteen years' of service. Approved on June 19, 1948, Public Law 810–80 raised the service requirement to twenty years and extended retirement privileges to Army and Air Force Reservists, thus making the retirement programs of all the services equal.[71]

A retired officer would receive 2.5 percent of his annual pay and longevity for the rank in which he retired multiplied by the number of years in service, not to exceed 75 percent. A reservist had to attain 60 years of age, complete 20 years of satisfactory Federal service as a member of the Reserve, and meet standards of performance established for such reserve components. The basic requirement was that he earn 50 points a year. The active reservist received 15 gratuitous points as a participating member. Thereafter, he earned points for attending authorized training sessions, serving on active duty, instructing, completing authorized extension courses, and completing flying training periods.[72]

Provision for Blacks and Women in the Air Reserve

Army Air Forces and War Department policy on the training of Blacks in the Air Reserve reflected the nation's attitudes on segregation of the races, and Black membership and training in the Air Reserve was on a segregated basis. An Air Defense Command policy directive of March 1947 reflected War Department policy as set down in Circular 124. The reserve training detachments were required to train Blacks as individuals until a sufficient number became available to form a unit. A composite organization could combine units consisting of Black and White Americans, but each component's members had to be of only one race. Blacks given active duty training tours were to be attached to an organized active force consisting of solely Black units in training. Within the constraints of military considerations, individual and unit active duty training of Blacks were conducted in localities where community attitudes were favorable. In June 1947 Headquarters Tactical Air Command agreed to conduct active duty training for about 1,500 Black air reservists during fiscal year 1948 at Lockbourne AFB, Ohio.[73] It would be another year before President Truman issued his Executive Order 9981 on July 26, 1948, which gave Black members of the Armed Forces "equality of treatment and opportunity," and another ten months after that before the Air Force fully implemented the policy.[74]

Meanwhile, Air Defense Command efforts to provide inactive duty training for Black Americans were often frustrated. On the one hand, the War Department prohibited assigning Blacks to existing reserve combat units; on the other, because of the funding crisis, in December 1947 the Air Staff suspended

Development of a New Program

the activation of additional Air Force Reserve combat units and limited the number of Air Force Reservists, regardless of race, who might participate in inactive duty training. If applied rigidly, these restrictions would prohibit the training of Black Air Force Reservists for the balance of fiscal year 1948.[75]

In February 1948, however, General Partridge suggested that the Air Defense Command organize sufficient provisional units within existing combat groups to accommodate all interested and qualified Black Air Force Reservists. He also authorized the command to provide all Black reservists assigned to such units the opportunity to participate in active duty training, subject to the availability of funds.[76]

The Air Defense Command's Second Air Force immediately organized the 1st and 2d Provisional Troop Carrier Squadrons at Chicago, Illinois, and Detroit, Michigan. The Chicago squadron was attached to the 84th Troop Carrier Squadron at Orchard Place Airport for training and administration, and the Detroit squadron, to the 5th Troop Carrier Squadron at Selfridge AFB. Headquarters Air Defense Command had to coerce the other numbered air forces into acting, but eventually they made some accommodation for the inactive duty training of Blacks.[77]

In June 1948 the Women's Armed Forces Integration Act designated the Women in the Air Force (WAF) program as an integral part of the U.S. Air Force (instead of being a separate corps) and granted permanent status to a Women's Reserve. This cleared the way for WAF participation in the Air Force Reserve.[78] Having anticipated this eventuality since January 1947, Capt. Marjorie O. Hunt, the Headquarters Air Defense Command WAF staff director for active force members, welcomed all former enlisted women to the Reserve WAF program. An August 1948 WAF training plan offered reserve commissions to Women Army Corps (WAC) officers then on active duty with the Air Force and those on active duty with the Army who had served with the Army Air Forces or its predecessor, former WAC officers who had served at any time in the top three grades, and civilians with particular specialties needed by the Air Force.

A WAF reservist could be assigned to any vacancy in an organized unit for which she was qualified, and mobilization assignee positions were also available. Captain Hunt anticipated that the majority of the WAFs would be assigned to the composite units. She also thought the emphasis in training would be placed initially on the development of leaders, both commissioned and noncommissioned, to permit rapid expansion of the WAF in an emergency.[79]

The Air Force Reserve

The Air Reserve and Service Unification

On September 18, 1947, the United States Air Force became a separate service under the Department of the Air Force when W. Stuart Symington was sworn in as the first Secretary of the Air Force and General Carl Spaatz as its first Chief of Staff. The U.S. Air Force was created by Public Law 253–80, The National Security Act of 1947, which President Truman signed on July 26. This act established the National Military Establishment with the Secretary of Defense as its head. The establishment consisted of the Departments of Army, Navy, and Air Force together with a number of other agencies created by the legislation. Transfer of personnel, property, records, and installations was to be accomplished in two years by the Departments of Army and Air Force under the direction of the Secretary of Defense.[80]

The staffs of the Army Chief of Staff and the Commanding General of the Army Air Forces developed about 200 agreements under the guidance of the Secretary of War to steer the actual separation of the two services. The Secretary of War and the secretary-designate of the Air Force approved the agreements, and Navy Secretary James V. Forrestal, who would become the first Secretary of Defense, quickly sanctioned their general intent and framework. He nevertheless cautioned the services that the agreements were only tentative until he implemented them by specific orders. The Army and Air Force staffs then consolidated the original agreements into eighty-eight major action projects.[81]

On September 26, Secretary Forrestal signed Transfer Order 1 which brought into the Department of the Air Force and the United States Air Force the greater part of the military personnel, bases, and equipment of the Army Air Forces, thus comprising the first substantive act in establishing the new branch of service. This placed the Air Force on an operating basis, but much remained to be done. Progress seemed slow, but in the end the task was completed on schedule. Within the next two years, Secretary Forrestal promulgated thirty-nine more orders. All-inclusive as well as final, Transfer Order 40 on July 22, 1949, consigned to the Air Force what were regarded as the remaining necessary and appropriate powers, functions, and duties.[82]

The act of establishing the Air Force Reserve occurred on April 14, 1948, when a joint Department of the Army and Department of the Air Force directive established the U.S. Air Force Reserve and the U.S. Air Force Honorary Reserve. The directive ordered the transfer of all officers and enlisted men of the Air Corps Reserve to the U.S. Air Force Reserve and it abolished the Air Corps Reserve Section of the Army of the United States.[83]

The instrument that effectively transferred the Air Reserve to the Air Force was Transfer Order 10 which became effective at noon on April 27, 1948. The order transferred to the Air Force those functions, power, and duties of the Secretary of the Army and the Department of the Army pertaining to the air

Development of a New Program

activities of the National Guard of the United States, the National Guard, the Officers' Reserve Corps, the Reserve Officers Training Corps, and the Enlisted Reserve Corps. It also transferred to the Air Force the air units of the National Guard of the United States, of the National Guard while in the service of the United States, and of the Organized Reserve of the United States.[84]

General Whitehead Evaluates the Program

In December 1950, on the eve of his departure for a new assignment, General Whitehead identified a number of weaknesses of the Air Force Reserve program to the Chief of Staff of the Air Force. Replaying an old refrain, he asserted that the basic weaknesses of the reserve program stemmed from the lack of a realistic reserve forces troop basis[*] and an Air Force mobilization plan. Until they were developed, he asserted, the Air Force was working in the dark. Lacking a firm mobilization requirements base, officials responsible for the reserve program could not define the necessary training. In his judgment, this single deficiency contributed most to the difficulties of the reserve forces.

Because the Air Force lacked proper plans for its reserve forces, its concepts for the organization and development of reserve forces were faulty. General Whitehead posted certain requirements and capabilities with respect to the reserve forces. Regular units had to be brought to wartime strength, Air Reserve Forces units had to be mobilized, and additional organizations had to be created from the Air Force Reserve. As he saw it, this meant that the Air Force had to establish a wartime strength for every Regular Air Force unit included in the troop program, and the unit had to fill the difference between its peacetime and wartime authorizations with mobilization assignees. The Air Reserve Forces units should comprise those additional units required within sixty days of M-Day, and they had to include all their prescribed organizational elements and be programmed, manned, and trained at their wartime strength during peacetime. Finally, the Volunteer Air Reserve should be programmed as a pool of reservists required after sixty days, and the timing of their utilization should dictate their administration and training.

General Whitehead dismissed the corollary flying units as not having warranted the effort, and the Category R[†] aspect of the flying center program

---

[*]The Air Staff had actually promulgated a reserve troop basis in May 1950 which, among other things, established a mobilization requirement of about 37,000 men for the Air Force Reserve. The individual recalls for the Korean War began less than two months later, and the concept never took effect (MFR, Dir/M&0, HQ USAF, subj: Composition of the USAFR Troop Basis and Grade Structure, May 25, 1950—AFRES X).

[†]Category R refers to reservists in the pre–Korean War era who were recalled to

The Air Force Reserve

as unsuccessful. He termed supervision of the existing reserve program as inadequate and proposed several innovations in structure including the establishment of geographical district headquarters, intended to get management closer to the reservists. He asserted that the Air Force had failed to invest adequate resources in the reserve programs, and had received commensurate value in return. He enumerated other problems, but he stressed inadequate planning, the failure to establish requirements, the need to spend money, and the need to promote a sense of mutual interdependence and understanding between the regular and reserve components.[85]

By June 1950, then, the U.S. Air Force was one year into its third post–World War II Air Force Reserve program. The first program had been, by definition, nothing more than a flying club, giving individual reservists the chance to fly in trainer aircraft. The second ostensibly included tactical units, but these were in reality nothing more than paper units equipped with trainers, and not much had changed. Intended as a three-year effort, the Air Force Reserve program for fiscal year 1950 lasted but one year, for in the latter half of 1950 the Air Force called upon its reserve forces to provide the initial manpower required to augment the regular force in a war in Korea and in an expansion required by a changing U.S. foreign policy.

---

extended active duty to help administer and train their units.

4

Mobilization for Korea and Expansion

> ... Nevertheless, we would not have been able to do the job we were ordered to do by the President if we had not used the Reserves; and even looking at it in hindsight, I don't see what else could have been done except to use them.
>
> —Thomas K. Finletter, September 1951

The 1950 Air Force Reserve Program, actually begun in May 1949, was to have extended for three years, but events in 1950 terminated it. Between July 1950 and June 1953, the U.S. Air Force called more than 146,000 Air Force Reservists and 46,000 Air National Guardsmen to active military service for periods ranging from one to three years. The recalls included the mobilization of all Air Force Reserve combat and corollary units and most Air National Guard units. The Air Force required these air reservists to augment its Korean police action and to feed its worldwide expansion.

Even though in July 1950, the Air Force still had not developed firm mobilization or war plans, the general expectation, particularly among reservists, was that they were susceptible to recall only in the event that the country became involved in another full-scale war. Instead, as a result of new U.S. foreign policy after World War II, 193,000 citizen airmen found themselves back on active duty for different purposes. Initially, a great many were recalled to active duty to participate in an action that their President did not even dignify as a war. Rather, he called it a United Nations police action to restore the status quo between the warring Democratic People's Republic of Korea and the Republic of Korea. The United States had played an important

The Air Force Reserve

As Secretary of the Air Force, Thomas K. Finletter, April 1950–January 1953, was deeply disturbed that reservists were being used to build up the peacetime Air Force. Finletter is conversing with Maj. Leonard C. Schultz, Commanding Officer, 58th Fighter-Interceptor Squadron.

role in creating the United Nations as a peacekeeping body, and viewing the attack on South Korea by North Korea in June 1950 as the first test for the international body, President Truman believed the United States was obligated to assist the United Nations. Later, still greater numbers of Air Force Reservists and Air National Guardsmen were recalled to address the intensified situation in Korea as the People's Republic of China entered the conflict and to guarantee the collective security of the Atlantic community as the United States joined another international body, the North Atlantic Treaty Organization.

Background of the Korean Mobilization

During World War II the United States and its allies had agreed to restore the independence of Korea, which Japan had annexed in 1910. At the end of the war in 1945 the USSR accepted the surrender of the Japanese forces north of the 38th parallel, and the United States, of those south of that latitude. Thereafter, entrenched political polarity between the southern followers of Syngman Rhee, a conservative autocrat, and northerners led by the communist Kim Il-Sung frustrated the efforts of joint commissions to unify the nation.

Korea and Expansion

When the North Koreans boycotted elections sponsored by the United Nations on August 15, 1948, Syngman Rhee established the Republic of Korea with himself as president. A few weeks later, the People's Republic of Korea established itself in the north and claimed authority over all Korea, and two antagonistic Koreas glared at each other across the 38th parallel.[1]

In the Cold War environment and the general insecurity of western European nations under the Soviet menace, the Truman administration turned the United States away from its traditional isolationist stance of nonentangling alliances toward a policy of collective security in Europe. On April 4, 1949, the United States and eleven other nations signed the North Atlantic Treaty in Washington, D.C. The United States joined Great Britain, France, the Netherlands, Belgium, Luxemburg, Canada, Norway, Denmark, Portugal, West Germany, and Iceland in the pact. Binding itself to a mutual security and aid agreement with western Europe, the United States accepted a degree of military collaboration far beyond anything it had ever considered in peacetime.[2]

As the United States' attention to Europe increased, its interest in the Far East diminished. When the Truman administration withdrew the bulk of U.S. forces from Korea on June 30, 1949, a military advisory group of about 500 men remained to complete the instruction of the 65,000-man Republic of Korea Army. By design, this army was really not much more than a constabulary. The United States wanted the South Korean force to be strong enough to repel invasion, but it did not want it so strong as to be tempted into attacking North Korea. Consequently, the new army was not issued tanks, heavy guns, or aircraft. It acquired some facility with small arms, but on the whole it was far from being a well-trained or well-equipped force. North of the 38th parallel, on the other hand, the Soviets had created a North Korean Army of 135,000 trained men organized around a core of veterans of the China civil war and equipped it with heavy arms, armor, and aircraft.[3]

President Truman further restricted the influence of South Korea on U.S. foreign policy on October 6, 1949, when he approved the Mutual Defense Assistance Act of 1949 which earmarked a mere $10.2 million for Korea. This amount reflected the importance of the commitment to Europe and the contrasting lower priority that the United States then accorded the threat in South Korea. Endorsing the U.S. military assistance program, the National Security Council confirmed that the program's purpose with respect to Korea was to create sufficiently strong forces to maintain internal order and secure the border.[4] In January 1950, six months after the United States had removed the bulk of its military forces from Korea, Secretary of State Dean Acheson publicly excluded Korea from the U.S. defensive perimeter in the Far East.[5] These developments gave the North Koreans some reason to anticipate that the United States would not intervene in a Korean civil war, or that if it did, its action would come too late to affect the outcome.

Clashes along the border separating the Koreas became common in early

The Air Force Reserve

1950, and communists infiltrated the south. When elections in the south in May 1950 did not advance the communist cause, North Korea demanded new elections with the intention of establishing a unified legislative body for all Korea. Syngman Rhee rejected the proposals, and on June 25, 1950, the North Koreans launched a full-scale attack on the Republic of Korea. Sustaining their initiative, within thirty-six hours the communists forced Syngman Rhee and his cabinet to abandon their capital at Seoul. At midafternoon on June 27, Korean time, President Truman and the Joint Chiefs of Staff authorized General Douglas MacArthur, Commander of the U.S. Far East Command, to commit U.S. naval and air forces to the defense of the Republic of Korea. Authority for the use of ground troops followed three days later, and on the same day, with the Soviet Union boycotting the session, the Security Council of the United Nations resolved to assist the Republic of Korea to repel armed attack and restore peace in the area. On July 7, the United Nations asked the United States to furnish a commander for all U.N. forces, and President Truman thereupon appointed General MacArthur to the position.[6]

On July 7, the Joint Chiefs of Staff approved the Air Force's projected deployment of units to the Far East. This would require the mobilization of one light bombardment and one troop carrier wing from the Air Force Reserve. As General Hoyt S. Vandenberg, the Chief of Staff, would later say, the United States Air Force in 1950 was "a shoestring air force." The active establishment's cupboard was bare, and to satisfy the needs of General Stratemeyer—now Commanding General, Far East Air Forces—it had to call upon the Air Force Reserve.[7]

In addition to providing the forces necessary to support the requirements of the Korean War, the Joint Chiefs of Staff also authorized a limited augmentation of the armed forces worldwide, and on July 24th the President asked Congress for a supplemental appropriation for this purpose. As enacted on September 17, the First Supplemental Appropriation Act of 1951 made an additional $11.7 billion available to the Defense Department. The Air Force's share included the costs of expanding from 48 to 58 wings through the mobilization of 10 Air Force Reserve wings. By that time, the Joint Chiefs had approved an Air Force buildup to 95 wings by June 30, 1954.[8]

On July 19, President Truman sought congressional approval of actions required to augment U.S. military forces and a program of support for the United Nations. The President asserted that the United States had to increase its military strength, not only to deal with the aggression in Korea but also to support its own military requirements elsewhere and to augment the military strength of other free nations. He had already authorized the Secretary of Defense to exceed the budgeted size of the military forces and to use the Selective Service System to the extent required to obtain the necessary increased strength. Since it would take some time for the Selective Service to react, he had also authorized the Defense Secretary to call into active federal

Korea and Expansion

As Chief of Staff of the Air Force during the Korean War, General Hoyt S. Vandenberg was careful to console reserve wing commanders whose units were used to provide filler personnel during the 1951 mobilizations and to explain to them the reasons the actions were necessary. Left to right *are Generals White, Twining, and Vandenberg and Secretary Talbott.*

service as many National Guard units and as many reservists and reserve units as were required. Congress immediately gave the Chief Executive strong bipartisan support and removed all military personnel ceilings for four years.[9]

The President could authorize reserve recalls because providentially Congress had just extended the military draft in a measure that also provided for reserve mobilization. Approved on June 30, 1950, the Selective Service Extension Act of 1950 extended for one year the Selective Service Act of 1948 which had expired the day before the North Koreans crossed the border. Citing increased international tensions, the President, looking east to Europe rather than west to Asia, had asked that the act be extended without amendment for three years. The Senate concurred, but a House amendment extended the draft for only one year and limited the period the President could recall units and members of the reserve components to twenty-one months, rather than the two

The Air Force Reserve

years that had previously been available to him.[10]

When the communists struck across the 38th parallel, the U.S. Air Force was about 5,000 people short of its 416,314 authorization for 1950, and it could not even maintain the 48 wings authorized by the President a few months earlier. Its officer strength, incidentally, included 35,126 Air Force Reserve officers on extended active duty who represented 62 percent of the officer force. Nowhere was the Air Force's presence more feeble than in the Far East. The Far East Air Forces, commanded since April by Stratemeyer, was organized for air defense rather than the air support role which the crisis in Korea required. Among his immediate needs, Stratemeyer wanted a B–26 wing and two additional B–26 squadrons to round out the 3d Bombardment Wing (Light) already in the theater. General MacArthur also wanted the Air Force to provide sufficient transport aircraft to drop the entire 187th Airborne Regimental Combat Team as a unit.[11]

The 1950 Unit Mobilizations

On July 28, 1950, the Air Staff directed Headquarters Continental Air Command to order the 452d Bombardment Wing (Light) at Long Beach MAP in California, and the 437th Troop Carrier Wing (Medium) at O'Hare IAP in Chicago to active military service on August 10 for twenty-one months unless sooner relieved. The headquarters was also directed to activate the motor vehicle, air police, food services, and installations squadrons originally withheld when the wings were organized in 1949. Additionally, the 452d's 731st Bombardment Squadron was to be reorganized as a light, night attack squadron, and the 86th Tactical Squadron of the 437th Troop Carrier Wing was to be inactivated.[12]

The reorganized wings were to be given sixty days' intense training before they deployed overseas. The 452d Light Bomb Wing was clearly the best prepared among the reserve wings, but lacking sufficient manpower, the 437th Troop Carrier Wing was not nearly as ready. These two were the first to be called primarily because each was collocated with another wing under its respective flying center. This collocation permitted the use of the second unit's personnel and equipment to replace shortages in its mobilized companion. In addition, in the expectation that the Korean emergency signaled a worldwide crisis, General Whitehead thought that some of his northern bases, including O'Hare at Chicago, should be cleared of troop carrier operations to make way for fighter units for air defense.[13]

On July 30, General Whitehead sent special instructions about the recalls to the Fourth and Tenth Air Forces which commanded the units under alert. He authorized them to transfer immediately to the Volunteer Air Reserve program any member of the two mobilized wings not qualified in his specialty who could not be upgraded within sixty days. The numbered air forces were to eliminate inefficient reserve officers and noncommissioned officers, and they could assign competent Category R personnel to the wings in their reserve grades.* General Whitehead made all personnel of the two collocated units available for assignment to the mobilized wings. Unit readiness was the paramount concern, and to assure full manning Whitehead directed the numbered air forces to recall all members of the four wings regardless of the number of dependents they claimed. This guidance contradicted published instructions on the individual recall program which excused all reservists with four dependents or more, but he correctly assumed there would be new dependency legislation before long.[14]

Two major problems dominated the mobilization of the 452d and 437th: the orders to reorganize the units concurrently with their mobilization, and the poor condition of individual and unit records. The guidance to retain all four of its flying squadrons while adding the four new support units more than doubled the 452d's authorized strength of 2,784. In addition to the personnel required to man the new component units, each flying squadron was authorized 12 additional combat crew members. However, the 437th Troop Carrier Wing could not simply redistribute the resources of its disbanded fourth tactical squadron to man its new support units. The surplus personnel were primarily rated officers who could not be matched to the new authorizations for ground support personnel. So it was not a simple matter of mobilizing the entire wing as it stood; selectivity and matching had to be exercised.[15]

Personnel officials of both mobilized wings criticized their supporting flying centers for the chaotic condition of the files that they received. Many of the individual files contained incorrect addresses for the reservists, and more than one hundred members of the 452d Bombardment Wing never received their mobilization telegrams. Airmen's records often contained incomplete forms, and many files were missing. On the other hand, two weeks after arriving at Shaw AFB, South Carolina, the 437th had files for hundreds of people not assigned to it.[16]

Suddenly acquiring dependents, critical job status, and ailments they had never had before, reservists of both mobilized units called in by the hundreds to claim ineligibility and request delays. Other calls came from distraught wives and employers. Both numbered air forces immediately set up deferment boards of five reserve officers called to active duty for that purpose. With no precedent to follow, the boards established rules and procedures as they went along until Headquarters Continental Air Command could declare some basic command policies.[17]

---

*Under the Category R program, reserve members of the reserve units serving as instructors and advisers were on extended active duty with the training centers (Air Force Letter 45–11, "Manning of Air Force Reserve Training Centers," May 9, 1949).

The Air Force Reserve

The boards acted quickly, and by August 8, telegrams were on the way to some reservists adjusting reporting dates. On August 10, however, and every day thereafter for a week, men reported in and sought deferment. In most cases, they applied immediately to the boards, which made quick decisions. In others, however, the men allowed themselves to be sworn in before they requested deferments, thereby creating some severe administrative complications. By August 16, when the O'Hare deferment board completed its work, it had granted 232 deferments and disapproved 195, referring only three cases to Headquarters Continental Air Command for resolution.[18]

Mobilization of the 375th and 433d Troop Carrier Wings

The mobilization of the Air Force Reserve 452d and 437th Wings, along with the recall of several thousand individual reservists, satisfied the Far East Air Forces' immediate need for reinforcements. Despite the guarantee written into the National Defense Act of 1916 that the National Guard would be called first in any expansion of the armed forces, the Air Force called upon the Air Force Reserve when the crisis in Korea arose. There seemed to be two reasons for this. One was that the Air Force Reserve had the specific resources General Stratemeyer needed. The other was that, on the premise the Korean incident would be the first in an international pattern of upheaval encouraged by the Soviet Union, national policy dictated that active and National Guard forces be withheld from the Far East in anticipation of a major conflict in Europe.

The Guard's turn came, however, along with that of additional reserve units in the summer of 1950 as the Air Force acted to expand to the interim 58-wing force approved by the President on July 17. On August 18, 1950, the Joint Chiefs of Staff approved the mobilization of two additional Air Force Reserve troop carrier wings and of four fighter-bomber and two tactical reconnaissance wings from the Air National Guard.

Confirming an earlier alert, Headquarters USAF officially advised Headquarters Continental Air Command on September 14 that the 375th Troop Carrier Wing at Greater Pittsburgh Airport, Pennsylvania, and the 433d Troop Carrier Wing at Cleveland MAP, Ohio, both equipped with C–46s, would be mobilized the following month. As in the case of the 437th mobilized in August, the fourth flying squadron of each wing was to be inactivated and the four additional support units activated. Implementing new unit recall procedures, Headquarters Continental Air Command recalled individuals from other reserve programs and reassigned them to bring the two wings up to authorized strength. Mobilized on October 15, the two units were to serve twenty-one months unless sooner relieved.[19]

By the time the 375th and 433d were ordered to active duty, the Continental Air Command had consolidated into new unit mobilization instructions for the numbered air forces the wisdom it had acquired when mobilizing the 452d Light Bomb Wing and the 437th Troop Carrier Wing. The guidance published on September 19, 1950, detailed the proper sequence to follow in bringing mobilized tactical units to their authorized wartime strengths. Fillers were to be drawn, in order, from corollary, combat, the command's active force units, the Volunteer Air Reserve, and Category R personnel.[20]

Upon mobilization, the 375th and 433d Troop Carrier Wings moved to Greenville AFB, South Carolina, which was soon renamed Donaldson AFB. Converting to C–119s and moving to Europe, the 433d set up operations at Rhein-Main Air Base (AB), Germany, on August 6, 1951, where it conducted routine troop carrier operations until it inactivated and reverted to reserve status on July 14, 1952. The 375th, meanwhile, converted to C–82s and remained at Donaldson until it too was inactivated on July 14, 1952. Following its conversion to C–82s, the 375th acquired the responsibility to support the U.S. Army Infantry School airborne training requirements at Fort Benning, Georgia.[21]

National Emergency and the 1951 Unit Mobilizations

The first phase of the Korean mobilization ended in November 1950. Air Staff operations and personnel officials determined that additional personnel requirements could be met from other sources without mobilizing additional reserve units. Except for a few officers in critical skills, the Air Force had stopped recalling individual reservists involuntarily.[22]

The suspension of the mobilization program reflected the state of the war itself. United Nations forces had reentered the South Korean capital, Seoul, on September 26 and crossed the 38th parallel on October 1. By October 26, they had reached the Manchurian border at Chosan on the Yalu River. Exactly a month later, however, Chinese troops opened a massive assault against United Nations troops in the Yalu Valley. U.S. troops abandoned Pyongyang on December 5 and had retreated south of Seoul to the Han River by January 4, 1951.[23]

On December 14, along with other measures to increase military strength, the National Security Council recommended the Air Force attain a strength of 87 wings by June 30, 1951, and 95 a year later. President Truman accepted these recommendations the next day and, proclaiming a national emergency on the 16th, established a new overall strength of 3,500,000 for the armed forces, of which the Air Force had 971,000. In the next 26 days, Air Staff officials defined manning policies to meet the new ceiling. They also disseminated mobilization procedures, including the phasing of recall orders and support arrangement, for the influx of new organizations and individuals.[24]

On January 18, 1951, the Department of Defense announced that the

The Air Force Reserve

remaining twenty-one Air Force Reserve combat wings would be recalled between March 1 and May 15. Six troop carrier wings would be retained at home station and assigned to the Tactical Air Command. The remaining fifteen—four light bomber and eleven troop carrier wings—would be recalled as filler units. Upon mobilizing, they would screen their personnel for retention eligibility, check their records, and provide medical exaninations. Within days, the personnel would be individually reassigned elsewhere in the Air Force, primarily to Strategic Air Command units, and their own units would be inactivated.[25]

With the 1950 experience behind them and fortified by consolidated recall instructions issued by Headquarters Continental Air Command in September, the command's numbered air forces conducted the 1951 unit mobilizations much more efficiently. Having mobilized three of the four wings in 1950, Tenth Air Force had borne the brunt of the earlier activities, and its procedures early in 1951 illustrate the progress made. Of the seven remaining wings in the Tenth Air Force area, six were to be used as fillers, and one, the 434th Troop Carrier Wing at Atterbury AFB, Indiana, was to be retained intact. The day after the announcement of the new recalls, the Tenth Air Force staff convened a conference of all reserve wing and flying center commanders to discuss mobilization plans.[26]

Visiting each of the reserve wings in February and March, personnel teams from Headquarters Tenth Air Force discovered personnel records in the usual disarray. Remaining with the units, they helped wing personnel restore the records and instructed them in proper personnel reporting. In turn, as it completed the processing of its assigned reserve unit, each center sent its own personnel officials to assist at other centers.

Although authorized to recall up to fifty people to assist in processing the main body, few units found this necessary because the advance notice enabled them to accomplish most of their processing on the training weekends preceding the mobilization. Consequently, in many instances the actual processing upon mobilization amounted to little more than a final records check. Since the Strategic Air Command had first call on all personnel mobilized with the six filler wings from the Tenth Air Force, its representatives met with officials at Tenth Air Force headquarters on January 30 to plan the selection of individuals. Integrated into the mobilization processing lines, Strategic Air Command screening teams separated the individuals they wanted as the people came through the line.[27]

The flying centers supporting the six wings bound for the Tactical Air Command continued to support their wings for about two months after mobilization. The six units were given the same supply precedence as Regular Air Force units. Every effort was made to obtain essential spares for the C–46s and properly equip the newly activated support squadrons, including the transfer of equipment from the filler units.[28]

Korea and Expansion

The Korean War gave a new emphasis to tactical air operations and resulted in the restoration of Tactical Air Command as a major air command on December 1, 1950. One of the resurrected command's immediate responsibilities was to assemble a tactical airlift force. By January 1951, the United States could count three troop carrier wings: the Regular Air Force's 314th at Sewart AFB, Tennessee, and the mobilized 375th and 433d reserve wings at Donaldson.

To fill the airlift void, six Air Force Reserve C–46 wings were identified for mobilization in January. On March 28, 1951, the Tactical Air Command activated the Eighteenth Air Force at Donaldson AFB, South Carolina, immediately assigning to it the 314th and 375th Troop Carrier Wings. As the six reserve wings came on active duty, they too joined the Eighteenth Air Force. The 435th Troop Carrier Wing at Miami IAP, Florida, the 403d at Portland MAP, Oregon, and the 516th at Memphis MAP, Tennessee, were mobilized on March 1, April 1, and April 16, respectively, while the 434th at Atterbury AFB, Indiana, the 514th at Mitchel AFB, New York, and the 443d at Hensley Field, Texas, all came onto active service on May 1.[29] The other fifteen reserve wings were recalled on various dates between March 10 and May 1 and were inactivated at home stations after their personnel had been reassigned.[30]

Mobilization and Inactivation of Filler Units 1951

Station	Wing*	Recalled	Inactivated
Dobbins AFB, Ga.	94 LBW	March 10	March 20
Birmingham MAP, Ala.	319 LBW	March 10	March 22
Tinker AFB, Okla.	323 LBW	March 10	March 17
Long Beach MAP, Calif.	448 LBW	March 17	March 21
Floyd Bennett NAS, N.Y.	63 TCW	May 1	May 9
L.G. Hanscom Field, Mass.	89 TCW	May 1	May 10
Hamilton AFB, Calif.	349 TCW	April 1	April 2
Scott AFB, Ill.	419 TCW	May 1	May 2
Standiford MAP, Ky.	436 TCW	April 1	April 16
Offutt AFB, Neb.	438 TCW	March 10	March 14
Selfridge AFB, Mich.	439 TCW	April 1	April 3
Minneapolis–St Paul IAP, Minn.	440 TCW	May 1	May 5

97

The Air Force Reserve

Filler Units, 1951—*Cont'd*

Station	Wing*	Recalled	Inactivated
O'Hare Field, Ill.	441 TCW	March 10	March 14
Olathe NAS, Kans.	442 TCW	March 10	March 12
New Castle County Airport, Del.	512 TCW	March 15	April 1

*LBW=Light Bombardment Wing; TCW=Tactical Control Wing.

The breaking up of the reserve units upon mobilization evoked a flurry of protest from the reservists and from congressmen representing the states in which the units were located. Reserve unit members believed the Air Force had promised that they would serve together upon mobilization—indeed recruiters of the period had at least implied if not actually asserted as much. In response to congressional queries, Secretary of the Air Force Thomas K. Finletter noted that the very purpose of the Air Force Reserve was to provide an augmentation force of units or individuals to meet the Air Force's emergency requirements for reinforcement or expansion. He insisted that, as much as the Air Force would like to retain mobilized units intact, it had never made any official commitment to do so. Secretary Finletter further explained that the Chief of Staff had to have absolute flexibility to employ Air Reserve Forces units and individuals in the best interests of national defense. Moreover, he noted that Public Law 599, under whose authority all mobilization during the Korean War took place, specifically authorized the President to order reservists to active duty as individuals or as members of units, with or without their consent.[31]

The Air Force Reserve Units on Active Service

Overcoming some initial shortfalls and recovering from temporary setbacks along the way, the ten wings mobilized and retained intact in 1950 and 1951 not only provided the Air Force an essential augmentation in a time of crisis but also performed their roles well in the first post–World War II test of the Air Force Reserve.

452d Light Bombardment Wing

Upon mobilization, the 452d Bombardment Wing ferried its B–26s and support aircraft to George AFB, California, and began accelerated aircrew training on August 10. Commanded by Brig. Gen. Luther W. Sweetser, Jr., the former

Korea and Expansion

Chief of the Reserve and National Guard Division on the Air Staff, the mobilized wing probably had more talent than any regular unit. As a civilian, its line chief, for example, held the same position at North American Aviation, and the maintenance and supply group commander was supply supervisor for Hughes Aircraft. As Douglas Aircraft Corporation employees, more than a hundred of the unit's mechanics were familiar with the B–26.[32]

On October 15, 1950, the first of five echelons of the 452d left George AFB for Itazuke AB, Kyushu, Japan. As projected, now trained in night operations, the 731st Bombardment Squadron was detached to the 3d Bombardment Wing (Light) at Iwakuni AB, Honshu, Japan. The First B–26 of the 452d arrived at Itazuke on October 25, and two days later the wing flew its initial B–25 interdiction mission to Korea, exactly seventy-seven days after recall. On the last day of the month, the aircrews of the 452d learned they were in a real shooting war, as three Yakovlev fighters jumped one of their B–26s and a Mosquito controller near Yangsi. The B–26 crew shot down one of the Soviet-designed fighters, and P–51s arrived to destroy the other two.[33]

Upon arrival in the theater, the 452d Bombardment Wing was the only B–26 unit conducting daylight operations. Until June 1951, it gave close support to ground units in Korea and engaged in interdiction of communist-held airfields, supply lines, and bridges, reaching peak operations in February 1951. The wing moved to Miho AB at Honshu, Japan, on December 10, and within a few days it suffered its first combat losses. Four B–26s and all their crews were lost, only one to hostile fire. One aircraft hit a cable on a power line during a low-level attack, a second flew into a mountain on takeoff in a snow squall, and a third dove out of the overcast into water. The fourth was knocked down by ground fire near Sunchon, Korea.*[34]

On April 23, 1951, the enemy began a spring offensive, and Fifth Air Force required an extensive effort of the 452d. For the next eight days the wing dispatched thirty to thirty-six sorties a day, getting maximum use from the approximately eighteen aircraft available each day. This required a refuel and rearm turnaround mission for each aircraft each day. The effort placed a heavy flying burden on all combat personnel as each crew was required to fly nine of ten days. As their effort began to exhaust the combat crews, pilots and observers serving in wing staff and support positions were pressed into service. This surge in operations also produced a sharp increase in maintenance activity as the aircraft sustained extensive battle damage. Three B–26s were lost behind enemy lines, and four others, only one of which was salvaged, sustained major battle damage.[35]

Following the April surge, the 452d Bombardment Wing underwent a remarkable 45-day period in which its commander was relieved, it moved from

---

*See Appendix 5 for detailed statistics on the wing's operations.

The Air Force Reserve

Brig. Gen. Luther W. Sweetser, Jr., the former Chief of the Reserve and National Guard Division on the Air Staff, expeditiously mobilized the 452d Light Bomb Wing at Long Beach, California, and had it in combat in Korea in 77 days.

Miho AB to Pusan East in Korea, and it completed a transition to night operations.[36] In April 1951, aircrew morale in the wing, which had been deteriorating, reached the point where four observers refused to fly. Their actions were the result of multiple reasons, but chief among them were misunderstandings regarding the policies for rotating combat aircrew members and separation of reservists in the Far East, difficulties related to operating the B–26 in the Korean hills, and a perception among aircrew members that the wing commander and other key personnel had no great interest in their day-to-day operational concerns.

The Far East Air Forces had recognized the requirement to establish a rotation policy immediately after hostilities began. However, extreme shortages of personnel had made it impossible to establish firm commitments for crew members. In the late summer of 1950, the command recommended a rotation policy based on a set number of missions, but the Air Staff rejected it, believing that such an Air Force policy would create difficulties for the Army whose rotation policy was based solely upon time served in the combat zone. Moreover, at that time Headquarters USAF simply could not assure the availability of sufficient additional personnel to the theater. Although desiring a more definitive combat crew rotation plan, the Air Force reluctantly included combat aircrews in the normal combat theater personnel rotation policy based on time in the theater.

Korea and Expansion

Headquarters USAF and Far East Air Forces emphasized the need for flexibility in rotation. The number of combat crew returnees would have to be directly proportionate to and contingent upon the replacement flow to the Far East. Personnel officials of the 452d Bombardment Wing committed a grave error when they not only failed to explain the flow requirement but actually advised aircrews that return to the United States was based on a fixed number of missions. When the crews were later informed of the error, a morale problem was born. The situation became more critical when the crews were then required to fly beyond the published planning standard because of lack of replacement personnel.[37]

Some of the dissatisfaction among the aircrews was also attributable to their misunderstanding of the different circumstances under which some went home earlier than others. Crew members recalled with the wing on August 10, 1950, had been ordered to serve for twenty-one months, whereas crew members who had been involuntarily recalled individually, from other Air Force Reserve wings, for example, to fill vacancies in the 452d incurred only a twelve-month obligation. Category R personnel, meanwhile, were obligated to serve for three years.

The morale problem among the 452d's shorthanded aircrew force also derived from the fact that the crews were being asked to fly difficult combat missions with no promise of relief in an airplane not suited for the task. The flying load could not be spread out because of severe shortages of both aircraft and experienced aircrews. In February 1951, General Partridge reported to a logistics official in the United States that "Our real shortage is B–26s . . . . Our shortages are considerable and unfortunately, our losses are heavy."[38]

At the beginning of the Korean War, the Air Force had no aircraft capable of detecting and destroying mobile enemy night ground traffic in the interdiction mission and no aircraft to conduct night intruder missions against the enemy's air forces. The Douglas B–26, designed as an attack bomber and employed in World War II as the A–26 in both light and medium bomber roles, represented the only, if less than satisfactory, potential for both roles. Not until the spring of 1951, after the entry of the Chinese threatened to extend the war, did an Air Staff board select the British-built Canberra B–57 jet bomber to replace the B–26, but even then the Far East Air Forces had to make do until sufficient quantities of the new aircraft could be delivered.[39]

The Far East Air Forces initially had no choice but to utilize the B–26s of the 3d Bombardment Wing, already in the theater, on both missions even though General Stratemeyer recognized the planes lacked a real ability to operate in bad weather or survive determined air opposition. Neither aircraft nor aircrews were available to expand the B–26 force in the Far East Air Forces in 1950 and 1951. The Tactical Air Command was operating a combat crew training school for B–25 crews, but its output could not keep pace with the need in the Far East. On the other hand, once the 452d and its B–26s were

The Air Force Reserve

brought on active duty and additional B–26s were drawn from other Air Reserve Forces units, they were depleted because the Douglas production line had been shut down immediately after World War II. Another problem involved in equipping combat units with the B–26 was that the fleet was replete with configuration changes and modification differences. A survey of the B–26 assets in the Far East Air Forces conducted by General Sweetser in April 1951 disclosed wide-ranging differences in communications, armaments, and fuel-carrying capabilities.[40]

The B–26s were effective in low-level attacks with machine guns, rockets, and bombs, but their crews found it difficult to maneuver at low altitudes in the small valleys of Korea, walled by hills rising from 500 to 5,000 feet. The moment of level flying needed to launch bombs and fire rockets made the light bombers vulnerable to ground fire, and combat losses soon forced them to bomb from medium altitudes.[41]

All of this operational difficulty recalled to the minds of the veteran pilots some of the Army Air Forces' early difficulties with the aircraft in World War II and the macabre ditty, "One a day into Tampa Bay!"[42] As another consideration, there were no B–26 bases in the United States to function as domestic rotational bases to support the overseas units with aircraft and trained personnel and provide a respite for combat-weary aircrews.

Commenting on the general demands of the B–26 mission and its physiological and psychological effects, the Fifth Air Force surgeon implied that B–26 aircrew morale rested on the razor's edge at best:

> The cramped quarters of the Douglas B–26 "Invader" aircraft being used, aggravated by the necessary carrying of parachutes, dinghies, and "Mae Wests" contribute to fatigue in flying personnel. Night missions and low-level strafing and bombing runs through mountains and unfamiliar terrain also contribute to nervous fatigue. It was felt that crews should have certain allotted areas in which to work consistently, so that they would become more familiar with the terrain, more confident, and thus more efficient.[43]

Finally, observing that their wing commander and other key personnel neither flew combat missions nor participated in mission debriefings, aircrewmen of the 452d concluded that these officials had no great interest in the airmen's day-to-day operational concerns.[44]

By April 1951, then, seeds of a serious morale problem in the 452d Light Bombardment Wing had been sown. When the unit's leadership failed to explain to the aircrews why they had to fly more combat missions in an unpopular airplane, a handful of crew members refused to do so. Directed by General Stratemeyer to get to the bottom of the problem, Lt. Gen. Earle E. Partridge, Fifth Air Force Commander, conducted a special investigation and an operational evaluation of the 452d. On May 10, on the basis of several indications that the morale of General Sweetser's unit had completely dissolved, General Partridge relieved him.[45]

Replacing General Sweetser on May 12, 1951, Col. Brooks A. Lawhon, formerly commander of the 35th Fighter-Interceptor Wing, swiftly stabilized the staggering unit. He entered in combat training many rated officers who had not been flying, getting them ready to take their places as combat crews. He also insisted on lead crew integrity and lead crew training, which soon proved its value. He reinstated military courtesy which, as it normally does, had accompanied morale out the door. He replaced key personnel as quickly as he could. As for the crew rotation problem which had started it all, Maj. Gen. Edward J. Timberlake authorized him to ground the flyers when they got up to seventy-five missions, even at the risk of decreasing the number of combat sorties.[46]

On June 18, 1951, the 452d completed converting to night operations. From the beginning of operations in Korea, the U.S. Air Force 3d Bombardment Wing and the Marine squadron VMF–513 had provided the only night intruder capability. Needing still more night effort, General Stratemeyer readily accepted General Vandenberg's advice to convert the 452d to night operations as well. Following its changeover, the wing flew more than 9,000 night combat missions.[47]

On May 10, 1952, having served its prescribed twenty-one months, the 452d Bombardment Wing was relieved from active military service, inactivated at Pusan East, and returned to the control of the Continental Air Command as an Air Force Reserve organization.[48]

731st Bombardment Squadron

The 452d's separated 731st Squadron completed its move from George AFB to Iwakuni AB, Honshu, on November 20, 1950. Four crews which had left George AFB as an advance echelon on September 15 participated in combat during October, and the unit put up its first complete squadron mission on November 24, 1950.[49]

The 731st filled a real need for General Stratemeyer. From the beginning of operations in Korea, the Air Force had been unable to attack moving targets at night. On September 6, General Vandenberg suggested that General Stratemeyer convert the 3d Group completely to night attack and assign the 731st Squadron, especially trained for low-level operations, to the understrength 3d Group. General Stratemeyer quickly implemented this solution to his night-attack problem. During its seven-month Korean tour, the 731st flew more than 9,000 hours of combat on 2,000 combat sorties. Its missions included high-, medium-, and low-level visual and radar bombing, front-line close support, flare drops, and armed reconnaissance—all under conditions of darkness. When the 3d Bombardment Wing was brought up to full strength by the acquisition of the 90th Bombardment Squadron as a third active force unit, the 731st was inactivated at Iwakuni June 25, 1951.[50]

The Air Force Reserve

437th Troop Carrier Wing

On August 15, 1950, the main contingent of the 437th Troop Carrier Wing, commanded by Brig. Gen. John P. Henebry, left O'Hare for Shaw AFB, South Carolina, by rail, air, and private automobile. At Shaw, personnel officials reconciled as best they could the number of persons on orders with the locator files and individual files, correcting errors in names, ranks, and serial numbers and trying to rectify malassignments. Commanders interviewed each man, making logical adjustments as they went along, immeasurably improving morale and efficiency. On September 2, personnel officials conducted a four-hour session in which commanders literally traded personnel back and forth. At that time 1,441 men were assigned to the 437th Troop Carrier Wing, acquired from the sources indicated in the following table.

437th Troop Carrier Wing Members September 1950

Source	No. of Members
Reservists called to active service at O'Hare	971
Reservists processing at O'Hare en route to Shaw	75
Regular Air Force members from O'Hare	187
Category R reservists from O'Hare	33
Reservists who volunteered for active service	8
Reservists from the 512th Troop Carrier Wing	95
Regular Air Force members from basic training	46
Personnel assigned to Continental Air Command	26

On October 15, the day before the 437th left Shaw, it got up to its full wartime strength of 1,569. Most of the additional men came from the Regular Air Force, including 60 from Sewart AFB, Tennessee, and another 59 fresh from basic training at Lackland AFB, Texas.[51] The 437th had sixteen C–46s at O'Hare. On August 10, it acquired the fifteen that belonged to the collocated 441st, and at Shaw it received seventeen others from various flying centers, bringing its aircraft complement to the forty-eight authorized. It began local flying at Shaw on August 22.[52]

Augmented by a few maintenance men, the command and operations elements of the wing deployed their C–46s to Japan. Delayed on the West

Korea and Expansion

Coast while the planes underwent modification for combat, they arrived at Brady AB, Kyushu, Japan, at sundown on November 8, just as the main body of the wing, which had crossed the Pacific aboard ship, marched in from the railroad station. The maintenance force quickly removed the long-range fuel tanks which had been installed for the overwater flight. Thirty-six hours after the first plane had landed, the 437th Troop Carrier Wing sent its first three planes on a routine combat cargo mission to Pyongyang Air Field in North Korea.*[53]

The 437th Troop Carrier Wing conducted operations for Combat Cargo Command, a provisional organization commanded by Maj. Gen. William H. Tunner. It was assigned to the Fifth Air Force, commanded by Lt. Gen. Earle E. Partridge, for support and administration. During the last 52 days of 1950, the wing flew almost 3,500 hours, conducting more than 1,500 effective combat sorties carrying passengers, cargo, or patients. When the 437th arrived in the theater, United Nations forces were driving north, and the U.S. Air Force was using airfields at Sinanju and Yonpo in the north. As the Chinese struck south, however, the 437th helped evacuate these bases. Soon 437th aircrews were helping move everything out of the airstrips near Pyongyang, and by year's end they were evacuating the Kimpo airstrip near Seoul.[54]

In December 1950, the 437th acquired the responsibility for conducting Combat Cargo Conmand's scheduled courier operation, a daily airline connecting all the major Japanese and Korean air bases and strips.[55] As the U.N. forces pressed their attack in the early months of 1951, it became necessary to augment the Army's overburdened supply system with airdrops of supplies. On February 24, therefore, the 437th conducted the first of many missions to resupply frontline U.S. Eighth Army troops.[56]

The 437th Troop Carrier Wing participated in its first combat personnel airborne drop on March 23, 1951, at Munsan-ni. The unit and the C–119-equipped 311th Troop Carrier Wing conducted a week's intensive training preparing to drop the 187th Regimental Combat Team at Chunchon. Then on March 21, forty-eight hours before it was to go, the mission was changed, not an unusual circumstance in fluid battlefield conditions. The 187th was now to be dropped at Munsan-ni instead of Chunchon, and that, on the morning of the 23d, not the 21st.[57]

Weather on the 23d was perfect, and for 30 minutes before the drop, B–26s of the 3d and 452d Bomb Wings softened up the objective area with 500-pound air-burst bombs and low-level strafing and rocket attacks. In addition to 55 C–46s, the 437th provided several crew members who had recently transitioned into C–119s to augment the 314th's crews. The wing's planes dropped 1,446 troops and 15½ tons of ammunition, food, and signal equipment. Enemy

---

*See Appendix 6 for for the wing's complete operations statistics while in the Far East.

The Air Force Reserve

interference was meager, and the wing suffered no injuries to personnel nor damage to aircraft. One aircraft dropped its troopers at the wrong place, incurring the displeasure of higher officials, but neither inordinate casualty nor tactical disadvantage resulted from the mischance.[58]

After the Munsan-ni drop, spring thaws and constant rains rendered roads virtually impassable, and the 437th resumed its supply drops to front line troops. When engine problems grounded all C–119s in the theater near the end of March, the entire aerial resupply burden fell upon the 437th and its C–46s. It dispatched 138 aircraft on paradrop missions during the last 10 days of the month, and the airdrops intensified in April. Early in April, most sorties were in support of Republic of Korea troops in the northeast sector. Later, as the Chinese again drove south, most of the drop missions were flown in direct support of the allied effort to thwart the communists' drive.[59]

437th Command Succession

As Brig. Gen. Luther W. Sweetser's star dimmed in Korea, Brig. Gen. John P. Henebry's brightened. Some sort of reorganization of Far East Air Force's airlift resources was imminent at the beginning of 1951, and Henebry, who had brought the 437th Troop Carrier Wing onto active duty and into the theater, always figured prominently in discussions of proposed realignments of key personnel.[60]

On January 25th, Far East Air Forces discontinued Combat Cargo Command and activated the 315th Air Division (Combat Cargo) with General Henebry as its commander. Like its predecessor, the 315th was directly subordinated to Far East Air Forces. When General Henebry became commander of the 315th Air Division on February 8, 1951, he was succeeded as wing commander initially by the wing executive officer, Col. John W. Lacey, and a month later by Col. John P. Roche, the 437th Troop Carrier Group conmanding officer.[61]

The 437th Troop Carrier Wing's tour of active military service ended on June 10, 1952, when it was inactivated and returned to the control of the Air Force Reserve. Its personnel, then all active force replacements, and its equipment were transferred to the concurrently activated 315th Troop Carrier Wing (Medium) at Brady AB, Japan.[62]

403d Troop Carrier Wing in the Far East

The 403d Troop Carrier Wing, one of the six units initially assigned to the Eighteenth Air Force, was eventually sent to the Far East. Commanded by Brig. Gen. Chester E. McCarty, the 403d mobilized on April 1, 1951, at Portland MAP, Oregon. The wing trained at home in its C–46s and participated in Eighteenth Air Force's routine training exercises for the next eleven months. On February 11, 1952, however, the Eighteenth Air Force directed it to transfer

Brig. Gen. Chester E. McCarty brought the mobilized 403d Troop Carrier Wing to Korea and succeeded General Henebry as commander of the 315th.

its C–46s and prepare to move overseas by March 25, 1952. By April 14, it was in place at Ashiya AB, Kyushu, Japan. There it acquired a second group and some independent squadrons as well as a new commander—General McCarty had been given command of the 315th Air Division a few days earlier.[63]

Upon arrival at Ashiya, the 403d immediataly converted to C–119s. This action finally solved the Far East Air Force's year-old problem of providing the Army with sufficient lift to handle the 187th Regimental Combat Team intact. The new arrangement was soon put to the test. In May 1952, the 403d airlifted the 187th Regimnental Combat Team to Pusan in an expedited movement incident to the quelling of a communist prisoner-of-war riot at Koje-do Island. The wing's subsequent operations encompassed airborne assault training, airdrop resupply, air landed resupply, and air movement of complete units in the Far East. It engaged in a number of airborne training missions with the 137th Regimental Combat Team. In October 1952 the wing participated in an airborne feint which was part of a United Nations Command amphibious demonstration off eastern Korea.[64]

After it had served the prescribed twenty-one months on active military service, the 403d Troop Carrier Wing was inactivated on January 1, 1953, and returned to reserve status.[65]

The Air Force Reserve

Employment of the Eighteenth Air Force Units

Other than the 403d, the reserve wings mobilized in 1951—the 435th, 516th, 434th, 514th, and 443d—remained with the Eighteenth Air Force for the balance of their active duty tours. They routinely trained in the troop carrier role, participated in several joint training exercises, and discharged the bulk of Tactical Air Command's troop-carrying responsibilities to other agencies. Among the major joint training exercises in which the units participated were Exercise SOUTHERN PINE in August 1951, Operation SNOWFALL in January–February 1952, and Exercise LONG HORN in March 1952.[66] On July 14, 1952, the 375th Troop Carrier Wing was relieved from active military service, and the other five were relieved at various times between December 1, 1952, and February 1, 1953.[67]

For one six-month period of its active duty tour, one of the reserve wings became something of a cold-weather outfit. In April 1952 the United States agreed to construct a weather station for Denmark a few hundred miles from the North Pole, a location inaccessible except by air. Ironically, the southern-most of the reserve wings, the 435th of Miami, drew the assignment to airlift the materials to the north country.[68]

Some Reserve Personnel Problems in the Far East Air Forces

The fact that Air Force reservists were recalled during the Korean War under three different prescribed lengths of service presented personnel officials of Far East Forces with severe challenges in administering them. Members of the 437th and 452d Wings recalled on August 10, 1950, were ordered to serve for twenty-one months. However, reservists involuntarily recalled to fill vacancies in the units incurred only a twelve-month obligation, and Category R cadre personnel were obligated for thirty-six months. Early in 1951, following President Truman's declaration of a national emergency, the Air Force encouraged an understanding among recalled reservists that they were needed for the overall expansion of the force, not merely as temporary replacements in the war zone.

Consequently, on April 24, 1951, in conjunction with this concept as well as to address the personnel problems caused in the Far East by the differing lengths of reserve tours, Headquarters USAF offered all reservists involuntarily recalled since June 25, 1950, the opportunity to remain on active duty for twenty-one months or to change to volunteer status and serve for an indefinite time. In July, Category R personnel were given the options of separating immediately, remaining on extended active duty, or enlisting in the Regular Air Force for three years.[69]

While giving individual reservists something tangible upon which to base their personal planning, these measures did little to relieve the immediate

Korea and Expansion

concerns of Far East Air Forces. The problem was posed by the presence in the Fifth Air Force of three reserve units—the 452d, 437th, and 731st—which had hundreds of involuntarily recalled reservists assigned to them as fillers and who would become eligible to go home on August 10, 1951. In March 1951 General Stratemeyer approved a Fifth Air Force plan to spread the twelve-month people around the theater in exchange for members of the Regular Air Force. Developed in response to requests of unit personnel officials for guidance, this plan would avoid the complete collapse of any individual unit by the simultaneous discharge of a host of men.[70]

Unfortunately, the exchange did not occur until May 17 when the 452d and 437th transferred about half of their twelve-month service people to other units in exchange for Regular Air Force men. Unit personnel officials conceded that was a good idea which would have been far better had it been implemented several months earlier when they had first asked for guidance. As it was, recipient units could anticipate only a few months' service from the reservists, and the exchange hardly seemed worthwhile. On July 9 about half the remaining twelve-month reservists started directly home to be discharged.[71]

In August 1951, a similar exchange was initiated for the reservists who had been recalled for twenty-one months. Since these people still had about nine months to serve, their new organizations were receiving a fairer return on the bargain, and wing personnel officials were more optimistic about the success of this exchange. As replacements arrived from the United States, these reservists were transferred to other units in the theater. Most being replaced at this point occupied key positions, and their release posed a hardship on the wings, but a simultaneous loss of all of them in March 1952 would have created even greater difficulties. In February 1952, the rotation home of the 21-month personnel who had not been exchanged in 1951 began, and the last of the personnel who had come overseas in October 1950 with the reserve wings went home.[72]

The Recall of Individual Air Force Reservists

The necessity of a partial mobilization in July 1950 raised a number of perplexing problems which became more difficult as the war progressed through its first year. The fundamental problem centered around the fact that the Air Force, requiring a substantial augmentation of reserve manpower in a circumstance no planner had ever envisioned, needed individual replacements and augmentees, not entire organized units.[73]

When the war broke out, aside from the two reserve wings it made available to General Stratemeyer in August, the Air Force's immediate need was for individuals to raise active force units to their authorized wartime strengths. National policy required preparedness for a conflict in Europe, and

109

The Air Force Reserve

the Air Force hesitated to withdraw manpower from the organized units of the Air Force Reserve and the Air National Guard, the only trained augmentation resource available. Therefore, discounting a handful of volunteers, the Air Force's individual replacements to satisfy the demands of the first phase of the Korean War as well as the expansion requirements came from reservists who, in the main, had not been participating in any organized program. The perceived unfairness of this circumstance aroused great bitterness among affected reservists and became the occasion for subsequent congressional legislation.

For nearly a month after American troops went into Korea, the Air Force strove to meet burgeoning personnel requirements with volunteers, offering its reservists and guardsmen opportunities for either enlistment or voluntary recall to active duty. The Air Force's first voluntary recall on June 30, 1950, sought communications and electronic officers, radar officers and specialists, telephone and radio operators and maintenance men, cryptographer operators and technicians, and wiremen and cablemen. Additional calls followed, and by July 20 the Continental Air Command had a consolidated recall requirement for almost 50,000 reservists. They included 2,000 pilots, 1,900 specialized observers, 4,326 nonrated officers, and 41,536 airmen.[74]

By this time, it was obvious that the need for men could not be satisfied by the voluntary recall which had produced only rated officers. Therefore, by July 19, President Truman had authorized involuntary recall of reservists for one year. The Continental Air Command directed its numbered air forces to select individuals from the Volunteer Air Reserve training program for assignment outside the command. Members of the command's corollary units and its mobilization augmentees and designees could be called up to fill the command's authorized vacancies. The mobilization augmentees of other commands could be recalled to fill any other vacancy in the Air Force. When feasible, corollary unit members were to be used to fill vacancies in their parent units. Members of the Volunteer Air Reserve could be recalled to fill a Continental Air Command vacancy when Organized Air Reserve sources were unavailable, but no member of an organized reserve unit at a flying center was to be individually recalled.[75]

Initiation of the involuntary recall immediately raised the question of deferments and delays. Air Staff and Continental Air Command officials agreed generally on the issues involved. It was the duty of all reservists to serve, but national interests might require some to defer their service. Such delays, however, did not exempt an individual indefinitely, and they were not to exceed six months. They were made on an individual basis; there were no blanket delays.

Reservists in medical, dental, and veterinary schools could be deferred as could employees of the Federal Bureau of Investigation, Civil Aeronautics Authority, and Atomic Energy Commission, along with others whose recall would critically affect community health or welfare. Finally, two-month deferments would be granted to those whose recall would work an undue hardship on either their dependents or themselves. If the condition of their hardship was not relieved within that time, these individuals would be transferred to the Inactive Reserve Section. Otherwise, no deferment was to exceed six months.[76] On September 8, 1950, President Truman signed the Dependency Assistance Act of 1950 which provided basic allowances to airmen with dependents. Thereafter, airmen in lower grades were no longer granted dependency deferments. After August 19, the numbered air forces had established appeal boards to which each reservist was entitled to present his case for deferment. The boards could defer if the conditions clearly met criteria. Either the board or the reservist could carry the case to a higher appeal board at Headquarters Continental Air Command, which served as the court of last resort.[77]

On October 24, 1950, as the fighting in Korea turned in favor of United Nations forces, Headquarters USAF directed the Continental Air Command to discontinue the involuntary recall of airmen immediately and to limit the recall of officers to certain critical specialties. The involuntary recall of officers was to be confined to individuals possessing skills not available from voluntary procurement or training resources. These men were to be drawn to the greatest possible extent from the organized Air Reserve. Officers with at least four dependents were not to be recalled, and any reservist with four or more dependents already recalled was to be separated upon application. No officer or airman was to be retained involuntarily for longer than twenty-one months.[78]

The entry of the Chinese into the war in November 1950, the resultant proclamation of a national emergency, and the accompanying military buildup early in 1951 required the Air Force to turn to its individual reserve resources again. Still desiring to preserve the effectiveness of existing units while rapidly expanding its manpower base, the Air Force needed the reservists to fill critical skill shortages and provide cadre for new units in the expanding force.[79]

The Air Force wished to fill as much of the new requirement as possible with volunteers. When volunteers did not materialize, the Air Force again started to draw members of the Volunteer Air Reserve involuntarily. Soon, however, the President's proclamation of a national emergency aroused a patriotic response, and the Air Force experienced a significant increase in enlistments in the active force. This permitted Headquarters USAF to slow its involuntary recall.[80]

The basic principle of the new recall program was that no reservist would be ordered into active military service until he had been found physically and administratively qualified, had undergone thorough reclassification, and his delay status had been determined. The Continental Air Command sought volunteers, but it selected reservists involuntarily from the Organized Air Reserve and the Air Force ROTC as well. The Air Staff also authorized the

The Air Force Reserve

command to recall all its own mobilization augmentees as well as those of all other commands. Medical personnel were inducted on a volunteer basis only. Under the new procedures, recalled airmen were retained in the United States until they demonstrated proficiency in their specialties.[81]

Even though restricted to the Organized Air Reserve, the involuntary recall of individuals in February and March 1951 was the heaviest of the war. The Continental Air Command recalled slightly more than 7,000 reservists in both February and March. About 4,000 were recalled in April, and the number leveled off thereafter at a slightly lower figure.[82]

In the fall of 1951, the Air Force again began releasing reservists from active duty. Anticipating that its recruiting program would continue to produce sufficient volunteers during the rest of fiscal year 1952, the Air Force reinstated its volunteer manning policy and directed the release of involuntarily recalled airman reservists and guardsmen as soon as possible. Recalled personnel who were surplus to the immediate requirements and who had six months or less remaining on their tours were released immediately. Otherwise, unless they applied to complete their current tours or to extend them, all involuntarily recalled airmen who had completed twelve months of service were to be released as soon as possible, but at least before December 15, 1951, in deference to the holiday season. Air Force Reserve and Air National Guard airmen with fewer than fourteen months retainability on extended active duty who wanted to stay on active duty were offered the opportunity to do so. They could accept immediate discharge for the purpose of enlisting or reenlisting in the Air Force Reserve and concurrent, voluntary entry into active military service for twenty-four months.[83]

About the same time, that is, the fall of 1951, the Air Force began to offer Air Force Reserve officers opportunities to leave active military service early. Officers who had come on duty voluntarily or involuntarily from a nonpay reserve element and who had served at least twelve months' active duty during in World War II and at least seventeen months since the start of the Korean War were eligible for immediate release or for the opportunity to remain on active duty in an indefinite status.[84]

Because of the several categories of service under which reserve officers were then serving, the instruction required some clarification. Part of the complexity was created by the passage of Public Law 51–82 on June 19, 1951, the Universal Military Training and Service Act. This legislation restricted the service of reservists recalled under its provisions to seventeen months.[*] As published on December 29, 1951, the new Continental Air Command instructions specifically exempted several groups of reserve officers then on active military service from early release. These groups included officers who

---

[*]Passage of the Universal Military Training and Service Act of 1951 is discussed in Chapter 5.

Korea and Expansion

had voluntarily or involuntarily entered active duty from pay status; those who had served less than twelve months during World War II; those who had voluntarily entered active military service between July 10, 1950, and June 18, 1951, and had subsequently signed a voluntary indefinite service statement; those who had voluntarily or involuntarily entered active military service on or after June 19, 1951, for any specified period of service in excess of seventeen months; and Air ROTC graduates on active duty who signed a deferment agreement and were required to serve for twenty-four months.[85]

The Air Force established a fiscal year 1953 recall requirement of more than 11,000 officers, but nothing like this number was called because the requirement dissolved. Late in March 1953, possibly reflecting the recent death of USSR Premier Josef Stalin, truce talks at Panmunjom intensified. Although the armistice would not be signed until July 26, the signal seemed clear: the war was over. By July 6, except to fill certain professional fields and school tours, the Air Force had suspended processing applications for or recalls to active duty.[86]

The "Fear of Flying" Incident

Along with a handful of others, 108 recalled Air Force Reserve officers between November 1951 and February 1952 at Randolph AFB, Texas, and other Air Training Command bases sought voluntary relief from flying for an expressed "fear of flying." Although some of these officers had been on extended active duty before the Korean War, most had been recalled for the Korean emergency. For one reason or another, they had reached the point where they did not want to fly in combat, if at all, and they did not want to be in the Air Force under any circumstance. In that frame of mind, they eagerly grasped what seemed a painless, legal way out.[87]

The painless means of being relieved of flying responsibilities was buried in a subparagraph of the Air Force regulation that prescribed flying status. Paragraph 9a(3) of Air Force Regulation (AFR) 35–16 read:

> *Fear of Flying.* The commanding officer of an Air Force Base will suspend a person assigned or attached for flying who exhibits a fear of flying, a fear of flying certain types of aircraft, or lack of incentive for flying, and will order his appearance before a a Flying Evaluation Board.[88]

Some of the rated personnel undergoing refresher B–29 training at Randolph AFB soon perceived that by merely submitting an application for relief on the basis of thir having become afraid of flying, they would immediately be grounded to await final disposition. Their example soon influenced many of their classmates to do the same thing, and voluntary groundings became epidemic. Training commitments were threatened, and Air Training

The Air Force Reserve

Command officials, along with those at Headquarters USAF and in the using commands, became deeply concerned.[89]

The Air Training Command was sufficiently disturbed to bring court-martial charges against six officers at Randolph AFB, Texas, and six at Mather AFB, California, for refusing to fly. Generating a wave of publicity, the six officers at Randolph—a pilot, two bombardiers, two navigators, and a radar observer—issued statements. They cited a fear of flying, pressure from their wives, the impact upon morale of crashes caused by poor maintenance, and a perception that reservists were doing all the combat flying as their reasons for refusing to participate. By this time, however, the Air Training Command was enforcing another provision of AFR 35–16 which made refusal to fly an act of official disobedience. This paragraph provided:

> Persons who desire suspension from flying will submit a letter through channels . . . . Commanders will forward requests through channels as expeditiously as possible, but will not suspend the person from flying status. Suspension of this nature will be made by Headquarters USAF only and will be based upon individual considerations of each case.[90]

The new policy provided that because of disruptions to training, all students would continue to fly until final action on grounding requests had been taken by the Air Force. Under this policy, refusal to fly became disobedience of orders.

The Vice Commander in Chief of Strategic Air Command, Lt. Gen. Thomas S. Power, was worried. His solution was "firm action." Although he was reluctant to establish hard-and-fast rules, he thought the existing circumstances required the Air Force to court-martial the airmen for refusal to obey orders. But the problem seemed more complex to General Vandenberg, Air Force Chief of Staff. He questioned the justice of court-martialing men who had been through two wars—some of those involved had already returned from Korea. Moreover, he thought that the situation reflected poor local command and that the pending court-martial cases should never have been brought to trial.[91]

In time, Air Training Command dropped the court-martial charges and simply dismissed the officers from the service. This course of action resulted from the gradual crystallization of a policy during the spring of 1952 which reflected, as much as anything else, the Air Force's constant quest for a truly volunteer force. First enunciated by General Vandenberg during a news conference at Randolph AFB on April 21, 1952, the new policy was codified by AFR 36–70 early in 1953. Incorporating General Vandenberg's very words, the operative paragraph stated:

> Training leading to an aeronautical rating has always been and must remain voluntary. Once an officer is rated, crew assignments, including refresher

training as needed, become military duties. Officers must be expected to assume this duty willingly for a considerable period of time. Efforts on the part of an individual, declared professionally and physically qualified, to avoid hazardous duty and in particular training for and actual combat, indicate he has failed to live up to the standards of an Air Force officer and he should be separated from the service. The length and character of officers' rated service will be considered when determining whether separation is appropriate . . . .[92]

In the end, then, the Air Force response was not as stern as the approach the Air Training Command had originally adopted nor the one preferred by officials such as General Power. For various reasons—an actual fear of flying, a desire to avoid combat, dissatisfaction with military service, and family pressure—a few of the rated reservists assigned to the Air Training Command for retraining in 1952 were willing to go to almost any length to avoid flying. Ultimately, the Air Force leadership accommodated them, deciding that an unwilling flyer did not contribute to force readiness.

Assessing the Mobilization

Between July 1950 and June 1953, the Continental Air Command processed 146,683 Air Force Reservists into active military service and 46,413 from the Air National Guard. Almost equally divided between officers and airmen (73,167 and 73,516, respectively), this number included twice as many Volunteer Air Reservists as it did members of the Organized Air Reserve. The Air Force called 98,782 reservists from the former category compared to the 47,891 (29,904 combat unit members, 8,781 mobilization assignees and designees, and 9,206 corollary unit members) who came from the latter.[93]

About 73.3 percent of all those mobilized were brought in during fiscal year 1951, including all those who came from the combat units. Much of the early evaluation, most of it highly critical, came from the unit level. The 452d Light Bomb Wing and the 437th Troop Carrier Wing bitterly criticized their supporting Air Reserve flying training centers for shoddy record keeping and a general lack of preparedness, an assessment with which Continental Air Command Deputy for Operations Brig. Gen. Herbert B. Thatcher agreed.[94]

A major investigation of the recall program was conducted by a committee under the chairmanship of Brig. Gen. Clyde H. Mitchell, appointed on November 6, 1950, by Continental Air Command Vice Commander Maj. Gen. Charles T. Meyers to investigate both the unit and the individual recall programs. Reporting on December 14, the Mitchell committee recommended corrective action in the areas of recall procedures, publicity, Air Force controls, Continental Air Command controls, the personnel processing squadrons, classification, adequacy of records, effects on major commands, the unit recall,

The Air Force Reserve

and additional specification serial numbers (forerunners to current Air Force specialty codes). The committee concluded that the greatest deterrent to a satisfactory recall had been deficiencies in the basic personnel records of the reservists. Lacking fundamental personal/career information, the records caused many difficulties. This led to an inability to locate reservists, inability to recall them in their best skills, lack of knowledge of probable physical conditions, and a minimum of information on changes in their personal affairs. Commending the records purification effort then going on, the committee recommended that all records administration be standardized at the numbered air forces and that the records be periodically reviewed.[95]

Lacking established recall procedures at the outset, the Air Staff and Continental Air Command bombarded the field with a succession of ad hoc instructions, passing more than 200 changes in procedures to the field in the first months. Many were minor, but the great number produced excessive confusion and often led to doubt as to the proper procedure to follow. Therefore, the committee recommended that the Air Force maintain current recall instructions at all times.

A major, visible part of the mobilization had involved the recall of twenty-five combat wings in fiscal 1951. The first ten were recalled between August 1950 and May 1951 to fill defined unit requirements. Despite the problems of the 452d Light Bomb Wing, each of these units fulfilled its intended role, and most were well-led. For that matter, even while suffering under weak

In the summer of 1950, Brig. Gen. Herbert B. Thatcher, Continental Air Command Deputy Chief of Staff, Operations, worked hard to assure that mobilized Air Force Reserve units were prepared to take on their role.

Korea and Expansion

leadership, the 452d's combat crews had done their jobs. Under a new commander, the unit stayed on to earn two Air Force Distinguished Unit Citations. The members of the dissolved units provided the Air Force a trained resource that otherwise simply would not have been available.

Illuminated by national newspaper publicity, the group of Air Force Reservists in Texas hurt the reservist community's overall reputation when they refused to fly after being properly ordered to do so. Their actions seemed to reflect the general societal attitudes of the time, and moreover, they represented but a small percentage of all reservists. In sum, if not without problems, the Air Force Reserve responded as well as it could have the first time the Air Force called upon it in an emergency. Speaking about a year after the Korean War ended, Air Force Vice Chief of Staff General Thomas D. White observed:

> We can all be proud of our Reserves during that emergency. Its individual training program provided the only quick source of reinforcement of our active forces. Our two leading jet aces were Reserve officers and of 31 jet aces, eight were Air Reservists, and four were Air National Guardsmen. Reserve officers alone shot down 66 enemy aircraft in Korea.[96]

The imperfections in record keeping, equipment shortages, and absence of mobilization procedures, to say nothing of basic war and mobilization plans, were irritants that the Air Force and the Continental Air Command overcame with great difficulty during the mobilizations of 1950–1952. Of far greater significance was the impact of a changing foreign policy on the fundamental concept of the citizen soldier in the United States. The Cold War and the concomitant policy of international collective security led the nation to employ its reserve forces out of the country in a time of peace, or at least during an undeclared war. The ramifications of this led civilian officials at the Departments of the Air Force and Defense into troubled thoughts as they tried to evaluate the mobilizations in the broader context of the United States on the post–World War II world stage.

The military services turned to their civilian components to satisfy the manpower demands of the Korean War and the worldwide expansion. In doing so, they often called up individual reservists who had been affiliated with the reserves in name only, while passing up other individuals who had actively affiliated and trained as well as the members of reserve and National Guard units. These practices created great bitterness among the affected reservists and their families and led to indignant questions from members of Congress. Consequently, civilian officials of the Departments of the Air Force and Defense began in the fall of 1950 to review reserve policies. Lead roles were taken by Thomas K. Finletter, Secretary of the Air Force, and Anna M. Rosenberg, Assistant Secretary of Defense.

The Air Force's dilemma seemed particularly acute to Finletter, who became the second Secretary of the Air Force on April 24, 1950. In September

The Air Force Reserve

1950, as the Air Force prepared to mobilize the second pair of Air Force Reserve wings, along with some Air National Guard units, Secretary Finletter became "deeply troubled" over the reserve situation. The basic difficulty was the reservists' perception, although the principle was not founded in law, that their commitment was to serve the country in all-out war. They certainly had not given the Air Force an option on their services if they should be called as part of the peacetime establishment of the United States.[97]

Secretary Finletter saw the peacetime establishment as being greatly increased, largely with reservists being recalled for that purpose. This was not their bargain, he thought, and while he did not think it would create a serious question while fighting was actually going on in Korea, he did believe the problem would become acute when the fighting ended and the United States returned to being at peace, or at least not being at war. Then, he thought, the Air Force would hear from the reservists with questions as to why they were being called to form part of what was really the regular establishment. And, he thought, they would have much justice on their side. The Air Force, therefore, had to find a legitimate solution to the problem.[98]

Finletter thought the people in the recalled flying units had great enthusiasm in anticipation that they would soon be in the combat zone. He did not think for a minute that they would retain that enthusiasm if the Korean situation calmed down. He wanted to release immediately anyone who wanted to go home, especially those who had been recalled involuntarily, and to replace them with individuals from other sources. Finally, he was concerned about another category of reservist, those who had not been called but remained subject to call. They were being subjected to serious uncertainties in their business and personal affairs. They were somewhat unemployable because of their readiness to serve their country. Finletter wanted to be in a position soon to announce that these people would not be recalled unless the war expanded to the point where everyone was needed. He hoped that the manpower requirement could be met by volunteers. If not, he wanted to rely on an intensified recruiting program and, if necessary, the draft. At any rate, short of an all-out war and a full-blown national emergency, he did not think the Air Reserve Forces should provide the buildup.

Despite his concern about these matters and his belief that the Air Reserve Forces should not provide the manpower for the authorized buildup, Secretary Finletter did not completely absolve the reservists of their responsibilities, nor did he examine what else could have been done to address the issues the military establishment faced in June 1950. Responding in 1950 and 1951 to scores of recalled reservists and guardsmen who complained to him of a "raw deal," he sympathized with the World War II veterans who protested being recalled for something short of an all-out war, especially those who had not been participating in reserve training. Nevertheless, even in hindsight, he did not see how the Air Force could have performed the job the President ordered it to do without using its reservists. This was especially true, he said, of the organized reserve units who took reserve training in peacetime and were therefore much more qualified to be of immediate service than those in the unorganized reserve.[99] But the fact that the Air Force had found itself in a position where it had to condone and accept inequitable treatment of its reservists so that it could expand in time of peace "seriously disturbed" the Secretary. As a result, by the end of 1950, Finletter and other Air Force officials were examining the whole rationale of the service's reserve programs.[100]

Anna M. Rosenberg became Assistant Secretary of Defense in December 1950, and she took the lead in dealing with some of the same concerns with respect to all the military reserves. Accepting the reserve problem as her top priority, Mrs. Rosenberg determined to do everything she could to prevent inequities and to relieve hardships that had already occurred.[101]

Secretary Rosenberg recognized that since practically all the individual reservists had been needed, in contrast to relatively few of the units, great recrimination resulted as almost every recalled reservist could point to other individuals and categories of individuals who he thought might more justifiably have been called. She insisted upon handling all her correspondence, maintaining that she had gained extremely important insight into the problem and that some of the most constructive and corrective measures the Defense Department had taken with respect to the recall problems had resulted from her personal review and interchanges with her correspondents. The reason the reservists had been called, of course, was that the need for trained men had manifested itself suddenly, and no other resource had been available. She hoped that the nation could build up a new trained reserve through the universal military training and service program the Defense Department was preparing to present to the Congress when it reconvened in January 1951.[102]

For its part, stimulated by the recalls of 1950 and the resultant protests and recriminations, Congress now prepared to exercise its Constitutional responsibility for "organizing, arming, and disciplining the Militia."

5

Development of Post-Korean War Policies for Reserve Forces

> Current war planning has established a firm mobilization requirement for 51 tactical wings in the Air Reserve Forces.
>
> —General Nathan F. Twining, Chief of Staff, USAF,
> December 1955

Reflecting the attitude of most reservists, by 1951 Congress and the Department of Defense were dissatisfied with the disorder and inequities that had marked the recall of reservists to active military service in the last half of 1950. Incomplete and outdated records of individual reservists had made administration of the recall difficult. Moreover, unable to call upon younger men who had never served, the nation had to send World War II veterans back to war. The Department of Defense requested universal military training legislation to provide the military services with a source of nonveterans. Thus motivated, Congress passed a series of laws in the first half of the 1950s to strengthen the reserve programs, and the Department of Defense established new reserve policies in April 1951 to guide the administration and training of all reserve components. For its part, the Air Force published a long-range plan for the Air Reserve Forces, and for the first time it established a mobilization requirement for fifty-one Air Reserve Forces wings. It also began the tedious task of matching individual reservists who were not members of organized units to mobilization positions.

The Air Force Reserve

Secretary of the Air Force Harold E. Talbott swears in General Nathan F. Twining as Chief of Staff, United States Air Force. In January 1955 General Twining issued a memorandum directing the Air Staff to take all appropriate actions to equip and train the fifty-one Air Reserve Force wings to take their places in the combat forces of the U.S. Air Force.

Universal Military Training and Service Act of 1951

In 1950, after a lifetime of advocating universal military training, President Harry S. Truman found himself in the strange position of recommending that Congress not establish such a program at that time because he believed that prosecution of the Korean War would require all the resources and energies of the armed forces. Nevertheless, as President he continued to advocate universal military training as a matter of long-range policy.[1]

Dissatisfied with an administration bill submitted in January 1951, Congress passed a substitute measure as the Universal Military Training and Service Act on June 19, 1951. Amending the Selective Service Act of 1948, the new law required every male citizen between eighteen and twenty-six years of age to register under the Selective Service System, and it made those between eighteen and one-half and twenty years of age eligible for training and service in the armed forces. The President was authorized to induct men into the armed forces in peacetime as well as in wartime. Each person inducted would undergo a four-month period of basic military training and then be transferred to an active force unit for twenty months' service. Everyone inducted, enlisted, or appointed in the armed forces would be obligated for a combination of eight years active and reserve service.[2]

The law directed creation of the National Security Training Commission to supervise the training of the National Security Training Corps, which was to be created to administer the training. Before any universal training or service could occur, however, Congress had to approve a National Security Training Commission plan specifying the types of basic military training; measures for the personal safety, health, welfare, and morals of the members; a code of conduct, including penalties for violation; recommendations with regard to disability and death benefits for members of the corps; and descriptions of duties, liabilities, obligations, and responsibilities to be imposed upon the members.

Even then, however, no person was to be inducted into the National Security Training Corps until Congress by concurrent resolution or the President by executive order eliminated the mandatory period of active service (contrasted with training) required of persons who had not attained their nineteenth birthday. This meant that when the government stopped inducting men younger than nineteen or all men, those under nineteen would be liable for universal military training.[3]

The universal military training provisions of the 1951 legislation never became effective, but passage of the act marked the first time in American history that Congress approved the principle of a universal military training program to be administered at the national level. Hearings pertaining to the law and various proposed substitutes set a new pattern of investigation into the subject of national military manpower. Not limited to military aspects of manpower utilization, they also embraced moral, religious, industrial, educational, agricultural, and scientific aspects as many organizations and segments of American society, crossing traditional political party lines, presented their views.[4]

The National Security Training Commission drafted a bill incorporating the plan required by the Universal Military Training and Service Act and turned it over to Congress where Carl Vinson, Chairman of the House Committee on Armed Services, opened hearings on January 15, 1952.[5] Augmented by interest groups which cut across regional lines, the old coalition of western and midwestern Republicans and southern Democrats, which had turned back earlier universal military training measures, now defeated the National Security Training Commission's plan for a training corps, and the bill was returned to

The Air Force Reserve

the House Armed Services Committee, never to reemerge.[6] Without an approved plan, universal military training could not go into effect, at least not under the auspices of the Universal Military Training and Service Act of 1951.

The failure to implement the universal military training provisions of the Universal Military Training and Service Act left only its selective service provisions applicable and created another unfair situation. Young men who would be drafted under it would be subject to two years of active duty followed by six years in reserve status and susceptible to a recall to active duty. Because the draft was selective, however, fully a third of the nation's available men would never be drafted, would never be trained, and would never serve.[7] The reserve forces of the United States would remain a reserve of veterans.

The Armed Forces Reserve Act of 1952

Whether the universal military training provisions were ever implemented or not, Congress and the military services had recognized for some time that definitive legislation was required to organize and guide the nation's reserve programs. In July 1951, after earlier attempts had foundered in the absence of unanimous service support, the Secretary of Defense proposed new legislation.

Completing its hearings on August 22, 1951, a subcommittee headed by Representative Overton Brooks concluded that the Defense Department bill was neither sufficiently concrete nor comprehensive, and it prepared its own draft bill. Developed in consultation with representatives of the Department of Defense and all the major reserve and veterans organizations, House Resolution (H.R.) 5426 was a complete revision of the Defense Department bill. The House of Representatives passed the measure as the Armed Forces Reserve Act of 1952 on October 15.[8]

For various reasons, including recesses and hearings related to the prosecution of the Korean War, the Senate Armed Services Committee did not consider H.R. 5426 until May 1952. By then, the House had rejected the plan for the National Security Training Corps, leaving the Universal Military Training and Service Act of 1951 nothing more than an extension of the Selective Service System. H.R. 5426, presented as a companion piece of the universal military training act, was now crippled.

Major General Ellard A. Walsh, president of the National Guard Association, thereupon revoked his earlier support, protesting that H.R. 5426 was unworkable without a universal military training and service training program. The executive director of the Reserve Officers Association, Brig. Gen. E. A. Evans, took a realistic approach to the matter. "We must stop all the wishful thinking that UMT [universal military training] is just around the corner," he said. "We must now present a program based on actual conditions. We still want UMT, but just because we do not have it is no reason to do nothing. This bill is the only true foundation for a UMT program." Colonel A. B. McMullen, the executive director of the Air Reserve Association, agreed with Evans and rejected the National Guard Association's stand. He supported H.R. 5426 as part of a four-point program to be completed before the reserve forces could be properly organized, trained, and integrated into the overall armed forces team. He identified the other parts as universal military training, an equitable reserve promotion policy, and equalization of benefits among the regular and reserve components.

Assistant Secretary of Defense Anna M. Rosenberg was disappointed by the National Guard's turnabout and, like General Evans, took a pragmatic view of matters. Naturally, she testified, the Defense Department wanted to build a reserve of nonveterans, but the fact was that without universal military training, the reserve would continue to consist almost entirely of veterans. The reality then facing the department was that men were coming off active duty with six-year reserve obligations, and a system was needed to accommodate them. She strongly endorsed the Senate bill which would let the veterans know exactly where they stood and was which designed to meet requirements with or without a universal military training system.[9]

President Truman approved H.R. 5426 as the Armed Forces Reserve Act of 1952 on July 9, 1952. In its final form, the new law appeared to most persons and organizations interested in reserve matters, the National Guard Association excepted, as a first concrete step in curing the ills of the national reserve program. It codified many existing laws, regulations, and practices; it gave the combat veteran some protection against being mobilized before others who had not served; and it removed several inequities of treatment of reservists. It was the first legislation ever passed that pertained exclusively to the reserve forces.

At its center, the law established Ready, Standby, and Retired Reserve categories within each reserve component to define liability for call to active duty. The Ready Reserve consisted of units or members who were liable for active duty in time of war, in time of national emergency declared by Congress or proclaimed by the President, or when otherwise authorized by law. The Standby Reserve consisted of units or members—or both—of the reserve components, other than members in the Retired Reserve, liable for active duty only in time of war or a national emergency declared by Congress or when otherwise authorized by law.

Except in time of war, no unit or member of the Standby Reserve could be ordered to active duty unless the appropriate service secretary determined that adequate numbers of the required types of units or individuals of the Ready Reserve were not available. Members of the Retired Reserve could be ordered to active duty involuntarily only in time of war or national emergency declared by Congress or when otherwise authorized by law. All other reservists not on the Inactive Status List Retired would be placed in the Ready Reserve. The strength of the Ready Reserve therefore was established by automatic action, for it would include all active status reservists who had not qualified for nor requested Standby Reserve status.*

The law's significant provisions, which all reservists and their advocates had sought since the end of World War II, were that each service establish an adequate and equitable system of promotion for participating reservists, appoint reserve officers for indefinite periods instead of the previous five-year terms, and give all reservists common federal appointments and written contracts while on active duty. The appointment of reserve officers for indefinite terms would reduce the loss of reservists by removal through the periodic renewal feature, promote savings by eliminating commission renewals, and eliminate the stigma of probationary scrutiny of reservists. The common federal appointment would make each member of the Air Force Reserve and the Air National Guard a reserve of the Air Force. Written contracts would give more security to reservists on active duty. Any member so contracted and released involuntarily, except for misbehavior or inefficiency, prior to the expiration of his agreement would be entitled to receive remuneration equal to that for one year's service.[10]

The Eisenhower Administration and National Reserve Policy

Campaigning as the Republican Party candidate for the presidency in 1952, Dwight D. Eisenhower criticized the Truman administration for failing to develop a strong reserve program despite the recent passage of the Armed Forces Reserve Act. He promised to establish a sound reserve program based on military needs which would encourage maximum participation by all qualified personnel and afford reasonable assurances to reservists as to their liability to recall. Eisenhower seemed committed to some form of universal military training, but he agreed with those who claimed that universal training and the draft were incompatible.[11] With the draft due to expire in 1955, President Eisenhower had to face the issue, and in doing so, he turned away from universal military training and service.

In July 1953, the President asked Julius Ochs Adler, publisher of the *New York Times*, whom he had just appointed Chairman of the National Security Training Commission, to advise him on three related issues by December 1, 1953. He sought remedies for the inequities in the existing method of securing men for the armed forces reserves and a recommendation on the desirability of conducting universal military training simultaneously with the draft. Eisenhower also wanted an estimate of how the establishment of a universal military

---

*It should be noted that the Air Force never established Standby Reserve units although it had a large reservoir of individual standby reservists.

As President, Dwight D. Eisenhower advocated new national reserve policies to adapt the reserve forces to a nuclear age.

training program would affect the building of a strong citizen reserve capable of rapidly expanding the regular forces from peacetime to wartime strength. A week later, the President asked Arthur S. Flemming, Director of the Office of Defense Mobilization, to study the availability of manpower to support a military training program and the active force peacetime manning along with the impact on the national manpower bank.[12]

The President's requests precipitated an internal struggle within his administration which, pitting the National Security Training Commission and the Selective Service System against the defense agencies, lasted for fifteen months before the latter defeated once and for all the notion of universal military training in favor of a reserve of veterans. The National Security Training Commission's report, *Twentieth Century Minutemen*, submitted on December 1, 1953, was an unabashed plea for universal military training. It determined that the country needed a trained reserve of nonveterans and concluded that all young men should share the obligation to serve the nation and that the existing reserve system was unfair and inadequate. The commission recommended that all fit young men eighteen years of age should register with the Selective Service System and enter the national security training pool. Young men would draw lots upon registering with Selective Service to determine whether they would be liable for service or training.[13] The commission declared past reserve policy not only morally wrong but also socially unfair and financially costly. It insisted the nation could not justly continue to place veteran reservists in double jeopardy while excusing nonveterans from both service and training.[14]

Lawrence A. Appley, whom Arthur Flemming had appointed to conduct the study of manpower issues requested by the President, delayed his final report until he had reviewed *Twentieth Century Minutemen*. Based on his belief that trained manpower to augment the armed forces could be provided more quickly by the reserve, Appley's report submitted on December 18, 1953, contravened the National Security Training Commission's report by calling for a reserve of veterans and rejecting universal military training. Appley questioned the desired size of the reserve components.[15] Therefore, in submitting the report to the President on January 6, 1954, Flemming asked that the national manpower program be more precisely defined. He asked that the National Security Council determine the size and composition of the required military reserve forces. He blocked any attempt to resuscitate the universal military training program by recommending that the administration defer, pending determination of the size, composition, and training of the reserve forces, any decision on putting into effect the universal military training provisions of the Universal Military Training and Service Act. Flemming thereby sidestepped the recommendations the National Security Training Commission had made to the President a few weeks earlier.[16]

Accepting Flemming's recommendations on January 8, 1954, President Eisenhower asked him to present them to the National Security Council no later than April 1, 1954. A few days later, giving the National Security Training Commission the kiss of death, the President asked Chairman Adler to work closely with Flemming on the new studies.[17]

Establishing the Mobilization Requirement

During the next six months, the Office of Defense Mobilization, the Department of Defense, and the National Security Council developed a paper outlining the desired size, organization, procurement, training, and mobilization process of the reserve forces. The paper asserted the imperative that ample reserve strength be established around a core of competent prior-service personnel. Reserve forces consisting of large numbers of relatively untrained individuals would not satisfy national security requirements, it said, because they would be unable to carry out the reserve forces' mission of mobilizing immediately. Refining one of the Appley report's proposals, the paper proposed a Service Callable Reserve of instantly available trained units and individuals to meet the need for expanded military manpower during the first six months of conflict or crisis. The Service Callable Reserve would be divided into a First Line Reserve and an Auxiliary Reserve on the basis of the required training participation rather than liability for service.

The First Line Reserve was to consist of individuals and units in training who would be immediately available for active duty. The Auxiliary Reserve would be composed of trained individuals and units in numbers which, together with the First Line Reserve, would meet requirements from the Reserve Forces of an expanded need for trained military manpower during the first six months of an emergency. Reservists not in the Service Callable Reserve would comprise the Selectively Callable Reserve and be liable for active duty only when authorized by Congress. On the basis of the strategic and mobilization plans of each of the services, the Department of Defense established a total Service Callable Reserve requirement of 3,055,894 (1,692,235 for the Army, 774,059 for the Navy, 200,000 for the Marine Corps, 39,600 for the Coast Guard, and 350,000 for the Air Force). Requirements for Selectively Callable Reserves were established at 635,150 for the Army, 52,601 for the Navy, 50,000 for the Air Force, and 22,000 for the Marine Corps.

The Defense paper assumed that all males entering the armed forces by any means would acquire a total military obligation of eight years and that upon entering the reserve forces they would become members of the Service Callable Reserve. Individuals who served with the active forces for four or more years would be transferred upon separation from active duty to the Service Callable Reserve.

Requirements for about 105,000 personnel with no previous military service validated by the services could be met by voluntary enlistments of youth below the draft age and by the induction of draft-eligible persons through the Selective Service System. All non–prior service personnel entering the reserve forces would be ordered to active duty for training. Upon completion of their initial training, they would be assigned to the First Line Reserve where they could be required to serve the remainder of their eight-year obligation.[18]

On June 17, 1954, the National Security Council suggested that the proposed reserve program should include sufficient veterans to build up the reserve forces to their required strength, but at the same time, men with service in World War II and Korea who did not wish to serve in the reserve forces should be released as expeditiously as possible. It was proposing, therefore, a reserve of veterans, but not necessarily combat veterans.[19]

The President, in a meeting with Defense Secretary Charles E. Wilson, Mr. Flemming, and other officials on July 26, approved the concept of the revised paper. He asked only that it specifically require that all inductees go into military service instead of some going into the National Security Training Corps, and that the pay and prerequisites of inductees be determined by length of service. Although the Selective Service System, which was not represented at the meeting, protested, by the late summer of 1954 sufficient signals had come from the White House to embolden the Defense Department and the National Security Council to ignore not only the National Security Training

The Air Force Reserve

Commission but the Selective Service System as well. On September 30, 1954, therefore, the National Security Council approved an Office of Defense Manpower–Defense Department report that closely resembled the paper the agencies had submitted to the White House on May 24, 1954.*[20]

The report calculated that after fiscal year 1956 an overall reserve requirement would exist for about 3.5 million men, just about double the size of the active forces, with an Air Force portion of 350,000. This Air Force Service Callable Reserve would be essentially an M-Day force and would be subjected to continuous training to maintain it in a high state of readiness. It was to be composed largely of flying units designed to be so highly trained and proficient that they could be immediately deployed as units or used as a source of replacements for early losses. Qualified individual reservists could be called to replace those members of the active force moved from support to combat units.

The report also stated the need for a Selectively Callable Reserve consisting of other reservists who would be liable for recall as authorized by Congress. The number of this force was established as about 750,000, but with so many unknowns about its procurement and training, the paper contained no definitive guidance about it.[21]

Development of the National Reserve Plan

Its major manpower issues settled and having opted for a reserve of veterans, the Eisenhower administration began to develop the specifics of a reserve program in 1954. On August 30, 1954, the President publicly confirmed his administration's commitment to the timely development of develop an equitable reserve program.[22]

The Office of the Secretary of Defense completed the promised program

---

*The National Security Training Commission made one last formal appeal for the National Security Training Corps and universal military training on November 15, 1954. The President listened, but did not react (Memo, NSTC to NSC, subj: Implementation of National Security Training, Nov 15, 1954–DDEL). On June 30, 1957, at the suggestion of Congress and with the concurrence of the President, the National Security Training Commission went out of existence. Although it maintained to the end that to be ready in fact as well as in name, all reservists should receive at least six months' active duty training. It admitted that the reserve programs were substantially under way and that the commission's mission had been accomplished. An intensive advertising campaign had helped build up reserve strength, and possibly of great surprise to the commission, the military services were highly sensitive to their responsibilities to the youth and the nation and maintained active oversight activities to discharge them (NSTC, *Final Report to the Congress* [Washington, D.C., 1957]–DDEL, Bryce N. Harlow Records, NSTC. Box 6).

by the first week in December 1954, and Carter L. Burgess, the Assistant Secretary of Defense, presented it to the President and several leadership groups within the administration. On each occasion, President Eisenhower set Burgess' briefing in the context of his defense philosophy. The United States now had to focus its security efforts, he thought, on retaliatory forces and continental defense. The President had reduced the Army and those parts of the Navy not involved in the deterrent or continental defense, but he asserted the new approach to the reserve forces would provide the backup they needed.[23]

The National Reserve Plan, as the Eisenhower reserve program was called, expanded upon the concept paper developed earlier in the year by the defense agencies. Secretary Burgess' presentations and ensuing discussions focused on four aspects: provision for a six-month active-duty training program, avoidance of universal military training, the need to have trained men other than those who had already served, and the status of the six-month trainees in later years.

Over the objections of the National Security Training Commission, whose officials recognized that passage of the legislation would toll the death of their agency, the Office of the Secretary of Defense incorporated the National Reserve Plan in a draft bill submitted to Congress on December 22, 1954. The proposed program would retain the Ready Reserve and Standby Reserve as established by the Armed Forces Reserve Act of 1952. Generally, reflecting the concepts of the Selectively Callable and Service Callable Reserves of the administration's earlier studies, the Ready Reserve would be a trained, organized force constituting the reserve manpower base for the initial phases of a general mobilization. Its members would be obligated to participate in reserve training.

The Standby Reserve, which would not be required to train, would be a reserve manpower pool of undetermined size from which individuals would be drawn for the follow-on phases of a general mobilization. The Ready Reserve would be continuously screened and its personnel moved to the Standby Reserve to assure a proper balance of military skills. The retention of individuals possessing critical civilian skills would be limited to a quota sufficient to maintain a basic manning requirement for those skills. In the event of mobilization, the Selective Service System would administer the recall of the Standby Reserve.

Men leaving active service with a remaining obligation would be the primary source of personnel for the reserve forces, but the National Reserve Plan also provided for direct entry of nonveterans into the reserve forces. Individuals younger than nineteen years of age and having no prior active military service could volunteer for a ten-year military obligation under certain conditions. They would receive six months of active duty for training and be paid $30 a month with no veterans' benefits accruing. After their initial training, continued deferment from induction would be contingent upon their satisfactory participation in the reserve training program.[24]

The Air Force Reserve

On January 13, 1955, President Eisenhower sent Congress a special message on national security requirements which, among other measures, requested that Congress enact legislation to implement the administration's National Reserve Plan. The President told Congress that under the new National Reserve Plan the draft and the reserve forces, in conjunction with the regular establishment, would fulfill the nation's security needs with the least possible disruption of the lives of individual citizens and of the civilian economy. This would require certain changes in reserve forces legislation, however, and he identified five principal areas where such changes were necessary.

First, noting that existing law divided reserve personnel into categories that did not lend themselves fully to strategic requirements, he asked that to meet the requirements of an immediate mobilization, the law provide one group of reservists who could be organized into a force maintained in a high degree of readiness, and that to meet the requirements of a general mobilization if one should be needed, it provide for a group of prior-service individuals to be called into military service by a selective process. Second, he recommended that legislation be adopted to permit young men seventeen to nineteen years of age to volunteer for six months' basic training followed by active reserve participation for nine and one-half years. Third, to assure that the National Guard receive an adequate flow of young men with appropriate basic training, he asked that men enlisting in the National Guard be required by law to receive basic training with the active services. He also recommended that legislation be adopted to induce participation in reserve training by a provision that men who had served fewer than two years on active duty might be recalled to active duty to maintain or restore their proficiencies. Finally, he recommended that Congress enact legislation permitting states in time of peace to raise and maintain organized militia forces that would take over the National Guard's domestic activities upon its mobilization.[25]

Passage of the Reserve Forces Act of 1955

When Secretary of Defense Charles E. Wilson testified before the Brooks subcommittee of the House Armed Services Committee on February 8, 1955, the reception was hardly cordial. Among other committee members, James E. Van Zandt, William G. Bray, and James P. S. Devereux resented the Department of Defense's failure to implement the Armed Forces Reserve Act of 1952 and were skeptical that the services would do better with a new reserve plan. Congressman Bray was also angry that the administration had asked the Senate not to consider the reserve promotion bill on which the House committee had worked so hard."[*][26]

On March 25, concluding that the administration's bill required drastic revision, Representative Brooks introduced H.R. 5297 as a substitute. The new bill encountered serious opposition in the parent Armed Services Committee, whose members inexplicably viewed it as a faintly disguised attempt to get universal military training or service, the last thing the Eisenhower administration wanted.[27]

Although the President emphasized a national need for the law during a press conference in June, the legislation remained bogged down, primarily over the definitions of reserve categories and the length of obligated service, and Representative Brooks introduced H.R. 7000, whose semantics promised flexible interpretation. It moved quickly through the House Armed Services Committee, and when Congressman Adam Clayton Powell, who had obstructed passage of the earlier bills by similar tactics, introduced an amendment forbidding assignment of reservists to segregated National Guard units, southern congressmen amended the bill to eliminate all mention of the National Guard.[28]

Although not satisfied that the law granted him everything he had asked for on January 13, the President signed the law on August 9, 1955, and conceded that it would definitely strengthen the reserve structure. It provided special enlistment programs with forced reserve participation intended to provide an input of the reserve components into Ready Reserve units and to keep such units vitalized. It amended the Universal Military Training and Service Act of 1951 to provide obligated tours to conform to such programs. In addition, the President was given limited authority to call a portion of the Ready Reserve to active duty without advance congressional action. Provisions were made for continuous screening of the Ready Reserves for mobilization availability and diversity of skills. In that connection, utilization of the Standby Reserve was restricted in mobilization because the Director of Selective Service first had to determine that such personnel were available for active duty.[29]

The Reserve Officers Personnel Act

Pending passage of the National Reserve Plan legislation, the Eisenhower administration tried to delay congressional consideration of the unrelated Reserve Officers Personnel Act. In fact, the President put his personal prestige on the line in an unsuccessful effort to defer consideration until 1955 when it was thought that Congress would have completed its work on the National Reserve Plan.

---

[*]The passage of the Reserve Officers Personnel Act of 1954 is discussed at the end of this chapter.

The Air Force Reserve

The Officer Personnel Act of 1947 had established a promotion system for the regular forces, and the reserve lobbies demanded that Congress establish a parallel system for the reserve forces. This was a complicated process involving integration of provisions from four different services for the commissioning, assignment, service in grade, limitations, release, and mandatory retirement of officers. The Department of Defense wanted uniformity; the services wanted individuality. The dispute led to lengthy internal delay as efforts were made to devise a comprehensive bill.[30]

Despairing of the services' ability to reach such a compromise, the House Armed Services Committee developed its own reserve officer promotion legislation in 1953. Assistant Secretary of Defense John Hannah boycotted the House hearings in April 1954, and defense officials prepared a substitute bill. The resultant substitute was developed too late for consultation with the Bureau of the Budget, and, not given an opportunity to study the details, the Reserve Forces Policy Board refused to take a position on it.* The Defense Department's bill consisted of four amendments to the House bill which would have the primary effect of making it more difficult for the Army's World War II veterans to be promoted. While conceding that their bill would hurt the World War II reservists, Department of Defense officials sought to transition to a new promotion system without creating an unworkable officer grade structure in the reserve forces by promoting more people to higher grades than were required.[31]

On the morning of July 27, with the Senate Armed Services Committee due to consider the House bill that very afternoon, President Eisenhower asked Senator Leverett Saltonstall, the committee chairman, to withhold action on the legislation in 1954. The White House request was intended to strengthen Saltonstall's hand in defeating the bill in committee.[32] Administration officials presumed that the Senate committee would not ride roughshod over the Defense Department position to pass the House bill. Normally, their position would be reasonable enough, but they did not account for the powerful force of Senator Strom Thurmond, World War II combat veteran, member of the Armed Services Committee, national president of the Reserve Officers Association, and strongest advocate on the committee of the House bill. Reviewing the history of the controversial subject, Senator Thurmond isolated a single issue for consideration: "that in time of war the Reserve is as good as the Regular. It is just that simple."[33]

Influenced by Thurmond, the Senate Armed Services Committee accepted the House bill with but one substantive amendment. As a conciliatory gesture, Saltonstall gave the Defense Department another chance to present its position. Intending to conduct extensive hearings on the entire subject of the reserve

---

*The Reserve Forces Policy Board was provided for by the "Department of Defense Policies Relating to the Reserve Forces," approved April 6, 1951, and discussed on pp 338–340.

Post–Korean War Policies

forces promptly upon the convening of the 84th Congress, he invited the military services to make any recommendations they wished concerning the reserve promotion bill at that time. In the meantime, the Senators had given voting reservists tangible evidence that at least the legislative branch had their interests at heart.[34]

Signed into law as Public Law 83–773 on September 3, 1954, the Reserve Officers Personnel Act was a complicated piece of legislation. Some of its general provisions applied universally to all the military services, but individual sections accommodated the services' idiosyncratic differences. In general, however, the law provided uniform systems for the promotion, precedence, constructive credit, distribution, retention, and elimination of officers of the reserve components. Its promotion and elimination features promised a revitalization of the Air Force Reserve by eliminating inactive and stagnant members and advancing the active and progressive.

Within the Air Force, officers of the Air Force Reserve and the Air National Guard of the United States would compete with one another and with reservists on extended active duty for promotion against the overall mobilization requirements. The officers would also be considered at certain points in their careers for promotion to unit vacancies. In addition to the attrition already provided by age-in-grade elimination, the act provided for elimination upon twice being passed over for promotion, the attainment of certain lengths of total service, and where certain excesses to the grade structure existed.[35]

The Reserve Officers Personnel Act of 1954 and the Reserve Forces Act of 1955 provided the nation's reserve forces with a legislative foundation on which to develop as combat-ready adjuncts of the active forces. Provision had been made for their buildup by both voluntary and compulsory means, some assurance of equitable recall had been made, promotion policies had been standardized, and an obligation existed to train. Many old laws, practices, and customs had been codified, and if some found the new combination of reserve legislation ineffective, it was sufficiently adequate that Congress would not change it for the next twelve years. It now became the responsibility of the Department of Defense and the military services to erect upon this foundation the reserve structure needed by the active forces.

Changes in the Reserve Policy and Management Structure

In the eighteen months following June 1950, when the Air Force Reserve was caught up in the mobilizations and recalls to expand the active force, the entire policy and management structure within which the organization existed changed. The changes reflected in varying degrees the prosecution of the Korean War, the establishment of the Department of Defense in August 1949, and the development of reserve policies. The changes were also manifested in

The Air Force Reserve

the legal definition of the organization and composition of the Air Force and in the reserve forces legislation. The first change from which the Air Force Reserve undoubtedly benefited in the long term was the Continental Air Command's loss of its tactical and defense missions, leaving it free to concentrate on its responsibilities for the civilian components. With the resurgence of the tactical air role in the Korean fighting, the Air Force restored the Tactical Air Command as a major command on December 1, 1950. Exactly one month later, with the departed Tactical Air Command's fighter forces no longer available to serve in common air defense roles, the Air Force separated the Air Defense Command from the Continental Air Command as well.[36]

The 1950's Air Force Reserve was also affected by fundamental legislation pertaining to the parent Air Force. Even after the Unification Act of September 1947 established the United States Air Force, much of the statutory authority upon which it operated still stemmed from various laws pertaining to the U.S. Army. To clarify the situation and provide both services sounder legal bases from which to operate, Congress passed the Army and Air Force Authorization Act of 1949 which became law on July 10, 1950. The law stipulated that the Air Force of the United States would consist of the U.S. Air Force (the Regular Air Force), the Air National Guard of the United States, the Air National Guard when it was in the service of the United States, and the U.S. Air Force Reserve. The Air Force of the United States was to have an authorized strength of not more than seventy groups with separate Air Force squadrons, reserve groups, and whatever supporting and auxiliary and reserve units as might be required.[37]

Approved in September 1951, the Air Force Organization Act of 1951 provided a more detailed internal structure for the Air Force and confirmed that it consisted of the Regular Air Force, the Air Force Reserve, the Air National Guard of the United States, and the Air National Guard while in the service of the United States. The law defined the Air National Guard of the United States as a reserve component of the Air Force and consisting of all federally recognized units and organizations of the Air National Guard of the several states, the territories, and the District of Columbia.[38] This language was doubly significant. Defined as reserve rather than as militia, the Air National Guard could be called up by the President under the "Army" rather than the "Militia" clause of the Constitution, and the component could clearly be used more freely than if it were restricted to being called up under the militia clause. Moreover, the Air National Guard was limited to organizing and training units only. Thus, if the Air Force required an augmentation of individual reservists, it had to turn to the second civilian component, the Air Force Reserve. Although active force officials were slow to recognize it, and the Air National Guard ignored it, the 1949 and 1951 legislation governing the organization of the armed forces firmly established the Air Force Reserve and Air National Guard as equal components of the Air Force.[39]

The first Special Assistant to the Chief of Staff for Reserve Forces was Lt.

Gen. Elwood R. Quesada, who served until his retirement in September 1949. His successor was Maj. Gen. Earl S. Hoag.* As intended, the Air Staff was to handle reserve forces matters the same way it handled Regular Air Force issues. When other elements of the Air Staff were slow in coordinating proposed actions in 1951, however, General Hoag's office forged ahead unilaterally as an action office.[40]

General Nathan F. Twining, as Vice Chief of Staff, revised the charter of the Office of the Special Assistant for Reserve Forces in September 1951. He made the special assistant directly responsible to the Office of the Chief of Staff for reserve affairs and established him as adviser to the Chief of Staff and the Air Staff on all reserve forces matters. He would be a Regular Air Force member on the Reserve Forces Policy Board. The appropriate Air Staff agencies were to develop all major programs, plans, and policies for the reserve forces, but they were to be coordinated with the Office of the Special Assistant before publication. The Air Force Assistant for Programming was to take the lead in developing a reserve program which would be realistically based upon foreseeable requirements. These changes in the special assistant's functions

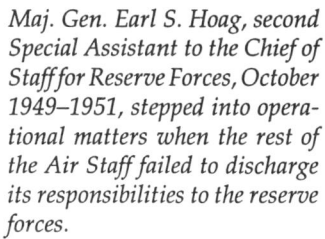

Maj. Gen. Earl S. Hoag, second Special Assistant to the Chief of Staff for Reserve Forces, October 1949–1951, stepped into operational matters when the rest of the Air Staff failed to discharge its responsibilities to the reserve forces.

*For a complete list of the incumbents of the Office of the Special Assistant for Reserve Affairs and its variously named predecessor and successor organizations, see Appendix 1.

The Air Force Reserve

became effective on October 1, 1951. If cosmetic in appearance, the changes in the directives reminded the Air Staff of the existence of the Special Assistant's office at a time when the Air Staff was beginning to ignore it.[41]

On April 6, 1951, the Secretary of Defense approved Department of Defense policies for the reserve forces to supersede the old War Department policies of October 1945. Reflecting the many recommendations for the reorganization and administration of reserve affairs, the policies provided for appropriate reserve forces oversight at the assistant secretary and chief of staff levels in each military department. In addition, each military department was to establish a reserve forces policy committee, half of its members to be reserve forces officers. At the Office of the Secretary of Defense level, a Reserve Forces Policy Board was to be established which would recommend reserve forces policies to the Secretary of Defense and coordinate policies and programs common to all the reserve forces.

Anticipating passage of reserve forces legislation, policies defined the reserve forces categories as consisting of Ready, Standby, and Retired Reserve and prescribed a reservist's eligibility and liability for each. Influenced by the difficulties being created by the concurrent mobilization, the policies required that each service publish priorities for recall. As military conditions permitted, a reservist ordered to active federal service was to be allowed at least thirty days from the time he was alerted until he had to report for duty. When units or persons from the reserve forces were ordered to active military service during a partial mobilization, military departments were to assure the continued organization and training of reserve forces not yet mobilized. In their attempt to forestall one problem revealed during the mobilizations of 1950 and 1951, drafters of Defense Department policies increased the potential for a more serious inequity. In any expansion of the active armed forces requiring the ordering of reserve units and persons to active military service, members of units organized and trained to serve as units were not, when feasible, to be ordered into active military service involuntarily as individuals. This did not preclude, however, reassigning such persons after they were ordered into military service. Application of this policy would preserve unit integrity during periods of mobilization, but it would also tempt the Air Force to recall reservists who were not participating in any program while it deferred the recall of individuals who had actively participated in and had drawn pay for training, just as it had during the Korean War. Defense Department policies of April 1951 pertaining to the United States Air Force Reserve were implemented by a revised AFR 45–1 in May 1952.[42]

The Air Force Long-Range Plan for the Reserve Forces

On June 4, 1951, following preliminary work by an Air Staff planning board, Assistant Secretary of the Air Force Eugene M. Zuckert formed a committee under the chairmanship of the Air Force Reserve's General Smith to examine the Air Reserve programs. General Smith was a reservist who had been associated with the Air Training Command during World War II, had served on several of the Air Defense Command's early reserve boards, and had been the first chairman of the Air Staff Committee on Reserve. Submitting a long-range plan for the Reserve Forces of the United States Air Force on July 27, 1951, General Smith asserted that its adoption would provide a balanced reserve force by 1958 to meet unit and individual requirements of the Intermediate-Range War Plan until post–D-Day training produced additional resources.

The plan provided for 27 Air National Guard and 24 Air Force Reserve tactical wings, 6 Air Force Reserve flying training wings, and almost 1,300 Air Force Reserve nonflying units. This structure would accommodate 250,000 members and provide flying and combat crew training for 38,000 in wing and squadron aircraft. Like most contemporary planning documents, the plan recommended that Air Staff planning for the reserve forces be continually integrated with that of the active force. It also proposed a revival of the Category R program in which reservists on extended active duty would man positions in the flying centers and hold compatible assignments in the flying units.

The plan recommended that a vigorous public relations program be undertaken to promote public acceptance of the necessity of the Air Reserve Forces. It urged that the Air Force seek a presidential statement emphasizing the increasingly vital role of the reserve in national security and that the Department of Defense undertake efforts with such agencies as the National Association of Manufacturers and the Chamber of Commerce toward relieving perceived job insecurity for reservists.[43]

Assistant Secretary Zuckert and General Twining approved the Long-Range Plan on August 9, 1951, and, accepting certain limitations, the Air Staff began its limited implementation in October. The Air Force Reserve had no aircraft, and none would be available until July 1952. Upon mobilization in 1950 and 1951, Air Force Reserve units remaining intact had kept their aircraft, while aircraft belonging to the mobilized "filler" units had been redistributed. As an additional limitation, new ground training centers proposed by the plan could not be constructed until fiscal year 1953. Until then, leased facilities and the old Volunteer Air Reserve training locations would be used. Training curricula and aids for specialized training would be phased in. Until they were available, equipment and materiel on hand would be utilized.[44]

The Air Force Reserve

The Reserve Program Review Board

Primarily because of the lingering influence of the mobilization, the revised Air Force Reserve program was slow to develop, and on July 7, 1953, General Twining, then Air Force Chief Staff, directed Lt. Gen. Leon W. Johnson, Commander of Continental Air Command as of February 1952, to evaluate the two-year-old, long-range plan. General Johnson's Reserve Program Review Board found nothing wrong with the long-range plan but concluded that the active establishment understood the reserve forces programs no better than it ever had.

The Johnson Board established a number of principles as essential to the success of any reserve forces program. Such a program had to be objective, fulfilling a requirement for national defense; it had to be accepted and supported at all levels of the Air Force; and it had to be within reserve capabilities, with the emphasis placed on quality training. The program had to be simple and stable; it had to be acceptable to reservists, encompassing incentives to attract reservists; and it had to have public acceptance and support. On the basis of these principles, the Johnson Board offered twenty-three recommendations to strengthen the Air Reserve Forces programs. They fell into five general categories: training structure, personnel, facilities, budget, and reserve information and public relations.

Most of the board's recommendations concerned the program's structure and nomenclature which the board thought essential to change in the interests of simplicity and understanding. It recommended that air reserve centers replace all the existing reserve training and administrative structure below the numbered air force level and become the hubs of all Air Force Reserve activity within given geographical areas.

The board recommended that Headquarters USAF replace the Special Assistant to the Chief of Staff for Reserve Forces with a new office, the Assistant Chief of Staff, Reserve Forces, to emphasize the policy of integrating reserve and regular program functions. Not overlooking the gaining commands' responsibilities to the individual training programs, the board recommended that all domestic major commands provide annual active duty training for reservists who held training designations with them.

The Johnson Board recommended that the existing long-range facilities construction program for the Air Force Reserve be approved for immediate implementation in accordance with program requirements. The board maintained that the availability of adequate facilities was paramount in the operation of a successful reserve program. Never recovering from its initial handicap as the youngest component of the military services, the Air Force Reserve had not accumulated sufficient facilities.

As Continental Air Command Commander, General Johnson did not believe that the Air Force gave sufficient attention to reserve information and

As Commander of Continental Air Command, in July 1953 Lt. Gen. Leon W. Johnson chaired the Reserve Forces Review Board which recommended many measures to improve the operation of the Air Force Reserve program.

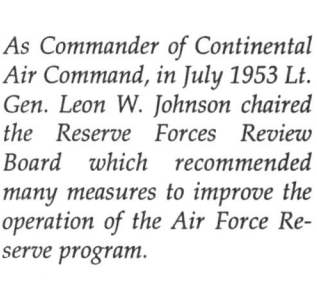

public relations. His board, therefore, suggested that these areas be given additional priority and that firm policy guidance was essential to the success of the reserve information program. To this end, the board recommended that an office to coordinate reserve information activities be established under the Director of Information in the Office of the Secretary of the Air Force. The board also recommended that the Air Force organize reservists having public information skills into units with a training objective of supporting and projecting Air Force information and public relations programs. It suggested establishing effective liaison with civic groups, legislative bodies, and industrial organizations to ensure better understanding of Air Force activities and cooperation in such problem areas as facilities and employee relations. In short, the Johnson Board called for the reserve forces to be "sold" to the active establishment and to the general public. The Air Force implemented most of the Johnson Board's recommendations by February 1954.[45]

The Twining Memo, January 1955

On November 24, 1954, Lt. Gen. Frank F. Everest, Air Force Deputy Chief of Staff for Operations, advised Assistant Chief of Staff for Reserve Forces Maj. Gen. William E. Hall that the Joint Mid-Range War Plan identified a D-Day requirement for fifty-one tactical Air Reserve Forces wings. General Hall

The Air Force Reserve

brought this requirement to General Twining's attention a few days later and recommended that the Chief of Staff direct the Air Staff to reorient all reserve policies, plans, and programs toward meeting the requirement.[46]

Issued on January 4, 1955, General Twining's resultant statement required Air Force officials to reexamine all pertinent Air Reserve Forces guidance:

1. Current war planning has established a firm mobilization requirement for 51 tactical wings in the Air Reserve Forces.
2. It is my desire, therefore, that within budget limits and consistent with the policy of attaining and maintaining maximum combat capability within the 137 wing force, all pertinent Air Staff actions be directed specifically toward: fully equipping Reserve units with aircraft capable of carrying out the D-Day mission; provision of adequate facilities and full unit equipment; and supervision and inspection of training programs with an end toward reaching an acceptable degree of combat capability at the earliest practicable date. In order to insure that this objective shall be met, it is necessary that all plans, policies, and programs pertaining to tactical and support units of the Air Reserve Forces be thoroughly reexamined.[47]

General Twining would observe later that the devastation caused by the Korean recall had forced the Air Force to start its Air Force Reserve program all over again in 1953.[48] Actually, the 1953 program was just an extension of the 1950 program from which the Air Force Reserve had entered the Korean War. The contemporary Air Force Reserve program got its real start in January 1955 from the impetus of General Twining's own memorandum.

The new mobilization requirement was for twenty-seven Air National Guard and twenty-four Air Force Reserve tactical wings. The latter included nine fighter-bomber, two tactical bombardment, and thirteen troop carrier units. The Mid-Range War Plan assigned specific D-Day missions for the guard and reserve units upon mobilization. The fighter-bomber wings initially would have an air defense role and later a tactical fighter role. The tactical bombardment and troop carrier wings would be assigned immediately to the Tactical Air Command. As General Twining often pointed out, airlift was one thing the Air Force needed on D-Day, and the thirteen Air Force Reserve wings would certainly add to the force's mobility.

On April 27, 1955, the Air Staff incorporated General Twining's guidance into a headquarters operating instruction requiring revision of the reserve forces' policies and programs. Of great significance to the Air Force Reserve, with Air Force Reserve wings now required to attain an acceptable degree of combat capability, the Air Reserve Forces were entitled to equal treatment with the Air National Guard in the designation of priorities for equipment.[49]

Equally significant, the new emphasis on the Air Reserve Forces was also reflected in a revision of Air Force Manual 1–2, *United States Air Force Basic Doctrine*, published April 1, 1955. The document defined the term *air power* as embracing the entire aviation capability of the United States, and stated that active military forces, reserve air forces, and their supporting facilities comprised a major component of air power. The definition had not appeared in the initial draft, but Vice Chief of Staff General Thomas D. White asked that it be incorporated into the final version to emphasize that the term *United States Air Force* included both the active and reserve air forces.[50]

In addition to providing units to augment the active force for limited or full-scale war, by mid-1955 the Air Force Reserve had a requirement to provide the Air Force with trained individuals in wartime to augment and replace the attrition in the active force. These personnel were to be recruited, matched against specific wartime requirements, and trained in specific skills. Basically the same as the Service Callable Reserve approved by the National Security Council on September 30, 1954, the total Air Force Reserve mobilization requirement was set at 349,000. Of that 349,000, the Air Staff identified 115,000 as the individual replacement and augmentation reserve.[51]

Finally, during the latter half of 1955, the Air Force published *Reserve Mobilization Recall Requirements*. This marked the first time in the history of the Air Force Reserve that definitive reserve requirements, based on Air Force war plans, could be announced. In November 1955, the requirements were given to the major commands by grade and skill, covering wartime augmentation, replacement, attrition, and overseas levies. The documents identified that portion of each command's Air Force Reserve Mobilization Recall Requirement to be trained by the command itself and that portion for which the Continental Air Command was responsible for administration and inactive duty training. On December 1, 1955, the Air Staff directed the major commands to align their current reserve training programs with the newly defined requirements.[*52] Thus provided with an adequate framework of national policy and Department of Defense guidance, the Continental Air Command and the major air commands which would gain the Air Reserve Forces units and individuals upon mobilization began to develop the force into a combat-ready mobilization asset.

---

[*]The alignment of the reserve force resources with active force requirements is discussed in Chapter 10.

6

Implementing the Revised Concepts and Programs

> ... with the understanding that the Department of the Air Force will carry out both in letter and spirit the commitment it has made and the safeguards it has promised to apply with respect to employees who would be affected by the Plan. It is also understood that the Department will comply fully and strictly with the requirements of the Veterans' Preference Act of 1944 and the Commission's Regulations under that Act in all of its activities under the Plan.
>
> —Harris Ellsworth, Chairman, Civil Service Commission,
> June 1957

Following the Korean War, the Air Reserve Forces were realigned to reflect more precisely the Air Force's mobilization requirement for fifty-one tactical wings, and the gaining commands cooperated with the Continental Air Command to develop combat-ready reserve units. The commands established training objectives and the Air Staff authorized additional flying training periods and overwater navigation training flights. As they matured, the Air Force Reserve troop carrier wings began to participate in Air Force transport missions, joint airborne training operations, and the relief of domestic emergencies. As a highlight of fighter unit development, aircrews of an Air Force Reserve F–84E fighter-bomber unit joined Air National Guard units in standing runway alert.

Faced with severe challenges in bringing post–Korean War reserve units to their authorized strengths, the Air Staff and the Continental Air Command

The Air Force Reserve

experimented with several manning programs. They included the successful non–prior service personnel and detached squadron programs and the unsuccessful selective assignment program. Acknowledging the universal demand to centralize reservists' records, the Continental Air Command established the Air Reserve Records Center. In 1957, the Air Force took a giant stride toward establishing combat-ready Air Force Reserve units when it authorized the Continental Air Command to initiate the Air Reserve technician program which provided the units with full-time civilian technicians who were also key reservist members of their units. To reflect changing Air Force mobilization requirements and operational considerations, the Air Force Reserve flying units were realigned late in the decade into an all troop carrier/rescue force.

Implementing the Long-Range Plan: A Divided Responsibility

The Joint Mid-Range War Plan distributed in late 1954 identified D-Day requirements for fifty-one tactical Air Reserve Forces wings, twenty-seven from the Air National Guard and twenty-four from the Air Force Reserve. The latter included nine fighter-bomber, two tactical bombardment, and thirteen troop carrier wings. This allocation of units required the Continental Air Command to revise the Air Force Reserve unit program, consisting at that point of seventeen tactical wings (including tactical reconnaissance, fighter-bomber, and troop carrier wings) and six pilot training wings.[1]

Established merely as peacetime training units, the six pilot training wings had no mobilization mission. In view of the prescribed mobilization mission and the sense of the Twining memorandum of January 1955, they were replaced by five tactical units. On May 18, 1955, the Continental Air Command discontinued the pilot training wings and activated three troop carrier wings and two fighter-bomber wings. At about the same time, it also redesignated the two tactical reconnaissance wings as tactical bombardment units.[2]

With these actions accomplished, the September 1955 Air Force Reserve flying wing force consisted of twenty-four combat wings with the missions and aircraft at the locations depicted in the accompanying table.[3]

Air Force Reserve Flying Wing Program September 1955

Location	Wing*	Aircraft
Scott AFB, Ill.	94 TBW	B–26
Long Beach MAP, Calif.	452 TBW	B–26
L. G. Hanscom Field, Mass.	89 FBW	F–80C/F–84E
Memphis MAP, Tenn.	319 FBW	F–80C/F–84E
Hamilton AFB, Calif.	349 FBW	F–80C/F–84E
Gen. Billy Mitchell Field, Wis.	438 FBW	F–80C/F–84E
Selfridge AFB, Mich.	439 FBW	F–80C/F–84E
Minneapolis–St Paul IAP, Minn.	440 FBW	F–80C/F–84E
Niagara Falls MAP, N.Y.	445 FBW	F–80C/F–84E
Dallas NAS, Tex.	448 FBW	F–80C/F–84E
Dobbins AFB, Ga.	482 FBW	F–80C/F–84E
Clinton County Airport, Ohio	302 TCW	C–46
Greater Pittsburgh Airport, Pa.	375 TCW	C–46
Portland IAP, Oreg.	403 TCW	C–46
Brooks AFB, Tex.	433 TCW	C–46
Bakalar AFB, Ind.	434 TCW	C–46
Miami IAP, Fla.	435 TCW	C–46
Floyd Bennett NAS, N.Y.	436 TCW	C–46
O'Hare IAP, Ill.	437 TCW	C–46
Grandview AFB, Mo.	442 TCW	C–46
Ellington AFB, Tex.	446 TCW	C–46
Andrews AFB, Md.	459 TCW	C–46
New Castle County Airport, Del.	512 TCW	C–46
Mitchel AFB, N.Y.	514 TCW	C–119

*TBW=Tactical Bombardment Wing; FBW=Fighter-Bomber Wing; TCW=Troop Carrier Wing.

For the first time, the Air Force Reserve possessed no trainer aircraft, and the units did all their flying in tactical models—B–26s, F–80s, F–84s, C–46s, and C–119s. With the missions and equipment finally determined, three other factors remained in the development of combat-ready Air Force Reserve units: training, which the Continental Air Command conducted in cooperation with

The Air Force Reserve

A C–46 of the 302d Troop Carrier Wing, Clinton County Airport, Ohio, prepares to leave Floyd Bennett NAS for Puerto Rico during August 1956 in Operation SIXTEEN TON, the Air Force Reserve's first institutional by-product mission.

the gaining commands; manning, which required great effort by the Continental Air Command and the reserve units and much cooperation from the Air Staff; and facilities, which required the understanding of the Bureau of the Budget and Congress as well as an Air Force resolve to use Air Force Reserve construction money for the purpose intended.

As recommended by the Johnson Board, the Continental Air Command regained its responsibility to conduct the active duty as well as the inactive duty training of the Air Reserve Forces units. Nevertheless, the gaining commands furnished the tactical doctrine and operating procedures and assistance in preparing training objectives and plans. Active duty training objectives that guided the summer training of the Air Force Reserve wings in 1955, 1956, and 1957 reflected the desires of the gaining commands. The Tactical Air Command wanted troop carrier units capable of participating in mass maneuvers and joint exercises involving two or more troop carrier wings in support of other Air Force and Army units. The Air Defense Command required fighter-bomber wings capable of supportting augmented tactical squadrons operating independently of the parent wing after mobilization and tactical squadrons capable of performing continuous air defense operations for indefinite periods. The command would also have to refine its interceptor techniques and perform realistic interceptor exercises.[4]

Revised Concepts and Programs

To become combat-ready in tactical aircraft, Air Reserve Forces aircrews needed additional training opportunities. In June 1954, the Air Staff Committee on National Guard and Reserve Policy recommended that the reserve aircrews be authorized full flight pay on inactive duty because they could not attain the required flying proficiency during the authorized 48 inactive duty drill periods and the annual 15-day active duty for training tours. Reluctant to authorize the reservists full flying pay, the Air Staff finally settled on 36 additional 4-hour flying training periods which became effective in fiscal year 1957. In August 1955, meanwhile, to increase the realism of Air Reserve Forces aircrew training, the Vice Chief of Staff authorized troop carrier units and navigation training squadrons to conduct overwater training flights.[5]

As the Air Force Reserve troop carrier units acquired proficiency, they began to participate in the relief of domestic emergencies. In August 1955, for example, reserve aircrews delivered chlorinated lime to New England for purifying the drinking water after an outbreak of typhoid fever, and in October reservists delivered tons of food and clothing to flood-stricken Tampico, Mexico, in the aftermath of Hurricane Janet. The post–Korean War Air Force Reserve really began to come of age, in the summer of 1956 when it conducted an independent major airlift. In SIXTEEN TON, as the operation was called, twelve Air Force Reserve troop carrier wings used their annual active duty training time to move U.S. Coast Guard equipment to the Caribbean.[6] The Air Reserve unit at Portland, Oregon, did not participate because of its distance from the onload station.

Participating units first flew from their home stations to Floyd Bennett NAS, New York, where they took on the cargo for the first leg to Miami IAP. From Miami, they transported their loads to either Isla Grande Airport, San Juan, Puerto Rico, or San Salvador in the Bahamas. The last aircraft was unloaded at San Salvador on September 13 and it returned to Miami the following day. The reserve crews flew 164 missions on which they transported 856,715 pounds of cargo. No significant delays were experienced except for four days lost due to Hurricane Betsy, and no flying safety incidents were incurred.

SIXTEEN TON's having established a precedent, the Air Force Reserve troop carrier units soon became involved in two rather continuous airlifts. The first, begun in April 1957, was Operation SWIFT LIFT, in which the reserve troop carrier units used inactive duty training periods to airlift personnel and cargo for the Tactical Air Command. Each Air Force Reserve troop carrier squadron provided one aircraft with crew in continuous support of the requirement. In addition to providing training for the reserve crews, SWIFT LIFT moved considerable high-priority cargo for the Air Force, saving significant amounts in transportation and procurement dollars. In the summer of 1958, reserve units initiated Operation READY SWAP, an open-ended airlift in which they

149

The Air Force Reserve

transported aircraft engines between Air Materiel Command depots.[7]

Along with the point-to-point airlifts, the reserve units began dropping paratroops. In August 1954, the 514th Troop Carrier Wing C-119s dropped troops during a joint maneuver with the 82d Airborne Division at Fort Bragg, North Carolina, in the first reserve paradrop during a joint Army/Air Force exercise.* Then, at the suggestion of the Tactical Air Command, five of the Air Force Reserve troop carrier wings culminated their 1956 active duty training by participating in the joint exercise Operation PINE CONE. This was the first large-scale exercise to combine Air Force Reserve and active forces.[8]

Originally apprehensive about using reserve aircraft and aircrews on paratroop exercises, the U.S. Army changed its collective mind after PINE CONE and thereafter requested the use of reserve airlift for basic paratroop training. On November 17, 1956, Air Force Reserve troop carrier units employing C-46s and C-119s began a regular program of weekend drops of paratroop trainees at Fort Bragg. Sometime during the following six months, they also began dropping student paratroops at Fort Benning, Georgia.[9]

Among the Air Force Reserve fighter-bomber units, the high-water mark of development was reached by the 319th Fighter-Bomber Wing at Memphis MAP. On July 1, 1956, upon the recommendation of the Air Staff Committee on Air National Guard and Air Force Reserve Policy and with the concurrence of the Secretary of the Air Force, the wing's qualified aircrews began standing F-84E runway alert under operational control of the 20th Air Division, joining Air National Guard units as part of the Air Defense Command's defense network.†[10]

Beginning in 1956 the Air Force Reserve flying unit program expanded to include air rescue squadrons equipped with the fixed-wing SA-16 aircraft. The Continental Air Command activated the first three squadrons in August and October 1956 at Miami, Long Beach, and Williams AFB, Arizona. The fourth squadron was organized at Portland IAP, Oregon, in November 1957 and the last, at Selfridge AFB, Michigan, in February 1958. The 301st Air Rescue Squadron at Miami conducted the first reserve rescue in January 1957, recovering three airmen from the sea when two B-47s collided off the coast of Cuba.[11]

The Air Force Reserve's aircrew training activities expanded when Headquarters USAF identified a requirement to train navigators to meet not

---

*The first Air Force Reserve drop of U.S. Army paratroopers under any circumstance probably took place at Camp Atterbury, Indiana, in July 1949.

†After an experimental program at Syracuse, New York, and Hayward, California, eight Air National Guard units began regularly to augment the Air Defense Command's runway alert on August 15, 1954 (Charles J. Gross, *Prelude to the Total Force: The Air National Guard, 1943–1969* [Washington, DC, 1985], pp 95–105).

only the Air Force's day-to-day needs, but also those of the Civil Reserve Air Fleet. Starting in January 1955, a Continental Air Command training program offered refresher and continuation academic and flying training to the navigators. As enrollment in the program reached 5,000 annually, the Continental Air Command established navigator replacement training squadrons at the site of each Air Force Reserve wing. Reservists took their monthly inactive duty training at these sites, and the Air Training Command offered them annual two-week active duty training tours. The program initially employed TC–45 and TC–47 aircraft until T–29s became available.[12]

The Air Force Reserve unit program had never been restricted to flying units, and in the mid-1950s nonflying support units proliferated. July 1956 saw nine aerial port operations squadrons in existence. An Air Force Reserve airways and air communications program consisted of three mobile squadrons, each with six detachments, to provide mobile facilities which could be put into operation with relatively short notice. The Continental Air Command activated thirteen air terminal squadrons in October 1956 and organized ten Air Force hospitals in April 1957.[13]

Manning the Air Force Reserve Wings

Manning of their units was a concern peculiar to the commanders of the reserve units of all military services. In the active force, units acquired the people they were authorized from basic or technical training schools or through reassignment from other organizations. The personnel system matched faces to spaces, and the active force unit commander simply monitored the quality of the people his unit was receiving. In common with all other reserve component unit commanders, however, commanders of Air Force Reserve units were responsible to man their units; like colonial militia captains, they had to comb their local areas for recruits. They received considerable help from the Continental Air Command, its numbered air forces, and especially the Air Reserve flying centers, but ultimately manning was their responsibility. Manning contributed to operational readiness, and their success in building up their units was reflected in their efficiency reports. Moreover, the commander's responsibility did not end with bringing in the reservists; he had to motivate them to participate in his unit's training programs.

The membership of the Air Force Reserve was in a state of transition as the Air Force started rebuilding its program after the Korean mobilization. Numerically reduced by the mass termination of commissions of World War II officers, the residual reserve membership was evolving into a hard-core volunteer group augmented by the vanguard of a generation of obligated servicemen. The Air Force Reserve units made some progress in recruiting after

The Air Force Reserve

the Korean War, but turnover in personnel held their membership down. One year, for example, the reserve flying units brought in 2,501 officers but lost 1,529; they gained 7,860 airmen and lost 3,785. In effect, units had to recruit two people to gain one.[14]

A panel of officers in Headquarters Continental Air Command studying the retention phenomenon concluded that the major contributing factors to the high drop-out rates were weak leadership and organization; inadequate facilities, equipment, and command support; and local economic conditions. The point about economic conditions was weighty. Many reservists were employed in industries offering good wages, and they could earn more money working overtime on their civilian jobs over a weekend than they could from reserve participation. Consequently, they failed to participate and ultimately became dropouts.[15]

Personnel officials in Headquarters Continental Air Command believed the only solution was for Headquarters USAF to authorize the command to man the reserve wings with non–prior service personnel. Despite earlier indications of Air Staff opposition, on September 29, 1952, General Johnson, the Continental Air Command Commander, asked Headquarters USAF to authorize the command to enlist a maximum of 14,000 non–prior service individuals in reserve flying units. At this time, obligated reservists were still subject to the draft, and General Johnson further recommended that when their draft became imminent, such individuals be given the option of enlisting in the Regular Air Force for four years or volunteering for a two-year period of active military service in the Air Force. Either option would prevent the loss of an Air Force–trained person to another service.[16]

Privy to General Johnson's proposal, the Air Staff Committee on National Guard and Air Force Reserve Policy asked the U.S. Air Force Deputy Chief of Staff, Personnel to establish a policy governing the enlistment of non–prior service personnel in the Air Force Reserve. This request coincided with a proposal by the Air Staff Directorate of Training to revise eligibility for enlistment in the Air Force Reserve. Discussion of the two issues soon disclosed a sharp divergence of opinion within the personnel agency on the matter of non–prior service enlistments. This disagreement among the action officers necessitated a determination of policy at the two-star level.[17]

On November 10, Maj. Gen. Morris J. Lee, the acting Assistant Deputy Chief of Staff for Personnel, rejected General Johnson's appeal for authority to enlist non–prior service individuals into the Air Force Reserve. General Lee conceded that the Air Force Reserve needed a recruiting system more extensive than one based solely on voluntary recruiting. He observed, however, that such a system would necessarily involve qualified, draft-eligible youths—the very group on which the Air Force depended to build up its active force. This group was rapidly diminishing, and national manpower policies placed an absolute,

Revised Concepts and Programs

first-priority claim on these individuals for active duty. Moreover, Lee noted that under existing law the reservists' term of active duty for training or service would be shorter than the established four-year period of enlistment in the Air Force. Finally, the Continental Air Command proposal was unacceptable to the Air Force, General Lee said, because the reserve units did not have the capability to conduct initial basic or technical training comparable in quality to that provided by the active force.

General Lee also disclosed that the Air Staff considered the manning of lower-ranking airman positions in reserve units as the least essential requirement that the combined active and reserve forces faced. "In the opinion of this Headquarters," General Lee wrote, "it would be more acceptable to Total Force posture to waive this requirement and accept this delay in reserve manning rather than to make the compromise required with the resultant loss of effectiveness in the Active Force." For that matter, he noted, facilities would become the limiting factor upon mobilization, and probably reserve units could be called to duty as units only at their peacetime locations. In that event, the entire basic airman problem would be satisfied almost immediately by establishing a pipeline from indoctrination training centers. That seemed to be the case.[18]

Headquarters Continental Air Command continued to press the issue, and a year later it finally persuaded the Air Staff to authorize the enlistment of 14,000 non–prior service individuals during fiscal year 1954. Still subject to the draft, an airman-level member of a reserve wing could enlist in the Regular Air Force for four years any time before he received his notice of induction under the Selective Service System. Continental Air Command was authorized an annual quota of 5,000 guaranteed enlistments in the Air Force to protect an airman upon notification of his impending induction.[19]

Thus stimulated, the reserve wings tripled their strength in a little more than two years. From 3,216 in June 1952, the number of assigned airmen increased to 11,587 in October 1954, including 4,500 non–prior service personnel. On June 30, 1955, however, again apprehensive of the program's effect upon four-year enlistments, the Air Staff withdrew the authority to enlist non–prior service individuals in Air Force Reserve wings. Three months later, with airman manning falling off, General Johnson asked the Air Staff to reinstate a modified non–prior service enlistment program. By this time, the Reserve Forces Act of 1955 had become law, and General Johnson recommended that the Air Force use its provisions to authorize the Continental Air Command to enlist youths who had not yet attained the age of 8½ years. These individuals would be required to serve three months on active duty for training and then complete the remainder of their service obligations in the Air Force Reserve.[20]

At that time, the Air Force's official position was that it would not enlist

The Air Force Reserve

non–prior service individuals in the Air Force Reserve as provided by the Reserve Forces Act of 1955. Some internal dissent existed, however. In January 1956, Maj. Gen. William E. Hall, Assistant Chief of Staff for Reserve Forces, warned the Deputy Chief of Staff, Personnel that Congress might no longer accept the Air Force's traditional explanations and would require more substantial and tangible data on Air Force Reserve manning trends. General Hall therefore suggested that the Air Force commission an independent study on the effect of the six-month legislation on its volunteer four-year enlistment program. At about the same time, the Air Force Director of Legislative Liaison suggested to David S. Smith, the Assistant Secretary of the Air Force for Manpower and Reserve Forces, that the Air Force resolve its internal differences quickly and establish a position on the matter. Such a position had to be defensible, and Air Force witnesses had to present uniform testimony to congressional committees. As keeper of the flame, however, the Deputy Chief of Staff for Personnel saw no need to go outside his area for additional studies, and he insisted that experience had validated the Air Forces' current manning policies.[21]

With the enlisted strength of the Air Force Reserve declining, the Air Staff approved another limited non–prior service reserve enlistment program. Under this program, youths 17 to 18½ years of age would be accepted into the Air Reserve, be given six months' active duty for training, and then be assigned to reserve units.[22] In March 1957, the age limit was raised to permit the enlistment also of persons between the ages of 18½ and 26 years. The non–prior service reserve enlistment program brought 6,589 enlistees into the Air Force Reserve program between October 1956 and June 1958. They included 1,979 17- to 18½-year-old enlistees without critical skills; 3,820 enlistees, ages 18½ to 26 without critical skills; and 790 critical-skill enlistees.[23]

The non–prior service programs were essential if the Air Force Reserve units were to fill their spaces for low-ranking airmen. Equal attention had to be given the higher-ranking skilled positions. In fiscal year 1954, the Assistant Chief of Staff for Reserve Forces spearheaded a drive to emphasize reserve recruiting, and he influenced the Air Force Recruiting Service to reinstate formal support of Air Reserve Forces recruiting programs employed before the Korean War mobilizations. Public relations activities in the Pentagon on the part of the reserve forces increased markedly in response to this initiative. The increase reflected the finding of the Johnson Board in the fall of 1953 that the general public had a grave lack of knowledge about reserve programs, and, for that matter, so did the reservists themselves.[24]

The dedicated, long-range public information effort soon produced many national magazine articles, major speeches before national organizations, preparation of fact sheets and similar materials for local use, data for radio-television presentations, and numerous other constructive activities, all

Revised Concepts and Programs

Maj. Gen. William E. Hall, Assistant Chief of Staff of Air Force Reserve (above), favored the Air Force's acceptance of the six-month reserve programs contained in the Reserve Forces Act of 1955. David S. Smith (shown at the right during his swearing in as Assistant Secretary of the Air Force for Manpower by Secretary of the Air Force Harold E. Talbott) supported General Hall and encouraged Air Force adoption of the six-month and air reserve technician progams, among others, to facilitate development of combat readiness in the Air Force Reserve.

The Air Force Reserve

designed to promote the successful manning of reserve units. Washington efforts were paralleled by those of the Continental Air Command, which initiated an Air Reserve recruiting and motivation program designed to add 100,000 participating air reservists. Encouraged by the Air Staff Committee on Air National Guard and Air Force Reserve Policy, and with the approval of the Air Staff, Headquarters Continental Air Command hired an advertising firm in March 1955 to service the motivation and recruiting programs. About the same time, the command undertook a major organization measure intended in part at least to increase the manning of the Air Force Reserve flying units.

The Detached Squadron Concept

During the first half of 1955, the Air Force began detaching Air Force Reserve squadrons from their parent wing locations to separate sites. As the Johnson Board had recognized, the concept offered several advantages: communities were more likely to accept the smaller squadrons than the large wings; separate squadron operations would ensure the training of the squadron as the basic Air Force unit, without the confusion of group and wing being superimposed upon squadrons; and the location of separate squadrons in smaller population centers would facilitate recruiting and manning.[25]

As it finally evolved in the spring of 1955, the Continental Air Command's plan called for placing Air Force Reserve units at fifty-nine installations located throughout the United States. Initially, the command detached troop carrier squadrons from Andrews AFB, Maryland, to Byrd Field, Virginia; from Portland, Oregon, to Paine AFB, Washington; and from Miami to Orlando AFB, Florida.[26] In time, the detached squadron program proved successful in attracting additional participants to the Air Force Reserve and producing combat-ready units.

The Selective Assignment Program

Not all the Air Force's ideas for manning the reserve units were fruitful. Among the least successful was the selective assignment program. The idea was to assign airmen coming off active duty with a remaining military obligation against appropriate vacant positions in the reserve units. The assignments were "selective" because some effort was made to geographically match the airmen and their units of assignment. The Air Force put great stock in this idea, but at best it never became anything more than another list of names.[27]

The major factor in the plan's favor, of course, was the fact that the reserve units would enter active service more nearly at full strength with personnel currently skilled in their specialties, thus nominally in a higher state of readiness. The Johnson Board had also thought identification with a specific unit might motivate individuals selectively assigned to participate voluntarily.

Revised Concepts and Programs

The plan had two major disadvantages. First, like many reserve measures, it was not applied universally. Its selective feature aroused resentment among reservists who were assigned when others were not. Then, too, even at its best, it never overcame the problem of manning the low-rank airman spaces. Airmen released from active duty after a four-year enlistment normally possessed higher grades and therefore could not be assigned to lower grades. Those who had not attained higher grades after a four-year enlistment were probably not worth signing up.[28] By the end of June 1956, the Continental Air Command had selectively assigned 21,498 airmen to Category A units. Of that number, a mere 434 were actively participating in the units to which they were assigned and 213 were participants in other program elements. Rather than showing an improvement, participation of the selective assignees declined steadily after that.

The Option Letters

While desperately trying every possible means to increase the membership of its reserve units, the Air Force also acted to assure the quality of the force and to increase participation in training. In April 1955, the Air Force took a step which Maj. Gen. William E. Hall called "ventilation" of the Air Force Reserve. He said, "Briefly, what we have set out to do, is to assure that the Reserve forces are manned by people who are physically, mentally, and in every other way ready to go if needed." To accomplish this, in May 1955 Headquarters Continental Air Command sent option letters to nonparticipating officers asking them to select one of three options. They could chose among assignment to an active program element, resignation, or retirement. Within a month, more than 50,000 officers responded. A remarkable 60 percent (33,418 officers) requested assignment to an active program element. Another 17,654 tendered their resignations, and 2,148 requested assignment to the Retired Reserve. Those not selecting an option numbered 1,015, 13,979 failed to reply at all, and (a demonstration that the Air Force Reserve inventory of its members was still far from perfect) 11,680 of the letters sent proved undeliverable.[29]

It was one thing for an officer to request assignment to an active program element; it was often quite another for him to get the assignment he desired. His geographical separation from a place where reserve training was available, possibly the very reason which had kept him inactive in the first place, could not be overcome by simple fiat. It was also necessary that the officer be offered a feasible reassignment quickly before he again lost interest. General Johnson, the Continental Air Command Commander, foresaw the danger of administrative lassitude obviating the purpose of the option letters, and he urged his numbered air force commanders to be equally attentive to the process. Moreover, he established the policy that each of the officers who had chosen to become active be assigned to an active program element.[30]

157

The Air Force Reserve

Establishment of the Air Reserve Records Center

The Korean mobilization convinced the entire Air Force that the individual records of air reservists were in chaos. The common recommendation for correcting the situation was to centralize the administration of reserve personnel records. Headquarters Continental Air Command took a first step in this direction in November 1951 by establishing a locator file in its headquarters to reflect the location of master and field personnel records of all Air Force Reservists not on active military service. Throughout the remainder of fiscal year 1952, the command inventoried reservists and corrected their records.[31]

Ideally, the reservists' records should have been centralized at Headquarters Continental Air Command, and until April 29, 1953, the headquarters budgeteers and engineers were planning the necessary modifications to allow the facility to meet this need. On that day, however, General Johnson returned from an Air Force commanders' conference with the news that the eastern seaboard of the United States, including the New York–Washington corridor, "was considered vulnerable and therefore is not a suitable location for the establishment of a records repository." He therefore decided to establish a records center at the place where Headquarters Continental Air Command would ultimately relocate.[*,32]

The Air Force retained the headquarters on the east coast, but pressure continued to centralize the records maintenance function. After reviewing a number of potential locations,[†] the Continental Air Command selected surplus facilities at the Air Force Finance Center in Denver, Colorado, purely on the basis of economics and availability. The command established the Continental Air Command Air Reserve Records Center as a detachment of the headquarters at Denver on November 1, 1953. When it officially opened its doors for business on March 1, 1954, the center had custody of 250,000 master personnel records. It quickly got the administration of reservists' records in hand and eventually evolved into the personnel center of the Air Force Reserve.[‡,33]

---

[*]At one point in 1950 the headquarters had been programmed to relocate to Grandview AFB (later, Richards-Gebaur AFB), Mo., but the Air Force budget contained too little money to permit the move.

[†]Among the sites surveyed were Pyote AFB, Tex.; Wendover AFB, Utah; Godman AFB, Ky.; Memphis MAP, Tenn.; Richards-Gebaur AFB, Mo.; Scott AFB, Ill.; Fort Snelling, Minn.; and the Montgomery Quartermaster Depot, Ala.

[‡]The center was redesignated as the Air Reserve Personnel Center on September 1, 1965, and on August 1, 1968, it became a separate operating agency in consequence of the reorganization of the management structure of the Air Force Reserve following the enactment of Public Law 90–168.

Revised Concepts and Programs

The Air Reserve Technician Program

From the very beginning of the post–World War II Air Reserve program, officials and observers at all levels endorsed the need to strengthen the program by integrating full-time personnel into the reserve combat wings in some manner. Early in 1948, a board of reserve officers under Brig. Gen. Lafeton Whitney recommended to Lt. Gen. George E. Stratemeyer that career reservists be assigned to the reserve units as instructors. Later that year, Secretary Gray's Committee on Civilian Components recommended that full-time personnel, preferably reservists on extended active duty, be assigned as members of reserve units in administrative positions. Observing that training had become the last consideration because of the demands of administration, the Gray committee insisted that full-time assistants were essential to an efficient operation.[34]

Implementing the Gray committee's recommendation, in 1948 the Air Force authorized the Continental Air Command to assign reservists to administrative positions on the flying center staffs. These Category R reservists, as they became known, were also members of the reserve unit. They were local residents voluntarily recalled to extended active duty for three years. The Category R program dissolved two years later in the throes of the Korean mobilization. Those two years may be insufficient to support an adequate evaluation, but clearly the program had many advantages, including the ones posed by the Gray committee. Category R personnel provided a continuity of administration and policy, and that stability reduced the number of active force officials required. Also, since the Category R program selected its participants rather than depended on assignment of personnel by the Air Force, the opportunity to assign qualified people existed. Category R personnel had the reserve perspective, and their program gave them the kind of training that was needed to prepare them to immediately assume their duties upon mobilization.[35]

The Category R program had its limitations as well. Too few Category R people were available, and some should have been attached to the wings during peacetime. The dual status of the Category R reservists—assigned to the wing but under the peacetime control of the flying center commander—worked a hardship on the wing commander because most Category R reservists were among his key personnel, and he needed them for wing planning and to support administration and training. Instead, they usually worked for the center commander who, of course, signed their efficiency reports. Most important, the question of their susceptibility to mobilization with their units remained unresolved, and at the moment of mobilization, when the wing commander needed them most, they worked with the center commander.[36]

Evaluating the Category R program in December 1950 from the perspective of the active Air Force and weighing its impact upon the traditional

The Air Force Reserve

military structure and the personnel system which supported it, General Whitehead, the Continental Air Command Commander, categorized it as unsuccessful. His major complaint was that military personnel should not enjoy indefinite exemption from overseas service, nor should they be granted what amounted to indefinite tenure at any location. "Benefits and privileges of the uniform can be granted only when all obligations are equally shared," he wrote. Nevertheless, he too agreed that a permanent group of reserve wing members was necessary to guarantee some sort of stability to the units. He suggested abandoning the Category R program and instituting a program of civilian employees such as the Air National Guard operated in its technician program, which he thought would meet the requirements of but not perpetuate the features he objected to in the Category R program.[37]

For three years after 1950, because of financial and manpower restrictions, the Air Staff reluctantly disapproved various recommendations to provide some form of permanent staff to the reserve units, based on either the Category R or the technician concept. In 1954, however, under the sponsorship of L. C. Lingelbach, its Director of Civilian Personnel, the Continental Air Command staff developed a plan envisioning the employment of Air Reserve technicians, that is, members of the Air Reserve units who were also civilian employees of the units during the normal work week. Evolving over a long period, the plan reflected ideas inherited from the Air Defense Command; the recommendations of the Gray and Smith committees and the Johnson Board; the concept and operation of the contemporary Air National Guard technician program; and discussions throughout the command, its numbered air forces, and reserve units.

After preliminary discussions with officials of the Civil Service Commission and the Air Staff, the Continental Air Command on August 18, 1954, recommended consideration of the plan briefed by the Air Force Director of Civilian Personnel. The objective was to establish maximum combat readiness of the Air Force Reserve units upon mobilization. It called for 9,500 technicians, about 20 percent of the total wing personnel requirement. In addition to combat readiness, it promised extensive savings in military and civilian personnel assignments in the operation of the reserve flying program, specifying savings of $7.25 million in permanent party costs. It suggested that increased administrative efficiency would result from greater stability and higher skill levels among the work force. The Air Staff submitted the proposal with minor revisions to the Civil Service Commission on October 3, 1954. The major concern at that time was to obtain commission approval of certain exceptions to its rules and regulations governing competitive service: selectees would have to become active members of the Air Force Reserve, and, for reduction-in-force purposes, separate competitive levels and areas would be established for Air Reserve technician positions.[38]

Revised Concepts and Programs

L. C. Lingelbach refined and advocated adoption of the air reserve technician program as early as 1954 and administered it from its adoption in 1958 to 1976 when he left Headquarters AFRES.

The Civil Service Commission promised to do everything legally possible to enable approval of the plan. Partially because adoption of the detached squadron plan had skewed the data on which the technician plan had been based, Civil Service Commission consideration of the plan was delayed throughout 1955 while the Department of Defense and the Air Force reconciled conflicting figures to satisfy Bureau of the Budget officials.[39]

The delay was also partially due to Assistant Secretary of Defense Burgess' withholding of approval for the technician plan that sought quid pro quo Air Force acceptance of the administration's six-month, non–prior service plan. In March 1956, Secretary Burgess pointedly told Air Force Secretary Donald A. Quarles, "I do not see why we should presently move on a proposal that is not provided by law [the Air Reserve technician plan], when we have one here that is pending and was urged into law at the personal insistence of the President, the Secretary of Defense, you and me [the six-month program]." Insisting that the six-month, critical skills program had more pertinence to the Air Force than to the other services, Burgess reminded Secretary Quarles that they themselves had played an essential role in its inclusion in the Reserve Forces Act of 1955.[40] Soon after, Assistant Secretary Smith worked out an agreement with Secretary Burgess by which the Air Force would accept 2,500 non–prior service enlistments for the balance of fiscal year 1957 in Air Force Reserve units. Secretary Quarles told Secretary Wilson that the Air Force had "reevaluated"

The Air Force Reserve

its position on the special enlisted programs and determined that Air Force Reserve units could advantageously use six-month non–prior service personnel.[41]

Subsequent to this agreement, in May 1956 Assistant Secretary Burgess visited Headquarters Continental Air Command where Lingelbach briefed him on the proposed program. On June 12, Burgess recommended that the Secretary of Defense approve the plan subject to certain limitations. Defense Secretary Charles E. Wilson thereupon authorized the Secretary of the Air Force to proceed subject to Civil Service Commission approval and the following limitations: the concept of requiring reserve status as a condition of employment was not to extended to any position other than to those enumerated in the plan then under consideration; the technicians had to meet the same service eligibility requirements as other reservists; no present Civil Service employee was to be displaced involuntarily; and the program had to be accomplished within existing funds and manpower ceilings.[42]

The Air Force accommodated the Office of Secretary of Defense's wishes with minor changes in the plan and resubmitted it to the Civil Service Commission. Thereupon, while not rejecting it, the commission declined to approve the plan, now believing that it required enabling legislation from Congress. Thus passed another year.[43] Lingelbach kept the lines open to Civil Service Commission staffers, however, and he managed to arrange one more meeting on the subject. Held on January 15, 1957, in the commission offices, the meeting of Burgess, Commission Chairman Philip Young, Commissioner Lawton, and Assistant Secretary of the Air Force Smith, produced agreement on all but one provision—the commission representatives would not accept any age limit, implied or explicit, for hiring civilian employees. This problem revolved about the fact that the law prohibited age limits for civilian employees of the government on the one hand, but specific age limits were involved in reserve service eligibility on the other.[44]

Secretary Smith discussed the commissioners' views with Maj. Gen. William E. Hall, Assistant Chief of Staff, Reserve Forces; Maj. Gen. William E. Stone, the Air Force Deputy Chief of Staff for Personnel; and John A. Watts, the Air Force Director of Civilian Personnel. They quickly agreed that the age problem could be circumvented by imposition of strict physical requirements on technician applicants. On January 23, Civil Service Commission staffers accepted this adjustment, and on January 29, Secretary Smith confirmed the Air Force's agreement to all this and offered to cooperate in the necessary public relations efforts and legislative proposals.[45]

On June 21, 1957, having consulted with interested veterans organizations, unions, and employee groups, Chairman Harris Ellsworth authorized Smith to proceed with the plan. Chairman Ellsworth said the commission approved with the understanding that the Department of the Air Force will carry out both in letter and spirit the commitment it has made and the safeguards it has promised to apply with respect to employees who would be affected by the plan. It is also understood that the Department will comply fully and strictly with the requirements of the Veterans' Preference Act of 1944 and the Commission's Regulations under that in all of its activities under the plan.[46]

The 1957–1958 budget cuts, necessitating reductions in both reserve and civilian personnel, restricted Air Force implementation of the plan. Nevertheless, on January 10, 1958, Lt. Gen. William E. Hall, Commander of the Continental Air Command, swore in MSgt. Samuel C. McCormack and TSgt. James W. Clark as the first two Air Reserve technicians in ceremonies at Headquarters Continental Air Command. The Air Force then initiated the plan in limited form at Ellington AFB, Texas, and Davis Field, Oklahoma. Full implementation of the program followed in two increments in April and October.[47]

The Air Reserve technician program was under way. In June 1957, the Civil Service Commission sent a letter to the Assistant Secretary of the Air Force approving the program. Its initiation had involved more than three years of study, negotiations, and compromise among government agencies, including an enormous amount of work from all echelons in the Continental Air Command. Despite the concessions that the Air Reserve had made to the Department of Defense and to the Civil Service Commission as well as the ones required for legal reasons, the plan that L. C. Lingelbach had briefed in the Air Staff in August 1954 remained essentially intact. It embodied the Air Force's goal of eventually building a combat-ready Air Force Reserve.

The basis of the plan was the employment of inactive duty reservists in Air Force Reserve flying units as civilian technicians five days a week. On training weekends or active duty periods, the technicians integrated into the unit, providing training and administrative continuity. The purpose, originally posited and never lost sight of, was to improve the combat readiness of the Air Force Reserve units by providing a core of skilled personnel. All else—improving wing manning, releasing active duty military personnel for use elsewhere, opening more positions for civilians—was peripheral to the main purpose of achieving and sustaining combat-ready reserve units.

The single greatest difficulty inherent in the Air Reserve technician program was the status quo problem. Those initial civil service personnel employed by the flying centers who could not or would not accept reserve status and technicians who subsequently involuntarily lost their Ready Reserve assignments were known as status quos. Later status quos were created by promotion to colonel while not occupying a colonel's position; by reaching eight years' commissioned service as a lieutenant colonel or below; by reaching 30 years' commissioned service or five years in grade, whichever came first,

The Air Force Reserve

as a colonel or brigadier general; or by becoming medically disqualified for military service. With the exception of the medical reason, these conditions usually caused the technician to reach his mandatory cutoff date for military participation before he was qualified to retire as a civilian. It was fundamental to the Air Force's agreement with the Civil Service Commission that no technician would lose his civilian job while he was otherwise eligible for the civilian aspects of the job under Civil Service Commission regulations. Of course, as soon as an Air Reserve technician became militarily ineligible, the Air Force began great effort to place him elsewhere in a suitable civilian position. The employee encumbered the civilian half of this position meanwhile, and usually another reservist was assigned to his reserve position.[48]

The status quo phenomenon contained the seeds of two problems: that of great numbers going status quo simultaneously and that of a key individual, a commander for example, becoming a status quo employee. The Air Force eventually learned how to circumvent the latter problem in various ways. In 1957, by terms of an agreement among officials of the commission, the Department of Defense, and the Air Force, the first condition soon ceased to be a problem. It had been agreed that the technician program could accommodate up to 10 percent of its members as status quos at any time. By the end of the program's first year, 18.3 percent of its members were status quos. Two years later, reflecting the reassignment and retirement of original status quos, the proportion had dropped to 6.6 percent, and it declined steadily thereafter until it stabilized around 1 percent in 1974. In the end, although it remained a frequent target of criticism, the status quo issue proved more of an irritant than a problem.

In time, the cost of the Air Reserve technician program would attract great criticism. Because of the perception that the technician's dual status as reservist and civilian (entitling him to dual retirement benefits) was unnecessarily costly, many budgetary and manpower study groups sought to have the technician program eliminated on grounds of economy and efficiency, but their argument lacked conviction and the mathematics involved proved faulty.[*49]

The Air Reserve technician program would stand the test of time and turn aside the slings and arrows of its critics to form, along with Public Law 90–168 passed in December 1967 and the Total Force Policy proclaimed in August 1973, the tripod on which the combat readiness of the Air Force Reserve rested in 1982.

---

[*]For a discussion of later attacks against the Air Reserve technician program, see Chapter 11, pp. 298–307.

Revised Concepts and Programs

The Reserve Facilities Problem

At a time when the Air Force Reserve program was finally achieving some success, the lack of adequate reserve facilities deterred greater progress. Late in 1953, Brig. Gen. James B. Burwell, the Continental Air Command Deputy Chief of Staff for Operations, described the acquisition of facilities as the "greatest single difficulty" confronting the command in implementing the Air Force reserve program. He warned:

> Without a decided improvement in the facilities situation we might be soon forced to reject aircraft now programmed and the Specialist Training Center program will be considerably delayed and reduced in scope. I know of no single problem in the Reserve Program as serious as this facilities question.[50]

General Johnson expressed equal concern, advising the Air Staff that the greatest delay in implementing the reserve flying training program had been the failure to reestablish permanent sites and facilities after the Korean War, and he asked the Chief of Staff to take "every possible action" to provide the essential reserve facilities.[51]

General Johnson's Reserve Program Review Board had recommended that the Air Force Reserve construction program be approved and that local civic

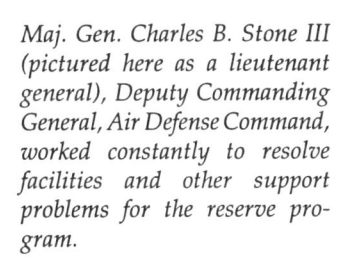

Maj. Gen. Charles B. Stone III (pictured here as a lieutenant general), Deputy Commanding General, Air Defense Command, worked constantly to resolve facilities and other support problems for the reserve program.

The Air Force Reserve

leaders and reservists be encouraged to share the responsibility for the construction program. Amplifying this recommendation, the Headquarters Continental Air Command staff pleaded with the Air Staff to enlighten the Department of Defense and the Bureau of the Budget on the realities of programming facilities for reserve use. As the fundamental problem in justifying budget requests, the Air Force could never calculate the exact number of reservists who would participate in any facility in a given locality. This could be done for active force units with pinpoint accuracy, but the fluctuating reserve population made it difficult to define the specific need for facilities in the reserve program. General Johnson urged Headquarters USAF to prevail upon the Department of Defense and the Bureau of the Budget to take this fact into consideration when seeking congressional authorization for acquisition of facilities and construction programs.[52]

Congress authorized the Air Force to spend $29.5 million to construct Air Force Reserve training facilities during 1952 and 1953. Nevertheless, because of revisions necessitated by approval of the Long-Range Plan produced by General Smith's committee and the diversion of funds intended for reserve construction to other purposes, Lt. Gen. Charles B. Stone III, who succeeded General Johnson as Continental Air Command Commander in December 1955, also reported that the lack of adequate facilities was seriously hampering the realization of an effective Air Force Reserve. Early in 1956, General Stone complained that although the Air Staff programmed the construction of facilities required for reserve units under a policy of first things first, it diverted the bulk of reserve construction funds made available by Congress to higher priority operations facilities for the Regular Air Force.[53]

In his last days as Chief of Staff, General Twining encouraged the construction of facilities for reserve forces. Recalling his memorandum of January 1955, he wanted the annual military construction program of the Air Force Reserve to be funded in the same proportion that the total amount appropriated for military construction was to the total approved construction program of the Air Force.[54] Twining was a lame duck, of course, and in June 1957, with General Thomas D. White as Chief of Staff, the situation had not improved. General Stone complained bitterly about the low priorities endured by the Air Force Reserve. He told the Chief of Staff that a great disparity existed in the precedence categories assigned Air Force Reserve and regular units in the continental United States having comparable D-Day tasks and missions. Unit precedence categories in the Air Force Operating Program formed the basis for the distribution and allocation of critical resources and were assigned depending upon each unit's relative importance to the overall force structure. With rare exception, Air Force Reserve units were in the very lowest of the assignable twenty-five categories, notwithstanding the fact that Air Force and gaining command war plans assigned D-Day tasks and missions

Revised Concepts and Programs

to specific units of the Air Force Reserve.[55] By that time, however, in common with the rest of the Department of Defense, the Air Force began reducing operations in the face of the Eisenhower economies, and soon the Continental Air Command would be eliminating, rather than increasing, Air Force Reserve facilities.

Changing Operational and Mobilization Considerations

Change and reorganization are endemic to the Air Force Reserve. As this story demonstrates, as a component settles into an organization of forces and missions and exhibits some degree of efficiency, external forces frequently impose change upon it, sometimes for good, sometimes for ill. So it was in the late 1950s. In 1957, with its twenty-four wings attaining reasonable degrees of operational readiness, with equipment and even facilities improving, and with the Air Reserve technician program on the eve of implementation, the Air Force Reserve flying unit program was drastically changed. Some of the initial changes were rooted in valid operational considerations, but economies initiated by the Eisenhower administration would have soon overtaken the entire program in any event.

By the summer of 1956, the Air Reserve Forces comprised twenty-seven Air National Guard (twenty-five fighter-interceptor and two tactical reconnaissance) and twenty-four Air Force Reserve (two tactical bomber, sixteen troop carrier and six fighter bomber) wings. In July 1956, however, the Air Staff put into motion a train of events that led to a sharply reduced wartime requirement for the reserve forces units. In concert with the Eisenhower administration's economy drive, it was eventually decided to reduce the Air National Guard to twenty-four wings and the Air Force Reserve to fifteen.

The July 1, 1956, version of the Joint Strategic Objectives Plan contained some new strategic concepts which reflected the anticipated nuclear nature of the next war and indicated that the combat-ready forces available on D-Day would probably be the only forces capable of making a significant contribution to the outcome of the initial and critical phase of a general war. That being so, the Air Force Director of Plans reexamined the proposed mobilization role of the Air Reserve Forces. He concluded that Air Force Reserve tactical bomb wings should be phased out by the end of fiscal year 1958 and its fighter-bomber wings, by the end of fiscal 1960.[56]

Concurrently, General Stone, as Commander of the Continental Air Command, questioned the validity of the planned use of the two Air Force Reserve B–26 tactical bomb wings on D-Day. He asserted that limitations on D-Day utility of the B–26 units, along with the lack of a suitable replacement for the B–26, invalidated the current reserve forces tactical bomber program.

167

The Air Force Reserve

To achieve validity in reserve forces programming, the general said it was essential that unit missions be realistically consistent with aircraft availability, mobilization requirements, and reserve training capabilities. Consequently, assuming that a modern tactical bomber would not become available, he recommended that Air Force Reserve tactical bomb wings be redesignated as troop carrier and that action be taken to provide suitable transport aircraft.[57]

Already pressuring the Air Force to provide more wartime airlift, the Joint Chiefs of Staff readily endorsed General Stone's suggestion to establish more reserve troop carrier units. Meanwhile, as an important consideration, about 150 C–119s had become available from the active force. Consequently, on November 19, 1956, General White, then Air Force Vice Chief of Staff, directed the Continental Air Command to convert three Air Force Reserve fighter-bomber wings to the troop carrier role in the first quarter of fiscal 1958.[58]

About the same time, the headquarters staffs of the Air Defense Command and the Tactical Air Command conducted a dialogue that would have far-reaching results for the Air Force Reserve. Initiated by the Air Defense Command on November 14, 1956, the participants ultimately concluded that the number of Air Reserve Forces fighter-bomber units then at hand greatly exceeded the commands' combined D-Day requirements for air defense augmentation. They jointly established requirements for only 70 Air Reserve Forces fighter and reconnaissance squadrons. The Air Reserve Forces' combined force of 96 units therefore clearly exceeded the mobilization requirement.[59]

Presented with this joint major command position, on March 8, 1957, Lt. Gen. Frank F. Everest, Air Force Deputy Chief of Staff for Operations, recommended that the entire Air Reserve Forces fighter program be given to the Air National Guard and the troop carrier program, to the Air Force Reserve. No decision was reached at the time, but all involved agencies and commands agreed to undertake still another study of the Air Reserve Forces structure. The seeds of a future action were sown, thefore, in a dialogue initiated by the Air Force's chief operating official, not by the National Guard Bureau as Air Force Reserve mythology has held.[60]

By August 1957, the Defense Department had instructed the Air Force to reduce its fiscal 1958 budget to $17.9 billion, nearly a billion less than the service had requested in April. Among other actions, General White, now Chief of Staff, directed his Deputy Chief of Staff for Plans and Programs to suspend all action to expand the Air Reserve Forces and conduct another study of the reserve programs to validate programming actions already in progress.[61]

As an initial restriction, the Air Staff advised the Continental Air Command that the 27,103 manpower spaces and $223.3 million authorized for its operations in the last quarter of fiscal year 1957 would become ceilings for

Revised Concepts and Programs

the indefinite future. The problem was that the part of the command's mission that absorbed the greatest share of its resources—support of the reserve flying wings—was precisely the part programmed for the greatest expansion. The 24 wings never had their 72 authorized squadrons. In July 1957, they comprised 55 tactical squadrons and another 17 to be activated at detached locations within the next 4 years. If these units were to be supported by flying centers, the Continental Air Command's requirements for permanent party personnel would increase to more than 30,000. Implementation of the Air Reserve technician program would help, but not enough. Besides, a 72-squadron program would demand a number of expensive construction projects, more aircraft and other equipment, and more flying hours, all of which would cost more than the Air Force could afford to pay.

The source of manpower and money required for completion of the planned Air Force Reserve program was never elucidated; now Defense Department guidance made it perfectly clear they would never be available. Abandonment of the 24-wing goal was therefore inevitable. The real question was how many wings would be eliminated. The Air Staff recommended a force of 15 wings, and the Chief of Staff said he was willing to consider an 18-wing plan proposed by the Continental Air Command if the command could support the effort with no additional resources. The command's requirement for manpower to manage a 15-wing program already exceeded its manpower ceiling, however. On September 9, General Hall accepted the 15-wing/45-squadron troop carrier program. Thus, it was settled that the Air Force Reserve would lose not only the 6 fighter-bomber wings, but also 3 troop carrier wings. The Air National Guard, meanwhile would be reduced to 24 wings.[62]

The Secretary of the Air Force approved the 1957–1961 reserve flying wing program on September 20, 1957. Once an additional three squadrons were activated, the flying program would consist of 15 troop carrier wings comprising 45 squadrons, all equipped with C–119s, and 5 air rescue squadrons equipped with SA–16s.

With the activation of the 78th Troop Carrier Squadron at Bates MAP, Alabama, in May 1959, the troop carrier squadron program was complete. At that point, the reserve troop carrier squadrons were located on eighteen Regular Air Force bases, three naval air stations, and fourteen civil airports. An air rescue squadron was the sole occupant of one location, and the other four rescue squadrons were collocated with reserve troop carrier units on either active force bases or civilian fields.[63]

At the end of fiscal year 1959, the Air Force Reserve flying force consisted of forty-five troop carrier and five air rescue squadrons. After a brave beginning following the Korean War, the flying force had fallen victim to the Eisenhower economies and a redirection of mobilization roles. Nevertheless, it emerged from the period a stronger structure, its Air Reserve technician

The Air Force Reserve

program became operative, and personnel assignments in the units stabilized. Unit manning was also strenthened by the influx of non–prior service personnel and the detached squadrons, which reached out into fresh recruiting markets. After a succession of weak, ill-defined, often feckless plans and programs stimulated by the Long-Range Plan of 1951 and the Twining memorandum of 1955, the post–World War II Air Force Reserve program had evolved into a concept and form that would carry it through the next ten years.

7

A Return on the Investment 1961–1965

> ... the President may, without the consent of the persons concerned, order any unit, or any member not assigned to a unit organized to serve as a unit, in the Ready Reserve of an armed force to active duty for not more than twelve consecutive months.
>
> —PL 87–117, August 1, 1961

In the early 1960s, the Air Force and the nation began to accrue a dividend on their investment in the Air Force Reserve. A number of factors coalesced to occasion this. Internally, the Air Force reorganized its system of managing the Air Reserve Forces, making the gaining commands more responsible for the training and readiness of the reserve units they would acquire upon mobilization. Placed in greater daily proximity to their reserve units, the commands soon realized the potential the reservists had for conducting productive peacetime missions. Consequently, the Air Force began to employ Air Force Reserve troop carrier units on all manner of daily missions.

The nation's reserve forces also acquired greater importance and utility as John F. Kennedy initiated a policy of flexible response to meet challenges to the national security with actions short of war and thus avoid nuclear confrontation. Since the military services did not have enough people on active duty to implement the President's policies and to meet the crises that arose over Berlin and Cuba in 1961 and 1962, they found it necessary to rely increasingly upon the reserve forces to augment their active forces in daily operations and contingencies. Finally, the Air Force Reserve met the ultimate challenge when

The Air Force Reserve

President John F. Kennedy and General Walter C. Sweeney, Jr., Commander, Tactical Air Command (right), visit Brig. Gen. John S. Bagby, commander of the mobilized 512th Troop Carrier Wing, Willow Grove NAS, Pennsylvania, and one of his C–119 crews at Homestead AFB, Florida, on November 20, 1962, during the Cuban missile crisis.

the President found it necessary to mobilize parts of it during the Berlin and Cuban crises.

Revisions to Air Reserve Forces Management

In May 1960, the Air Force revised its system of managing and training the Air Reserve Forces. The Continental Air Command retained command of all Air Force Reserve units, but the gaining commands became more responsible for the operational readiness of the Reserve Forces units they would gain upon mobilization and acquired the responsibility to inspect the units and supervise their training.

The reorganization resulted from the recommendations of the Reserve Forces Program Review Group under the chairmanship of Maj. Gen. Sory Smith, Continental Air Command's Fourth Air Force Commander. General

White, Air Force Chief of Staff, appointed the Smith group on October 1, 1959, at a time when a number of Air Reserve Forces issues demanded resolution. These included an assertion by an Air Staff study committee that the Air Force Reserve needed a long-range program in place rather than annual programs devised in fits and starts; a request from Under Secretary of the Air Force Malcolm A. McIntyre that the Air Staff justify each segment of the reserve structure in terms of its actual support of the active force's mission; and agitation within the Air Force Association for a merger of the Air Force Reserve into the Air National Guard.[1] Then, in the summer of 1959, the Department of Defense directed the Air Force to reduce its 1961 budget estimates, reductions which would have to affect the Air Reserve Forces as well as the active force.[2]

On September 25, 1959, Vice Chief of Staff General Curtis E. LeMay threw a lighted match into this flammable atmosphere. Speaking at a Reserve Forces seminar at the Pentagon, he suggested that it was inefficient and costly to have two reserve components. The Vice Chief did not stop here. Observing that there might not always be time to mobilize, he remarked, "Weekend soldiers will not do. We can't afford to man our tremendously costly weapons with part-time help." General LeMay acknowledged the need for a single air reserve, but he insisted that it had to be good and be able to help in case of war. "A stronger and tighter Reserve would be more effective and permit funds to be diverted to the Regular establishment," he said. The Vice Chief of Staff concluded by saying that his remarks were intended to stimulate creative thinking within the Air Reserve Forces about restructuring the force. They stimulated, instead, a firestorm of protest from the Air National Guard. Perceiving a threat to the guard's existence, the National Guard Association suggested that General LeMay was "flying off course" and that his "qualifications and continued usefulness be reevaluated."[3]

At least in part because of the conflagration ignited by General LeMay, a week later General White established General Smith's group to study the long-range requirements and missions for the Air Reserve Forces. Representing all three components of the Air Force, the fourteen-member group convened at the Pentagon on October 19 and completed its deliberations on November 18.

The Reserve Forces Review Group recommended that the gaining commands assume greater responsibility for the training and readiness of the Air Reserve Forces, that the Continental Air Command be discontinued, that the Air Reserve Records Center be assigned to the Deputy Chief of Staff, Personnel in Headquarters USAF, and that the Office of the Assistant Chief of Staff, Reserve Forces be expanded to include a staff comparable to that of the National Guard Bureau's Deputy for the Air National Guard. The group recommended continued modernization of Air Reserve Forces units and the assignment of additional defense and reconnaissance missions.[4] Having said all this, the group hedged:

The Air Force Reserve

Intending to stimulate creative thinking within the Air Force Reserve on restructuring the force, General Curtis E. LeMay, speaking at a Reserve Forces seminar, remarked, "A stronger and tighter Reserve would be more effective and permit funds to be diverted to the Regular establishment."

> These proposals can succeed only if the highest Air Force officials insist that the Air Staff and major commands conscientiously and understandingly accept their responsibilities for imaginative, objective, and enlightened guidance and management of the Reserve Forces unit and individual mission.[5]

In other words, without the goading advocacy of an agency like the Continental Air Command, the necessary "enlightened guidance and management" might not materialize.

On January 7, 1960, the Air Force Council approved an embodiment of the group's findings presented by Maj. Gen. Robert E. L. Eaton, Assistant Chief of Staff for Reserve Forces. The refined proposal included a concept of developing a post–nuclear attack recovery role for the Reserve Forces. This Reserve Forces structure for the 1960s would retain basically the same combat flying and support units, as well as the organization necessary to conduct the postattack mission. Under the revised management structure, the Continental Air Command would be eliminated and the gaining commands would work directly with the reserve units. By virtue of his position, General Eaton was required to present the plan to the council. Since he did not agree with it completely, however, he presented an alternate plan that would retain the Continental Air Command.[6]

Called to a special meeting on January 25–27, the Air Reserve Forces Policy Committee rejected the presentation the Air Force Council had accepted

174

and recommended further consideration by the Air Staff. The committee wanted to hear the views of the commanders of the gaining commands and their plans for implementing the proposals. Insofar as possible, committee members wanted the revised individual training program organized into a structure of combat units instead of the proposed training structure. Also, with the suspicions engendered by bitter experience with shifting Air Force winds, Air Reserve and Air Guard members of the committee wanted some assurance that the manpower and funds necessary to support the plan would be available.[7]

Secretary of the Air Force Dudley C. Sharp, who recalled a year later when he left the office that he had "never been very enthusiastic about the Reserve program,"[8] disapproved the policy committee's recommendations for further Air Staff study. On February 2, Secretary Sharp approved the basic plan for the future development, employment, and management of the Air Reserve Forces. Sharing the committee's reservations about the proposed management plan, he asked the Chief of Staff to ensure the proper supervision, control, and manning necessary to its successful implementation. Sharp said that the manpower requirements would be subject to continuous review, but he assured the policy committee "that the manpower and funds necessary to support the program will be available," a promise the Air Force could not keep.[9]

General White approved the Air Staff's implementing plan to revise the management and employment of the Air Reserve Forces on May 17, 1960. In a compromise engineered by General Eaton, the Continental Air Command continued to exist, but it lost its responsibilities for the supervision of training and inspection of Reserve Forces combat units to the gaining commands. This, incidentally, ended the relationship between the command and the Air National Guard, inasmuch as its only responsibility toward the Guard had been inspection and supervision of training. The revised management plan also introduced the concept of giving Air Force Reservists a more active role in management of their programs. This was to be achieved in two ways. First, although it survived as an organization, the Continental Air Command lost its numbered air forces. Their place at the command's intermediate management level was taken by six organizationally comparable Air Force Reserve regions. Reservists would occupy 85 of the 117 personnel spaces authorized each regional headquarters. Second, the new postattack recovery program was managed entirely by reservists.[10]

With regard to the tactical unit program, the Air Force defined supervision of training as the process by which the gaining commands observed, evaluated, and guided Air Reserve Forces units to make them operationally ready. The gaining commands exercised this supervision by formulating training objectives and programs; appointing air advisers with the authority to supervise Air Reserve Forces training; and conducting tests, training exercises, and staff visits.[11] Explaining the objective of the new system, Chief of Staff General White declared that to be truly effective in the modern era the Air Force had to

The Air Force Reserve

be able to count on active reserve forces as being something more than a manpower pool. Their members had to be active participants, comparable in readiness and effectiveness to the first-line active force units.[12]

While training for their wartime mission, certain reserve units could perform day-to-day peacetime functions for the Air Force, thereby conserving manpower and money. Air Force objectives published in September 1961 demanded that the active force capitalize on the potential of the Air Reserve Forces to augment active units in peacetime. The Air Reserve Forces were to provide the flying units needed to augment the Air Defense Command with fighter interceptors; the Tactical Air Command, with tactical fighter, troop carrier, and tactical reconnaissance; and the Military Air Transport Service, with airlift, aeromedical transport, and air rescue. The Air Reserve Forces were also to support all the major commands with nonflying support units as well as units to conduct postattack recovery and reconstitution operations.[13]

As the Air Force was thus accentuating the role of its reserve forces, the presidential administration of John F. Kennedy took office in 1961 with a new approach to national defense. The President defined a defense policy of flexible response, but he found the defense establishment lacked sufficient conventional forces and airlift to apply the policy. At the same time, Robert S. McNamara, his new Secretary of Defense, developed serious questions about the role and adequacy of the nation's reserve forces. Before these two men could do much

As Secretary of Defense, Robert S. McNamara recommended that the President recall reserve forces during the Berlin and Cuban missile crises of 1961 and 1962.

about either problem, however, the United States became involved in successive international crises which required the use of the reserve forces, including Air Force Reserve troop carrier units.

The Berlin Crisis of 1961 and Mobilization

World War II had left Berlin 100 miles deep within East German territory, controlled by the Soviets, and divided into Russian, British, French, and American zones administered under local agreements which did not guarantee Western access to the city. Responding to a series of Soviet actions in 1948, the three western allies consolidated their zones. For ten years the western powers maintained a tenacious hold on West Berlin under periodic harassment of the Soviets. Then, in 1958, Soviet Premier Nikita Khrushchev demanded a German peace treaty to authenticate the division of the country and to end western occupation rights inside East German territory. Nothing came of his demand at the time, but the threat existed.[14]

It was President Eisenhower's policy to refrain from treating each instance of Soviet harassment in Berlin as a cause for a "Berlin crisis." He anticipated that the Soviets would sustain their efforts to keep the United States off-balance over Berlin for a good many years. The essence of the Kennedy administration's Berlin policy, on the other hand, was to guarantee the freedom of the citizens of Berlin and the right of the western allies to maintain access to the city.[15]

President Kennedy's problem was to fit his policy on Berlin into his overall views on national defense. As a candidate in 1960, he had called for strengthening both the conventional and nuclear forces of the United States. As President, on March 28, 1961, he outlined his defense policies for Congress, declaring in part, "Our defense posture must be both flexible and determined . . . our response . . . suitable and selective."[16] Among the defense issues that Secretary McNamara found requiring immediate action were the need to modernize the conventional forces, strengthen airlift capabilities, and define the role of the reserves.[17]

Premier Khrushchev vowed on January 6, 1961, to "eradicate the splinter from the heart of Europe," but he also agreed to meet the new U.S. President in Vienna, Austria, in June 1961, implying that he would take no action on Berlin until after their meeting. Nevertheless, the Kennedy administration prepared for varying levels of action in response to a Berlin crisis, and the U.S. Army developed plans for a much more rapid deployment of a major portion of its reserve forces.[18] The June meeting between President Kennedy and Premier Khrushchev intensified the tension over Berlin. The Soviet Premier confirmed his intention to sign a unilateral treaty with East Germany and said he would never recognize American rights in West Berlin afterward. If the

The Air Force Reserve

President insisted on occupation rights after a treaty and violated German borders, the United States should expect Russia to meet force by force.[19]

Faced by the intransigence of the Soviet Premier, President Kennedy himself returned home determined not to yield. By mid-July, he was trying to unravel a skein of options. At a National Security Council meeting on July 13, the Joint Chiefs of Staff and the Secretaries of State and Defense took a militant stand. Among other measures, they urged the President to declare a national emergency, call up reserve and National Guard forces, extend the terms of service of members of the armed services, request additional money for defense, and refrain from negotiating to ease the tension. Although rejecting such militancy as unnecessary, the President, nevertheless, asserted that "two things matter: our presence in Berlin, and our access to Berlin."[20]

The President wanted to avoid the appearance of overreacting to the crisis. He had suffered a personal loss of respect four months earlier when he had condoned an abortive landing of Cuban exiles at the Bay of Pigs, and he needed to establish some international confidence in his leadership and judgment. He did not want to signal a strong sense of national alarm by declaring a national emergency. He thought it better to undertake a sustained global effort rather than adopt an instant program oriented toward Berlin alone that might produce a dangerous climax. Llewellyn Thompson, U.S. ambassador to Russia, and Henry A. Kissinger, a consultant to the National Security Council, were also advising him that the Russians would be more impressed by a long-range buildup of U.S. forces than by frantic improvising.[21]

On July 19, the President and McNamara put the finishing touches on a program of gradual military response which the National Security Council confirmed the same afternoon.[22] If Kennedy was going to react to the Russian threats over Berlin without declaring a national emergency, and all that went with such a decision, he had no choice but to respond gradually. The United States simply was not prepared to do otherwise. Only three of the Army's fourteen active divisions were prepared for combat. The others had trained cadres of 4,000 to 6,000 men, approximately 40 percent of normal divisional strength, and were fleshed out with draftees and recruits. This was a constant condition as groups of trainees followed each other through the organizations before being dispersed worldwide as replacements. It might take as long as a year to prepare the divisions being used for training for deployment to Europe. To increase the strength of the Strategic Reserve in the United States, it would be necessary to mobilize reserve units. In addition, the Kennedy administration's strategy of a flexible, mobile military posture required additional tactical fighters and strategic airlift, and the Air Reserve Forces were the only available source of immediate augmentation.[23]

On July 25, President Kennedy went to the nation with his program on the Berlin crisis. He told the people that the U.S. right to be in Berlin and its commitment to the city had to be defended if the Soviets attempted to curtail them unilaterally. The President told the nation that he would ask for mobilization authority, an increase in the draft, higher military strength authorizations, and a supplemental military appropriation of approximately $3.25 billion. He disclosed that he initially intended to recall a number of Air Force Reserve air transport squadrons and Air National Guard tactical fighter squadrons, but that he would call others if needed.[24]

The principal objective of the military expansion proposed by Secretary McNamara was to make possible a significant increase in U.S. military strength by January 1, 1962, and in the months immediately thereafter. His program focused on building up the nation's conventional military power. He intended to call up and intensively train reserve ground, tactical air, and antisubmarine units and to deploy additional ground and air units to Europe. The Berlin crisis served to support the new administration's contention that the nation lacked sufficient military airlift capability.

Major increases in air strength would be provided by calling up twenty-one fighter and eight reconnaissance squadrons from the Air National Guard and five transport squadrons from the Air Force Reserve to be available for deployment by January 1, 1962. The Joint Chiefs of Staff believed that this partial mobilization and the European deployment, along with an anticipated contribution from the NATO allies, would enable U.S. commanders in Europe to do a number of things. They would have the capability to reopen access to Berlin if necessary, wage conventional war on a scale to indicate U.S. determination, and provide the additional time to begin negotiations before resorting to nuclear warfare. They would also gain the time to prepare for the use of nuclear weapons should that become necessary.[25]

Congress gave the President the requested powers on August 1, 1961, authorizing him to order reserve units and individual reservists involuntarily to active duty for not more than twelve consecutive months. The joint resolution further authorized the President and the Secretary of Defense to extend service obligations in any reserve component that would expire before July 1, 1952, for not more than twelve months.[26]

Shortly thereafter, the crisis in Berlin escalated. Despite legal and psychological obstacles, thousands of East Berliners were streaming daily into West Berlin, seeking freedom in the West and, in the process, draining the depressed economy of the East. The communists responded on August 13 by sealing off the border between East and West Berlin, first with a fence and then with a concrete wall topped with barbed wire. Buildings along the border were also incorporated into the barrier by closing their apertures with bricks.[27]

Convinced that some response was required, if only to restore morale among the stunned Berliners, President Kennedy acted. He conceded the right of East Germany (the German Democratic Republic) to close its borders with West Germany (the Federal Republic of Germany) and would not posit that as a casus belli. But the President would not accept denial of United States/NATO

The Air Force Reserve

access to West Berlin. It was to protect against that contingency alone—the denial of access—that on August 14 President Kennedy directed McNamara to take his military actions. Kennedy moved an armored battalion into West Berlin and sent Vice President Lyndon B. Johnson along with retired General Lucius D. Clay, whom the Berliners considered one of the heroes of the airlift of 1948 and 1949 when he was military governor of the U.S. zone, to Berlin to show the flag and bolster the spirits of the West Berliners.[28]

On August 25, with the Wall acquiring greater permanence as each day passed and amid rumors that the Russians were about to resume atmospheric testing of nuclear weapons, President Kennedy approved Defense Department plans to order Army, Navy, and Air Force Reserve and National Guard units to active duty with 76,542 men. These included the five Air Force Reserve C–124 units.[29] Six days later, the Air Staff advised Headquarters Continental Air Command that the recall would take place on October 1, and the headquarters immediately alerted the affected units.[30]

On October 1, 1961, as their gaining command, the Tactical Air Command mobilized the C–124 units, which had been alerted on September 1, and the Air Reserve Records Center recalled 2,666 filler personnel for the mobilized Reserve and Guard units. In all, 5,613 Air Force Reservists came on extended active duty for the Berlin crisis.[31]

Of all the Air Force Reserve troop carrier units, the five groups assigned to the mobilized 435th and the 442d Troop Carrrier Wings were the least prepared for active duty because they had just begun converting from C–119s to C–124s. The Air Force Reserve received its first C–124A at Donaldson AFB, South Carolina, about the time that President Kennedy took office in January 1961. Its five C–124 squadrons were organized on May 8, not a month before the President's meeting with Khrushchev in Vienna. Whether the units were ready or not, the President needed C–124 troop carrier units, and the reserve units were the only available augmentation.[32]

Upon mobilization, the two C–124 wings concentrated on readiness training. The 442d Troop Carrier Wing, commanded by Col. James E. McPartlin, attained combat readiness on March 1, 1962. Thereafter, the wing participated in a wide variety of missions and exercises directed by the Tactical Air Command, and it conducted extensive overwater training on flights to Hawaii, Newfoundland, Bermuda, and the Azores. Commanded by Col. Forest Harsh, the 435th Troop Carrier Wing became combat-ready in January 1962. Its crews flew missions that took them to England, South America, Iceland, California, and points between.[33]

In December 1961, the Kennedy administration began to review the question of retaining the reserve units on active military service. The President wanted to do a number of things that were not entirely compatible. He wanted to return all the recalled reservists to inactive status as soon as possible without having to call up others to replace them. At the same time, for both political

Return on Investment, 1961–1965

An enclosed maintenance stand provided some protection against the icy winds for the maintenance men of the mobilized 442d Troop Carrier Wing working on a C–124 during the winter of 1961–1962 at Richards-Gebaur AFB, Missouri.

and military reasons, he thought it advisable to maintain the strength of the U.S. Army in Europe at essentially the existing level for some time to come. He also wanted to maintain strong Army forces in strategic reserve in the United States ready to deploy to Europe or any other threatened area. Finally, he wanted to accomplish all these things within a 1963 active Army strength of 960,000.[34]

When queried during his press conference on March 21 about the possibility of releasing the reservists early, President Kennedy emphasized that they would be released as early as possible consistent with national security. They had been called up because of the crisis in Berlin and because of threats in Southeast Asia, and he could see no evidence of these threats abating.[35] A few weeks later, however, he was able to announce that the mobilized National Guard and reserve units probably would be released in August. Administration officials thought the permanent buildup had progressed sufficiently that unless the international situation deteriorated, the recalled units would be released. They emphasized that the release would be possible because of the buildup of permanent strength rather than because of any marked change in the international situation.[36]

The Air Force released the 435th and 442d Troop Carrier Wings from active military service on August 27, 1962. President Kennedy, who had so urgently needed their numbers and presence a year earlier, saluted them:

> On your return to civilian life, I wish to convey my personal appreciation for the contribution that you have made to the defense of this Nation during the past year. I am keenly aware that your active duty has involved inconvenience and hardships for many individuals and families. For the fortitude with which these difficulties have been borne, I am deeply grateful.[37]

All things considered, the mobilization of Air Reserve Forces in October 1961

The Air Force Reserve

was accomplished with a minimum of confusion and compromise with requirements. The total Air Reserve Forces recall significantly augmented the Air Force at a time when the cupboard was otherwise bare—a 17 percent augmentation in troop carrier forces, 28 percent in heavy transport, 28 percent in tactical reconnaissance, and 37 percent in tactical fighter strength.[38]

Although not recalled to extended active duty, about one hundred reservists from the Air Force Reserve's five Aerospace Rescue and Recovery Squadrons voluntarily came on active duty to provide rescue coverage for deployment of the jet fighters from the mobilized Air National Guard units to Europe. Four crews and SA–16 aircraft were stationed at Goose Bay, Labrador, and four at Prestwick, Scotland, to reinforce coverage of the northern route; additionally, two crews deployed with their aircraft to Eglin AFB, Florida, to provide against the contingency that bad weather might necessitate a southerly crossing.[39]

The Air Force's interpretation of the language of Public Law 87–117 incurred some congressional criticism for its handling of the mobilization. The passage in question stated that

> the President may, without the consent of the persons concerned, order any unit, or any member not assigned to a unit organized to serve as a unit, in the Ready Reserve of an armed force to active duty for not more than twelve consecutive months.[40]

Deciding that this language permitted it to recall individuals from organized units that were not themselves mobilized, the Air Force recalled about 160 members of units other than the C–124 squadrons. Most were non–prior service individuals but a few were not. Among the latter group was a lawyer in civilian life, now recalled as a filler to serve as a stenographer in the 442d Troop Carrier Wing. He applied in the U.S. District Court for a writ of habeas corpus for his immediate release from the service. He based his petition on the ground that the statute empowered the President to recall only units and individuals not assigned to units.[41]

The Air Force responded that the non–prior service individuals it called possessed needed skills; that Congress intended that airmen who had not served on active duty should be called up before those who had; and that since relatively few persons were being called from other units, the integrity of these units was not impaired. The U.S. District Court of Missouri sustained the Air Force's contention when the airman's case was heard on April 17, 1962.[42]

The Air Force amplified its position during hearings conducted on the recall the same month by a subcommittee of the House Armed Services Committee. Benjamin W. Fridge, Special Assistant to the Secretary of the Air Force for Manpower, Personnel, and Reserve Forces, testified that most individual reservists ordered to active duty were non–prior service enlistees. They had voluntarily enlisted in a component of the Air Reserve Forces and acquired a military obligation of six or eight years under the Universal Military

Return on Investment, 1961–1965

An Air Force Reserve SA–16 crew conducting water rescue exercises in the late 1950s.

Training and Service Act. Those who changed their residences or for any reason could no longer participate in training with their units were placed in a Ready Reserve pool. Many of these people were called as fillers because they had unfulfilled military service obligations. Others were draft-exempt persons who had served on active duty for less than twelve months.[43] The District Court in Missouri accepted the Air Force's argument, but the House subcommittee scolded the service for bending the law. The committee declared that statute clearly limited recall authority to either units or individuals not assigned to an organized unit.[44]

The mobilization for the Berlin crisis was a new departure for the United States in its use of the reserve forces. Assistant Secretary of Defense Carlisle P. Runge noted that the President had recalled reservists in this instance to prevent a war. The modern reserve forces had to be capable of satisfying three requirements, he said. They had to be able to augment the active forces significantly on short notice, provide a base for large-scale mobilization, and provide the initial loss replacement for the active forces which would bear the brunt of the first attack.[45]

The mobilizations of Air Force Reservists for the Korean War in 1950–1952 and the Berlin crisis of 1961 admit to little comparison. Only 5,600 were involved in 1961 contrasted to the 148,000 a decade earlier. In the nine years since the Korean War, the Air Force had refined its administration of the Air Force Reserve so that it could quickly identify reservists who were available and ready. The major problem involved in the Berlin crisis mobilization of the Air Force Reserve was the fact that the mobilized units were caught converting to a new aircraft, the very one the Air Force needed at the moment. The requirement that the mobilized units become accustomed to entirely new sets of directives, especially with respect to personnel and maintenance

The Air Force Reserve

functions, was troublesome. The units had trained with Continental Air Command directives but they "went to war" with Tactical Air Command directives. Furthermore, no sooner had the units mobilized than they had to reorganize, and it took the Tactical Air Command several months to refine the new manning documents. This last concern was probably the major lesson of the Korean mobilization that the Tactical Air Command and the Air Force ignored during the 1961 mobilization of Air Reserve Forces units.[46]

Concluding his account of the Berlin crisis in *Kennedy*, Theodore Sorensen noted that the Wall still stood in Berlin, but so did the Americans. That, ultimately, was what the President had sought to demonstrate by his response in the summer and fall of 1961, when he mobilized certain Air Reserve Forces units.[47]

The Cuban Missile Crisis, October–November 1962

By August 22, 1962, when the Air Force released the reservists it had mobilized in October 1961, a second crisis had arisen to involve other Air Force Reserve units. The focus of the new problem was Cuba, where a revolution had installed Fidel Castro as president. Socialist in nature, the Castro government soon placed itself in the communist group of nations, and relations between the new republic and the United States deteriorated. In the summer of 1960 Castro seized U.S.- and British-owned oil refineries, the United States reduced imports of Cuban sugar, and Castro nationalized all sizable Cuban and foreign businesses. On January 3, 1961, after Castro had restricted the U.S. diplomatic presence in Cuba to eleven persons, President Dwight D. Eisenhower broke off diplomatic relations with Cuba, protesting against "a long series of harassments, baseless accusations, and vilification."[48] On the night of April 17, a force of about 1,500 Cuban emigres supported by the United States landed at the Bay of Pigs in the fruitless expectation of inspiring an uprising against Castro.[49]

On September 1, 1962, the Soviets announced a new treaty with Cuba under which the island country was to receive Soviet arms and technicians "to resist the imperialists' 'threats.'" Replying to Khrushchev's announcement that any U.S. military reaction against the buildup would unleash war, President Kennedy restated the U.S. intention to do what it must to protect its security.[50]

With a large segment of the U.S. press and many congressmen urging the administration to act, the President accepted renewed standby mobilization authority from Congress. The second joint resolution within fourteen months authorized the President to mobilize any unit or member of the Ready Reserve for no more than twelve consecutive months, provided that no more than 150,000 members were involuntarily serving under this authority at any given time. The resolution gave the administration the same options as the 1961 resolution had to strengthen the active forces by extending tours of duty. Under its terms, the law excluded from liability to involuntary recall all reservists who had involuntarily served on active duty during the Berlin crisis.[51]

The new resolution, Public Law 87-736, differed significantly from the earlier joint resolution which had authorized the President to act in the Berlin crisis. The 1961 resolution had been directed specifically toward the Berlin crisis; the new resolution was not designed to meet a single threat, but it acknowledged that U.S. interests were threatened in many areas including Berlin, Cuba, and Southeast Asia. While conceding that the armed forces had become stronger during the preceding year, Congress anticipated certain contingencies that might require the President to have access to additional manpower while it was in recess. The President could proclaim a national emergency, thereby acquiring authority to mobilize a million reservists, but congressional leaders did not want such an important step to be taken in their absence.

The new resolution differed in another way. At the insistence of the Senate Committee on Armed Services, it dispelled any uncertainty about its intentions concerning the mobilization of members of units not mobilized intact. The House Armed Services Committee version of the resolution would have prevented the call-up of individuals who were members of units not being called, but the Senate committee insisted that those in drill-pay status whose previous service had been limited to six months for training should be liable to recall. Even so, the House committee did not yield until assured by McNamara that the power to call individuals from units would be exercised very selectively. The Senate version became law as part of the joint resolution passed as Public Law 87-736.[52]

On October 16, President Kennedy reviewed aerial photographs showing that the Soviets were installing offensive missiles in Cuba. Ordering daily reconnaissance flights over the island, the President and his advisers met regularly to consider military options while he mustered diplomatic support around the world. Among the actions they considered for removing the missiles were air strikes, naval landings, airborne landings (which would employ the Air Force Reserve), and amphibious operations. On October 22, the President established an Executive Committee of the National Security Council (ExCom) to control the Executive Branch actions related to the missile crisis.[53]

On the evening of October 22, explaining to the nation and the world that U.S. policy demanded the withdrawal of the missiles, the President declared that he would quarantine all offensive military equipment under shipment to Cuba. He directed the armed services to be prepared for any eventuality and reinforced the U.S. post at Guantanamo Bay. He ordered continued surveillance of the island, called for emergency meetings of the Organization of American States Council and the United Nations Security Council, and appealed to Khrushchev "to halt and eliminate this clandestine, reckless, and provocative

The Air Force Reserve

threat to world peace and to stable relations between our nations." The President also asserted that any missile launched from Cuba at the United States would be considered tantamount to a missile launched from the Soviet Union and would require an appropriate response.[54]

The Organization of American States supported the President with a resolution that its member states take all actions individually and collectively, including use of armed force, to ensure that Cuba could not receive any additional military materials and related supplies which might threaten the peace and security of the continent. On the basis of that resolution and the joint congressional resolution, President Kennedy ordered U.S. military forces, beginning at 2:00 P.M. Greenwich time, October 24, 1962, to interdict the delivery of offensive weapons and associated materiel to Cuba. On that day, the President delegated his mobilization powers to the Secretary of Defense.[55]

Thereafter, the crisis stretched out as the world watched Russian merchant ships steam toward Cuba. The first, a tanker, was allowed to pass about noon on the 25th. By the 27th, Soviet vessels were either sitting dead in the water or seemed to have turned back. While this and some formal and informal signals from the Soviet Union suggested that the tension might lessen, there was still much cause for concern in the midst of which the Air Force Reserve troop carrier units were participating in preparations for an invasion of Cuba.

They did not know it then, but Headquarters Continental Air Command and its reserve troop carrier wings became involved in the Cuban missile crisis at 5:42 P.M., October 12, a typical Friday, about an hour after the headquarters' quitting time. Major Wesley C. Brashear, on duty in the command post, received a telephone call from Maj. Gen. Stanley J. Donovan, Deputy Chief of Staff for Operations at Headquarters Tactical Air Command. Donovan needed Air Force Reserve help to airlift cargo from as yet undetermined points all over the United States. The operation was to begin the next morning, when specific requirements and destinations would be furnished, and it would be completed by Monday, October 15. Major Brashear immediately rounded up a sufficient number of operations staff officers from their homes, the officers' club, and the golf course so that decisions could be made. The operations staff quickly agreed that on the basis of the number of reserve troop carrier units training that weekend, the command could furnish as many as 328 aircraft. Talking around a classified subject over an open telephone line restricted the flow of information, but, assured by Headquarters Tactical Air Command that the mission was valid and vital, Lt. Col. W. L. Spencer, Chief of the Current Operations Division, committed the Air Force Reserve troop carrier force. In the end, 80 C–119s flew 1,232 hours that weekend carrying materiel into Key West Naval Air Station and Homestead AFB, Florida. The buildup of military forces in the southeast United States had begun.[56]

Much of the buildup was carried out under the cover of PHIBRIGLEX 62, a major amphibious exercise conducted in the Southeast United States and

Caribbean. The exercise obsured the initial military preparations related to the Cuban crisis. Many actions that would have been ordered by the Joint Chiefs of Staff had already been set in motion by PHIBRIGLEX 62. For example, more than forty ships involved in the exercise got under way October 15. At scattered posts, 40,000 marines were loaded on ships heading toward the Caribbean to augment the 5,000 at Guantanamo Bay, if necessary. The 82d and 101st Airborne Divisions were made ready for immediate deployment. Altogether the Army gathered more than 100,000 troops in Florida. Strategic Air Command bombers left Florida airfields to make room for tactical fighters flown in from bases all over the country.[57]

Air Force Reserve airlift support of the Tactical Air Command continued at an exceptionally high rate. The Continental Air Command increased its normal daily aircraft support to the Tactical Air Command from ten to twenty-five. Between October 20 and 28, Air Force Reserve C–119s, C–123s, and C–124s delivered cargo and military personnel into the southeast and flew priority missions for Air Force Logistics Command, Air Force Systems Command, and Air Defense Command.[58] Having watched the President's telecast the night before, reserve troop carrier wing officials were not surprised on October 23, at 4:00 P.M. when the Headquarters Continental Air Command directed them to activate their command posts and operate them around the clock, seven days a week. The command posts did not have to be elaborate, but someone had to be on duty at all times who was in immediate contact with key personnel of the wing.[59]

In Washington meanwhile, President Kennedy and the ExCom continued their nervous management of the crisis. A letter to the President from Premier Khrushchev on October 26th seemed to suggest a resolution based on U.S. desires, but a second letter, broadcast from Moscow at 10:00 A.M. on the 27th, was colder in tone and proposed a quid pro quo. The Soviet Union now said it would remove its missiles from Cuba and offer a nonaggression pledge to Turkey if the United States would remove its missiles from Turkey and offer a nonaggression pledge to Cuba. Shortly thereafter, the ExCom learned that the Cubans had shot down a U–2 reconnaissance plane, killing its pilot, Maj. Rudolph Anderson.[60]

Demonstrating that the Cubans had some air defense capability, the Anderson incident convinced Secretary McNamara that the United States would not be able to get away with a limited airstrike on Cuba. During an ExCom meeting at 4:00 P.M. on the 27th, he suggested that the President consider an invasion preceded by a major airstrike. A decision to invade would require immediate mobilization of the Air Force Reserves. The ExCom met again at 9:00 P.M. for the sole purpose of reviewing the request to mobilize the reservists. McNamara said the call-up was necessary to meet invasion plans and that it would also put some pressure on the Russians. Without much additional

The Air Force Reserve

discussion, President Kennedy approved McNamara's recommendation to mobilize 24 Air Force Reserve troop carrier squadrons—about 14,000 reservists and 300 planes.[61] This was the flashpoint of the crisis. The President's brother Robert, the Attorney General and a member of the ExCom, recalled:

> I returned to the White House. The President was not optimistic, nor was I. He ordered twenty-four troop carrier squadrons of the Air Force Reserve to active duty. They would be necessary for an invasion. He had not abandoned hope, but what hope there was now rested with Khrushchev's revising his course within the next few hours. It was a hope, not an expectation. The expectation was a military confrontation by Tuesday and possibly tomorrow [Sunday].[62]

Although conducted without formal warning, the mobilization did not catch the Air Force Reserve unaware. Many key personnel of reserve units heard the Office of Secretary of Defense announcement at 9:30 Saturday evening that it had authorized the Secretary of the Air Force to mobilize twenty-four Air Force Reserve troop carrier squadrons. Typical reactions were those of Col. Stanley Rush, the senior Air Reserve technician of the 512th Troop Carrier Wing at Willow Grove NAS, Pennsylvania, and of Col. Joseph J. Lingle, Commander, 440th Troop Carrier Wing at General Billy Mitchell Field, Milwaukee. Upon hearing the announcement, Colonel Rush called other technicians in the wing,

Cuban Mobilization. Mobilized 434th Troop Carrier Wing passes in review prior to being mustered from active service at Bakalar AFB, Indiana, on November 27, 1962, following the Cuban missile crisis.

alerting them to the possibility of a no-notice callup. Thus, when he received the actual notice by telephone from Headquarters Continental Air Command about 1:20 the next morning, his key people were psychologically prepared.[63]

At Milwaukee, Colonel Lingle was attending the wing's annual Airman's Ball at the Schroeder Hotel when newsmen apprised him of the Secretary's announcement. A telephone call to the information officer at Headquarters Tactical Air Command only confirmed that there had been such an announcement. Having moved on to the Halloween Ball at the base by 11:00 P.M., and still without official word, Colonel Lingle ordered a wing practice alert for 9:00 the next morning. Thus, his unit too, was prepared when, five hours later, Continental Air Command's retransmission of the Air Force alert message came in.[64]

Operations officials at Headquarters Continental Air Command were hearing the same broadcasts and began drifting in to work about 10:00 P.M. at Robins AFB. They called all wing commanders to alert them to the imminence of the recall and to relay a Headquarters Tactical Air Command request that had just come in that the wing commanders attend a meeting at Langley AFB, Virginia, the next day to review certain Tactical Air Command contingency plans. The official recall message came in from Headquarters USAF at 2:23 A.M. The command post immediately telephoned all affected troop carrier and aerial port units and retransmitted the message as confirmation. Consequently, all Air Force Reserve units had the pertinent information two hours and twenty minutes before Headquarters Tactical Air Command dispatched its official call.[65] The message ordered one C–123 and seven C–119 troop carrier wings along with six aerial port squadrons to extended active duty at 9:00 A.M. October 28, 1962, for no more than twelve consecutive months.[66] The following table shows the reserve units mobilized during this time.

Air Force Reserve Units Mobilized During the Cuban Missile Crisis

Location	Unit*	Detachment
L. G. Hanscom AFB, Mass.	94 TCW	
L. G. Hanscom AFB, Mass.	731 TCS	
Grenier Field, Manchester, N.H.	732 TCS	
Hill AFB, Utah	733 TCS	
Willow Grove NAS, Pa.	512 TCW	
Willow Grove NAS, Pa.	326 TCS	
Willow Grove NAS, Pa.	327 TCS	

Air Force Units Mobilized, Cuban Crisis—*Cont'd*

Location	Unit*	Detachment
Niagara Falls MAP, N.Y.	328 TCS	
Gen. Billy Mitchell Field, Wisc.	440 TCW	
Gen. Billy Mitchell Field, Wisc.	95 TCS	
Minneapolis–St. Paul IAP, Minn.	96 TCS	
Paine Field, Everett, Wash.	97 TCS	
Hamilton AFB, Calif.	349 TCW	
Hamilton AFB, Calif.	312 TCS	
Portland IAP, Oreg.	313 TCS	
McClellan AFB, Calif.	314 TCS	
Clinton County AFB, Ohio	302 TCW	
Clinton County AFB, Ohio	355 TCS	
Clinton County AFB, Ohio	356 TCS	
Bates Field, Ala.	357 TCS	
Selfridge AFB, Mich.	403 TCW	
Selfridge AFB, Mich.	63 TCS	
O'Hare IAP, Ill.	64 TCS	
Davis Field, Muskogee, Okla.	65 TCS	
Bakalar AFB, Ind.	434 TCW	
Bakalar AFB, Ind.	71 TCS	
Bakalar AFB, Ind.	72 TCS	
Scott AFB, Ill.	73 TCS	
Dobbins AFB, Ga.	445 TCW	
Dobbins AFB, Ga.	700 TCS	
Memphis MAP, Tenn.	701 TCS	
Memphis MAP, Tenn.	702 TCS	
McGuire AFB, N.J.	11 APS	1
Ellington AFB, Tex.	14 APS	1, 2
Donaldson AFB, S.C.	15 APS	1, 2
Bakalar AFB, Ind.	16 APS	1, 4, 5, 6
Paine Field, Wash.	17 APS	1, 3, 4, 5
Pope AFB, N.C.	18 APS	1, 3, 5, 6

*TCW=Troop Carrier Wing; TCS=Troop Carrier Squadron; APS=Aerial Port Squadron.

One week later, Headquarters Tactical Air Command amended its original orders to include the recall of ten additional detachments of the aerial port

Return on Investment, 1961–1965

The 512th Troop Carrier Wing musters on November 29, 1962, at Willow Grove NAS, Pennsylvania, to demobilize following the Cuban missile crisis.

squadrons.[67] The mobilized Air Force Reserve units brought 14,220 people and 422 aircraft on active duty with them on October 28, 1962.[68]

About the time the mobilized troop carrier wings came on active military service at 9:00 A.M. October 28, the White House received a new message from Premier Khrushchev. Conciliatory in tone and accepting President Kennedy's terms, it promised removal of the missiles and verification of the fact by the United Nations. Although this definitely relieved the crisis, the President decided that U.S. ships would stay on station and that the recalled Air Force Reserve units would remain on active duty pending satisfactory United Nations arrangements. Not wanting the United States to appear too anxious to return to normalcy, the President and Secretary McNamara wanted the Soviets to understand that Washington would not consider the matter ended until the missiles were gone.[69] Not until November 20, therefore, did the President announce that he was lifting the quarantine and that the mobilized air reserve units would be released before Christmas.[70]

On November 22, the Air Force directed the Tactical Air Command to release the units at midnight, November 28.[71] The units' aircrews were given the opportunity to remain on active duty voluntarily for an additional 15 days, to help the Air Force redeploy the military forces that had been dumped on the southeastern United States during the preceding 45 days. Electing to do so were 442 crew members—290 pilots, 64 navigators, and 88 flight engineers.[72]

The mobilization exposed some administrative problems as usual, and communication between the Continental Air Command and the gaining commands needed to improve—for that matter, the Air Staff at times had kept the Continental Air Command in the dark—but none of this impeded the real

The Air Force Reserve

operation nor suggested that the reservists could not have carried out an invasion role. The problem of the reserve units being responsible to two sets of reporting and records requirements still needed resolution, but yielding to the blatant objections of the Continental Air Command staff, the Tactical Air Command did not commit the egregious error of reorganizing the reserve units upon mobilization. The most far-reaching problem involved the incompatibility between reserve and active force statistical reporting, as the Air Force Reserve would continue to lag at least one generation behind in the equipment to automate personnel reporting.[73]

The Air Force Reserve did absolutely all that was asked of it between October 13 and December 29, 1962. It augmented the active force in assembling materiel in the southeastern corner of the country. When the President thought he might need an invasion force and the Department of Defense mobilized Air Force Reserve troop carrier units as essential to the task, they responded quickly and were prepared to do their part. Then, individual crew members stayed on to help redeploy the assembled force.

Along with the placement of the strategic missile force on alert and the visible movement of tactical air forces to Florida, the mobilization of Air Force Reserve troop carrier units played a part in persuading Premier Khrushchev that the United States was serious about getting those missiles out of Cuba. A *London Times* editorial of December 23, declared:

> Looking back over that fateful week, some officials are disposed to believe that the mobilization of 24 troop carrying squadrons finally persuaded Mr. Khrushchev that war would be inevitable if the missiles were not withdrawn.[74]

The *Times'* assertion has been supported by one scholar, who observed that the blockade was the first of several possible U.S. moves; the next was the invasion of Cuba as evidenced by the mobilization of the troop carrier forces. In his *Essence of Decision: Explaining the Cuban Missile Crisis*, Graham T. Allison asserts that the presence of the mobilized reserve troop carrier force demonstrated the seriousness the United States attached to its cause and its probable willingness to escalate to achieve it.[75] Although the resolution of the Cuban missile crisis and the stabilization of the situation in the Caribbean seemed in 1963 to signal a lessening of tension between the United States and the Soviet Union, other developments beyond the Pacific were drawing the Air Force and its reserve components into new military activity.

Military Air Transport Service Use of Reserve C–124s

When the Military Air Transport Service replaced the Tactical Air Command as the gaining command for Air Force Reserve C–124 units in July 1963, its commander, Lt. Gen. Joe W. Kelly, told Lt. Gen. Edward J.

Return on Investment, 1961–1965

In 1963 Lt. Gen. Joe W. Kelly, Commander, Military Air Transport Service (shown here as General), and gaining commander of reservists, began using the C–124 reserve units to conduct airlift missions worldwide.

Timberlake, Continental Air Command Commander, that he was planning to use the reserve units to conduct airlift missions worldwide. General Kelly's command soon put that philosophy to work. The latter half of 1963 became a period of unprogrammed exercise participation for the Military Air Transport Service as the entire defense establishment responded to a Secretary of Defense directive to conduct a series of strategic mobility exercises. To sustain some degree of its normal transpacific cargo capability while it was thus engaged, the Military Air Transport Service arranged through the Continental Air Command for the Air Force Reserve's C–124 units to begin flying missions on the Pacific routes in September 1963.[76]

In the process of training themselves to full operational readiness in their unit equipment, the C–124 units produced a by-product of available aircraft space. The Air Force commonly capitalized on this potential by arranging through the Continental Air Command for the reserve units to carry passengers and cargo on their training flights. For a long time the resulting airlift was an unwritten secondary mission of the troop carrier units.[77]

Each reservist assigned to a Category A unit, such as a troop carrier squadron, was authorized 24 days of inactive duty and 15 days of active duty training annually. Aircrewmen were authorized an additional 36 days inactive duty a year to sharpen their flying skills. It was this training availability, coupled with the airlift potential, that the Military Air Transport Service wished

The Air Force Reserve

to use. If his normal training availability was exhausted, a reservist could participate in man-day status (a man-day was a day of duty for which a reservist was entitled to be paid). If the day was occasioned by reserve training requirements, the reservist was paid from reserve funds. If, however, a major command, or Headquarters USAF itself, imposed a requirement over and above the requirements of reserve proficiency, as the Military Air Transport Service was doing, the reservist was paid from active Air Force funds.

With each unit flying about 1 trip per month, by April 1964 the 5 reserve groups had completed 22 missions to Tachikawa AB in Japan and 19 to Hickam AFB, Hawaii, for the airlift command. These trips, or missions, took about 8 days, home station to home station, during which the aircraft were in the air for slightly more than 75 hours and on the ground for 136. A typical trip would originate at home station about noon on a Saturday and land at Travis AFB, California, in the late afternoon to pick up cargo and passengers. There, too, the Military Air Transport Service assumed operational control of the mission. Departing about sunrise the next day, the plane would make Hickam 12 hours later, in time for supper. After the necessary crew rest, it was off again early Monday morning for Wake Island, a trip that was 1½ hours shorter than the Sunday leg but which also lost a day to the International Dateline, so that the crew put its plane down on Wake Island a little before 5:00 on Tuesday afternoon. Off by 8:00 Wednesday morning, they normally made Tachikawa by 3:30 in the afternoon. Then, after a 36-hour turnaround, before dawn on Friday, the C–124 started back the way it came—Wake to Hickam—picking up the lost day—and home station somewhere in the late afternoon or early evening of Sunday, the ninth day.[78]

Between September 1963 and April 1964, the reservists flew the Pacific missions on an irregular basis dictated by the Military Air Transport Service's changing needs. When cargo began to accumulate at the West Coast ports in April, however, the command called for reserve help on a more sustained basis. At that point, the Continental Air Command guaranteed 15 C–124s per quarter for the Pacific routes.[79] This assistance did not eliminate the cargo backlog, and early in August 1964 the Military Air Transport Service returned to the Continental Air Command for additional airlift. This time, the 442d Troop Carrier Wing, to which all 5 C–124 groups were then assigned, provided 12 C–124 trips over and above the 7 already scheduled between August 9 and September 23, 1964. By October 2, the reservists had reverted to the 15-trips-a-quarter schedule. In all, from September 1963, when first called upon by the Military Air Transport Service, until the end of 1964, the 442d Troop Carrier Wing's five C–124 groups and their 20 aircraft flew at least 98 trips to Tachikawa or Hickam.*[80]

---

*The number is at least 98, but it could possibly be 102. The question is how many trips were launched during the first eight days of August 1964 and

Return on Investment, 1961–1965

POWER PACK *and the C–119s' Offshore Mission*

In April 1965, when a political crisis in the Dominican Republic boiled over into active revolution, President Lyndon B. Johnson dispatched U.S. marines and soldiers to the island to protect American citizens. To support this force, as well as provide emergency relief supplies to the islanders, the United States conducted an emergency airlift into the island. Participating voluntarily between April 30 and July 5, Air Force Reserve aircrews flew approximately 1,850 missions and 16,900 hours in Operation POWER PACK, as the emergency airlift was called. About 185 of the missions were flown into the island itself. With the Air Force Reserve C–124 units already heavily committed in support of Southeast Asia operations, the C–119 units bore the primary burden of the Air Reserve's participation in the POWER PACK operation, although there were a few C–123 and C–124 missions as well.[81]

After POWER PACK had confirmed the capability of the Air Force Reserve C–119 units, the Military Air Transport Service immediately requested their

Great numbers of Air Force Reserve C–119s participated in the active force's Exericse EXOTIC DANCER *in the Far East in May 1969.*

---

during the last eight days of September 1964. In each case, there could have been none or as many as two.

195

The Air Force Reserve

use on missions along the coasts of North and Central America. This freed the airlift transport service's own four-engine aircraft for direct support of the Southeast Asia requirement. In the seven years beginning in fiscal year 1966, C–119s conducted 3,648 offshore missions for the airlift command, flying 27,138 hours and carrying 8,418 tons of cargo and 3,155 passengers. At peak periods during 1966 and 1967, the C–119s flew 16 offshore missions weekly—from Dover AFB, Delaware, to Goose Bay and Argentia, Newfoundland; from Patrick AFB, Florida, to Grand Turk and Antigua, West Indies; and from Norfolk NAS, Virginia, to Puerto Rico and Guantanamo Bay, Cuba, among other locations. The C–119 support of this Military Airlift Command[*] mission ended only when the aircraft left the Air Force Reserve inventory in March 1973.[82]

In the early 1960s the Air Force revised the management structure of its civilian components to draw the major commands more actively into the process of training the gaining reserve units upon mobilization. The gaining commands quickly took advantage of this new relationship and involved the reserve forces more in active force exercises and in peacetime missions and when the Dominican operation developed, in actual contingency operations.

Also during this period, President Kennedy twice called upon the Air Force Reserve twice to extend his policies: in 1961, to gain time while the Department of Defense rebuilt its conventional tactical forces during the Berlin crisis, and in 1962, to provide an airborne invasion force should an invasion of Cuba prove necessary during the missile crisis. On the other side of the world, Air Force Reserve C–124 units had begun to augment the Military Air Transport Service on its Pacific routes. In 1965, just before POWER PACK was conducted, these missions were extended to Vietnam, and the Air Force Reserve's decade-long commitment to the Air Force's Southeast Asia mission had begun.

---

[*]The Military Air Transport Service was redesignated the Military Airlift Command on January 1, 1966.

8

The Air Force Reserve in the Vietnam Era, 1965–1975

> The question arises, at what levels of conflict and under what circumstances would it become necessary to call the Reserve forces to active duty . . . Our Reserve Forces can best serve the nation in a conflict of this type by remaining in an inactive status but performing genuine "active duty" functions as part of their training programs. The important point here is that, pending the decision to bring them to active duty, the Reserve forces must fill the gap left by those regular forces which have been assigned to combat . . .
>
> —General John P. McConnell, June 1966

By the time John F. Kennedy took office in January 1961, the United States had become deeply involved in Southeast Asia. The new administration soon perceived that the burden of resisting communism in Asia had fallen on the United States. Outgoing President Dwight D. Eisenhower warned the President-elect that if Laos fell to the communists, inevitably the rest of Southeast Asia would follow. Eisenhower urged unilateral intervention by the United States if necessary to sustain Laos.[1] International agreements signed in Geneva in July 1962 apparently neutralized Laos, but Vietnam remained a problem.[2]

In South Vietnam, the United States had tried to stabilize the government and train its military forces to subdue internal guerrilla activity by the Viet Cong and resist invasion from North Vietnam. The northerners had declared their intention to extend the "national democratic revolution" to South Vietnam and unify Vietnam under the communist regime. Dispatched by President

The Air Force Reserve

Kennedy on a tour of Southeast Asia, India, and Pakistan in May 1961, Vice President Lyndon B. Johnson promised support to those who would resist communism and he recommended to the President that the United States promptly undertake a major effort to help the people of Southeast Asia.[3]

Distracted by the Berlin crisis and the concurrent revitalization of the United States' conventional military forces, President Kennedy approved only limited military assistance to the Republic of Vietnam.[4] Nevertheless, for the next thirteen years the U.S. Air Force would be actively engaged in combat operations in Southeast Asia. The Air Force Reserve's place in all of this had three aspects to it: whether the President would mobilize any or all of the reserve components, which underlay all the administration's considerations of military policies and measures (mobilization was always an issue after July 1965); the inactive duty contribution to the Air Force's mission throughout the war (the Air Force began to employ the Air Force Reserve on operational missions in 1965); and the actual mobilizations, when they did occur (limited mobilizations came in 1968).

The Question of Mobilization for Southeast Asia

In 1976 the Defense Manpower Commission, created by Congress to study defense manpower needs, charged that the failure to mobilize elements of the Selected Reserve during the war in Southeast Asia placed an inordinate burden on the active forces, damaged the prestige and morale of the National Guard and the reserve forces, and caused the public to question the worth of the reserve components.[5] The commission was right. Throughout the period of U.S. Air Force operations in Southeast Asia and for some years thereafter, active force members criticized the decision not to commit the reserve components. Maj. Gen. William Lyon, Chief of Air Force Reserve, observed in 1979 that even then some Air Staff officials were reluctant to commit aircraft and equipment to a force when their use might be denied when needed most.[6] The prestige of the reserve components certainly suffered, publicly as reflected in *The Congressional Record*, and within the Air Force community as frequent letters to the *Air Force Times* editorial pages attested. Maj. Gen. Richard Bodycombe, who succeeded General Lyon as Chief of Air Force Reserve, remembered his neighbors and business associates in Michigan challenging him as a career reservist in the 1960s to explain why reservists were withheld from Vietnam.[7]

The United States did not mobilize reservists for use in Southeast Asia before 1968, and then it mobilized relatively few, because Lyndon B. Johnson, the President of the United States, did not wish to do so. His reasons for not mobilizing reserve forces were many. Primarily, he did not believe that the war in Vietnam, in which the United States merely sought to stabilize the political

The Vietnam Era, 1965–1975

By refusing to make very extensive use of the reserve forces during the Vietnam War, President Lyndon B. Johnson allowed them to be viewed as a draft haven, and the active force came to distrust their availability in a crisis.

division of North and South Vietnam as it had existed in 1962, justified the dramatic act of mobilizing reserve forces. He accepted the need to fight the war, but he wanted to prosecute it as quietly as possible, not attracting too much attention at home and risk jeopardizing his domestic programs. He also wanted to avoid drawing the Chinese into the war. Moreover, recalling reservists' complaints of inactivity following the mobilization of 1961, he was reluctant to recall reservists without the assurance that their employment would significantly affect the course of the war, an assurance no official in his administration could provide.[8]

The issue of mobilization for Southeast Asia was first raised in October 1961 when the Joint Chiefs of Staff suggested that introducing U.S. forces into Vietnam should require expanding the mobilization that the Kennedy administration had just initiated as part of its response to Soviet threats in Berlin. About a year later, General Maxwell D. Taylor, Chairman of the Joint Chiefs of Staff, recommended that the United States put combat forces into Vietnam. Such forces would have to come from the already weakened Strategic Reserve, and he suggested that they be replaced by mobilized reserve forces.[9]

President John F. Kennedy was assassinated in November 1963, and the war became Lyndon B. Johnson's. The new President got through his first year as chief executive without escalating U.S. actions in Southeast Asia. Following a visit to Southeast Asia by Secretary McNamara and General Taylor in 1964, National Security Action Memorandum 288 defined the U.S. objective as reinforcing South Vietnam as an independent noncommunist nation. President Johnson accepted the memorandum's conclusion but rejected its central

The Air Force Reserve

recommendation that the United States expand its commitment to South Vietnam with additional troops and materiel. He thought it probable that the enemy would retaliate to the U.S. action and that the South Vietnamese would be unable to prevail. He also thought it possible that the Russians and Chinese would respond to any such action as well.[10]

Nevertheless, the President authorized a moderate increase in the U.S. effort, and he sought some way to rally the public to the flag. It was he who had gone to Southeast Asia in 1961, promised aid to the Saigon government, and urged President Kennedy to take firm action to protect the freedom of the South Vietnamese. He felt a deep personal and national commitment to redeem his promise and awaited the opportunity to bring the American public and Congress along. On June 2, 1964, he defined U.S. policy in Southeast Asia as faithfulness to its commitments:

> America keeps her word. Here as elsewhere, we must and shall honor our commitments. The issue is the future of Southeast Asia as a whole. A threat to any nation in that region is a threat to all, and a threat to us. Our purpose is peace. We have no military, political or territorial ambitions in the area.[11]

When the U.S. destroyer *Maddox* clashed with North Vietnamese patrol boats in the Gulf of Tonkin in August, the President seized the occasion to persuade Congress to authorize him to take necessary measures to protect U.S. resources and the peace in Southeast Asia. In a special message to Congress on August 5, 1964, he repeated the public commitment he had made on June 2 as the keystone of U.S. policy in Southeast Asia.[12]

When Lyndon Johnson was reelected in November 1964, 23,000 American troops were in Vietnam. At that point, the United States was concentrating on getting South Vietnam to pull its own weight, intended to resort to air strikes only on a contingency basis, and had no plans to deploy major ground forces. In February 1965, however, the Viet Cong seized the initiative with an attack on a U.S. advisory compound and airstrip near Pleiku which killed eight Americans and wounded several others, and the President had to respond. [13]

The United States initiated a program of limited air strikes against North Vietnam and limited air action in the south. The deployment of offensive air forces to South Vietnam required ground forces to protect them, and on February 25, the President approved a Joint Chiefs of Staff recommendation to deploy two battalion landing teams of U.S. Marines to Da Nang. The bombing of the north did not cause the ground situation in the south to improve, and on April 1, the President accepted the recommendations of the Joint Chiefs and Maxwell Taylor, U.S. Ambassador to the Republic of Vietnam, to deploy two additional Marine battalions and up to 20,000 more men in U.S. support forces. These deployments raised U.S. military strength in Vietnam to approximately 82,000.[14]

With U.S. retaliation and escalation failing to deter the enemy, in June

The Vietnam Era, 1965–1975

1965 President Johnson pleaded with his advisers to define the U.S. purpose in Vietnam, the likelihood of achieving it, and its ultimate cost. The contention of McNamara and Secretary of State Dean Rusk that the United States sought stalemate in the south to demonstrate to the north that it could not win did not comfort the President. Forecasting doom if the United States undertook too active a role in Vietnam, Under Secretary of State George Ball wanted South Vietnam to take a larger share of the war and observed that the United States would pass the breaking point if it committed substantial troops to combat.[15]

The President was assailed by three different sets of advice. McNamara endorsed a Joint Chiefs of Staff recommendation that U.S. forces in Vietnam be increased to 179,000, with deployed forces being replaced by a substantial call-up of reserves. Under Secretary Ball urged a negotiated withdrawal, and William Bundy, an assistant to the Secretary of State, suggested a limited initial commitment followed by a choice among options after a summer test period.[16]

To resolve his dilemma, the President sent Secretary McNamara back to South Vietnam for another firsthand assessment of the situation. While in Saigon, McNamara communicated some preliminary findings to his deputy, Cyrus Vance, confirming the need for a substantial troop reinforcement for General William C. Westmoreland, commander of U.S. Military Assistance Command, Vietnam. Thereupon, administration officials convinced themselves that the President intended to authorize a substantial buildup of U.S. forces in Vietnam supported by a major mobilization of the reserve forces. Their conviction was so firm that the Office of the General Counsel of the Department of Defense prepared several alternative drafts of legislation to permit the President various reserve recall and service extension options, and Vance initiated planning for mobilization, extension of military tours, and an increased number of draft calls.[17]

Upon his return on July 20, McNamara reported to the President that the situation was steadily worsening in Vietnam. He recommended that the President ask Congress to authorize the call-up of approximately 235,000 reservists and guardsmen to provide 36 maneuver battalions and support forces by the end of the year.[18]

The President and his advisers discussed McNamara's recommendations through the week of July 21–26. They had three basic options: withdraw, maintain the status quo, or deploy additional forces to Vietnam. If there were to be additional troops, another decision was required to identify their sources and whether they would be furnished by the draft, the active force, reserve mobilization, or a combination thereof. The President and his advisers agreed that General Westmoreland should be provided the 125,000 troops he wanted. Only George Ball dissented and favored withdrawal. When his military advisers admitted that the additional troops could be made available from other sources—Europe and the Strategic Reserve, for example—the President seized the moment to state his decision against mobilization.

The Air Force Reserve

As commander of U.S. forces in Vietnam, General William C. Westmoreland's increasing requests for troops kept the question of a reserve mobilization alive throughout the Vietnam War.

Before he would resort to mobilization, the President demanded that defense officials explain fully what had changed in Vietnam to require a massive infusion of U.S. troops and what results they anticipated from a mobilization. Secretary McNamara's paper promised no military victory; it simply implied a continuing stalemate. The President wanted to restrict the United States to as limited a role as possible in Southeast Asia short of withdrawal. That being so, and always conscious of the 1961 uproar among mobilized reservists who complained that they had not been employed properly, he was extremely reluctant to inject mobilized reservists into Vietnam simply to sustain stalemate. He needed something more spectacular. If he were to resort to the dramatic step of mobilization, he demanded a virtual guarantee of results. This was undoubtedly the key consideration for him. In defining the stalemate objective, McNamara and Rusk conceded that the war would be long. Even if the President gave them the massive infusion of additional manpower they sought, the Secretaries could not promise him that it would shorten the war because North Vietnam would certainly counter any escalation by the United States. This, the President instinctively knew, was not the circumstance in which to mobilize several hundred thousand reservists involuntarily and disrupt their lives. He sought other alternatives, possibly a greater use of third-country troops.[19]

On the evening of July 27, the President explained his decision to the National Security Council and congressional leaders. He outlined five options that he and his advisers had considered during the preceding week. He noted that many of his advisers favored declaring a national emergency, raising the necessary appropriations, and mobilizing the reserves. He explained that he thought if he did this, North Vietnam would turn to China and Russia for help, which they would have to give. Therefore, he wanted to avoid dramatic actions that would increase international tension. He would give General Westmoreland the forces he requested at that time, with the promise of more in the future. There would be no mobilization, however. The additional forces required would be drawn from active force dispositions around the world. Draft calls would be doubled over time from 17,000 to about 35,000 a month, and the drive for voluntary enlistments would be intensified.[20]

General Earle G. Wheeler, Chairman of the Joint Chiefs, had gone into the meetings on July 21 seeking mobilization and, before yielding to the President, presented the case for a recall. General Wheeler later explained that all of the Joint Chiefs' contingency plans were based upon the assumption that if the United States made a sizable military commitment anywhere in the world, the Strategic Reserve would be reconstituted by calling up reserve units. General Wheeler also observed that continued reliance upon the regular forces as augmented by the draft diluted the leadership, officers and noncommissioned officers alike, by spreading them too thin. The initial supply of officers for World War II had come from reservists, and the same would have to be true of any major expansion of forces in Southeast Asia. General Wheeler also cited the psychological factor a reserve call-up would play in assuring the public's understanding that the country was in a real war and not engaged in "some 2-penny military adventure."[21]

So it was that the President announced at a press conference on July 28, 1965, for the third time that month, that he did not then think it necessary to order reserve units to active service.[22] Through the remainder of 1965, the Johnson administration publicly explained that it was preserving the reserve for some other use, that it did not wish to dissipate it in the Southeast Asian conflict. Instead, it had decided to meet the immediate needs in Vietnam by selective service and enlistments while preserving, and strengthening, the reserve for other crisis or possible future use in Southeast Asia.[23]

During a discussion of military manpower requirements in Honolulu in February 1966, McNamara explained why the subject of a reserve call-up would receive intensive study over the next few months and that it was important that they all understand why. The problem was very complicated and—despite the fact that mobilization had been under consideration for several years—all the necessary financial data was not at hand. It was also, he said, an extremely delicate issue politically. Several strong bodies of opinion were at work in the country. One school of thought had it that the country was overextended economically and could not afford the current level of activity in Vietnam; another held that the United States should not be in Vietnam at all, whether it could afford to or not. A third view held that although the United States had a right to be in Vietnam, it was mismanaging the war and heading straight for war with China. Others wanted to place the country on a war footing, complete with national emergency, mobilization, extended tours of duty, and higher taxes.

Moreover, McNamara asserted that, regardless of one's views, the economy of the country was beginning to run near or at its capacity, with the resulting probability of a shortage of certain skills and materiel, which could lead to wage and price controls, excess profits taxes, and so on. With all these conflicting pressures, the administration would find it very difficult to maintain the required support to carry on the war properly. In other words, the Secretary told them, consideration of a reserve call-up involved extremely serious problems in many areas, and decisions could not be made overnight.[24]

Throughout 1966, the Joint Chiefs of Staff urged the President to mobilize reserve forces. At first, they talked of selective mobilization, but by the end of the year they sought mass mobilization. On March 1, 1966, they recommended that the U.S. presence in Vietnam be increased with a selective call-up of reserve units and an extension of terms of service to about 600,000 by the end of 1966. In October 1966, they advised McNamara that without reserve call-ups and extensions of service tours, it would be difficult to meet the 1967 requirements for the Commander in Chief, Pacific. The Army would suffer the most, but after the required deployment, the Air Force would not have a residual capability for rapid deployment of any combat-ready tactical fighter force. A capability could be established for the Air Force by mobilizing twenty tactical fighter squadrons from the Air National Guard while the Air Force Reserve could relieve shortages of troop carrier aircraft and individuals.

At this time, the Joint Chiefs were urging McNamara and the President to institute a large mobilization to add 688,500 reservists to the armed forces by December 1966. In pushing the mobilization issue once again, the Joint Chiefs of Staff argued that requirements in the Pacific could not be met otherwise and that only with the proposed infusion of aerial firepower in the north and manpower in the south could the war possibly be ended in the shortest possible time at the least cost. While admitting to a long war and recommending expansion of the forces and other measures to the President, McNamara avoided the question of a reserve call-up.[25]

As the administration increased the size of U.S. military force in Vietnam, Congress began to take a more active interest in the rationale and conduct of the war. Conducting hearings in February 1966 on an administration request for supplemental foreign aid, Senator J. William Fulbright, chairman of the Foreign Relations Committee, could not conceal his opposition to the war, which he believed would lead the United States to a confrontation with China. Committee member Wayne Morse was even more adamant in his denunciation of the United States' unilateral intervention in Vietnam.[26]

The Vietnam Era, 1965–1975

As Congress reviewed the conduct of the war and America's increasing involvement in it, many members questioned the rationale for withholding the reserves. Senator Ernest Gruening of Alaska and Oregon's Wayne Morse cosponsored legislation that would have forbidden sending anyone but volunteers to South Vietnam. Introducing the legislation, Senator Gruening read into the record seventy-one letters from citizens criticizing the insulation of the reserves from the draft. These were, he said, "a small sampling" of those he had received.[27]

In April, Representative Bob L. F. Sikes of Florida criticized the Department of Defense for apparently disregarding the reserves as a source of trained manpower. He thought it obvious that additional involvement anywhere in the world or a general broadening of the conflict in Southeast Asia would require a general mobilization. Yet, he observed, for some reason it seemed to be administration policy not to use the trained reservists in Vietnam. Placing the blame at the wrong door, Sikes demanded that the Defense Department spell out its plans for using the reserves.[28]

As the administration continued to rely on the Selective Service System to supply manpower for the war, and as Congress began to reevaluate the draft, issues of favoritism in the reserve components and the use of reserve status as a haven for draft dodgers were raised. In December 1966, Congressman L. Mendel Rivers asked McNamara to investigate charges that favoritism was being shown professional athletes in enlisting them into the Army Reserve or the National Guard after a national magazine had reported that only 2 of 960 professional football players had been drafted in 1966 although many were in the eligible age group and obviously in good health. In addition to looking into the charge of favoritism, the Department of Defense ordered National Guard and reserve units to fill vacancies on a first-come, first-served basis rather than by picking and choosing among the most desirable candidates. As the demand for manpower in Vietnam grew, waiting lists for reserve and guard units were growing, and recruiters and commanders no longer had to enlist the first qualified man who volunteered. As this phenomenon developed, newsmen and congressmen observed that reserve force units appealed to potential draftees because the chance seemed remote that such units would be called to active service, and even more remote that they would go into combat.[29]

Both the White House and Congress appointed groups to study the draft. The two groups completed their work and released their reports in the first week of March 1967. A panel under retired Army General Mark W. Clark called for a crackdown on draft evaders, draft-card burners, and men who joined reserve and guard units to avoid the draft and combat. Declaring the selective service system to be essentially fair, the Clark group directed its main reservations at the six-month reserve programs. Clark observed that when a youth enlisted in a six-month program, he effectively ensured himself against having to serve initially on active duty for two years for training combat, or

The Air Force Reserve

other full-time military service. The enlistee also ensured against additional active duty since neither reserve units nor individuals were being called to active service. These conditions provided reserve enlistees probable means of avoiding certain service to which draftees were vulnerable Clark said.

The six-month program inequities seemed to be especially prevalent in the Army's Reserve Enlistment Program. Clark's panel found the the Army was retaining more than 42,000 reserve enlistees in control groups. These men were not assigned to drilling units and therefore were performing no significant training or other duty while still enjoying their draft deferments. Clark recommended therefore that the Selective Service System order to active duty any reserve enlistee who was not, for whatever reasons, participating satisfactorily in reserve or guard training.[30]

The phenomenon which disturbed General Clark's panel, as well as the legion of other critics of the operation of the draft, groups and individuals alike, was the perfectly legal opportunity created by law for young men to discharge their entire military obligation in reserve status. In 1951 the Universal Military Training and Service Act imposed an eight-year service obligation on any man who assumed military status of any kind before the age of twenty-six. The young man could discharge this on active duty, in active reserve status, or any combination of the two. The Reserve Forces Act of 1955 reinforced the earlier act, specifically providing that a young man who had not yet attained eighteen and one-half years of age could join any organized unit of the reserve components and, contingent upon satisfactory participation in unit training, be deferred from induction into the active armed forces until his draft liability ceased at age twenty-eight.[31]

Without question, during the 1960s hundreds of young men took advantage of the legal opportunity to join a reserve unit, gambling that the unit would never be called to active duty, thereby reducing their chances of being exposed to danger in what was becoming an unpopular war. They were avoiding the draft, certainly, and the law provided the reserves as a haven for them to do so. The perception that the reserve units had been created to provide a haven from the draft was unfair, however. The Air Force Reserve units of the 1960s, some of which had existed for more than a decade, consisted of many more people than the directly enlisted non–prior service members. In the first place, never enthusiastic about the non–prior service programs, the Air Force limited the Continental Air Command to inflexible quotas for enlistment of such people in the Air Force Reserve. In fiscal 1967, when General Clark was conducting his investigation, that quota was 6,508, the largest it would ever be, not quite 16 percent of the authorized total of 41,080 men in the Air Force Reserve units.[32]

Although the Air Force Reserve did accept a controlled influx of individuals without prior service who might been draft dodgers, most men on the units' rosters were veterans, and many had fulfilled their military obligations. In 1966–1967, the reserve units still included many members who had

The Vietnam Era, 1965–1975

served in both World War II and Korea and, depending upon their specific unit, had been recalled for either the Berlin or the Cuba crisis. They were in the units because they wanted to be, enjoying the camaraderie of a common band, the sense of belonging, and the call of the drum, and they aspired to an Air Force Reserve retirement, understanding full well that part of the investment in that retirement might be another recall. They had taken the king's shilling, and they would serve.[33]

Reporting concurrently with the Clark panel, the President's National Advisory Committee on Selective Service under Burke Marshall, vice president of the International Business Machines company, asserted that men eligible for the draft should not gain immunity by enlisting in guard and reserve units. The committee also recommended that vacancies in reserve forces units be filled by the draft operating on random selection procedures.[34]

Giving President Johnson the kind of legislation he requested, Congress passed the Military Selective Service Act of 1967, which the President approved on June 30, 1967. It provided for priority enlistment for the 17- to 18½-year age group not then eligible for the draft into reserve units. The law authorized the President to call to active service any member of the Ready Reserve who was not participating satisfactorily in a Ready Reserve unit, had not fulfilled his statutory reserve obligation, and had not served on active duty for a total of twenty-four months.[35]

The discussion of national strategy continued through the summer and fall of 1967, but it did not consider how to win the war, or what was the U.S. goal in Vietnam in the first place, as much as it did the size of the force that could be put into Vietnam without requiring mobilization of reserves. By 1967, the war was decidedly unpopular and administration motives for waging it were obscure to the public. To mobilize at this late period to support this distasteful war would acerbate growing political and social unrest and was unthinkable to President Johnson.[36]

By the fall of 1967, protests raged across the land, many occurring on the same college campuses where two years earlier students had supported the war. By this time, the issue of the unfairness of the draft to Blacks had driven the civil rights and peace movements into each other's arms. Crowds protested outside draft induction centers and often engaged in physical struggles, with policemen arriving to disperse the combatants. It all came to a grand climax in the nation's capital on October 22, 1967, when thousands of demonstrators from among the 50,000 or so who had marched on the Mall in an orderly fashion stormed the Pentagon in nearby Virginia. One of the more striking images of the war emerged from this clash—the newspaper photograph of a young woman placing a flower into the muzzle of a rifle held by a hapless soldier in that meeting of the sublime and the ridiculous.[37]

The President implored the Joint Chiefs of Staff to search for imaginative ideas to bring the war to a conclusion. He did not seek more bombing and

The Air Force Reserve

troops; he wanted the Chiefs to come up with some entirely new programs. He anticipated that when Congress returned in January 1968, its members would press to end the war, either by withdrawal or a significant escalation.[38]

Equally obvious by that time was the certitude that the country simply could not afford the war. If, as the President's military advisers insisted, winning the war required mobilization and increased draft calls, the cost of the war would probably rise from $30 billion to about $42 billion in 1969. This would probably result in wage and price controls, politically objectionable at any time, but especially during a presidential election year.[39] The uncertainty and debate continued through 1967, and when, early in the new year, mobilization did occur, it was the result of an unforeseen development.

As a member of the Joint Chiefs of Staff, General John P. McConnell supported the body's frequent recommendations for partial or complete mobilization to meet the demands for military forces in Southeast Asia. Yet, as Air Force Chief of Staff, he could afford to be ambivalent about the need to mobilize Air Force Reserve airlift units. The Air Force's position on the question was based largely on data developed by the Continental Air Command. Asked in May 1965 by the Air Staff for a position on a proposal to recall reserve troop carrier units to support contingency airlift operations, the headquarters staff recommended against recall. Among other reasons, the command staff concluded that to recall one C–119 unit for 30 days would cost $500,000, and that to provide 60 aircraft in the airlift system daily would require the recall of five C–119 units at a monthly expense of approximately $2.5 million. As an alternative to mobilization, the command offered a system whereby volunteer crew members on inactive duty could guarantee 60 aircraft for 30 days. The total cost for aircrew and maintenance and other support personnel would be about $235,000, compared with about $500,000 to recall one C–124 unit for 30 days.

Should the same voluntary approach be taken, the command could provide four C–124s daily for $33,600 per month. For this reason, the Continental Air Command strongly recommended that it be authorized to continue the existing mode of operation and be granted the man-days to support it. For the moment, the man-days were made available.[40] Thus, with airlift units contributing substantially to the war effort while still on inactive duty, the Air Force could take something other than an either-or approach to the question of mobilization. General McConnell explained the point during a major address in June 1966:

> The question arises, at what levels of conflict and under what circumstances would it become necessary to call the Reserve forces to active duty .... Our Reserve Forces can best serve the nation in a conflict of this type by remaining in an inactive status but performing genuine "active duty" functions as part of their training programs. The important point here is that, pending the decision to bring them to active duty, the Reserve forces must fill the gap left by those regular forces which have been assigned to combat.[41]

The Vietnam Era, 1965–1975

The Southeast Asia Contribution of Reservists on Inactive Duty

General McConnell asked that the Air Reserve Forces contribute to the Southeast Asia conflict by performing genuine missions as part of their inactive duty training. For more than twelve years, Air Force Reservists met the Chief of Staff's guideline. From January 1965, when the C–124 units extended their transpacific missions for the Military Air Transport Service to Vietnam, until June 1975, when medical personnel staffed the refugee relocation center at Eglin AFB, Florida, reservists voluntarily participated in the Air Force mission of supporting U.S. objectives in Southeast Asia while remaining on inactive duty.

By the end of 1964, the U.S. military force in Southeast Asia had increased to about 23,000.[42] As U.S. combat forces in Southeast Asia increased, so did their logistics tail, and that was what drew in the Air Force Reserve C–124 units. Before January 1965, the reservists generally had not gone beyond Japan on missions for the Military Air Transport Service, but in that month they were called upon to go farther. Late in the afternoon of January 23, 1965, a Military Air Transport Service caller asked Maj. Boyce N. Pinson, on duty in the Continental Air Command's operations division, if the Air Force Reserve C–124 force could provide urgently needed airlift into Vietnam. Scratching rapid calculations on a yellow legal pad, Major Pinson committed the Air Force Reserve to provide the Military Air Transport Service with thirteen trips into Saigon. Upon formal confirmation of Pinson's promise, twenty days later a C–124 of the 935th Troop Carrier Group was en route to Saigon from Richards-Gebaur AFB, Missouri, initiating the Air Force Reserve's Southeast Asia commitment.[43]

The thirteen trips committed by Major Pinson were flown in February and March. In mid-April the airlift command again called for help, this time for all the C–124s that the Air Force Reserve could offer, and reserve crews flew thirty more flights into Saigon by the end of June 1965.[44] Although not seeming like much, the provision of thirty flights in two months was considerable because the combined strength of the five Air Force Reserve C–124 groups involved was a mere twenty aircraft.

During the first six months of fiscal year 1965, as the Military Air Transport Service's need for reserve augmentation continued, the Air Force Reserve C–124 groups flew another forty-one missions into Tachikawa and Saigon, primarily to Saigon.[45] Thereafter, from January 1966 through November 1972, when the last C–124 left the reserve inventory, the Air Force Reserve C–124 crews on inactive duty flew 1,252 missions into Southeast Asia for the Military Air Transport Service and the Military Airlift Command, as the command was renamed in January 1966. These were airlift missions the Military Airlift Command could not have otherwise conducted; they therefore comprised a significant Air Force Reserve contribution to the Air Force mission.[46]

The Air Force Reserve

By mid-1966, Air Force Reserve support of the Southeast Asia mission settled into a routine of C–124 trips to Saigon and C–119 offshore missions. The pace quickened in 1968 when the North Koreans seized the USS *Pueblo*. The United States sent about 150 fighter-bomber, interceptor, and reconnaissance aircraft from the Strategic Reserve to stabilize South Korea. In the subsequent readjustment of forces, Air Force Reserve C–124 units helped redeploy elements of the U.S. Strategic Reserve within the United States and overseas. The reservists initially moved cargo from MacDill AFB, Florida, and from Goldsboro, North Carolina, to Southeast Asia.[47] Their maximum effort came between February 14 and March 11 when they flew 186 missions to help move the Army's 82d Airborne Division and more than 3,000 U.S. marines to Korea and South Vietnam.[48]

The Associate Unit Contribution

By 1968, the Military Airlift Command was operating modern jet C–141s and preparing to receive C–5s as well. No longer was it economical or operationally feasible for the command to continue its support of the reserve airlift force's obsolescent piston-driven C–124s. Therefore, in March 1968, the Air Force inaugurated the Air Force Reserve's associate airlift program. Reminiscent of the corollary unit program that had dissolved in 1951, the associate program provided for Air Force Reserve units to maintain and fly aircraft assigned to collocated active force units which the reservists would augment upon mobilization. The associate units initially flew C–141s, but some transitioned into C–5s in 1973. On August 14, 1968, the first all-reserve C–141 associate crew left Norton AFB, California, on a Southeast Asia mission. Captain William Maxey served as aircraft commander, and the group commander, Col. Richard P. McFarland, who had promised such a flight within six months of activation, was aboard as an additional crew member.[49]

Sharing the experience of their active force partners, the reserve associate units participated in airlift operations into and out of Southeast Asia at varying levels between Captain Maxey's maiden flight in August 1968 and the last flight out of Saigon almost seven years later. The average associate C–141 trip into Saigon from either coast lasted anywhere from six to thirteen days as aircrews staged at Elmendorf AFB, Alaska; Yokota AB, Japan; Kadena AB, Okinawa; and U-Tapao AB, Thailand.[50]

The greatest surge occurred during an April and May 1972 spring offensive by the North Vietnamese. Drawing upon its reservoir of active, reserve, and civil airlift, the Military Airlift Command moved a tactical fighter wing, complete with 3,195 people and 1,600 tons of cargo, from Holloman AFB, New Mexico, to Takhli AB, Thailand, in nine days.[51] The missions were arduous; the crew duty-day stretched from 16 to 18 hours as crew rest periods conversely shrank to 10 hours from the previous 12. In addition, perennially short of navigators, the Military Airlift Command desperately sought additional reserve augmentation. Reserve navigators from all six associate groups responded, volunteering for tours of active duty up to 60 days long.[52]

In February and March 1973, the North Vietnamese released American aviators who had been shot down and taken prisoner during the war. In Operation HOMECOMING, as the repatriation effort was called, the freed prisoners were airlifted to Clark AB in the Philippines before being returned to the United States for thorough medical examinations. The Air Force Reserve contribution to HOMECOMING included aircrews, doctors, nurses, medical technicians, general casualty assistance, and intelligence personnel.[53] Air Force Reserve C–141 associate crew member participated in five Operation HOMECOMING flights. Also, one loadmaster and eighteen medical technicians of the 938th Military Airlift Group (Associate) at Travis AFB participated in twelve airlift missions with active duty crews, and thirty aeromedical personnel from the 939th Military Airlift Group (Associate) at McChord AFB, Washington, served on various HOMECOMING legs with both reserve and active crews. Other aeromedical evacuation crew members, nurses and technicians, from the 68th (Norton), 40th (McChord), and 55th (Travis) Aeromedical Evacuation Squadrons as well as the 73d Aeromedical Airlift Squadron (Associate) at Scott AFB individually volunteered as crews on the HOMECOMING flights. Twenty reserve physicians also voluntarily participated in the Prisoner of War/Missing in Action, Next of Kin Program developed by the Air Force Surgeon General to counsel families of the missing and imprisoned men.[54]

The Air Force Reserve Intelligence Specialists

Lacking sufficient intelligence specialists, in May 1966 the Air Force used reservists on extended active or inactive duty tours to augment the intelligence function at the National Military Intelligence Center and the Military Airlift Command's Indications and Warning Center on a continuing basis.[55] Then in 1972, Air Force Reservists in the intelligence function began to counsel families of prisoners and the missing, interrogate released prisoners, and analyze the prisoners' experiences. Expanded from its original medical orientation, the surgeon general's counseling program evolved into an effort designed to provide counseling, guidance, and referral assistance to families who requested help in coping with a broad spectrum of physical, emotional, or adjustment problems. Air Force Reserve intelligence personnel who were additionally qualified in medicine provided these services in locations where there were many families of prisoners but too few resources to accommodate them.[56]

In a third program, 114 intelligence reservists were trained as debriefers under the Operation HOMECOMING plan for the processing of returned prisoners. Reservists were placed on 72-hour alert to perform 30-day special tours of active duty upon implementation of the plan when a few prisoners were released in 1968. When the greatest number of prisoners returned in February 1973, seventy-five reservists participated in debriefings at ten military hospitals in the United States.

In the summer of 1973, as a follow-on to HOMECOMING, reserve Majors Frederic F. Wolfer and Willis A. Bruninga served several extended tours of active duty helping the Escape and Invasion/Prisoner of War Branch of the Directorate of Intelligence analyze debriefing information. They devised a program to develop a series of multidisciplinary studies of the prisoner experience. Following Air Force establishment of the program, the Department of Defense adopted it as well.[57] Designated the Prisoner of War Experience and Analysis Program, the activity collated relevant data from prisoner of war debriefings into reports on escape and evasion. The program also studied interrogation and resistance techniques experienced by U.S. prisoners, storing the resultant data in computers for instant retrieval. Between 1973 and 1975, 372 reservists participated in the project.[58]

Operations NEW LIFE and BABY LIFT

As its penultimate act in the Southeast Asia period, the Air Force Reserve participated in the whole range of activities associated with Operation NEW LIFE, the Indochina Refugee Airlift. The contribution took several forms. Associate aircrews, including 101 reserve flight nurses and medical technicians, flew missions in support of NEW LIFE, and the 906th Tactical Airlift Group prepared a camp on Guam as a refugee staging site.

Between April 4 and June 30, 1975, 108 complete Air Reserve C–5/C–141 crews flew 773 sorties airlifting evacuees and refugees or placing aircraft in position for the missions. In addition, 197 individual crew members and reserve aeromedical evacuation personnel performed duties on 811 sorties augmenting Military Airlift Command aircrews or completed medical crew requirements on evacuation missions flown by all-reserve associate aircrews. Crew duty-days were often as long as 20 hours with rest periods of no more than 12 hours on missions that ran as long as 14 days. Other reserve associate aircrews indirectly supported NEW LIFE by flying Military Airlift Command channel, exercise, and special missions, thus freeing active force crews to participate in the evacuation.[59]

On May 13, 1975, the Air Staff directed Headquarters AFRES to provide a detachment of two UC–123K aircraft to Guam to rid an interim refugee camp site of dengue fever–bearing mosquitoes. Ten days later, the 355th Tactical Airlift Squadron sprayed 3,535 gallons of Malathion over a 40,000-acre area of Guam.[60]

During the period April 29 to May 21, 1975, Air Force Reserve C–130s

The Vietnam Era, 1965–1975

flew 231 sorties in support of the Military Airlift Command as that command sought to fill the airlift vacuum created by the dedication of its strategic airlift fleet to the U.S. evacuation of South Vietnam. These sorties expended 776 hours and airlifted 517.9 tons of cargo and 170 passengers.[61]

The Air Force Reserve 40th, 65th, and 68th Aeromedical Evacuation Squadrons on the West Coast played an important role in NEW LIFE and the associated Operation BABY LIFT; 40 of their flight nurses and 61 medical technicians flew as medical crew members. When the first C–5A BABY LIFT flight from Saigon crashed on takeoff on April 4, 1975, SSgt. James A. Hadley, one of the 65th's medical technicians, although injured himself, stayed with the wreckage and administered oxygen to the surviving orphans.[62]

Besides flying live-patient missions as medical crew members, individuals from various aeromedical evacuation units supported Operation NEW LIFE at Eglin AFB, Florida, where one of the temporary refugee relocation centers was established. These volunteers began their service at the U.S. Air Force Regional Hospital at Eglin AFB on May 18, 1975, and, depending on the need, remained for two or three weeks. Aside from the intelligence officers whose prisoner-of-war analysis could go on indefinitely, the medics were the last Air Force Reservists directly involved in the United States Air Force Southeast Asia mission, ten years and five months after Boyce Pinson committed that first C–124.[63]

Other Air Force Reserve Support

The Air Force Reserve provided the Air Force with various other forms of support during the Vietnam period. More than 270 nurses and medical technicians served volunteer tours as long as 240 days evacuating and treating U.S. servicemen who developed drug abuse problems while in Vietnam. Other Air Force Reservists ferried 185 aircraft between the United States and Southeast Asia and provided flying and maintenance training to Vietnamese air force personnel both in the United States and in South Vietnam. Air Force Reserve aerial port units sent 60 volunteers to U-Tapao AB in Thailand in 1974 on tours of 85 to 120 days to alleviate shortages there. Reserve lawyers supported the Air Force effort in Southeast Asia by providing the entire range of legal assistance to servicemen and their dependents, including help with difficult legal problems encountered when the returning prisoners of war reunited with their families. Likewise, reserve chaplains supplied the entire spectrum of ministerial services and assistance to servicemen, their families, and their survivors.[64]

Hundreds of mobilization augmentees served tours as individuals each year, adding to the active force in command headquarters and units in the United States and in the theater. Suffering a lack of reserve unit parental care and divided administrative interests of the Air Reserve Personnel Center and their active force command of assignment, these individuals tended not to present a definable presence, and their contributions were little acknowledged.[65] Nevertheless, contributions by Air Force Reserve individuals and units to the Air Force's Southeast Asia mission from 1965 to 1975 as a by-product of their training was real and effective. Conceived as a post–Korean War mobilization force in the U.S. Code, in 1968 the Air Force Reserve finally became caught up in two minor mobilizations.

The 1968 Mobilizations

On January 23, 1968, a date President Johnson would characterize as symbolic of the turmoil his administration experienced throughout 1968, North Korea seized the USS *Pueblo*, a small, intelligence ship, and interned its crew. The United States responded by sending a mixture of fighter-bombers, interceptors, and reconnaissance planes to Korea to reassure the South Korean government. Fearing another invasion by the North Koreans, South Korea was considering withdrawing its forces from Vietnam. U.S officials believed that the South Korean Army could take care of itself, but that there was no point in tempting the larger North Korean air force to take advantage of the situation.[66] To make the action possible, the President approved the mobilization of about 15,000 air and naval reservists and their units to replace those deployed from the dwindling Strategic Reserve.[67]

Colonel Cecil W. Alford, Deputy to the Chief of the Air Force Reserve, received a telephone call from Maj. Gen. Winston P. Wilson, Director of the Air National Guard, at about 10:30 P.M. on January 24, 1968, asking that he and Maj. Gen. Tom E. Marchbanks, Jr., Chief of the Air Force Reserve, come to the Pentagon as soon as possible. Upon arrival, they learned that the Air Reserve Forces were to be recalled. The Air National Guard was to furnish tactical fighters and the Air Force Reserve, airlift and rescue forces. To avoid any sort of a political protest, no unit that served in 1961 was to be recalled, and no more than one unit was to be recalled from any one state.[68]

With that information in hand, General Marchbanks assembled his staff and worked into the morning hours selecting units. The precise requirement for Air Force Reserve units was five C–124 military airlift groups and an HC–97 aerospace rescue and recovery squadron. Aside from the Chief of Staff's restrictions, General Marchbanks' staff had another measure to guide them in their selections. Certain of the Air Force Reserve units were in a special category in terms of readiness. These were the Beef Broth units, so designated by the Department of Defense in August 1965 as high-priority units. Required to become fully capable of responding to any requirement on short notice, they had been given priorities for manning, supply, and equipment.

The Vietnam Era, 1965–1975

An Air Force Reserve C–124 crew of the 349th Military Airlift Wing, Hamilton AFB, California, awaits clearance at Hickam AFB, Hawaii, to continue its cargo mission to Southeast Asia early in 1967.

Fitting in Beef Broth units with the Chief's strictures, insofar as possible, General Marchbanks selected the 305th Aerospace Rescue and Recovery Squadron at Selfridge AFB, Michigan; the 938th Military Airlift Group and its collocated 349th Military Airlift Wing at Hamilton AFB, California; the 921st Military Airlift Group at Kelly AFB, Texas; the 941st Military Airlift Group at McChord AFB, Washington; the 918th Military Airlift Group and its collocated 435th Military Airlift Wing at Dobbins AFB, Georgia; and the 904th Military Airlift Group at Stewart AFB, New York, the only unit selected outside the Beef Broth listing.[69]

Selection is more easily described than accomplished, of course, and not until daylight could General Marchbanks submit his recommendations. About the time the official notification process lumbered into motion (6:00 A.M. or 7:00 A.M. on the 25th), the Office of the Secretary of Defense released the news to the newspapers, and affected reservists and units learned of their impending mobilization through news reports as opposed to through official channels. About 8:00 that morning, for example, while visiting a dentist, Brig. Gen. Rollin B. Moore, Jr., 349th Military Airlift Wing Commander at Hamilton AFB, California, received word of the mobilization by telephone from another reservist who worked at a radio station. As General Moore was returning to the base, his car radio carried a newscast that not only confirmed a reserve callup but also identified his own 349th Wing as one of the units being mobilized.[70]

When finally dispatched at 5:12 P.M., the Headquarters USAF mobilization message directed the mobilization of the selected Air Force Reserve units no later than midnight local time, January 26, 1968, for a period of not more than 24 months. The mobilized units placed 4,851 reservists on active duty and brought 52 aircraft with them. By midnight of the first day, 4,717, or 97.8

215

The Air Force Reserve

percent, had responded to this no-notice mobilization; the other 2.2 percent were in hospital, school, or travel status.[71]

C–124 Units on Active Duty

The five mobilized C–124 units were immediately integrated into the Military Airlift Command's worldwide system in which they actually had been operating for three years. In July, they began operating a detachment at RAF Mildenhall, England, to augment U.S. Air Force airlift operations in Europe with aircraft and aircrews. This allowed the Air Force to redeploy a C–130 wing from Europe to Southeast Asia. The Military Airlift Command formed the 1648th Provisional Squadron (Alpha Rotational) at RAF Mildenhall, England, on July 7, 1968, to operate a sixteen-aircraft rotational squadron. The first C–124 arrived from Dobbins AFB the next day with the vanguard of aircrews and maintenance technicians, and the rotational squadron began incrementally replacing a Tactical Air Command C–130 squadron. The squadron complement amounted to 16 C–124s and 388 officers and airmen, with the individuals' rotation periods ranging from 2 to 6 months long.[72] In addition to supporting the Mildenhall operation, aircrews from the mobilized groups also rotated to Rhein-Main AB, Germany, for two or three months at a time to support the 52d Military Airlift Squadron. The squadron closed down officially at noon on May 16, 1969.[73]

305th Aerospace Rescue and Recovery Squadron

The mobilized 305th Aerospace Rescue and Recovery Squadron augmented the Aerospace Rescue and Recovery Service around the globe, deploying its HC–97s in one- and two-ship elements to such widely scattered places as Iceland, Spain, Okinawa, Libya, and the Philippines. The reserve rescue crews stood alert and flew rescue missions as required, flying at least 849 sorties on search and rescue and airlift missions as they increased the Aerospace Rescue and Recovery Service's fixed-wing capability in the United States by a third and worldwide by 8 percent.[74]

The 305th placed two aircraft and crews each on temporary duty at Wheelus AB, Libya, and Keflavik Air Station, Iceland. At Wheelus, the 305th supported the 58th Aerospace Rescue and Recovery Squadron while it transitioned from HU–16s to HH–3s. The Wheelus mission terminated on November 15 after the reserve crews had conducted eight search missions. The squadron placed single aircraft at Hickam AFB, Hawaii, and Hamilton AFB, California, during the July–September 1968 quarter. On October 22, 1968, Squadron Commander Lt. Col. John C. Riley took two planes to Naha AB, Okinawa, to augment the 33d Aerospace Rescue and Recovery Squadron while it too converted from HU–15s to HH–3s.[75]

In April 1969, the aircraft stationed at Okinawa participated in the search

The Vietnam Era, 1965–1975

for a Navy EC–121 shot down by the North Koreans over the Sea of Japan. One of the 305th's aircraft flew primarily night search missions on which it operated as the communication controller and flare dropper. On one of these night missions, a flare whipped back into the aircraft and landed near a stack of the devices. Sergeant William C. Smolinski, a pararescueman, grabbed the errant flare and threw it from the plane. Then he wrapped his glove around some smoldering magnesium that remained and threw it out too, preventing the probable destruction of the airplane.[76]

By the time the squadron's Iceland detachment left in May 1969, it had expended nearly 400 hours on 79 actual search and rescue missions. As practitioners of such missions attest, search and rescue is mostly search and very little rescue, but on March 25, 1968, a deployed crew of the 305th was instrumental in saving the life of a downed Air Force pilot. While flying a precautionary orbit off the coast of Iceland in support of an Air Defense Command mission, Capt. John F. Wood and his crew heard an F–102 pilot declare a flameout emergency. Captain Wood established visual and radio contact with the ejected pilot 15 minutes after he had landed on a riverbank. The pilot was unharmed and declined paradrop assistance because of gusty winds. Captain Wood remained on the scene and directed a Navy H–34 helicopter into the area. The helicopter required escort around mountains into the river valley pickup point. Wood and his crew thereafter escorted the H–34 back to the base through periodic rain showers and winds gusting to 45 knots.[77] About a year later, on March 6, 1969, Capt. Charles M. Srull's aircraft escorted a Navy helicopter carrying firemen and a medic 60 miles to sea to aid a burning ship. With the help thus afforded, all but five of the ship's crew could be saved.[78]

Utilization of Mobilized Personnel

Soon after mobilization, one of the effects of recalling whole Air Force Reserve wings and groups for active duty at their home stations on which they were tenants became obvious. The reserve units were organized with base support elements but they were mobilized on stations where complete support structures already existed. Although the communications flights and the U.S. Air Force dispensaries were immediately assimilated by their gaining commands in accordance with standing mobilization orders, in exactly one of the scenarios that President Johnson had foreseen, hundreds of support personnel became superfluous to base needs. Consisting primarily of civil engineers, aerial porters, and supply personnel, these people eventually received reassignment worldwide to alleviate Air Force personnel shortages.[79]

An example of the reservists's discontent with this system is the suit brought by seven members of the 904th Military Airlift Group at Stewart AFB, New York, to prevent the Air Force from reassigning them from their units involuntarily. Conforming to the general pattern of such cases, a judge in

The Air Force Reserve

305th Mobilization. Aircrew members (above) of mobilized 305th Aerospace Rescue and Recovery Squadron processing on to active duty at Selfridge AFB, Michigan, on January 26, 1968. Maintenance men (below) of the mobilized 305th Aerospace Rescue and Recovery Squadron change engines on an HC–97 in the desert heat at Wheelus AB, Libya, July 1968.

The Vietnam Era, 1965–1975

305th Mobilization. Lt. Col. John C. Riley (left), commander of the mobilized 305th Aerospace Rescue and Recovery Squadron, is greeted at Naha AB, Okinawa, by Lt. Col. R. E. Ingraham (right), commander of the 33d Aerospace Rescue and Recovery Squadron.

305th Mobilization. All in a day's work, Sgt. William C. Smolinski (left) recognized earlier for hurling a burning flare from an HC–97, participates in homecoming ceremonies at Selfridge AFB, Michigan, in March 1969.

The Air Force Reserve

Federal District Court upheld the Air Force's right to move its people around. Dr. Theodore C. Marrs, Air Force Deputy Assistant Secretary for Reserve Affairs, defended the reassignment, noting both congressional and Air Force authority for such actions.[80]

Secretary of the Air Force Harold Brown explained the Air Force's position on these matters to the Congress on July 18. He noted that immediately after the *Pueblo* incident in January, the Air Force had sent a number of personnel to Korea on temporary duty. These people then had to be replaced, so the Air Force was sending over about 2,200 reservists for this purpose. The Secretary further explained that the Air Reserve Forces were part of the Strategic Reserve, and inherent in its rationale was the concept that its members were in a ready status for immediate deployment. Since the *Pueblo* matter was not resolved and the United States was continuing to augment its air forces in Korea, it was not possible to project where recalled reservists would serve.[81]

Circumstances of the May 1968 Mobilizations

Within a week of the *Pueblo* incident, on the weekend of Tet, the Vietnamese national holiday celebrating the Chinese lunar new year, about 70,000 North Vietnamese and Viet Cong troops struck at more than a hundred cities and towns in South Vietnam. Demonstrating that North Vietnam was not a beaten enemy on the verge of collapse, the Tet offensive demoralized the U.S. public. Anticipating that the President would want to give General Westmoreland the resources he wanted, and believing that the United States faced communist threats in Korea, Berlin, and possibly elsewhere, the Joint Chiefs of Staff tried to coerce the President into calling up reservists. General Wheeler saw Tet as the opportunity to attain the long-sought goal of mobilization. Vietnam would be the excuse for but not necessarily the beneficiary of a reserve mobilization.[82]

On February 12, McNamara directed the Joint Chiefs to deploy one brigade of the 82d Airborne Division and one Marine regimental combat team with a total strength of 10,500 to Vietnam. Even while complying, the Chiefs reemphasized earlier recommendations that it would be necessary to mobilize 46,300 reservists to replace and sustain the deployed troops.[83]

In the end, in the midst of a general assessment of U.S. objectives in Southeast Asia led by Secretary of Defense Clark Clifford (successor to Robert McNamara in the Johnson administration), the President approved the deployment of 30,000 troops to Vietnam in addition to the 10,500 already deployed as an emergency measure in January. This would substantially meet General Westmoreland's initial package request. The Air Force would support the initial deployment with slightly more than 4,000 men—a tactical fighter squadron, forward air controllers, an airlift package, and support troops. The President approved two reserve call-ups, the first to support the 30,000 deployment and the second to reconstitute the Strategic Reserve which had been seriously depleted by the January deployments.[84]

On May 11, Secretary Clifford announced that approximately 24,500 men in 88 reserve units of all services would be mobilized on May 13 for 24 months or less. The official alert notification followed the next day. In addition to a tactical airlift group for which a specialized mission was envisioned, the second mobilization of Air Force Reserve units in 1968 included three aerial port squadrons, a medical service squadron, and an aeromedical evacuation squadron required to support the deployed combat forces.[85]

On April 11, Headquarters USAF directed the Continental Air Command to alert certain Air Force Reserve units for recall on May 13. Coming on extended active duty on the appointed day with 755 people were the 930th Tactical Airlift Group, less certain support elements; the 34th Aeromedical Evacuation Squadron; the 52d Medical Service Squadron; and the 82d, 86th, and 88th Aerial Port Squadrons.[86]

The Air Force Reserve Units on Active Duty

Fifteen days after it was mobilized, the 34th Aeromedical Evacuation Squadron, commanded by Capt. Charles J. Kittell, went to Yokota, Japan, on temporary duty for 179 days. Its personnel flew medical evacuation routes from Vietnam to the United States, taking part in 1,262 combat missions in Southeast Asia and 948 evacuation missions from Japan to the United States.[87] The 52d Medical Service Squadron remained at its home station, Scott AFB, Illinois, and helped alleviate the base hospital's increased patient load from Southeast Asia, handling about 2,000 patients a month. The average base hospital and casualty staging flight workload doubled in early 1968 with a surge in the number of C–141 aeromedical evacuation flights coming in from the Pacific. The additional 52d Squadron personnel at the Scott hospital reduced a 67-day patient backlog in the facility's ophthalmology clinic to 12 days by January 1969. Similarly, the backlog of the ear, nose, and throat clinic, which had consistently run to 25 days before May 1968, was reduced to four days.[88]

The three aerial port squadrons were assimilated into the Military Airlift Command port operations at their home stations at Travis AFB, California, McChord AFB, Washington, and McGuire AFB, New Jersey. Individual members of the 88th Aerial Port Squadron, however, deployed to the Republic of Korea in July 1968 to augment the aerial port function there. From mid-July to December 1968, they comprised more than half the entire military aerial port work force in Korea.[89]

On June 15, 1968, about a month after the 930th Tactical Airlift Group had been mobilized at Bakalar AFB, Indiana, with eighteen C–119Gs, its 71st Tactical Airlift Squadron moved to Lockbourne AFB, Ohio, and converted to

The Air Force Reserve

gunship operations. On that same date, the 71st was redesignated as the 71st Air Commando Squadron, a name that lasted less than a month, as the unit became the 71st Special Operations Squadron on July 8.[90]

Conversion from tactical airlift to gunship operations in the AC-119 brought significant changes. The crew composition increased from five to eight as the crew acquired a second navigator and two gunners while the loadmaster cross-trained as an illuminator operator. Also, a change in the ratio of crews to airplanes increased total crew requirements from sixteen to twenty-four. By November 21, 1968, the crews had formed and were ready. The aircrews left for Vietnam on December 5; four days later, other elements of the squadron left via C-141s. The unit was reassigned to the 14th Special Operations Wing on December 20, 1968.[91]

The 71st got away very cheaply for having flown more than 6,000 hours in six months in a combat zone. It lost no aircraft, and only six received any kind of battle damage in the air. The most serious incident involved an aircraft struck by about six rounds of 12.7-mm fire which put 19 holes in the aft part of the fuselage and caused minor lacerations in the neck and back of a gunner. This active force man was augmenting the basic reserve crew; nevertheless he became the first combat casualty aboard an Air Force Reserve aircraft since the 452d Light Bomb Wing was relieved at Pusan East Air Base, Korea, on May 8, 1952.[92]

Release of Mobilized Reservists

Just like the mobilizations earlier in the year, the ones in May evoked protest. This second round was broader based, however. In January, reservists had protested the breaking up of mobilized units and the reassignment of individuals, but in the summer of 1968 some reservists protested the very concept of mobilization itself. The U.S. Army Reserve had the most dissidents, but the Air Force Reserve had problems too.[93]

For its own reasons, however, the Air Force soon began reviewing its requirements to retain reservists on active duty. In July 1968, with the Air Force pressed for funds, the military situation in South Vietnam stabilizing, and some movement occurring toward peace talks, the Air Staff began discussing the feasibility of releasing the mobilized Air Reserve Forces units. An operational analysis showed that early release of the aerial port units would have limited impact. Release of the C-124 units would force the Tactical Air Command to look elsewhere to replace the C-130 capability in England and Germany. Early release of the medical service squadron would reduce the capability of the hospital at Scott AFB to care for casualties returning from Southeast Asia who staged through the base en route to other stateside hospitals. The Pacific Air Force's capability to evacuate Southeast Asia casualties by air would be restricted by the release of the aeromedical evacuation squadron. With the Air Force facing a troop reduction of 10,000 in fiscal year 1969, on September 19 General McConnell approved an Air Force Council recommendation to release the units early.[94]

Headquarters Military Airlift Command released the 82d, 86th, and 83th Aerial Port Squadrons from extended active duty on December 12, 1968, and the C–124 units on June 1, 1969. Finally, on June 18, 1969, the Military Airlift Command released the 34th Aeromedical Evacuation Squadron, the 52d Medical Service Squadron, and the 305th Aerospace Rescue and Recovery Squadron. On the same day, the Tactical Air Command released the 930th Special Operations Group, its maintenance squadron and aerial port flight, and the 71st Special Operations Squadron. These actions meant that the 305th Aerospace Rescue and Recovery Squadron had served the longest stint on extended active duty: it was mobilized on January 26, 1968, and released on June 18, 1969.[95]

Evaluation of the 1968 Mobilizations

The 1968 mobilizations understandably disclosed problems. Aside from accommodating the excess support personnel placed on active duty at Military Airlift Command bases (reminiscent of the Korean mobilization), major problems in 1968 related to the processing of personnel and their records. However, the problems of the two eras were quite different.

Eighteen years earlier, the Air Force had mobilized Air Force Reserve units for the Korean War without any mobilization plans. In January 1968, plans were in place, but they did not address the circumstances of a no-notice mobilization. The basic Air Force and Continental Air Command directives were predicated upon a 30-day alert notice preceding any mobilization. Both directives spelled out detailed, time-phased actions, but in the no-notice January mobilization, the guidance was invalidated by the press of events, including the actions taken in Washington on the night of January 24, 1968, and the Military Airlift Command's delay in getting its mobilization instructions to the field.[96] On the basis of the units' experiences in the January mobilization, the Continental Air Command staff revised its mobilization plan to provide guidance for both types of mobilizations. The May mobilization, which incorporated a 30-day alert, therefore proceeded more smoothly.[97]

Air Force directives failed to include procedures for stopping normal losses to units at the time of mobilization, and this became a serious concern for some reserve unit commanders. When no method was established to extend enlistments and service obligations automatically upon mobilization, separations continued as enlistments and service obligations expired. The resulting personnel losses compounded skill shortages. The Air Force revised its

The Air Force Reserve

There they are!! Relatives react to the return of the mobilized 71st Special Operations Squadron to Bakalar AFB, Indiana, on June 18, 1969.

directives to incorporate procedures to stop such losses during all mobilizations.[98]

The Korean mobilization eighteen years earlier had disclosed that personnel records maintained for Air Force Reservists were inaccurate and inadequate. In 1968, their records were present and accurate, but they were not fully compatible with the active force records system. It was this incompatibility between reserve force and active force personnel data systems that received the most extensive attention during postmobilization evaluations.[99]

Nothing stirs more resentment in a soldier, or an airman, than to reach the end of the pay line and find that his name has been red-lined or does not appear on the pay roster. The pay lines of World War II were gone, but the absence of a check or deposit slip in the mail still aroused the same resentment. And for sundry reasons—its no-notice nature, the incompatibility of personnel records, and problems in the consolidated base personnel office—the January mobilization produced an indeterminate number of instances of delayed pay. This is another example of how Air Force procedures governing pay were made obsolete by the centralized computerization of Air Reserve Forces pay that occurred on January 1, 1968.[100]

Aside from personnel matters, all components of the Air Reserve Forces complained about being restricted by obsolete weapons and equipment. The 1968 mobilizations illustrate the point. In their nonmobilized, inactive duty status, Air Reserve Forces units maintained an acceptable state of readiness in obsolescent aircraft according to their aircraft's capabilities and the peacetime flying-hour utilization rates. The logistics system could not support the higher flying-hour rates required by the reserve aircraft once they came on active duty. Neither could it support the daily maintenance of reserve aircraft due to the rapid deterioration of aging parts.[101]

After Richard M. Nixon became President of the United States in January 1969, he quickly declared his intention to turn the war over to South Vietnamese and reduce U.S. forces in Vietnam. He later said that he began his presidency with three fundamental premises regarding Vietnam: he would prepare public opinion for the fact that total military victory was no longer possible; he would act on the basis of his conscience, his experience, and his analysis on the need to keep U.S. commitments; and he would end the war as quickly as was honorably possible. He stressed reducing U.S. commitments, not only in Southeast Asia but elsewhere in the world as well. In May 1969, the new administration offered a peace plan for Vietnam, and, although the war would continue for another six years, the issue of a reserve mobilization for Southeast Asia was never seriously raised again.[102]

9

A Bill of Rights, the Dual Hat, and Total Force

> There is in the executive part of the Department of the Air Force an Office of Air Force Reserve which is headed by a chief who is the adviser to the Chief of Staff, on Air Force Reserve matters.
>
> —Public Law 90–168, December 1967

Countering a Department of Defense move to merge the reserve components, late in 1967 Congress passed Public Law 90–168, Reserve Forces Bill of Rights and Vitalization Act, which among other things guaranteed the existence of the individual components. As the new Office of Air Force Reserve struggled to assert itself in the management of the Air Force Reserve, the Air Force, followed by the Department of Defense, applied a concept of total force to the planning and employment of the reserve forces. In 1975 the Air Force and its reserve components reconciled apparent contradictions posed by the provisions of Public Law 90–168 and the demands of the Total Force Policy.

General LeMay Reopens the Merger Issue

For about a year beginning in January 1964, the Air Staff discussed the issue of merging the Air Force's two reserve components. Its considerations were stimulated in part by its own Chief of Staff and in part by related developments in the U.S. Army. For one thing, General LeMay, who as Vice Chief of Staff in 1959 had advocated eliminating one of the two Air Reserve Forces

The Air Force Reserve

components still thought it was a good idea,* and as Chief of Staff he revived the issue in January 1963. His greetings to the members of the Air Reserve Forces Policy Committee of Headquarters USAF at their regular meeting on January 15 were not garden-variety, stroke-the-Reservists, show-the-flag remarks. He had a more serious purpose; he wished to stimulate the committee to consider the ramifications of merging the two Air Reserve Forces components.[1]

It still made no sense to him to have two different reserve systems duplicating recruiting, pay, training, and other activities. He wanted to change the system, but because of the political uproar that erupted every time the active force talked about merger, LeMay asked the policy committee to consider it because he did not believe that merger could occur unless reservists themselves advocated it. Thus, while still failing to accept the inadvisability of raising the issue of merging the two air reserve components, General LeMay had at least become wise enough to realize that there could be no merger without the cooperation of reserve leaders.

As a body that met semiannually unless called into special session, the Air Reserve Forces Policy Committee customarily moved at a little more than glacial speed, and a year passed before the Air Force Secretariat arranged a special meeting to consider the feasibility of establishing a single Air Reserve force. When the committee met at the Pentagon on the morning of January 15, 1964, General LeMay was there to greet it and expanded upon the remarks he had made exactly a year earlier. This time, in addition to restating the Air Force's need for a single, strong Reserve, he suggested that the Air Force had a better chance of getting more money through one appropriation for a single reserve force than in continuing to divide the available money between two components.[2]

Following the Chief of Staff's lead, the committee endorsed the concept of a single Air Force Reserve and recommended that a series of preparatory studies be conducted. At the least, these were to include an analysis of changes in the basic law that merger might require; an examination of the roles, missions, and composition of the components to ensure that they were in fact complementary; and a cost-effective survey of the single Air Reserve Forces concept. Framed by active force and Air National Guard members, the committee's recommendation was not unanimous. While regarding the concept of merger with the guard as abhorrent, the five Air Force Reserve members, seduced by the Lorelei's promise of increased funding for a single reserve component, insisted upon the provision for the studies before they reluctantly joined the majority.

The Secretariat approved the Air Reserve Forces Policy Committee's

---

*General LeMay's earlier comments on the desirability of merging the two reserve components are discussed in Chapter 7.

Bill of Rights, Dual Hat, and Total Force

In company with Lt. Gen. Bryan M. Shotts, former Strategic Air Command Commander in Chief General Curtis E. LeMay visits Col. Ronald R. Blalack, Commander, 452d Air Refueling Wing, in May 1978.

recommendations on February 11, but the Air Staff was preoccupied with other matters, and not until the Secretary of Defense stimulated them nine months later did they seriously consider the issue.[3]

On the morning of October 28, 1964, McNamara asked Secretary of the Air Force Eugene M. Zuckert for a plan to phase the Air Force Reserve into the Air National Guard. Passing the request to the Air Staff, Theodore C. Marrs, Deputy for Reserve and ROTC Affairs who served under the Special Assistant to the Secretary of the Air Force for Manpower, Personnel, and Reserve Forces, asked for several cost-study options involving the two components. Inferring that such a request implied approval, the Air Staff prepared confidently to merge the Air Force Reserve into the Air National Guard.[4]

Secretary Zuckert thought it would be a simple matter to transfer Air Force Reserve units into the Air National Guard, but Lt. Gen. Edward J. Timberlake, the Continental Air Command Commander, knew better. Discussing the subject with Secretary Zuckert on November 13, General Timberlake predicted that merger would create personnel turbulence sufficient to cause Air Force Reserve units to lose their combat effectiveness. More than half of the enlisted personnel in the reserve units (about 13,400) were men with no prior service, and the Air Force could not force them to transfer to the Air National Guard; indications were that very few would voluntarily cross over. General Timberlake also anticipated that only about half of the Air Reserve technicians would transfer into the Air National Guard. Most technicians had at least ten years of

The Air Force Reserve

In 1965 Secretary of the Air Force Eugene M. Zuckert supported the move to merge Air Force Reserve units into the Air National Guard.

federal civil service for retirement purposes, had veterans' preference rights, and probably would exercise bumping rights as civilians, leaving the Air Force Reserve if necessary. Prior-service reservists, representing 32 percent of the force, presented another problem. Reserve wing commanders believed that many of these people, so essential to combat readiness, would be unwilling to change to Air National Guard and state militia status.[5]

On November 4, the Air Staff submitted a study to the Secretariat that favored eliminating the Continental Air Command, transferring Air Force Reserve units to the Air National Guard, and reassigning Air Force Reserve individuals to the Air Reserve Records Center. The next day, Lt. Gen. Hewitt T. Wheless, the Deputy Chief of Staff for Programs and Requirements, presented the study to General LeMay and recommended that the Air Staff and the National Guard Bureau continue to measure the impact of placing all Air Force Reserve units in the Air National Guard. One of the criteria posited for the study of options to achieve a single Air Reserve was that the ultimate management structure provide the Chief of Staff of the Air Force with undisputed control over all Air Reserve Forces. Since the Chief of Staff could never exercise undisputed control over Air National Guard forces in peacetime, this criterion should have prejudiced the study toward transferring Air National Guard units into the Air Force Reserve.[6]

General LeMay rejected the briefing and directed the Air Staff to restudy the issue, particularly examining manpower and cost implications and

Bill of Rights, Dual Hat, and Total Force

Alone among the major air commanders, Lt. Gen. Edward J. Timberlake, Commander of Continental Air Command (July 1962–June 1965), resisted a move to merge Air Force Reserve units into the Air National Guard in 1965.

concentrating on the objective of a single force under either the Air National Guard or the Air Force Reserve.[7] Although he left the options of guard or reserve merger open in his instructions to the staff, in forwarding the study to the Air Force Secretariat on November 27, LeMay opted for merging the Air National Guard into the Air Force Reserve. Secretary Zuckert, however, asked the Air Staff to refine the option of transferring reserve units only to the Air National Guard.[8]

By this time (November 1964), Air Force considerations of merging reserve components were being influenced by concurrent developments in the Army. The Kennedy administration's military response to the Berlin crisis demonstrated that both the active and the reserve forces were too rigidly structured to permit the deployment flexibility the President thought necessary. Flexible response required the existence of relatively small, highly ready reserve units. McNamara's initial review disclosed, however, that it was far easier to conduct a mass mobilization than to recall certain units selectively. He therefore proposed to create highly ready, limited mobilization forces while reducing the large-scale mobilization forces. His 1963 budget recommended that the Army Reserve components' authorized paid strength be reduced from 700,000 to 670,000.[9]

On April 4, 1962, ignoring opposition from its General Staff Committee on Army National Guard and Reserve Policy, several governors, and numerous congressmen, the Army declared its intention to inactivate eight Army Reserve

The Air Force Reserve

independent brigades and to reduce four National Guard and four Army Reserve divisions to headquarters status. The proposed realignment would eliminate 58,900 paid drill spaces, reducing the total to 642,000. The announcement provoked extensive opposition outside the Department of Defense. State governors and the reserve organizations joined the adjutants general and the appropriations and authorizations committees of both houses of Congress in objecting. The congressional action at least temporarily blocked part of the proposal by maintaining the level of drill-pay spaces at 700,000 in the 1963 appropriations act.[10]

The issue was no longer simply that of the organization and readiness of the Army's reserve components; it had become a conflict of wills between McNamara and Congress. Attributing an ad hominem motivation of power to him, committee chairmen resisted what they perceived as the Secretary's effort to usurp their constitutional role "to provide for organizing, arming, and disciplining the Militia." For his part, McNamara would concede nothing to the congressmen. This standoff would prevail for more than five years, from August 1962 when Representative F. Edward Hébert picked up McNamara's gauntlet, to December 1967 when President Johnson signed the Reserve Forces Bill of Rights and Vitalization Act.

The administration's proposals encountered great resistance in Congress. Many congressmen as well as their staffers were reservists and saw Secretary McNamara's proposals as threats to their components, particularly those who belonged to the Army Reserve. McNamara's first deputy secretary, Roswell L. Gilpatric, recalled with awe the entrenched reserve element he and the secretary encountered in seeking to reform the reserve program:

> We had something like twenty-seven or thirty-two divisions; some of them only on paper. But they all had their commanding officers, and they all had plans for fleshing out the units. And we found that we couldn't count on our own people, far less the people on the Hill, to back any major reform. . . . McNamara spent a tremendous amount of blood, sweat, and tears, backed up by Cy Vance, and later by Paul Ignatius. . . . we didn't realize how deeply dug in the Guard Association and the Reserve Association and all the state adjutant generals and the governors [were]—and the fact that two-thirds of the congressional staffs on the Armed Services and Appropriations Committees belonged to the reserves. . . . Dozens of congressmen and senators were members of the reserve.[11]

Opposition in August 1962 from the House Armed Services Committee and the National Governors Conference forced the Secretary to develop a compromise proposal to realign the structure and eliminate some units within the drill-pay strength of 700,000. The reorganization eliminated approximately 1,850 company- or detachment-sized units, added about 1,000 of a different nature, and replaced four divisions each of the guard and reserve by separate

Bill of Rights, Dual Hat, and Total Force

brigades. To strengthen the top-priority, mobile, fast-reacting units, their authorization of civilian technicians was increased and their overall manning levels were raised. McNamara therefore achieved his basic goal of bringing the Army's reserve components into closer alignment with mobilization requirements and by the end of fiscal 1963 had come a step closer to achieving the Kennedy strategy of flexible response.[12] Then on December 12, 1964, McNamara announced that the Army intended to merge all Army Reserve units into the National Guard, leaving only individual reservists in the Army Reserve.[13]

These developments in the Army added a new dimension to the restudy of the merger issue in the Air Staff. Announcement of the proposed merger of the Army's reserve components did not imply that the Air Force had to do likewise, but the new Air Force study group wanted to avoid having the Air Force place the Secretary of Defense in the untenable position of supporting two different courses of action based on conflicting rationale. As the Reserve Forces Policy Board and the Reserve Officers Association resisted the consolidation, the group also learned from the *Washington Post* that public and congressional opinion opposed the merger as well. Whatever the study group proposed would be subject to critical and scrutinizing evaluation. On January 6, 1965, the group's director, Col. John R. Kern, Jr., Chief of the Organization Branch in the Manpower and Organization Directorate, recommended that only Air Force Reserve units be integrated into the Air National Guard. Colonel Kern's group asserted that the option would require less legislative change and have less impact on the rights and benefits of individuals.[14]

On the same day, Maj. Gen. Curtis R. Low, Assistant Chief of Staff of the the Reserve Forces, independently recommended the same course of action to the Chief of Staff. General Low cited the collocation of the National Guard Bureau with Headquarters USAF and its situation as both a command headquarters and an extension of the Air Staff as giving the Air National Guard a great advantage over the Air Force Reserve. He also noted that the National Guard enjoyed strong political support, which usually resulted in its acquiring better equipment and a larger budget. He asserted that through its accomplishments, its political support, and an active public information program, the Air National Guard had created a better image in the minds of many active force officers than the Air Force Reserve had, with its legacy of the Reserve Officer Personnel Act of 1954 promotions and its "Little Red School House" programs. Primarily for these reasons, General Low recommended that Air Force Reserve units be transferred to the Air National Guard, but that the individual program be retained in the Air Force Reserve.[15]

The separate Kern and Low recommendations were submitted in time to be considered at the Air Force commanders' conference convening at Ramey AFB in Puerto Rico on January 7, 1965. McConnell, Vice Chief of Staff and due to become Chief of Staff upon General LeMay's retirement at the end of

The Air Force Reserve

In January 1965 Maj. Gen. Curtis R. Low, Assistant Chief of Staff for Reserve Forces (here as a colonel), recommended to the Chief of Staff that units of the Air Force Reserve be merged into the Air National Guard.

the month, chaired the opening session. In a surprise move, he suspended the published conference agenda to put the question of the creation of a single reserve component before the commanders. The Air Force had to present its position to McNamara the next day, and General McConnell wanted the commanders to give him their thoughts.[16]

Instructing Colonel Kern to withhold his recommendations until the end of his briefing, McConnell asked General Timberlake for his views. Repeating the warning he had given to Secretary Zuckert on November 13, 1964, that the merger would result in great personnel turbulence and destroy the Air Force Reserve, the Continental Air Command Commander then declared:

> In our business it is fatal if we ever consider sacrificing principle for expediency. It appears to me that if we put the Reserves into the Guard we are doing just that. Taking the apparently easy way out. My sole concern is to maintain absolute control of Reserve units—in peacetime as well as war—particularly those units vital to National Defense.
>
> I am concerned about the possibility of placing these units in a political atmosphere, commanded in peacetime by one organization [State] and in wartime by another [Air Force]. The object of the exercise was to create a single Reserve component. Neither option . . . accomplishes this.*[17]

---

*Timberlake had also spoken out against merger and the proposed Air Force Reserve

McConnell then asked the commanders of the gaining command for their views. General John K. Gerhart, Commander in Chief of the North American Air Defense Command, and Lt. Gen. Herbert B. Thatcher, Commander of the Air Defense Command who had no Air Force Reserve units except the inactivating recovery units, thought the Reserve should be absorbed by the Guard. General Howell M. Estes, Jr., Commander of the Military Air Transport Service which would gain all the heavy airlift units, and Lt. Gen. Charles B. Westover, Vice Commander of the Air Defense Command, agreed with Timberlake in principle, but they thought it would be better not to upset the Guard and went on record as favoring the merging of the Reserve into the Guard. Maj. Gen. Kenneth P. Bergquist, Commander of the Air Force Communications Service, unequivocally favored retaining the Guard because its units were better equipped and manned. With only General Timberlake voting to transfer the Guard into the Reserve, McConnell declared that the position of the Air Force was to transfer all Air Force Reserve units into the Air National Guard.[18]

When General LeMay appeared the next day and convened an executive session, General Timberlake asked him if the vote the day before represented the official Air Force position. General LeMay replied that he did not agree with it, but it was the Air Force position. The Chief of Staff said that if any change was made, he preferred that the Air National Guard should be absorbed by the Air Force Reserve for better and continuous command and control. He added that when briefed in Washington, he had asked the staff what would be the best for the Air Force in the absence of outside pressures, and they had all agreed that, discounting outside pressures, the best thing would be to transfer the Guard into the Reserve. They thought that the National Guard could not be reconciled to this, but LeMay insisted that if he were staying he would challenge the National Guard Bureau and undertake to transfer the Guard into the Reserve.[19]

Upon returning to Washington, McConnell formally recommended to the Secretary of the Air Force that Air Force Reserve units be merged into the Air National Guard but that individual reservists be retained in the Air Force Reserve. Zuckert endorsed the recommendation to the Secretary of Defense on January 11, projecting a completed merger by July 1966, if McNamara approved it.[20]

Secretary McNamara never approved it. The Air Staff hurried out with a preliminary program, the General Counsel of the Air Force examined the legal and fiscal implications, and the National Guard Bureau distributed some initial

---

Bureau as a "good way to kill off the Air Force Reserve" during an informal session with the reserve members of the Air Reserve Forces Policy Committee at a Sunday supper session at the Bolling AFB Officers Club (Remarks, Lt Gen E. J. Timberlake, Bolling AFB Officers Club, 1800, Nov 25, 1964 [Sunday]—AFRES VC4).

planning instructions to the state adjutants general and key unit personnel. On January 18, President Johnson advised Congress of the steps the Army was preparing to take in merging the reserve components, but he never mentioned the Air Reserve Forces. Meanwhile, although continuing to oppose merger, General Timberlake began to prepare Air Force Reserve commanders and his staff for the inevitable.[21] All of this transpired without any announcement from the Office of the Secretary of Defense, because McNamara was engaged in a bitter battle with various congressional committees over the proposed Army merger, and he was not sanguine about his winning it.

Testifying before the House Armed Services Committee on February 19, 1965, McNamara stated that the existence of two Army Reserve components made no better sense in 1965 than it had in 1948 when the Gray committee had recommended merger. He said that the choice to transfer the Army Reserve units into the National Guard was based on two major considerations. The governor of each state needed a military force to deal with natural disasters and to preserve law and order. Moreover, as the lineal descendants of the state militia, the guard units were deeply imbedded in the constitutional tradition and were entitled to preference as the senior reserve component.[22]

When McNamara insisted that the merger should occur in fiscal year 1966, Congressman Hébert, a champion of reservists rights, objected to being "told" rather than "consulted" about the merger plans. He asked McNamara to give Congress the opportunity to discuss the matter and settle once and for all the division of authority between the executive and legislative branches. The committee chairman, L. Mendel Rivers, supported Hébert, insisting that the Department of Defense was obligated to consult Congress on any proposed merger.[23]

When Senator John C. Stennis' Subcommittee on Preparedness took up the matter on March 1, 1965, he opened hearings with the assertion that no change would be made to the reserve structure until Congress had studied the proposal. Undaunted, McNamara again denied the necessity of new legislation to implement merger and claimed the authority to assign reservists with a service obligation involuntarily to the National Guard for training.[24] Subsequent sessions changed no one's position. Defense witnesses insisted that the merger decision had been made in the best interests of national defense. While quibbling about how the decision was reached and who had proposed it in the first place, the Senators never disproved the assertion that a single Army Reserve component would be more efficient than the existing two.[25]

When Congressman Hébert's subcommittee reconvened on March 25, the most effective witness against the proposed merger was John T. Carlton, the executive director of the Reserve Officers Association, which had taken a public position against merger earlier in the year. Faced with the eventual loss of his constituency if the National Guard absorbed the Army Reserve, Carlton attacked the merger proposal. Playing to his congressional audience, he accused the Department of Defense of waiting until Congress was not in session to announce its plan in the hope of attracting public support for merger before the legislators had a chance to evaluate its merits. Carlton charged, as had other critics of merger, that the plan had not been fully staffed and that McNamara had attempted to get the General Staff Committee on Army National Guard and Army Reserve Policy to rubber-stamp it.[26]

The chairman of that policy committee, Maj. Gen. J. W. Kaine, confirmed that the policy committees were often asked to approve proposed Department of the Army policies or actions affecting the reserve components without having been given the opportunity to review or participate in the drafting of such policies. This left them with the options of only rubber-stamping or nonconcurrence. General Kaine testified that his committee had opposed the proposed merger for many reasons, among them that no alternate plans had been considered, the reorganization would destroy unity of command rather than simplify it, most reservists would not transfer to the National Guard, and experienced personnel would be lost for development as leaders as positions were deleted. General Kaine also noted that the plan had not originated in standard Army channels and, therefore, did not have the considered views of the overall professional Army, including the Continental Army Command, the administrator of the Army Reserve.[27] The hearings ended with McNamara agreeing to propose legislation to clarify the proposed merger. The Senate Appropriations Committee meanwhile delayed merger for a season by setting an Army Reserve strength of 650,000 for the coming fiscal year.[28]

Secretary McNamara soon submitted the promised legislative proposal incorporating a merger plan, which Congressman Hébert's subcommittee began to consider on August 2, 1965. In McNamara's absence due to illness, Deputy Secretary of Defense Cyrus R. Vance reasserted that a merger would achieve the department's objectives, specifically increasing the combat power and readiness of the reserve forces, producing a balanced structure, retaining only those units required by contingency plans, and simplifying management by eliminating duplicate channels. Vance insisted that the time had come to act on the Army's proposal to merge its reserve components. However, he withdrew the proposal to merge the Air Force's Reserve components. Conceding a truth that frequently characterized Air Force studies of its reserve components, Vance noted that its current proposal dealt solely with the peacetime management of the Air Reserve Forces and was not pertinent to their wartime readiness.[29]

Concluding its hearings on August 12, the Hébert subcommittee rejected the Department of Defense's proposal to merge the Army's reserve components and announced congressional intention to enact definitive legislation governing the organization of reserve components.[30]

The Air Force Reserve

Public Law 90–168 and a "Bill of Rights"

Congressman Hébert introduced H.R. 2, the Reserve Forces Bill of Rights and Vitalization Act, on January 10, 1967. The House had passed a comparable measure in September 1966, but it had been too late in the session for the Senate to act on it. The purpose of the legislation was to guarantee in law a structure for each of the reserve components. Unable to dissuade the Department of Defense by counsel, Hébert now intended to erect legal barriers against the merging of the reserve and guard components of the Army and the Air Force.[31]

The Reserve Officers Association, the Air Force Association, and various other service associations and veterans' groups endorsed the house resolution. Advising Mr. Hébert that the Office of the Secretary of Defense position on the merger was unchanged, Deputy Secretary Vance declined an invitation to testify. The bill moved quickly through the chamber and passed on February 20, 1967, by a vote of 324 to 13. Following reconciliation with a Senate amendment, the legislation was approved as Public Law 90–168 and became effective on January 1, 1968.[32]

With respect to the Air Force (and containing comparable provisions applicable to the Army), the law provided that there would be a fourth assistant secretary, that is, for manpower and reserve affairs; that the role of the Air Reserve Forces Policy Committee would be expanded to enable it to comment upon major policy matters directly affecting the reserve components of the Air Force; that an Office of Air Force Reserve would be created, led by the Chief of Air Force Reserve, a reservist nominated by the President and confirmed by the Senate; that the Secretary of the Air Force was responsible to provide the personnel, equipment, facilities, and other general logistic support necessary to enable Air Force Reserve units and individuals to satisfy their training and mobilization requirements; and that there be a Selected Reserve, that is, a Ready Reserve consisting of units and individuals, whose strength would be mandated annually by Congress. Addressing the issue that had started it all, the law mandated that there be units in both components, thereby precluding any merger of the Air Force Reserve and the Air National Guard.[33]

When Lt. Gen. Horace M. Wade, Air Force Deputy Chief of Staff for Personnel, suggested that the Reserve Policy Council participate in the selection of the first Chief of Air Force Reserve, that body nominated Brig. Gen. Tom E. Marchbanks, Jr. A Reserve Officers Association activist, Marchbanks was a member of the Policy Council and Commander of the 433d Troop Carrier Wing at Kelly AFB, Texas, and had flown as a fighter pilot in World War II and the Korean War. Pending his confirmation by the Senate, General Marchbanks was brought on a special tour of active duty to participate in establishing the new agency. The Senate confirmed his nomination as Chief and promotion to major general on February 16, 1968.[34]

Bill of Rights, Dual Hat, and Total Force

On February 23, Marchbanks briefed McConnell and several Air Staff personnel and manpower officials on his proposal for organizing his office and the field structure of the Air Force Reserve. The essential features of the option he recommended were that the Office of Air Force Reserve would have a staff of about 113 people and that Headquarters Continental Air Command would be replaced at Robins AFB, Georgia, by Headquarters AFRES. The new organization would be a separate operating agency established as a field extension of the Office of Air Force Reserve and would be commanded by another reserve major general recalled to active duty for the purpose. The Air Reserve Personnel Center would be retained, but as another separate operating agency responsible to the Office of Air Force Reserve. General Marchbanks and his reserve advisers did not want to retain the large Regular Air Force Continental Air Command as a link in the new Air Force Reserve chain of command. Career reservists such as he held as an article of faith that the Continental Air Command had always been more obstructive than productive in developing combat-ready Air Force Reserve units. Nevertheless, some kind of a field agency with the prerogative of command was necessary to administer the nationwide network of reserve units, and a separate operating agency, which would function as an extension of the office of the Chief, seemed to be the appropriate solution to the command question. McConnell accepted the recommendation, and the proposal was endorsed by the Air Reserve Forces Policy Committee on March 18 and approved shortly thereafter by Secretary of the Air Force Harold Brown.[35] Secretary Brown especially agreed with the appropriateness of placing the Air Reserve Personnel Center under the supervision of the Office of Air Force Reserve.*[36]

On August 1, 1968, the reorganization of the field management structure of the Air Force Reserve became effective. Headquarters Continental Air Command was discontinued at Robins AFB, Georgia. Replacing it was Headquarters AFRES, constituted and activated as a separate operating agency with the procedural functions and responsibilities of a major command. The Air Reserve Personnel Center ceased functioning as an organizational element of Continental Air Command and became a separate operating agency. On July 30, 1968, McConnell presided over ceremonies at Robins AFB marking the retirement of Lt. Gen. Henry Viccellio as the last commander of the Continen-

---

*General Marchbanks' immediate tasks were to organize his office and to decide the nature of the operating headquarters in the field. The only pressure to do anything about the Air Reserve Personnel Center came from an Air Staff proposal that the center be aligned under the Air Force Deputy Chief of Staff, Personnel, which was beginning to cast covetous glances toward the center and its Air Force Reserve personnel accounting apparatus. To set the question aside while he dealt with the major issues, yet still protect the center, General Marchbanks persuaded the Chief of Staff to designate it as a separate operating agency responsible to his office.

The Air Force Reserve

tal Air Command. During those ceremonies, the Continental Air Command was discontinued, Headquarters AFRES was established, and Maj. Gen. Rollin B. Moore, Jr., received his second star and assumed command of the Air Force Reserve. Two days later, activation ceremonies for the Air Reserve Personnel Center as a separate operating agency occurred at Denver, Colorado.

Thus passed the Continental Air Command from the management structure of the Air Force Reserve. Often maligned for its efforts, the organization had struggled in cooperation with the Air Staff and the gaining commands for nearly twenty years to develop the Air Force Reserve into a combat-ready component. General Marchbanks' generation of Air Force Reserve leaders perceived that the Continental Air Command impeded their progress toward combat readiness and obstructed the development of the component as an effective force, but the converse was more accurate. During sundry Air Force and Department of Defense economy drives, the command had often labored with insufficient financial resources and materiel to complete its tasks. Working with the gaining commands, however, it developed several programs and operations in which Air Force Reservists participated to augment the active force in its daily peacetime operations—rescue, SWIFT LIFT, READY SWAP, POWER PACK, CONTAC, the C–119 offshore missions, and the C–124 Southeast Asia missions. Often the Continental Air Command was the Air Force Reserve's only advocate in the Pentagon. For that matter, Deputy for Reserve Marrs in the Office of the Secretary of Defense, once scolded the command for its sponsorship of the Air Force Reserve recovery program and its penchant for "weak plans not based on actual requirements but instituted to make jobs for the reserves." Whatever the perception in the field, the Continental Air Command never stinted on its effort to develop a ready reserve force.[37]

General Moore was already on extended active duty as Commander of the mobilized 349th Military Airlift Wing[*] when he was selected to be the first Commander of Headquarters AFRES. A World War II veteran, Moore joined the California Air National Guard and progressed through its ranks, becoming a wing commander in 1951 and a brigadier general the following year. When the Air Force Reserve initiated the Air Reserve technician program in 1958, General Moore transferred over and became the Commander of the 349th Troop Carrier Wing at Hamilton AFB, California. He brought the wing on active duty in 1962 during the Cuban missile crisis and again in January 1968 in the *Pueblo* crisis. An active member of the National Guard Association and the Reserve Officers Association, Moore served on the Air Reserve Forces Policy Committee from 1961 to 1964.[38]

---

[*]The mobilization is discussed above in Chapter 8.

Bill of Rights, Dual Hat, and Total Force

General John P. McConnell (second from left), Air Force Chief of Staff, presides over ceremonies at Robins AFB, Georgia, on July 31, 1968, marking the retirement of Lt. Gen. Henry Viccellio (left) as the last commander of the Continental Air Command on that day, the discontinuation of the Command and establishment of Headquarters Air Force Reserve the next day, and the appointment to command of the new organization and promotion to major general the next day of Brig. Gen. Rollin B. Moore, Jr. (second from right).

Some Growing Pains and the Dual Hat

By 1970, the Office of Air Force Reserve and Headquarters AFRES actively disagreed over their respective responsibilities for the management of the Air Force Reserve. Headquarters AFRES was established as a separate operating agency "with the procedural functions and responsibilities of a major air command," but it quickly became obvious to the Air Force Reserve staff that the assignment of duties was not going to be that simple. The issue was indeed complicated. By normal Air Force standards, the specialized mission of Headquarters AFRES and the need for organizational placement of Air Force Reserve units and bases would have given it unquestioned status as a separate operating agency. However, the management of the Air Force Reserve was made unique by Congress' intention that the Chief of Air Force Reserve be the focal point for supervision, operation, and readiness of the Air Force Reserve.

241

The Air Force Reserve

For that reason alone, Headquarters AFRES would have to complement and respond to the Office of Air Force Reserve. Headquarters AFRES would manage the field operation of Air Force Reserve units under the guidance of the Office of Air Force Reserve.[39]

There was no question in General Marchbanks' mind that his office was competent to guide and control the Air Force Reserve program. His Washington staff made many decisions of the type normally the prerogative of field commanders, such as selection of unit commanders and increased control of the Air Force Reserve budget, and passed them to Robins AFB for implementation. For his part, although as a member of the Air Reserve Forces Policy Committee he had been an ardent advocate of an Air Force Reserve Bureau, General Moore now frequently opposed the bureau-like Office of Air Force Reserve. With time, he tried to gain for his headquarters the major air command status that the Continental Air Command had enjoyed and make it preeminent in Air Force Reserve management. The congressional intent to place the management responsibility for the Air Force Reserve in the Office of Air Force Reserve notwithstanding, as commander of a separate operating agency, General Moore was entitled to communicate directly with the Chief of Staff and Vice Chief of Staff of the Air Force, and he did, especially with Vice Chief General John C. Meyer. By the same token, the Air Force Reserve staff had direct access to the Air Staff and did not hesitate to avail itself of the opportunity. Moreover, some Air Staff officials abetted the Air Force Reserve staff in bypassing General Marchbanks' office and dealt directly with the headquarters at Robins AFB on many issues.[40]

The relationship between the two reserve agencies was made more explicit by the publication of two new directives by the Air Staff in July 1970. A new Headquarters USAF standard operating procedure stipulated that Headquarters AFRES had to advise the Office of Air Force Reserve of all matters it intended to communicate to the Air Staff concerning Air Force Reserve program resources. Then, on July 28, almost two years after activation of Headquarters AFRES, Headquarters USAF published the mission directive for the organization. Delayed by often contentious coordination in the Air Staff, AFR 23–1 was a blow to the advocates of major command status for the Air Force Reserve at Robins AFB. The directive left no doubt that the Office of Air Force Reserve was the office of primary responsibility for Air Force Reserve matters and the only channel for Air Force Reserve dealings with other Air Staff agencies on Air Force Reserve matters.[41]

The new directives notwithstanding, the Air Force Reserve agitation for major command status continued. After visiting Headquarters AFRES in October 1970 and receiving command, daily operations, status of forces, and functional briefings of the command, Maj. Gen. Ernest T. Cragg, Headquarters USAF Program Review Committee Director, agreed with General Moore that the Air Force Reserve was a separate operating agency with major air command

Bill of Rights, Dual Hat, and Total Force

Maj. Gen. Tom E. Marchbanks, Jr. (left), the first Chief of Air Force Reserve, and Maj. Gen. Rollin B. Moore, Jr. (right), the first Commander of Headquarters AFRES. Their tandem leadership of the Air Force Reserve component was hindered by disagreements.

prerogatives.[42] On February 26, 1971, Moore suggested to General Meyer that the Reserve's status as a separate operating agency ought to be reviewed. Moore conceded that while implementation of AFR 23–1 caused the Reserve some difficulties, the major one was its status as a separate operating agency as distinguished from Continental Air Command's role as a major command. He argued that the Air Force Reserve simply did not fit the pattern of the other five separate operating agencies, which had specialized and restricted missions requiring a high degree of supervision by the Air Staff.* Pointing to the Reserve's broad mission, extensive liaison with the Air Staff, hundreds of assigned units, extensive aircraft operations, eleven air bases, and its role as an Air Force planning agent with the Army and Navy in certain areas, General Moore asserted that his command had all the functions, responsibilities, and duties of a major command and that it should be so designated.[43]

At this time, ill health forced General Marchbanks to retire. As first Chief of the Air Force Reserve, he had influenced the direction of his component in many ways. He shared the questionable perception of most career reservists that the Continental Air Command had allowed its secondary missions to dilute its attention to the Air Force Reserve. Shortly after it was announced that

---

*These other agencies were the USAF Academy, the Air Force Accounting and Finance Center, the Air Reserve Personnel Center, the Air Force Data Systems Design Center, and the Aeronautical Chart and Information Center.

The Air Force Reserve

Headquarters AFRES would replace the Continental Air Command at Robins AFB, therefore, General Marchbanks promised that the Air Force Reserve would exist in fact as well as in name and would be "operationally and administratively managed by reservists as a reserve command."[44]

In his first presentation to the Air Force Reserve unit commanders during his only visit to Headquarters AFRES in August 1968, he said that "the words 'Air Force Reserve' should be painted on every wall down here!" Moreover, not only did he want the Air Force Reserve headquarters staff to emphasize Air Force Reserve in its thinking, he demanded that the component itself realize its potential. The new Chief did not believe that the Air Force and the Continental Air Command had ever realized the potential of the Air Force Reserve. General Marchbanks told the field commanders that he and General Moore were dedicated to the objective of giving the Air Force that full capability, and that they would be perfectly willing to abandon commanders who could not come along.[45]

General Marchbanks broke new ground for the Air Force Reserve in fostering a career progression system that would permit reservists from both the unit and individual programs to progress through the Air Force Reserve structure, in grade and assignment, from squadron to the Air Staff and his office. To do this without disturbing the career planning of the regular or reserve officer on extended active duty, he arranged with the Air Force Secretariat to allot a number of Section 265 and 8033 positions to the reserve management structure.[*] In November 1969, believing that the Air Force Reserve pilot force was aging too rapidly, he secured from the Air Staff a handful of spaces in the Air Force undergraduate pilot training program, which trained the Air Force's pilots, with the promise of more training positions to come.[46]

In the final analysis, perhaps General Marchbanks' greatest accomplishment as the first Chief was to retain a flying force in the Air Force Reserve. Subsequent chiefs would fight to modernize and resist forced reorganizations; in General Marchbanks' case it was more a matter of accommodation and endurance. He inherited, for example, great turbulence in a C-119 program comprising fourteen groups. By July 1968, a series of announcements from the Office of the Secretary of Defense implied that all fourteen might be inactivated by the end of fiscal 1969. The Nixon economies dictated that the Department of Defense slash $3 billion from its budget. The Air Force Reserve had no

---

[*]Sections 265 and 8033, Title 10, U.S. Code, provide that additional officers could be placed on extended active duty—not for training—to advise commanders at Headquarters USAF and command headquarters on reserve affairs. Ultimately, the Office of Air Force Reserve and Headquarters AFRES were authorized 40 percent of their officer strength to be 265 officers (AFR 45–22, *Reserve Component Responsibilities*, Oct 31, 1969).

Bill of Rights, Dual Hat, and Total Force

immunity, and the Air Force announced discontinuation of units and the closing of several Air Force Reserve bases. Not all of these inactivations came to pass, but the threat and turbulence were there to challenge the mettle of the Air Force Reserve's first chief. It was the prospect of a dwindling C–119 force that reversed his instinctive opposition to the associate program in which a reserve unit shared the aircraft of a collocated active force unit and augmented it with aircrews and maintenance personnel. Rather than see units inactivated as they lost the C–119s, Marchbanks accepted the associate role for them.[47]

On April 5, 1971, the Senate confirmed the President's nomination of Maj. Gen. Homer I. Lewis to succeed General Marchbanks, and on April 19 General Lewis took the oath of office as Chief of Air Force Reserve.[48] General Lewis had been an active Air Force Reservist since 1937. His most recent assignment had been Reserve Deputy to the Commander, Headquarters Command. He had served on the Air Reserve Forces Policy Committee and had been president of the Reserve Officers Association in 1968 and 1969.[49]

Whatever his anticipations might have been, General Lewis quickly realized that his tour as Chief of Air Force Reserve was to be no sinecure handed to the faithful reservist headed toward the sunset of retirement. He inherited a program pulsating with turbulence. The discord between the Office of Air Force Reserve and Headquarters AFRES, in which the latter was often abetted by some Air Staff officials, had become an embarrassment to General John D. Ryan, Air Force Chief of Staff since August 1969. Thus, he directed the Air Force Inspector General to inspect the Air Force Reserve. Consequently, one of the first documents General Lewis reviewed as Chief was the inspector's report declaring, "There was confusion and controversy throughout the reserve organization concerning the exact role of HQ USAF (AF/RE) and HQ AFRES in the overall management of the Air Force Reserve."[50]

Reinforcing the inspector's report, the only guidance General Lewis received as the new chief from General Meyer was to straighten out the command and management relationships of the two reserve agencies. "You've got to stop this in-house conflict between AF/RE and AFRES," the Vice Chief told Lewis. "That guy down there can come straight to me anytime he wants to; the charts say so. But it's not good business. He ought to come to you, and you straighten it out!"[51] Then, on May 17, 1971, not one month after General Lewis had taken over, General Meyer directed the major air commands and the separate operating agencies to review all support staff functions at numbered air forces and other intermediate headquarters for elimination or reduction in fiscal year 1973.[52]

Influenced by the Air Force inspection, General Cragg's observations, and General Meyer's guidance, General Lewis directed his deputy, Brig. Gen. Donald J. Campbell, to form a study group to evaluate the management structure of the Air Force Reserve once again. Submitted to the Air Force Directorate of Manpower and Organization on September 7, 1971, General

The Air Force Reserve

Campbell's report recommended making the Chief of Air Force Reserve and certain of his directors also Headquarters AFRES officials. This concept was suggested to General Lewis by Col. Zane C. Brewer, his Chief of Plans, Programs, and Resources, as a means of eliminating the conflict between the Robins and Pentagon agencies by unifying their leaders in one person.[53]

Negotiations between the Office of Air Force Reserve and the Directorate of Manpower and Organization resulted in only General Lewis acquiring the second role. The two agencies agreed that the Chief of Air Force Reserve would serve in a dual capacity as the principal adviser to the Chief of Staff on all Air Force Reserve matters and as Commander of the Air Force Reserve Command which would replace the Air Force Reserve at Robins AFB. Although the most effective and economical approach called for organization at a single location under a single manager, certain practical considerations ruled this out for the moment. Because too few facilities were available in the Washington, D.C., area among other reasons, major military headquarters were barred from moving there. Consequently, the dual-hat option, as it became known, was based on the headquarters' remaining at Robins AFB.[54]

On February 26, 1972, the Vice Chief of Staff formally approved the proposal that the Chief of Air Force Reserve also be designated Commander, Air Force Reserve. However, the agreement that the Reserve would become a major air command was deleted during the Air Staff coordination process. Anticipating approval of command status, General Lewis had already reorganized the Office of Air Force Reserve, deleting its operations, logistics, and medical functions. Thereafter, the Air Force Reserve staff at Robins AFB met many of the Air Staff's requirements for information in these areas by funneling them through designated officials on General Lewis' staff.[55]

The dual-hat decision was timely, because on January 26, 1972, General Moore completed his tour of extended active duty as Air Force Reserve Commander and, exercising his civilian employee return rights as an Air Reserve technician, became Commander of the Western Air Force Reserve Region at Hamilton AFB in California. During his 3½-year tour as a commander, the Air Force Reserve flying force expanded from an airlift/rescue force to one that included special operations and fighter units, with many units going into jet operations. Six new aircraft entered the reserve inventory as nineteen squadrons converted to new missions. Yet during this transition, only three major aircraft accidents occurred, and 1969 was accident-free. The units flew their authorized hours and made their new readiness ratings on schedule. General Moore manned the force by virtue of a comprehensive, never-ending recruiting/retention program. In July 1969, Air Force Reserve unit manning was at 84 percent, but by year's end the command had surpassed its authorized strength.[56]

On March 16, 1972, General Lewis assumed command of the Air Force Reserve while retaining his Air Staff role. He declared the goal of achieving unity of component as symbolized by the concentration of the two roles in one man. "There is only one Air Force Reserve and realistically there should be but one commander," he declared.[57] Lewis authorized Brig. Gen. Alfred Verhulst, Air Force Reserve Vice Commander, to act in his name in all matters pertaining to the field operation of the Air Force Reserve except those duties required of the commander by public law and higher headquarters.[58]

Deeming General Lewis' actions insufficient, in July 1972, General Horace M. Wade, the Vice Chief of Staff, directed Lt. Gen. George S. Boylan, Jr., Deputy Chief of Staff for Programs and Resources, to examine the entire Air Force Reserve management structure and the Air Staff functional relationships for possible revision. On September 13, 1972, Brig. Gen. John R. Kern, Jr., then the Director of Manpower and Organization, circulated a draft study which offered five reserve management structure options with sundry alternatives.[59]

Although not recommending any particular option, the study clearly pointed toward adoption of an option under which Headquarters AFRES would be dissolved and the gaining commands would assume reserve training, command, and administration, leaving the Chief of Air Force Reserve with only his advisory role. Challenging the accuracy, objectivity, completeness, and responsiveness of the study, on September 21 General Lewis warned General Boylan that he would not concur in any significant change to the Air Force Reserve management structure.[60]

General Lewis and the Air Reserve staff protested that the proposal would

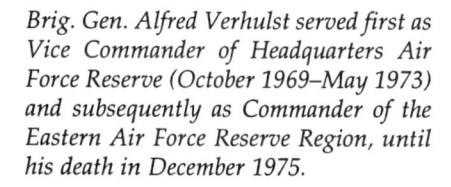

Brig. Gen. Alfred Verhulst served first as Vice Commander of Headquarters Air Force Reserve (October 1969–May 1973) and subsequently as Commander of the Eastern Air Force Reserve Region, until his death in December 1975.

not improve the structure for managing the reserve forces because it was based on unrealistic assumptions. To implement this option would decentralize the management of the Air Force Reserve among thirteen major commands, with a consequent escalation of cost. The gaining commands would undoubtedly relegate reserve missions to a secondary priority, and the Chief of Air Force Reserve would lose his statutory responsibility to control Air Force Reserve funds and facilities. The Air Force Reserve officials argued that management and direction of their force required an expertise that the major commands lacked. But probably the greatest effect of reorganization would be to deter reserve career progression and dilute reserve management opportunities. This would undoubtedly raise a furor of protest and charges of bad faith within the Congress and the professional reserve societies. It would be unlikely that the Office of the Secretary of Defense and the Air Force would welcome the resultant uproar over a proposal that promised no observable advantages.[61]

Never really coordinated through the Air Staff, the study was nevertheless briefed to the Air Force Council on October 13, 1972. As he had promised, General Lewis stood firm on the existing organization and resisted implementation of any of the options. General Lewis' position notwithstanding, the council wanted to approve a new management structure that would eliminate the Air Force Reserve. The members clearly recognized, however, that none of the options would be workable without the full support of the Reserve which, to judge from General Lewis' stance, would not be forthcoming. Their position became academic when General Wade rejected the study and the council's recommendation because it proposed to re-create a system of active force management of the Air Reserve that had been discarded as ineffective. Conceding that nothing was wrong with reservists managing the Air Force Reserve, General Wade promised General Lewis that the management structure would therefore not change.[62] General Lewis' successful defense of the reserve management structure secured the dual-hat concept and completed the work of Public Law 90–168. The law became the second leg—after the Air Reserve technician program—of the tripod on which the Air Force Reserve's stature and excellence eventually rested. The law guaranteed the component's existence under a chief who was a reservist and who became the Chief of Staff's primary adviser on Air Force Reserve matters. Now dual-hatted, the Chief of Air Force Reserve not only represented the force in Headquarters USAF as adviser to the Chief of Staff, but he commanded the force in the field as well. He provided the one voice speaking for the Air Force Reserve that General Meyer had demanded.

Personalities still influenced the level of cooperation, but the ranking reserve official at Robins AFB was merely a vice commander, and everyone in the Pentagon understood that. Years later, General Lewis confirmed his belief that the dual-hatting "was a great idea, and the only way to go!" He said that the initial separation of chief and commander was too dependent upon

Bill of Rights, Dual Hat, and Total Force

personalities. The first two incumbents had clashed, both had access to the Chief of Staff, and the Air Force Reserve structure appeared to be in disarray. It was hard enough to make it work under the dual hat, he said.[63]

Actually, such breakdown in relations as occurred between the Robins and Pentagon Reserve staffs resulted not so much from the dual-hatting of the Chief of Air Force Reserve as it did because staff members in Washington behaved as though they, too, were dual-hatted. As observed by one of General Lewis' successors, Maj. Gen. Richard Bodycombe (whose tenure spanned 1979 to 1982), a conscientious colonel in the Office of Air Force Reserve in his determination to do a good job would try to accomplish more than simply completing his staff work and advising the chief. He would try to execute plans and policies, bypassing Headquarters AFRES and communicating his decisions directly to field units. He would thus be doing the work of the reserve official who was being paid to do that job, which produced confusion and conflict. It was more confusion—and duplication—than conflict because, building upon the foundation laid by General Lewis, his successors, Maj. Gen. William Lyon (1975–1979) and General Bodycombe, kept the joint staffs meeting on a regular basis. The staffs developed an effective working relationship over the years, and the occasional wounded ego was a small price for the effective Air Force Reserve management system that developed after 1972.[64]

By 1973, the early turbulence accompanying the Air Force Reserve management system emplaced by Public Law 90–168 had subsided for the most part, and General Lewis' new challenge was to guide the component under the mantle of Total Force, a concept declared by Secretary of Defense Melvin R. Laird in August 1970.[65]

The Total Force Concept and Policy

In September 1966, stimulated by a number of issues—level of active forces in Southeast Asia, Defense Department initiatives to eliminate some Air Reserve Forces units, and continued uncertainties about the proper role of the Reserve Forces—General McConnell called on the RAND Corporation (a civilian contract study organization frequently used by the Air Force) for help. He asked it to review the roles and missions of the Air Reserve Forces with respect to force structure planning of Air Force by the mid-1970s.[66]

Completing its study in July 1967, RAND declared that regular and reserve forces were complementary systems of a total force. The central problem was to determine the cost and effectiveness of alternative mixes of regular and reserve forces in various mission areas. RAND asserted that the reserve forces should be considered for part of the planned force mix in many mission areas in the 1970s. The study found that the general-purpose forces and related tactical airlift seemed particularly promising mission areas for reserve role, but

The Air Force Reserve

that strategic areas offered less.[67] The Air Reserve Forces Policy Committee and the Air Force Secretariat endorsed the RAND study in September.[68]

On February 17, 1968, General McConnell submitted a seminal paper to the Secretariat summarizing several basic concepts for force development that he had refined into guidance for the Air Staff. He recommended that the Secretary of the Air Force consider his guidance as basic force structure doctrine. McConnell stated that, because of the lower activity of Air Reserve Forces units and the cost of support programs for active personnel, the Air Reserve Forces offered the Air Force significant potential for monetary savings during peacetime. Consequently, where the threat did not require immediate deployment or employment of active forces, the Air Staff intended to have the Air Reserve Forces assume part of the Air Force's total capability in the given mission area. Then, when the regular units were committed, the reserve units could be alerted and made available for either commitment to other contingencies or as follow-up forces. McConnell said the Air Reserve Forces would therefore play an important role in virtually all areas of Air Force responsibility as an integral part of the total Air Force and would be a valuable instrument of national policy. He defined the Total Force concept as "the concurrent consideration of the Total Force, both regular and reserve, to determine the most effective mix which will support the strategy and meet the threat," and he declared that "This Total Force Concept will be employed by the Air Force in all considerations of force structure development and analytical studies leading to force structure size and mix recommendations."[69]

The Chief of Staff was careful to note that the Air Reserve Forces could not be justified solely on their productivity during peacetime. Rather, their justification was their lower peacetime sustaining costs, while at the same time providing skilled resources, operationally ready equipment, and the base from which the regular forces would be expanded in wartime. Moreover, he observed, the Air Reserve Forces should not be tasked for extended periods to provide the total Air Force capability in any single mission area during peacetime. This would merely represent civilianization of the forces and offer no advantage in cost or capability. The Air Reserve Forces could be used, however, to perform certain Air Force functions as an adjunct of their required training. This would result in legitimate manpower and monetary savings to the Air Force.

McConnell posited five general mission areas for the reserve forces—general-purpose and tactical support forces, air defense, the training base, strategic airlift, and support units. He also advised the Secretariat that the Air Staff had validated several alternative missions for the reserve units programmed for inactivation between 1969 and 1973.[*] He said that continuous reviews would

---

[*]On April 17, the Air Staff advised all concerned that ten Air Force Reserve and Air National Guard C–119 units previously programmed for inactivation in fiscal 1969

Bill of Rights, Dual Hat, and Total Force

be conducted to identify additional missions for the Air Reserve Forces and validate their existing missions in the interests of providing the most effective total force possible.[70]

On the same day, Lt. Gen. Hewitt T. Wheless, the Assistant Vice Chief of Staff, directed the Air Staff to apply the Total Force concept to the development of requirements for the Air Reserve Forces. Positing strong, viable Air Reserve Forces to be an important segment of the total Air Force capability, the directive declared it essential that "the total force concept be applied in all aspects of planning, operations, programming, manning and equipping."[71] Thus, by the summer of 1970, the Air Force had adopted a Total Force concept in programming its Air Reserve Forces units.

The Air Force Concept Becomes Defense Policy

When Richard M. Nixon assumed the presidency of the United States on January 20, 1969, his evolving foreign and defense policies affected the Air Force Reserve. His Secretary of Defense, Melvin R. Laird, defined the administration's defense policy as effective deterrence based on a balanced force structure of strategic and theater nuclear weapons and adequate U.S. and allied conventional defenses. The Nixon administration's view of effective deterrence included a high degree of reliance upon the total capabilities of all U.S. forces—active and reserve—and the forces of its allies in a Total Force concept.[72]

In applying this Total Force concept to all U.S. Reserve Forces, on August 21, 1970, Secretary Laird used the very words of the Air Force's various directives in asserting:

> Guard and Reserve units and individuals of the Selected Reserves will be prepared to be the initial and primary source for augmentation of the active forces in any future emergency requiring a rapid and substantial expansion of the active forces.[73]

The Secretary of Defense noted that President Nixon's effort to reduce expenditures would require the Department of Defense to reduce overall strengths and capabilities of the active forces while increasing reliance on the National Guard and reserve units. Consequently, in an approach strikingly similar to the Air Force's, which cited the lower peacetime sustaining costs of reserve units, Secretary Laird directed his department to take a total-force approach to programming, equipping, and employing the forces.

---

would be retained pending further study of new roles and missions (Msg, AFOAPDA to NGB et al, subj: Retention of Reserve Forces, 171701Z Apr 68—AFRES 6C).

251

The Air Force Reserve

As President, Richard M. Nixon (left) advocated defense policies that his Secretary of Defense Melvin R. Laird (right) articulated in the Total Force Concept and the All-Volunteer Force.

The Nixon administration's application of the Total Force concept represented more than just simple economy measures. Reflecting upon his predecessor's failure to call upon the reserve forces during the Vietnam War, the President asserted that the United States would not rely solely upon draftees in future wars. It would call upon reservists who were being paid and trained for just such contingencies.

In January 1973 the Air Staff began an effort to consolidate three directives pertaining to the mission, management, and equipping of the Air Reserve Forces in the name of Total Force and management efficiency. Before the consolidation was effected in March 1975, skeptical reservists and congressmen had induced a new Secretary of Defense to elevate the concept of total force to a policy-level issue.[74] In June 1973, Representative O. C. Fisher complained to William P. Clements, Jr., acting Secretary of Defense, that the authority, responsibility, and, consequently, effectiveness of the chiefs of the various reserve components seemed to be eroding. He noted that the trend had been particularly evident during recent hearings conducted to establish the 1971 Selected Reserve strengths, when witnesses avoided giving direct answers to specific questions and appeared to lack firsthand knowledge about service plans and policies in certain important areas of guard and reserve management.[75]

Congressman Fisher reminded Secretary Clements that it had been the intention of Congress in passing Public Law 90–168 that the chiefs of the reserve components be managers of reserve affairs and that they be solely responsible for administering and supervising the guard and reserve programs.

Bill of Rights, Dual Hat, and Total Force

He suggested that it was time to reemphasize to the armed services their responsibility for full implementation of the Total Force concept and to restate the policy that funds, equipment, management emphasis, and assistance in manning be provided to the degree that would assure proper levels of readiness of the reserves.

In response, in August 1973 James R. Schlesinger, who had become Secretary of Defense on July 2, elevated the Total Force concept to Total Force Policy and initiated an examination of the viability of the reserve forces as part of the total force. He stated that the Total Force Policy integrated the active, guard, and reserve forces into a homogeneous whole. Secretary Schlesinger further declared:

> An integral part of the central purpose of this Department—to build and maintain the necessary forces to deter war and defend our country—is the Total Force Policy as it pertains to the Guard and Reserve. It must be clearly understood that implicit in the Total Force Policy, as emphasized by Presidential and National Security documents, the Congress and Secretary of Defense policy, is the fact that the Guard and Reserve forces *will* be used as the initial and primary augmentation of the Active forces.[76]

Secretary Schlesinger confirmed that the National Guard and the Reserve Chiefs would be staff-level managers of the guard and reserve programs, budgets, policies, funds, force structures, plans, and so on. They would be provided the authority, responsibility, and resources to accomplish their functions effectively. Their management responsibility would be supported by all other appropriate staff agencies.

The Secretary that same day sent Congressman Fisher a copy of his Total Force Policy memorandum. He promised he would make it a point to ensure that as the Defense Department programs proceeded through the planning, programming, and budget cycle that year, proper emphasis would be placed on Selective Reserve readiness. He would further expect all members of his staff and the military departments to contribute actively to the development of reserve forces capable of being the initial and primary augmentation of the active force in wartime.[77]

Also on August 23, the Secretary directed his staff to undertake a study of the guard and reserve forces to include consideration of the available force mix and limits, and the potential of the Selected Reserve in a national emergency.[78] The Total Force study group was to have submitted its report in August 1974, but staffing problems delayed its work, and it did not circulate a comment draft until the end of the year.[79]

The draft study troubled the Air Force in several respects, and its comments to the Office of the Secretary of Defense reflected more than a little institutional paranoia. Inferring some criticism from the group's observation that modernization of the reserve forces was necessary, the Air Force replied

The Air Force Reserve

that it had taken the lead in modernizing its reserves. The Air Force also took strong exception to a number of subjective judgments such as "the attitude of regular forces toward the Reserves ranged from indifference to disdain," "the active forces have generally had a negative attitude toward the Reserves," and the "public image of the Reserves has been poor—a haven for draft dodgers during Vietnam, street patrols in Watts and Wilmington, and impulsive shooters at Kent State." The service protested that such statements were "unjust and untrue." Unjust, perhaps, but some certainly were true—coming out of the Vietnam decade, the public's perception of the reserve forces was exactly as described by the study.[80] The Air Staff should have taken comfort from the study's finding that the Total Force Policy was closer to reality in the Air Force than in any other service and that Air Reserve Forces units had proven readiness and capability.

Although he did not release the Total Force report until September 9, 1975, on the basis of its findings, Secretary Schlesinger issued program guidance on June 21 to the General Counsel of the Offices of the Secretary of Defense, the Secretary of the Army, and the Secretary of the Navy. Because Total Force was further advanced in the Air Force than it was in the other departments, the Secretary issued no guidance to the Air Force other than some generally applicable to all services regarding the Individual Ready Reserve.[81]

Revision of AFR 45–1 in the Name of Total Force

In January 1973, General Wade, Air Force Vice Chief of Staff, directed General Boylan to consolidate several Air Force regulations pertaining to the mission, organization, and equipping of the Air Reserve Forces.[82] The first attempt to combine the directives encountered strong objection from the Office of Air Force Reserve and the National Guard Bureau, thus delaying publication for more then two years. The initial objective seemed simple enough, but two diametrically opposed approaches immediately put the whole process into tension. Waving the Total Force banner and supported by the gaining commands, the Air Staff programs community ventured to invest the latter with greater responsibilities for supervision, training, safety, and inspection. For its part, invoking Public Law 90–168 and the authority it invested in the chief, the Air Force Reserve tried to reclaim some of the management and supervisory responsibilities the Continental Air Command had lost to the gaining commands in 1960. Wary of proposed changes to a system in which the Air National Guard generally fared well, Guard officials sided with their Reserve colleagues.

Objecting to a third draft of the proposed consolidation in April 1973, General Campbell, who had overseen the group in 1971 that prepared the initial dual-hat report, protested that the draft passed great authority to the gaining commands and eliminated proven procedures for managing the Air Force Reserve. He insisted that the responsibilities for training and safety were inherent to command, and splitting them for training, safety, and operational readiness violated the management principle that responsibility be accompanied by authority. Campbell asserted no evidence existed that the proposed changes would improve the combat capability or the responsiveness of the component, and he saw no advantage in combining the three directives.[83]

Six months later, as the revised directive neared final Air Staff coordination, the Office of Air Force Reserve and the National Guard Bureau jointly prepared a substitute version of the proposed regulation. In offering the reserve forces substitute, Air National Guard Director Maj. Gen. I. G. Brown objected that the Air Staff version contained major ambiguities in defining responsibilities for operational readiness of the Air National Guard and in what constituted "supervision of training." General Brown also objected to the omission of certain passages guaranteeing the National Guard Bureau's traditional role as an integral part of the Air Staff and as the channel of communication for all Air National Guard matters between the Air Force and the several states. Otherwise, he and General Lewis noted that the language the Air Staff wanted to change derived from the experience of almost thirty years which had included successful mobilizations of the two components by the Air Force during the Korea, Berlin, Cuba, *Pueblo*, and Southeast Asia contingencies. Protesting that the objective of the Air Staff's proposal was not simple consolidation but was revision of the basic legal structure and operation of the components, the two reserve leaders demanded a comprehensive explanation of the shortcomings, and how the revised directive would correct them. Expressing their desire to cooperate with the Air Staff, the two officials asserted that many of the problems could have been avoided if the two agencies had been invited to participate in the Air Staff's deliberations from the beginning. Finally, Generals Lewis and Brown recommended that the proposed directive be presented to the Air Reserve Forces Policy Committee and then to the Secretary of the Air Force for approval.[84]

After hearing another explanation of the subject from General Boylan, and under some prodding by the Air Force Secretariat, Chief of Staff General George S. Brown reluctantly accepted the recommendation for policy committee review. When the committee met on June 20, 1974, primed by activist Air Force Reservists in the field, the guard and reserve members expressed skepticism about what the real issue was. They questioned why the Air Staff was advocating major changes in the policy relations among the Air Force and its two successful reserve components. They rejected the explanation of the active force members that the proposal did not represent a major policy change—that it was simply an attempt to clear up the ambiguities of organization responsibilities and authority, clarify the roles of the gaining commands and the Air Reserve Forces, and set the whole down in writing.[85]

The Air Force Reserve

Before it would take any position, the policy committee appointed a subcommittee to clarify five issues: responsibility for operational readiness, supervision of training, channels of communication, coordination of directives, and deletion of items covered in other directives. After meticulous review of each of the basic issues, on June 21, the policy committee recommended a revision that retained some duplication with other directives in the interests of emphasis, confirmed the right of the gaining commands to assure that Air Reserve Forces units were ready to function effectively upon mobilization, made the Commander of the Air Force Reserve responsible to the Chief of Staff of the Air Force for the operational readiness and efficiency of the total Air Force Reserve program, and defined the Chief of the National Guard Bureau and the Commander of the Air Force Reserve as the channels of communication on all matters pertaining to their units.[86]

The leaders of the two reserve components and the director of plans accepted the proposed regulation as revised by the Air Reserve Forces Policy Committee and recommended its approval for publication. Although delayed in the process as some Air Staff agencies awaited the outcome of the Department of Defense Total Force studies before adding their imprimatur, the consolidated directive was published as AFR 45–1 on March 3, 1975. The new regulation set forth the purpose, policy, and responsibilities for the Air Force Reserve within the context of the Total Force Policy. The directive defined the mission of the Air Reserve Forces as providing

> combat units, combat support units, and qualified personnel for active duty in the Air Force to support augmentation requirements and to perform such peacetime missions as are compatible with ARF training requirements and the maintenance of mobilization readiness.[87]

The regulation asserted that the Total Force Policy and the concomitant reliance on the reserve forces in an emergency emphasized the importance of having combat-ready Air Reserve Forces ready to perform missions when needed. To ensure the proper composition of the total Air Force, the Air Reserve Forces structure and programs were to be reviewed each year as an integral part of the planning-programming-budgeting process. These reviews were to occur in the Air Staff Board structure with full participation of Air Reserve Forces members. Finally, the directive included the revision put forth by the Air Reserve Forces Policy Committee, confirming the responsibility of the Air Reserve Forces for their command, training, and readiness.

With the publication of AFR 45–1 in March 1975, the Air Force and the Air Force Reserve reached the accommodation they had sought to reconcile the implications of Public Law 90–168 with Total Force. The law gave the reserve component the right to manage itself and command its forces in peacetime. Reservists trained themselves, but conceding that the active force had the right to ensure the readiness of the forces it would call upon in an emergency, the Air

Bill of Rights, Dual Hat, and Total Force

Force Reserve agreed, as it always had, that the gaining commands were entitled to set standards and evaluate reserve performance against these standards. As concept or policy, Total Force pertained to the programming, planning, and employment of Reserve Forces, not to their management or command in peacetime. That was the benefit of Public Law 90–168.

As a group, the Chiefs of Air Force Reserve have agreed that the greatest benefit the Air Force gave the Air Force Reserve was the management structure in which all key positions were held by reservists—the only service in which this is true. By accepting the intent and rationale of Public Law 90–168, if reluctantly, the Air Force permitted a succession of reserve leaders to rise to leadership positions and bring their perspective and experience as career reservists to bear to produce a ready, responsive Air Force Reserve.

Upon retirement in 1975, General Lewis acknowledged that ". . . the Air Force took 90–168 and they did it 100 percent properly. They took the law, and they saluted smartly, and they did it. That's what we have today—management of reserves by reserves."[88] General Bodycombe always insisted that the Air Force did three very important things for the Air Force Reserve which made the component strong. The first was to implement Public Law 90–168, giving the Reserve a strong management structure and establishing the Office of the Chief of Air Force Reserve as a viable agency. The other two were to provide modern equipment and the real-world missions to go with it. "The Air Force gave us the management structure, the equipment, and the real-world missions, and then it let us perform them all around the world," he frequently remarked.[89]

What Lewis and Bodycombe said publicly and for the record was correct. As long as the Reserve Chiefs maintained their vigilance, the Air Force, if reluctantly so, honored the underlying philosophy of the law. What the Air Force gave, however, it could take away. With justification, the Air Force insisted that it control its components. The law, on the other hand, gave the reserve components a degree of autonomy. It was necessary, therefore, for the Air Force and its civilian components to establish the accommodation that was to unify them as a whole. In succeeding years the economic complexities of manpower management would bring down external challenges upon the Air Force, and only a unified establishment was able to resist them.

10

Administering and Training Individuals, 1953–1981

> The lesson to be learned here is that an attempt to have half a program was far worse than no program at all. A decision to correctly fund and back the program would have allowed units to develop and maintain an important deterrent in the defense posture of our country. On the other hand, disbanding the program in the beginning would have saved millions of dollars which could have been utilized in other reserve programs which were considered an important aspect of the overall Air Force mission. By choosing the middle road, we committed one of the worst errors in the history of the reserve program.
>
> —Col. William F. Berry, Cmdr, 8574 AFRRG

In addition to organized combat units, the Air Force Reserve included various programs for training reservists as individuals. Sometimes the Air Force grouped these individuals into administrative units for the convenience of managing them. Such organizations were never intended to be mobilized, and their members were managed strictly as individuals. The program structures under which these people were administered and trained changed from time to time, but really only two categories of individual reservists existed: those specifically assigned to an element of the active force for mobilization in wartime, and those who had no specific mobilization assignment and were considered as replacements for casualties. The first group was known successively as Part I augmentees, mobilization assignees, and mobilization

The Air Force Reserve

augmentees. They were authorized pay for inactive duty and active duty training which was supposed to be conducted by their active force unit of assignment. The other individuals were the Part II or III augmentees or reinforcement designees. They trained with the Air Defense Command, the Continental Air Command, or Headquarters AFRES; were authorized inactive duty training pay only briefly in the mid-1950s; and were authorized active duty training tours when funds were available. Programs for the administration and training of the two categories of individuals paralleled one another for about thirty years, until 1975, when, having fallen into disuse, the last program for the unassigned reservists was discarded.

The Unassigned Air Force Reservists

By July 1953, the administration and training of individual members of the Air Force Reserve had become chaotic. Unappealing as it was, the Volunteer Air Reserve training program was, nevertheless, competing for members in specialist training centers under the approved Long-Range Plan recommended by General Smith's committee in 1951. Meanwhile, another provision of the Long-Range Plan, a network of air reserve districts to administer the individual programs on a geographic basis, was proving too costly.*

General Nathan F. Twining, who had become Chief of Staff in June 1953, appointd General Johnson, the Continental Air Command Commander since December 1952, to chair the Reserve Program Review Board to assess the reserve program. General Johnson recognized that the structure of the training program for individuals could not be left in the disarray then perceived by reservists and that its organization had to be simplified. Adopting a plan the Continental Air Command staff had developed, his Reserve Program Review Board recommended that the Air Force consolidate the Volunteer Air Reserve training structure, the specialist training centers, and the districts into air reserve centers. The Air Force approved the consolidation and directed the Continental Air Command to organize the first fifty of a planned ninety-three centers on April 1, 1959.[1]

The Air Reserve Center Program

The new air reserve centers were Regular Air Force units responsible to organize, administer, and train reserve units and individuals and to conduct local Air Force public relations programs through the discarded Volunteer Air

---

*The Volunteer Air Reserve Training program and the approved Long-Range Plan of the Smith committee are discussed in Chapters 3 and 5.

Administering and Training Individuals, 1953–1981

Reserve training program's network of air reserve units.[2] The centers conducted specialized and general individual training. Specialized training was refresher training in specific Air Force specialties or career fields. It consisted of lecture, shop, and laboratory instruction conducted by permanent party personnel, reservists, or civilian instructors. Mobilization assignees who participated in specialized training were authorized twenty-four paid drills and fifteen days of active duty for training annually. Technical courses were taught by contract instructors as were, for the most part, all courses conducted at air reserve squadrons and groups geographically detached from their parent air reserve centers.

As the descendent of the composite and Volunteer Air Reserve training programs, general training emphasized orientation training in Air Force policies and organization. It consisted of staff exercises, lectures, films, and field trips. Reservists enrolled in general training were not paid for the twelve two-hour training periods they attended annually. Course materials were prepared by the Air University, and instructors included reservists, military and civilian guest speakers. The general training program included professional training for reservists who did not require additional schooling in the rudiments of their career fields. These included physicians, lawyers, and public relations experts whom the Air Force wished to draw into reserve activities to keep them current in Air Force practice in their respective fields.[3]

Professional training was usually organized into professional flights and practical projects in lieu of attending general training sessions. The information services flights, for example, often helped the center commander discharge his public relations responsibilities. Although contributing generously of their time and energy, like other general trainees, members of the professional flights earned retirement points but not pay for training.

Specialized training courses of the air reserve center program became popular and recruiting was comparatively simple. Initially, the program contained a basic dichotomy. A specialized training course was open to any reservist in the corresponding Air Force specialty if he met time-in-grade, physical, and availability requirements. Even if he were in a pay status, he did not have to be assigned to a specific mobilization position. As a result, some courses, notably those for flight operations and administrative officers, had far more enrollees than were needed, while others had too few.

In 1955, however, reflecting the tenor of a January 4 Twining memo, the Air Force finally attempted to design a reserve program based upon mobilization requirements. In May, Headquarters USAF set an annual ceiling on officers in pay status and soon forbade further assignments to specialized training in any status. Thereafter, the specialized training program was bound by restrictions, and headlong recruiting for it was halted.[4]

The Air Force Reserve

Mobilization Requirements and the Match-Merge

During the latter half of 1955, the Air Staff declared that all reservists occupying M-Day positions, regardless of program element, had to be in the Ready Reserve and available on M-Day. The Ready Reserve included all Category A units, all mobilization assignees and designees, and all training designation positions in the air reserve center program.[5]

In November, the Air Staff also provided the major air commands their mobilization requirements for individual reservists by grade and skill. This number was derived from the requirement established for M-Day combat-ready Air Reserve Forces to augment the projected 137-wing Air Force. The numbers for the Air Reserve Forces were based upon the established mobilization requirement of 349,000—the Service Callable Reserve of the National Reserve Plan—which included the 51 units defined by General Twining's January 4 memorandum. The war strength manpower requirements calculated to be met by the Air Reserve Forces unit programs was 234,000, leaving 115,000 personnel to be provided by the Air Force Reserve[*] through such individual training programs as mobilization assignee/designee, air reserve center, and aircrew replacement training programs. On December 1, 1955, the Air Staff directed the major commands to align their reserve training programs with their actual requirements. Their completed actions left the Continental Air Command with the responsibility to train about 94,000 reservists through its air reserve centers.[6]

The process of matching the reservists enrolled in the Continental Air Command's air reserve center program against the Air Force's actual mobilization requirement for individuals became known as the Match-Merge. After testing the concept in 1956, the Air Force conducted actual matching in three of the next four years. The war mobilization requirement was divided in three formal parts. Part I consisted of the major commands' mobilization assignees, which they recruited and trained themselves. Part II was the portion of the major commands' requirement that was beyond their capability to train and, therefore, underwent inactive duty training in Continental Air Command's air reserve centers. Part III comprised all the rest, that is, individuals the Air Force calculated it would need to replace attrition in wartime. Part III reservists were assigned to the Continental Air Command for training in the air reserve centers. Any reservist not matched against a Part I or II requirement after June 30, 1957, became ineligible for active duty training, and those who had not procured a Ready Reserve position by early August were reassigned to a nonpay element.[7]

---

[*]The Air Force Organization Act of 1951 limited the Air National Guard to units. The Air Force Reserve, therefore, provided the entire individual requirement.

Administering and Training Individuals, 1953–1981

The withdrawal of pay from reservists not assigned to mobilization positions devastated their morale. Many reserve airmen would not participate in any training program without pay. For their part, on the other hand, possessing fourteen or fifteen years' service toward a twenty-year retirement at age sixty, most officers hung on regardless. But they did so with a mixture of resignation and defiance, resigned to the fact that more blows would follow, but defying the Air Force to do its worst.[8]

Match-Merge had a confusing and harsh effect upon reservists, especially Part II participants in the air reserve centers. The process of matching seemed to proceed without rhyme or reason as the major commands continually changed their requirements. The process was so fluid at times that even officials in Headquarters Continental Air Command and the Office of the Assistant Chief of Staff for Reserve Forces had a difficult time in keeping up with the status of the alignment.[9]

It was in the conduct of Match-Merge that the Continental Air Command took a fruitless stand on one of the thornier issues of Air Force Reserve participation. In August 1956, Lt. Gen. Charles B. Stone III, General Johnson's successor in December 1955 as commander, appointed Maj. Gen. Robert E. L. Eaton, Tenth Air Force Commander, to examine the individual training programs. General Eaton's board included representatives from Headquarters Continental Air Command and its numbered air forces, a few air reserve center commanders, and several senior reservists. In addition to making significant recommendations for the development of noncommissioned officer management and leadership courses, the Eaton Board asserted that everything possible should be done to enable Part III reservists to remain active. The board specifically urged that general training be retained and improved, that all forms of center training be open to all categories of reservists, and that, funds permitting, Part III reservists be given annual, paid two-week tours of active duty for training. Despite its obvious irrelevance to mobilization requirements, the Eaton Board urged the retention of general training. Applying some of General Stratemeyer's arguments for retaining older reservists in the program to perform general training, the board asserted that the elders supported the active establishment and helped them inform the general public on the need for a strong and ready Air Force. To retain this large group of reservists, Eaton insisted that it was necessary to develop a program that was broad in nature, qualitative in content, and presented in a stimulating manner. His board believed that with relatively minor changes, the general training program could attain these objectives.[10]

Maj. Gen. Maurice R. Nelson, the Continental Air Command Vice Commander, presented the Eaton Board's appeal to the Air Staff in November 1956. He pointed out that about 30,000 reservists were then in general training and that the number would increase under the stimulus of the reserve legislation of 1952 and 1955. He asserted that the language of the Armed

The Air Force Reserve

Maj. Gen. Robert E. L. Eaton, as Commander of the Tenth Air Force before becoming the Assistant Vice Chief of Staff for Reserve Forces, headed the individual Reserve Training Board which fruitlessly recommended several far-reaching steps to invigorate the Air Forces individual reserve training programs.

Forces Reserve Act of 1952 imposed a legal obligation upon the Air Force to train Standby Reservists.

General Nelson also pointed out that the Air Force Vitalization and Retirement Act of 1948 offered paid retirement to reservists at 60 years of age who had 20 years of satisfactory service and had served on active or inactive duty. Since thousands of reservists then in the Standby Reserve were participating in training with the promised goals of promotion and retirement, General Nelson argued that the Air Force was obligated to continue the general training program. The Continental Air Command could no longer sustain the program within its own resources; therefore, Nelson urged the Air Staff to define a requirement for reservists in the general training program and provide the command the necessary budget and manpower authorization to support the requirement.[11]

Eaton and Nelson, of course, based their whole case on the perceived obligation to ensure that reservists had good years for retirement. Some Air Staff officials were sympathetic to the problem, but the new policy regarding mobilization requirements, along with the developing budget crisis, forced Headquarters USAF to reject the command's plea. Replying in June 1957, Brig. Gen. Cecil E. Combs, the Air Force Deputy Director of Personnel Procurement and Training, rejected the arguments that the Air Force had an obligation to provide training for Standby Reservists. Agreeing it would be desirable to continue general training, he urged the command to try to provide some form of general training within the framework of facilities, manpower support, and

Administering and Training Individuals, 1953–1981

funds provided for required Ready Reserve programs.[12]

In the spring of 1959, the Air Staff declared a year's moratorium on major changes in the individual war augmentation requirement, and the next alignment did not occur until the summer of 1960. By that time, the Air Force had extensively reviewed the conduct and management of its reserve programs and had devised a new management structure for the Air Force Reserve as a whole, and an entirely new program for individual reservists.

Revision in 1960 and the Air Force Reserve Recovery Program

Along with transferring greater responsibility to the gaining commands for the training of Air National Guard and Air Force Reserve units, the 1960 reorganization of the Air Reserve Forces was significant for its effect upon the Air Force Reserve's individual program. In its most trenchant recommendation, the Reserve Forces Review Group, chaired by Maj. Gen. Sory Smith, Fourth Air Force Commander, suggested the formation of reserve aircraft recovery and alternate base units to conduct postattack missions. The primary mission of a reserve recovery unit would be to augment Air Force bases during a crisis. The recovery units would provide disaster assistance to Air Force units and operate civilian airports suitable for the recovery of Air Force aircraft dispersed during an attack.[13]

In September 1960, the Continental Air Command activated six base support units and seven Air Force Reserve recovery groups to test the feasibility of reserve units performing the general mission of survival, support, and recovery following an attack. The command recruited, trained, and administered the base support units with the cooperation and assistance of the base commander concerned. Unit members received on-the-job training on the base using available equipment and facilities.[14]

The recovery units were to provide emergency medical assistance and disaster control augmentation for Air Force units and installations damaged during an initial nuclear exchange. They were required to be capable of organizing and regrouping residual Air Force resources and resuming Air Force proficiency, providing emergency support for aircraft and aircrews dispersed or recovered at civilian airfields, and providing a domestic emergency backup communications system. The program gave reservists complete responsibility for their recovery units, including manpower, facilities, management, and operations. Since the reserve operation would depend on civilian support for supplies and equipment, the program drew the communities in which the units were located into the defense of the United States. It was all very nebulous, though. Specific details about the units' mission, their manning documents, training standards, facilities requirements, and equipping policies had to be developed.[15]

The Air Force Reserve

As Fourth Air Force Commander, Maj. Gen. Sory Smith headed the Reserve Program Review Group which recommended in 1959 that the gaining commands assume much of the Continental Air Command's responsibility for training the Air Force Reserve. In addition, he promoted a reserve recovery program.

Carlisle P. Runge, Assistant Secretary of Defense for Manpower, sanctioned the program, authorizing the Air Force to activate an additional 75 Air Force Reserve recovery groups and 193 squadrons on July 1, 1961. Almost immediately, however, Deputy Secretary of Defense Roswell L. Gilpatric asked for extensive additional information on the program and restricted its members to only 24 paid drills annually, except for the original test groups which were still authorized 48 paid drills.[16] Joseph V. Charyk, Under Secretary of the Air Force, submitted the requested additional information in the form of a revised program on August 28, 1961, and defended the need for 48 paid drills, claiming that the recovery mission was a valid military requirement for which the units required a high degree of proficiency.[17]

Upon conducting further analysis, Secretary Runge's staff protested that the Air Force Reserve recovery program did not represent a valid military requirement, that the program's concept had been inadequately coordinated with the plans of other Air Force and government agencies, and that the Air Force should be directed to phase out the program. The Air Force official who bore the brunt of liaison with the Office of the Secretary of Defense on the recovery program was Benjamin W. Fridge, Reserve Deputy to Lewis S. Thompson, the Air Force's Special Assistant for Manpower, Personnel, and Reserve Affairs. Although Mr. Fridge thought that the program made much more sense than the classroom training the reservists had been receiving, he called up the political argument to justify its retention. An Air Force Reserve activist, he knew that the recovery program was strongly endorsed by such organizations as the Reserve Officers Association and the Air Force Association, and it had the active support of many congressmen. The Air Force had introduced the program in a blare of publicity, and he believed that it would be a political mistake to discontinue it out of hand.[18]

For his part, Secretary Runge actually agreed that the reserve components should provide a recovery capability for military purposes and should support civil defense. His question was whether the requested expansion of the program was necessary to meet the postattack airfield requirement. He got no help from the Joint Chiefs of Staff who gave the program superficial support and recommended that the Secretary of the Air Force provide the answers. Runge also knew that neither the Secretary nor the Deputy Secretary of Defense was disposed to invest more money in any reserve program, and that both were particularly reluctant to support the Air Force Reserve recovery program. Nevertheless, well briefed by Benjamin Fridge, Runge understood the political ramifications of a precipitate cut in the program and offered what he thought was "the most feasible solution from a political standpoint." On November 30, he recommended that the program be continued at the 1962 level pending the submission of additional data by the Air Force, thereby postponing the hard decisions.[19]

Secretary Gilpatric accepted Mr. Runge's advice and continued the Air Force Reserve recovery and base support programs on a provisional basis within the 1962 budget level of $11 million, specifically limiting the participants to 24 paid drills annually. In addition, as suggested by the Joint Chiefs of Staff, Secretary Gilpatric asked the Secretary of Air Force to rejustify the programs.[20] The Air Force submitted a revised program on April 25, 1962, justifying an increase of 5,555 drill pay spaces in the recovery program for fiscal 1964 along with the requested 48 paid drills and funds in the amount of $17.3 million to support these increases. Secretary Gilpatric initially approved the proposal, but late in November, still dubious of the program's efficacy, Secretary McNamara directed that the program be continued on the same interim basis of 20,000 people, 24 paid drills, and $10.8 million in funds.[21]

Secretary McNamara's ruling coincided with a concerted Air Force effort to demonstrate that the Air Force Reserve recovery program had already proved itself. During the Cuban missile crisis of October and November 1962 the Strategic Air Command and the Air Defense Command dispersed aircraft to several civilian airfields including some where reserve recovery units were located. Thereupon, 349 reservists from 34 recovery units and 7 other Air Force Reserve units expended 6,313 man-days in support of those dispersed units. Most of this support was conducted by individuals or, at best, teams of individuals, as unit effort was initiated at only three locations. At one of these locations the recovery unit did not receive notice of the dispersal until after the first aircraft had landed, and owing to the lack of specialist personnel and

The Air Force Reserve

equipment, it was unable to satisfy the complete needs of the dispersal aircraft and crews. Although recovery units were located at or near other airports to which active force units dispersed, they either were not asked to or did not provide support. At one location, a recovery unit offered to provide support, but it was turned down by the commander of the dispersed unit.[22]

Nevertheless, asserting that this slight action had demonstrated the worth of the program, Secretary Zuckert appealed to Secretary McNamara to authorize the requested $17.3 million for fiscal 1964. Unimpressed, Secretary McNamara continued the restricted program defined on November 30.[23] To trim the total program to the reduced authorization of people, the Air Force discontinued the test base support groups on December 31, 1962.[24]

By the spring of 1963, two developments were under way which would have the cumulative effect of ending the Air Force Reserve recovery program within two years: the General Accounting Office was reviewing the program at the request of Congress, and the Air Force had finally moved to develop an active force survival, recovery, and reconstitution program. Pending completion of these actions, the Air Force Reserve recovery program drifted uncertainly through 1963.

A team of the 9223d Air Force Reserve Recovery Squadron, Port Columbus, Ohio, simulates decontaminating a crew of the Strategic Air Command's 900th Air Refueling Squadron from Sheppard AFB, Texas, in 1962.

Administering and Training Individuals, 1953–1981

The Comptroller General submitted his report on the program to Congress and the President on February 17, 1964. The report criticized the Air Force for establishing reserve recovery squadrons at 200 airports nationwide without ascertaining the needs of the major Air Force commands the squadrons were intended to serve. The Air Force was then reassigning or was considering reassigning more than 100 of the reserve squadrons to airports that were located in areas of high vulnerability to enemy attack, had inadequate facilities or otherwise did not meet the needs of the major commands, were unreasonably long distances from the home cities of the units, or were already occupied by military units capable of performing the recovery mission.

Consequently, more than half the reserve recovery squadrons would be of little value to the Air Force in an emergency. Moreover, unless the Air Force could find some way of adequately utilizing these squadrons, more than half of $30 million appropriated to date for the reserve recovery program would have been largely wasted. The report also charged that the Air Force had never demonstrated the need for reserve recovery squadrons to provide ground support to aircraft dispersed from their home bases to less vulnerable airports during periods of increased tension. It also observed that the unlikelihood of effectively using recovery units during a prehostility period to support dispersal of aircraft and aircrews was demonstrated during the Cuban missile crisis when the Air Force operating commands dispersed their aircraft with only minor assistance from a few recovery units.

The Comptroller General, therefore, recommended that the Secretary of Defense immediately inactivate Air Force Reserve recovery squadrons that had no foreseeable need and inactivate additional units indicated in a study under way by the Air Force. Also, since planning for survival in the event of an enemy attack would concern the Army and the Navy as well as the Air Force, the comptroller recommended that the Joint Chiefs of Staff review the Air Force survival plans in conjunction with the plans of the other military services.[25]

Completed on February 21, 1964, just a few days after the Comptroller General issued his report, the long-awaited Air Force–revised Air Force Reserve recovery program confirmed 131 units as unnecessary to Air Force recovery requirements. After some discussion between Secretaries McNamara and Zuckert, the Continental Air Command discontinued the units at various times before August 25.[26]

By the time it inactivated the last of these units in August, the Air Force had abandoned any hope of retaining the remaining 155. Refinement of the Air Force's formal survival, recovery, and reconstitution plan confirmed what Secretary Runge's staff had claimed all along: that the Air Force Reserve recovery program did not have a valid mission. On December 9, Secretary Zuckert conceded that the units should be phased out, and the Continental Air Command completed this action on March 25, 1965.[27]

The Air Force Reserve

Reflecting the bitterness of the reservists eliminated by the inactivations, the terminal histories of the discontinued units included frank condemnation of inadequate planning and infidelity by defense officials. Typical were the remarks of Col. William F. Berry, Commander of the 8574th Air Force Reserve Recovery Group at Decatur, Illinois:

> At the beginning of the recovery program morale was at the highest the reserve program had ever known. Here was something reservists could get their teeth into while at the same time enjoy the feeling that their contribution to the overall Air Force mission was an important cog in the defense of this country. Enthusiasm, excitement, initiative, desire and confidence were contagious from Maine to California. Today, among the reservists who have been associated with the recovery program, morale is at a low ebb. Failure of the program and the disintegrated morale [have] been the result of what seemed to many a slow but continuous bleeding of resources and personnel.
>
> It is almost as if the plan to disband was an annex to the plan which conceived, but the decision was to bleed a little each month until there was nothing left. Half pay, inferior equipment, curtailed strength and ultimate deactivation have sapped our initiative and killed our morale.
>
> There is no way to place the guilt; I was among the worst offenders in building hope on promises I could not deliver, in maintaining confidence where all the signs pointed to failure.[28]

At the core of the reservists' bitterness and disillusionment over the demise of the Air Force Reserve recovery program was their perception that, finally, the Air Force Reserve had had a program for individuals that actually amounted to something. They had gotten out of the classrooms and meeting halls and had actually done something. They trained to provide minor aircraft maintenance, messing and billeting facilities for aircrews, decontamination of aircraft, emergency operation of airfields, crash and rescue services, weather information, communication services, information services, supplies, medical support, ground transportation, and basic intelligence services. In the civilian communities they found sources of the supplies and equipment they needed to perform these services, and for more than three and one-half years they practiced performing these services, sometimes in cooperation with such major air commands as the Military Air Transport Service, but mostly on their own. In 1964, many units participated in a Federal Aviation Agency civil defense airlift exercise designed to test the nation's general aviation fleet in a national emergency. The agency's administrator, Najeeb E. Halaby, was effusive in his praise of the reservists' performance.[29]

Some Air Force officials blamed the Secretary of Defense for allowing the program to fail. During the period of the recovery program, Lt. Gen. William E. Hall, successively Assistant Chief of Staff for Reserve Forces and Commander of the Continental Air Command, charged officials in the Office of the Secretary of Defense with breaking faith with the Air Force Reserve because

Administering and Training Individuals, 1953–1981

they had known from the outset that the recovery program would require more drill-pay spaces than were ever forthcoming. General Eaton, also Assistant Chief of Staff for Reserve Forces during part of the period, thought that Defense Department officials simply did not understand the need for a recovery program.[30]

Whatever the merit of these accusations, sufficient blame existed for the program's failure that the Air Force could share in some of it. This was a classic case of the Air Force rushing into a reserve program without properly defining the parameters for the endeavor and providing it with the proper resources. Lacking input from the major commands, the Air Staff never developed the definitive requirement which the Office of the Secretary of Defense sought throughout, and following its natural bent to put programs where the reservists were, the Air Force established scores of recovery units at places where there was no need. It was easy for such agencies as the Air Force Auditor General and the General Accounting Office to identify these locations.

Reserve Element Training

About 8,200 people remained in the Air Force Reserve recovery program when it ended, and the Continental Air Command tried to accommodate all of them within its reserve programs. About 1,500 went into organized units, 253 acquired Part I augmentation positions, and about 2,900 yielded to the inevitable and retired. This left about 3,600 reservists who drifted back into the Part III program and tried to hang on. Because of geographical dispersion and other reasons, 6,808 members of the individual training program had not been absorbed by the recovery program in 1961 and were placed in an approved program element called Reserve Element Training in July 1961. It was this program that assimilated the remaining of 3,600 reservists from the recovery program in March 1965.[31]

Although the Continental Air Command proposed on several occasions thereafter that the Part III program be removed from its life-support systems and be allowed to die, the Air Staff sustained it for another ten years. In 1962 and 1963, the Reserve Element Training program offered project training in the legal, information, medical, intelligence, and research and development career fields as well as classroom training with courses in education and training, administrative services, personnel, and individual survival and recovery.[32]

At Air Staff direction, the Continental Air Command experimented with specialty training, reminiscent of the specialist training centers of 1952 and 1953. Lasting until September 1967, specialist training failed because junior and noncommissioned officers did not participate. They were simply reluctant to put the same effort they had invested in the recovery program into the new program while its future depended upon the outcome of a test program.[33]

The Air Force Reserve

When the Office of Air Force Reserve was established in Headquarters USAF, and Headquarters AFRES replaced Continental Air Command at Robins AFB in 1968, the two new agencies energetically tried to vitalize the individual training programs. On June 30, 1970, fewer than 6,000 reservists were active in the Part III program. At this point, reservists were offered opportunities to participate in the Staff Development Course and the National Security Management Course as well as in seven varieties of project training. The Air Force Reserve introduced an ROTC assistance program availing the opportunity to gain training credit by offering liaison and counseling to ROTC units. Other reserve officers participated in judge advocate and chaplain area representative programs and in the Air Force Academy liaison officer program. Finally, some reservists received training credit for their roles as staff and training officers in the reserve squadrons and flights of the Reserve Element Training program.[34]

Nothing that the Office of Air Force Reserve or Headquarters AFRES did, however, could breathe life back into the dying Reserve Element Training program. Decline in participation was reflected in the organizational structure of the program as the Reserve found it necessary to discontinue air reserve squadrons. The Air Force prescribed that each squadron have a membership of at least twenty-five reservists, and as mandatory retirements continued to have their effect, squadrons fell below the minimum manning standard, and the reserve element discontinued them. Attrition accelerated in the early 1970s as World War II veterans with thirty years of service retired and were not replaced by youngsters for whom the lifeless program held no attraction.[35]

On April 15, 1975, the 9342d Air Reserve Squadron in Los Angeles became the last unit remaining in the program. The 9342d was still well above minimums, but the Chief of Air Force Reserve approved the recommendation of the Air Force Reserve Vice Commander that the unit be disbanded on September 30, 1975. On June 4, 1975, when the Reserve published the order advising the squadron of its intention, the 9342d Air Reserve Squadron had thirty-five members. Displaying remarkable tenacity, when it submitted its final report on September 5, 1975, it had lost only one additional member.[36]

The discontinuance of the Part III Reinforcement Designee training program left two training vehicles for the individual Air Force Reservists: the professional squadrons and the mobilization augmentee programs. Sixteen air reserve squadrons remained as administrative vehicles for reservists engaged in project training, school, or intern training in the public affairs, legal, chaplain, and medical career fields until the Air Reserve Personnel Center inactivated the public affairs squadrons on July 1, 1981.[37] While having great difficulty in developing and administering programs for the unassigned reservists, the Air Force had a slightly easier time with the mobilization assignees/augmentees.

Administering and Training Individuals, 1953–1981

Evolution of the Mobilization Augmentee Program

In April 1947, with training programs for Air Reserve units under way, Lt. Gen. George E. Stratemeyer, the Air Defense Command Commander, turned his attention to reservists unable or unwilling to affiliate with a unit program. With a view toward capitalizing on reservists who lived near his command's management headquarters, he directed the staffs of his headquarters at Mitchell Field and those of the numbered air forces to use reservists to expand their operations.[38] This prompted Maj. Gen. Earle E. Partridge, Army Air Forces Assistant Chief of Staff for Operations, to protest that the only real justification for a reserve program was to make up the difference between peacetime and war strength. He said that training should be directed toward preparing the people needed to fight a war and that it was out of the question to absorb all reservists just because they were available to participate.[39]

In December 1947, with little progress having been made in organizing a program for individual reservists, Air Staff and major command officials meeting at Air Defense Command headquarters agreed that all elements of the Air Force should train individual reservists in peacetime for specific wartime mobilization duties. There followed in February 1948 publication of the Air Force's first directive governing the placement of reservists in a mobilization assignment program. Backing away from General Partridge's philosophy of training only reservists who would be needed in wartime, the guidance allowed bases to train the maximum number of air reservists within the installations' capabilities.[40] Later in 1948, the Air Staff assigned quotas of mobilization assignees by grade to the major commands and established procedures to develop an inventory of qualified Air Force Reserve officers for mobilization assignments through continuous screening and cataloging.[41]

In May 1949, the U.S. Air Force Reserve Fiscal Year 1950 Program included mobilization assignees as part of the Organized Air Reserve and authorized them pay for inactive and active duty training. The 1950 program also introduced the category of mobilization designees. These were reservists who by virtue of either military or civilian experience required very little training to maintain their proficiency. Mobilization designees did not train and therefore received no pay.[42]

Disappointed by the lack of progress made by the new mobilization assignment program, in December 1949 General Quesada's deputy, General McConnell, directed the major commands to initiate new procedures. He told them to examine the quality of training to assure it was interesting and effective, and to make training available at night and on weekends for reservists not otherwise able to participate. The commands were to give mobilization assignments with pay only to reservists who needed and could participate in regular training. An individual unable or unwilling to participate was to be relieved of his mobilization assignment. General McConnell also issued preliminary instructions for reallocating major command quotas for mobilization assignees on the basis of the availability of their assigned reservists for training.[43]

General Whitehead, Commander of Continental Air Command since April 1949, opposed the concept of permitting the availability of funds and the willingness of individuals to participate to determine training requirements, instead of the converse. He insisted the Air Force must determine the number of mobilization assignees required by grade and skill on the basis of a war plan. Disagreeing with so many of McConnell's instructions, General Whitehead asked the Air Staff to rescind them and establish a war plan, a troop basis for the Air Force Reserve, and a mobilization plan.[44]

The uncertainty raised in the Air Staff by this disagreement between the two Air Force agencies most responsible for reserve training delayed definition of the mobilization assignment program. In June 1950, the Korean War intervened to postpone further any serious Air Staff consideration of the program. Then, in November 1954 a new directive simply restated the guidance General McConnell had disseminated in 1949. Retaining the policy General Whitehead had protested, the Air Staff determined the number of mobilization positions for each command only in part on the basis of mobilization requirements. For the most part, each command's quota of individual mobilization requirements was still determined by its capability to train them and the availability of qualified reservists. Two methods were available for the commands to fill their mobilization positions. Ideally, they accepted applications from interested reservists; in the absence of such applicants, they requisitioned names of personnel by grade and skill from the Air Reserve Records Center.[45]

At the end of fiscal year 1954, only 5,806 mobilization assignee/designees were assigned against the 15,000 positions authorized throughout the Air Force. The Air Staff Committee on National Guard and Reserve Policy thought the primary reason for the deficiency was that most reservists were unaware of the program and the using commands had failed to provide realistic training for those who did participate. The committee also believed that the major commands abrogated their responsibilities to the Continental Air Command, allowing too many of their reservists to train in the air reserve center program. For their part, Continental Air Command officials were convinced that the deficiency was due at least in part to a Secretary of Defense decision to pay mobilization assignees for only half of their required twenty-four drills. The Air Staff made four fruitless attempts during fiscal year 1954 to have that ruling overturned.[46]

In November 1964, with Secretary of the Air Force Eugene M. Zuckert questioning the validity of the mobilization assignment program, the Air Staff validated the major commands' requirements for mobilization assignees and confirmed the policy that each augmentee had to meet a wartime need and not merely contribute to accomplishing the commands' peacetime tasks.[47] In April 1966, however, the Air Staff liberalized its position to the extent it authorized the commands to employ mobilization augmentees, as they were then called, to administer and train reservists in peacetime when they could be used more economically than active force members.[48]

In the mid-1960s war again intervened, and the Air Staff paid little attention to administering the mobilization augmentees while it coped with the demands imposed by the Air Force's involvement in Southeast Asia. At the same time, Continental Air Command officials and Air Force Reserve leaders were also preoccupied with other matters. Their energies and resources were absorbed in establishing the Office of Air Force Reserve in the Pentagon and Headquarters AFRES at Robins AFB. The new management structure required time to mature, and the reserve flying force needed to be modernized. The Air Staff and the major commands meanwhile continued to conduct the mobilization augmentee program under existing directives. The efforts applied and the results obtained were uneven, however; managing and operating such programs proved challenging.

It was difficult to train and use an individual reservist. Catching up on regulations and new policies and practices consumed only a small portion of the training period, especially if the reservist was on a two-week tour. Providing the mobilization augmentee with practical training for the balance of the period was a challenge to even the most conscientious of supervisors, especially in view of the restrictions dictated by Air Force manpower officials against employing the reservist to perform a peacetime Air Force function. A certain chemistry had to exist between the active duty supervisor and reservist to make the arrangement work. General Bodycombe recalled his tour as a mobilization assignee in Headquarters Tenth Air Force in the mid-1950s as succeeding because he had served on active duty with his supervisors, had skills they wanted to use, and had a civilian schedule flexible enough to allow him to commit the extra time. Other mobilization assignees in that same headquarters "sat there gathering dust," he recalled, because no personal chemistry existed in their cases.[49]

Aside from the difficulty in training and administering the mobilization augmentees, the program in the early 1970s had to overcome a lingering disdain, justified or not, for the reservists within active force organizations in the field. When reserve field grade and staff officers turned up at major command headquarters overweight, wearing ill-fitting, outmoded uniforms, and generally lacking in military bearing, they brought disdain upon themselves and upon the entire Air Force Reserve program. Active force officials had no enthusiasm for taking these unsatisfactory people to war with them, and hesitated to define mobilization requirements. In time, the problem was dealt with as one of the benefits of the centralization of Air Force Reserve leadership in the Office of Air Force Reserve when Generals Lewis and Lyon began

The Air Force Reserve

encouraging unsatisfactory reservists to conform to standards or separate from the Air Force Reserve.[50]

The individual reservist also had to overcome a certain amount of disdain within the Air Force Reserve itself. With the stabilization of the Air Force Reserve unit program after 1958 and its acknowledged contribution to the Air Force mission, its members took on an élan and superior attitude in which they treated the individual reservists as country cousins. Becoming Chief of Air Force Reserve in 1975, General Lyon, a former individual mobilization augmentee for several years, thought that the worst effect of this attitude was that it fostered a similar disparaging opinion about individual reservists among the active force members. One of his objectives as chief, then, was to vitalize the individual mobilization program as a means toward improving the image of the Air Force Reserve as a unified, disciplined component.[51]

When General Lewis left office in 1975, he could single out some commands that were conducting excellent programs, in spite of the problems the individual mobilization program encounterd in the early 1970s. They included the Aeronautical Systems Division at Wright-Patterson AFB, Ohio, and the Air Force Intelligence Service at Fort Belvoir, Virginia. Both of these programs employed a unitized approach; that is, they assigned their reservists to administrative units to facilitate their management.

In 1971, the Aeronautical Systems Division found that its reserve training program was not very vital. Training was too loose and individual officers had no sense of belonging. Refusing to let the program die and rejecting a patchwork solution, the division commander, Lt. Gen. James T. Stewart, adopted a new approach to reserve training. With Rafael L. Marderosian, serving in the Plans and Programs Office and Brig. Gen. Byron K. Boettcher, General Stewart's mobilization augmentee, as principal architects, the division initiated a unitized program of reserve training in May 1973. Formed into two groups that met at different times and under the guise of training, the reservists worked on projects desired by the division.[52]

By 1979, about 360 individual mobilization augmentees were participating. Under the leadership of Brig. Gen. Donald A. McGann, as mobilization augmentee to the commander, the reservists conducted important studies for the division. Among them were a review of energy conservation and management programs in the Air Force's industrial plants, a study of the effects on the propulsion industry of shortages of such critical materials as cobalt and titanium, and an assessment of the Air Force's tanker aircraft requirements through the year 2000. The reservists worked on active duty as teams at seventeen detachments and operating locations around the country. Possessing advanced degrees and technical and professional skills, they gave the command a pool of talent representing such fields as engineering, business management, science, and education.[53]

Continuing in the programs they developed during the Korean and

Administering and Training Individuals, 1953–1981

Maj. Gen. Homer I. Lewis leaves Headquarters AFRES at Robins AFB, April 4, 1975

The Air Force Reserve

Southeast Asia wars, the reservists assigned to the Air Force Intelligence Service managed their own activities and turned their training into very productive activities for the Air Force. Their program was vitalized in January 1974 with the establishment of the Directorate of Intelligence Reserve Forces as a staff element of the Air Force Intelligence Service. In approving this approach, Maj. Gen. George J. Keegan, Jr., Air Force Assistant Chief of Staff for Intelligence and also the commander of the Intelligence Service, was motivated by his experiences in the wars in Southeast Asia. In each instance, rapidly escalating hostilities had revealed a shortage of trained intelligence specialists in the armed forces. This resource had been allowed to slip back into civilian life after World War II and Korea, and General Keegan did not want to see it happen yet a third time.

Under its first director, Col. Ronald H. Markarian, the program developed dramatically within eighteen months. With its authorized strength tripling from 300 to 888 on the basis of intelligence billets contributed by other Air Force organizations, the program doubled its assigned strength from 565 to 1,100. What had been basically a human intelligence program became multidisciplinary, encompassing the full spectrum of Air Force intelligence specialties. In September 1974, after a test at Langley AFB, Virginia, demonstrated the feasibility of the idea, the Intelligence Service authorized increased numbers of sensitive, compartmented information clearances to members of the Intelligence Reserve program. Reserve linguists contributed to studies on Soviet military thought and Soviet civil defense systems. They also participated in the development and teaching of courses in targeting and science and technology at the Armed Forces Air Intelligence Training Center at Lowry AFB, Colorado. The revised program's development and operations during its first year earned it the Air Force Organizational Excellence Award for exceptionally meritorious service.[54]

Although chartered to manage the unit force, Headquarters AFRES itself conducted a highly successful mobilization augmentee program. It originated in the responsibilities that Headquarters AFRES inherited from the Continental Air Command to assist civil authorities in civil defense and disaster relief. Before 1960, the Continental Air Command had discharged these responsibilities through its numbered air forces. Replacing the numbered air forces, the reserve regions inherited the role. In March 1962, the region reservists were put on pay status as individual mobilization assignees in the civil defense function.[55] In time, these programs evolved into the Base Disaster Preparedness Augmentation, Federal Preparation Liaison Officer, and State Preparation Augmentation programs. The responsibility for planning and coordinating Air Force support for these programs, along with operational control of the resources with the exception of aircraft, was assigned to Headquarters AFRES which delegated their conduct to the reinstated numbered air forces. A lieutenant colonel and a noncommissioned officer administered these programs through networks of about 225 reservists. The reservists were assigned in peacetime to the numbered air forces with mobilization assignments to civil defense and disaster relief agencies.[56]

These were isolated islands of success, however. By July 1974, the dwindling mobilization augmentee program had less than half of its authorized 16,500 positions occupied. Rather than sit back and allow the program to erode, Secretary of the Air Force John L. McLucas asked General Lewis to step in and revitalize the program. Air Force Chief of Staff General David C. Jones approved the resultant revitalization plan on June 12, 1975, when General Lyon had become Chief of Air Force Reserve. General Jones directed the major commanders to involve themselves in the program so the Air Force could realize the maximum benefit from its individual reserve resource.[57]

The objective of the new program was to improve the management, manning, and training of the mobilization augmentees. One feature of the new program significantly distinguished it from its predecessors. It required each command's senior mobilization augmentee and senior reserve adviser to create a team to oversee the administration and training of the command's mobilization augmentees. The revised program also reinstated the requirement that the commands offer training on the weekends when most reservists were available.[58] When the Office of Air Force Reserve became the focal point of the revitalization effort, General Lyon made the reserve recruiting system, previously dedicated to recruiting for the units, responsible for recruiting for the mobilization augmentee program as well.[59]

The matter of a focal point for direction of the individual mobilization augmentee program had always been subject to dispute. Support always existed for the major commands to administer the individual augmentee program because they were mandated to establish requirements for it. Others insisted that the program's management should be centralized in the interest of efficiency. Many who argued for centralization maintained that the focal point should be within the Air Force Reserve, more specifically at the Air Reserve Personnel Center.

General Lewis, however, thought that the effort within the Air Force Reserve should be returned to Headquarters AFRES where it had been before 1970. The argument for placing the responsibility at the Air Reserve Personnel Center was based on the center's orientation toward individuals. General Lewis thought that since the augmentee program was a training program, it ought to be assigned to headquarters, whose business was training, but he never succeeded in arousing any support for the concept. Therefore, in developing the revitalization plan, he reluctantly agreed to place the focal point for program guidance in the Office of Air Force Reserve while leaving responsibility for direction of the reserve aspect of the program at the center.[60]

As Chief of the Air Force Reserve, in 1979 General Bodycombe invited the Air Force Inspector General to conduct a functional management inspection of

The Air Force Reserve

Returning recruiting responsibilities to unit commanders at Hamilton AFB, California, on August 1, 1974, Maj. Gen. Homer I. Lewis, Chief of Air Force Reserve, emphasizes the commanders' responsibility to deliver for him.

When a Department of Defense budget decision in December 1975 apparently doomed the Air Force Reserve regions, General David C. Jones, Air Force Chief of Staff, gave Maj. Gen. William Lyon, Chief of the Air Force Reserve, the opportunity to determine the management structure he thought best for the Air Force Reserve.

the augmentee program. The inspector did so, and early in November 1979 he issued a long report in which, among other findings, he criticized the Chief of Air Force Reserve for failing to delegate authority for the program's management. He recommended that management of the entire program be transferred from the active force to the Air Reserve Personnel Center and that the authorizations for augmentees should be centrally identified at the Air Force rather than at the user's level.[61]

Rejecting the idea that the active force's role in the program should be limited, General Bodycombe observed that mobilization augmentees were something more than mere wartime fillers, replacing personnel lost to attrition. They were trained before mobilization to fill specific positions in time of war or national emergency. In peacetime, they performed a variety of tasks for the Air Force as part of their overall proficiency training. General Bodycombe might have observed as well that the historical underlying weakness of the individual reserve programs had been the failure of the active force to identify specific mobilization requirements, recruit the reservists to meet them, and train the reservists. Air Force Reserve could handle the recruiting, but through its war plans, the active force had to identify the requirements and subsequently train the reservists to meet them. The Chief of Air Force Reserve insisted these functions could not be centralized.

General Bodycombe also took strong exception to the inspector's criticism of "lack of adequate guidance and procedural direction" in the program and comment that "lack of program control can be attributed to the failure of the Chief of Air Force Reserve to delegate authority for MA [Mobilization Augmentee] Program Management." Bodycombe asserted that if the Air Force Reserve were to be successful, it could not assume total management for a program that required strong active force management at all levels of command.[62]

For the most part, the Air Staff supported General Bodycombe in his rejection of the inspection report's major recommendations. An Air Staff working group chaired by Maj. Gen. William R. Usher, Director of Personnel Plans, disagreed that the lack of program control was caused by General Bodycombe's failure to delegate appropriate authority for managing the program. General Usher asserted that the key to a successfully managed mobilization augmentee program included active force leadership and responsibility at all levels of command. He also rejected the idea of assigning the mobilization resource to the Air Reserve Personnel Center for central management. He asserted that the reservists should be assigned to specific active force positions identified, justified, and approved by the active force. He agreed that the Reserve should continue to recruit and assign the individuals, but thereafter it remained the responsibility of the organization of assignment to administer and train the reservists.[63]

General Bodycombe's position, as supported by General Usher, was legally

The Air Force Reserve

correct, but the mobilization augmentee program consisted of reservists. Therefore, when it suited its purposes in management and unit programs, the Air Force Reserve historically argued that reservists were best suited to manage reservists. Consistency suggested that the Air Force Reserve accept the challenge of managing the individual augmentee program.

In 1980, recognizing that the gaining organizations of mobilization augmentees were generally unwilling to surrender management prerogatives, the Air Reserve Personnel Center tried to get around the issue of centralized management. To improve program management, the center staff revised its system for tracking the status of mobilization manning to give Air Reserve recruiters more accurate information. At the same time, they began to test a system of base level coordinators for mobilization augmentees. The test employed enlisted reservists recalled to extended active duty at four locations with large concentrations of mobilization augmentees—the Pentagon; Bergstrom AFB, Texas; Scott AFB, Illinois; and MacDill AFB, Florida. The coordinators counseled the augmentees and the base personnel officials on program technicalities and administration.[64] The test went well, and in September 1981 the Air Force Manpower and Personnel Center expanded the program to eight additional locations, with the expectation of including another eleven bases in the program soon.[65] Center officials thought that placing trained specialists at the bases to administer mobilization augmentees would at least standardize program administration in the absence of absolute centralization.

By 1988, those specialists were known as base individual mobilization augmentee administrators. Their main responsibility was to assist the readiness of individual mobilization augmentees. The principal means of doing so was by educating the reservists' commanders, supervisors, and trainers. They occupied Title 10, U.S. Code, Section 678 senior master sergeant positions which were established at bases where there were between 100 and 199 mobilization augmentees. Additional positions could be added as the population grew.[66]

The Air Force had believed from the beginning that it would need a large body of individual reservists to augment the active force and replace combat losses. Insofar as it could, it devised a program to administer and train reservists who were matched against a mobilization requirement. On the other hand, the Air Force never really defined the precise requirement for the attrition replacement. In the mid-1950s when it established the policy that mobilization requirements had to be identified for all Air Force Reservists, individuals as well as unit members, the Air Force found itself with a surplus of individual reservists who could no longer be trained. The reservists who continued with the Air Force Reserve individual training program through the reserve's composite unit, volunteer air reserve unit, specialty training, air reserve center, and recovery program stages in 1965 suddenly found themselves without a program, and they faded away. It need not have been. Between the extremes of

Administering and Training Individuals, 1953–1981

training only reservists who possessed defined mobilization requirements and of maintaining reservist replacements in a large pool that the Air Force felt obliged to carry to retirement, another alternative seems to have been available, one the Air Force approached from time to time in the 35 years after World War II.

The individual programs should have had an advocate on the Air Staff from the beginning. The alignment of reserve programs under the successors to General McConnell's office in the Air Force's operations community, with its natural predilection for unit programs, did not result in effective oversight of individuals. Such an official should have led the Air Staff to accept without equivocation a program for individuals that might not always have a defined requirement. If only active duty training pay and provisions for retirement were involved, the cost would not have been great, certainly far less than that of many misguided programs the Air Force embraced over the years. Especially during the first two decades after the war, a sufficient number of reserve advocates were seated in Congress to ensure the program would receive a friendly hearing.

This is not to deny the apparent contradiction in the failure of the Chiefs of Air Force Reserve to provide for the individual programs. Since the Office of the Chief of Air Force Reserve came into being in 1968, the Chiefs have discharged their responsibilities with respect to the overall component and the unit programs exceedingly well, but they have not been completely successful in providing for individuals. This is not to say that they did not try. Two elements were basic to their failure: Of prime significance was their unanimous insistence that the individual programs were the province of the active Air Force to administer and train, since the reservists would accrue to it upon mobilization. This was self-serving and merely passing a difficult problem on to someone else. The same argument which might be applied to the administration and training of units, which also comprise an augmentation force, was rejected by Air Force Reserve leaders at every turn of the road on the proper grounds that reservists should manage reservists. If the traditional cry that the active force did not know enough about reservist matters to administer them had any merit at all, it was certainly most pertinent to individuals, who were the most reservist of all reservists, especially those without defined mobilization roles. Air Force Reserve leaders proudly proclaim that active duty reserve units cannot be distinguished from the regulars, and they make the same claim for the mobilization augmentees. These mature in the security of the combined Air Force Reserve and active force management structures; it is the orphaned individual reservists who have required and have been denied the most parental care.

The second common misguided tendency has been to place the individual programs under the Air Reserve Records Center. With all respect, program management has not been the center's long suit. Institutional jealousy led to the

The Air Force Reserve

withdrawal of the individual programs from Headquarters AFRES when it replaced the Continental Air Command. General Lewis's instinct to return their management to the headquarters at Robins AFB in 1974 was sound. Training and management of Air Force Reserve programs are a function of that headquarters; the Chiefs should not have allowed its natural preference for the more glamorous unit programs to stand in the way.

Clearly, the Air Force had a need to define its mobilization requirements for individuals and provide them with realistic training. Quite aside from any sense of moral obligation, it would seem prudent not only to administer those without assignments but also to utilize them in the conduct of the Air Force's daily business. In denying the Air Force the use of unaligned reservists to perform peacetime functions simply for the sake of maintaining precise manpower requirements, its manpower officials performed a great disservice to the Air Force. Historically, the best reserve programs for individuals were those in which the reservists performed a service, that is, did something tangible—the professional training flights under the air reserve centers and the Air Reserve Personnel Center, the recovery units, the civil defense/disaster relief network of mobilization augmentees under Headquarters AFRES, and the unitized programs for mobilization augmentees of the Aeronautics Systems Division and the Intelligence Service, among others. These programs benefited the reservists, the Air Force, and the nation.

So the Air Force might have conducted a program for unaligned reservists precisely in the manner in which General Stratemeyer directed that they be used in the Air Defense Command in 1947. Even if not employed in the precise tasks they might eventually perform when mobilized, such reservists would be keeping current on changing Air Force customs, policies, and practices as they performed some function for the peacetime Air Force. Furthermore, it is not uncommon for an active force member trained in one job to be transferred into another as shortages or other contingencies dictate, especially in support or administrative roles. It should not be unthinkable, therefore, to place an experienced reservist into a different job upon recall, as was common practice during the Korean mobilization.

Such a program could have incorporated from the beginning the policy and practice initiated in 1975 of a reserve team approach to overseeing the administration and training of mobilization augmentees within each major command. The same approach, involving the senior mobilization augmentee and the reserve adviser in each headquarters, could have been applied to the unaligned reservists, under any designation.

Among all the Air Force's notable successes in managing and conducting its Air Force Reserve programs, the individual mobilization augmentee reservist program was obviously unsuccessful. Given more enlightened and dedicated guidance, programs for individuals could have joined the mainstream of successful Air Force efforts. Instead, without Hera to guide them, they drifted uncontrolled between Scylla and Charybdis, frequently colliding with the one before ultimately disappearing into the vortex of the other.

11

*M*anning Considerations in the Volunteer Force

The heart of the reserve unit was its members. Unless the unit commander went out into the community and convinced patriots to join his organization, all the plans, money, organization, equipment, and good will in the world would avail him nothing in producing a unit. In the mid-1960s, however, the Air Force Reserve unit commander's recruiting burden eased as American youth took advantage of the provisions of the Reserve Forces Act of 1955 to discharge their military obligations in the reserve forces and avoid active service in the Vietnam decade.

When President Nixon advocated an all-volunteer military force and sought to end the draft and the Defense Department and Congress moved to implement his ideas, reservists lost their draft-exempt status, and as the Headquarters AFRES Vice Commander observed, "Everybody is back in the recruiting business!" Moreover, Public Law 90–168 made the chiefs of the reserve components responsible to attain congressionally mandated manning levels. In the mid-1970s, one of the Air Force Reserve's major challenges was to man its force as an unpopular war wound down, and its leaders had to reexamine their approach to recruiting and retention. They also had to defend the Air Reserve technician program against criticism of its being an uneconomical system.

An End to the Draft and the Advent of the Volunteer Force

Campaigning for the presidency in October 1968, Republican candidate Nixon declared his intention to end the military draft once the nation had extricated itself from the Vietnam War.[1] On becoming President in January 1969, he

The Air Force Reserve

moved quickly to do so. Instructing Secretary of Defense Melvin R. Laird to prepare to operate without conscription, the President appointed a commission to develop a plan for eliminating conscription and he asked Congress to amend the draft law.[2]

It would take some time to develop an all-volunteer force, and the country would still require some kind of selective service program. In the interim, the President wanted to limit the disruption the draft caused. Congress responded to his request for revised draft legislation with the Selective Service Amendment Act of 1969. Signing the measure on November 26, 1969, the President observed that so long as there was a draft, there would be inequities, and some young men would serve and some would not, but he was pleased to sign a bill that removed much of the suspense from the process and reduced the period of uncertainty from seven years to one.[3]

The new system would feature a national drawing under which each of the 365 days of the year would be scrambled and matched with a new sequential number to determine the order of induction. Individuals drawing the lowest numbers would have the greatest vulnerability for induction. A second national drawing would determine the order of induction for those registered with the same local board and born on the same date. This sequence would be accomplished by a random selection of the letters of the alphabet.

All 19- and 20-year-olds would remain in the prime vulnerable group for a year, after which, if not inducted, they would move to a less vulnerable category. No youth would know at the time of the drawing whether or not he would be called, but he would have a good idea of his vulnerability to the draft. Students and others then deferred past the age of 20 would be put in the 19- to 20-year-old age group for the purpose of receiving a number on the first drawing. The drawing would not change their deferments, but when their deferment expired they would be placed in the 19- to 20-year-old group based on the vulnerability of the number they had previously acquired. The amendment had no effect on registration, classification, deferments, or exemptions, which remained as before.[4]

On March 27, 1969, President Nixon appointed a commission under former Secretary of Defense Thomas S. Gates, Jr., to develop a comprehensive plan for eliminating conscription and moving toward an all-volunteer armed force. In conducting its deliberations, the commission was to give serious consideration to the national requirements for an adequate reserve forces program. Significantly, the President did not charge Mr. Gates to determine whether an all-volunteer program should be undertaken, but rather to plan how such a program should be implemented.[5]

Submitting its report to the President on February 21, 1970, the Gates Commission concluded that the draft should be phased out at the point when the government was confident of its ability to maintain an armed force of the required size and quality through voluntary means, a point the commission

Manning Considerations in the Volunteer Force

thought would be reached by July 1, 1971. The commission had come to a consensus slowly, if not reluctantly, because several of its members, including the chairman, initially opposed or were highly skeptical of the all-volunteer concept.[6]

With the Gates Commission report in hand, the White House staff prepared an all-volunteer program for the President to present to Congress and the public. Pending realization of such a program, the staff continued to develop additional draft reform proposals. Believing that opposition to the draft was the one issue that unified all groups on the nation's campuses, the President's staff seized upon elimination of the draft as the perfect opportunity for the President to identify with students and other young people. The chief executive sent his program to Congress on April 23, 1970, announcing that the administration sought to end the draft and reform it as well in the interim. He pledged, "From now on, the objective of this Administration is to reduce draft calls to zero, subject to overriding consideration of national security."[7]

On October 12, 1970, Secretary Laird, who thought the Gates Commission's projection of ending the draft by July 1971 unrealistic, established a Defense Department goal of ending the draft by July 1973. Outlining the actions necessary to achieve this end, he asked the service secretaries to identify the priority steps to be taken to ensure success.[8]

On September 29, 1971, President Nixon approved Public Law 92–129, a comprehensive military manpower measure. Along with a score of administrative provisions pertaining to the composition and operation of local draft boards, the new legislation extended to July 1, 1973, the President's authority to induct persons into the armed forces. It gave the President discretionary authority to end college undergraduate deferments, it changed the exemptions to deferments for divinity students, and it provided for the suspension of state and local quota systems to enable the President to establish a uniform national call in selecting persons for induction. It also permitted a high school student who reached his 20th birthday during his senior year to graduate before induction and imposed a ceiling of 150,000 inductions for fiscal years 1972 and 1973, with authority for the President to exceed the ceiling under certain conditions. The measure also extended the Dependents Assistance Act for E–4s with fewer than four years' service and all ranks below that.[9]

Manning the Air Force Reserve in the All-Volunteer Era

The end of the draft and the all-volunteer force created problems for reserve forces units. Between 1957 and 1969, Air Force Reserve flying units had been manned at generally between 80 and 85 percent of their authorized strengths. Occasional recruiting drives had been held, and in the halcyon days of the air reserve center program, the entire Air Force Reserve sometimes surpassed its authorized strength. Even then, however, Category A reserve unit strength hovered around 80 percent.[10] The average wing commander found this figure

The Air Force Reserve

to be perfectly satisfactory. As long as he had his aircrews and maintenance force, he did not fret about shortages of lower grade airmen or nonflying specialties. He knew that when he had to mobilize his unit, the Air Force Military Personnel Center would open its pipeline, and his vacancies would be filled as would those of any unit on active duty. Meanwhile, he could make his readiness ratings, pass inspections, and sustain short contingency and exercise operations.[11]

By 1969, however, things changed. The immensely popular air reserve center program was no longer present to buttress the manning figures, and the 1968 reorganization had shifted all responsibility for manning from the Continental Air Command to the component. In winning the right to run its own program, the Air Force Reserve had also acquired other responsibilities. One hundred percent manning may not have been important to reserve wing commanders, but it was to congressional committees and the Office of the Secretary of Defense, especially with the President demanding a voluntary military force, reserve as well as active.[12]

When Congress established an average Air Force Reserve strength of 45,526 for fiscal year 1969, the Air Force Secretariat indicated its desire to reach that level at year's end. Major Generals Tom E. Marchbanks, Jr., Chief of Air Force Reserve, and Rollin B. Moore, Jr., Commander of Headquarters AFRES, took definitive actions to bring the reserve units up to full strength. Despite strenuous efforts by General Moore, the Air Reserve fell about 2,500 short of its authorized drill strength for 1969.[13]

General Moore and his headquarters staff maintained the pressure on the units throughout fiscal year 1970. No fewer than seventeen of his weekly commander's letters during the last half of the year included exhortations to sustain the manning drive. On numerous other occasions staff officials dispatched ad hoc letters and messages dealing with specific aspects of the problem. The intensive campaign bore fruit. At year's end 46,180 reservists were assigned in drill-pay status against an authorization of 46,129.[14]

The momentum generated by this manning effort carried over into the new fiscal year, and on June 30, 1971, 46,265 Air Force Reservists were assigned, 99 percent of the authorized 46,727. These figures were deceptive, however. In 1969, with the wholesale conversions of units to C–130 and C–141 operations, the Air Force Reserve had entered a six-year period of constant programmatic upheaval. By June 30, 1974, the Air Force Reserve's fifty-four flying squadrons were operating the EC–121, C–7, C–123K, C–130, F–105, A–37, HC–130, C–141, C–5, C–9, and various rescue helicopters. Moreover, the U–3A and O–2 had come and gone as four units had converted to an interim tactical air support role pending assignment of new missions.[15]

This dramatic turnover of the force between 1968 and 1975 demonstrated the practical meaninglessness of the authorized and assigned manning figures during a period of turbulence. Drill pay for any given year was authorized on

Manning Considerations in the Volunteer Force

the basis of some percentage of the authorized manning document strength of the units in the program that year. Although Congress tried to reflect reality by establishing average strengths, such an approach really presumed fully manned and converted units at year's end. Not all conversions started on July 1 and ended on June 30; they could start up at any time of the year on the basis of aircraft availability and other factors. In the meantime, units did some advance hiring for necessary preconversion training and schooling and exercised loyalty to their reservists by keeping those who were displaced on the rolls for at least six months pending their settlement into new positions or some other disposition of their status.

The local commander knew what his new manning document required, and his personnel officer could explain where everybody was and why. With a liberal use of asterisks, he could develop a reasonable briefing to depict his manning status—including overhires, advance hires, and delayed losses—to Headquarters AFRES. By the time the headquarters staff consolidated fifty-four such reports, however, the asterisks outnumbered the entries, and all the Air Staff really gained was a gross manning figure. If this figure was close enough to the authorized figure to satisfy the budget community and congressional committees, the Air Force Secretariat was satisfied as well. It was no measure of reality, however, and the Air Staff and congressional emphasis on meeting the drill-pay authorization was not necessarily the most reliable management approach.

This approach to manpower management had another aspect. The practical effect of a slight increase in the overall Air Force Reserve authorized strength for fiscal 1971 was distorted by geographic and skill disparities. In 1972, the programed conversion of eight units to different aircraft and the reorganization of aircraft units would reduce authorizations by an additional 2,500 people. Foreseeing a steady erosion of the Air Force Reserve's reservoir of skilled people, including aircrew members and highly qualified aircraft maintenance supervisors, General Moore thought it imperative to act. In April 1971 he asked General Lewis for immediate authority to form surplus reservists into combat support squadrons, units featuring a wide variety of nonflying skills, pending their assignment to combat units or individual mobilization positions on requirements. Even though General Moore sought interim relief of the problems of surplus reservists at the airlift locations, illustrative of the major essential difference between the active and reserve forces, he still had serious shortages of people elsewhere in the country which could not be relieved by surplus, immobile reservists, bound to other locations by civilian careers and avocations.[16]

General Lewis replied on July 2 with a consolidated Air Staff position rejecting General Moore's proposal. Basically, the Air Force simply did not need the surplus reservists Moore was trying to salvage. Aside from the overriding reality of shrinking budgets, the Air Staff identified several factors

The Air Force Reserve

contributing to the reduced personnel requirements. One was the allocation of fewer aircraft per unit. Only enough C–130s were available to provide six per unit unless the total number of reserve units was to be reduced. Another factor was the reduction in wartime utilization rates. When the reserve flying-hour program was reduced concurrently with a reduction in the active force flying program, fewer reservists were needed to maintain and fly the planes. Moreover, the C–130s and A–37s that were replacing the C–119s and C–124s required fewer navigators and maintenance personnel. Finally, under the approved concept of operation for reserve tactical and military airlift forces, the wartime requirement for these forces to deploy and operate from other than main operating bases was deleted. All this resulted in significant reductions in the manpower resources required in supply and other support areas.[17]

Recruiting was only one factor of the manning equation, retention bearing equal weight, especially in the volunteer environment. On November 13, 1970, responding to a letter from General John D. Ryan, Air Force Chief of Staff, soliciting suggestions to improve active and reserve force retention, General Moore suggested several measures. They covered personnel policies, travel, incentives, publicity, training, retirement, and benefits. The Department of Defense and Air Force legislative proposals for 1970 sought authority and funding for many of the retention incentives suggested by Headquarters AFRES and the other commands to advance the all-volunteer force. The Reserve was given great latitude to modernize traditional recruiting and retention procedures, and the Air Force Military Personnel Center took steps to involve separation counselors at active force bases in reserve recruiting.[18]

On June 29, 1973, with the draft to end two days later, Maj. Gen. Homer I. Lewis, General Marchbanks' successor as Chief of Air Force Reserve on April 19, 1971, and, as well, Reserve Commander after March 16, 1972, wrote his commanders to reemphasize his concern. He noted that congressional and defense officials were "becoming increasingly alarmed at the apparent inability of the Reserve components to meet desired manning levels." Insisting that recruiting and retention receive priority attention, he directed several specific actions. First, he imposed on each recruiter in the field a quota of one individual with no prior service per week. Second, he made each commander down to squadron level additionally responsible to recruit one non–prior service person a week. Placing equal emphasis on retention, he established the objective of a 15 percent reenlistment rate for all eligible first-term enlisted personnel.[19]

By this time, Headquarters AFRES personnel officials had become convinced that although unit commanders were primarily responsible for recruiting, they needed help, and the command recruiting effort required centralization. After some early experimentation with recruiting program organization, the Air Force Reserve began fiscal 1973 with a recruiting force of ninety-six recruiters, half of whom were Air Reserve technicians, assigned at the units. The nontechnicians worked under man-days. On April 1, 1973, Headquarters AFRES established the Directorate of Reserve Recruiting under the Deputy Chief of Staff, Personnel to manage the new Air Force Reserve recruiting program. With the exception of one officer and one civilian typist, the new agency was manned by reserve recruiters working under various man-day programs. Aside from two in the headquarters to assist in monitoring the program, reserve recruiters were placed on duty in unit personnel offices and in units with peculiar personnel problems.[20]

In part, the new dedicated reserve recruiting force was created to participate in a test of the feasibility of integrating reserve and regular recruiting forces. In February 1973, General Lewis convened a meeting of personnel officials from the Air Staff, the Air Force Reserve, the Air Reserve Personnel Center, the Air Training Command, and the Air Force Military Personnel Center to review the problem of reserve recruiting. Lt. Gen. Robert J. Dixon, the Air Force Deputy Chief of Staff for Personnel, recited the active force recruiters' article of faith that "Reserve recruiting would never succeed until it was brought under the umbrella of the Regular Air Force Recruiting Service."[21]

The concept had been invalidated by a test in 1964, but the only way to prove or disprove the hypothesis in the all-volunteer period would be to conduct another test. Consequently, the Reserve was authorized to organize a recruiting structure similar to the one employed by the Air Force Recruiting Service so that General Dixon's hypothesis could be evaluated.

The test began on October 1, 1973, and evaluated various reserve and regular recruiting combinations. In the northeast, it was business as usual: reservists recruited reservists, and their active force counterparts sought active force enlistees. Around Charleston AFB, South Carolina, reserve recruiters worked from the Air Force Recruiting Service offices and sought active force candidates, and active recruiters solicited reserve enlistments. Recruiters remained under their respective headquarters at Tinker, Carswell, and Richards-Gebaur AFBs in Oklahoma, Texas, and Missouri, recruiting enlistments for both reserve and regular units. At Norton, Travis, and McClellan AFBs in California, the reserve recruiters remained on station and were controlled by the active force recruiting group commander.[22]

During the test year of fiscal 1974, Air Reserve recruiters brought in 8,393 people, including 184 for the active force. Nevertheless, the per capita production of its recruiters was lower than it had been with the original group that had been active between October 1, 1972, and June 30, 1973. In the earlier period, an average of 45 recruiters a month brought in 3,678 recruits for the Air Force Reserve, a per capita production of 9.1 recruits per month. By comparison, the average force of 98 recruiters in the field during fiscal 1974 had a per capita production of 7.1 per month. The test itself contributed to this decline. In areas of the United States where reserve recruiters were required to recruit

The Air Force Reserve

for the active force, a distinct dip in production coincided with the beginning of the test on October 1, 1973. Production did not return to pretest levels in those areas until May 1974.[23]

At Hamilton AFB on the night of August 1, 1974, as they prepared to convene a commander's conference the next morning, Maj. Gen. Earl O. Anderson, the Air Force Reserve Vice Commander, gave General Lewis a position paper recommending significant change to reserve manning concepts. The proposals were based upon experience gained during the previous year, especially as it pertained to the recruiting integration tests. General Anderson explained that two valuable lessons had been learned: effective manning of reserve units required recruiting, retention, and loss control; and a successful manning program required active participation by each reserve unit commander.[24]

The combined efforts of active and reserve recruiters had brought more than 9,000 people into the Air Force Reserve, but the end result was still unsatisfactory because recruiting had been overemphasized and the recruiting responsibility had been removed from the unit commanders. General Anderson had concluded that a separate recruiting organization with a large management structure patterned after the Air Force Recruiting Service was unnecessary for reserve recruiting. He recommended, instead, a streamlined permanent force of full-time reservists expert in the intricacies of reserve personnel administration. Such specialists would monitor and service specific reserve units and would report to the senior local reserve unit commander instead of the reserve recruiting detachment.

While the recruiters had been busy bringing in the 9,000 reservists, 7,000 other reservists had left the program for various reasons through the first three-quarters of the fiscal year. The Air Force Reserve staff conceded that additional emphasis on retention programs would help, but it noted that fully one-third of the unit losses were uncontrollable losses, reflecting reservists ineligible to reenlist in their unit. These included those whose positions were lost to program actions, those who moved from the unit area, and those who voluntarily retired.

Consequently, in addition to sustaining emphasis on recruiting and retention, General Anderson believed Air Force Reserve officials had to initiate what he called stop-loss management. He believed that the Reserve had the recruiting expertise and with more counseling assistance its commanders could improve retention, but an integrated, commandwide stop-loss program was necessary to reduce uncontrolled losses. Therefore, he urged that the integrated recruiting test be concluded on schedule at the end of September and that General Lewis concurrently adopt the total manning concept.

When the conference convened the next morning, it was quickly apparent that the field commanders supported General Anderson's recommendations. Although conceding that the dedicated recruiting force was indeed helpful, the

Manning Considerations in the Volunteer Force

Maj. Gen. Earl O. Anderson, Vice Commander of Headquarters AFRES (May 5, 1973–October 12, 1976), urged General Lewis to return recruiting responsibility to unit commanders in August 1974.

Air Force Reserve Leadership Conference, Hamilton AFB, California, August 1–2, 1974. During this conference, the Air Force Reserve leadership agreed that the recruiting responsibility should be returned to unit commanders. Seated left to right are Brig. Gen. James D. Isaacks, Jr., Mobilization Augmentee, Air Force Reserve Chief of Staff; Maj. Gen. Alfred Verhulst, Commander, Eastern Region; Maj. Gen. Rollin B. Moore, Jr., Commander, Western Region; Maj. Gen. Homer I. Lewis, Chief of Air Force Reserve; Maj. Gen. Earl O. Anderson, Vice Commander, Air Force Reserve; and Maj. Gen. John W. Hoff, Commander, Central Region.

The Air Force Reserve

Air Force Reserve Commanders' Conference, Hamilton AFB, California, August 1–2, 1974. Top row, left to right, are Col. John E. Taylor, Commander, 301st TFW, Carswell AFB, Texas; Brig. Gen. Roy M. Marshall, Commander, 403d TAW, Selfridge ANG Base, Michigan; Col. Donald F. Beyl, Commander, 446th MAW, McChord AFB, Washington; Col. James L. Wade, Commander, 349th MAW, Travis AFB, California. Bottom row, left to right, are Brig. Gen. Sidney S. Novaresi, Commander, 434th TFW, Grissom AFB, Inidana; Brig. Gen. William G. Hathaway, Commander, 452d TAW, Hamilton AFB, California; Col. James E. McAdoo, Commander, 514th MAW, McGuire AFB, New Jersey; Col. Richard P. McFarland, Commander, 315th MAW, Charlston AFB, South Carolina.

commanders unanimously insisted that control of the recruiters must be returned to them. Taking them at their word, General Lewis complied, noting that his credibility as Chief of Air Force Reserve went with it, and they now had to produce for him.[25]

Meeting in Washington on August 13, the recruiting-test steering committee agreed to terminate the exam in September. On October 1, 1974, the Air Force Reserve and the Air Force Recruiting Service agreed that reserve recruiters would serve under reserve unit commanders, attend Air Training Command recruiting schools, augment active force inspection teams, and participate with active force training teams. For their part, the active force recruiters would provide referrals to the reserve recruiters and other assistance when possible.[26]

In March 1975, Headquarters AFRES placed fifty-one recruiters on active

Manning Considerations in the Volunteer Force

Air Force Reserve Commanders' Conference, Hamilton AFB, California, August 1–2, 1974. Top row, left to right, are Col. Leonard F. Deist, Commander, 445th MAW, Norton AFB, California; Col. Charles R. Corcilius, Commander, 440th TAW, General B. Mitchell Field, Wisconsin; Col. Donald H. Balch, Commander, 512th MAW, Dover AFB, Deleware; Col. Justin L. Townsley, Commander, 302d TAW, Rickenbacker AFB, Ohio. Bottom row, left to right, are Col. Ronald C. Dunn, DO, 439th TAW, Westover AFB, Massachusetts; Brig. Gen. Cecil T. Jenkins, Commander, 94th TAW, Dobbins AFB, Georgia; Brig. Gen. Alvin J. Moser, Commander, 442d TAW, Richards-Gebaur AFB, Montana; Brig. Gen. Harry J. Huff, Commander, 433d TAW, Kelly AFB, Texas.

duty for two years. In October 1976, in one of the more significant steps taken to support reserve recruiters, Maj. Gen. William Lyon, who succeeded General Lewis as Chief of Air Force Reserve in April 1975, persuaded the Air Staff to award proficiency pay to qualified reserve recruiters. To boost retention, the Reserve staff assigned trained career advisers to the reserve units. The headquarters also acted to offset one of the traditional causes of uncontrolled losses: reservists moving beyond the area of their units. In August 1974, the staff enunciated a four-point policy designed to retain such people. Essentially the policy required units to advise departing reservists of reserve units existing in their projected new locations, assist them to contact such units, and establish contact with the prospective gaining personnel offices to expedite reassignment. To facilitate reassignment, the Reserve authorized gaining units to carry the new people as overages if they required retraining. Also, by the end of fiscal 1975, Air Force Reserve units were applying a reserve career motivation program developed by the Air Staff which included career counseling.[27] In the final analysis, however, retention was a day-by-day, case-by-case proposition that required constant counseling and attention to young airmen.

The Air Force Reserve's attainment of its fiscal 1975 manning objectives reflected a good retention effort as well as a productive recruiting effort. The first-term reenlistment rate rose from 25 percent in 1974 to 37 percent in 1975 while the career reenlistment rate dropped a single point, to 89 percent. The Air Force Reserve recruited 12,068 people in fiscal year 1975, an increase of about half over the 1974 production that numbered 8,209. The Air Force Reserve units exceeded their drill-pay strength for the first time since fiscal 1970. On June 30, 1975, 45,497 Air Force Reservists were assigned against the 44,828 authorized in the units.[28]

Congressionally imposed budget restrictions in fiscal years 1976 and 1977 forced the Reserve to limit its recruiting efforts, and by the end of the latter year, Air Force Reserve drill-pay manning was 2,909 below its authorized strength of 53,298. Nevertheless, reflecting General Lyon's year-long emphasis on recruiting and retention, the trend of losses established in 1976 was reversed and the manning deficit, reduced. Lyon's emphasis was further reflected at the end of fiscal 1978 when the Air Force Reserve exceeded its drill-pay floor of 53,000 by 800. The attainment of the Selected Reserve's drill-pay floor on September 25, 1978, as Lyon swore in SMSgt. Rudell Dutton as a mobilization augmentee, was the highlight of the year for him; no other reserve component had been able to reach its manning objective.[29] After achieving the breakthrough, the Air Force Reserve sustained the momentum and annually attained at least 100 percent drill-pay manning.*

The Air Reserve Technician System Under Attack

The Air Reserve technician program, in which reserve members of units who were also full-time civilian technicians formed a combat-ready cadre, had proved to be an effective, efficient personnel and force management system since its inception in 1958. Nevertheless, there began in 1973 significant efforts to change its operation and character.

The Excepted Service Controversy

In January 1973, to neutralize what it perceived as the "status quo" problem, the Office of Air Force Reserve began to seek legislation that would give the Air Force Reserve more flexibility in managing the technician force. The status

---

*As of fiscal 1986, the Air Force Reserve has exceeded its congressionally authorized drill-pay floor every year since. To trace this phenomenon, see Appendix 2.

quo situation was inherent in the dual nature of the technician's employment condition: he was at once a Ready Reservist subject to military regulations and administration and also an Air Force civilian employee subject to U.S. Civil Service Commission regulations and administration. By virtue of the original agreement between the Air Force and the commission, a technician who lost his Ready Reserve eligibility or status through his own fault could be removed from his civilian position by the Air Force. However, one who lost reserve eligibility for reasons beyond his control could not be removed until the Air Force was able to offer him a comparable civilian job elsewhere. Therefore, until the Air Force could place him, he retained his status as a civilian employee. The two predominate reasons for going status quo—medical ineligibility or mandatory military retirement—were both deemed to be beyond the member's control.

More a problem of perception than of reality, the status quo issue had been historically overstated. The phenomenon contained the seeds of two potential problems: one, great numbers of personnel going status quo simultaneously, and the other, a key individual, for example, a wing commander, becoming a status quo employee. By the terms of an original agreement between Civil Service Commission and Air Force officials in 1957, the first condition ceased to be a problem after the program was two years old. The principals had agreed that the technician force could accommodate up to 10 percent of its members being status quo at any time. At the end of the first year, 18.3 percent of the program's members were status quo. Two years later the rate had dropped to 6.6, and it declined steadily until it reached less than 1 percent in 1974, a rate subsequently sustained.[30]

From 1972 to 1973, potential problems, primarily commanders in key positions encumbered by status quos, troubled General Lewis' staff. It was a concern shared by the gaining commands, especially in the total force environment. The presence of a commander who could not be mobilized and sent off to war, they reasoned, invalidated the basic concept of a Ready Reserve. Therefore, the Air Force proposed legislation on January 12, 1973, to amend Title 10 of the U.S. Code to give the Army and Air Force more flexibility in managing their technician forces.[31]

In early 1974, a reserve study group recommended that if the pending legislation failed, the technician program should be established as an excepted service, as was the National Guard technician program.* General Anderson initially thought it undesirable to place the Air Reserve technician program in an excepted service category, and Headquarters AFRES staff members insisted

---

*Broadly speaking, excepted service is contrasted to competitive civil service in that those in the former group are subject to more singular rules of recruitment, employment, and termination in their separate program. They do not compete with other civil service employees for their positions.

The Air Force Reserve

that excepted service would bring with it more liabilities than assets. They thought that adoption of excepted service would increase the cost of administration, impair union–management relations, and create problems resulting from the interim administration of two systems until existing technicians either left the program or went under excepted service. Staff members also thought it would restrict opportunities for technicians to advance because of their smaller competitive group, invite congressional hearings on the program in view of the extreme union positions, and reverse society's current trend of employee rights.[32]

In November 1973, the Office of Air Force Reserve began coordinating a new legislative proposal through the Air Staff to establish excepted service and require secretarial review before a technician could be separated.[33] The proposal immediately became an emotional, controversial issue that permitted no unanimity within the Air Force Reserve. After observing the situation beyond personal considerations, General Lewis and his Washington staff favored the change and judged the question strictly on its merits as a management measure that might produce a more efficient program. Field commanders, viewing the question subjectively from their perspective as reservists and civilian employees, opposed excepted service for its restriction of career opportunity. As an intermediate body organizationally placed between the Washington office and the field units, the Air Reserve staff reflected the diversity of views. L. C. Lingelbach, Air Force Reserve Director of Civilian Personnel, who had advocated a technician program in 1954 and had administered it since its inception in 1958, rigidly opposed excepted service. His own staff, on the other hand, was divided, some favoring and some opposing.

Beset by conflicting advice when he succeeded General Lewis, General Lyon withheld immediate judgment on the issue. Mr. Lingelbach urged him to retain the technician program under competitive civil service. Arguing that the program as it then stood had been fundamental in the development of the successful Air Force Reserve unit program, Lingelbach declared it risky to open a Pandora's box of congressional, civil service, and labor review over a handful of people. He asserted that the technician program operating under competitive Civil Service Commission regulations was far superior to excepted service, and logical improvements and refinements were possible administratively, if properly supported and presented.[34]

Meanwhile, the views of many Air Force Reserve officials were being influenced by the findings of the Defense Manpower Commission. The commission was a bipartisan body chartered on November 16, 1973, by Congress to determine defense manpower needs for the near and far terms. The commission investigated such questions as whether more economical ways existed for providing the necessary manpower without sacrificing effectiveness; whether the manpower could be structured, developed, trained, educated, compensated, and used more effectively; and whether the management of defense manpower programs could be improved. Finding that the nation was spending more money for fewer people who were increasingly located more in headquarters and support structures than in combat units, Congress had developed deep concerns about the increasing cost of defense manpower.[35]

Submitting its report on April 19, 1976, the Defense Manpower Commission concluded, with respect to the Air Reserve technician program, that the objectives of the program could be accomplished at substantial savings by replacing the technicians with full-time active duty guardsmen and reservists. The commission believed that while preserving the citizen-soldier concept basic to the guard and reserve systems, implementating this change would eliminate dual pay and retirement for what in essence was the same job.[36] Cautioning against rushing into a drastic revision, the commission also recommended that active duty guardsmen and reservists should replace technicians gradually to protect employment for the technicians.

On March 22, 1977, responding to the Defense Manpower Commission report as well as to a request by the House Armed Services Committee for a review of the Naval Reserve programs, the Deputy Assistant Secretary of Defense for Reserve Affairs appointed a multiservice group under Maj. Gen. Francis R. Gerard of the Air National Guard to study the full-time training and administration of the Selected Reserve. The Gerard group submitted its report on October 25, 1977. It conceded that the Army's and the Air National Guards' excepted service personnel systems had some advantages over the competitive service features of the Air Force Reserve's Air Reserve technician program. Nevertheless, the group recommended retaining the latter with the provision of certain safeguards. In general, disregarding additional manpower requirements such as those to operate bases, the group decided that the difference between a full-time military force and the technician force was not sufficient to justify changing the existing technician system. Moreover, the Gerard group thought that all the existing full-time support systems could, when properly funded, managed, and manned, produce the desired combat readiness. The group found the technician programs of the National Guard and Air Force Reserve to have been particularly effective, and it recommended their retention without significant change.[37]

The Deputy Secretary of Defense accepted the Gerard study on June 8, 1978. The Defense Department's General Counsel drafted legislation authorizing the service Secretaries to employ all reserve technicians in excepted service and to retain a reserve officer in active status for an undefined, reasonable limited period beyond the statutory limitations for his grade, up to age 60. This would give him sufficient creditable service for immediate civil service retirement by the time he reached the statutory limitation on active reserve service.[38]

When it seemed inevitable that Air Reserve technicians would be drawn into a system of excepted service in August 1978, a new Air Force initiative produced a development that negated any need for excepted service legislation. The Air Staff endorsed Office of Air Force Reserve proposals to the Office of Personnel Management to change Federal Personnel Manual 930–71, which prescribed the general operating instructions for the Air Reserve technician program.[39]

Accepting the Air Force proposals on January 24, 1979, the Office of Personnel Management revised its supplement to the manual to include significant changes in the procedures for appointing and retaining Air Reserve technicians. The effect was to establish military requirements as the paramount condition for appointment and retention. The new procedure also established an age restriction to preclude appointment to a technician position unless the candidate could accrue 20 good years of service for military retirement before the age of 60, revised mobility requirements for technician officer positions to require that new appointees, should they become status quo, be subject to mandatory placement in a nontechnician position at the same grade at any Air Force activity in the continental United States, applied qualification requirements to in-service and competitive appointments, and allowed a veteran to be passed over on the basis of certification that the candidate did not qualify for membership in the active Air Force Reserve.[40]

These changes eliminated the status quo problem, and since this was the only technician problem that ever really concerned the Air Force, excepted service was not needed. Consequently, the Assistant Secretary of the Air Force for Reserve Affairs asked the Office of the Secretary of Defense to withdraw the legislative proposal. On November 16, 1979, the Secretary's office notified the Air Force that it had done so.[41] Now, a new threat to the Air Reserve technician program had appeared.

The Militarization Test

Dissatisfied with the findings of the Gerard committee on full-time training and administration of the reserve components, the Defense Subcommittee of the House Appropriations Committee revived the issue of technician program costs during the 1979 Department of Defense budget hearings in July 1978. Focusing on Army and Air Force Reserve testimony that they would not be able to attract and retain qualified full-time personnel in military status, the subcommittee proposed a series of tests to evaluate the various military employment options that could be used by the two components. The Senate Appropriations Committee recommended against the House position because it would disrupt management and administration of the reserve, and the Secretary of Defense recommended that the test apply only to the Army because it had the least effective program and was adding a large number of new technician positions that could be militarized for the test. Nevertheless, the proposal slipped through in the confusion attendant to the late passage of a 1979 appropriations act. The measure required all reserve components in fiscal 1979 to test their abilities to attract and retain active duty military personnel for technician positions which would be converted from civilian to military authorizations. The test initially required the Air Force Reserve to convert sixty-eight positions.[42]

General Lyon was apprehensive about the test and seized upon every appropriate opportunity to argue circumspectly against it, both within the Department of Defense and in congressional hearings. The Air Force Reserve was manned and combat-ready, and he suggested that if the Army was having trouble preparing its reserve components, it should conduct the tests. Benjamin S. Catlin III, an official of the Reserve Officers Association, suggested less elegantly, "If the Army is sick, don't give the Air Force the pill." General Lyon was in a difficult position, for his was the only component to resist the test. Conducting small reserve programs with active duty people, the Navy and Marine Corps were indifferent. The Army was desperate and welcomed any kind of help it could get. Even the Air National Guard, influenced by the National Guard Bureau which shared the Army Reserve's anxiety, was not the usual staunch ally.[43]

If the Air Force Reserve's sister reserve components did not rally to its cause, its parent organization did. The 1979 appropriations bill directing all reserve components to test the militarization concept became law in November 1987, but responding to indications that the test would be extended to future years, the Air Force hierarchy rallied to General Lyon's side. Air Force Chief of Staff General Lew Allen, Jr., and Secretary of the Air Force James C. Stetson supported Reserve Chief Lyon on the issue and succeeded in winning the support of Secretary of Defense Harold Brown as well. All accepted the minimum test of fifty-eight spaces in 1979 but were opposed the addition of any thereafter.*[44]

General Allen went public with his opposition to the test in February 1979, telling the House Appropriations Committee:

> The Air Force has reservations regarding the appropriateness of such a venture given the record of our technician program. Were we to realize the full implementation of this concept, I believe that we would see a highly skilled nucleus replaced by a largely unskilled cadre, a stable force replaced by a transient force, and low readiness replacing our existing high readiness status. In the long term, we also anticipate recruiting and retention difficulties as well as higher costs. Thus, it appears that implementation of such a program for the Air Force presents us with an opportunity to lose much and gain little.[45]

Testifying before the House Armed Services Committee, Antonia Handler Chayes, Assistant Secretary of the Air Force for Manpower, Reserve Affairs,

---

*Apparently, budget officials in the Office of the Secretary of Defense were not listening, for they soon established a figure of 229 for 1980.

The Air Force Reserve

Col. Benjamin S. Catlin III, Commander, Air Reserve Personnel Center (February 1970–December 1974), led the organization through a great expansion of services to reservists and guardsmen and established the Personnel Mobilization Center.

and Installations, struck still another chord. Noting that for twenty years the technicians had been the principal vehicle by which the Air Force Reserve had maintained a readiness that matched the active force, Secretary Chayes warned that

> currently serving technicians will perceive this test as a threat to their status and will seek other employment. A further concern is that the Air Reserve Forces will be unable to fill these new full-time military, reserve positions and would then incur delays in attaining combat-ready status in units converting to new weapon systems. We are especially concerned about whether we can attract enlisted personnel to these full-time reserve positions at pay levels substantially less than for technicians.[46]

But it was General Lyon, in his last congressional appearance as Chief of Air Force Reserve, who cast the opposition in the strongest and bleakest terms. He told the House Armed Services Committee's Subcommittee on Personnel that the test was the "one black cloud" on the horizon for the Air Force Reserve, and he wanted to call it to the committee's attention "in the strongest terms I can state." He was concerned, he said,

> about the outstanding record of the Air Force Reserve being adversely affected by the conversion of Air Reserve Technicians to full-time reserve military billets. . . .

Manning Considerations in the Volunteer Force

Supporting General Lyon in his opposition to the congressionally directed test to militarize positions in the full-time training force of reserve programs, General Lew Allen, Jr., Chief of Staff of the Air Force, testified to the House Appropriations Committee that such a program would cause the Air Force Reserve more harm than good.

I don't think that the Air Force Reserve should be saddled with an Army problem and included in a test that, as all of you well know, is being thought of well beyond a test; it's going to be a fact! They're going to militarize those technicians, and I'm here today to tell you that when you do that with the Air Force Reserve, you run the risk of degrading that readiness over the years. . . .

I'm very peaked up on this subject, but I think it's important, and it's my last chance to talk about it . . . I think there is no other feature in the Air Force Reserve that is more critical than this. We have the manning; we have the equipment; we have the know-how; we can do the job; and to take this force and turn around and sunder it of the thing that makes it go seems to me to be unbelievable. I cannot understand why anybody would want to do this.[47]

Becoming Chief of Air Force Reserve in April 1979, General Bodycombe took up the fight. Testifying the following month before the House Appropriations Committee, he expressed his concerns about the effect the test might have on combat readiness and its long-range effect on the overall program. He would reemphasize these points more strongly during his 1980 testimony.[48]

While trying to fend off its extension beyond fiscal 1979, General Lyon moved to implement the test at Grissom AFB, Indiana, and Homestead AFB, Florida, on March 1, 1979. The 931st Air Refueling Group at Grissom AFB and the 915th Tactical Fighter Group at Homestead were converting to different aircraft which meant that they would have personnel turnover and many vacant spaces. The test affected 41 spaces at Homestead and 21 at Grissom in 26 Air

The Air Force Reserve

Force specialties in grades from airman first class to lieutenant colonel. Reminiscent of the pre–Korean War Category R program, reservists would be called to active duty, remain assigned to the same unit throughout their tours, be administered by the reserve unit's personnel office, and be mobilized with their units if such a call came. With a great deal of skepticism among veteran Air Reserve technicians, who equated it with the excepted service drive and other recent actions which seemed to portend doom for the technician program, the test got under way.[49]

The 1980 appropriations act required the Air Force to add 161 positions to the test, for a total of 229. Headquarters AFRES filled 142 of the positions by June 1980 when the test ended. Since nearly 50 percent of the critical enlisted positions in the maintenance functions had gone unfilled, the Air Force Reserve considered that the test had demonstrated failure of the militarization effort, and it continued its vigorous opposition to any changes in the Air Reserve technician program. A task group under Brig. Gen. Sloan R. Gill, Deputy to the Chief of Air Force Reserve, explained that the Air Force Reserve problems did not involve issues of unionism and status quo, and that the common perception of an inordinately costly technician dual-status system was ill-founded. Only 1 percent of Air Reserve technicians were status quo the day the test ended. There was no union problem in the Air Force Reserve on June 30, 1980, nor had there ever been one in the 23-year history of the Air Reserve technician program. The cost effectiveness of the Air Reserve technician force had been extensively studied, and the technician program proved to cost no more than, if as much as, a full-time military force. However, the fundamental issue insofar as the Air Force Reserve was concerned was operational readiness, and the Air Force Reserve, with the technician as its wellspring, had been proved ready, day after day, year after year, in peace and war.

The technician militarization test had established the difficulty of attracting skilled people to the low military grades that accompanied the wage board maintenance positions constituting 75 percent of the Air Reserve technician force. This was the very question the test had been conducted to answer. The Air Force Reserve evaluation concluded that the Air Reserve technician program was a good system and worked well. It asserted that a full-time military conversion program would dilute Air Force Reserve unit combat readiness, nullify efforts to improve the quality of the technician program, and cause an unnecessary attrition of highly skilled personnel from the technician force. The Air Force Reserve, therefore formally suggested that it be relieved of the requirement to continue the test.[50]

On September 12, Deputy Assistant Secretary for Reserve Affairs George M. McWilliams forwarded the reports of the test submitted by the Air Force Reserve and the Air National Guard to the Office of the Secretary of Defense and recommended that the two air components not convert technicians to military personnel.[51] The Office of the Assistant Secretary of Defense for

Manning Considerations in the Volunteer Force

Manpower, Reserve Affairs and Logistics reported to Congress on December 30, 1980. Like the Defense Manpower Commission report of December 1976, the report treated all reserve components differently. Noting that the full-time support structures of the reserve components took five forms, the Defense Department explained the unique service recommendations and suggested that each component's full-time reserve support questions be answered independently. It recommended that the two Army components and the Air National Guard increase, in varying degrees and mixes, their support of reserve programs by reservists on active duty. The recommendation for the Air Force Reserve was, however, that it not convert any additional technician positions, and as the converted positions became vacant, that they be reconverted.[52] Thus, the Department of Defense report to Congress on the technician militarization test incorporated all Air Force positions. Congress did not take nor recommend further action on the subject, and the converted positions were reinstated to technician status as they became vacant.

By 1982, the Air Force Reserve had enjoyed several consecutive years of successful manning, and for the time being, the Air Reserve technician program seemed secure. Critics of the technician program still characterized the dual role of the technicians as too costly, but a series of examinations and challenges in the context of the overall military manpower environment of the United States failed to fault the program's effectiveness or identify a better substitute.

12

The Air Force Reserve Matures in the Total Force

> The Air Reserve Forces present a textbook case of success for the total-force policy. . . . A measure of this success is reflected in the fact that these units have repeatedly demonstrated their capability to mobilize and deploy within seventy-two hours. Using the standards applied to active Air Force units, operational readiness inspections confirm the readiness of these units.
>
> —W. Standford Smith,
> *The Guard and the Reserve in the Total Force,*
> National Defense University, 1985

In 1968 the Air Force Reserve began to change as a force through the acquisition of more modern aircraft. With the new aircraft came new missions, and the nature of the benefit the Air Force received from its reserve component changed as well. The traditional by-product of airlift training flights remained, but the Air Force Reserve also began to conduct directed missions for the Air Force in such areas as early warning surveillance, weather reconnaissance, aerial spray operations, and air refueling, among others. The ultimate demonstration of the Air Force Reserve's ability to fit into active force operations occurred in the 1973 Arab-Israeli War, when aircrews of the reserve associate units flew hundreds of missions into Israel and elsewhere in the Middle East. The component's participation in Air Force exercises and deployments was extensive, and it perfected its mobilization and mobility capabilities through its own Redoubt series of mobilization/deployment

The Air Force Reserve

exercises. The Air Force Reserve comprised significant percentages of the Air Force's total capability in many mission areas, and a National Defense University study in 1985 declared it, along with the Air National Guard, the epitome of the Total Force Policy in action. Nevertheless, the component could not take its newly won stature and status for granted, and its leadership had to be alert to active force desires to regain greater control of this component in which, after all, it had invested great resources.

Modernization and Expansion of the Reserve Role

When Maj. Gen. Tom E. Marchbanks, Jr., became the first Chief of Air Force Reserve in January 1968, the Air Force Reserve flying force consisted of 15 troop carrier and military airlift wings with 45 C–119 and C–124 squadrons assigned. There were also five aerospace rescue and recovery squadrons which flew HC–97s and SA–16s. Actions were already under way to change the composition of the force, however, and two aircraft conversions would begin on March 25.

On July 1, 1967, Defense Secretary McNamara authorized the Air Force to convert three Air Force Reserve C–119 units programmed for inactivation to new missions. One was the 944th Tactical Airlift Group, which would move down the freeway from March to Norton AFB, California, in the third quarter of fiscal year 1968 as the first Air Force Reserve airlift associate C–141 unit. At the same time, the 924th and 925th Tactical Airlift Groups would convert to C–130s at Ellington AFB, Texas. Later, Secretary McNamara approved the conversion of four additional groups to C–141 operations in the associate program in fiscal year 1969.[1]

The Air Force Reserve Airlift Associate Program

As the Military Airlift Command converted its strategic fleet from obsolescent piston-driven C–124 aircraft to modern jet transports, it could no longer provide the Air Force Reserve's C–124s with en route and overseas station maintenance support. Consequently, in January 1966 General Howell M. Estes, Jr., Commander, Military Airlift Command, proposed that the reserve forces operate the C–141s and C–5s in a corollary mode, that is, that they share aircraft owned by collocated active force units. Secretary McNamara endorsed the corollary concept as he continued his search for greater economy and efficiency.[2]

Acceptance of what would become the Air Force Reserve airlift associate program was neither rapid nor unanimous. Recalling the failure of the original corollary program of 1949–1951, Continental Air Command officials did not rush to embrace the new concept, and they influenced General Estes to rename the new venture as the associate program. Air Force Reservists and Air

The Air Force Reserve Matures

National Guardsmen expressed reservations about the associate concept as they learned their units would not own the new C–141s and C–5s but would merely contribute aircrews and maintenance talent to collocated active force units. The reservists believed the new program was nothing more than a glorified individual program and feared they would eventually lose their identity. But, as General Marchbanks later acknowledged and as most Air Force Reserve officials came to realize, the Air Force Reserve really had no choice. Continued operation of the C–124 was impractical, and in the pre–Total Force period, neither the Air Force nor Congress was inclined to make the expensive new aircraft directly available to the Air Force Reserve.[3]

On January 15, 1968, the Continental Air Command organized the 944th Military Airlift Group (Provisional) as an associate group at Norton AFB with Col. Richard P. McFarland as commander. Under the provisions of a Continental Air Command programming plan and a Military Airlift Command program action directive, the associate program test got under way. In the absence of an overall Air Force regulation or manual to govern the associate program, ad hoc local agreements broke new ground in the increasingly complex arrangements between the two commands and their subordinate units. The commander of the 63d Military Airlift Wing, the active force parent wing, assumed operational control over the group during unit training assemblies and active duty training periods as well as aircrew members any time they integrated into the active wing for training purposes.[4]

The test quickly confirmed the soundness of the associate concept, and the new unit, now designated the 944th Military Airlift Group (Associate), held its first training assembly on the last weekend of March 1968. A few days later, on April 4, TSgt. John P. Stappler became the first reservist to serve as an aircrew member on a C–141 operational mission. Two days later, Maj. Ronald D. Blalack, Capt. Woodrow T. Fail, and Capt. Anthony Colange flew a C–141 on a mission to Tinker AFB, Oklahoma, as the first all-reserve associate crew. The program made rapid strides. On August 14, 1968, the first all-reserve C–141 associate crew left Norton AFB on a Southeast Asia mission. Captain William Maxey was aircraft commander and Colonel McFarland, who had promised such a flight within six months, went as an additional crew member.[5]

A number of factors contributed to the initial success of the 944th. General Estes tolerated no resistance to the program within his headquarters, and Brig. Gen. Gilbert L. Curtis, 63d Military Airlift Wing Commander, enthusiastically supported the program. General Estes gave the 944th top priority for aircrew training spaces at the C–141 transition school, and General Curtis assured the reservists priority access to aircraft for training flights when possible. Of great importance, the two local commanders, General Curtis and Colonel McFarland, cooperated to make the unusual program work.[6]

By January 2, 1974, the Air Force Reserve airlift associate program had grown to include wings at Norton, Travis, and McChord AFBs on the West

The Air Force Reserve

Coast, and McGuire, Dover, and Charleston AFBs in the East. Aligned under these wings were four C–5 squadrons and thirteen C–141 squadrons which greatly augmented the Military Airlift Command's aircrew and maintenance resources. This reserve force routinely participated in the Military Airlift Command's worldwide operations. Although it was not an airlift unit, the 932d Aeromedical Airlift Group (Associate) was developed as a C–9 unit at Scott AFB, Illinois, as part of the overall associate program.[7]

Revision of the Tactical Airlift Force

The tactical airlift buildup in the Air Force Reserve begun in 1968 with the C–130 continued through 1974. The C–7 entered the reserve inventory in December 1971, and the C–123 returned to the Air Force Reserve in the modified jet-assisted K model on October 12, 1971.

Headquarters AFRES learned on October 2, 1969, that Air Force Reserve units would convert to the C–130A models "sometime in December." The Secretary of Defense notified Congress on October 29, and two days later Headquarters AFRES established December 6 and 13 as the effective dates of conversions at New Orleans and Minneapolis.[8] This Air Staff practice of retaining conversion information as classified data and withholding public and congressional announcement of the conversions until virtually the eleventh hour was the only factor that troubled the Reserve's programmers and planners throughout the mass conversions of 1969–1974. By treating the information as classified, the Pentagon staff made it impossible for Headquarters AFRES to initiate public hiring, training, and construction arrangements.[9]

Fiscal year 1975 marked the first year that no aircraft conversions occurred. By then, sixteen Air Force Reserve tactical airlift squadrons were equipped with C–130s.[10] The C–123 returned to the Air Force Reserve on December 1, 1971, when the 906th Tactical Airlift Group converted at Lockbourne AFB, Ohio. Conversion of three other groups followed: at Pittsburgh in March 1972; at L. G. Hanscom AFB, Massachusetts, in October 1972; and another group at Lockbourne in April 1973.[11] The Air Force Reserve tactical airlift force of the mid-1970s was rounded out by the acquisition of the C–7A at Maxwell AFB, Alabama, and at Dobbins AFB, Georgia, in December 1971 and April 1972. These units were selected to receive the C–7A because the planned use of the aircraft to support U.S. Army airborne and special forces training dictated its assignment in the southeastern United States.[12]

The Jet Fighter Returns to the Air Force Reserve

In July 1970 the 930th Special Operations Group (which had moved to Grissom AFB, Indiana, after Bakalar AFB closed in that state seven months earlier) received A–37s, the first Air Force Reserve unit to be assigned single-jet aircraft since the F–86H left the Reserve inventory in 1957. When the A–37A

The Air Force Reserve Matures

became available, the Air Staff decided to convert the 930th because its 71st Special Operations Squadron had just acquired considerable combat experience, even if in another mission. Subsequently, the 930th's sister organization, the 931st Special Operations Group at Grissom, and Air Force Reserve groups at Youngstown Municipal Airport, Ohio, and Barksdale AFB, Louisiana, also converted to A–37s.[13]

Even though the little A–37 was deprecated in some circles as the Tweetie Bird that not even the Vietnamese Air Force thought was combat-worthy, it was capable of speeds in excess of 400 miles an hour and it could carry more than 4,800 pounds of ordnance. The Air Force Reserve was glad to have it. Air Force Reserve officials were even more excited, therefore, to learn in January 1972 that the component would acquire a *real* jet fighter. The F–105 was becoming surplus to U.S. requirements in Southeast Asia, and reserve C–124 units at Tinker AFB, Carswell AFB in Texas, and Hill AFB in Utah would convert to it.[14]

When the fact of the assignment of the F–105 to the Air Force Reserve appeared in the Five-Year Defense Plan in January 1972, the Chief of the National Guard Bureau protested on the basis of the traditional assignment of fighters to the Air National Guard and, if nothing else, that the Guard ought to

Members of the 9633d Air Force Reserve Recovery Squadron practice decontamination of an F–86 at the Fresno Air Terminal in California.

313

The Air Force Reserve

get them first. General John D. Ryan, the Air Force Chief of Staff, sustained the decision, however, telling the Guard's Chief that it was in the best interests of the Air Reserve Forces to assign the F–105s to the Air Force Reserve. General Ryan thought the assignment would ease the Air National Guard's already heavy facilities construction requirements and the acquisition would improve the Air Force Reserve's appeal and image without damaging those aspects of the Air National Guard.[15]

A high-performance, sophisticated airplane, the F–105 provided the Air Force Reserve with its most demanding conversion yet. The immediate problem was the usual lack of notification. From rumor on January 11 to organization of the first unit at Tinker on May 20, the Air Force Reserve had slightly more than four months in which to prepare. Moreover, declassification of the action on March 29 left fewer than two months for open preparations. At any rate, on May 20, 1972, the C–124-equipped 937th Military Airlift Group at Tinker was replaced by the 507th Tactical Fighter Group which began transitioning into F–105Ds and Fs.[16]

The time-phasing of other Air Force programs involving the F–105 indicated that the first reserve group accept at least one aircraft in June and the first two groups be fully equipped by the end of July 1972.[17] In view of the pressing need for the Air Force Reserve to accept aircraft before the 507th Tactical Fighter Group would be prepared to inspect and maintain them, General Lewis agreed to accept immediately at Tinker eight aircraft if Tactical Air Command personnel conducted the acceptance inspections. The first aircraft arrived on April 14, and a seven-man Tactical Air Command team performed the acceptance inspection and placed the aircraft in flyable storage. The 506th Tactical Fighter Group, which converted on July 8, received its first F–105D at Carswell AFB on May 10 under similar circumstances.[18] The 506th Tactical Fighter Group was activated at Carswell on July 8, and on July 25 the 301st Tactical Fighter Wing was also activated at Carswell, where the 506th and 507th were assigned to it. On January 1, 1973, the wing was rounded out by the activation at Hill AFB of the 508th Tactical Fighter Group.[19]

The Airborne Early Warning and Control Group

When the Air Force's force of EC–121s for airborne early warning and control was programmed to be reduced from 46 to 18 at the end of fiscal 1972, Air Staff officials feared the United States would be left with only minimum surveillance capability in the Caribbean and Gulf of Mexico regions. A potential solution appeared when Representative Bob F. Sikes asked Air Force Reserve officials to investigate the possibility of stationing a reserve unit at Eglin AFB in his Florida panhandle district. On March 10, 1971, Deputy Secretary of Defense David Packard approved an Air Staff proposal to convert an Air Force Reserve airlift unit at Homestead AFB, Florida, to EC–121s instead of to its programmed C–130s, and to assign those C–130s to a new

The Air Force Reserve Matures

tactical airlift unit at Eglin. These actions enabled the Air Force to solve the surveillance problem and honor Congressman Sikes' request.[20]

Headquarters AFRES activated the 79th Airborne Early Warning and Control Squadron at Homestead and assigned it to the redesignated 915th Airborne Early Warning and Control Group on July 30, 1971. The unit was equipped with six strategic EC–121D aircraft and two transport-configured C–121s for transition and support. Soon after its conversion, the 79th began flying active surveillance missions in the Caribbean and Gulf of Mexico, and its declared C–3 readiness as programmed in March 1973.[21]

Acquisition of Other Missions

Discounting the A–37 units' earlier interlude, the Air Force Reserve became engaged in special operations in April 1974 when the 302d Aerospace Rescue and Recovery Squadron converted from HH–34 rescue operations to CH–3Es at Luke AFB, Arizona. The squadron's new special operations mission required it to become proficient in helicopter day/night infiltration, exfiltration, reinforcement, and resupply operations.[22] A second special operations unit was created when the 919th Tactical Airlift Group and its 711th Squadron converted from C–130Bs to AC–130As at Duke Field, Eglin AFB, on July 1, 1975. The AC–130A was a close support version of the C–130A and had more powerful engines. It was armed with 7.62-mm miniguns and 20-, 40-, and 105-mm cannon and equipped with searchlight and sensors, including infrared target acquisition and direct-view intensification sights.[23]

The Air Force Reserve also acquired an aerial spray mission with the C–123Ks in 1973. The responsibility for conducting insect aerial spray operations in the United States had resided with the Tactical Air Command before it was delegated to the 302d Tactical Airlift Wing and its 906th Tactical Airlift Group at Rickenbacker AFB, Ohio. The 906th maintained three UC–123Ks equipped with an information systems program plan, mini-max spray system ready for deployment on 72-hour notice, and it kept six A/A45Y–1 defoliant dispenser (Ranch Hand) systems available for immediate installation. In the event of an emergency spray mission requiring its total operable assets, the 906th would have a three-day capability of spraying 1.2 million acres—an area half again as large as the state of Rhode Island but not quite as large as Delaware.[24]

From the very beginning, the Air Force called upon the unit to conduct special spray operations along with its routine mosquito and Japanese beetle control missions. On April 1, 1973, for example, six days after it became operationally ready, the group flew missions to control an infestation of Mediterranean fruit fly in Managua, Nicaragua, after a major earthquake. Also, in May 1975, Headquarters AFRES deployed a detachment of UC–123K aircraft to Guam to control dengue fever-bearing mosquitoes while preparing a camp for refugees from Vietnam.[25]

The Air Force Reserve

Crews of the 302d Special Operations Squadron at Luke AFB, Arizona, conduct wet drills with their CH–3E in March 1982.

An AC–130 gunship of the 919th Special Operations Group at Duke Field, Eglin AFB, Florida, firing during a night mission

The Air Force Reserve Matures

General Lyon's Perception of Modernization

When Maj. Gen. William Lyon became Chief of Air Force Reserve in April 1975, his immediate objectives were to modernize the component's attitudes, unify it as an entity, and expand its missions. His concept of modernization extended beyond the mere acquisition of new airplanes and tactical missions. He had come to the position of Chief after consecutive tours as mobilization assistant to the commanders of the Sacramento Air Materiel Area and the Fifteenth Air Force and as Commander in Chief of the Strategic Air Command. The perceptions he brought with him were those of the individual reservist performing his duties in an active force environment rather than those of a member of a formed reserve unit operating in the reserve environment. From this perspective, he was not convinced that the attitude of the Air Force Reserve as a whole, about 85 percent of which comprised the unit force, was sufficiently mature to meet its expanding Total Force obligations. In the preceding thirty years, the Air Force had brought the reserve component a long way from its flying club days, but General Lyon was skeptical that the Air Force Reserve itself had made the transition. His views reflected those of the active force officers he had met during his five years at various headquarters. While conceding the Air Force Reserve's ability to perform the operational tasks assigned it, the active force officials with whom he had dealt in command and field headquarters harbored doubts about the discipline and tough-mindedness of this component in which, in a Total Force world, they were required to invest more and more resources and faith.[26]

The Air Force Reserve claimed to accept the concept of Total Force, but General Lyon thought it remained generally set in its ways, clinging to traditional methods of serving. The Air Force Reserve had helped prove the efficacy of the associate unit concept, but the component resisted active force overtures to explore new ways to discharge the reserve mission of augmenting the active Air Force.

Finally, building on his predecessor's considerable success in unifying the Office of Air Force Reserve, the Air Reserve Personnel Center, and Headquarters AFRES into a more coherent management structure, General Lyon wished to extend the unification process to the unit and individual programs which often seemed to be two separate Air Force Reserves. This resolve, too, had been fostered during his three preceding assignments as mobilization assistant. He had observed that since members of organized Air Force Reserve units often treated their colleagues in the individual programs as country cousins, it was easy for the active force to adopt a similar, disparaging attitude.

Given the choice, General Lyon probably would have emphasized revitalization of the Air Force Reserve individual program as his initial priority, but events soon forced him to deal simultaneously with all three objectives. Although an Air Staff manpower study of 1974 validated retention of the Air

317

The Air Force Reserve

Maj. Gen. William Lyon, Chief of Air Force Reserve (April 1975–April 1979), introduced many management innovations, reinstated numbered air forces to the management structure, accepted nontraditional missions, and strongly resisted a move to militarize the air reserve technician program.

Force Reserve regions in the management structure, it recommended that the number of regions be reduced from three to two, primarily as an economy measure. General Lyon would not concur in reducting his management structure as one of his first official acts, but on December 12, 1975, an Office of the Secretary of Defense budget decision eliminated all three regions; reduced air reserve strength by 620 active duty military, civilian, and reserve spaces; and reduced the Air Force Reserve fiscal 1977 budget by $4.9 million.[27]

General Lyon was successful in convincing Air Force Chief of Staff General David C. Jones that the Air Force Reserve should have the opportunity to define its own organizational needs, and the Chief of Staff intervened with the Secretariat to give General Lyon that chance. A revised budget decision confirmed the $4.9 million reduction, but it deleted the reference to the regions and allowed the Air Force to identify the source of the savings.[28]

In May 1976, General Lyon accepted the recommendations of a study team under Maj. Gen. Gwynn H. Robinson that three numbered air forces replace the regions in the Air Force Reserve management structure, that they be organized functionally with an emphasis on operations and logistics, and that they be oriented toward the gaining commands to encourage mutual endeavor to improve reserve unit readiness. The Secretary of the Air Force approved the concept on August 4, 1976.[29]

Headquarters AFRES reactivated the Fourteenth, Tenth, and Fourth Air Forces on October 8, 1976, to replace the concurrently inactivated Eastern, Central, and Western Air Force Reserve Regions at Dobbins AFB, Georgia; Ellington AFB, Texas; and Hamilton AFB, California. The Fourth and Fourteenth Air Forces were oriented toward Military Airlift Command's

The Air Force Reserve Matures

Twenty-second and Twenty-first Air Forces, and Tenth Air Force was associated with the Aerospace Defense Command, the Strategic Air Command's Eighth and Fifteenth Air Forces, and the Tactical Air Command's Ninth and Twelfth Air Forces.[30]

At the same time that he was preserving an intermediate management structure to guide the Air Force Reserve field program, General Lyon suddenly found it necessary to replace a number of key officials in the Air Force Reserve management structure. The management team he had inherited was an experienced group of professional airmen, reservists, and Air Reserve technicians that promised great stability to the force. Within the first year, however, a series of events depleted this team. The first was routine when Maj. Gen. Rollin B. Moore, Jr., retired on schedule as Commander of the Western Air Force Reserve Region in September 1975, and Brig. Gen. Sidney S. Novaresi, Commander of the 434th Tactical Fighter Wing, replaced him. In the eight months that followed, however, Brig. Gen. Alfred Verhulst, Eastern Air Force Reserve Region Commander, died suddenly, and Central Region Commander Maj. Gen. John T. Hoff and Air Force Reserve Vice Commander Maj. Gen. Earl O. Anderson retired prematurely, both because of ill health.[31]

Maj. Gen. Sidney S. Novaresi, who replaced Maj. Gen. Rollin B. Moore, Jr., as Commander of the Western Air Force Reserve region, is shown here flanked by Col. James C. Wahleithner on his right and Col. Charles B. Coleman on his left at the dedication of the 403d Rescue and Weather Reconnaissance Wing at Keesler AFB, Mississippi, on April 29, 1978.

319

The Air Force Reserve

Maj. Gen. John W. Hoff, Commander, Central Air Force Reserve Region, visits deployed units at Volk Field, Wisconsin, in July 1973.

These developments gave General Lyon the opportunity to raise the stature of some reserve generals who were not Air Reserve technicians by assigning them to positions of command. Pending selection of permanent commanders, in the summer of 1976 he chose for interim appointments the nontechnicians, Maj. Gen. Edwin R. Johnston and Brig. Gen. Joe A. Thomas as Commanders of the Eastern and of the Central Regions. Extending his philosophy to its logical conclusion, on July 22, 1976, he assigned Brig. Gen. Roy M. Marshall as Commander of the Central Region. This last appointment was significant

Maj. John J. Closner explains some of the difficulties of the 507th Tactical Fighter Group's conversion to F–105s at Tinker AFB, Oklahoma, to Maj. Gen. Earl O. Anderson, Vice Commander of Headquarters AFRES, in the summer of 1972.

The Air Force Reserve Matures

Maj. Gen. Roy M. Marshall, Reservist Commander of the Tenth Air Force, with an appropriate apprehensive expression, observes the progress of an operational readiness inspection of one of his units.

because, like Generals Johnston and Thomas, General Marshall was not a technician; unlike the previous assignments, however, this appointment was permanent. General Lyon's confidence in selecting General Marshall was strengthened by the fact that Marshall had commanded the 403d Tactical Airlift Wing as a reservist for several years.[32]

The most significant personnel action was yet to come. When it became evident in the summer of 1976 that poor health would force General Anderson to retire as Vice Commander, General Lyon persuaded Maj. Gen. Richard Bodycombe, another reservist, to come on active duty and take the job. Like Lyon, Bodycombe had served successive tours as mobilization assistant within the Strategic Air Command. During their common Strategic Air Command service, Generals Lyon and Bodycombe found they shared similar views on major Air Force Reserve issues. When General Bodycombe accepted the vice commander's position on November 1, 1976, the top two command positions in the Air Force Reserve were then held by men who had never been Air Reserve technicians but had risen in the structure as reservists.[33] This circumstance may have neither strengthened nor weakened the Air Force Reserve, but it did signal that in a period when the Air Reserve technicians had proved themselves as strong managers and commanders and the component was being drawn into the Total Force, room remained at the top in the Air Force Reserve for purely reservists.

321

The Air Force Reserve

Maj. Gen. Richard Bodycombe, Chief of Air Force Reserve (center), and his party (including the author, to his right) listen to the theater briefing upon arrival at Howard AFB, Panama, on September 18, 1982, preparatory to flying down-country on a two-day mission the next day.

Training By-product Becomes Directed Missions

With the active encouragement he received from General David Jones, Air Force Chief of Staff from 1974 to 1978, General Lyon accepted a variety of operational missions for the Air Force Reserve in the Total Force environment. The traditional airlift and rescue missions continued as the by-product of required training, as did those generated by the more recently acquired aerial spray training. Beginning in 1976, however, the Air Force Reserve became more involved in the Air Force's day-to-day operations in other mission areas.[34]

Extension of the Airborne Surveillance Mission

In 1975, still seeking ways to economize on its operations, the Air Force programmed the withdrawal of the EC–121 surveillance mission from Iceland. When the U.S. State Department protested the action as politically unacceptable because it would leave Iceland without warning of intruders into its airspace, the Office of the Secretary of Defense asked the Air Force to retain three EC–121s in Iceland pending the availability of the Airborne Warning and Control System E–3A airplane or some politically and militarily acceptable alternative. The Air Force solved the problem by establishing an Air Force Reserve rotational mission in Iceland with augmentation by active force aircrews and support personnel in what was often referred to as a reverse associate arrangement. On March 1, 1976, the Aerospace Defense Command

The Air Force Reserve Matures

activated a detachment to augment the 79th Airborne Early Warning and Control Squadron at Homestead AFB. From there, the 79th rotated crews and support personnel to Iceland to conduct the mission. Although occasionally stumbling over its organizational peculiarity, the integrated organization accomplished its mission. The A–3E was to assume the North Atlantic airborne early warning and control mission from the EC–121 on October 1, 1978. When acquisition of the A–3E was delayed, however, the Air Staff directed the reserves to retain one EC–121 on station for another six weeks. Except for the responsibility of maintaining that single aircraft in Iceland, the Homestead AFB EC–121 mission, in Florida and in Iceland, ended on September 30, 1978.*[35]

The Weather Surveillance Mission

In January 1976, the Air Force Reserve's 920th Tactical Airlift Group at Keesler AFB, Mississippi, converted to WC–130Hs and was redesignated as a weather reconnaissance unit. The unit's major peacetime mission was to locate, identify, and track hurricanes, assuming 70 percent of the Department of Commerce's responsibility for that function. The group also sought out winter storms on the East Coast, supported transatlantic fighter deployments, and met Department of Defense weather reconnaissance requirements on the West Coast.[36]

The Air Refueling Mission

In fiscal year 1976, the Strategic Air Command reluctantly began to transfer 128 KC–135s to the Air Reserve Forces. The Air Force Reserve received 24 of the KC–135s compared with the Air National Guard's 104. The disproportion in the allocation was created because the Guard already had an aerial refueling mission, and the KC–135s would replace the KC–97s assigned to its tanker units.[37]

The first Air Force Reserve units to convert to the tanker mission were the 452d Tactical Airlift Wing and its 336th Squadron. The honor fell to them by geographic and programming accident. Believing that further upkeep and maintenance of the old station would be too costly, the Air Force decided to close Hamilton AFB and move the 452d farther south in California to March AFB. Since General Lyon wanted the converting Air Force Reserve units to be collocated with Strategic Air Command units to take advantage of their experience, support, and, where necessary, facilities, the 452d and the 336th acquired the tanker mission by virtue of their move to March AFB, home of Strategic Air Command units.[38]

---

*Even as the one-ship Iceland force was extended, however, the EC–121 unit at Homestead began its conversion as the first Air Force Reserve F–4C unit.

The Air Force Reserve

Preconversion training and joint Strategic Air Command–Air Force Reserve preparations began in the latter half of 1975. Typifying its professionalism, the Strategic Air Command took pains to expedite and facilitate the conversions in an atmosphere of friendly partnership. On October 1, 1976, the actual conversion date, the Commander in Chief welcomed the 452d, now commanded by Brig. Gen. James L. Wade, as the first Air Force Reserve unit to convert to the KC–135 and join the Strategic Air Command tanker force. A few weeks earlier, the 452d's host unit at March AFB had organized an orientation visit to Headquarters Strategic Air Command for Wade and members of his staff.[39]

Moving to March AFB on January 12, 1976, with only 28 percent of its Hamilton complement, the 452d Air Refueling Wing accelerated its conversion timetable through the efforts of its own personnel and the cooperation of the host 22d Bomb Wing, which loaned the converting wing an aircraft that first day. So successful was the cooperative venture that on October 1, 1976, the official conversion date, the wing had 63 percent of its crews trained and ready for mission certification, five crew chiefs fully qualified, and 85 percent of its technicians trained. By the end of December 1976, the wing had received all its aircraft, and four of its eight formed aircrews were combat-ready.[40]

The 452d Air Refueling Wing assumed tanker alert duties, providing one alert crew and aircraft to the active force at March AFB on October 1, 1977, one year after its conversion. The wing's second unit, the 940th Air Refueling

Before assuming command of the first Air Force Reserve unit to convert to the KC–135, Brig. Gen. James L. Wade had commanded the 507th Tactical Fighter Group, which in May 1972 was the first Air Force Reserve unit to have converted to the F–105.

The Air Force Reserve Matures

The first Air Force reservists of the 452d Air Refueling Wing to stand tanker alert for the Strategic Air Command on October 1, 1977, are (left to right) Capts. Tom Frank, Francis Bott, and Ron Bird. (Photo, courtesy MSgt. James Alexander, Air Reservist, *Nov. 1977.)*

Group, meanwhile completed its conversion ahead of schedule at Mather AFB, California, in preparation for assuming its own alert commitment on New Year's Day 1978. The Reserve activated the 331st Air Refueling Group at Grissom AFB, Indiana, on July 1, 1978, as the third group of the wing.[41]

In addition to providing Strategic Air Command a daily line of alert, each of the Air Force Reserve air refueling units began participating in the European Tanker Task Force in 1979. The wing augmented the task force at RAF Mildenhall, United Kingdom, with 12 aircraft and aircrews and 550 support personnel during a 44-day period in August and September. Each of the wing's three units provided four aircraft, crews, and support personnel for two-week periods.[42] The Air Force Reserve's air refueling mission expanded in November 1981 when the 78th Air Refueling Squadron (Heavy) (Associate) was activated as a KC–10 associate unit at Barksdale AFB, Louisiana, the first of three such KC–10 associate units.[43]

The Air Force Reserve

Rescue Operations in the Later Period

Second only to airlift, air rescue was the oldest of the Air Force Reserve's missions. In July 1972, the 303d and 305th Aerospace Rescue and Recovery Squadrons converted from HC–97s to HC–130Hs at March AFB, California, and Selfridge Air National Guard Base (ANGB), Michigan. In June and July 1971 the 301st and 304th converted to the HH–34J helicopter, and in July 1974 the 301st added HH–3Es.[44]

By December 1980, Air Force Reserve units were credited with saving 547 lives in rescue and disaster relief operations. Most saves resulted from locating Air Force fighter aircraft with single crew members or small civilian planes with three or four occupants. However, many hikers and hunters also lived to tell their stories because of reservists' rescue and recovery efforts.[45] Some rescues were spectacular, and at least one operation was bizarre.

Two spectacular operations occurred in 1980. Situated in the wilderness of Washington State, but near recreation and logging interests, the Mount Saint Helens volcano had lain dormant for 125 years. When it erupted on May 18, 1980, the 304th Aerospace Rescue and Recovery Squadron at Portland, Oregon, was in the midst of a monthly training session. Unbidden, the unit responded to the emergency, and within minutes its helicopters were en route to the mountain. On that first day, the 304th rescued 51 persons on 32 sorties. In all, at the end of ten days, the 304th had flown 111 sorties and saved 61 lives. Also participating in the rescue operations were the 304th's sister rescue squadrons, the 303d from March AFB and the 305th from Selfridge; maintenance men from all over the Air Force Reserve; and the 129th Aerospace Rescue and Recovery Group of the California Air National Guard.[46]

The other spectacular operation in 1980 occurred in the early morning hours of November 21, 1980, when fire engulfed the MGM Grand Hotel in Las Vegas, Nevada. Unable to rescue numerous persons trapped on the upper floors, civil authorities requested assistance from the consolidated command post at nearby Nellis AFB in Nevada. Deployed to Nellis for a Red Flag exercise, crews from the Air Force Reserve 302d Special Operations Squadron quickly responded. Using the hoist system integral to their CH–3E helicopters, the reservists saved fifteen hotel guests who had been trapped on isolated balconies, beyond the reach of any other means of rescue, and two other guests from the hotel roof.[47]

The operation characterized as bizarre occurred late in 1978. In mid-November in Jonestown, Guyana, members of the Peoples Temple cult killed Congressman Leo Ryan and four members of his fact-finding party, wounded four other people, and then, all 900 men, women, and children committed mass suicide by poisoning. At the State Department's request, the Air Force launched a humanitarian airlift to Georgetown, the Guyanese capital, on the 18th to retrieve the wounded and the dead among the congressman's party as well as the bodies of Americans among the cultists who had committed suicide. Air Force Reserve participation consisted of two HC–130N tankers and 38 personnel—two 7-person teams from the 31st Aeromedical Evacuation Squadron at Charleston AFB; nineteen aircrew members and two maintenance personnel of the 305th Aerospace Rescue and Recovery Squadron at Selfridge ANGB; and one person each from the 46th, 58th, and 59th Aerial Port Squadrons at Dover and Westover AFBs in Delaware and Marrachusetts, respectively.

One team from the 31st went to Timehri IAP, Guyana, where it picked up casualties and survivors from Congressman Ryan's party and returned them to U.S. bases. The second 31st team recovered the bodies of Congressman Ryan and three other individuals and delivered them to Charleston AFB. The lack of fuel, quarters, and ramp space at Timehri forced the Reserve HC–130s to refuel the HH–3Es and rotate crews, parts, and maintenance personnel between Timehri and Roosevelt Roads Naval Station in Puerto Rico. The two HC–130N tankers of the 305th Squadron refueled airborne helicopters nineteen times. Meanwhile the reserve aerial port personnel supplemented personnel at Dover AFB for six days, unloading and loading the ten C–141s that were returning the human remains of the Guyana tragedy.[48]

Support of Israel in the Yom Kippur War

Aside from the Southeast Asia wars, the only major international hostility in which the Air Force Reserve participated in the 1970s was the Arab-Israeli conflict in October 1973, variously known as the Yom Kippur War, the October War, or the War of Ramadan. The war broke out on October 6 when Egyptian and Syrian forces attacked Israel. By the fourth day of the fighting, it was clear to the Nixon administration that the Israelis had lost so much in armor, aircraft, and ammunition that their losses would have to be restored with supplies from the United States. Private insurance companies in the United States balked at covering the aircraft of the Civil Reserve Air Fleet, commercial carriers which had contracted to support the Military Airlift Command. As a result, President Nixon directed that the Department of Defense conduct a military airlift, and the Air Force responded with its first flight at 3:30 P.M. on Sunday, October 13.[49]

The Military Air Command's C–141s and C–5s provided most of the U.S. airlift, with the Air Force Reserve associate aircrews participating heavily. Although the war ended on October 20, reservists were involved in associate unit operations to the Middle East from October 14 to November 15. In all, 650 Air Force Reserve associate unit aircrew members volunteered to fly there, and 286 did so. Included were 24 all-reserve crews and 183 reservists who flew into Israel itself. Meanwhile, 1,495 reserve crew members flew routine channel

The Air Force Reserve

missions, freeing other active and reserve personnel to participate in the airlift.[50]

In all, the U.S. C–141s and C–5s conducted 588 missions into the Middle East and carried 22,395 tons. The cargo included some that could only be carried by C–5s, such as M–60 and M–48 tanks weighing about 100,000 pounds each, CH–53 helicopters, 175-mm cannon, assembled F–4E aircraft fuselages and tail sections, and 155-mm howitzers. The Soviets meanwhile flew 900 missions on shorter routes, delivering about 15,000 tons to the Arab states.[51] The routine response of Air Force Reserve aircrews not only validated their proficiency, it also demonstrated the confidence the Air Force and the Defense Departments had in the Air Force Reserve associate units during worldwide military crises.

The Postal Mobilization of March 1970

There occurred in March 1970 an incident in which the Air Force exceeded its authority and briefly mobilized two Air Force Reserve air postal and courier groups. On March 23, after some U.S. postal workers had struck for more pay and better working conditions, President Nixon declared a national emergency because the work stoppage impeded critical government and commercial functions. He authorized the Secretary of Defense to use any military forces necessary to assist the Postmaster General to restore national postal service. The President's order specifically authorized the Secretary to mobilize Army and Air National Guard units if necessary; it was silent about the Army and Air Force Reserve.[52]

In addition to recalling certain Air National Guard units, the Air Staff also ordered the mobilization of two Air Force Reserve postal and courier groups with their eight flights, consisting of about 200 men in all. The 1st Air Postal and Courier Group located at Dobbins AFB, Georgia, had flights at Greensboro, North Carolina, Memphis, Tennessee, and Maxwell AFB, Alabama. The 2d Air Postal and Courier Group was situated at Hamilton AFB, California, with four flights at Alameda NAS, California.[53]

Dr. Theodore C. Marrs, Deputy Assistant Secretary for Air Force Reserve Affairs, soon determined that the Air Staff had exceeded its authority in calling up the Air Force Reserve units, and he arranged their release. As it was, the postal crisis soon abated, and the units would not have been required much longer in any event. Otherwise insignificant, the brief mobilization demonstrated the readiness and responsiveness of the reserve postal units in reacting quickly and efficiently to a mobilization order.[54]

The Air Force Reserve Matures

Air Force Reserve Exercises/Deployments

Long before the advent of the Total Force Policy, Air Force Reserve individuals and units participated in training exercises. With the advent of Total Force, the Air Staff and Headquarters AFRES strove to increase Air Reserve Forces participation in joint exercises. Various levels of exercise activity were available to Air Force Reserve units and individuals. Some deployments were sponsored by the units themselves; for example, fighter units in the north deployed crews and aircraft to southern bases to escape prohibitive winter flying weather. The Joint Chiefs of Staff sponsored joint exercises involving forces from all the services, usually in overseas areas. The Tactical Air Command sponsored the Flag series—Red, Green, and Blue—simulating various threat and electronic warfare environments. By 1981 the Air Force Reserve tactical fighter units were preparing to begin regular deployments to their European wartime bases under the Checkered Flag program. Days when everyone participated in the traditional mass unit summer encampment exercises had become memory, and pending initiation of the Checkered Flag wartime base deployments in 1982, the Flag series offered the most realistic training. The Joint Chiefs exercises offered the least to Air Force Reserve units because U.S. Army training objectives imposed an artificial role upon the air forces.[55]

In fiscal year 1981 Air Force Reserve aircrews and aircraft participated in seventeen exercises sponsored by the Joint Chiefs of Staff including five Red Flags, two Blue Flags, and a substantial number of unit-level exercises. In addition, nonflying units and individual reservists augmented active forces in ten field exercises of various types.[56]

The exercise that gave General Lyon the greatest emotional lift during his tour as Chief of Air Force Reserve was CORONET POKER/OKSBOEL, the deployment of the 301st Tactical Fighter Wing to Norvenich Air Base in the Federal Republic of Germany in August 1977. In the first overseas deployment of an Air Force Reserve fighter unit, Brig. Gen. John E. Taylor, Jr., led 20 F–105s and 292 people from Carswell AFB to Germany. At Norvenich, the wing was employed in Exercise OKSBOEL, a Danish operation with multinational participation.[57] General Lyon characterized participation of the Air Force Reserve F–105s in the NATO exercise as the epitome of Total Force.[58]

The REDOUBT Series of Mobilization Exercises

In many respects, CONDOR REDOUBT 81, the culminating exercise of an Air Reserve mobilization series, was the most important and significant of the exercises that the Reserve engaged in fiscal year 1981. General Bodycombe conceived the idea of the REDOUBT series of Air Force Reserve mobilization exercises shortly after he became the Vice Commander in November 1976. With the reinstatement of the numbered air forces into the chain of command

The Air Force Reserve

a few weeks earlier, he concluded that the Air Force Reserve ought to review and, if necessary, revise its command and control procedures to accommodate the new organizations. So was conceived Operation REDOUBT, a series of exercises and tests sponsored by Headquarters AFRES to improve command and control, mobilization and deployment capability, and crisis reaction capability. Under Phase I of REDOUBT in 1977, Headquarters AFRES tested its ability to deploy its battle staff to the alternate headquarters site and monitored the results of a commandwide unit notification test. Phase II in May 1978 unified the entire alert, notification, mobilization, mobility, deployment, employment, redeployment, and demobilization process into one continuous operation. All units scheduled for unit training assemblies on the May 6–7 weekend were put through the alert, recall, and mobilization phases, and some deployed and redeployed. Using new processing procedures developed as a result of the Phase I experience, Headquarters AFRES processed more than 18,000 reservists through mobilization at 31 locations with an average processing time of 45 seconds.[59]

In 1979, Phase III of REDOUBT expanded the testing of mobilization procedure as reserve aircraft deployed about 1,000 people to exercise bases. The 924th Tactical Airlift Group at Bergstrom AFB, Texas, tested streamlined mobilization procedures developed during the critique of Phase II. When the unit processed 251 personnel with an average time of 17 seconds each, Headquarters AFRES recommended adoption of the new procedures and elimination of the mobilization line which in its best modified form took an average of 108 seconds per person. Besides providing a realistic training environment to increase readiness, Phase III of Operation REDOUBT met congressional and Defense Department guidance to test and improve reserve mobilization and deployment capabilities.[60]

Exercise PAID REDOUBT 80 in 1980 expanded upon everything that had gone before. Covering three training weekends in June, it fed units into the Joint Chiefs of Staff Exercise POSITIVE LEAP, a Red Flag exercise, and a tanker overseas deployment. The Air Staff coordinated mobilization directives; the gaining commands participated in the mobilization process; the Air Reserve Personnel Center, Air Force Military Personnel Center, and Headquarters AFRES collaborated on providing personnel filler action; the Military Air Command tested a concept of replacing deploying members of its numbered air force staffs with reservists; the Air Force Accounting and Finance Center tested new procedures; and Headquarters AFRES coordinated postmobilization procedures with the gaining commands.[61]

Reflecting the reserve experience in the REDOUBT series to a great extent, a new AFR 28–5 was published in May 1980. The new directive consolidated all Air Force mobilization guidance into a single, formal document and included chapters on general information, logistics, medical, personnel, information, and legal arrangements. Incorporating the philosophy that individuals need only "sign in and go to work," it eliminated the mobility processing line.[62]

In addition to demonstrating Air Force Reserve unit readiness in August 1981, CONDOR REDOUBT 81 confirmed the utility of Westover AFB, Massachusetts, as an aerial port of embarkation and included the largest Air Force Reserve field medical exercise ever conducted. In conjunction with this exercise, the Air Force Inspector General also conducted a functional management inspection of the Air Force's capability to mobilize, absorb, and sustain reserve forces.[63]

All Air Force Reserve units on unit training assembly weekends or annual tours mobilized all available personnel using the new AFR 28–5 procedures. Of 47,002 people available, the units mobilized 34,054 in 24 hours. Of this number, 3,674 individuals deployed to various U.S. bases as well as to bases in Canada, England, Denmark, Panama, and the Azores. Combat logistics support squadrons deployed to three bases where they performed maintenance on F–4s, F–15s, and F–111s. Nine aerial port units deployed 136 people to 6 locations, ranging in scope from the major embarkation port at Westover AFB to a small forward operating base at Goose Bay, Labrador. CONDOR REDOUBT 81 also provided a stage for the Air Force Reserve to exercise newly acquired skills in communications jamming and chemical warfare defense for the first time.

The Air Force Surgeon General proclaimed the medical field training exercise an outstanding training experience for the 890 Air Force Reserve medics and 236 other participants. It incorporated tactical and strategic aeromedical evacuation, operation of an aeromedical staging facility, squadron medical element training, augmentation by tactical hospital and clinic personnel of an air transportable hospital, and a comprehensive combat medicine course for all. The medics conducted 96 tactical, 16 strategic, and 12 helicopter evacuation missions, attended 230 litter and 250 ambulatory patients, and treated 211 actual outpatients and 2 inpatients.[64]

As CONDOR 81 was winding down in the last days of August 1981, some Air Staff officials, as well as the Tactical Air Command Commander, suggested the Air Force Reserve had carried the REDOUBT series far enough and should begin to participate more actively in Air Force exercises. The point was not well taken since Air Force Reservists had participated in fifty-four exercises sponsored by the Joint Chiefs of Staff and forty-six by the major air commands over the REDOUBT period of 1978–1981, and until very recently the Tactical Air Command's Red Flag series had been ill-suited for airlift forces. Nevertheless, General Bodycombe agreed that REDOUBT had served its purpose and discontinued the series.[65]

Responding to his initial guidance, the Air Reserve staff had devised ways to refine and test the whole spectrum of unit response—alert, notification, mobilization, deployment, employment, redeployment, and demobilization.

The Air Force Reserve

Air Force Reserve members of the 919th Special Operations Group at Duke Field, Eglin AFB, Florida, learn to function while wearing protective chemical warfare clothing during a weekend training session in the autumn of 1981.

Mobilization and mobility procedures were honed to a fine edge, with the mobilization line eventually eliminated by the publication of AFR 28–5. Although it had not been part of his original intention, General Bodycombe also utilized REDOUBT to attract coverage of the Air Force Reserve in the national press. Finally, by virtue of bringing such agencies as the Air Force Accounting and Finance Center, the Air Force Military Personnel Center, and the gaining commands into exercise play, the Reserve and REDOUBT made the Air Force realize that there just might be more involved in the mobilization process than it had remembered in the thirteen-year interval since the recalls of 1968.

Exercising the Rescue Force

For all its benefits to the Air Force combat forces as a whole, the REDOUBT series of mobility and deployment exercises failed to satisfy one element of the combat units. Just as the joint exercises with the Army had failed to employ the Air Force Reserve troop carrier–airlift forces adequately, so the REDOUBT series neglected the Air Force Reserve rescue units. While the REDOUBT series permitted the rescue units to exercise mobilization, mobility, and deployment, it made no provision for their realistic employment. The typical REDOUBT exercise scenario called for two rescue helicopters to perform runway alert throughout the exercise.[66]

Consequently, members of the 305th Aerospace Rescue and Recovery

Squadron at Selfridge ANGB, Michigan, with the encouragement of their collocated parent unit, the 403d Rescue and Recovery Wing, began to conduct their own combat rescue exercises. Following modest squadron efforts at Savannah, Georgia, in 1977, Wing Commander Col. James C. Wahleithner approved the concept, and the wing staff assumed the planning and conduct of subsequent exercises. The concept evolved progressively during phases at Gulfport, Mississippi, and Phelps Collins ANGB, Michigan, in 1978 and 1979, employing increasing numbers of units beyond the wing's purview to add realism and dimension to the exercise.[67]

It all came to a grand climax in northern Michigan in May 1982 as the wing, now commanded by Col. Richard L. Hall, conducted the combat rescue-training exercise (CRTE) CONDOR CRTE 82. CONDOR CRTE's primary objective was to create a realistic and comprehensive combat environment such as would be experienced in war. Phelps Collins ANGB was the forward operating location, and nearby Camp Grayling was base for the aggressor force. Representatives of 67 active and reserve units of all U.S. military services participated, either directly or in support roles. The 1,137 participating personnel were drawn from the U.S. Air Force, the Air Force Reserve, the Air National Guard, the U.S. Army, the U.S. Coast Guard, the U.S. Marine Corps, and Canadian rescue and infantry forces. Aside from C–130s and C–141s used to deploy the participants, forty-five aircraft were employed—HC–130Ns and Hs, HH–3Es, UH–1Ns, HH–1Ns, UH–1Ms, A–10s, C–130Es, a KC–135, and an OA–37. The aircraft and their crews accounted for 556 sorties and 880.2 flying hours during the employment phase of the exercise. The combat scenarios became increasingly complex as the exercise developed and the crews gained experience. An aggressor threat intensified as the scenario evolved. Although exposing some minor support problems that any similarly sized exercise would likely incur, CONDOR CRTE 82 was judged by both the Air Force Reserve and Aerospace Rescue and Recovery Service officials to have been fully successful in attaining its objectives. More important, aircrews of the Air Force Reserve's four rescue squadrons agreed with this assessment because they now thought they were receiving adequate and realistic combat rescue training.[68]

Assessing the Air Force Reserve Within the Total Force

The Defense Department's Total Force study of 1975 had found that the Total Force philosophy was more advanced in the Air Force Reserve and the Air National Guard than it was in the other reserve components. Assessing the first decade of the concept ten years later, a study published by the National Defense University found that integration of the Air Reserve Forces into the Total Force was more complete and that "The Air Reserve Forces presented a text book

The Air Force Reserve

case of success for the total-force policy."[69]

The study cited a near unanimous belief within both the reserve and active forces that the Air Reserve Forces components were models of what reserves could contribute to the national security if given sufficient means and support. The authors found this perception all the more convincing because it was freely stated by uniformed personnel of other regular and reserve components. They posited several reasons for this successful integration of the Air Reserve Forces by the Air Force under the Total Force Policy. Included were the major command's emphasis on the need to manage reserve components effectively and employ them in accomplishing the Air Force mission; the close relationships between gaining commands and reserve units; a low percentage of non–prior service personnel in reserve units and a corollary high level of experience among prior-service personnel; an Air Force willingness to provide additional flying training for reserve units; and that the Chief of Air Force Reserve, himself a reservist, actually commanded the Air Force Reserve.[70]

The study's observation that the Air Force Reservist was indistinguishable from the Regular Air Force member out on the flight line was well taken and was emphasized many times by Air Force Reserve leaders. General Lyon often made the point that when he went out on exercises or climbed into an associate unit C–141, he could not tell the difference between the reserve and the regular serviceman, except perhaps for the relative youth of the latter. Everyone, including the non–prior service reserve servicemen, had been trained in the same schools. Reservists left active duty for various reasons and reentered civilian society, but they continued to apply their Air Force training and schooling in the reserve.[71]

Major General Sidney S. Novaresi, who retired as a reserve numbered air force commander in 1982 after a long and varied active career as an Air Force Reservist, once shattered the aplomb of a group of senior Strategic Air Command officers in making the same points albeit more colorfully. In 1976, when the Air Force Reserve was preparing to acquire its first KC–135 refueling unit at March AFB, General Lyon sent General Novaresi down to a planning meeting hosted by Lt. Gen. B. M. Shotts, Fifteenth Air Force Commander, "to guard the candy store." Trying to dispel the Strategic Air Command officials' concerns about turning over their KC–135s to the "raggedy-ass militia," General Novaresi told them that they would find the reservists to be very professional, proud of their heritage, and proud of their blue suits:

> We weren't spawned by the side of the river; we came out of your system, we run no technical schools. You run those. All of our people go through them and graduate from them. All of us came out of your force. I came out of your force with about 14 years of active service.... If you don't like what you see, you'd better take a good look in the mirror because that's what you've created, because you're responsible for each and every one of us. You are responsible for the training we've received. You are responsible for the

The Air Force Reserve Matures

character, the integrity, and everything else that we display.... So don't look at the reservists and say, Boy, where did those guys come from?... You're going to find we fly airplanes better than you and we maintain them better than you do. We maintain our facilities better than you do. That's not because we are smarter than you are. That's because our maintenance people have about 15 years of maintenance experience. Yours have 4. My pilots have about 3,500 hours of experience. Yours have 1,500.... .so that's the kind of force you're getting and that's what we are.[72]

The Air Force Reserve Mobilization Capabilities

As prescribed by the U.S. Code, the fundamental purpose of each reserve component was "to provide trained units and qualified persons for active duty in the armed forces, in time of war or national emergency and at such other times as the national security requires."[73] In 1975, the Air Force incorporated this prescription into the formal mission statement of its Air Reserve Forces in the following words:

> The mission of the ARF [Air Reserve Forces] is to provide combat units, combat support units, and qualified personnel for active duty in the Air Force to support augmentation requirements and to perform such peacetime missions as are compatible with ARF training requirements and the maintenance of mobilization readiness.[74]

The Air Force Reserve's readiness and capability to fulfill this purpose and mission were gauged from a number of perspectives. Fully integrated into the Total Force, as depicted in the accompanying table, in 1981 the Air Force Reserve provided a large share of the Air Force's total capability in specific mission areas.[75]

Mission Forces Furnished by the Air Force Reserve Fiscal Year 1981

Air Force Reserve Component	Percent of Air Force Mission Forces Supplied
Strategic Airlift Aircrews	50
Strategic Airlift Maintenance Force	35
Aeromedical Airlift Crews	30
Tactical Airlift Force	36

The Air Force Reserve

Mission Forces Furnished, 1981—Cont'd

Air Force Reserve Component	Percent of Air Force Mission Forces Supplied
Weather Reconnaissance Force	35
Helicopter Rescue and Recovery Force	21
Aerial Spray Capability	100
Military Airlift Command Medical Crew	64
Aerial Port Capability	47
AC–130 Gunship Force	50
Tactical Fighter Force	8
KC–135 Refueling Force	4
KC–10 Aircrews	50
Combat Logistics Support Capability	60
Civil Engineering Capability	15

As another manifestation of its readiness, the Air Force Reserve surpassed its congressionally mandated drill-pay floor in fiscal year 1981 for the fourth consecutive year. Given a floor of 60,754, on September 30, 1981, the Air Force Reserve had 61,565 reservists assigned, including 52,304 in its units.[76]

Finally, measured in terms of operational readiness, the only Air Force Reserve units rated less than substantially combat-ready were flying units that were converting to new missions and a handful of nonflying units that were also experiencing certain Air Force–wide equipment shortages. Moreover, the force was flying its missions and numbers of hours and was passing its inspections. Indeed, as General Bodycombe told his commanders and staff in Washington in February 1982, by any of the conventional indices, as a military mobilization force, the Air Force Reserve was at a historical peak of readiness. Moreover, the Air Force Reserve could quickly assemble its forces and make them available to the Air Force.[*77] The Air Force Reserve could deliver itself upon mobilization. But once the units had responded and mobilized themselves, the rest was up to other agencies, that is, the gaining commands that acquired them upon mobilization and the bases that had to support them, at least for the moment.

---

[*]Understandably, each of General Bodycombe's successors has truthfully made the same statements ever since.

The Air Force Reserve Matures

Presidential Recall Authority

In 1970, Secretary of Defense Melvin R. Laird and Congress let the mobilization authority granted the President by the Russell Amendment of 1967 lapse. As matters stood in 1974, the President was authorized by the National Code to mobilize up to 1 million reservists involuntarily after a declaration of war or national emergency.[78] Early in 1974, Senator Sam Nunn became concerned about the Defense Department's planned uses of its reservists as well as the limited access the department had to them. He therefore asked the department to prepare a legislative proposal permitting the President to recall limited numbers of reservists to active duty for short periods under certain circumstances without declaring a national emergency.[79]

President Gerald R. Ford, successor to Richard Nixon in 1974, and his White House staff found the proposed bill satisfactory when it was prepared in November, but they asked that it be withheld until after the upcoming congressional elections.[80] It was then too late for the 93d Congress to act upon

Maj. Gen. Richard Bodycombe, Chief of Air Force Reserve, in a Pentagon ceremony on June 21, 1982, presents Air Force Reserve plaques of appreciation to General Lew Allen, Jr., Chief of Staff, U.S. Air Force (center), and General David C. Jones, Chairman of the Joint Chiefs of Staff (right), in recognition of their support of the Air Force Reserve in the Total Force.

337

The Air Force Reserve

it, and the bill was resubmitted in March 1975 as S–2115. As the Defense Department's chief witness, Secretary of Defense James R. Schlesinger emphasized the importance of the legislative proposal for the Total Force Policy. He noted that existing law forced the United States to make a massive response and declare a national emergency if it wanted to mobilize the Guard and Reserve forces. There were, of course, substantial diplomatic reasons for avoiding "massive response," and the Vietnam experience had demonstrated that there could be political inhibitions in employing reserve forces during a period of national involvement overseas. For these reasons, Secretary Schlesinger said, the Defense Department sought the flexibility of a more measured response as a means of strengthening the nation's deterrent posture.[81]

Delayed by amendments and discussion in both houses, the bill did not pass until May 3. As submitted to the White House for approval, it gave the President the requested limited authority to recall involuntarily up to 50,000 reservists of all or any service for up to 90 days. Once he did so, the President was required to transmit to both houses immediately the reasons for his actions and the intended use of the recalled reservists. This authority was not to be used during a domestic disturbance, and it was clearly not intended to permit the Department of Defense to circumvent manpower limitations by resorting to consecutive call-ups. The bill also provided that the service of the recalled reservists could be terminated either by order of the President or by a concurrent resolution of Congress.[82]

In its final form, the legislation expressed congressional concern that the reserve forces were less vital than they should be. The Armed Services Committees of both houses intended this legislation to ease access to a specific portion of the forces in a manner that would energize the entire program. The senators perceived that the failure to call the reserves during the Vietnam conflict planted doubts among the active force leaders as to the availability of the reservists, and it prejudiced these leaders against properly training and equipping the reservists. The new legislation addressed this perception by providing the authority to use the reserve forces for operations without the declaration of a national emergency. The senators thought this authority would underwrite the usefulness of the reservists in time of need and encourage the active force to provide modern equipment and meaningful missions to the reserve components.[83] In signing the measure as Public Law 94–286 on May 14, 1976, President Ford promised the nation that its provisions would be invoked only when clearly warranted, and then, most judiciously.[84]

Concluding from exercise experience that 50,000 reservists might not be enough under certain circumstances, in April 1980 the Defense Department requested legislation to extend the authority to 100,000. The proposed legislation passed both Houses of Congress early in December, and President

The Air Force Reserve Matures

Jimmy Carter signed it as Public Law 96–584 on December 23, 1980.*[85] After May 1976, therefore, the President had full authority to order the recall of limited numbers of reservists under certain circumstances.

The Management Assistance Group and Its Implications

Despite the development of the Air Force Reserve as a valuable component which conducted practical missions on a daily basis and promised a combat-ready mobilization resource (or possibly because of it), the active force was not loath to tinker with the structure of the reserve element. After investing heavily in the Air Force Reserve, the Air Force insisted on a full return and would not hesitate to step in and assert control if the Reserve showed signs of weakness. Such an instance occurred in 1982.

In November 1981, although invalidating some alleged improprieties in the Headquarters AFRES management practices, Maj. Gen. William R. Usher, Director of Personnel Plans for the U.S. Air Force, recommended that the Air Force Inspector General review the management of the Air Force Reserve. During his visit at headquarters, General Usher learned that—shades of the discord between Generals Marchbanks and Moore—General Bodycombe and Headquarters AFRES Vice Commander Maj. Gen. Edward Dillon did not always conceal differences in policy and operating philosophy. Uncertain about how far the differences between these two reserve officials extended, and concerned that they could dilute the effectiveness of the component upon which the Air Force had learned to depend so much in the Total Force environment, Usher returned to Washington with his reservation.[86]

General Robert C. Mathis, Air Force Vice Chief of Staff, thereupon constituted the Air Force Management Assistance Group on January 29, 1982. After receiving preliminary briefings, the group spent a week visiting officials in the Office of Air Force Reserve. Thereafter, the 28-person group visited Headquarters AFRES and other active and reserve organizations and agencies, interviewing officials and employees, evaluating directives, and assessing the effectiveness of management practices.[87] The Air Force Management Assistance Group submitted its final report on April 30. As its major finding it said:

> Air Force Reserve units, except those in conversion status, are combat ready and consistently received high ratings during inspections by the Gaining Commands. Reserve units participated daily with the active force in several major operational areas and have repeatedly proven to be highly qualified,

---

*Public Law 99–661, Department of Defense Appropriations Authorization Act, 1987, increased the recall authority to 200,000.

The Air Force Reserve

Maj. Gen. Edward Dillon served as Vice Commander, Headquarters AFRES, from April 16, 1979, to April 28, 1982.

often demonstrating greater skills than active force personnel. The Total Force Policy is implemented effectively and working well in areas such as operations, programming, and logistics. Personnel at reserve units are competent and conscientious managers and technicians.[88]

The report then inexplicably recommended 249 changes to the Air Force Reserve management structure, system, and procedures, many of which would have been devastating. It recommended stripping the Chief of Air Force Reserve of his role as Commander of Headquarters AFRES and redistributing some Office of Air Force Reserve functions within the Air Staff to emphasize reserve participation in the Air Staff planning, programming, and budget system. It recommended Headquarters AFRES be redesignated as a major command to recognize its divers missions and its partnership in the total force. The Headquarters AFRES Commander would be a reserve major general reporting to the Chief of Air Force Reserve, who held the rank of lieutenant general and who would remain the principal adviser to the Chief of Staff on Air Force Reserve matters. The group recommended that the Air Force Reserve Vice Commander be a regular officer and the Chief of Staff a reservist. Further, the Air Reserve Personnel Center should revert to separate operating agency status and report to the Headquarters USAF Deputy Chief of Staff for

The Air Force Reserve Matures

Manpower and Personnel.* Finally, the group recommended that the 2600th Reserve Recruiting Group be divested from the Air Force Reserve and aligned under the the Air Force Recruiting Service.[89]

Whatever their merits, the major recommendations of the Air Force Management Assistance Group would require thorough staffing as well as consideration by the Air Reserve Forces Policy Committee before they could be implemented. Public Law 90-168, Reserve Forces Bill of Rights and Vitalization Act, provided that the committee review and comment on all major policies affecting the reserve forces.[90]

Quite aside from the law's built-in safeguards, ever alert to the threats against the reserve components, the Reserve Officers Association protested implementation of the group's major recommendations. Charging that these actions would return the Air Force Reserve to the unsatisfactory status it had endured before the passage of Public Law 90-168, the association protested to Congress and civilian officials in the Pentagon. It noted the irony of the Air Force's considering this reorganization at the very time the Senate Armed Services Committee had directed the Secretary of the Army to consider realigning the Army Reserve along the lines of the Air Force Reserve.[91]

Civilian officials of the Air Force and Defense Department also questioned the proposed actions. On May 3, Tidal W. McCoy, Assistant Secretary of the Air Force for Manpower, Reserve Affairs, and Installations, advised Lt. Gen. Hans H. Driessnack, Assistant Vice Chief of Staff of the Air Force, of his intention to assure that the Air Staff fully considered the ramifications of the group's proposals. This would be particularly critical, he said, "if any major functional or command realignments are ultimately proposed which could be interpreted as diminishing the public stature now enjoyed by the Guard and the Reserve."[92]

Discussing the matter the same day with Air Force Secretary Verne Orr, McCoy observed that the Air Staff's apparent perception that increasing the integration of the Air Force Reserve into the active force as the key to better management was not substantiated by the successful peacetime operation of the Air Force Reserve. McCoy also reminded Orr of the relevance of Public Law 90-168 on the matter; he emphasized the provision for review of proposed major policy changes by the Air Reserve Forces Policy Committee. He noted the law certainly implied that returning to the old management system and divesting the Air Force Reserve of some of its power and authority would almost certainly generate not only congressional resistance but also a strong

---

*In July 1978 in consonance with other Air Force organization changes, Headquarters AFRES became a direct reporting unit and the Air Reserve Personnel Center an organizational element of the Air Force Reserve (Ltr, DAF/PRM 167q, Col Harold S. Gillogy, Dep Dir/M&O, to AFRES & ARPC, subj: Organization Changes Affecting Certain Air Force Reserve Units, Jun 14, 1978—as Document 2, Hist, AFRES, 1978).

The Air Force Reserve

reaction from such groups as the Air Force Association, the National Guard Association of the United States, and the Air Force Sergeants' Association, in addition to the Reserve Officers Association which had already spoken up. Finally, he noted that Dr. Edward Philbin, his counterpart in the Office of the Secretary of Defense, had already conveyed his desire to be kept abreast of developments by his encouragement of the Army and the Navy to model their reserve programs along Air Force lines.*[93]

On June 17, General Bodycombe submitted the Air Force Reserve's views on the management assistance group's report to Secretary Orr. Since the report was 186 pages long and included 249 recommendations, he restricted his remarks to several major recommendations which, if implemented, would damage the Air Force Reserve. First, however, he expressed dismay over the dichotomy in the report, which at once praised the combat readiness of the flying force but promised to destroy the management structure that fostered it. He also questioned the management assistance group's intention to return the Air Force Reserve to an organizational structure found lacking in the past.

He rejected the idea of divesting the Chief of Air Force Reserve of his role as Commander of the Air Force Reserve. He recalled the history of the early years in the implementation of Public Law 90–168 and the problems when the Chief of Air Force Reserve and the Commander at Headquarters AFRES reported separately with differing views to the Chief of Staff. He protested the management assistance group's proposal to decentralize certain elements of the Office of Air Force Reserve operations and personnel staffs to other Air Staff functions. Like the duality of his position and the major command issue, the fundamental question, he said, was whether the authority to manage the Air Force Reserve rested in the Chief's office or at the operating headquarters at Robins. General Bodycombe did not concur in designating the vice commander's position at Headquarters AFRES for a regular force brigadier general because that would be incompatible with retaining the dual-hat concept.

General Bodycombe also rejected the Management Assistance Group's recommendation that the Air Force Reserve be divested of its personnel center and recruiting service. He could not concur in reinstating the Air Reserve Personnel Center as a separate operating agency with its commander reporting to and receiving guidance from the Air Force Deputy Chief of Staff for Manpower and Personnel. He argued that the mission of the Air Force Reserve was to provide trained people to the active force in time of war; it dealt in people, and the Air Reserve Personnel Center managed them. Management of reservists by reservists was key to the Air Force Reserve's success. Reservists had to be managed and serviced differently from active force personnel. They were a high priority to the Air Force Reserve, but that priority would be lost

---

*In a telephone conversation in early May during this time, Dr. Philbin promised the author that "the Air Force Reserve would be dismantled over my dead body."

The Air Force Reserve Matures

under active force management.

With respect to the 2600th Reserve Recruiting Group's being aligned under the Air Force Recruiting Service, Bodycombe asserted that the Air Force Reserve militia concept made local commanders responsible to man their units, and recruiters worked under the operational control of the senior local commander. This forced the local commanders to work personally in the community to make recruiting programs successful. In addition, each member of the unit was expected to refer candidates to the recruiters. It was this close relationship among reserve recruiters, commanders, and unit members that had produced fully manned reserve units for several years. Moreover, experiments to merge the active and reserve recruiting forces had failed twice in the past.[94]

When General Bodycombe submitted the Air Force Reserve's response to the management report to the Inspector General, he repeated the fundamental positions he had outlined to Secretary Orr, and he insisted that his position be an essential part of any evaluation. He also suggested that these issues be included in the Air Reserve Forces Policy Committee's review.[95]

Thereafter, not much more happened to the Air Force Management Assistance Group's recommendations. A steering group appointed by General Mathis met once and disposed of twenty-two of the lesser recommendations.[96] It was to have met again in August, but it never did. Along the way, General Dillon was reassigned, and General Bodycombe was granted early retirement. In the only major recommendation ever implemented, Headquarters AFRES and the Air Reserve Personnel Center were reinstated as separate operating agencies reporting to the Chief of the Air Force Reserve.[97] By the time Maj. Gen. Sloan R. Gill succeeded General Bodycombe as Chief of the Air Force

Before succeeding General Bodycombe as Chief of Air Force Reserve in November 1982, Maj. Gen. Sloan R. Gill successfully defended the Air Reserve technician program as a dual-status system.

343

The Air Force Reserve

Reserve in November 1982, General Charles A. Gabriel was Chief of Staff of the Air Force, and the Management Assistance Group's finding that the Air Force Reserve and its people were operationally ready satisfied him. Except for some continued pressure by the personnel community of the Air Force to assimilate the Air Force Reserve recruiting structure, the Management Assistance Group episode of Air Force Reserve history was concluded.[98]

The episode brought about the reassignment of the vice commander and hastened the retirement of the Chief, However, aside from the restoration of the Air Force Reserve and the Air Reserve Personnel Center as separate operating agencies, it produced no change in the Air Force Reserve management structure or in the way it did business, hardly a significant return on the great investment in time and personnel. Nevertheless, the experience contained some lessons for both the Air Force Reserve and the Air Force about the nature of their relationship, lessons that may require reinforcement from time to time. The Air Force had to accept the fact that the existence of the Office of Air Force Reserve and the function of the Chief of Air Force Reserve as a reservist were established by law at the express wish of Congress. The same law also strengthened the Air Reserve Forces Policy Committee as an advisory body to the Secretary of the Air Force. The assistant secretaries for reserve affairs, whose positions rested in the law, opposed arbitrary efforts by the active force to curtail the agencies. For its part, however, the Air Force Reserve leadership was reminded that while guaranteeing the Air Force Reserve's existence, Public Law 90–168 did not give it autonomy.

The law gave the component the right to exist, manage itself, and command its forces in peacetime. Reservists trained themselves, but the Air Force, exercising its right to assure the readiness of the forces it would call upon in an emergency, set the standards and evaluated reserve performance against them. As concept or policy, Total Force pertained to the programming, planning, and employment of reserve forces, not to their management or command in peacetime. That was the benefit of Public Law 90–168.

The Air Force Reserve leadership contained the seeds of its own destruction. If it could not present a unified front, it invited problems. The force would be there and would continue to respond as it always had. However, when leadership becomes disorganized and cannot present a unified front for obtaining equipment and missions, the force will have less with which to respond.

13

From Flying Club to Total Force*

One of the two civilian components of the U.S. Air Force, the post–World War II Air Reserve (which became the U.S. Air Force Reserve) began in 1946 as an acknowledged flying club with little purpose other than to allow reserve pilots to fly. Over the years, benefiting from changing reserve policies, the air reserve component evolved into a taut, fully ready operational force upon which the Air Force could, and did, depend for instant augmentation in times of national crisis. In the process of its training, the Air Force Reserve has paid a handsome dividend to the parent force and the nation in its daily operational missions.

Evolution of the Structure

The Army Air Forces was never sure of what should comprise its reserve force, how large a force it should be, or what place the reserve forces should have in its overall war plans. In the face of these uncertainties, the Army Air Forces initially developed an umbrella reserve program to include all air reservists under its coverage. A number of problems were inherent in this approach. It was very costly, and the Army Air Forces (later, the U.S. Air Force) could not

---

*Portions of this chapter were prepared in 1995 by the staff at Headquarters AFRES Directorate of Historical Services at the request of Dr. Richard P. Hallion, Air Force Historian. He wished to have Mr Cantwell's original narrative expanded to include more recent events of the 1982–1994 period. Contributors include Dr. Charles F. O'Connell, Jr., Command Historian, Headquarters AFRES; Dr. Kenneth C. Kan; Ms Margaret L. MacMackin; and Mr. Christiaan J. Husing. These authors dedicate their work to the memory of Gerald T. Cantwell, who died in 1994.

345

The Air Force Reserve

define precise mobilization requirements; neither could it justify the large expenditure of funds. Pressed for funds, its leaders tried to conduct an inexpensive program, and they obtained commensurate results. Thousands of air reservists did some flying in trainer airplanes, while others experienced very little satisfactory participation.

In 1949 there occurred the first of four definitive program changes that would shape and benefit the Air Force Reserve. Responding to complaints from reservists, service associations, congressmen, and even the White House regarding the inadequacies of the Air Force Reserve program, the Air Staff developed a more structured program to include tactical units and a program of mobilization assignments for individuals. The tactical units appealed to reservists who, assisted with trainers and training doctrine from the Continental Air Command, developed themselves into recognizable combat units. Mobilization in 1950 and 1951 disrupted the peacetime reserve structure, making it necessary for the Air Force to reestablish the Air Force Reserve, a process that lasted from 1953 through 1958. The initial post–Korean War Air Force Reserve was a balanced force of troop carrier, reconnaissance, light bombardment, fighter, and rescue flying units augmented by a number of nonflying support units.

In 1958, however, the second change in conceptual direction to benefit the Air Reserve occurred. Reflecting demands for economy in the Defense Department and force changes necessitated by the Eisenhower administration's defense policy of massive nuclear retaliation, the Air Force Reserve flying program was restructured as an all-troop, carrier-rescue force. Unlike their predecessors, however, these units had mobilization missions defined in Air Force war plans. Their readiness was assisted by implementation of the Air Reserve technician plan in 1958. Under this program, civilian technicians who also occupied key reserve positions in their units provided an administrative and training continuity previously lacking. Implementation of the Air Reserve technician program became the first sure step toward the development of a truly operationally ready Air Force Reserve.

Another beneficial change occurred in 1960. Although the Continental Air Command had done its job well, the Air Staff, in seeking to develop fully ready units responsive to Air Force needs, decentralized training of the reserve units to the major commands that would gain them upon mobilization. Taking a greater interest in the units they would acquire in wartime, the gaining commands supervised training more intently and provided frequent operational and exercise experience.

Developments in 1968 increased the stature of the Air Force Reserve. Public Law 90–168 mandated the establishment of the Office of Air Force Reserve under the Chief of Air Force Reserve, a reservist recalled to active duty, as the Air Force Chief of Staff's primary adviser on Air Force Reserve matters. When the second Chief of Air Force Reserve assumed the additional role, Commander of Headquarters AFRES (the successor to the Continental Air Command), he unified the command structure of the component. The Air Force's full acceptance and implementation of the provisions of Public Law 90–168, which had the effect of giving the Air Force Reserve a degree of management autonomy under its own leaders, became the second leg of the tripod upon which readiness of the Air Force Reserve rested.

As the war in Southeast Asia subsided, the Air Force began to pass more modern equipment to the Air Reserve Forces and include the reserve in force planning and daily use as part of the total Air Force. By 1973, the Department of Defense had expanded the Air Force's Total Force concept into departmental policy.

Air Force implementation of the Total Force Policy, the full integration of its reserve forces into the plans and operations of the active force, became the final leg of the tripod upon which the readiness of the 1981 Air Force Reserve rested. Adapting to the demands of Total Force, the Air Force Reserve soon demonstrated its ability to employ modern airplanes and equipment. In the associate programs, the reservists maintained and flew C–141s, C–5s, C–9s, and KC–10s. The equipped force included F–4 and KC–135 units. Ground technicians and support personnel kept pace, accepting new roles and complex technical equipment. Through more efficiently managed mobilization augmentee programs, individual reservists contributed as well. In cockpits, on the line, in the shops, and in headquarters offices it was impossible to distinguish the Air Force Reservists of the Total Force from their active force counterparts.

In the Air Force Management Assistance Group review of 1982, Air Force Reserve leaders expressed their conviction that the management structure in place provided the nation with a vibrant, combat-ready Air Force Reserve. With more than a decade of Total Force experience behind them, these leaders shared a common belief that, given adequate support, Air Force Reservists could respond effectively to any challenge.

The 1980s proved to be a period of expansion for almost every aspect of the Air Force Reserve program. Defense policies in the administration of President Ronald W. Reagan channeled additional funds to the nation's military, and a percentage of this money reached Air Force Reserve coffers. The command's operation and maintenance budget grew from $511.4 million in fiscal year 1980 to $1.07 billion in fiscal 1989, while the assigned strength of the reserve unit and individual mobilization augmentee programs grew from 58,921 to 82,489. The operation and maintenance budget supported a fleet of 478 assigned aircraft that flew about 139,000 hours in fiscal year 1980. By fiscal 1989, the fleet had grown only slightly (to 504 assigned aircraft), but the flying-hour program had grown to 497,000 hours.[1]

These numbers reflected the Reagan administration's commitment to rebuild a defense establishment that had, in the administration's view, been

The Air Force Reserve

allowed to become hollow in the years following the end of the Southeast Asia conflict. On taking office, President Reagan and his Secretary of Defense, Caspar W. Weinberger, asked Congress for funds to improve readiness, modernize conventional and strategic forces, and improve the quality of life of military personnel. While the final defense budgets submitted by the Carter administration had reversed the downward trend of defense spending throughout the 1970s, Secretary Weinberger and the services sought funds to accelerate the turnaround. Congress generally supported these requests, at least through fiscal year 1985.[2]

In Secretary Weinberger's words, the Reagan administration pursued a military strategy that was "simple to state and very difficult to achieve; it was to regain, as quickly as possible, sufficient military strength to convince our friends to stay closely aligned with us and to convince the Soviets they could not win any war they might start against us or our allies."[3] Thus deterrence remained firmly in place as the cornerstone of American defense policy throughout the decade. While discussions of deterrence generally focused on strategic nuclear weapons, the Reagan administration committed itself to strengthening the nation's conventional forces as a way of reducing reliance on these weapons. An extended debate over when and how those forces might be used (sparked by Secretary Weinberger's November 1984 speech to the National Press Club in Washington where he enunciated six tests that should be applied before the United States decided to commit conventional forces to combat) did little to slow the revitalization of these forces that occurred throughout the decade.[4]

The defense buildup of the early 1980s affected the Air Force Reserve in many ways. The Air Force followed through on the force modernization commitment central to Total Force, an effort that saw six Air Force Reserve wings and ten Air Force Reserve groups undergo some type of major equipment conversion. The command's tactical airlift units continued to swap their C–7s and C–123s for C–130s while fighter units turned in their A–37s and F–105s for A–10s, F–4s, and in January 1984, the Air Force Reserve's first F–16s. The strategic airlift force added its first unit-equipped C–5s in December 1984 and its first unit-equipped C–141s in July 1986. The associate force added the KC–10A to its roster in November 1981.[5]

These and other force structure changes contributed to an increase of almost 40 percent in the number of personnel assigned to the reserve unit program. However, new manning policies introduced in 1987 forced the Reserve to pursue a markedly different recruiting philosophy. Before then, Air Force Reserve units recruited to a personnel strength floor which left recruiters and commanders some leeway to exceed minimum strength levels, otherwise known as overmanning. Congress turned the process around in 1987, imposing a personnel strength ceiling on the command that provided money for a not-to-exceed end-strength.[6]

Flying Club to Total Force

Meeting the demands of the Total Force, the Air Force Reserve demonstrated its ability to employ and maintain modern aircraft and equipment. Airplanes that Reservists in the associate's program flew include those shown here:

C–141

C–5

The Air Force Reserve

C–9

KC–10

Flying Club to Total Force

A KC–135 refueling an F–4

F–4

The Air Force Reserve

C–119

C–123

Flying Club to Total Force

C–124

This policy change forced the command to impose new and more stringent manpower policies on its units. All were expected to pursue recruiting, retention, and training policies yielding the highest possible readiness levels; however, commanders were required to reduce overmanning. The personnel community conducted an aggressive review of participation records and transferred members whose participation had not met standards to the Air Reserve Personnel Center for reassignment to other reserve categories. The review also targeted individuals who were "not tasked under a UTC [unit type code] and/or whose loss does not adversely affect the unit's 'C' ratings."[7] These personnel were also subject to transfer to the Air Reserve Personnel Center. Commanders found themselves much more limited in their ability to create and fill positions not established on gaining, major command–approved unit manning documents. When valid vacancies did occur, units attempted to level their personnel resources by transferring manpower within the unit before adding new members to the rolls (a process that tended to limit the number of reservists who found themselves involuntarily separated from the program as a result of the floor-to-ceiling switch).[8]

Air Force Reserve leaders expressed concern with the new policy. During hearings before the Senate on the Department of Defense Appropriation for fiscal year 1988, Maj. Gen. Roger P. Scheer, Chief of Air Force Reserve, voiced reservations about the manning ceiling. He stated that since the Reserve had already reached its personnel ceiling, it could not keep "people in the total force—[that is,] when they want to leave active duty, [by] bringing them into

353

The Air Force Reserve

Maj. Gen. Roger P. Scheer, Chief of Air Force Reserve (November 1, 1986–October 31, 1990)

the Reserve Forces." General Scheer's remarks received a sympathetic reception from one senator who stated it made sense to raise the guard and reserve end-strength in order to accommodate individuals leaving active duty as a result of budgetary and end-strength reductions; nevertheless the ceiling remained in place.[9]

General Scheer's misgivings notwithstanding, the Air Force Reserve usually met its mandated ceiling throughout the 1980s, but manpower issues regularly attracted the attention of General Scheer and his staff. In fiscal year 1984, Reserve retention rates (the measure of the command's ability to keep personnel) exceeded command goals for the first time, but this success was short-lived. Two years later in fiscal 1986, the Air Force Reserve lost more than 10,000 of the members it had hoped to keep, the largest loss noted since 1977 when the command began tracking retention. Reassignment to inactive status because of unsatisfactory participation (an outgrowth of the imposition of the manpower ceiling) accounted for most of the losses. In 1988, General Scheer emphasized that retention was critical to maintaining combat readiness. He enjoined commanders to make every effort to retain trained and experienced reservists, whose loss was a blow to the program.[10]

In 1988, General Scheer directed Maj. Gen. Alan G. Sharp, Headquarters AFRES Vice Commander, to convene a panel to examine retention issues. While it acknowledged the validity of General Scheer's broad concerns, the group recommended imposing stringent new policies on unexcused absences and unit training, assembly absence procedures. In short, reservists could not exceed a stipulated number of absences before being reassigned to individual Ready Reserve status.[11] On a more positive note, the group recommended an expansion of existing programs that paid bonuses to members who reenlisted or voluntarily retrained to undermanned career fields. By the end of the decade, the command added bonuses for former active duty personnel in selected career fields who joined the reserve program, refined the reenlistment bonus program to enable it to respond to periodic shortages in targeted fields, and established a participation awards program. By the end of the decade, retention levels again exceeded command goals.[12]

The Air Force Reserve paid particular attention to Air Reserve technician pilot manning. During the late 1980s, the active duty Air Force experienced significant losses of trained aircrew members. In fiscal year 1989, the Air Force lost 1,000 more pilots than it produced in its Undergraduate Pilot Training program. In contrast, reserve pilot manning overall remained steady, but Air Reserve technician pilot retention became a matter of concern. In 1985, the command responded to this longstanding problem by instituting an intern recruiting effort under the auspices of the Air Force Civilian Personnel community's Palace Acquire program. Although the program was small (six slots in fiscal year 1989), the intern program provided the means for a newly recruited Air Reserve technician pilot to advance from the entry level position of airplane pilot to a better-paid flight instructor position.[13]

The Reserve also pursued a number of initiatives to bolster Air Reserve technician pilot recruiting and retention levels. These actions included aggressively recruiting active duty pilots who had left the service and advertising job openings in commercial publications (efforts that supported the recruitment of aircrew personnel who also served as traditional reservists). Retention incentives included establishing new position classification standards which enabled commanders to upgrade positions; attempting to reduce pilot workload by adding additional administrative positions to unit manning documents; offering relocation service assistance to Air Reserve technicians who accepted positions at other units; and pushing back mandatory separation dates so Air Reserve technicians could retain their technician status until they became eligible to retire from the federal civil service.[14]

Another long-standing Air Reserve technician issue—the status quo question—moved toward resolution during the decade. Although it had long since ceased to be the burning issue it once was, the Air Force Reserve staff continued to work the issue. In 1987, the Air Force Reserve finally won Office of Personnel Management approval to amend the basic technician agreement. Among the amendment's provisions was the stipulation that officer and enlisted technicians in a variety of categories who were no longer eligible for reserve membership through no fault of their own were to be enrolled in the Department of Defense's priority placement program for nontechnician positions. Anyone who did not accept a position offered through this program

The Air Force Reserve

at the same or higher grade would be separated.[15]

Issues affecting traditional reservists also attracted command attention. In October 1986, Reserve officials began work on a detailed study of enlisted force issues. The review included a wide range of topics such as recruiting, retirement, separation, strength by grade, and promotions. Brig. Gen. Dale R. Baumler, Fourteenth Air Force Commander, chaired the study group, which also included enlisted personnel, numbered air force, Air Reserve Personnel Center, field unit, and statutory tour representatives. The panel convened in April 1987 and eventually developed a list of twenty-six action items. By April 1989, all the group's issues had been worked to some resolution, although resolution did not always mean that the recommendations had become Air Force Reserve policy. In some cases (such as formalizing recruiting and retention bonus programs), policy changes recommended by the panel were incorporated into new or revised Air Force regulations. In others (such as high year of tenure), the command developed a program that accommodated the panel's recommendations. A few issues (such as promotion based on length of service, the establishment of an Air Force Reserve professional military education facility, and changes in the way retirement points were calculated) were not implemented because they would have violated federal law or because the Air Force, gaining major command, or Air Force Reserve staff felt the issue did not warrant implementation.[16]

Despite the turmoil brought on by force structure, force modernization, and personnel policy changes, the Air Force Reserve successfully met all the operational challenges it faced during the 1980s. The command had long since outgrown its flying club past, but in some circles it was still seen as an organization of flagpole flyers who provided that Air Force little more than the proverbial one-weekend a month. The beginning of the Total Force era in the early 1970s highlighted the passing of this view at the highest levels, but stereotypes are rarely erased overnight. As Secretary of Defense Melvin R. Laird noted in 1970, the Air Force Reserve generated a significant amount of airlift capability as a by-product of its normal training operations. During fiscal year 1980, such by-product airlift produced 5,394 missions that moved 4,058 tons of cargo and 37,402 passengers. At the end of the decade, the command's 5,720 by-product airlift missions moved 41,487 tons of cargo and 127,367 passengers.[17] The gaining major commands, and especially Military Airlift Command, came to rely increasingly on the Air Force Reserve as a provider of routine airlift support on a day-to-day basis. Other Air Force components looked to the Air Force Reserve for assistance to support a wide range of contingency, rescue, and humanitarian operations during the decade. Events demonstrated that their confidence was well-founded.

Flying Club to Total Force

Emergency Relief and Contingency Operations

Throughout its metamorphosis through various organizational and conceptual structures, the Air Force Reserve returned an operational dividend on the parent Air Force's investment in training and equipment dollars. As the post–Korean War troop carrier units acquired proficiency, they began to participate in domestic emergency relief and airlift operations. Early airlift programs included Operation SIXTEEN TON, the transport of Coast Guard equipment to the Caribbean in 1956; Operation SWIFT LIFT the following year, when the troop carrier units used inactive duty training time to airlift personnel and cargo for the Tactical Air Command; and Operation READY SWAP, an open-ended airlift in which units transported aircraft engines between the Air Force's depots. Along with point-to-point airlifts, reserve units began dropping paratroops, ultimately participating with active and reserve Army and Air Force units in joint exercises.

Late in 1963, with its active airlift units overwhelmed by burgeoning requirements in the Far East, the Air Force called upon the Air Force Reserve for help. Beginning with a handful of monthly missions, reserve C–124 units flew missions to Southeast Asia until 1973, when this aircraft left the Air Force Reserve inventory. By significantly augmenting the Air Force even while remaining on inactive duty during the early Vietnam war years, the Air Force Reserve helped make it possible for President Johnson to conduct the war without resorting to a mobilization of reserve forces until 1968.

Air Force Reserve troop carrier units equipped with the smaller C–119 and C–123 aircraft contributed to the active-force mission as well. In April 1965, when Johnson intervened in a political crisis in the Dominican Republic, the Air Force conducted an airlift into the island to support U.S. forces and provide emergency relief supplies to the populace. Participating in the operation voluntarily between April 30 and July 5, Air Force Reserve aircrews flew approximately 1,850 missions. With C–124 units already committed to the Southeast Asia missions, C–119 units bore the brunt of Air Force Reserve participation. A few C–123s and C–124s were there as well. Undoubtedly the mission could have been performed without the Air Force Reserve, but the reserve organization's participation facilitated the Air Force's discharge of the airlift as required by presidential policy.

The Dominican operations had demonstrated the capabilities of the reserve C–119 units, and the Air Force began to use them on missions along the coasts of North and Central America. During the next eight years C–119 units conducted more than 3,600 offshore missions. This freed the active force's four-engine aircraft to support the Southeast Asia requirement.

In October 1973, when Arab forces attacked Israel, the United States came to the aid of the Jewish state with a mammoth airlift of military equipment. Military Airlift Command C–141s and C–5s conducted the bulk of the airlift,

The Air Force Reserve

with Air Force Reserve associate unit aircrews participating heavily. In all, 650 air reservists volunteered to fly to the Middle East, and 286 did so. These included 24 all-reserve crews and 183 reservists who flew into Israel itself.

From August 1968 to the very last flight from Saigon in May 1975, aircrews of the associate units were involved in Air Force airlift operations into and within Southeast Asia. Air Force Reserve support of the War in Southeast Asia was not confined to air operations. From May 1966 on, reservists on extended active duty and inactive duty tours augmented the Air Force's intelligence function. Beginning in 1972, intelligence reservists also participated in the Surgeon General's counseling program for families of the prisoners and the missing, interrogated released prisoners, and analyzed prisoner experiences.

Other Air Force Reservists provided various forms of support throughout the Vietnam period. Nurses and medical technicians served volunteer tours of duty by staffing hospitals in the United States throughout the war. Some ferried aircraft between Vietnam and the United States and provided flying and maintenance training to Vietnamese personnel in the United States and in Vietnam. Volunteers from aerial port units operated at U-Tapao AB in Thailand in tours as long as 120 days to alleviate shortages there. Reserve lawyers and chaplains supported the Air Force effort in Southeast Asia by providing the entire spectrum of legal and religious procedures to servicemen and their dependents. Notable as its inactive duty contributions were, the Air Force Reserve was perceived as a mobilization force, and on several occasions over the years, parts of it did mobilize.

Humanitarian operations in other forms have long afforded Air Force Reserve units an opportunity to serve their communities directly. In May 1980, the 304th Aerospace Rescue and Recovery Squadron, Portland IAP, Oregon, assisted by a handful of other Air Force Reserve units, rescued ninety-one people after Mount Saint Helens erupted in Washington State. Later that year, members of the 302d Special Operations Squadron, stationed at Davis-Monthan AFB, Arizona, but deployed to Nellis AFB, Nevada, for training, rescued fifteen guests trapped on balconies of the blazing MGM Grand Hotel in Las Vegas. Aircraft and crews of the 907th Tactical Airlift Group, Rickenbacker ANGB, Ohio, provided the Air Force with its only aerial spray capability. The unit sprayed millions of acres each year, combating both weeds and insect pests. The group helped put down infestations of encephalitis-bearing mosquitoes in Minnesota in 1983 and grasshoppers in Idaho in 1985.[18]

Other Air Force Reserve units provided a range of additional services. The 815th Weather Reconnaissance Squadron, part of the 403d Tactical Airlift Wing, Keesler AFB, Mississippi, worked with active duty hurricane hunters to track threatening storms in the western Atlantic and eastern Pacific Oceans. Reserve units responded to a drought in the southeastern United States by airlifting hay in 1986. A Reserve C–141 flew tents to Soviet Armenia following

Flying Club to Total Force

an earthquake there in 1988. Strategic and tactical airlift units helped transport relief equipment and supplies to California after an earthquake there in 1989, while California reservists helped operate emergency command posts, disaster shelters, and medical facilities. The command provided similar services, albeit on a smaller scale, following earthquakes and other natural disasters in Central and South America. In the summer of 1987, two Air Force Reserve F–4s operating from Iceland intercepted a pair of Soviet Bear bombers over the north Atlantic.[19]

Air Force Reservists also responded to a variety of contingency operations during the decade. In 1983, associate aircrews and aeromedical evacuation teams flew seven missions to assist in the evacuation of dead and wounded marines following the destruction of their barracks in Beirut, Lebanon, in mid-October 1983; reservists flew the aircraft that evacuated the first twelve wounded marines. Just a few days later, reservists supported Operation URGENT FURY, the invasion of Grenada. Most of the 20 strategic airlift missions flown by reserve crews brought troops to the island and flew American citizens home. An associate C–141 crew from the 315th Military Airlift Wing, Charleston AFB, South Carolina, brought the first group of students evacuated from the island back to Charleston. Reserve medical units provided aeromedical evacuation personnel on these flights, while other personnel supported the operation, both directly and indirectly, from their home stations.[20]

Command personnel began to demonstrate their skills more effectively at Air Force competitions held throughout the decade. With a few exceptions, Air Force Reserve teams had not performed well at these events earlier than about 1983, when the 301st Tactical Fighter Wing captured the award, Best A–10 Maintenance, at Gunsmoke 83, the Tactical Air Command's fighter weapons competition. At Volant Rodeo 84, the Military Airlift Command's airlift competition, Air Force Reserve units took Best C–141 Aircrew and Best Maintenance Team awards.[21] Then, in 1985, the Air Force Reserve embarked on a string of superlative performances at these competitions. It captured Top Gun awards at Gunsmokes in 1987 and 1989,[22] Top Team awards at Gunsmoke 85 and Volant Rodeo 85, and Best KC–135 Unit at the Strategic Air Command's Bombing and Navigation Competition in 1985, in addition to other category awards at these competitions.[23] This string of successes would continue into the 1990s.

Two events, both close to home, highlighted the extent to which the Air Force Reserve had integrated itself almost seamlessly into day-to-day operations of the U.S. Air Force by the end of the 1980s. Both suggested, in varying degrees, the role the Air Force Reserve would play in the Air Force of the 1990s. In September 1989, Hurricane Hugo struck South Carolina. In December of the same year, American forces invaded Panama.

Hurricane Hugo highlighted virtually all of the Air Force Reserve's peacetime roles. The 815th Weather Reconnaissance Squadron, Keesler AFB,

The Air Force Reserve

Mississippi, first began tracking the storm that would become Hugo on September 14. The squadron eventually flew twenty-one sorties into the storm as it approached the mainland. Crews from Military Airlift Command's 437th Military Airlift Wing and the Air Force Reserve's 315th Military Airlift Wing (Associate) evacuated C–141s from their home station, Charleston AFB, South Carolina, in the face of the storm. Hugo, which had already caused heavy damage in the U.S. Virgin Islands and in Puerto Rico, struck the Carolinas on September 22, the eye passing over the city of Charleston. The storm devastated the city and the air base, which shared facilities with the city's municipal airport. Personnel from the 315th responded immediately to the crisis and were soon joined by hundreds of other reservists. Air Force Reserve units, already flying relief missions into the Caribbean, increased the tempo of their operations to begin moving volunteers and relief supplies into Charleston. Eleven Air Force Reserve C–130, C–141, and C–5 units flew relief mission to areas hit by the storm while volunteers from reserve aerial port, civil engineer, medical, and service units aided relief efforts at their home stations and in the damaged areas. On October 12th the Centers for Disease Control in Atlanta reported that unusually large numbers of mosquitoes were hampering recovery operations, and on the 19th the Federal Emergency Management Agency asked the Department of Defense for spray support. The 907th Tactical Airlift Group, Rickenbacker ANGB, Ohio, conducted spray operations around Charleston from mid-October through mid-November, eventually treating more than 855,000 acres.[24] At approximately the same time, reservists on the West Coast were assisting in recovery operations following the October 17 earthquake that had shaken the San Francisco Bay area in California.

The Mobilized Reserves

In 1950 the Air Force Reserve was, along with the Air National Guard, the only resource available when President Truman ordered the Air Force to meet the dual challenge of fighting in Korea and expanding to counter the communist threat in Europe. Initially, four Air Force Reserve wings came on active duty, two for combat in Korea. Thousands of individual reservists were also recalled to fill Air Force personnel shortages worldwide. With the entry of the Chinese into the Korean War and the President's declaration of a national emergency in 1951, the component emptied itself to meet the new challenge as 21 other units and about 100,000 individuals were called. Thus, although no specific mobilization or emergency plans foresaw the conditions that arose in 1950 and 1951, the Air Force Reserve permitted the Air Force to comply with the President's policies.

President Kennedy entered office in January 1961 with a new approach to national defense. He defined a defense policy of flexible response to crisis, as opposed to the nuclear retaliation that his predecessor, Dwight D. Eisenhower, had espoused. Among the defense issues he and Secretary of Defense Robert S. McNamara found to require immediate attention were the need to modernize the conventional forces and strengthen the nation's strategic airlift capabilities. Before Kennedy or McNamara could do much about either, the United States became involved in successive international crises, the resolution of which included the recall of Air Force Reserve units.

The first crisis involved Berlin, still being jointly administered in 1961 by the United States, Great Britain, France, and the USSR. President Kennedy's response to the situation there included plans to expand the active military forces. To gain time for his action to mature, the President authorized Secretary McNamara to mobilize certain Army and Air Force Reserve and National Guard units. Five Air Force Reserve C–124 troop carrier groups came on active duty in October 1961 and developed into efficient, dependable units. In addition to training, the groups conducted scores of operational missions for the Air Force, transporting active units and their equipment throughout the Western Hemisphere. Most important, in augmenting the active force, they and other mobilized reserve and National Guard units gave President Kennedy and Secretary McNamara the time they needed to expand the active conventional force. The President would say he conducted the mobilization to prevent a war rather than to wage one, and taken with his other actions, the mobilization succeeded in gaining that end.

Shortly after the Air Force released the reservists it had mobilized in 1961, a crisis arose in Cuba which involved other Air Force Reserve units. On September 1, 1962, Premier Khrushchev announced a new treaty under which the Soviets would provide arms and technicians to Cuba and declared that any U.S. military reaction would unleash war. The confrontation intensified on October 16 when the United States discovered the Soviets had installed offensive missiles on the island. On October 28, as the crisis reached its flashpoint, the President ordered eight Air Force Reserve troop carrier wings and supporting aerial port units to active duty. Their role was simple: Prepare to carry a U.S. invasion force to Cuba. The Soviets soon agreed to withdraw their missiles. Ample evidence exists to support the contention that this mobilization of citizen reservists to participate in an invasion force demonstrated the seriousness of the U.S. resolve and led the Soviets to withdraw.

President Johnson tried to fight the war in Southeast Asia without declaring a national emergency or mobilizing reserve forces, but he ultimately resorted to mobilization twice in 1968. In January, North Korea seized the USS *Pueblo*, a small intelligence ship. The United States responded by sending a force of fighter-bomber, interceptor, and reconnaissance airplanes to Korea to reassure the South Korean government. To support this action, Johnson authorized mobilizing about 15,000 air and naval reservists and their units. Among those

The Air Force Reserve

called were five C–124 military airlift groups and an aerospace rescue and recovery squadron from the Air Force Reserve.

The other mobilization occurred in May, the result of a January attack by North Vietnamese and Viet Cong forces on more than a hundred cities and towns in South Vietnam. Eventually, as the United States deployed additional troops to Vietnam, the President authorized the mobilization of reservists to replace support forces withdrawn from the Strategic Reserve. Called from the Air Force Reserve were an aeromedical evacuation squadron, a medical service squadron, three aerial port squadrons, and a tactical airlift group.

Operation JUST CAUSE

The invasion of Panama, Operation JUST CAUSE, demonstrated the Air Force Reserve's ability to participate in combat operations. Relations between the United States and the government of Panama headed by Manuel Antonio Noriega had been deteriorating for months. In mid-1989, responding to various threats and provocations from Panamanian security forces, the United States augmented its forces at bases in the Panama Canal Zone in a brief airlift operation called NIMROD DANCER. Unit-equipped and associate strategic airlift units supported the movement of forces, while Air Force Reserve C–130 units, deployed in regular, continuing rotations with their Air National Guard counterparts to Howard AFB, Panama, as part of Operation CORONET OAK provided tactical airlift within the Canal Zone and throughout the region.[25]

On December 19, 1989, American forces attacked from their bases in the Canal Zone, augmented by airborne forces dropped into Panama from bases in the United States. While no Air Force Reserve units were called up to support the operation, more than 6,500 reservists participated before JUST CAUSE officially ended on January 31, 1990. At least one 8-member Air Force Reserve associate C–141 crew, from the 446th Military Airlift Wing (Associate), McChord AFB, Washington, flew in a formation that dropped U.S. Army Rangers in the initial assault on December 19th.[26] Two 14-member crews from the 919th Special Operations Group, Eglin Auxiliary Airfield No. 3 (Duke Field), Florida, already in Panama on a routine deployment with 27 maintenance and support personnel, flew 21 combat sorties in their AC–130A Spectre gunships from December 19, 1990, through January 6, 1991, when they returned to Florida.[27] Two other Air Force Reserve units, the 403d Tactical Airlift Wing from Keesler AFB, Mississippi, and the 934th Tactical Airlift Group from Minneapolis–St Paul IAP, Minnesota, had C–130s deployed to Panama on VOLANT OAK rotations that coincided with JUST CAUSE.[28]

During the six weeks of JUST CAUSE, Air Force Reserve associate strategic airlift, associate air refueling, unit-equipped strategic airlift, special operations, and tactical airlift units flew a total of 621 sorties and more than 1,500 hours in direct support of the operation. They moved more than 5,000 passengers and 1,385 tons of cargo. Tankers delivered more than 1.1 million pounds of aviation fuel to 18 receivers. In combat operations, the 919th's AC–130As expended 220 rounds of 40-mm and 2,000 rounds of 20-mm ammunition.[29] In addition, 207 volunteers from three Air Force Reserve medical units provided more than 1,000 man-days of support at the Wilford Hall Medical Center in Texas, while personnel from 5 mobile aerial port and 10 aerial port squadrons and 2 security police units served at locations around the country. By the end of January 1991, approximately 1,760 Air Force Reservists had served on the ground in Panama or had flown missions in direct support of Panamanian operations, while another 4,760 volunteers had supported operations from their home stations.[30]

A study of lessons learned conducted not long after the operation ended revealed that reserve units and personnel encountered many irritants during JUST CAUSE, but the nature of these complaints showed that, on the whole, the Air Force had made substantial progress in integrating the Air Force Reserve into its operations in the two decade-long Total Force era. None of the units queried complained seriously about outdated equipment or untrained personnel; virtually all reported they could have done more had they been asked. Their complaints generally focused on operational issues, such as long crew duty-days and in-flight communications problems, delays encountered while getting aircraft serviced at en route stops, various agencies (up to and including Headquarters AFRES) being left out as the operation unfolded, and a flight and operations planning system swamped because of the need to restrict access to information in the days immediately before the operation began. Medical units complained that the distinction between tactical and strategic medical activities had become blurred during the operation and that both sides suffered culture shock when they found themselves working outside their normal environment. Aerial port personnel complained of the difficulty of supporting increased operations while relying only on volunteers; planners had only a general idea how many personnel they might have available from day to day. Even so, Air Force Reserve units generally reported that they had more volunteers available than they needed to support their mission taskings.[31]

In his own assessment of the operation, General Scheer noted that the command's participation in JUST CAUSE "culminated a decade that saw us cement our strong relationship with all components of the U.S. Armed Forces." He noted, "Missions like these are the paybacks—both to those of us in the Air Force Reserve and to the nation. These missions are what every one of us in the Air Force Reserve has trained for; they're what make all those training periods meaningful." Finally, he asked reservists not to forget the support the regular Air Force had provided to the Air Force Reserve during the decade and during JUST CAUSE:

The Air Force Reserve

> For the most part, in Operation JUST CAUSE, it really didn't matter what component of the Air Force was flying a mission; what mattered was [that] the Air Force was delivering assists as needed. We can be justifiably proud of our Air Force Reserve contributions to Operation JUST CAUSE. But we should remember that, in a military operation like this, what matters is that air forces contributed properly to the success of the operation. That's Total Force Policy at its best.[32]

The Air Force Reserve and the Persian Gulf War

On August 2, 1990, Iraqi armed forces invaded Kuwait. The next day, Iraqi armored units reached the northern border of Saudi Arabia. The United Nations Security Council met to condemn the invasion and demand that Iraq withdraw all its forces from Kuwait. On August 7, 1990, President George H. W. Bush ordered American combat forces to Saudi Arabia to help defend the kingdom. Although some units began moving almost immediately, the full-scale deployment began on August 9. The Air Force Reserve faced its most significant operational challenge since the outbreak of war in Korea in 1950.[33]

By the summer of 1990 the Air Force Reserve had attained a high state of operational readiness. Most units met or exceeded manning goals, their personnel trained and combat-ready according to the standards established by the gaining major commands. Flying units were equipped with a variety of modern, front-line weapon systems. Headquarters Air Force Reserve at Robins AFB, Georgia, and its three subordinate numbered air forces (Fourth Air Force at McClellan AFB, California; Tenth Air Force at Bergstrom AFB, Texas; and Fourteenth Air Force at Dobbins AFB, Georgia) oversaw the operation of 21 wings, 36 groups, and 335 squadrons, 58 of which were flying squadrons. These reserve units and personnel contributed significantly to the Air Force forces available for deployment to the Persian Gulf. For example, reservists provided fully 50 percent of the Air Force's strategic airlift aircrews and aerial port capability, roughly 33 percent of its aeromedical evacuation aircrews, and 25 percent of its tactical airlift forces, in addition to 12 percent of its strategic airlift aircraft, 8 percent of its tactical fighters, and 5 percent of its KC–135 tanker force. The United States Air Force could not fight a protracted war in the Persian Gulf without relying heavily on its reserve forces.[34]

As the United States began marshaling its forces for the operation that became known as DESERT SHIELD, Headquarters AFRES took preliminary steps to ascertain what level of support the Air Force Reserve could provide under what circumstances. Many reserve units conducted unit training assemblies—their "one-weekend-a-month"—on August 3–4, 1990. There, commanders began to ask which of their personnel might be available to serve as volunteers if they were needed during the crisis. The units also looked closely at the state of their equipment and the readiness of their personnel to deploy on short notice if they were mobilized. Initial calls for volunteers came soon thereafter, and reservists responded in large numbers. By August 20, more than 15,300 had volunteered to serve, about 22 percent of all Air Force Reservists.[35]

Operations and maintenance personnel from the Air Force Reserve's associate units were among the first reservists to become actively involved in the crisis. Air reserve technicians assigned to Military Airlift Command–gained associate strategic airlift units at Travis and Norton AFBs, California; McChord AFB, Washington; Charleston AFB, South Carolina; Dover AFB, Delaware; and McGuire AFB, New Jersey, took their places with their active duty counterparts at these bases, their numbers quickly supplemented by traditional reservists who had volunteered to serve. The first reservists to reach the theater were members of a C–141 crew that landed in Saudi Arabia the morning of August 8, 1990. Reservists supported the airlift flow that moved the first American units into the theater; they remained in the forefront of the deployment effort as it unfolded.[36]

Air Force Reserve KC–135Es with volunteer crews and support personnel, built around a cadre from the 940th Air Refueling Wing, Mather AFB, California, formed part of a composite tanker force deployed to the theater on August 11. A few days later an Air Force Reserve C–130 unit, built around the 94th Tactical Airlift Wing, Dobbins AFB, Georgia, and staffed completely by volunteers from multiple reserve units, left American bases for the theater, although this unit spent several weeks in the United Kingdom while planners decided where it would be stationed in the Gulf. While in England, the C–130s supported the move of an F–111 unit from its base in England to the Gulf. A second group of reserve C–130s, drawn largely from the 440th Tactical Airlift Wing, Milwaukee, Wisconsin, replaced the initial package in mid-September. By August 22, reserve volunteers had logged more than 4,300 flying hours and had moved 7 million tons of cargo and 8,150 passengers to the theater.[37]

The effort was not without cost. On August 29 an active duty C–5 flown by an all-reserve, all-volunteer crew from the 68th Military Airlift Squadron of the 433d Military Airlift Wing, Kelly AFB, Texas, crashed on takeoff from Ramstein AB, Germany. The aircraft, carrying medical supplies and other equipment, had seventeen men and women on board. Thirteen died and four were injured. Ten of the seventeen were reservists. Of these ten, nine died and one was injured. The reservist who survived, SSgt. Lorenzo Galvan, Jr., a loadmaster, subsequently received the Airman's Medal for his efforts to rescue the other victims of the crash. The nine who died in this crash were the only reservists to lose their lives during the conflict.[38]

Although many reservists served as volunteers throughout the war, the Department of Defense soon realized it needed the authority to recall portions of its reserve components to support the rapidly expanding commitment of forces in the Persian Gulf. On August 22, 1990, President Bush authorized the

The Air Force Reserve

call-up of 200,000 reservists for 90 days under the authority of Title 10, U.S. Code, Section 678b. The next day Secretary of Defense Cheney granted the Air Force authority to call up 14,500 members of the selected reserve, either those assigned to the unit program or individual mobilization augmentees.[39]

This decision, the first significant, conflict-related call-up of the reserve component since 1968, marked the beginning of a process that would eventually see more than 20,000 Air Force Reservists called to active duty. Reserve C–5 and C–141 units, both associate and those equipped with aircraft of their own, were among the first called, and further call-ups through late October focused on strategic airlift units. The first C–130 tactical airlift units were called up for deployment in early October. These units soon took the place of the volunteer C–130 unit in the theater.[40]

The terms of the recall eventually changed twice over the course of the war. On November 13, 1990, the President extended the recall from 90 to 180 days. Two months later, on January 19, 1991, he declared a national emergency and ordered the partial mobilization of the Ready Reserve for up to twelve months, an act that affected 360,000 personnel in all services. Secretary Cheney authorized the Air Force to mobilize 52,000 of its personnel, although it never called that number. He also directed that all units and personnel previously recalled or serving as volunteers be switched to partial mobilization status.[41]

While attention focused on the flying units and their maintenance personnel, thousands of other reservists in all functional areas supported DESERT SHIELD from bases in the United States, Europe, the Middle East, and the Gulf region. Firefighters, security police, aerial port supply, transportation and administrative specialists, civil engineers, cooks, doctors, lawyers, and chaplains, among others, were involved. They served at their home stations, at other bases left short of personnel by the deployment of their active duty forces, at staging bases throughout the world (where they augmented facilities overburdened by the flow of personnel and equipment), and in the theater of operations itself. In percentage terms, reserve medical personnel were among the most heavily involved. In expectation of massive casualties that never came, all Air Force Reserve medical units were called to duty. As with their counterparts in other specialties, they served throughout the world, including in the Gulf.[42]

By mid-November 1990, Air Force Reserve aircraft and crews had flown more than 63,000 hours, moved about 80,000 passengers and 132,000 tons of cargo, and delivered 3 million pounds of fuel. By mid-January 1991, on the eve of DESERT STORM, these totals had become 107,000 hours, 135,000 passengers, 235,000 tons of cargo, and about 5 million pounds of fuel.[43]

In late November the Air Force Reserve's first (and, as it turned out, only) tactical fighter unit to be recalled was alerted for call-up. The 706th Tactical Fighter Squadron of the 926th Tactical Fighter Group, an A–10 unit stationed at Naval Air Station New Orleans, Louisiana, deployed to Saudi Arabia in mid-

Flying Club to Total Force

January, just before the beginning of the air campaign against Iraq. In early December the 439th Military Airlift Wing was activated at its home station, Westover AFB, Massachusetts. Wing personnel had been operating Westover as an East Coast staging facility since August 17, 1990; the recall brought all unit personnel to duty to support the operations there.[44]

The last and largest block of recalls came during the first two weeks of January when about 7,000 Air Force Reservists received orders. By about the first of February 1991, more than 17,500 reservists were on active duty. About 3,800 were officers and 13,700 were enlisted personnel. Roughly one in four was a woman. Approximately 1,800 were Air Reserve technicians, 1,300 were individual mobilization augmentees, and more than 500 were members of the individual Ready Reserve. More than 7,800 of these reservists were in medical specialties.[45]

The onset of the war in mid-January found Air Force Reserve units in action throughout the theater. The strategic airlift forces continued to shuttle personnel and equipment into Europe and on to bases in the Gulf. Tactical airlift forces played a major role in the redeployment of forces in northern Saudi Arabia as commanders set up what became the dramatic left hook into Iraq. The A–10s, operating from bases close to the front lines, attacked a full range of ground targets that included Iraqi Scud missiles. Reserve AC–130s and

An AC–130 from the 919th Special Operations Group is readied for battle during the Gulf War.

367

The Air Force Reserve

A 706th Tactical Fighter Squadron A–10 receives repairs for battle damage.

HH–3E helicopters also supported special operations as well as search and rescue missions.[46]

In combat, reservists claimed a handful of noteworthy firsts during the war. Captain Bob Swain, a pilot from the 706th Tactical Fighter Squadron, scored the first-ever A–10 air-to-air kill when he destroyed an Iraqi helicopter. Crews from the 1650th Tactical Airlift Wing (Provisional), a unit composed of aircraft, aircrews, and maintenance and support personnel drawn largely from the Reserve's 914th Tactical Airlift Group, Niagara Falls IAP, New York, and the 927th Tactical Airlift Group, Selfridge ANGB, Michigan, made the first tactical resupply airdrop of the war, delivering eight pallets of food and water to marines dug in along the Kuwait border. Another 1650th crew flew the first C–130 into liberated Kuwait IAP, delivering communications equipment. Yet another C–130 crew flew the first tactical aeromedical evacuation mission of the ground campaign for a number of wounded marines. During one day of combat, Lt. Col. Greg Wilson of the 706th and 1st Lt. Stephan K. Otto of the Tactical Air Command's 354th Tactical Fighter Wing, Myrtle Beach AFB, South Carolina, destroyed ten mobile Scud launchers and a pair of ammunition dumps and helped F/A–18s destroy ten more Scuds.[47]

In three months (January–March 1991), the 16 C–130s of the 1650th flew more than 5,000 hours and 3,200 sorties. In 42 days of combat (from mid-January through the end of February), the 18 A–10s of the 706th flew more than 2,100 hours and 1,000 sorties. They expended nearly 85,000 rounds of 30-

mm cannon ammunition, 300 Maverick air-to-ground missiles, 430 cluster bombs, and 1,200 Mark–82 iron bombs. While a number of the A–10s sustained varying degrees of damage in combat, no Air Force Reserve aircraft were lost during the war, nor were any reservists killed in combat.[48]

The mobilization reached its peak on March 12, 1991, with almost 23,500 Air Force Reservists on duty. Of these, more than 20,000 were assigned to 215 reserve units, 2,300 were individual mobilization augmentees, and 960 were members of the individual Ready Reserve or retirees. Most members of the Ready Reserves were medical personnel. The Department of Defense authorized the commanders of the gaining major commands to demobilize reservists, consistent with military requirements, on March 8, 1991. Most reservists had been demobilized by late June, but a handful remained on active duty through August (and beyond).[49]

The end of the Persian Gulf War in April 1991 did not signal any significant drop-off in the tempo of Air Force Reserve operations. The command, like the rest of the Air Force, had begun to anticipate force structure cuts, base closures, and other adjustments before the war began, changes the war neither delayed nor halted. Even as it adjusted to these realities, the Air Force Reserve began a detailed examination of its experiences during the war with an eye toward changing policies and procedures in an already dynamic environment.

From a practical standpoint, circumstances gave the Air Force Reserve the opportunity to concentrate its energies more on people issues than on operational considerations. Total Force dictates that reservists train to active duty standards, but it leaves those standards in the hands of the gaining major commands. Thus, to the extent that the Gulf War contributed to any fundamental reconsideration of how the Air Force as a whole accomplishes its wartime mission, the Air Force Reserve made its views known to the gaining major commands through a number of lessons-learned processes, and it reviewed the application of these lessons learned since the war's end.[50]

The Air Force Reserve conducted its most significant internal review of Gulf War lessons learned in Denver, Colorado, August 21–22, 1991, when it hosted the Operation DESERT STORM/SHIELD Hotwash. The event, organized in response to a request raised at the first postwar Commanders' Conference in July 1991, brought together commanders from most Air Force Reserve units, including all whose units had been mobilized during the war. The group broke into three teams along numbered air force lines that were chaired by the numbered air force commanders. Each team entered its Gulf War issues at some point on a 36-element matrix that broke the war into six phases (volunteerism, 200K call-up, mobilization, employment, redeployment, and demobilization), each of which included six factors (people, administration, logistics, operational, command and control, and "others"). The numbered air force teams initially developed 144 issues, a list later reduced to 68 points, each assigned

The Air Force Reserve

to a Headquarters AFRES staff agency for resolution.[51]

One question raised repeatedly during the war and again during the Hotwash suggested that reservists serving as volunteers did not receive the same legal protection as those called up or mobilized. The Air Force Reserve Judge Advocate reported that this was not true, and that the Veterans' Reemployment Rights Act and other provisions of the U.S. Code provided the same protection to volunteers as it did to those called to duty involuntarily. The Judge Advocate and personnel staff revised their emergency action checklists to ensure that members were properly informed of this "during the next declared contingency." On the other hand, volunteers who served tours of less than 31 days were eligible for fewer military benefits than those recalled to active duty.[52]

In some cases it was difficult to do more than explain the rationale behind actions viewed as irritants. Commanders wanted Headquarters AFRES to control a pool of military personnel–account man-day money. Its financial management staff reported that Department of Defense policy prohibited the Air Force from allocating military personnel account funds to the major commands. In other cases, Headquarters AFRES or the gaining major commands could only explain why, in retrospect, things that might have seemed inefficient or inappropriate at the unit level were done. The Military Airlift Command Plans and Operations staff, responding to a concern that stage managers were not responsive to aircrew suggestions, noted: "During a surge, each aircrew has a microscopic view of the whole operation. What may seem illogical to a particular aircrew may make sense when viewed in the larger context." The Military Airlift Command staff agreed that stage managers should be able to answer the crews' questions, but it noted that "too few command and control people trying to do too much during surges makes the smooth flow of 'why' to individual crews 'iffy.'"[53]

Reservists noted that the "failure to place AFRES commanders in command of AFRES units created morale problems and made problem solving ... difficult." This contributed to "(1) a feeling of 'second class' citizenship and (2) a feeling that our people were pawns which [the] active duty could use without any accountability." Reserve leadership acknowledged the issue, voiced after every significant reservist call-up. All parties agreed that "when the next large scale contingency occurs," an Air Force Reserve request to place a Reserve general officer on the theater air commander's staff would be "thoroughly considered," although the staff also noted that "Currently no AF war-fighting commander will obligate in writing that we will get our share of the command action; however, the point has been made and well received."[54]

Other points were the decision to "tailor" unit type codes rather than to call up units as a whole, limitations imposed during the 200K call-up, the lack of comprehensive and consistent theater redeployment and major command demobilization policies, problems with the extended use of volunteers in place

Flying Club to Total Force

of an early presidential call-up, dissatisfaction with the first in, first out policy implemented in the theater after the war, excessive reporting requirements, communications breakdowns, and interface problems between the active duty personnel and pay systems.[55]

These questions had no easy answers. The decision to tailor the unit type codes, for example, reflected a desire to deploy the greatest possible capability consistent with conservative allocations under the 200K call-up authority, in-theater host-nation personnel limits, and the needs of the theater Commander in Chief. Dissatisfaction with the first in, first out policy was rooted in the long-held belief among reservists that "Civilian job requirements and continued employer support remain [the] driving principle to return reservists first following cessation of hostilities and diminished threat." Reserve employers echoed this sentiment. Neither reservists nor their civilian employers could understand why reservists were still on active duty (and away from their peacetime jobs) when active duty units had already come home. The Air Force Reserve leadership was sympathetic and proposed changes to Air Force mobilization policy, but they had no way to predict how theater commanders would respond in future crises.[56]

Pay and personnel problems proved somewhat easier to solve. The Air Force Reserve created a two-member, Personnel Support for Contingency Operations (PERSCO) unit type code package after the war so that reserve personnel could be assigned to active duty PERSCO teams managing reservists, providing reserve payroll expertise that the active duty organization admitted it did not have. The Defense Finance and Accounting Service—Denver Center admitted incompatibility between the active duty and reserve Joint Uniform Military Pay System and directed that, during future contingencies, reservists would be paid by the reserve system, with a long-term goal of standardizing the active duty and reserve pay systems.[57]

The question of how much support the Air Force Reserve could provide on a voluntary basis during a crisis became an issue that received great attention during and after the war. Experience gained during earlier operations, and during the Gulf War itself, suggested that between 20 and 35 percent of all reserve capability could be made available by relying on volunteers, but that this source of personnel would generally be exhausted within 30 to 45 days as the volunteers used up their individually determined availability. Neither the Air Force Reserve nor the gaining major commands could accept this level of uncertainty, so headquarters undertook to develop volunteer force packages that could be made available to major command planners and theater commanders during crises.[58]

Press reports and speculation during the war suggested that large numbers of reservists would abandon the program once the war ended. This did not happen. Reserve units reported no significant loss of personnel following demobilization. Recruiting dropped off somewhat during the war, but it picked

The Air Force Reserve

up again soon thereafter, and the Air Force Reserve closed out fiscal years 1991 and 1992 at, or very close to, its manning goals. The Persian Gulf War had no significant long-term effect on the Air Force Reserve's ability to recruit and retain quality personnel or to meet its end-strength goals.

Recruiters noticed a drop-off in accessions when the war began, a trend that continued through July 1991. Approximately 3,000 applicants withdrew paperwork or delayed processing it between August 1990 and July 1991, and recruiting leads decreased through February 1990. The implementation of Stop-Loss on January 2, 1991, also affected recruiting, since it eliminated the pool of individuals with prior service from which Reserve recruiters drew a significant percentage of their total production. Average accessions dropped to a low of 14 per day in January 1991; by June 1991, the daily number had risen to 33, close to normal production. This return to normal rates, plus a significant effort to work the larger than normal prior-service personnel pool that developed when the Defense Department lifted Stop-Loss and accelerated the drawdown of active duty units, sparked an upsurge in accessions between July and September 1991. Recruiters had signed up only about 56 percent of their annual goal by the end of June; they ended the year with 90 percent of their goal.[59]

The Air Force Reserve's senior leadership moved to address retention as soon as it became obvious that the Reserve would be heavily involved in the Gulf. The war marked the sixth major call-up of Air Force Reserve units and personnel since the activation of the Air Force Reserve on April 14, 1948, the seventh if the brief mobilization of a few of aerial port personnel during a mail strike in 1970 is included. Many factors influenced an individual's decision to stay with the reserve program following a crisis, but two elements seemed most crucial: reservists tended to stay if they thought their service had been worthwhile and they had been well cared for during and after their service. Armed with this knowledge, the Air Force Reserve set about to do all it could to make the Gulf War experience as satisfactory as possible for all mobilized reservists.[60]

No issue threatened more discomfort and confusion for mobilized reserve personnel than the absence of Family Support Centers at Air Force Reserve bases. Such facilities existed on active duty bases, but the Reserve had seen no need for the centers on reserve bases because they supported no resident military population. The first call-ups in late August 1990 demonstrated the need, but the Air Force Reserve was ill-equipped to meet it. The same call-ups also showed that reserve units on active duty bases were in only marginally better shape, since the active duty Family Support Centers were not organized to meet a much larger pool of eligible families' requests for services.

Local reserve units responded to their own pressing family support needs in a variety of ways. At each location some individual or organization stepped (or was pushed) forward to act as a focal point for family support matters. In many cases unit chaplains and public affairs offices provided a cadre of personnel and equipment around which other efforts, led by officers' and enlisted wives' clubs and similar bodies, often coalesced. In some cases these reserve groups attempted to assist local, active duty Family Support Centers, but for the most part the system that developed tended to split along active and reserve lines, each side looking after its own as best it could. Regardless of who took the phone calls; published the newsletters; arranged for health care, child care, or car care; or distributed the goods donated by local merchants, the ad hoc family support organizations that evolved generally received the highest praise from reservists whose families availed themselves of their services.[61]

When the war ended many who did the most to develop the family support functions during the war took the forefront in expressing concern that the Air Force Reserve needs to do more in the future to prepare reservists and their families for call-ups. Significant numbers of reserve units had not been mobilized since 1968, so extremely few reservists had had experience with transitioning from reserve to active duty service. In practical terms, some reserve families were unprepared legally, financially, and psychologically for what happened when the call went out. Tales of spouses who could not balance their checkbooks (if they knew where they were) or put gas in their families' cars—most stories were almost certainly apocryphal—made the rounds in many units. Some reserve families had little information about benefits that became available to them during call-ups. Reserve Judge Advocates processed thousands of wills and powers of attorney on the mobility processing line. Family members had little idea of whom to turn to for information or rumor control at many points during the crisis.

It became obvious that some reservists had never given much credence to the possibility that they would be called to active duty. They had never thought much about what such a call would mean to them or their families. To help focus their thinking, in early 1992 the Reserve published *What's Next: A Guide to Family Readiness*, a 62-page booklet that laid out what the Air Force Reserve was, how it worked, and what happened before, during, and after call-ups and mobilizations. The narrative dealt with many basic ideas presented in sections entitled, for example, "What Does the Air Force Reserve Expect of Reservists" and "Making a Personal/Financial Business File." It also covered weightier issues, such as benefits, entitlements, and reemployment rights. It provided ten pages of worksheets for inventorying key documents and personal property.[62]

Many of those most active in providing ad hoc family support for reservists during the war, especially spouses, lobbied aggressively after the war for a more formal reserve family support system tailored to the needs of reservists. In response to these pressures, relayed to the Air Force leadership by unit commanders, the headquarters personnel community developed the Reserve Family Support Program, formally implementing it on July 15, 1992, with the

The Air Force Reserve

publication of Air Force Reserve Regulation 30–2, *Family Support Program.* The new program established Family Support Centers at Air Force Reserve bases and established procedures that reserve units assigned to active duty bases could use to forge closer links with active duty centers. Headquarters AFRES formally established a Command Family Support Program Manager to oversee this effort. Reserve bases received authorization to hire a full-time Family Support Director, while all locations received authorizations to hire traditional reservists dedicated to family support services and training. Reserve units on active duty bases each received two authorizations; host units on reserve bases received one authorization for every 500 people assigned to the base.[63] The new regulation recognized the link between its members' readiness and the well-being of their families—"The single greatest contributor to the Reserve member meeting mission requirements is [the] family"—and assigned to the new Family Support Program the mission of supporting Reserve readiness and retention "by helping families adapt to the demands of Reserve life and assist commanders in responding to family concerns."[64]

Comments received during and after the war revealed that employers were confused about their responsibilities as well. Most wanted to be as helpful as possible toward their reservist employees, but neither side was as well-informed as it should have been. The Air Force Reserve had heard comments from its own people and their families during and after the call-up, but no system was in place to give employers a way to voice their concerns. To ensure that the employers received a full hearing, the Air Force Reserve invited a large number of employers, nominated by the units, to participate in a Headquarters AFRES–sponsored Employer Support Meeting at Robins AFB, Georgia. Thirty-seven people, representing companies large and small, participated in the event held March 4–6, 1992. Employers, joined by members of the Reserve staff, split into three teams to develop lists of problems, questions, and comments. One focused on medical issues, one on problems facing larger employers, and one on those facing smaller companies.[65]

The broadest concerns related to what employers considered identity questions about the organization and mission of guard and reserve units; the "general lack of communication between the military, the employer, and the reservist"; the failure of reservists to identify themselves to their employers; and a lack of information concerning the role (even the existence) of the National Committee for Employer Support of the Guard and Reserve. Medical participants raised more specific issues including the financial hardships mobilization imposed on medical professionals, the failure of the reserve system to recognize and use the specialties of mobilized physicians (who were classified as general doctor), and the difficulties some health care professionals faced when their civilian professional license expired while they were on active duty. The problem of the small, rural medical facility left without a practitioner because of the call-up also made the list, although small organizations of many types expressed the same concern. Specific remedies considered often involved attempts to keep everyone better informed. The need for better communications became the most frequently heard plea from the employers (as it had been from the commanders at the Hotwash).[66]

Before DESERT STORM, few reservists knew what their job rights were. DESERT STORM rapidly changed that. As unprecedented numbers of reservists volunteered or were called to duty, employers and reservists alike wanted facts on reemployment rights. The 54-year-old Veterans' Reemployment Rights law stated that a veteran's reemployment rights were automatically protected whether the individual worked for state or federal governments or for privately owned businesses. On October 13, 1994, President Bill Clinton signed the Uniformed Services and Reemployment Rights Act of 1994 that completely rewrote and replaced the previous legislation. The new law strengthened the provisions ensuring that reservists cannot be refused hiring, denied promotion, or fired because of their military service. Most American employers strongly support reservists commitments, but this law was intended to protect individuals who nevertheless experienced discrimination when serving their country.[67]

The Air Force Reserve in the 1990s

The Air Force Reserve was justifiably proud of its work during the Gulf War, and it took great satisfaction in the efforts it made after the war to correct problems the call-up revealed. Events, however, gave the command little time to savor its success or rest on its laurels. The pace of operations remained high after the war, while the pace of organizational change accelerated dramatically.

On October 30, 1990, General Merrill A. McPeak became Chief of Staff of the Air Force.[68] The Air Force he inherited was responding to Iraqi aggression in the Gulf, but it was also on the verge of a significant reduction in its force structure. The Soviet Union and the Warsaw Pact were in their death throes, leaving the United States the world's only global superpower and one that faced, in some eyes, no credible military threat. The Reagan-era defense buildup had been predicated on a desire to counter an expanding Soviet threat. If that threat was gone, the American people had reason to expect a defense dividend in the form of reduced military expenditures that could be applied to either a reduction in the federal budget deficit or to a range of new or expanded social programs.

There was no escaping the fact that cuts were coming. On August 2, 1990 (the day Iraq invaded Kuwait), in a speech to the Aspen Institute Symposium in Colorado, President Bush acknowledged that the "threat of a Soviet invasion of Western Europe launched with little or no warning is today more remote than at any other point in the postwar period." Defense leaders faced a challenge:

> Our task today is to shape our defense capabilities to these changing strategic circumstances. In a world less driven by an immediate threat to Europe and the danger of global war — in a world where the size of our forces will increasingly be shaped by the needs of regional contingencies and peacetime presence — we know that our forces can be smaller. Secretary [of Defense Richard B.] Cheney and General [Colin L.] Powell [Chairman of the Joint Chiefs of Staff] are hard at work determining the precise combination of forces that we need. But I can tell you now, we calculate that by 1995 our security needs can be met by an active force 25 percent smaller than today's. America's Armed Forces will be at their lowest level since the year 1950.[69]

If, as President Bush suggested, the active force could be cut, the reserve component would be forced to assume a greater role in the nation's military structure. But, as the President noted, the reserves could anticipate changes as well: "The need to be prepared for massive, short-term mobilization has diminished. And we can now adjust the size, structure and readiness of our reserve forces to help us deal with the more likely challenges we will face."[70]

In August 1991, President Bush, in a report on the evolving national security strategy, suggested that the emerging "New World Order" would force the United States to move toward a force mix that allowed the nation "to respond initially to any regional contingency with units—combat and support—drawn wholly from the active component, except for a limited number of support and mobility assets."[71] The restructured reserve component would include support units ready for use in extended confrontations, combat units designed to supplement active duty units, and some reserve combat units maintained in a cadre status. As President Bush suggested,

> This approach will allow us to maintain a Total Force appropriate for the strategic and fiscal demands of a new era: a smaller, more self-contained and very ready active force able to respond quickly to emerging threats; and a reduced but still essential reserve component with emphasis on supporting and sustaining active combat forces, and—in particularly large or prolonged regional contingencies—providing latent combat capability that can be made ready when needed.[72]

These concepts had been evolving for some time, as had discussions that focused more closely on the structure of the base force the United States would field in the 1990s, the size of the reserve component as a portion of the base force, and ways the reserve component could be used more effectively under any circumstance.[73]

General McPeak was cognizant of this debate and the effect it would have on the Air Force, but he and Secretary of the Air Force Donald B. Rice also had their own ideas about how the Air Force should be organized in the post–Cold War era. In June 1990 Secretary Rice outlined a new direction for the Air Force in a policy paper, "The Air Force and U.S. National Security: Global Reach—Global Power," which established the philosophical and doctrinal basis for the changes to come. To implement the concepts inherent in Global Reach—Global Power, General McPeak sought to streamline the chain of command, reduce organizational layering, and clarify and decentralize responsibility and authority. Sweeping organizational changes began in 1991 and were largely completed (at least on paper) by the end of fiscal year 1992. The effect of these changes on the Air Force Reserve was dramatic.[74]

The first change came on February 1, 1992, when most major Air Force Reserve units were redesignated. General McPeak suggested that new designations would better reflect the units' missions, as fighter and airlift units routinely conducted operations that blurred traditional distinctions between tactical and strategic. Tactical fighter organizations became fighter units, while the distinction between strategic and tactical airlift units was eliminated entirely.[75] Soon thereafter, the Air Force inactivated the Military Airlift Command, the Strategic Air Command, and the Tactical Air Command and activated the Air Combat Command and the Air Mobility Command in their places. On the same date, June 1, 1992, the Air Force Reserve's Tactical Air Command–gained units became Air Combat Command–gained; the Military Airlift Command–gained units became Air Mobility Command–gained; and the Strategic Air Command–gained units (all tankers) became Air Mobility Command–gained.[76] One month later, on July 1, 1992, the Air Force Reserve's Air Force Logistics Command–gained units became Air Force Materiel Command–gained after the Air Force Logistics Command and the Air Force Systems Command were inactivated and consolidated into a single, new major command, the Air Force Materiel Command.[77]

By far the most significant organizational change to affect the Air Force Reserve during fiscal year 1992 was the Air Force–wide implementation of the objective wing structure. As early as 1990, Secretary Rice and General McPeak had begun to consider how to reshape the Air Force to reflect the changing geopolitical and economic realities of the new decade. They developed the Quality Air Force concept to describe their approach to "reorienting, restructuring, and resizing aerospace forces." The new structure that grew out of this thinking was based on principles grounded in quality principles common to modern corporate management.[78]

The restructuring of the Air Force Reserve covered five actions: realignment of some wing/group/subordinate unit relationships; reorganization

The Air Force Reserve

of Headquarters AFRES wings/groups according to the objective wing model; redesignation of Headquarters AFRES organizations to more closely reflect mission capability; identification of revised unit-gaining major commands; and realignment of units at each base under one wing or group.[79] A series of orders published between August 31 and November 18, 1992, officially implemented these changes. Two years later, the final steps in the process saw the elimination of the term *associate* from the official designation of Air Force Reserve associate units (although the associate concept remained unchanged) and the redesignation of all geographically separated flying groups as wings.[80]

A series of mission changes expanded the scope of Air Force Reserve operations even as the command struggled to adapt to its new structure. On April 1, 1991, the command assumed sole responsibility for the weather reconnaissance mission. It activated its first C-17 associate squadron (the 317th Airlift Squadron [Associate] assigned to the 315th Airlift Wing [Associate] at Charleston AFB, South Carolina) on April 1, 1992. With the activation of the 7th Space Operations Squadron at Falcon AFB, Colorado, on January 1, 1993, the command added satellite operations to its mission palette, while the activation of the 93d Bombardment Squadron assigned to the 917th Wing at Barksdale AFB, Louisiana, added B-52H heavy bombers to the command's force structure. The activation of the 931st Air Refueling Group at McConnell AFB, Kansas, on October 1, 1994, marked the beginning of the KC-135 associate mission.[81]

Despite the addition of these new missions, the Air Force Reserve faced structural pressures on several fronts throughout the first half of the decade. The Base Realignment and Closure Commission (established by the Secretary of Defense in 1988 to review all continental United States military installations and make realignment/closure recommendations) announced decisions in 1991, 1993, and 1995 that affected reserve units at more than a dozen bases.[82] Periodic Air Force and Air Force Reserve force structure announcements (driven by the commission, budget pressures, and the results of a "bottom-up review" of the nation's "defense strategy, force structure, modernization, infrastructure, and foundations" conducted in 1993 by Secretary of Defense Les Aspin) mandated further changes.[83] As a result, between 1990 and 1994 the Air Force Reserve inactivated four flying groups and one flying wing, converted one fighter and one airlift group to tankers, moved several units (some more than once), and assumed responsibility for three former Air Force facilities (with more transfers forthcoming). The command assigned its first Air Reserve technicians and traditional reservists to the headquarters in February 1991. The organization considered a proposal to streamline its structure by eliminating its numbered air forces in 1990 and 1991, but it settled on a substantial reduction in the size of these organizations instead. On July 1, 1993, the Air Force inactivated the command's Fourteenth Air Force headquarters at Dobbins Air Reserve Base, Georgia, transferred the designation to the active Air Force, and

Flying Club to Total Force

activated Headquarters Twenty-second Air Force in its place.[84]

Despite this organizational turbulence, Air Force Reserve units contributed significantly to all operations undertaken by American forces after the end of the Gulf War. The end of the war did not see the end of Air Force Reserve activity in Europe or the Gulf. PROVIDE COMFORT, the effort to deliver relief supplies to Kurdish refugees in southern Turkey and northern Iraq, began on April 7, 1991, supported by reservists from the 302d Tactical Airlift Wing, Peterson AFB, Colorado, and the 32d Aeromedical Evacuation Group and the 74th Aeromedical Evacuation Squadron, both from Kelly AFB, Texas. Operation ARC WIND, the use of Reserve C–130s to move personnel returning from Gulf War operations to their home stations, also began at this time.[85]

Not all of the events of 1991 were war-related. The 944th Tactical Fighter Group, Luke AFB, Arizona, was the best F–16 unit and took second place overall at Gunsmoke 91. The command added another Top Gun to its list as well. In June, crews of the 445th Military Airlift Wing (Associate), Norton AFB, California, participated in Operation FIERY VIGIL by helping evacuate those fleeing from the eruption of Mount Pinatubo near Clark Air Base in the Philippines. The 446th Military Airlift Wing, another associate unit, also assisted in the operation when its home station, McChord AFB, Washington, became a processing area for nearly 13,000 evacuees from the Philippines. The 67th Aerial Port Squadron, Hill AFB, Utah, and the 440th Mobility Support Flight, General Mitchell International Airport, Wisconsin (at McChord for training), also responded to the call for volunteer support. They worked around the clock, doing everything from unloading aircraft to assisting families with food and clothing and caring for and entertaining the children.[86]

In the aftermath of the Persian Gulf War, the Air Force Reserve became heavily involved in humanitarian relief efforts in the former Soviet Union, eastern Europe, Africa, and the Persian Gulf region. The 445th Military Airlift Wing flew the first humanitarian aid mission to Mongolia, airlifting almost 20 tons of emergency medical supplies. On another humanitarian mission in mid-December, a C–5 from the 439th Military Airlift Wing, Westover AFB, Massachusetts, carried almost 140,000 pounds of aid including blankets, cots, and medical supplies to Moscow to help meet critical shortages in the crumbling Soviet Union. In February, 1992, reservists participated in Operation PROVIDE HOPE, transporting food and medicine to the newly formed Commonwealth of Independent States. By July, 1992, the command turned its attention to the Balkans, when the United States, with PROVIDE PROMISE, joined the United Nations' relief mission to the components of the recently sundered Yugoslavia. Reserve aircrews, aerial port, and maintenance personnel operated out of Rhein-Main AB, Germany, airlifting supplies and medicine to Sarajevo, Zagreb, and other locations. By the time C–130 operations ended in May 1994, reserve units flew 2,872 sorties for more than 5,900 flying hours while deployed units transported over 17,500 tons of cargo and carried more

The Air Force Reserve

than 5,000 passengers. After C-130 missions ended, reserve associate unit aircrews flew active duty C-141s from Rhein-Main on PROVIDE PROMISE support missions. As tensions mounted in the former Yugoslavia, reserve fighter units began participating in DENY FLIGHT, the enforcement of the no-fly zone over the troubled land. Reservists flew combat air patrol and reconnaissance missions from Aviano AB, Italy. In April, 1994, Reserve air refueling units contributed two KC-135 tankers and about 100 Air Force Reserce personnel as an additional part of the Air Reserve component's involvement in DENY FLIGHT operations.[87]

Reservists also contributed to relief efforts in Somalia. Reserve aircraft and aircrews initially operated out of Mombassa, Kenya, and other locations and flew in supplies to help alleviate the plight of millions of starving Somalians. Reserve C-130 units contributed 99 sorties and 226.4 flying hours and carried 812.3 tons of cargo. In November 1992, the United Nations launched RESTORE HOPE, a massive relief effort for Somalia. Reservists flying C-130s, C-5s, C-141s, and tankers moved supplies and provided aerial refueling support. In addition, medical and aerial port personnel also participated in the operation. During RESTORE HOPE, reserve flying units, primarily associate, carried more than 16,000 tons of cargo and transported more than 14,000 passengers.[88]

Reservists also participated in PROVIDE COMFORT II, the enforcement of another no-fly zone, this time over northern Iraq, and the associated airlift of humanitarian supplies to Iraqi Kurds. Reserve rescue, airlift, and special operations units flew HC-130s, C-130s, and MH-60Gs from Incirlik AB, Turkey. Reservists also supported SOUTHERN WATCH, the enforcement of the United Nations' no-fly zone over southern Iraq, with HH-60Gs and HC-130s. Beginning in August 1994, reserve strategic airlift and aerial refueling units took part in SUPPORT HOPE, the United Nations' Rwandan relief efforts. During a 7-week period, reserve units carried 6,930 tons of relief supplies and 4,481 passengers and flew 350 sorties for 1,880 flying hours. In mid-September 1994, Air Force Reserve forces were poised, alongside their active duty counterparts, for the military restoration of democracy in Haiti. Once the operation changed from an invasion to a peaceful occupation, their participation focused on airlifting personnel and supplies. By the time Air Reserve support ended in mid-October, reservists had flown 390 sorties for 1,086 hours, delivered 3,358 passengers, and transported 2,435 tons of cargo. More than 1,100 Air Force Reserve personnel from 37 units and 60 aircraft took part in Haitian operations.[89]

Reservists also played major roles in natural disaster relief efforts. In late August 1992, Hurricane Andrew devastated south Florida. The massive storm had a particularly large impact on the Reserve community because Homestead AFB (home of the 482d Fighter Wing and the 301st Rescue Squadron and several active duty units) was destroyed. In the days immediately following the storm, the 301st Rescue Squadron's HH-60 helicopters and crews saved 137 lives, operating from the unit's temporary location, Kendall-Tamiami Airport. Other reservists ranging from civil engineers to medical personnel to security police provided varying forms of aid. Reserve units from around the country flew in relief supplies. During a 3-week period following the storm, reservists flew 266 missions, transported 4,387 passengers, and carried 7,315 tons of cargo. In March 1993, a massive, late winter storm struck west central Florida. The 301st Rescue Squadron responded again, rescuing 93 people. Hurricane relief efforts also went on in the Pacific region. In late August 1992, the 445th Airlift Wing, Norton AFB, California, flew emergency generators to Guam following a storm. The next month, another storm struck the Hawaian islands of Kauai and Niihau. Reserve associate aircrews responded by flying in disaster relief personnel and supplies and by evacuating hundreds of people.[90]

Reserve units continued to do well in Air Force–level competitions. In 1992, the 446th Airlift Wing (Associate), McChord AFB, Washington, took home the General William G. Moore, Jr., award as Best Air Mobility Wing at the Air Mobility Command's Rodeo 92. After achieving a perfect score, a crew from the 79th Air Refueling Squadron, March AFB, California, won the first Best KC–10 Air Refueling Crew trophy ever offered at the competition. The 440th Airlift Wing, General Mitchell IAP, Wisconsin, won the Best Air Mobility Wing trophy during Rodeo 93, as well as four other first-place awards. The 446th Airlift Wing also did well again, taking five C–141 awards. In Rodeo 94, the same unit repeated as best C–141 wing and won several other awards, as did the 916th Air Refueling Group (Associate), Seymour Johnson AFB, North Carolina, and the 934th Airlift Group, Minneapolis–Saint Paul IAP Air Reserve Station, Minnesota.[91]

Air Force Reservists participated in all of these activities as volunteers. By the end of 1991, virtually all reservists who had been recalled to active duty during the war had been demobilized. To meet the Air Force's continuing and expanding operational requirements, the Air Force Reserve time and again asked its personnel to volunteer for an extraordinary range of activities. Some of their participation exposed the reservists to hostile action. This degree of reliance on the willingness of reservists to respond to informal taskings quickly became a topic of great concern to the Air Force Reserve's senior leadership, which believed that some theoretical limit existed on the amount of support the command could provide on a voluntary basis, even if that limit had not yet been reached.[92] With each additional crisis, the senior leaders' concern became more palpable. Chief of Air Force Reserve Maj. Gen. John J. Closner spoke of a bank account of trust and confidence the Air Force Reserve had developed with the reservists, their employers, and their families, and he worried that each episode withdrew capital from that account.[93]

Events, however, do not yet support this concern. A survey conducted by the Headquarters AFRES Public Affairs Directorate revealed that, as of February 1995, approximately 80 percent of all reservists were willing to

The Air Force Reserve

Maj. Gen. John J. Closner, as Chief of Air Force Reserve, oversaw the recall to active duty of thousands of Air Force Reservists during the Gulf War.

volunteer more time than they had in the past, although only 65 percent of aircrew personnel expressed a willingness to do more. Not surprisingly, the survey revealed that most were more willing to volunteer for short periods (one to four weeks) perhaps once or twice a year for overseas humanitarian and domestic relief missions. Most expressed concerns that longer or more frequent service might cause problems with their employers.[94]

The Air Force Reserve has always been concerned with issues that affect its personnel on- and off-duty. Commanders recognized the whole-person concept, but little was made to improve the quality of life as it impacted off-duty areas before the late 1980s. Before then, quality of life generally equated to on-duty or postretirement benefits. In the 1980s these benefits included issues involving education, retirement, base exchange and commissary privileges, medical and dental care, pay, and life insurance. During the 1990s, the focus of quality of life issues has broadened to include on-duty and off-duty concerns such as housing, the environment, and an effective family support system (in addition to the more traditional concerns).[95] In December 1994, not long after he became Chief of Air Force Reserve, Maj. Gen. Robert A. McIntosh highlighted six quality of life issues high on his agenda for the mid-1990s: improve lodging for reservists at their home station, improve entitlements available during contingencies, fully fund the family support program, obtain tax relief for employers of reservists and expand deductible expenses for reservists, obtain affordable health insurance for reservists, and for

The present Chief of Air Force Reserve, Maj. Gen. Robert A. McIntosh, has advanced quality-of-life issues to the forefront of contemporary Air Force Reserve planning.

spouses of Air Reserve technicians who are civil service employees, secure placement considerations similar to those offered active-duty spouses.[96]

In the early 1980s, Representative G. V. "Sonny" Montgomery proposed legislation that would expand educational benefits available to reserve personnel. In 1985 this legislation became the Montgomery GI Bill—Selected Service (Title 10, U.S. Code, Section 106).[97] Among its many provisions, the bill allowed personnel in vocational training programs to qualify for benefits. Similar to the active duty GI Bill, it was originally intended for reservists who did not have a bachelor's degree and was limited to one four-year degree per reservist. In 1990 it was expanded to include availability for obtaining advanced degrees.[98] President Bush declared the "Montgomery GI Bill among the most practical and cost-effective programs ever devised."[99] Congress and the Department of Defense have expanded the scope of services available to reservists in other ways as well. They have extended the range of medical and dental care available to authorized personnel, provided expanded access to base exchange and commissary facilities, increased life insurance coverage, and opened access to the full range of Morale, Welfare, Recreation, and Services facilities.[100]

Participation by women in the Air Force Reserve can be traced to 1948, when the Women's Armed Integration Act granted permanent status to a women's reserve, created the Women in the Air Force program, and integrated it as part of the Air Force rather than as a separate corps. As of March 1950,

The Air Force Reserve

1,127 female reservists were on the rolls (about 1.6 percent of the force): 491 were officers and 636 were enlisted. Male and female reservists had to meet the same eligibility requirements except for a dependent provision, which made any woman ineligible for service if she had a dependent younger than 18 years of age. Also, any member who became pregnant was involuntarily discharged. The Air Force Reserve Technician program opened to women on April 15, 1971. On December 31, 1975, eligibility criteria became the same for all potential members. By late 1994, 12,367 women were in the Air Force Reserve (18.7 percent of the force): 2,020 were officers and 10,347 were enlisted.[101]

Female reservists took advantage of the increased opportunities available to them and their active duty counterparts. In July 1976, 2d Lt. Kathleen A. Rambo became the first female Air Force Reservist selected for undergraduate pilot training. On April 28, 1993, General McPeak announced that women would be eligible to fly any aircraft in the Air Force inventory. Shortly thereafter, 1st Lt. Leslie DeAnn Crosby became the first woman in the Air Force Reserve selected to attend F–16 training at Tucson, Arizona. Increased opportunities brought the prospect of higher rank. Colonel Frances I. Mossman, mobilization assistant to the Director for Programs and Evaluations, Deputy Chief of Staff for Programs and Resources, Headquarters USAF, became the first woman in any reserve component to achieve the rank of brigadier general in August 1983. In 1991, CMSgt. Faye Whitehead was selected as senior enlisted adviser, 94th Airlift Wing, Dobbins AFB, Georgia, the first woman to hold that position in any reserve unit. On March 11, 1993, Maj. Gen. Alice Astafan became the first woman in any reserve component to achieve that rank. In November 1993, Col. Betty L. Mullis became the first female commander of an Air Force Reserve flying squadron (the 336th Air Refueling Squadron, March AFB, California). Five months later, she became the first female vice commander of an Air Force Reserve wing (the 452d Air Mobility Wing at March).[102]

Black Americans also found opportunities to serve in the Air Force Reserve from its inception. As early as March 1947, Headquarters Air Defense Command established policies to increase recruiting and improve training of African-American reservists in an Air Force that was still officially segregated. One year later, Air Defense Command began to investigate the possibility of activating up to four Air Force Reserve fighter squadrons for Black personnel. On April 28, 1948, the command activated two Provisional Troop Carrier Squadrons, one at Chicago and one in Detroit, to train minority members. In August 1948, President Truman officially ended segregation in the American armed forces, a move that marked the beginning of two decades of steady growth in the number of African-Americans serving as Air Force Reservists in one category or another. By June 1968, the Air Force Reserve had 108 Black officers and 1,106 Black enlisted personnel on its unit rosters (1.72 percent of all officers and 3.39 percent of all enlisted members). In 1994, members of all

Flying Club to Total Force

minority groups accounted for 24.36 percent all Air Force Reserve personnel; 924 (10.32 percent) were officers and 15,884 (27.71 percent) were enlisted. Of this number, 436 were African-American officers and 10,944 were African-American enlisted personnel. Colonel William C. Banton II, mobilization assistant to the assistant Surgeon General at Headquarters USAF, was the first Black promoted to brigadier general in the Air Force Reserve in March 1973. On January 17, 1995, Brig. Gen. Joseph A. McNeil became Commander, Twenty-second Air Force. He was the first African-American to serve as a numbered air force commander in the Air Force Reserve.[103]

Underpinning the activities of the Air Force Reserve in the mid-1990s was the command's implementation of the quality initiative. The Reserve's senior leadership mandated that the entire AFRES community undergo a culture change and embrace quality as a decision-making and management tool. All reserve personnel from Headquarters AFRES down to the unit level were to be trained in the quality process through the cascade procedure. Teams consisting of personnel from across the command prepared several publications that specified the organization's immediate and long-range goals. These documents ranged from annual plans developed by the smallest work groups to documents applicable to the command as a whole, such as the *Air Force Reserve Road Map to the Future*, the Total Quality Implementation Plan, and the Long Range Plan. Each document detailed the goals all members of the Reserve community were to strive for while employing quality tools in the workplace.[104]

In Summation

By any standard of military effectiveness, the U.S. Air Force Reserve was well prepared to participate fully in the Air Force's daily operations around the world and respond when mobilized. In February 1982, the component chief, General Bodycombe, could stand before his commanders and staffs and proclaim the incontestable excellence of this force of reservists and technicians.

In November 1994, when Maj. Gen. Robert A. McIntosh became the eighth Chief of Air Force Reserve and the seventh person to serve concurrently as Commander, Air Force Reserve, the Air Force Reserve, in all its complexity, was approaching its fiftieth anniversary with a sense of pride in its accomplishments and confidence that it would remain a strong partner in the Total Force in years to come. The challenges the command faced at that point in its history were daunting, but reservists had already demonstrated a remarkable resilience and flexibility that served them and their command well. Events of the 1980s and 1990s showed that the Air Force Reserve long ago shed the last vestiges of its flying club past and has matured into a valued partner in the Total Force. However it may be that future administrations

The Air Force Reserve

choose to employ the Air Force Reserve, the component grew from Flying Club to an essential element of Total Force, employable in peace or war as an integral part of the United States Air Force.

APPENDICES

APPENDIX 1

AIR FORCE RESERVE OFFICIALS, 1946–1994

Chief of National Guard and Reserve Affairs Division

Brig. Gen. John P. McConnell
    June 1947–March 1948

Chief, Civilian Components Group (DCS/Operations)

Brig. Gen. John P. McConnell
    March 1948–November 1948

Special Assistant to the Chief of Staff for Reserve Forces

Lt. Gen. Elwood R. Quesada
    Decmber 1, 1948–September 30, 1949

Maj. Gen. Earl S. Hoag
    October 1949–October 1951

Maj. Gen. Robert L. Copsey
    October 1951–September 1953

Assistant Chief of Staff for Reserve Forces

Maj. Gen. William E. Hall
    October 1953–June 1957

Maj. Gen. Richard A. Grussendorf
    July 1957–August 1959

Maj. Gen. Robert E. L. Eaton
    August 1959–December 1961

Maj. Gen. Chester E. McCarty
    January 1962–January 1963

Maj. Gen. Chester R. Low
    February 1963–July 1966

Maj. Gen. John H. Bell
    August 1966–October 1966

Maj. Gen. Richard S. Abbey
    November 1966–December 1967

Appendices

Chief of Air Force Reserve

Maj. Gen. Tom E. Marchbanks, Jr.
January 18, 1968–February 1, 1971

Maj. Gen. Homer I. Lewis[*]
April 19, 1971–April 8, 1975

Maj. Gen. William Lyon
April 16, 1975–April 16, 1979

Maj. Gen. Richard Bodycombe
April 17, 1979–November 1, 1982

Maj. Gen. Sloan R. Gill
November 1, 1982–October 31, 1986

Maj. Gen. Roger P. Scheer
November 1, 1986–October 31, 1990

Maj. Gen. John J. Closner
November 1, 1990–October 31, 1994

Maj. Gen. Robert A. McIntosh
November 1, 1994–

Commander of Air Defense Command

Lt. Gen. George E. Stratemeyer
March 21, 1946–November 30, 1948

Commander of Continental Air Command

Lt. Gen. George E. Stratemeyer
December 1, 1948–April 15, 1949

Lt. Gen. Ennis C. Whitehead
April 15, 1949–December 14, 1950

Maj. Gen. Willis H. Hale
December 14, 1950–February 20, 1952

Lt. Gen. Leon W. Johnson
February 21, 1952–December 15, 1955

Lt. Gen. Charles B. Stone III
December 15, 1955–Junuary 30, 1957

Lt. Gen. William E. Hall
July 1, 1957–September 30, 1961

---

[*] Beginning on March 16, 1972, Lewis and his successors were dual-hatted as Chief and Commander, Headquarters Air Force Reserve.

The Air Force Reserve

Lt. Gen. Gordon A. Blake
    October 1, 1961–June 30, 1962

Lt. Gen. Edward J. Timberlake
    July 1, 1962–June 15, 1965

Maj. Gen. Albert T. Wilson, Jr.
    June 15, 1965–August 18, 1965

Lt. Gen. Cecil H. Childre
    August 18, 1965–May 18, 1966

Maj. Gen. J. S. Holtoner
    May 28, 1966–July 31, 1966

Lt. Gen. Henry Viccellio
    August 1, 1966–July 31, 1968

Commander of Headquarters Air Force Reserve

Maj. Gen. Rollin B. Moore, Jr.
    August 1, 1968–January 26, 1972

Brig. Gen. Alfred Verhulst
    January 26, 1972–March 16, 1972

Maj. Gen. Homer I. Lewis
    March 16, 1972–April 8, 1975

Maj. Gen. William Lyon
    April 16, 1975–April 16, 1979

Maj. Gen. Richard Bodycombe
    April 17, 1979–November 1, 1982

Maj. Gen. Sloan R. Gill
    November 1, 1982–October 31, 1986

Maj. Gen. Roger P. Scheer
    November 1, 1986–October 31, 1990

Maj. Gen. John J. Closner
    November 1, 1990–October 31, 1994

Maj. Gen. Robert A. McIntosh
    November 1, 1994–

Vice Commander of Headquarters Air Force Reserve

Brig. Gen. Alfred Verhulst
    October 1, 1969–May 4, 1973

Maj. Gen. Earl O. Anderson
    May 5, 1973–October 12, 1976

Appendices

Maj. Gen. Richard Bodycombe
   Nov 1, 1976–April 15, 1979

Maj. Gen. Edward Dillon
   April 16, 1979–April 28, 1982

Maj. Gen. Sloan R. Gill
Maj. Gen. John E. Taylor
Maj. Gen. James E. McAdoo
   Rotating duty between April 29 and December 1, 1982

Maj. Gen. James E. McAdoo
   December 2, 1982–November 30, 1986

Maj. Gen. Alan G. Sharp
   December 1, 1986–November 30, 1990

Maj. Gen. Robert A. McIntosh
   December 1, 1990–June 30, 1993

Maj. Gen. James E. Sherrard III
   July 1, 1993–

APPENDIX 2

The Air Force Reserve

USAF RESERVE PERSONNEL STATISTICS, FISCAL YEARS 1947–1994

YEAR	CAT A UNITS	ART	IMA	MD	VAR	VARTU	IRR	AUTH	ASGN	READY	STANDBY	RETIRED	TOTAL
1947													429,000
1948	43,320				375,962	41,911							419,282
1949	28,412				390,642				28,412				419,054
1950	58,442				315,814				58,442				374,256
1951			4,902	2,086	303,971	47,855			4,902				315,242
1952	5,149		3,352	2,505	299,447	42,139	308,362		8,501	316,863	5,046	3,687	325,596
1953	10,843		2,974	2,617	223,683	36,963	205,405		13,817	219,222	18,278	3,126	240,626
1954	13,783		4,026				202,665		17,809	220,474	32,119	3,081	255,674
1955	21,655		5,207	2,991			139,593		26,862	166,455	75,072	4,047	245,574
1956	22,566		5,366	2,300			260,775		27,932	288,707	51,000	5,533	345,240
1957	22,828		6,207	1,554			188,811		29,035	217,846	204,052	6,518	428,416
1958	21,333		9,295				184,181	63,000	30,628	214,809	275,179	8,972	498,960
1959	24,720	3,133	9,839				191,260	65,000	34,559	225,819	316,041	10,908	552,768
1960	26,452	3,635	7,943	2,247			168,111	67,000	34,395	202,506	303,677	14,566	520,749
1961	33,745	3,891	6,579	2,306			173,547	63,000	40,324	213,871	265,593	20,548	500,012
1962	31,318	3,495	6,766	3,113			165,392	59,000	38,084	203,476	184,766	26,888	415,130
1963	31,645	3,682	5,612	4,178			131,125	61,000	37,257	168,382	116,874	34,052	319,308
1964	35,399	3,977	6,076	3,969			135,982	61,000	41,475	177,457	129,623	41,839	348,919
1965	38,991	3,800	5,633	4,845			148,884	48,820	44,624	193,508	141,341	48,916	383,765
1966	38,735	3,873	4,857	3,649			165,867	47,440	43,592	209,459	145,440	56,613	411,512
1967	41,419	4,096	2,522	4,381			159,767	48,865	43,941	203,708	143,667	63,779	411,154
1968	38,833	3,595	4,904	3,990			147,430	45,145	43,737	191,167	101,214	124,905	417,286
1969	38,498	4,216	4,508				183,151	48,785	43,006	226,157	89,239	153,089	468,485
1970	46,180	4,441	4,026				210,540	50,820	50,206	260,746	88,467	171,188	520,401

DRILL PAY

392

Appendices

USAF RESERVE PERSONNEL STATISTICS, FISCAL YEARS 1947–1994—Cont'd

YEAR	CAT A UNITS	ART	IMA	MD	VAR	VARTU	IRR	AUTH	ASGN	READY	STANDBY	RETIRED	TOTAL
1971	46,265	4,922	6,576				192,534	59,655	52,841	245,375	107,446	189,839	542,660
1972	43,670	5,108	6,136				154,929	58,854	49,806	204,735	64,088	211,296	480,119
1973	43,382	5,714	6,920				130,290	53,811	50,302	180,592	45,968	231,062	457,622
1974	42,001	6,234	5,279				120,024	51,503	47,280	167,304	46,442	238,984	452,730
1975	44,215	6,548	5,638				88,235	50,165	49,853	138,088	44,575	228,201	410,864
1976	41,983	6,616	8,201				81,087	53,210	50,184	131,271	44,047	273,807	449,125
1977	41,932	6,640	8,356				63,503	52,417	50,288	113,791	44,237	280,000	438,028
1978	46,246	6,457	8,816				44,619	53,000	55,062	99,681	42,932	270,993	413,606
1979	46,188	6,437	8,463				46,252	53,900	54,651	100,903	44,146	270,084	415,133
1980	49,800	6,385	9,121				46,234	58,219	58,921	105,155	41,359	270,714	417,228
1981	52,304	6,641	9,261				44,015	60,754	61,565	105,580	37,119	252,556	395,255
1982	54,053	7,308	9,833				43,946	63,736	63,886	107,832	32,514	234,564	374,910
1983	55,622	7,610	11,116				43,353	66,600	66,738	110,091	28,939	221,833	360,863
1984	58,196	7,634	11,633				42,445	69,880	69,829	112,274	29,543	211,518	353,335
1985	62,962	8,064	11,682				46,554	74,829	74,644	121,198	28,321	200,003	349,522
1986	65,653	8,354	12,254				49,321	77,400	77,907	127,228	25,823	195,855	348,906
1987	66,613	8,612	12,969				49,121	79,562	79,582	128,703	24,479	206,679	359,861
1988	69,031	9,123	12,292				56,707	82,400	81,323	138,030	21,772	212,620	372,422
1989	69,594	9,189	12,895				53,842	83,615	82,489	136,331	17,299	218,167	371,797
1990	69,811	9,517	13,315				69,401	84,900	83,126	152,527	15,369	217,786	385,682
1991	69,934	9,526	12,669				80,617	85,591	82,603	163,220	14,234	221,955	399,409
1992	69,420	9,914	11,784				108,857	82,400	81,204	190,061	13,573	263,554	467,188
1993	68,267	9,816	11,668				112,875	80,741	79,935	192,810	11,271	271,973	476,054
1994	66,282	9,595	12,288				99,899	81,500	78,570	178,469	9,926	270,706	459,101

CAT A=Reserve Combat/Combat Sustaining Units (train, receive points, and are paid); IMA=Individual Mobilization Augmentees (CAT B); ART=Air Reserve Technicians (included in CAT A data); VAR=Voluntary Air Reserve; VARTU=Voluntary Air Reserve Training Units; IRR=Individual Ready Reserve (not required to train but subject to mobilization); Auth=Autorized; Asgn=Assigned (receive pay, points, assigned to unit); Ready=Ready Reserve (CATs A and B, subject to recall); Standby= Standby Reserve (do not train, not assigned to unit); Retired=Retired Reserve (receive retirement pay as a result of Active or Reserve duty, subject to involuntary recall).

APPENDIX 3

DEPARTMENT OF THE AIR FORCE
AIR FORCE RESERVE DIRECT OBLIGATIONS ($000)

FISCAL YEAR	3700 RPA OBLIGATIONS	3730 1/3/MCP BUDGETS	3740 O&M OBLIGATIONS	TOTAL
1947	15,339			15,339
1948	39,426			39,426
1949	69,500			69,500
1950	26,167			26,167
1951	31,968			31,968
1952	19,264			19,264
1953	21,339			21,339
1954	22,879			22,879
1955	21,194			21,194
1956	32,811			32,811
1957	40,504			40,504
1958	41,991			41,991
1959	42,400			42,400
1960	45,455			45,455
1961	44,213			44,213
1962	44,997	12,613		57,610
1963	42,089	5,000		47,089
1964	50,057	4,000		54,057
1965	47,943	5,000		52,943
1966	49,891	4,000		53,891
1967	54,675	3,600		58,275
1968	53,898	3,900		57,798
1969	56,233	4,300		60,533
1970	72,505	5,300	128,059	205,864
1971	87,700	4,000	155,872	247,572
1972	96,170	6,581	172,220	274,971
1973	104,075	7,000	186,619	297,694
1974	103,564	10,000	238,901	352,465

Appendices

DEPARTMENT OF THE AIR FORCE
AIR FORCE RESERVE DIRECT OBLIGATIONS ($000)—*Cont'd*

FISCAL YEAR	3700 RPA OBLIGATIONS	3730 1/3/MCP BUDGETS	3740 O&M OBLIGATIONS	TOTAL
1975	120,305	16,000	295,537	431,842
1976	129,857	18,000	331,630	479,487
1977T**	44,724	1,000	85,190	130,914
1977	135,952	10,773	355,088	501,813
1978	158,599	11,200	383,640	553,439
1979	173,220	13,000	390,866	577,086
1980	199,151	12,000	511,389	722,540
1981	246,196	21,600	599,072	866,868
1982	292,743	37,375	675,580	1,005,698
1983	362,116	35,412	761,923	1,159,451
1984	389,311	40,750	782,978	1,213,039
1985	570,048	65,936	877,847	1,513,831
1986	580,180	58,008	857,355	1,495,543
1987	570,868	58,780	924,633	1,554,281
1988	616,564	79,031	999,721	1,695,316
1989	655,819	70,365	1,072,505	1,798,689
1990	663,749	45,764	1,018,103	1,727,616
1991	597,410	31,473	1,084,349	1,713,232
1992	721,642	7,287	1,154,726	1,883,655
1993	706,790	24,349	1,229,322	1,960,461
1994	785,812	45,027	1,357,749	2,188,588

The Air Force Reserve

APPENDIX 4

AIR FORCE RESERVE AIRCRAFT, FISCAL YEARS 1947–1994

A/C TYPE	47	48	49	50	51	52	53	54	55	56	57	58	59	60	61	62	63	64	65	66	67	68	69	70
AT-7/11	315																							
AT-6	918	1320		491		59	58	16	4															
P/F-51						8	91	4																
B-26		82						18	27	89	8													
C-46		120				101	102	152	184	194	172	20												
C-47		42																						
T-28							48	53	61	61	13													
F-80									172	175	167	71												
T-33									96	99	95	64												
C-45									62	69	69	58	10											
C-119									31	35	39	201	517	622	653	614	669	616	601	578	399	344	269	190	120
F-84									11	53	63	68												
TC-47								26	37	44	44	37	32	32	30	30	30	18	16					
F-86										36														
SA/MU-16										13	14	20	21	24	20	20	20	20	19	19	22	22	18	
C-123B												46	45	47	47	41	41	18						
C-124												45	28	20	20	29	105	158	118	115	136			
HC-97																			2	18	9	9	20	
KC-97																			4					
C-130																					8	9	27	
U-3A																						9	51	
O-2A																							20	
HH-34																								
A-37																								
C-7																								
C-123K																								
EC-121																								
F-105																								
HC-130																								
HH-1H																								
HH-3H																								
HH-3E																								
CH-3E																								
KC-135																								
WC-130																								
AC-130																								
F-4																								
UH-1H																								
UH-1N																								
A-10A																								
C-5																								
C-141																								
HC-130																								
MH/HH-60																								
B-52																								
F-16																								
OA/A-10																								
Total	1233	1320	244	491	0	168	299	615	733	814	748	605	725	751	762	794	727	712	663	545	539	426	354	392

396

Appendices

AIR FORCE RESERVE AIRCRAFT, FISCAL YEARS 1947–1994—Cont'd

A/C TYPE	71	72	73	74	75	76	77	78	79	80	81	82	83	84	85	86	87	88	89	90	91	92	93	94
AT-7/11																								
AT-6																								
P/F-51																								
B-26																								
C-46																								
C-47																								
T-28																								
F-80																								
T-33																								
C-45																								
C-119	34	13																						
F-84																								
TC-47																								
F-86																								
SA/MU-16	8	4	1																					
C-123B																								
C-124	100	21																						
HC-97	3	1																						
KC-97																								
C-130	74	107	106	110	120	137	125	117	117	119	110	128	139	142	143	143	119	122	124	126	127	123	116	111
U-3A	30																							
O-2A																								
HH-34	3	30	29																					
A-37	62	62	64	55	80	93	93	93	91	86	25													
C-7		36	32	32	32	32	32	32	32	36	36	18	11											
C-123K		33	67	63	63	63	64	63	63	63	34	40	4	4	4	4								
EC-121		9	7	6	7	10	7																	
F-105		14	78	61	74	72	70	67	65	72	50	25	18											
HC-130		10	10	10	14	14	14	14	14	15	15	15	15	14	14	8	22	14	14	14	10	11	10	
HH-1H		16	18	18	18	18	18	18	5	5	5	5	5			5	5	5	5	5				
HH-3H			1																					
HH-3E				6	6	6	5	7	7	8	8	8	8	12	12	12	13	12	17	17	8			
CH-3E			7	6	7	7	8	7	8	6	6	6	6	2	2	2	7	5	1					
KC-135					8	16	24	24	24	24	24	24	26	24	24	24	24	24	30	30	30	52	62	
WC-130					7	7	7	7	6	7	7	7	7	7	7	12	8	4	4	12	12	12	10	
AC-130				10	10	10	10	10	9	10	10	10	10	10	10	10	10	10	10	10	10	11	10	
F-4					10	20	24	60	110	113	112	112	113	86	107	65	43							
UH-1H												5	5											
UH-1N							3	5	5	5	5	5	5											
A-10A								2	42	76	96	100	100	99	98	97	97	87	98	103				
C-5													5	5	11	24	32	32	32	32	32	32		
C-141													2	8	8	8	8	8	8	15	24	38		
HC-130											15	15	15	14	14	8	22	14	14	14	10	11	10	
MH/HH-60																					21	29	25	
B-52																								9
F-16												26	26	25	42	58	104	117	171	171	212	136		
OA/A-10																						81	62	
Total	314	330	410	363	416	477	469	468	478	452	442	456	476	481	483	480	445	527	518	508	538	545	591	515

APPENDIX 5

452d Light Bomb Wing Operations, Korea: October 1950–May 1952

Date	Aircraft Poss	Aircraft Cr	Aircraft Asgd	Aircraft Avail	Crews Cr	Crews Hours	Sorties	Aircraft Losses Enemy	Aircraft Losses Other	Crew Member Losses KIA	Crew Member Losses KNIA	Crew Member Losses MIA
Nov 50	47	34				2,210			1			
Dec 50	43	32				4,371		1	3	3	9	
Jan 51	42	28				2,721						
Feb 51	42	24				2,137		3	1	18		
Mar 51	39	26				1,609		4				9
Apr 51	29	18	55	43	43	3,614	686	2	1			6
May 51	29	21	50	36	33	2,921	591	3				1
Jun 51	40	24	69	66	42	5,187	684	1	1			
Jul 51	45	31	65	45	35	3,884	759		2	3		
Aug 51	52	38	66	66	51	4,124	785		3	1	1	5
Sep 51	51	39	67	67	56	4,657	942		6	7	10	12
Oct 51	49	40	60	60	54	4,428	930		2	3		
Nov 51	50	42	53	53	42	4,543	904		1			3
Dec 51	50	41	42	52	40	4,612	863					
Jan 52	53	43	53	53	38	4,257	738					
Feb 52	53	43	54	54	39	3,841	664	1				3
Mar 52	52	42	64	64	38	4,239	767	1				5
Apr 52	53	40	67	67	49	4,121	757					
AVG/TOT	45.5	33.6	59.9	55.8	43	67,476	10,070	16	21	35	20	44

Source: Fifth Air Force Commander's Review.
Flying hours for March 1951 reflect only the 728th and 729th squadrons.

APPENDIX 6

\multicolumn{6}{	c	}{OPERATIONS OF 437TH TROOP CARRIER WING ON ACTIVE MILITARY SERVICE, AUGUST 1950–JUNE 1952*}
Period	C–46s on Hand	Hours	PAX	Tons	In Comm Rate (%)
22 Aug–Oct 50	43	4,561			
10 Nov–31 Dec 50	37	3,471	7,699+		
Jan 51		3,257:25	14,992	5,178.3	65
Feb 51		4,118:10	10,221	4,713.8	79.9
Mar 51	62	4,120:45	15,127	3,383.6	
Apr 51	51	4,224	12,870	4,188	
May 51	49	5,578:05	15,072	5,124.4	76.2
Jun 51	49	5,629:10	16,743	5,018.2	77.7
Jul 51	55	5,027:10	13,958	2,923.3	82.1
Aug 51	57	6,207:20	15,999	3,437.8	73.6
Sep 51	59	2,697	5,516	1,624.9	86.7
Oct 51	60	4,939	17,125	2,968.8	74.9
Nov 51	61	5,900	13,626	3,864.8	79
Dec 51	61	6,968	13,508	4,072.4	81
Jan 52	60	7,640	14,387	3,914.4	78.1
Feb 52	58	7,389	15,000	3,536.7	75.6
Mar 52	56	6,973	12,904	3,083.4	67.3
Apr 52	56	8,506	12,714	2,220.9	73.8
May 52	54	6,215	12,081	2,097.8	72.3
1–9 Jun 52	56	1,735	2,815	592.1	73.9
AVG/TOT	54.6	105,155:25	242,357	61,943.6	

*Sources: Histories of 437th Troop Carrier Wing.
+Also, 5,501 patients moved during this period.

The Air Force Reserve

APPENDIX 7

AIR FORCE RESERVE FLYING UNITS, 1958–1967		
BASE	WING	SQUADRON
TROOP CARRIER UNITS		
Hamilton AFB, Calif.	349	312
Portland MAP, Oreg.		313
McClellan AFB, Calif.		314
Paine AFB, Wash.		97
Long Beach MAP, Calif.	452[1]	728[1]
Long Beach MAP, Calif.		729[1]
Long Beach MAP, Calif.		730[1]
Hill AFB, Utah		733
Bakalar AFB, Ind.	434	71
Bakalar AFB, Ind.		72
Scott AFB, Ill.		73
Gen. B. Mitchell Field, Wis.	440	95
Minn–St. Paul IAP, Minn.		96
Selfridge AFB, Mich.	403	63
O'Hare IAP, Ill.		64
Richards-Gebaur AFB, Mo.	442	303
Richards-Gebaur AFB, Mo.		304
Tinker AFB, Okla.		305
Davis Field, Okla.		65
Brooks AFB, Tex.	433[2]	67[2]
Brooks AFB, Tex.		68[2]
NAS Dallas		69[2,3]
Ellington AFB, Tex.	446	70
Ellington AFB, Tex.		705
Barksdale AFB, La.		706[4]
NAS New Orleans		357[5]
Mitchel AFB, N.Y.	514	335[6]
Mitchel AFB, N.Y.		336[7]

400

Appendices

AIR FORCE RESERVE FLYING UNITS, 1958–1967—*Cont'd*		
BASE	WING	SQUADRON
TROOP CARRIER UNITS		
Bradley Field, Conn.		337[8]
L. G. Hanscom Field, Mass.	94	731
Greiner AFB, N.H.		732[9]
NAS Willow Grove, Pa.	512	326
NAS Willow Grove, Pa.		327
Niagara Falls MAP, N.Y.		328
Clinton County AFB, Ohio	302	355
Clinton County AFB, Ohio		756
Andrews AFB, Md.	459	756
Youngstown MAP, Ohio		757
Greater Pittsburgh Airport, Pa.		758
Dobbins AFB, Ga.	445 (Assault)[10]	700[10]
Memphis MAP, Tenn.		701[10, 11]
Memphis MAP, Tenn.		702[10, 11]
Miami IAP, Fla.	435[12]	76[12]
Donaldson AFB, S.C.		77[13]
Bates Field, Ala.		78[14]
AIR RESCUE SQUADRONS		
Miami IAP, Fla.		301[15]
Williams AFB, Ariz.		302[16]
Long Beach MAP, Calif.		303[1]
Portland MAP, Oreg.		304
Selfridge AFB, Mich.		305
1. Moved to March AFB, Calif., November 1960.		
2. Moved to Kelly AFB, Tex., May 1960.		
3. Moved to Carswell AFB, Tex., January 1963.		
4. Moved to NAS New Orleans, May 1961.		
5. Moved to Bates Field, Ala., May 1961.		
6. Moved to McGuire AFB, N.J., March 1961.		
7. Moved to Stewart AFB, N.Y., March 1961.		
8. Moved to Westover AFB, Mass., March 1966.		
9. Inactivated, January 1966.		

The Air Force Reserve

AIR FORCE RESERVE FLYING UNITS, 1958–1967—*Cont'd*
10. Equipped with C–123s, September 1958.
11. Discontinued, December 1965.
12. Moved to Homestead AFB, Fla., July 1960; inactivated December 1, 1965.
13. Moved to Carswell AFB, Tex., April 1963.
14. Moved to Barksdale AFB, La., May 1961.
15. Moved to Homestead AFB, Fla., July 1960.
16. Moved to Luke AFB, Ariz., November 1960.

APPENDIX 8

UNITED STATES CIVIL SERVICE COMMISSION
Washington 25, D.C.

June 21, 1957

Honorable David F. Smith
Assistant Secretary of the Air Force
Department of the Air Force
Washington 25, D.C.

Dear Mr. Smith:

The Civil Service Commission has completed its review of the Air Reserve Technician Plan as it has been presented by the Department of the Air Force. This letter authorizes the Department to proceed with the implementation of the Plan. The Commission will issue instructions to its operating offices in the near future regarding their part in this program. I request that the Department of the Air Force coordinate as closely as possible with the Commission's staff in the work involved in putting the program into full effect.

The approval of this Plan by the Commission is given with the understanding that the Department of the Air Force will carry out both in letter and spirit the commitments it has made and the safeguards it has promised to apply with respect to employees who would be affected by the Plan. It is also understood that the Department will comply fully and strictly with the requirements of the Veterans' Preference Act of 1944 and the Commission's Regulations under that Act in all of its activities under the Plan.

By direction of the Commission:

Sincerely yours,

s/t

Harris Ellsworth
Chairman

The Air Force Reserve

APPENDIX 9

Public Law 90–168
90th Congress, H.R. 2
December 1, 1967

AN ACT

To amend titles 10, 32, and 37, United States Code, to strengthen the reserve components of the armed forces, and for other purposes.

Be it enacted by the Senate and House of Representatives of the United States of America in Congress assembled, That this Act may be cited as the "Reserve Forces Bill of Rights and Vitalization Act."

SEC. 2. Title 10, United States Code, is amended as follows:

(1) Section 136(b) is amended by inserting below the first sentence the following: "One of the Assistant Secretaries shall be the Assistant Secretary of Defense for Manpower and Reserve Affairs. He shall have as his principal duty the overall supervision of manpower and reserve component affairs of the Department of Defense."

(2) Section 136 is amended by adding at the end thereof a new subsection as follows:

"(f) Within the Office of the Assistant Secretary of Defense for Manpower and Reserve Affairs there shall be a Deputy Assistant Secretary of Defense for Reserve Affairs who shall be appointed from civilian life by the President, by and with the advice and consent of the Senate. Subject to the supervision and control of the Assistant Secretary of Defense for Manpower and Reserve Affairs, the Deputy Assistant Secretary shall be responsible for all matters relating to reserve affairs within the Office of the Assistant Secretary of Defense for Manpower and Reserve Affairs."

(3) Section 175(a)(2) is amended to read as follows:

"(2) the Assistant Secretary of the Army for Manpower and Reserve Affairs, the Assistant Secretary of the Navy for Manpower and Reserve Affairs, and the Assistant Secretary of the Air Force for Manpower and Reserve Affairs;"

(4) Section 175 is amended by striking out subsections (b), (c), (d), and (e), and inserting in lieu thereof the following:

"(b) Whenever the Coast Guard is not operating as a service in the

Appendices

Navy, the Secretary of Transportation may designate an officer of the Regular Coast Guard or the Coast Guard Reserve to serve as a voting member of the Board.

"(c) The Board, acting through the Assistant Secretary of Defense for Manpower and Reserve Affairs is the principal policy adviser to the Secretary of Defense on matters relating to the reserve components.

"(d) This section does not affect the committees on reserve policies prescribed by section 3033, 5251, 5252, or 8033 of this title.

"(e) A member of a committee or board prescribed under a section listed in subsection (d) may, if otherwise eligible, be a member of the Reserve Forces Policy Board.

"(f) The Board shall act on those matters referred to it by the Chairman and, in addition, on any matter raised by a member of the Board."

(5) Section 262 is amended by striking out "the reserve components" and inserting "each reserve component" in place thereof.

(6) Section 264 is amended to read as follows:

"§ 264. Reserve affairs: designation of general or flag officer of each military department; personnel and logistic support for reserves; reports to Congress.

"(a) The Secretary concerned may designate a general or flag officer of the armed force under his jurisdiction to be directly responsible for reserve affairs to the Chief of Staff of the Army, the Chief of Naval Operations, the Chief of Staff of the Air Force, the Commandant of the Marine Corps, or the Commandant of the Coast Guard, as the case may be. This subsection does not affect the functions of the Chief of the National Guard Bureau, the Chief, Office of Army Reserve, or the Chief, Office of Air Force Reserve.

"(b) The Secretary concerned is responsible for providing the personnel, equipment, facilities, and other general logistic support necessary to enable units and Reserves in the Ready Reserve of the Reserve components under his jurisdiction to satisfy the training requirements and mobilization readiness requirements for those units and Reserves as recommended by the Secretary concerned and by the Joint Chiefs of Staff and approved by the Secretary of Defense, and as recommended by the Commandant of the Coast Guard and approved by the Secretary of Transportation when the Coast Guard is not operated as a service of the Navy.

"(c) The Secretary concerned shall submit a written report to the Committees on Armed Services of the Senate and the House of Representatives each year regarding the extent to which units and Reserves in the Ready Reserve of the Reserve components under his jurisdiction have satisfied the training and mobilization readiness requirements pursuant to subsection (b) of this section for the year with respect to which such report was submitted. Reports under this subsection shall be made on a fiscal

The Air Force Reserve

year basis and the report for any fiscal year shall be submitted within 60 days after the end of the fiscal year for which it is submitted."

(7) The section analysis at the beginning of chapter 11 is amended by striking out "264. Reserve affairs: responsibility for." and inserting in lieu thereof "264. Reserve affairs: designation of general or flag officers for each military department; personnel and logistic support for reserves; reports to Congress."

(8) Section 268 is amended by inserting the designation "(a)" at the beginning thereof and by adding the following new subsections:

"(b) Within the Ready Reserve of each of the Reserve components defined in section 261 of this title, there is a Selected Reserve, consisting of units, and, as designated by the Secretary concerned, of Reserves, trained as prescribed in section 270(a)(1) of this title or section 502(a) of title 32, United States Code, as appropriate.

"(c) The organization and unit structure of the Selected Reserve shall be approved—

"(1) in the case of the Coast Guard Reserve, by the Secretary of Transportation upon the recommendation of the Commandant of the Coast Guard, and

"(2) in the case of all other Reserve components, by the Secretary of Defense based upon recommendations from the military departments as approved by the Joint Chiefs of Staff in accordance with contingency and war plans."

(9) Section 269(e) (1)–(6) is amended to read as follows:

"(1) he served on active duty (other than for training) in the armed forces for an aggregate of at least five years; or

"(2) he served on active duty (other than for training) in the armed forces for an aggregate of less than five years, but satisfactorily participated, as determined by the Secretary concerned, in an accredited training program in the Ready Reserve for a period which, when added to his period of active duty (other than for training), totals at least five years, or such shorter period as the Secretary concerned, with the approval of the Secretary of Defense in the case of a Secretary of a military department, may prescribe for satisfactory participation in an accredited training program designated by the Secretary concerned."

(10) Section 270(a)(1) is amended to read as follows:

"(1) participate in at least 48 scheduled drills or training periods each year and serve on active duty for training of not less than 14 days (exclusive of traveltime) during each year;"

(11) Section 511(d) is amended to read as follows:

"(d) Under regulations to be prescribed by the Secretary of Defense or the Secretary of Transportation with respect to the Coast Guard when it is not operating as a service in the Navy, a non-prior-service person who is under 26 years of age, who is qualified for induction for active duty in an armed

Appendices

force, and who is not under orders to report for induction into an armed force under the Military Selective Service Act of 1967 (50 App. U.S.C. 451–473), except as provided in section 6(c)(2)(2)(A) (ii) and (iii) of such Act, may be enlisted in the Army National Guard or the Air National Guard, or as a Reserve for service in the Army Reserve, Naval Reserve, Air Force Reserve, Marine Corps Reserve, or Coast Guard Reserve, for a term of six years. Each person enlisted under this subsection shall perform an initial period of active duty for training of not less than four months to commence insofar as practicable within 180 days after the date of that enlistment."

(12) The text of section 3013 is amended to read as follows:
"There are an Under Secretary of the Army and four Assistant Secretaries of the Army in the Department of the Army. They shall be appointed from civilian life by the President, by and with the advice and consent of the Senate. One of the Assistant Secretaries shall be the Assistant Secretary of the Army for Manpower and Reserve Affairs. He shall have as his principal duty the overall supervision of manpower and reserve component affairs of the Department of the Army."

(13) The first sentence of section 5034(a) is amended by striking out "three" and inserting in lieu thereof "four."

(14) Section 5034(b) is amended by adding at the end thereof the following: "One of the Assistant Secretaries shall be the Assistant Secretary of the Navy for Manpower and Reserve Affairs. He shall have as his principal duty the overall supervision of manpower and reserve component affairs of the Department of the Navy."

(15) The text of section 8013 is amended to read as follows: "There are an Under Secretary of the Air Force and four Assistant Secretaries of the Air Force in the Department of the Air Force. They shall be appointed from civilian life by the President, by and with the advice and consent of the Senate. One of the Assistant Secretaries shall be the Assistant Secretary of the Air Force for Manpower and Reserve Affairs. He shall have as his principal duty the overall supervision of manpower and reserve component affairs of the Department of the Air Force."

(16) Chapter 303 is amended by adding at the end thereof a new section 3019 as follows:
"§ 3019. Office of Army Reserve: appointment of Chief.

"(a) There is in the executive part of the Department of the Army an Office of the Army Reserve which is headed by a chief who is the adviser to the Chief of Staff on Army Reserve matters.

"(b) The President, by and with the advice and consent of the Senate, shall appoint the Chief of Army Reserve from officers of the Army Reserve not on active duty, or on active duty under section 265 of this title, who—

"(1) have had at least 10 years of commissioned service in the Army Reserve;

"(2) are in grade of brigadier general and above;

"(3) have been recommended by the Secretary of the Army.

"(c) The Chief of Army Reserve holds office for four years but may be removed for cause at any time. He is eligible to succeed himself. If he holds a lower reserve grade, he shall be appointed in the grade of major general for service in the Army Reserve."

(17) The following new item is added to the analysis of chapter 303: "3019. Office of Army Reserve: appointment of Chief."

(18) The text of section 3033 is amended to read as follows:

"(a) There is in the office of the Secretary of the Army an Army Reserve Forces Policy Committee which shall review and comment upon major policy matters directly affecting the reserve components of the Army, and the Committee's comments on such policy matters shall accompany the final report regarding any such matters submitted to the Chief of Staff and the Assistant Secretary responsible for reserve affairs.

"(b) The Committee consists of officers in the grade of colonel or above, as follows:

"(1) five members of the Regular Army on duty with the Army General Staff;

"(2) five members of the Army National Guard of the United States not on active duty; and

"(3) five members of the Army Reserve not on active duty.

"(c) The members of the Committee shall select the Chairman from among the members of the Committee not on active duty.

"(d) A majority of the members of the Committee shall act whenever matters affecting both the Army National Guard of the United States and Army Reserve are being considered. However, when any matter solely affecting one of the reserve components of the Army is being considered, it shall be acted upon only by the Subcommittee on Army National Guard Policy or the Subcommittee on Army Reserve Policy, as appropriate.

"(e) The Subcommittee on Army National Guard Policy consists of the members of the Committee other than the Army Reserve members.

"(f) The Subcommittee on Army Reserve Policy consists of the members of the Committee other than the Army National Guard members.

"(g) Membership on the Committee is determined by the Secretary of the Army and is for a minimum period of three years. Except in the case of members of the Committee from the Regular Army, the Secretary of the Army, when appointing new members, shall insure that among the officers of each component on the Committee there will at all times be two or more members with more than one year of continuous service on the Committee.

"(h) There shall be not less than 10 officers of the Army National Guard of the United States and the Army Reserve on duty with the Army General Staff, one-half of whom shall be from each of those components. These officers shall be considered as additional members of the Army General Staff while on that duty."

Appendices

(19) Chapter 803 is amended by adding at the end thereof a new section 8019 as follows:

"§ 8019. Office of Air Force Reserve: appointment of Chief

"(a) There is in the executive part of the Department of the Air Force an Office of Air Force Reserve which is headed by a chief who is the adviser to the Chief of Staff, on Air Force Reserve matters.

"(b) The President, by and with the advice and consent of the Senate, shall appoint the Chief of Air Force Reserve from officers of the Air Force Reserve not on active duty, or on active duty under section 265 of this title, who—

"(1) have had at least 10 years of commissioned service in the Air Force;

"(2) are in grade of brigadier general and above; and

"(3) have been recommended by the Secretary of the Air Force.

"(c) The Chief of Air Force Reserve holds office for four years, but may be removed for cause at any time. He is eligible to succeed himself. If he holds a lower reserve grade, he shall be appointed in the grade of major general for service in the Air Force Reserve."

(20) The following new item is added to the analysis of chapter 803:

"8019. Office of Air Force Reserve: appointment of Chief."

(21) The text of section 8033 is amended to read as follows:

"(a) There is in the Office of the Secretary of the Air Force an Air Reserve Forces Policy Committee on Air National Guard and Air Force Reserve Policy which shall review and comment upon major policy matters directly affecting the reserve components of the Air Force and the Committee's comments on such policy matters shall accompany the final report regarding any such matters submitted to the Chief of Staff, and the Assistant Secretary responsible for reserve affairs.

"(b) The Committee consists of officers in the grade of colonel or above, as follows:

"(1) five members of the Regular Air Force on duty with the Air Staff:

"(2) five members of the Air National Guard of the United States not on active duty;

"(3) five members of the Air Force Reserve not on active duty.

"(c) The members of the Committee shall select the Chairman from among the members of the Committee not on active duty.

"(d) A majority of the members of the Committee shall act whenever matters affecting both the Air National Guard of the United States and Air Force Reserve are being considered. However, when any matter solely affecting one of the Air Force Reserve components is being considered, it shall be acted upon only by the Subcommittee on Air National Guard Policy or the Subcommittee on Air Force Reserve Policy, as appropriate.

"(e) The Subcommittee on Air National Guard Policy consists of the members of the Committee other than the Air Force Reserve members.

The Air Force Reserve

"(f) The Subcommittee on Air Force Reserve Policy consists of the members of the Committee other than the Air National Guard members.

"(g) Membership on the Air Staff Committee is determined by the Secretary of the Air Force and is for a minimum period of three years. Except in the case of members of the Committee from the Regular Air Force, the Secretary of the Air Force, when appointing new members, shall insure that among the officers of each component on the Committee there will at all times be two or more members with more than one year of continuous service on the Committee.

"(h) There shall be not less than 10 officers of the Air National Guard of the United States and the Air Force Reserve on duty with the Air Staff, one-half of whom shall be from each of those components. These officers shall be considered as additional members of the Air Staff while on that duty."

(22) Section 8850 is amended by inserting before the period at the end of the first sentence "and who are not assigned to a unit organized to serve as a unit."

SEC. 3. Section 404(a) of title 37, United States Code, is amended by striking out "and" at the end of clause (2), striking out the period at the end of clause (3) and inserting in place thereof "; and", and adding the following new clause:

"(4) when away from home to perform duty, including duty by a member of the Army National Guard of the United States or the Air National Guard of the United States, as the case may be, in his status as a member of the National Guard, for which he is entitled to, or has waived, pay under this title."

SEC. 4. The last sentence of section 502(b) of title 32, United States Code, is amended to read as follows: "However, to have a series of formations credited as an assembly for drill and instruction, all parts of the unit must be included in the series within 30 consecutive days."

SEC. 5. From December 1, 1967, through June 30, 1969, appointments and promotions may be made without regard to the authorized strength in grade prescribed by or under chapter 831 of Title 10, United States Code, to fill vacancies in units of the Air National Guard, and in units organized to serve as units in the Air Force Reserve, as follows:

(1) Before July 1, 1968, in the Air National Guard, 250 in the grade of lieutenant colonel and 340 in the grade of major, and in the Air Force Reserve, 270 in the grade of lieutenant colonel and 240 in the grade of major, and

(2) After June 30, 1968, in the Air National Guard, 220 in the grade

of lieutenant colonel and 300 in the grade of major, and in the Air Force Reserve, 125 in the grade of lieutenant colonel and 175 in the grade of major.

SEC. 6. Section 412 of Public Law 86-149, as amended, is amended by adding at the end thereof a new subsection as follows:

"(c) Beginning with the fiscal year which begins July 1, 1968, and for each fiscal year thereafter, the Congress shall authorize the personnel strength of the Selected Reserve of each Reserve component of the Armed Forces; and no funds may be appropriated for any fiscal year beginning on or after such date for the pay and allowances of members of any Reserve component of the Armed Forces unless the personnel strength of the Selected Reserve of such Reserve component for such fiscal year has been authorized by law."

SEC. 7. The provisions of this Act shall become effective on the first day of the first calendar month following the date of enactment.

Approved December 1, 1967.

LEGISLATIVE HISTORY—
HOUSE REPORTS: No. 13 (Comm. on Armed Services) and No. 925 (Comm. of Conference).
SENATE REPORT No. 732 (Comm. on Armed Services).
CONGRESSIONAL RECORD, Vol. 113 (1967):

Feb. 20: Considered and passed House.
Nov. 8: Considered and passed Senate, amended.
Nov. 15: House agreed to conference report.
Nov. 16: Senate agreed to conference report.

The Air Force Reserve

APPENDIX 10

THE SECRETARY OF DEFENSE
Washington, D.C. 20301

Aug 21, 1970

MEMORANDUM FOR Secretaries of the Military Departments
    Chairman, Joint Chiefs of Staff
    Director, Defense Research and Engineering
    Assistant Secretaries of Defense
    Department of Defense Agencies

SUBJECT: Support for Guard and Reserve Forces

    The President has requested reduced expenditures during Fiscal Year 1970 and extension of these economics into future budgets. Within the Department of Defense, these economies will require reductions in overall strengths and capabilities of the active forces, and increased reliance on the combat and combat support units of the Guard and Reserves. I am concerned with the readiness of Guard and Reserve units to respond to contingency requirements, and with the lack of resources that have been made available to Guard and Reserve commanders to improve Guard and Reserve readiness.
    Public Law 90–168, an outgrowth of similar Congressional concern, places responsibility with the respective Secretaries of the Military Departments for recruiting, organizing, equipping, and training of Guard Reserve Forces. I desire that the Secretaries of the Military Departments provide, in the FY 1972 and future budgets, the necessary resources to permit the appropriate balance in the development of Active, Guard and Reserve Forces.
    Emphasis will be given to concurrent consideration of the total forces, active and reserve, to determine the most advantageous mix to support national strategy and meet the threat. A total force concept will be applied in all aspects of planning, programming, manning, equipping and employing Guard and Reserve Forces. Application of the concept will be geared to recognition that in many instances the lower peacetime sustaining costs of reserve force units, compared to similar active units, can result in a

Appendices

larger total force for a given budget or the same size force for a lesser budget. In addition, attention will be given to the fact that Guard and Reserve Forces can perform peacetime missions as a by-product or adjunct of training with significant manpower and monetary savings.

Guard and Reserve units and individuals of the Selected Reserves will be prepared to be the initial and primary source for augmentation of the active forces in any future emergency requiring a rapid and substantial expansion of the active forces. Toward this end, the Assistant Secretary of Defense (Manpower and Reserve Affairs) is responsible for coordinating and monitoring actions to achieve the following objectives:

—Increase the readiness, reliability and timely responsiveness of the combat and combat support units of the Guard and Reserve and individuals of the Reserve.

—Support and maintain minimum average trained strengths of the Selected Reserve as mandated by Congress.

—Provide and maintain combat standard equipment for Guard and Reserve units in the necessary quantities; and provide the necessary controls to identify resources committed for Guard and Reserve logistic support through the planning, programming, budgeting, procurement and distribution cycle.

—Implement the approved ten-year construction programs for the Guard and Reserves, subject to their accommodation within the currently approved TOA, with priority to facilities that will provide the greatest improvement in readiness levels.

—Provide adequate support of individual and unit reserve training programs.

—Provide manning levels for technicians and training and administration reserve support personnel (TARS) equal to full authorization levels.

—Program adequate resources and establish necessary priorities to achieve readiness levels required by appropriate guidance documents as rapidly as possible.

MELVIN R. LAIRD

The Air Force Reserve

APPENDIX 11

THE SECRETARY OF DEFENSE
Washington, D.C. 20301

Aug 23, 1973

MEMORANDUM FOR Secretaries of the Military Departments
    Chairman, Joint Chiefs of Staff
    Director, Defense Research and Engineering
    Assistant Secretaries of Defense
    Director, Defense Program Analysis and Evaluation
    Directors of Defense Agencies

SUBJECT: Readiness of the Selected Reserve

    An integral part of the central purpose of this Department—to build and maintain the necessary forces to deter war and to defend our country—is the Total Force Policy as it pertains to the Guard and Reserve. It must be clearly understood that implicit in the Total Force Policy, as emphasized by Presidential and National Security Council documents, the Congress and Secretary of Defense policy, is the fact that the Guard and Reserve forces will be used as the initial and primary augmentation of the Active forces.
    Total Force is no longer a "concept." It is now the Total Force Policy which integrates the Active, Guard and Reserve forces into a homogenous whole.
    As a result of this policy, the Selected Reserve has moved towards timely responsiveness and combat capability. Application of this policy has improved equipping, funding, facilities, construction, programming and some training areas.
    I recognize and appreciate the great amount of effort that has been made to develop the Guard and Reserve. Progress has been made. However, gross readiness measurements (which should be improved) indicate that we have not yet reached a level consistent with the objective response times. It is clear that we should move as much post-mobilization administration as possible to the pre-mobilization period and streamline all remaining post-mobilization administrative and training activities.
    We must assure that the readiness gains in the Selected Reserves are

Appendices

maintained and that we move vigorously ahead to reach required readiness and deployment response times in areas still deficient.

I want each Service Secretary to approach affirmatively the goals of producing Selected Reserve units which will meet readiness standards required for wartime contingencies. Each Secretary will provide the manning, equipping, training, facilities, construction and maintenance necessary to assure that the Selected Reserve units meet deployment times and readiness required by contingency plans. You will have my support and personal interest in overcoming any obstacles in these areas.

The Assistant Secretary of Defense for Manpower and Reserve Affairs is charged by statute and by Defense policy and Directives with the responsibility for all matters concerning Reserve Affairs. It is my desire that the Assistant Secretary of Defense for Manpower and Reserve Affairs, as a matter of priority, take such actions as are necessary to bring the Selected Reserve to readiness goals. In this respect, the Services, the other Assistant Secretaries of Defense, the Joint Chiefs of Staff, the Director of Defense Program Analysis and Evaluation and other Defense Agencies will provide support on a priority basis. Particular emphasis will be placed on assistance in manning, equipping and training. The Deputy Assistant Secretary of Defense (Reserve Affairs) will continue to function in accord with current statutes and directives.

To emphasize and to strengthen Selected Reserve management, I suggest a civilian Deputy Assistant Secretary for Reserve Affairs in the office of each of the Assistant Secretaries of the Military Departments for Manpower and Reserve Affairs. This Deputy should be supported by an adequate staff and be assigned responsibilities and functions similar to those assigned the Deputy Assistant Secretary of Defense for Reserve Affairs.

At the military level, the Navy has been given specific guidelines for developing the new office of Chief of Naval Reserve. The Air Force and Marine Corps management structure has produced combat readiness and that is the vital test. I expect that the Army's reorganization, with strong command emphasis and good selection of leaders will produce demonstrably visible improvement and I shall follow the results with interest.

The Chiefs of the National Guard and Reserve components will be the staff level managers of the Guard and Reserve programs, budgets, policy, funds, force structure, plans, etc. They will be provided the authority, responsibility and means with which to accomplish their functions effectively. The overall management responsibility of the Chiefs of the Selected Reserve, under the Service Chiefs, will be supported by all other appropriate staff agencies.

In addition to the foregoing emphasis on Reserve Force policy and management, I am asking my Deputy Assistant Secretary for Reserve Affairs, with your support, to manage a study covering the issues of

The Air Force Reserve

availability, force mix, limitations and potential of Guard and Reserve Forces.

In summary, strong management with achievement of readiness levels in the Selected Reserve is among our highest priorities—we must and will accomplish this objective as soon as possible.

JAMES R. SCHLESINGER

Appendices

APPENDIX 12

DEPARTMENT OF THE AIR FORCE
Headquarters US Air Force
Washington DC 20330

AF REGULATION 45-1

3 March 1975

Reserve Forces

PURPOSE, POLICY, AND RESPONSIBILITIES FOR AIR RESERVE FORCES (ARF)

Defense Planning and Programming Guidance under the total force policy specifies that guard and reserve forces will be the initial and primary source of augmentation of the active forces in future emergencies requiring rapid and substantial expansion of the active forces. This guidance further assures that these forces will be manned, trained, and equipped with adequate resources to deploy with active forces.

In an increasingly austere budgetary environment, the capabilities inherent in the ARF must be fully developed to optimize their contributions to our national defense. To assure and exploit the responsiveness of ARF during emergencies, their peacetime management, command and control, and training must be continually tested and refined. This regulation states the purpose, policy, and responsibilities of the Air National Guard (ANG) and the Air Force Reserve (USAFR). It applies to all Air Force activities which are responsible for the support and training of units or individuals of the ARF. This regulation establishes Air Force policy and assigns responsibilities to comply with: 10 U.S.C. 262, 264, 280, 715; 32 U.S.C. 105, 501, 708; and DOD Directives 1000.3, 20 March 1972, 1225.6, 18 April 1970, and change 1, 7180.1, 24 May 1971, and changes 1 and 2. Policy contained herein reflects the Department of Defense total force policy.

1. Terms Explained:
    a. Air Force Advisor. An active duty commissioned Air Force officer (Regular Air Force, ANG, or USAFR) detailed to duty with a unit of the air reserve forces. He represents the active Air Force and advises personnel of the ARF on Air Force philosophy, tactics, administration, logistics (including requirements for unit mobilization), mobility, and support.

The Air Force Reserve

b. Air Force Technical Advisor. An Air Force active duty noncommissioned officer, detailed for duty with an ARF unit to assist the Air Force advisor, or, in cases where an Air Force advisor is not assigned to the unit, to perform those functions listed in paragraph la.

c. Advisory Unit. A unit of the active force designated by its major command to advise and assist in training a specific unit of the ARF gained by that command when mobilized.

d. Advisory Team. A group of active duty personnel designated by the gaining command or one of its subordinate headquarters to perform the function of advising an ARF unit.

e. Gaining Command. A major command of the Air Force to which an ARF unit will be assigned upon mobilization.

f. Selected Reserve. Those units and individuals within the Ready Reserve designated by their respective services and approved by the Joint Chiefs of Staff as so essential to initial wartime missions as to require priority over other reserves. These reservists are either:

(1) Members of units who:

(a) Regularly participate in drills and annual active duty for training, or

(b) Are on initial active duty for training, or

(2) Individuals who participate in regular drills and annual active duty for training on the same basis as members of ARF units.

2. General:

a. Total Force Policy:

(1) Within the Department of Defense, all elements of our armed forces, both active and reserve components, are considered to be a part of a single United States military resource. In determining the most advantageous mix of forces to assure our national security, concurrent consideration is given to all elements of these forces in terms of their contribution to national security versus the cost to equip and maintain them.

(2) ANG and USAFR units and individuals of the Selected Reserves will be prepared to be the initial and primary source of augmentation of the active forces in an emergency requiring a rapid and substantial expansion of the active forces. Additionally, these forces perform peacetime missions as an adjunct to, or corollary of, training.

(3) Within the Department of the Air Force, this total force policy will be applied in all aspects of planning, programming, manning, equipping and employing active, ANG and USAFR forces. To optimize total force capabilities, the structure of units of the ARF will be as similar as possible to comparable active force units. Training and evaluation of ARF units will be conducted under the same standards as active force units to the maximum extent possible. An integrated approach to equipping, supporting, and exercising reserve and active forces will be taken.

b. The Secretary of the Air Force provides the personnel, equipment,

Appendices

facilities, and other logistic support to enable units and individuals in the Ready Reserve of the ARF to fulfill their training and mobilization readiness requirements. The Secretary is required to submit an annual written report to the Committees on Armed Services of the Senate and the House of Representatives regarding the extent to which these units and individuals have satisfied their training and mobilization readiness requirements.

   c. The total force policy and the concomitant reliance to be placed on the reserve forces in time of emergency emphasize the importance of having combat-ready ARF prepared to assume assigned missions when needed. To ensure the proper composition of the total Air Force, the ARF structure and programs are reviewed each year as an integral part of the HQ USAF Planning-Programming-Budgeting process. These reviews occur in the Air Staff Board Structure with full participation of ARF representatives.

   d. The Air Reserve Forces Policy Committee in the Office of the Secretary of the Air Force reviews and comments on major ANG and USAFR policy matters which directly affect the ARF.

3. Purpose. Section 262 of Title 10, United States Code, prescribes the purpose of reserve components as follows:

   "The purpose of each reserve component is to provide trained units and qualified persons available for active duty in the armed forces, in time of war or national emergency and at such other times as the national security requires, to fill the needs of the armed forces whenever, during, and after the period needed to procure and train additional units and qualified persons to achieve the planned mobilization, more units and persons are needed than are in the regular components."

4. Mission. The mission of the ARF is to provide combat units, combat support units, and qualified personnel for active duty in the Air Force to support augmentation requirements and to perform such peacetime missions as are compatible with ARF training requirements and the maintenance of mobilization readiness.

5. Policy. Authority and responsibilities for operational readiness, administration and support of ARF units are:

   a. Command:

   (1) Command jurisdiction of all nonmobilized units of the ARF is vested in the Governors or other appropriate authorities of the several States, the District of Columbia and Puerto Rico for ANG units and the Commander, HQ Air Force Reserve (AFRES) for the USAFR units.

   (2) When units or individuals are ordered to extended active duty (EAD), command jurisdiction is vested in the commander of the gaining command.

   b. Operational Readiness:

   (1) Governors or other appropriate authority of the several States, the District of Columbia and Puerto Rico, and the Commander, AFRES are

The Air Force Reserve

obligated to ensure that the training of their respective units conforms to that established by the gaining commands for similar units of the active force.

2) Major commands are responsible for training their individual mobilization augmentees and for ensuring the readiness of the augmentees to assume mobilized tasks and responsibilities.

(3) The Commander, AFRES, is responsible to the Chief of Staff for the operational readiness and efficiency of the total Air Force Reserve Program.

(4) Major commands must ensure that ANG and USAFR units are in a state of readiness to function effectively when mobilized to support the missions of the gaining commands.

(5) The commanders of units to be gained by the major commands are responsible for attaining and maintaining operational readiness, together with scheduling and conducting the training required to achieve this readiness.

c. Logistics:

(1) Air reserve forces units of the Selected Reserve will be provided combat serviceable equipment and logistical support to satisfy approved training and mobilization readiness requirements. Withdrawal, diversion, or reduction of equipment for reassignment to the active force, for NATO or SEATO commitments, or for the Security Assistance Program will be made only with written approval of the Secretary or Deputy Secretary of Defense. Proposals for such actions will be according to DOD Directive 1225.6.

(2) Air reserve forces units will be authorized the mobility equipment (ME) and unit support equipment (SE) required to support the assigned wartime mission. This equipment will be provided in balance with the aircraft (or other primary mission equipment for nonflying units), troop, and installation programs and will be phased to reach 100 percent as soon as possible.

(3) Equipment and supplies will be provided to support individual reserve training programs.

d. Personnel: ARF personnel policies will be in conformity with those established by the Secretary of the Air Force and the DCS/Personnel, HQ USAF.

e. Comptroller:

(1) The Comptroller of the Air Force is responsible for the Air Force budget. The Chief, National Guard Bureau (NGB), and the Chief of Air Force Reserve (AF/RE), will be responsible for justifying requirements through the Planning-Programming-Budgeting process and will man-age funds appropriated and allocated for their personnel, operations and maintenance, and construction programs.

(2) Budgeting for ARF investment material will be in the active Air

Appendices

Force procurement appropriations.

    f. Manpower and Organization:

    (1) ARF units will be organized in a manner similar to like type units of the active force. This is, as far as is practical while providing for the types of units needed to meet full mobilization requirements or selective recall requirements of partial mobilization [sic].

    (2) Manpower required for assigned wartime missions and for peacetime responsibilities in support of ARF training will be programmed as an integral part of the HQ USAF annual Planning-Programming-Budgeting process.

    g. Training Facilities:

    (1) Air Force commands will cooperate in making training facilities available. The ARF units and individuals will make maximum use of the Air Force facilities available for training.

    (2) Commanders of Air Force installations will provide training and logistical support to the ARF if requested by the NGB or AFRES and sanctioned by the gaining command.

6. Regulations and Directives:

    a. Applicable gaining command regulations and directives prescribe what the ANG and AFRES units must do to become mission-capable; the units implement those applicable gaining command regulations and directives to achieve the desired level of capability.

    b. ANG and USAFR regulations and directives should be written to complement those of the active force or to provide required additional direction in areas which are not covered by them (such as, the operation of bases and support facilities which are not gained by the major command and certain functions associated with resources provided by the NGB or AFRES). Such actions will avoid possible conflict in implementation at unit level and minimize the transition for ANG and AFRES units at the time of mobilization.

7. Channels of Communication:

    a. The Chief, NGB is the channel of communication to the States, the District of Columbia, and Puerto Rico on all matters pertaining to the ANG.

    b. The Commander, AFRES, is the channel of communication on all matters pertaining to USAFR units.

    c. Headquarters Air Reserve Personnel Center (ARPC) is the channel of communication on matters pertaining to individual USAFR personnel not assigned to units.

    d. Notwithstanding the above, direct communication is authorized between active and reserve forces elements when mutually agreed upon by the gaining commands, NGB, adjutant generals, and AFRES, as appropriate.

8. Specific Responsibilities:

    a. HQ USAF:

The Air Force Reserve

(1) Air Staff offices are functionally responsible for the reserve components as they are for the active force. The reserve components will receive full consideration with the active force in all aspects of Air Force planning and programming.

(2) The Chief, NGB and the Chief, AF/RE are directly responsible to the Air Force Chief of Staff for providing advice concerning their respective components.

(3) The NGB and AF/RE are co-equal air staff agencies responsible to the Chief of Staff. Because there is no single office responsible for ARF, matters pertaining to both reserve components are the joint responsibility of the NGB and AF/RE.

(4) Operating within departmental policies, the NGB and AF/RE meet with other air staff agencies to formulate plans and programs for their respective reserve components.

b. The NGB and AFRES:

(1) Are responsible for administration, personnel, logistical, and budgetary support of their respective units.

(2) Will identify in the ANG and AFRES publication indexes those gaining command regulations which are applicable to their respective units. The ANG publication index will also identify Air Force regulations which apply to ANG units. All Air Force regulations apply to the USAFR.

(3) Will notify their respective units when applicable Air Force and gaining command regulations are published.

(4) Will provide the appropriate gaining commands copies of their respective indexes, regulations, and directives published pertaining to units gained by that command.

NOTE: Detailed functions are contained in AFR 45-17 for the NGB and AFR 23-1 for AFRES.

c. ARPC is responsible for the administration of the individual mobilization augmentees assigned to gaining commands and the total management of all other air reserve forces individuals not assigned to gaining commands and the total management of all other air reserve forces individuals not assigned to units. Detailed ARPC functions are in AFR 23-29.

d. Gaining Commands:

(1) In fulfilling their responsibilities for ensuring operational readiness, the gaining commands will:

(a) Establish the training standards and objectives for ARF units and furnish suitable training manuals.

(b) Assign sufficient advisors to ARF units to advise and assist as appropriate, select and assign airmen to technical advisor positions, and coordinate with the NGB or AFRES, as appropriate, nominations of officers for assignment to ARF units prior to selection.

(c) Provide advisory units for each ARF wing, group, or separate unit

Appendices

for which the gaining command is responsible.

(d) Provide advisory team, to advise and assist units in training and with special problems involving command, staff, and support functions.

(e) Evaluate the effectiveness of training, readiness, and safety of ARF units through inspections.

(f) Provide guidance, advice, and assistance to ARF units to aid in solving specific problems associated with operational readiness.

(g) Establish and maintain, in coordination with the NGB and AFRES, safety programs compatible with those practiced by the gaining commands.

(h) Inform the NGB and AFRES of new techniques, procedures, tactics, and doctrines so that they may be incorporated, where applicable, in current or planned training.

(2) Coordinate, prior to publication, all gaining command directives and regulations applicable to ANG and USAFR units with the NGB and AFRES, respectively, and distribute approved publications to the NGB, AFRES, and units. Unresolved issues will be forwarded to HQ USAF for resolution.

(3) Review the organizational structure of ARF units to ensure their capability to perform wartime missions. If organizational changes are necessary as a result of this review, forward recommendations with supporting data to HQ USAF.

(4) Include ANG and USAFR units in programming, contingency planning, and exercise planning and execution.

(5) Approve the active duty training plans prepared by the ARF units.

(6) Approve unit mobility, mobilization and contingency plans, and host-tenant agreements that are effective upon mobilization, and assist in formulating and negotiating required agreements and licenses.

(7) In conjunction with Air Force Logistics Command (AFLC), assisted by NGB or AFRES, ensure the conduct of periodic equipment allowance reviews related to each type unit. Also, the gaining command will perform on-the-spot reviews of organizational equipment authorizations and assets to ensure adequate and valid equipping of the units programmed to be gained. These on-the-spot reviews will be accomplished by scheduling gaining command Equipment Management Teams to visit both ANG and USAFR units.

(8) Provide budgeting and funding support for USAFR associate units operating active force aircraft or equipment when augmenting the active force beyond prescribed drill periods funded by USAFR appropriations.

The Air Force Reserve

BY ORDER OF THE SECRETARY OF THE AIR FORCE
OFFICIAL
JACK R. BENSON, Colonel, USAF
Director of Administration
DAVID C. JONES, General, USAF Chief of Staff

SUMMARY OF REVISED, DELETED OR ADDED MATERIAL

This regulation supersedes AFRs 45–1, 45–6 and 5–60 providing a single source of basic policy and responsibilities for the management of the ARF. Details included in the previous three regulations that are also covered by other publications (AFRs 23–1, 23–29, 45–17, 45–9, 50–9, 50–29, 205–7, 400–24 and AFMs 11–1, 26–1, 67–1, 100–15, 172–1) have been deleted. The total force policy has been incorporated into this regulation including the implementation of DOD Directive 7180.1 regarding program and budget support of the ARF. This regulation defines the responsibilities of the gaining commands for ensuring the operational readiness of their ARF units.

NOTES

Owing to the author's death, some footnote abbreviations are not defined but remain as a part of the original citation.

Chapter 1

1. MR, Gerald T. Cantwell, subj: General Bodycombe's closing remarks at conclusion of Commanders Conference, Feb 17, 1982, as doc 8; memo, Bodycombe to OASD/MRA&L, subj: First Year Assessment, Jan 8, 1982, as doc 7—both in hist, Air Force Reserves, FY 1982.

2. Juliette A. Hennessy, *The United States Army Air Arm, April 1861 to April 1917*, U.S. Air Force Historical Study (hereafter, USAFHS) No. 98 (Montgomery, Ala., 1958 [New Imprint, USAF History Office: Washington, D.C., 1985]), p 15.

3. Martha E. Layman, *Legislation Relating to the Air Corps Personnel and Training Programs, 1907–1939*, Army Air Forces Historical Study (hereafter, AAFHS) No. 39 (Washington, D.C., 1945), pp 7–10, 122–23; Hennessy, pp 109–11, Appendix 13.

4. Hennessy, pp 14, 129; *Congressional Record* (hereafter, *Cong. Rec.*), chap. 418, p 129.

5. Hennessy, pp 131–32.

6. An interesting description of the group comprising the Prepardness Movement can be found in *The Soldier and State*. Samuel P. Huntington, "The Failure of the Neo-Hamilton Compromise, 1890–1920," chap. 10 in *The Soldier and State* (Cambridge, Mass., 1959). The group included Theodore Roosevelt, Henry Cabot Lodge, Elihu Root, Albert J. Beveridge, A. T. Mahan, Herbert Croly, Leonard Wood, Henry Adams, and Brooks Adams. See also Russell F. Weigley, *Towards an American Army* (New York, 1962), pp 207–20; "The Statement of a Proper Military Policy for the United States," in *War Department Annual Report* (hereafter, WDAR), *1915* (Washington, D.C., 1916), pp 114–30; Arthur S. Link, *Wilson: The Struggle for Neutrality, 1914–1915* (Princeton, 1960), pp 137–40.

7. Albert Shaw, ed., "Wilson's Second Annual Message," in *The Messages and Papers of Woodrow Wilson*, 2 vols (New York, 1917 [3d ptg]), vol 1, pp 76–80. Woodrow Wilson's struggle to maintain U.S. neutrality is traced in Link, *Struggle for Neutrality,* pp 586–93. See also Russell F. Weigley, *History of the United States Army* (New York, 1967), pp 343–44.

8. For a view of the opposing bodies of opinion in the nation on pacifism and preparation and Wilson's evolving attitude toward both, see Ray Stannard Baker, *Woodrow Wilson, Life and Letters: Facing War, 1915–1917* (Garden City, New York, 1937), vol 6, pp 40–47, 327–34. For the Senate debate, see *Preparedness for National Defense*, Hearings before the U.S. Senate Committee on Military Affairs, on *Bills for the Reorganization of the Army and for Creation of a Reserve Army, 1916*, 64th Cong., 1st sess.; and Link, *Wilson: Confusion and 1915–1916*, pp 327–34. For congressional resolution of the issue, see *Cong. Rec.*, 64th Cong., 1st sess., 1916, vol 53, pts 1–3, pp 458–5565, and pts 7–9, pp 7494–5.

9. *The National Defense Act of 1916* (Stat 39: 174–97); Edwin L. Williams, Jr., *Legislative History of the AAF and USAF, 1941–1951*, USAFHS No. 84 (Maxwell AFB, Ala., 1955), p 2.

10. For this point see, for example, Weigley, *History of the United States Army*, pp 348–49.

11. See note 9.

12. Ibid.

13. Layman, pp 49–54.

14. Hennessy, p 155.

15. Layman, pp 122–23.

16. "Report of the Secretary of War," *WDAR, 1916* (Washington, D.C.: War Department, 1916), p 29.

17. "Report of the Chief Signal Officer," *WDAR, 1916* (Washington, D.C., 1916), p 864.

18. "Report of the Adjutant General," in *WDAR, 1918* (Washington, D.C., 1919), p 174.

19. WD GO 43, May 3, 1917; Maurer Maurer, ed., *Combat Squadrons of the Air Force, World War II* (Maxwell AFB, Ala., 1967), pp 133–34; Hennessy, pp 183–84; HQ Eastern Dept SO 132, May 23, 1917; "Final Report of the Chief of Air Service, American Expeditionary Forces," in *United States Army in the World War 1917–1919* p 237; US Steel Corp Record of Service of Raynal C. Bolling, in Bolling papers, 1100 ABW/HO.

20. Hennessy, pp 183–85.

21. Wesley Frank Craven and James Lea Cate, ed., *Plans and Early Operations, January 1939 to August 1942,* vol 1 of *The Army Air Forces in World War II* (Chicago, 1958), p 7; Alfred Goldberg, ed., *A History of the United States Air Force, 1907–1957* (Princeton, 1957), p 7; "Recent Aero Statistics Show Growth of Service," *Air Service News Letter,* Dec 14, 1918, p 2; "Final Report of the Chief of Air Service, American Expeditionary Forces," in *United States Army in the World War 1917–1919: Reports of Commander-In-Chief, A.E.F., Staff Sections and Services, Washington, 1948,* pp 236, 266.

22. "Reserve Officers to Be Permitted to Fly Each Year," in *Air Service Weekly News Letter,* Dec 14, 1918, p 2; Air Service Dir/Mil Aeronautics, "Flying for Discharged Aviators," *Weekly News Letter,* Feb 8, 1919, p 11.

23. Ltr., Maj Gen C. T. Menoher, Dir/Air Svc, to SecWar, subj: Report of Air Service for 1919, Sep 25, 1919. See I. B. Holley, Jr., *General John Palmer, Citizen Soldiers, and the Army of a Democracy* (Westport, Conn., 1982), pp 444 ff, for discussion of some of the issues reflected in the War Department approach; Weigley, *Towards an American Army,* pp 224–39; *The Army Reorganization Act of 1920* (Stat 41: 759); Williams, *Legislative History of the AAF and the USAF, 1941–1951,* p 3; Chase L. Mooney, Martha E. Layman, *Organization of Military Aeronautics, 1907–1935 (Congressinal and War Department Action),* AAFHS No. 25 (Washington, D.C., 1944), pp 47–48; General Peyton C. March, *Annual Report of Chief of Staff, USA, WDAR, 1919* (Washington, D.C., 1920), pp 476–77; Weigley, *History of the United States Army,* pp 396–402.

24. "To Benefit Reserve Officers," *Air Service News Letter,* Jul 20, 1920, p 19.

25. "Annual Report of Chief of Air Service," *WDAR, 1922,* p 41.

26. Ibid., p 117; "America's First Airway," *Air Service News Letter,* Feb 3, 1921, p 1. "Annual Report of Chief of Air Service," *WDAR, 1922,* p 31.

27. "Report of Secretary of War," *WDAR, 1921,* pp 8–16.

28. "Report of Chief of Air Service," *WDAR, 1921,* p 39; "Annual Report of Chief of Air Service," *WDAR, 1924,* p 73.

29. "Air Service Organized Reserves in the Middle West," in *Air Service News Letter,* May 18, 1922, p 4; "Annual Report of Chief of the Air Service," *WDAR, 1923,* p 22.

30. "Crissy Field, Presidio of San Francisco, California," *Air Service News Letter,* Jan 6, 1922, pp 18–19.

31. "316th Reserve Squadron Gets Under Way," *Air Service News Letter,* May 13, 1922, p 10.

32. "Reserve Officers Participate in Big Cross-Country Flight," *Air Service News Letter,* Mar 17, 1925, p 11.

33. "The U.S. Air Service Reserve of Southern California," *Air Service News Letter,* Jan 19, 1924, p 1; "Air Service Reserve Activities In Southern California," *Air Service News Letter,* Feb 14, 1925, p 13.

34. "Annual Report of Chief of Air Service," *WDAR, 1921,* pp 6–8, 38–39; "Annual Report of Chief of Air Service," *WDAR, 1922,* pp 42–43.

35. "Annual Report of Chief of Air Service," *WDAR, 1922,* p 30.

36. See, for example, "Summer Training Conducted at Chanute Field," *Air Service News Letter,* Oct 22, 1922, pp 7–8, and "Air Service Reserve Officers Get Feel of the Air Again," *Air Service News Letter,* Sep 27, 1922, p 9.

37. "Annual Report of Chief of Air Service," *WDAR, 1925,* p 176.

38. "Annual Report of Chief of Air Service," *WDAR, 1923,* p 75; "Annual Report of Chief of Air Service," *WDAR, 1924,* p 134.

39. PL 446, *Air Corps Act of 1926* (Stat 41: 780), Jul 2, 1926. For some back-

ground, see Thomas H. Greer, *The Development of Air Doctrine in the Army Air Arm, 1917–1941*, USAFHS No. 89 (1955; reprint, Washington, D.C., 1985), pp 26–27.

40. "Annual Report of the Asst SecWar, Hon. F. Trubee Davison," *WDAR, 1929*, p 87.

41. "Annual Report of Chief of Air Corps," *WDAR, 1927*, p 43.

42. "Annual Report of Chief of Air Corps," *WDAR, 1931*, p 49; Maj Gen James E. Fechet, Ch/AC, "The Training of Air Corps Reserve Officers," *Aero Digest*, Feb 1930, p 53; *Air Corps News Letter*, Jan 16, 1930, p 6.

43. "Annual Report of the Asst SecWar, Hon. F. Trubee Davison," *WDAR, 1928*, p 69; "Annual Report of Chief of Air Corps," *WDAR, 1931*, pp 50–51.

44. "Annual Report of Chief of Air Corps," *WDAR, 1933*, p 33.

45. "Reserve Officers in Training at Selfridge Field," *Air Corps News Letter*, Oct 15, 1927, p 301.

46. "The Training of Reserve Officers at Selfridge Field," *Air Corps News Letter*, Apr 18, 1930, pp 113–14; "Sixth Corps Area Reserve Camp," *Air Corps News Letter*, Jul 19, 1932, p 311.

47. "Diversified Training of Reserve Officers at Boston Airport," *Air Corps News Letter*, Apr 21, 1928, p 142.

48. "Boston Airport, Mass., Oct. 1st," *Air Corps News Letter,* Sep 18, 1931, pp 472–73; "Boston Airport, Mass., Feb. 1st," *Air Corps News Letter*, Feb 13, 1932, p 68.

49. "Annual Report of Chief of Air Corps", *WDAR, 1931*, p 49; Fechet, "Training of Air Corps Reserve Officers," p 53.

50. "Annual Report of Chief of Air Corps," *WDAR, 1926*, pp 149–50. For the background of the Air Force ROTC program, see William C. Stancik, USAFR, and R. Cargill Hall, "Air Force ROTC, Its Origins and Early Years," *Air University Review*, Jul–Aug 1981, pp 38–51.

51. Stancik and Hall, "Air Force ROTC," pp 38–51; "Annual Report of Chief of Air Corps," *WDAR, 1927*, p 46; "Annual Report of Chief of Air Corps," *WDAR, 1928*, p 49. See also "Annual Reports of Chief of Air Service," *WDAR, 1922*, p 34.

52. "Annual Report of Chief of Air Corps," *WDAR, 1932*, pp 61–52.

53. See note 38.

54. "430th Pursuit Squadron, Kansas City, Mo.," *Air Corps News Letter*, Sep 21, 1932, p 388.

55. See note 52.

56. "Annual Report of Chief of Air Corps," *WDAR, 1934*, p 29.

57. "Reserve Activities on the West Coast," *Air Corps News Letter*, Apr 15, 1937, p 4.

58. *The Encyclopedia of Military History: From 3500 B.C. to the Present*, 2d rev ed. (New York, 1975), s.v. "World War II and the Dawn of the Nuclear Age, 1925–1945."

59. Press release, War Department, subj: Information for the Press Relative to Bill No. S. 4309 to Increase the Efficiency of the Air Corps Reserve, n.d. [ca. Mar 1936], Aubrey Moore papers, Air Force Historical Research Center (hereafter, AFHRC); Williams, *Legislative History of the AAF and USAF, 1941–1951*, p 8; "A Bill to Increase the Efficiency of the Air Corps Reserve," S. 4309, Feb 24, 1936, 74th Cong., 2d sess.

60. These figures were extracted from the "Annual Reports of the Chief of the Air Corps" in the *War Department Annual Reports* of 1927–1934.

61. "Reserve Officers Compete for Regular Commissions," *Air Corps News Letter*, May 1, 1938, p 15; ltr (AG 2102 ORC, Res), Maj Gen E. T. Conley, AG, to Corps Area et al., subj: Promotion of Second Lieutenants, Air Corps Reserve, on Extended Active Duty with the Air Corps, Nov 14, 1936; ltr (AG 580), Brig Gen Frank C. Burnett, Actg AG, to CGs All Corps Areas & Depts et al., subj: Extended Active Duty, Air Corps Reserve Officers, Aug 10, 1936—both in AFRES 7.

62. Ltr (AG 210–313, Air Res), Conley to Corps Areas, subj: Extended Active Duty for Air Corps Reserve Officers, Jan 11, 1938; ltr (AG 210–313), Maj Gen E. A. Adams, AG WD, to Corps Areas, subj: Extended Active Duty for Air Corps Reserve Officers, Jul 23, 1938—both in AFRES 7; "Refresher Course for Reserve Officers," *Air Corps News Letter,* Oct 15, 1938, p 6; "Refresher Reserve Officers Leave for New Stations," *Air Corps News Letter* Jan 15, 1939, p 9; "Last of Reserve Officers Complete Refresher Course at

The Air Force Reserve

Kelly Field," *Air Corps News Letter* May 1, 1939, p 2.

63. "Army Trains Half of Airline Pilots," *Air Corps News*, Jul 15, 1937, p 4.

64. Memo, Brig Gen Ira C. Eaker, to Dep Ch of Staff, [strength of Air Corps], Mar 31, 1940, Eaker, Box 4, Library of Congress (hereafter, LOC); staff study, GHQ Air Force [agency unknown] subj: Office Personnel Expansion Program, date obscured [ca. Aug 1939], Aubrey Moore papers, AFHRC; memo, Lt Col N. N. Young, Ch Res Div, to Gen Yount, subj: Air Reserve Personnel Status for Emergency, Submitted in Accordance with Verbal Instruction, Aug. 21, 1939, Aubrey Moore papers, AFHRC.

65. Williams, *Legislative History of the AAF and USAF, 1941-1951*, pp 27-29; PL 18-46, Apr 31, 1939.

66. Ltr (AG 210-313 Air Res [4-15-39] Res A), Adams to Corps Areas et al., subj: Extended Active Duty, Air Corps Reserve Officers, May 24, 1939; ltr (AG 210-313 Air-Res [6-27-39] Res), Adams to Corps Areas et al., subj: Extended Active Duty, Air Corps Reserve Officers, Jul 7, 1939—both in AFRES 7.

67. Williams, *Legislative History of the AAF and USAF l941-1951*, p 28; Craven and Cate, vol 6, *Men and Planes* (Chicago, 1958), p 451.

68. Craven and Cate, vol 6, *Men and Planes*, p 452; ltr (AG 221.99 Flying Cadets R-A), Adams to Corps Areas et al., subj: Agreement of Air Corps Cadets to Serve Three Years as Second Lieutenants, Air Corps Reserve, Aug 8, 1940, AFRES 7.

69. Williams, *Legislative History of the AAF and USAF, 1941-1951*, p 28; Craven and Cate, vol 6, *Men and Planes*, p 452.

70. Ltr (210-332 Air Res R-A), Adams to Corps Areas, subj: Transfer of Officers to Air Corps Reserve, Nov 15, 1939; ltr (AG 210-332 Air-Res), Adams to Corps Areas et al., subj: Transfers to and Appointments in Air Corps Reserve for Nonflying Duties, Aug 5, 1940; WD press release, subj: Steps to Build up U.S. Army Air Corps Reserve Officer Strength, Jun 9, 1940—all in AFRES 7.

71. Strength Report, Army Air Corps, Sep 30, 1940; atch to Cmt #2, R&R, A.N.D. Col, Ch Mil Pers Div, Total Reserves—Extended Active Duty, Jun 30, 1941; Total Reserves on Extended Active Duty with Air Corps, Dec 31, 1941; Strength Report, Reserve Officers BI on Duty with Air Corps, Dec 31, 1941—all in K141.24-10, AFHRC.

72. "Report of Secretary of War," in *WDAR, 1928*, pp 11-13; Organized Reserve Air Corps station list, Aubrey Moore papers, AFHRC.

73. Craven and Cate, vol 6, *Men and Planes*, p 450.

74. For the Reserve Officers Association's (ROA's) account of its work, see John T. Carlton and John F. Slinkman, *The ROA Story: A Chronicle of the First 60 Years of the Reserve Officers Association of the United States* (Washington, D.C., 1982). The origin and some of the early activities of the Air Reserve Association may be traced in *Air Corps News Letter*, Jul 19 and Dec 30, 1932, Feb 15 and Nov 1, 1939, and Jan 1, 1941; *Air Corps News*, Dec 30, 1932, p 491; and *Air Corps News Letter*, Feb 15, 1939, p 4, Nov 1, 1939, pp 3, 11, and Jan 1, 1941, p 2. See also Col Troy W. Crawford, "The Effectiveness of the Air Reserve Program," May 1947, a paper submitted to the Air War College.

Chapter 2

1. Message to the Congress on the State of the Union and on the Budget for 1947, Jan 21, 1946, in *Public Papers of the Presidents of the United States: Harry S. Truman, 1946* (Washington, D.C., Office of the Federal Register, National Archives and Records Service, 1962), p 42 (hereafter, Truman, *Public Papers*); "Address in Chicago on Army Day," Apr 6, 1946, in ibid., p 185.

2. "Special Message to Congress Presenting a 21-Point Program for the Reconversion Period, Sep 6, 1945," in Truman, *Public Papers, 1945*; diary, Harold D. Smith,

Jan 4, 1946, Harry S. Truman Library (hereafter, HSTL), Box 1; "The State of the Union Message from the President of the United States," Jan 6, 1945, in H.R. doc No. 1, 79th Cong., 1st sess., p 13; "The President's News Conference with the Keen Teen Club of Chicago," Apr 6, 1946, Truman, *Public Papers, 1946*, pp 181–82; intvw, with Harry H. Vaughan, Jan 14–15, 1963, HSTL.

3. See for example, the speech, "Universal Military Training and Peace," delivered by Marshall before the House Select Committee on Postwar Military Policy on June 16, 1945, in H. A. De Weerd, ed., *Selected Speeches and Statements of General of the Army George C. Marshall, Chief of Staff United States Army*, pp 258–59, and George C. Marshall, *Biennial Report of the Chief of Staff of the United States Army, July 1, 1943, to June 30, 1945, to the Secretary of War* (Philadelphia, 1947), pp 291–97 (hereafter, *War Reports*).

4. The definitive work on John M. Palmer is I. B. Holley, Jr., *General John M. Palmer, Citizen Soldiers, and the Army of a Democracy* (Westport, Conn., 1982). Its chapters 50 and 51 are perceptive expositions of the concept of the citizen army as perceived and expounded by Palmer. See also James E. Hewes, Jr., *From Root to McNamara: Army Reorganization and Administration, 1900–1963* (Washington, D.C., 1975), pp 131–37; Forrest C. Pogue, *George C. Marshall: Education of a General, 1880–1939* (New York, 1963), p 107.

5. Hewes, *From Root to McNamara*, pp 131–37.

6. Outline of Post-War Military Establishment, Apr 15, 1944, incl memo, Col G. E. Textor, GSC, Dep Dir/SPD, to Asst CS/G–1, et al., subj: Approved Assumptions for Post-War Planning, Apr 29, 1944; R&R sheet, Col F. Trubee Davison, Ch, SPO, to AC/AS, Materiel, et al., subj: Outline of a Post-War Permanent Military Establishment, Aug 19, 1945—all in RG 18, Box 577, Modern Military Branch (MMB), NA; Weigley, *Towards An American Army*, p 244.

7. War Department Circular No. 347, Aug 5, 1944.

8. Memo, Col G. F. Textor, Dep Dir/WD SPD, to CSA, subj: Training Policies for the Postwar Organized Reserve Corps, Mar 6, 1945, RG 18, 320, Box 38, MMB, NA; memo, Maj Gen W. F. Tompkins, Dir/SPD, to Brig Gen Edward A. Evans, subj: Procedures of War Department Reserve Committees, Oct 5, 1944, RG 18, 334, Box 51, MMB, NA; Holly, *General John M. Palmer*, pp 623, 655; R&R sheet, Col Luther W. Sweetser, Ch, Res & NG Div, to AC/AS–4, subj: General Staff National Guard and Reserve Policy Committees, Aug 7, 1945, Comment No. 1, w/atch, AFRES 5D1; memo, Maj Gen Ray E. Porter, USA, Dir/SPD, to A/CS G–1, et al., subj: General Staff National Guard and Reserve Policy Committees, Jul 28, 1945, AFRES 5D1; memo, Tompkins to CG AAF, subj: Administration of the Postwar National Guard, Feb 10, 1945, RG 18, NG 325, Box 116, MMB, NA; Report of Special Plng Div [mission of Postwar Reserve Corps], n.d. [ca. Jan 12, 1945], K145.86–6, AFHRC.

9. Approved War Department Policies Relating to Postwar Organized Reserve Corps, Oct 13, 1945, RG 18, 344, Box 165, MMB, NA. Charles Joseph Gross, in his *Prelude to the Total Force: The Air National Guard 1943–1969* (Washington, D.C., 1985), p 19, discusses the implications and implementation of the "Policies" from the National Guard perspective.

10. Memo, Lt Gen Idwal H. Edwards to CG AAF, subj: Postwar Planning, Apr 14, 1943; memo, Gen H. H. Arnold to Spec Proj Off, AAF, subj: Post-War Plans for the Army Air Forces, Apr 21, 1943—both in RG 18, 380, Box 99, MMB, NA; Craven and Cate, vol 7, *Services Around the World* (Chicago, 1958), pp 549–50; memo, Maj Gen George Grummert, DCS for Svc Cmds, to Lt Gen Somervell, subj: Demobilization Planning, Jul 10, 1943, RG 18, 380, Box 100, MMB, NA.

11. Memo, AC/AS, Plans, Post War Div, to CG AAF, subj: Long Range Planning for an Efficient Air Reserve–Air National Guard–Air ROTC in Post-War Period, n.d. [ca. Feb–Mar 1945], K145.86–87, AFHRC; comment No. 2, Maj Gen C. C. Chauncey, actg C/S, to Vandenberg et al., Jul 17, 1945, to ltr, Lt Gen Ira C. Eaker, Dep Cmdr and C/AS, to C/S, subj: Our Policies with Respect to ROTC and the Air Reserve, Jul 15, 1945, K145.86–76, AFHRC; study,

The Air Force Reserve

AC/AS, Plans Post-War Div, [plans to provide flying opportunities for reserve officers], Jul 24, 1945, K167.91-23, AFHRC; studies, AC/AS Plans, Post-War Div, "Plan to Outline a Definite and Concrete Program for Air ROTC Units and Instructors in Colleges," Jul 24, 1945, and "Revival of Air Reserve Association," Jul 26, 1945—both in K145.86-760R, AFHRC.

12. Memo, Arnold for Eaker, subj: Plans for Training Reserve Officers, Sep 22, 1945; R&R sheet, Chauncey to AC/AS-1, subj: Reserve Officers, Sep 25, 1945—both in RG 18, 320, Box 88, MMB NA; daily diary, Res & NG Div, Oct 2, 1945, K123.310, AFHRC; memo, Brig Gen William E. Hall, Actg AC/AS-1, to Col Jacob E. Smart, Sec A/S, subj Reserve Officers, Oct 17, 1945, RG 320, Box 88, NA; R&R sheet, Vandenberg to AC/AS-3, Tng Div, subj: Reserve, National Guard, and ROTC Affairs, Oct 30, 1945, RG 18, 320, NA; R&R sheet, Sweetser to C/AS, subj: Reserve Officers, Oct 2, 1945, RG 18, 320, box 88, NA; daily diary, Res & NG Div, Oct 2, 1945, K123.310, AFHRC.

13. Army Air Forces Letter (hereafter, AAF Ltr) 20-91, "Interim and Peacetime Air Force Plans," Dec 15, 1945; Herman S. Wolk, *Planning and Organizing the Postwar Air Force, 1943-1947* (Washington, D.C., 1984), pp. 74-76.

14. Memo, Brig Gen C. H. Caldwell, USA, actg Ch, Tng Div, AC/AS-3, to AC/AS-3, subj: Revised AF Plan for Air ROTC, Air Reserve, and Air National Guard, Nov 9, 1945, w/Tabs A&C, RG 341, 326.2, Box 43, NA; daily diary, Res & NG Div, Nov 19, 23-25, 1945, K123.310, AFHRC; memo, Eaker to C/S, subj: AAF Plan for Air National Guard, Air Reserve, and Air ROTC, Nov 26, 1945, w/ atch, RG 18, 381, Box 189, NA; memo, Caldwell to Ch/Staff, subj: Weekly report of AC/AS-3 for Chief of Staff, Nov 29, 1945, K123-4, AFHRC; ltr, Vandenberg to Arnold, Ch AAF, subj: Daily Activity Report of AC/AS-3, Nov 21, 1945, K123-4, AFHRC.

15. Memo, Brig Gen William F. McKee, Dep AC/AS, OC&R, to AC/AS, subj: Provisions for Inactive Non-Rated Personnel—Post War Period, w/atch, Jun 29, 1945, NA 189-381.

16. Memo, Lt Gen Thomas T. Handy, Dep CSA, to CG AAF, subj: Army Air Forces Plan for Air National Guard, Air Reserve and Air ROTC, Dec 4, 1945, RG 18, 381, Box 189, NA.

17. Memo, Brig Gen G. L. Eberle, Actg G-3, to CG AAF, subj: Activation of the Air Reserve Training Program, Apr 10, 1946; memo, Eberle to CG AAF, subj: Air Reserve Program, Apr 18, 1946, both in RG 18, 326, Box 607, NA; R&R sheet, Col B. H. Merchant for Sweetser, to Tng Div, AC/AS-3, subj: Army Air Forces Plan for the Air Reserve, Apr 24, 1946; ltr, Sweetser to Lt Clifford H. Pope, subj: Air Force Reserve Training, Apr 19, 1946, NA 1518-325.

18. Daily diary, Res & NG Div, Jun 12 and 20, 1946, K123.310, AFHRC; DF, Eberle to CG AAF, subj: Army Air Forces Plan for the Air Reserve, Jul 12, 1946 NA 18-326.

19. For the definitive study of the reestablishment of the Air National Guard after World War II, including the accommodation reached by Generals Ellard A. Walsh and George C. Marshall, see Gross, *Prelude to the Total Force*, chap 1.

20. Staff study, Air Defense Command (ADC), "Comparison of Approved War Department Policies Relating to the Postwar National Guard and Organized Reserve Corps," ca. Dec 1946, MF A4003, AFRES.

21. Memo, Partridge to Maj Gen Hugh J. Knerr, Sec Gen Air Board, subj: Air Reserve and Air National Guard, Nov 6, 1946, 1516, Box 325, RG 341, NA.

22 Intvw, Cantwell with Lt Gen Edward J. Timberlake, Sep 29, 1983, Hilton Head, S.C.

23. Ltr, Streett to Spaatz, subj: Administration of Reserve Forces, Aug 13, 1946, AFRES 9A.

24. *Army Air Forces Plan for the Air Reserve*, AC/AS-3, Jul 12, 1946, AFRES 5C2.

25. AAF Ltr 20-9, "Activation of Headquarters Continental Air Forces," Dec 16, 1944; ltr, AG 322 Maj Gen Edward F. Witsell, TAG, to CGs AAF & CAF, subj: Establishment of Air Defense, Strategic Air and Tactical Air Commands, Redesignation of the Headquarters, Continental Air Forces and Certain Other Army Air Forces Units, and Activation, Inactivation and As-

432

Notes

signment of Certain Army Air Forces Units, Mar 21, 1946, RG 18, NA.

26. Wolk, *Planning and Organizing the Postwar Air Force*, p 117; Robert Frank Futrell, *Ideas, Concepts, Doctrine: A History of Basic Thinking in the United States Air Force* (Maxwell AFB, Ala., 1971; 1974) 105, 114.

27. ADC GOs No. 1, Mar 27, 1946, No. 23, Mar 27, 1946, No. 25, Jun 6, 1946, and No. 27, Jun 13, 1946; ltr, Gen Carl Spaatz, CG AAF, to CG ADC, subj: Interim Mission, Mar 12, 1946, AFRES 9A.

28. Ltr, Maj Gen Charles B. Stone III, CS ADC, to CG AAF, subj: Activation of the Air Reserve Program, Jun 3, 1946, AFRES 9A; ltr, Lt Gen George E. Stratemeyer, CG ADC, to Maj Gen C. C. Chauncey, DC/AS, subj: Plan for Activating Air Reserve Program, May 15, 1946; *ADC Plan to Activate the Air Reserve*, May 15, 1946; ltr, Chauncey to CG ADC, subj: Activation of the Air Reserve Program, May 22, 1946, AFRES 9A; daily diary, Res & NG Div, May 16 and 22, 1945, K123.310, AFHRC; hist, ADC, Mar 46–Mar 47, pp 61–75; ADC Air Reserve Plan, 2d ed., Sep 5, 1946, AFRES 9A.

29. Ltr, Lt Col R. B. Travis, Actg Asst AG ADC, to CG AAF, subj: Activation of the Air Reserve Program, Mar 27, 1946, 1518, Box 325, RG 341, NA.

30. ADC GOs No. 33, Jun 21, 1946, and No. 35, Jun 24, 1946.

31. Hist, 14th AF, Jul–Dec 46, p 68; daily diary, Res & NG Div, Jul 8, 1946, K123.310, AFHRC; hist 554th AAFBU-(RT), Oct 45–Jul 46, p 39.

32. Ltr, Stratemeyer to CG AAF, subj: Problems Confronting Air Defense Command in Dealing with Civilian Air Components, Apr 16, 1946, AFRES 9A; R&R sheet, Col Monro MacCloskey, Ch, Res & NG Div, AC/AS-3, to Air Installations Div, AC/AS-4, subj: Facilities for Air Reserve Activities, Jun 13, 1946, 1518, Box 325, RG 341, NA; daily diary, Res & NG Div, Jun 4, 6, 19, 20, and 26, 1946, K123.310, AFHRC; ltr, Stone to NAFs, subj: Selection of Airfields for the National Guard and Reserve, Sep 10, 1946, w/3 incls, AFRES 9A.

33. Daily diary, Res & NG Div, Jun 25, 1946, K123.310, AFHRC.

34. Hist, 1st AF, Mar 21–Dec 31, 1946, pp 57–63; daily diary, Res & NG Div, Jul 26–28, 29 and Aug 15, 20, 26, 28, 1946, K123.310, AFHRC.

35. Hist, ADC, Mar 46–Mar 47, vol 1, p 72.

36. Weekly rpt, AC/AS-3 for C/AS, May 31, 1946, K123-4, AFHRC; daily diary, Res & NG Div, Jul 12, Aug 9–11, 22, 1946, K123.310, AFHRC; daily diary, Training Div, Sep 25, 1946, K123.310, AFHRC; ltr, Col Leon W. Armour, Ch, Disposal Sect, HQ AMC, to CG AAF, subj: Air National Guard, Reserve Officers Corps, and Civil Air Patrol Training Programs, Aug 27, 1946, 1st ind (Armour ltr), Brig Gen E. H. Alexander, Ch, Tng Div, AC/AS-3, to HQ AMC, Sep 30, 1946, 1517, Box 325, RG 18, NA.

37. Daily diary, Res & NG Div, Jul 11, Aug 9–11, 1946, K123.310, AFHRC.

38. Minutes, Air Board, 4th mtg, Dec 3–4, 1946.

39. Monthly ltr, Stratemeyer to commanders, Apr 18, 1947, AFRES 9B.

40. Weekly rpt, AC/AS-3 to C/AS, May 3, 1946, K123-310, AFHRC; WD Bul No. 21, Jul 24, 1946.

41. Memo, Eaker to Asst SecWar for Air, subj: Air Reserve Budget Estimates for Fiscal Year 1948, Dec 2, 1946; memo, Partridge to MacCloskey, subj: Reduction in the Reserve and National Guard Program, Dec 31, 1946, 607, Box 326, RG 18, NA; memo, Brig Gen H. I. Hodes, Asst D/CSA, to CG AAF et al., subj: Presentation of War Department Budget Estimates to the Congress, Dec 5, 1946; ltr, Spaatz to Stratemeyer, subj: Air Reserve Program for FY 1948, Apr 17, 1948—both in K410.161–22, AFHRC; ltr, MacCloskey to Partridge, subj: Hearings on Air Reserve and Air ROTC Budget Estimates for FY 1948, Sep 25, 1946, 607, Box 326, RG 341, NA.

42. Memo, Spaatz to Asst SecWar for Air, Jan 7, 1947, Subj: Air Reserve, Air ROTC, and Air National Guard Budget Estimates for Fiscal 1948 and Effects of Reduction upon Morale within the Civilian Components, Jan 7, 1947, 607, Box 326, RG 18, NA.

43. ADC Release, "Reserve Program Curtailed," n.d. [ca. Feb 22, 1947]; msg, Spaatz to CG ADC, subj: Retention of Air Reserve Training Units, AFACC 182210Z

433

The Air Force Reserve

Feb 47; ADC GO 18, Feb 17, 1947, a/a GO 23, Feb 27; list, "Airfields under 70 Base Program" Mar 5, 1947; worksheet, "Bases to Be Retained (41) a/o 28 Feb 47," Mar 18, 1947, all in AFRES 9B.

44. Air Force Reserve Statistical Summary, end FY 1948, AFRES 9C; Remarks, Stratemeyer, at Commanders Conference, Oklahoma City, Nov 15, 1947, AFRES 9B; ltr, Brig Gen John P. McConnell, Ch, NG & Res Div, to CG ADC, subj: Air Reserve Program, Mar 3, 1948, w/incl, AFRES 9C.

45. Statement cited in Wolk, *Planning and Organizing the Postwar Air Force*, p 117.

46. Daily diary, Res & NG Div, May 29–30, 1946, K123.310, AFHRC; ltr, Col C. R. Landon, AG ADC, to NAFs, subj: Responsibility for Administration of the Air Reserve, Jun 26, 1946, w/ind; ltr, Landon to NAFs, subj: Responsibility for Administration of the Air Reserve, Jul 19, 1946, AFRES 9A.

47. 1st Ind (ltr, Landon to NAFs, Jun 26, 1946), Col Charles Mylon, Ex AC/AS–1, to ADC, Jul 26, 1946—both in 1417, Box 325, RG 341, NA; memo, Brig Gen Reuben C. Hood, Jr., DC/AS, to AC/AS–1, subj: AAF Matters for Presentation to Army Commanders, Apr 16, 1946, 1513, RG 18, NA; ltr, Capt William Patrick Walsh, Jr., Ofc of Air Liaison Off, 1st Mil Area, to ALO, Hq 5th Svc Cmd, subj: Monthly Report as Directed by Letter Headquarters Army Air Forces, Apr 22, 1946, Jun 6, 1946, AFRES 9A; ltr, Symington to Sen. Joseph C. Mahoney, subj: Air Forces Records, Aug 23, 1946; memo, Symington for Brig Gen Leon W. Johnson, subj: Air Forces Personnel Records, Aug 23, 1946—both in Symington Papers, Box 3, HSTL.

48. Ltr, Stratemeyer to CG AAF, subj: Problems Confronting Air Defense Command in Dealing with Civilian Air Components, Apr 16, 1946; ltr, Stratemeyer to Spaatz, subj: Obstacles to Expediting Air Reserve Program, Jul 19, 1946, AFRES 9A; ltr, Eaker to Stratemeyer, Obstacles to Implementing the Air Reserve Program, Jul 29, 1946; ltr, Spaatz to CG SAC, subj: Air Reserve Training, Jul 31, 1946; daily diary, Res & NG Div, AC/AS–3, Aug 26, 27, 1946, K123.310, AFHRC; ltr, Brig Gen Reuben C. Hood, Jr., DC/AS, to CG ADC, subj: Activation of AAF Base Units for Air Reserve Training, Sep 9, 1946, w/ind; ltr, Maj Gen St. Clair Streett, Dep CG SAC, to CG 15th AF, subj: Reserve Flying at Regular Army Air Force Stations, Sep 16, 1946—all in AFRES 9A.

49. Ltr, Streett to Stratemeyer, subj: Cooperation with Air Defense Command, Aug 13, 1946; ltr, Streett to CG 15th AF, Sep 16, 1946, in note above; ltr, Stratemeyer to Streett, subj: Major Command Cooperation, Aug 16, 1946; ltr, Stratemeyer to Streett, subj: Major Command Cooperation, Aug 21, 1946, w/incl—all in AFRES 9A.

50. Lt Col Philip Doddridge, AG TAC, to 9th and 12th AFs, subj: Air Reserve Training Program, Jan 21, 1947; TAC Ltr 50–7, "Training of Air Reserve Personnel by Regular Army AAF Stations," Apr 14, 1947—both in AFRES 9B.

51. Minutes, HQ AAF Commanders Meeting, Mar 20, 1947, entry 213, Box 34, RG 341, NA.

52. Ltr, Partridge to CG ADC, subj: Training of Reserve Personnel by Regular AAF Stations and Units, Apr 15, 1947, AFRES 9B.

53. Foreword to *ADC Air Reseve Plan*, 2d ed., Sep 5, 1946.

54. Minutes, Air Board, 4th mtg, Dec 3–4, 1946.

55. Ltr, Col Kenneth P. Bergquist, Dep AC/AS–3, to CG ADC, subj: Allocation of Air Reserve Units, May 9, 1946, 326, Box 607, RG 341, NA.

56. ADC Mobilization Plan (ADC MP–47), Jan 30, 1947, MF A4003, AFRES.

57. Ltr, Stone to Douglass, subj: ADC Mobilization Plan, Jan 30, 1947, MF A4003, AFRES.

58. Brig Gen John P. McConnell, Ch Civ Comps Gp, HQ USAF, "The United States Air Force Reserve: An Analysis," n.d. [ca. Sep 1948], MF A4003, AFRES.

59. Ltr, Landon to NAFs, subj: Activation of Air Reserve Combat Units, Nov 5, 1946, w/incl—AFRES 9A; ltr, Chauncey to WDGS, subj: Combat Units of the Air Reserve, Jul 19, 1946, 1517, Box 325, RG 18, NA; ltr, AG 322 (27 Dec 46) AO–I–AFCOR (385e), WD to ADC, subj: Reconstitution, Redesignation, and Activation of Certain Army Air Forces Units of the

Notes

Organized Reserves, Dec 31, 1946, AFRES 9A; ADC GOs No. 5, Jan 10, 1947, and No. 1, Jan 7, 1947. Beginning in 1948, table of organization wings became the combat arm of the Air Force and had one or more combat groups, an airbase group, a maintenance and supply group, and a medical group assigned. The combat group exercised control over at least one assigned or rotational tactical mission squadron. The group was often used at a small base where no other support for the mission squadron was available. The combat squadron was the basic air unit of the Air Force. In 1952 the Strategic Air Command inactivated its combat groups and assigned the combat squadrons directly to the wings which replaced the groups as the basic combat element. The rest of the air forces soon emulated this example. Charles A. Ravenstein, *The Organization and Lineage of the United States Air Force*, (Washington, D.C., 1986); AFP 210–2, *Guide to Lineage and Unit History*, Jun 2, 1975; Woodford Agee Heflin, ed., *The United States Air Force Dictionary* (Maxwell AFB, Ala., 1956).

60. ADCR 20–15, *Formation of Composite Air Reserve Units*, Oct 15, 1947, MF A4002, AFRES.

61. Ltr, Stone to CG AAF, subj: Civilian Components, Jun 16, 1947, AFRES 9B.

62. Ltr, Lt Col Louis B. Grossmith, Jr., Dep for Tng, Mil Pers Div, AMC, to CG 14th AF, subj: Activation of AMC Composite Air Reserve Units, Apr 9, 1948, w/3 incls—similar letters to all ADC NAF Commanders, MF A4002, AFRES; ltr, Lt Col H. L. Fuller, Asst AG ADC, to CG, 14th AF, subj: Active and Inactive Duty Training of Technical and Specialized Personnel During Fiscal Year 1948, Apr 30, 1947, MF A4002, AFRES; ltr, Landon to CG AMC, subj: Revised Training Plan for AMC Specialized Air Force Reserve Personnel, Feb 5, 1948, incl inds 1 & 2; M/U, ADC and AMC, subj: Revised Training Plan for AMC Specialized Reserve Personnel, Mar 12, 1948—both in MF A4002, AFRES; ltr, Capt Lee W. Spitler, Actng Asst AG ADC, to ATC et al., subj: Training of Air Force Reservists on Mobilization Assignment, Mar 19, 1948; ltr, Maj James F. Rhodes, Asst AG ATC, to ADC, subj: Composite Units (ATC) Air Reserve (Joint ADC–ATC Agreement), Mar 15, 1948, w/ind, MF A4001, AFRES.

63. Ltr, Stratemeyer to Douglas et al., subj: Training of Individual Air Reservists, Apr 8, 1947, AFRES 9B.

64. TAC Ltr 50–7; "Training of Air Reserve Personnel by Regular Army Air Forces Stations," Apr 14, 1947; ltr, Stratemeyer to Spaatz, subj: Air Force Reserve Training, Dec 31, 1947, both in AFRES 9B.

65. Ltr, Spaatz to Stratemeyer, subj: Reserve Training Responsibilities, Jan 23, 1948, AFRES 9C.

66. AF Ltr 20–32, "Mobilization Assignments for Air Force Reserve Personnel at all USAF Bases," Feb 3, 1948, MF A4002, AFRES.

67. Ltr, Stone to Quesada, subj: Misinterpretation of Policy, Jun 26, 1947, AFRES 9B.

68. Speech, Stratemeyer, Commander's Conference, Oklahoma City, Nov 15, 1947, AFRES 9B.

69. Memo, Eaker to Dir/Info, subj: Publicity Campaign for the Air Reserve Training Program, Aug 14, 1946, 1517, Box 325, RG 18, NA; ADC Ltr 47–1, "Air Reserve Publicity," Aug 15, 1946, AFRES 9A; Orville S. Splitt, "The Army's Civilian Air Force: Air National Guard and Air Reserve Will Back Up the Regular Air Force," *Flying*, Sep 1946; daily diary, Res & NG Div, Jul 30, Aug 9–11, 1946, K123.310, AFHRC.

70. These letters, literally by the hundreds, can be found in the files of correspondence originated by War Department and Army Air Forces officials and now held in government repositories. See, for example, 1518, Box 325, RG 18, NA for HQ AAF correspondence; Spaatz, Box 256, LOC for correspondence of Secretary Symington; and AFRES 9A for General Stratemeyer's correspondence.

71. Memo, Spaatz to Symington, subj: Report of Progress of the Air Reserve and Air National Guard Plans and Public Relation Plans for the Civilian Components Program, Aug 7, 1946, Spaatz, Box 256, LOC; daily dairy, Res & NG Div, [report of progress of Air Reserve and Air National Guard], Aug 10, 1946, Spaatz, Box 256, LOC; memo, Eaker to AC/AS–3, subj: Information for the Assistant Secretary of War for Air in Regards to Air Re-

serve and Air National Guard, Aug 12, 1946, 1514, Box 325, RG 18, NA.

72. Ltr, Col Raymond C. Lewis to Stratemeyer, subj: Participation of Air Reservists, Sep 24, 1947; ltr Stratemeyer to Lewis, subj: Participation of Air Reservists, Oct 7, 1947—both in AFRES 9A.

73. Ltr, 1st Lt Fred A. Huston, AFRES, to Editor, *The Reserve Officer*, subj: Information about the Air Reserve, Jul 23, 1946; ltr, Capt MacArthur H. Manchester, ed., *The Reserve Officer*, to CG ADC, subj: Lack of Information about the Air Reserve Program, Jul 26, 1946; ltr, Stratemeyer to Huston, Information about the Air Reserve Program, Aug 7, 1946—all in AFRES 9A.

74. IRS, HQ ADC, Col Candee to CG ADC, CG to Candee, subj: Meeting of Reservists, Sep 24, 1948, MF A4002, AFRES.

75. Ltr, Gen Dwight D. Eisenhower, CSA, to Gen Jacob L. Devers, subj: Cooperation between Members of Regular and Reserve Components, Apr 28, 1947; Louis Galambos, ed., *The Papers of Dwight D. Eisenhower*, 8 vols (Baltimore, Md., 1978) pp 1668–69; ltr, Eisenhower to Spaatz, same subject, Apr 28, 1947, AFRES 9B; ltr, Spaatz to Eisenhower, same subject, May 2, 1947, Spaatz, Box 256, LOC.

76. Memo, Col T. Q. Graff, Actg PRO ADC, to Stratemeyer, subj: Reservists Meeting at Eglin Field, Apr 14, 1947, MF A4001, AFRES.

77. Monthly ltr, Stratemeyer to Commanders, Apr 1947, AFRES 9B.

78. Release, Brig Gen E. A. Evans, Ex Dir ROA, Oct 15, 1946.

79. Ltr, Col Theron B. Herndon, Senior VP, ARA, to Spaatz, subj: Air Reserve Program, Oct 1, 1946; ltr, Spaatz to Herndon, subj: Air Reserve Personnel and Administrative Problems, Nov 8, 1946, 1516, Box 325, RG 18, NA.

80. Remarks, Partridge, ARA Convention, Memphis, Nov 10, 1946, Partridge Collection, K168.7014, AFHRC.

81. James P. Straubel, *Crusade for Air-*

power: The Story of the Air Force Association (Washington, D.C., 1982), pp 34–35; recommendation, Committee on Resolutions, First National Convention of AFA, "Statement of Policy and a Program of Supporting Action," atch to ltr, Doolittle to Arnold, subj: AFA Convention, Sep 19, 1947, Arnold, Box 215, LOC.

82. "The United States Air Force Reserve: An Analysis." Based on the internal evidence, sometime after August 8 but before September 30, 1948, Brig Gen John McConnell, Chief of the Civilian Components Group, and his staff prepared a comprehensive analysis of the Air Reserve/Air Force Reserve Program as conducted by the Army Air Forces and the Air Force between July 1946 and June 1948. That analysis became the baseline for subsequent Air Staff studies and revisions of the program. A copy of this document is in the AFRES microfilm collection, roll A4002. McConnell subsequently presented compressed versions of the paper in talks at the ARA convention at Orlando on October 16, 1948 (AFRES 30A), and the Air War College on November 29, 1948 (McConnell papers, AFHRC). Except as otherwise indicated, this concluding section is based on my analysis of these three documents. See also Air Force Reserve Statistical Summary at the end of FY 1948, cited earlier in note 44, this chapter.

83. Air Force Reserve Statistical Summary, end FY 1948, AFRES 9C.

84. *ADC Plan to Activate the Air Reserve*, May 15, 1946, as cited earlier in note 28, this chapter.

85. Air Force Reserve Statistical Summary, end FY 1948, AFRES 9C.

86. The aircraft and flying-hour figures may be found in appendices 3 and 4 of the AFRES history for FY 1982. For the figure on pilots, see the attachments to the point paper, Lt Col Bryan Cary, Ofc of AF Res, subj: USAFR Rated Manning, Aug 4, 1981, doc 551, in hist, AFRES, FY 1981.

Chapter 3

1. "Special Message to the Congress on the Threat to the Freedom of Europe," Mar 17, 1948, Truman, *Public Papers, 1948*, pp 182–86; "St. Patrick's Day Address in New

Notes

York City," Mar 17, 1948, Truman, *Public Papers, 1948*, pp 186–90.

2. See note 1 above. For the President's recommendation to let the earlier draft lapse, see "Special Message to the Congress on Discontinuing the Selective Service," Mar 3, 1947, Truman, *Public Papers, 1947*, pp 163–64.

3. *The Selective Service Act of 1948* (Stat 62: 606).

4. Legislative History, *The Selective Service Act of 1948, U.S. Code Congressional Service*, 80th Cong., 2d sess., vol 2, 1948, p 1989 ff; *The Forrestal Diaries*, pp 418–21.

5. Memo, Brig Gen R. C. Lindsay to Symington, subj: Civilian Components of the Armed Forces, Nov 4, 1947, RG 340, Box 209, NA; ltr, F. M. Dearborn, Jr., Ex Sec, Cmte on Civ Comps, to Mrs. Douglas Horton, subj: Civilian Components Committee, Jan 16, 1948, 338, RG 341, NA; memo, Forrestal to Gray, subj: Committee on Civilian Components, Nov 20, 1947, Box 156 (PSF), HSTL.

6. Memo, C. V. Whitney to John Ohly, Spec Asst to SecDef, subj: Suggested Consideration by the "Inter-Service Committee to Study the Problem of the Civilian Components," Nov 6, 1947, RG 340, Box 209, NA.

7. Rpt, Committee on Civilian Components, *Reserve Forces for National Security* to the Secretary of Defense, Jun 30, 1948, (Washington, D.C., 1948); see also memo, Gray to Forrestal, subj: Synopsis of Major Recommendations of the Gray Board, Jul 2, 1948, Box 156 (PSF), HSTL.

8. Ltr, Truman to Forrestal, subj: Gray Committee Report, Aug 12, 1948, Box 156 (PSF), HSTL.

9. Intvw, with Gordon Gray, Jun 18, 1973, HSTL.

10. Air Staff Summary Sheet (ASSS), Partridge, subj: Training of Reserve and National Guard Personnel, Feb 11, 1948, w/2 incls, AFRES 9C.

11. Ltr, Stratemeyer to Spaatz, subj: Civilian Components Group, Feb 3, 1948, MF A4002, AFRES.

12. Ltr, Smart to McConnell, subj: Reserve Board of Officers, May 7, 1948; atch 2 (ltr, Whitney to Stratemeyer, subj: Report of Board of Officers, Apr 21, 1948, w/2 atchs); ltr, Stratemeyer to CSAF, subj: Report of Air Force Reserve Officers' Board, May 18, 1948, w/3 incls—all in MF A4002, AFRES.

13. Ltr, Smart to McConnell, subj: Revision of Air Force Reserve Program, Feb 27, 1948, AFRES 9C; R&R, Smart, subj: Revision of the AF Reserve Plan and Program, Feb 18, 1948, and incl, Policies for Revision of Air Force Reserve Plan and Programs, Feb. 17, 1948 [annotated, "Approved 19/2/48, George E. Stratemeyer"]; memo, Graff to McConnell, subj: Analysis of Air Force Reserve Program, Jun 8, 1948; memo, McConnell to Graff, subj: Analysis of Air Force Reserve Program, Jul 10, 1948—all in MF A4002, AFRES.

14. Memo, McConnell for DCS/O, subj: Reserve, National Guard and ROTC Programs, Mar 3, 1948, AFRES 9C.

15. Memo for Dir/Tng & Rqmts et al., subj: DCS/O Meeting, 5 February 1948, Feb 5, 1948, 213, Box 34, RG 341, NA; ltr, Spaatz to Stratemeyer, subj: National Guard and Reserve Division, Mar 22, 1948, AFRES 9C.

16. Ltr, McConnell to ADC, subj: US Air Force Reserve Program for FY 1949, Oct 6, 1948, MF A4002, AFRES; Presentation, DAF to JCS Cmte on Development of the Air Force during FY 1950, Aug 23, 1948, pp 37–42, 186, Box 2, RG 330, NA.

17. Ltr, Col. William H. Neblett, ROA official, to Maj Gen Harry H. Vaughan, subj: USA, Mil Aide to President Truman, Reorganization of Reserve, Jun 28, 1948, Box 156 (PSF), HSTL.

18. Memo, Truman to SecDef, subj: Request for Information on Reserve Programs, Jul 2, 1948; ltr, Forrestal to Truman, subj: Organization of Reserve Components, Aug 2, 1948, both in Box 156 (PSF), HSTL.

19. Draft ltr, Truman to Forrestal, subj: Synopsis of Report, [mid-Aug 48], Box 156 (PSF), HSTL.

20. Memo, Truman to John R. Steelman, Spec Asst Pres, subj: Draft Executive Order on Reserves, Oct 5, 1948, w/atch, Box 156 (PSF), HSTL.

21. Ltr, Forrestal to Truman, subj: Proposed Executive Order, Oct 6, 1948, Box 1643 (PSF), HSTL.

22. Memo, Steelman to Truman, subj: Proposed Executive Order, Oct 6, 1948; memo, Pace to President Truman, subj:

The Air Force Reserve

Proposed Executive Order, Oct 8, 1948, both in Box 1643 (PSF), HSTL.

23. Ltr, Pace to Attorney General, subj: Draft of Executive Order, Oct 8, 1948, w/incl; ltr, Tom C. Clark, Atty Gen, to President, subj. Proposed Executive Order, Oct 8, 1948—both in Box 1653 (PSF), HSTL.

24. Draft ltr, Truman to SecDef, subj: Proposed Executive Order, Oct 9, 1948, Box 1653 (PSF), HSTL. The letter was edited; Truman made marginal comments and handed it to Forrestal.

25. Ltr, Forrestal to President Truman, subj: Proposed Executive Order, ca. Oct 10, 1948, Box 1653 (PSF), HSTL.

26. Ltr, Forrestal to Truman subj: Proposed Executive Order, Oct 15, 1948; memo, Steelman for the President, subj: Proposed Executive Order, Oct 15, 1948, both in Box 1653 (PSF), HSTL.

27. Robert J. Donovan, *Conflict and Crisis: The Presidency of Harry S. Truman, 1945–1948,* (New York, 1977), p 425; EO 10007, Harry S. Truman, Oct 15, 1948.

28. Ltr, Truman to Forrestal, subj: Implementation of EO 10007, Oct 15, 1948, AFRES 13A.

29. Statement. Pres Harry S. Truman, Issuance of EO 10007, Oct 15, 1948, AFRES 13.

30. Carlton and Slinkman, *The ROA Story,* pp 404–11.

31. Ltr, Forrestal to Truman, subj: Implementation of EO 10007, Oct 19, 1948, Box 145 (PSF), HSTL; memo, Symington for Forrestal, subj: Report to the President under Executive Order No. 10007, Dec 8, 1948, AFRES 9C.

32. Memo, Brig Gen R. B. Landry, Pres Aide, to the Pres, subj: Comments and Recommendations on the Air Force Report to the President on Executive Order #10007, Jan 5, 1949, Box 1653 (PSF), HSTL.

33. Ltr, Symington to Truman, subj: Appointment of General Quesada, Nov 17, 1948, 1285Q, Box 1653 (OF), HSTL; ltr, Vandenberg to CG ADC, subj: The Reserve Forces, Nov 26, 1948; USAF Headquarters Operating Instruction (HOI) 45–5, "Assignment of Responsibilities to Offices of Headquarters USAF with Respect to Reserve Forces," Dec 1, 1948; memo, Col L. L. Judge, Air AG, to all offices at HQ USAF, subj: Office of Special Assistant to the Chief of Staff for Reserve Forces, Dec 1, 1948; memo, Gen Hoyt S. Vandenberg, CSAF, to Quesada, subj: Office of the Special Assistant to the Chief of Staff for Reserve Forces, Mar 1, 1949, AFRES 5/5A.

34. DeWitt S. Copp, *A Few Great Captains: The Men and Events That Shaped the Development of U.S. Air Power* (Garden City, N.Y., 1980), p 269.

35. Intvw, Lt Col Steve Long and Lt Col Ralph Stephenson with Lt Gen Elwood R. Quesada, May 13, 1975, K239.0512–838, AFHRC.

36. Memo, Symington to Shaw, subj: Merger of Components, Nov 23, 1948, 326, Box 253, RG 340, NA.

37. Ltr, Judge to personnel concerned, subj: Ad Hoc Committee on Reserve Forces, Jan 5, 1949, w/incl, Symington Papers, Box 3, HSTL; paper, "Presentation on 'The Reserve Forces of the Air Force of the United States,' by Lt Gen E. R. Quesada before Secretary of Defense," ca. Jan 1949, Symington Papers, 1946–50, Q, General, Box 10, HSTL.

38. Legislative History, *Army and Air Force Authorization Act of 1949,* Jul 10, 1950, and House Armed Services Committee, *Hearings on the Bill to Authorize the Composition of the Army of the United States and for Other Purposes,* 81st Cong., 1st sess. pp 201–17. See also Gross, *Prelude to Total Force,* pp 35–43.

39. DAF Ltr 322 (AFOOR 9Y9e), subj: Establishment of the Continental Air Command and Designation of Air Defense Command and Tactical Air Command as Operational Air Commands, Nov 19, 1948; AFR 23–1, *Organization of Continental Air Command,* Jan 11, 1949, AFRES 31A; memo, Symington to Forrestal, subj: Report to the President under Executive Order No. 10007, Dec 8, 1948; CONAC GO 1, Dec 1, 1948; R&R, Col Clarence D. Wheeler, Dep Dir/Tng & Rqmts, to Dir/Tng & Rqmts, subj: Report of the Department of the Air Staff Committees on Reserve Policies, May 16, 1949, all 319, Box 5, RG 341, NA; Hist, CONAC, Dec 1, 1948–Jun 30, 1949, sec 2, pp 27–30; DAF release No. 90, "Continental Air Command Is Organized," Nov 18, 1948, as doc 1 in hist, CONAC, Dec 1948–Dec 1949; hist,

Notes

CONAC, 1952, ch 1; Informal notes, Commanders Conference, Continental Air Command, Nov 30, 1948; memo, Col Allen R. Springer, Actg Ch, Org Div, Dir/Tng & Rqmts, CONAC, subj: Organizational Concept for the Continental Air Command, Dec 1, 1948—both in AFRES 32A. Initially, the official abbreviation for the Continental Air Command was "CONAC." On August 1, 1966, it became "CAC."

40. Ltr, Gen Jacob E. Smart, USAF (Ret), to Thomas A. Sturm, subj: Organization of Postwar Air Force, Jan 18, 1973, AFRES 10.

41. Hist, CONAC, Dec 48–Jul 50, vol 2, p 6.

42. Ltr, McConnell to Stratemeyer, subj: USAF Reserve Program for FY 1950, Mar 7, 1949, w/4 incls, AFRES 10; ltr, Frank Pace, Jr., Dir/DOD, to SecDef, subj: Revised Air Force Reserve Program, Apr 20, 1949; memo, Quesada to Symington, subj: Air Force Reserve Budget Delay, Apr 14, 1949; memo, Quesada to Symington, subj: Air Force Reserve Budget Delay, Apr 25, 1949—all in 326, Box 254, RG 340, NA.

43. Ltr, McConnell to CONAC, subj: Implementation of the Air Force Reserve Training Programs for Fiscal Year 1950, May 5, 1949, w/3 incls; AFP (Spec Asst CSAF/RF), *The United States Air Force Reserve: Brief of Program Fiscal Year 1950*, ca. 1949, AFRES 10; hist, HQ USAF, Jun 1949–Jun 1950, pp 80–84.

44. Ltr, McConnell to CG CONAC, subj: The USAF Reserve Programs for Fiscal Year 1950, May 9, 1949, w/3 incls, AFRES 10.

45. Memo, Quesada to Symington, subj: Air Force Reserve Program Status, Mar 18, 1949, 326, Box 253, RG 340, NA.

46. AF Ltr 45–12, "Corollary Units, United States Air Forces Reserve," May 9, 1945, AFRES 20A.

47. AFR 45–33, *United States Air Force Reserve Training Centers*, Oct 3, 1949, AFRES 15B.

48. Hist, CONAC, Dec 1948–Dec 1949, vol 2, p 119; 1st ind (ltr, McConnell, May 6, 1949), CONAC to 12th AF et al., May 12, 1949, AFRES 10.

49. Ltr, AFCAG–13 334, 1st Lt W. J. Goninan, Asst Air AG, to pers concerned, subj: Department of the Air Force Air Staff Committee on National Guard and Reserve Policy, Mar 31, 1948, MF A4000, AFRES; memo, Brig Gen Robert J. Smith, USAFR, et al., to CSAF; subj: Report of the Department of the Air Force Air Staff Committee on Reserve Policy, ca. Jul 1, 1948, 14, Box 30, RG 341, NA.

50. Memo, Smith to SecAF, subj: Report of the Department of the Air Force Air Staff Committee on Reserve Policy (4–9 Apr 1949, Inclusive), Apr 1949, AFRES 14C1.

51. Ltr, McConnell to CONAC, subj: The AFRTC Program, USAF Reserve, Fiscal Year 1950, May 6, 1949, w/4 incls and 1 ind, AFRES 10.

52. Ltr, McConnell to CONAC, subj: Relocation of Reserve Units and Aircraft, Dec 3, 1949, MF A4002, AFRES; DAF Ltr 322 (AFOOP 211f) to CONAC, subj: Constitution, Reconstitution, Redesignation of AFRTC Units, May 10, 1949; DAF Ltr 322 (AFOOR 215f) to CONAC, subj: Constitution, Redesignation, and Activation of the Hq & Hq Squadron, 439th Troop Carrier Wing, Medium, and Other AFRTC Units, May 19, 1949; DAF Ltr 322 (AFOOR 225f) to CONAC, subj: Activation of Air Force Reserve Units, Jul 1, 1949; DAF Ltr 322 (AFOOR 287f) to CONAC, subj: Activation of Air Force Reserve Units, Aug 4, 1949—all in AFRES 19C.

53. CONAC Ltr 45–13, "Volunteer Air Reserve Training Units," Aug 15, 1949; AFR 45–23, *United States Air Force Volunteer Air Reserve Training Units*, Jul 8, 1949; VAR Training Program Curriculum, 1950–1951—all in 50–10878 AF, AFRES 16A; ltr, Gen Hoyt S. Vandenberg, CSAF, to Maj D. W. Jewett, subj: The Volunteer Air Reserve, Jan 14, 1950, Vandenberg Papers, Box 33, LOC.

54. Ltr, Whitehead to Gen Muir S. Fairchild, VCSAF, subj: VARTU Program, Sep 14, 1949, w/incl; 1st Ind (ltr, HQ USAF/RF to CONAC, subj: Volunteer Air Reserve Training Units, Sep 1, 1949), Col Neal J. O'Brien, CONAC AG, to HQ USAF/RF, Sep 23, 1949; ltr, Maj Gen William F. McKee, Asst VCSAF, to CONAC, subj: Liaison Personnel for VARTUs, Oct 12, 1949, w/incl—all in AFRES 16A.

55. Ltr, Lt Col C. O. Moffett, Ch, Org & Equip Auth Ofc, HQ AMC, to HQ USAF, subj: Volunteer Air Reserve Training Units, Sep 23, 1949; AF Ltr 67–43, "Vol-

The Air Force Reserve

unteer Air Reserve Supply and Accounting Procedures," Jun 29, 1950—both in AFRES 16A.

56. Ltr, Maj Gen Charles T. Myers, VCmdr CONAC, to Maj Gen Harry A. Johnson, CG 10th AF, subj: VARTU Program, Oct 21, 1950; same ltr to 1st AF, 4th AF, and 14th AF—all in AFRES 16A.

57. AF Ltr 45-5, "Mobilization Assignment for Air Reserve Personnel," Jul 19, 1948.

58. Ltr, Col C. W. Schott, Dep Spec Asst CSAF/RF, to CONAC, subj: Mobilization Assignment for Air Reserve Personnel, Dec 13, 1948, AFRES 14K.

59. R&R, Schott to the Air Inspector & Dir/P&O, subj: Mobilization Assignment Program, Oct 25, 1949; memo, Hardin to McConnell, subj: MA Program, Oct 24, 1949; memo, Col Don H. Yielding, Ch, Svcs & Div, Spec Asst/RF, to Air Force Reserve Div, subj: Mobilization Assignment Program, Oct 25, 1949—all in 210.3, Box 3, RG 341, NA; ltr, McConnell to SAC et al., subj: USAF Reserve Mobilization Assignment Program, Dec 7, 1949, 210.3, Box 3, RG 341, NA.

60. 1st ind (McConnell ltr), Whitehead to CSAF, ca. Jan 1950, K419.161-6, AFHRC.

61. DAF Ltr 322 (AFOOR 212f) to CONAC, ATC, and MATS, subj: Designation and Organization of Corollary Table of Distribution Units, May 17, 1949; DAF Ltr 322 (AFOOR 213f) to SAC, CONAC, and AMC, subj: Constitution, Reconstitution, Redesignation, Activation, and Reorganization of Corollary Units, May 16, 1949, a/a ltr 322 (AFOOR 222f)—both in AFRES 20A; hist, CONAC, Dec 48–Dec 49, pp 240–43.

62. Hist, CONAC, Dec 48–Dec 49, pp 240–43; ltr, Whitehead to Fairchild, subj: Corollary Unit Program, Nov 2, 1949; ltr, Fairchild to Whitehead, Corollary Unit Program, Jan 16, 1950—both in Fairchild Collection, Box 2, LOC; 2d ind (ltr, CONAC to NAFs, subj: Activation of Reserve Corollary Aircraft Control and Warning Units, Jan 23, 1950); ltr, Myers to DCS/O USAF, Feb 8, 1950, K419.161-27, AFHRC; ltr, Whitehead to Fairchild, Elimination of Tactical Corollary Units, Feb 20, 1950, K419.161-26, AFHRC; ltr, Maj Gen John E. Upston, CG 4th AF, to Brig Gen Herbert B. Thatcher, Actg VCmdr CONAC, subj: Corollary Unit Program, May 25, 1950, K419.161-23, AFHRC; memo, Maj Gen Earl S. Hoag, Spec Asst CSAF/RF, to CSAF, subj: Visits of Maj General Earl S. Hoag to Summer Training Activities of Civilian Components, Jun 30, 1950, Vandenberg Papers, Box 36, LOC; Comment No. 1, R&R, Col Dolf E. Muehleisen, Dir/Ops & Tng, CAC, subj: Corollary Programs, Sep 13, 1950, AFRES 20A.

63. *United States Air Force Statistical Digest, January 1949–June 1950*, tables 174, "USAF Reserves Corollary Units by Command," and 179, "USAF Reserve Corollary Units."

64. The Naval Reserve Act of 1938 (Stat 52: 1184) authorized training pay for naval reservists, and the National Defense Act of 1916 (Stat 39: 174–97) did the same for national guardsmen.

65. PL 80–460, *Organized Reserve Corps—Inactive Duty Training Pay* (Stat 62: 87), Mar 25, 1948; Legislative History, PL 80–460, pp 1317–20.

66. Ltr, Lt Gen Lauris Norstad, DCS/O, HQ USAF, to CG ADC, subj: Inactive Duty Training Pay for USAF Reserve Personnel, Apr 29, 1948, w/ind, MF A4002, AFRES; AFR 45–10, *Air Force Reserve Inactive Duty Training Pay and Allowances*, Oct 11, 1948.

67. Hist, CONAC, Dec 48–Dec 49, pp 67–72.

68. Diary, HQ CONAC, Jan 31, 1949.

69. Ltr, 46th Bomb Sq (L), to 2230 AFRTC, subj: Navigation Training Flight, Jan 27, 1949, AFRES 14B.

70. AFR 45–10, *Air Force Reserve Inactive Duty Training Pay and Allowances*, Mar 22, 1949.

71. Legislative History, PL 810, 80th Cong., 2d sess. (Sep 27, 1949), *Army and Air Force Vitalization and Retirement Equalization Act of 1948, United States Code Congressional Service*, pp 2161–71.

72. PL 810, 80th Cong., 2d sess. (Sep 27, 1949), *Army and Air Force Vitalization and Retirement Equalization Act of 1948*.

73. Daily diary, Res & NG Div, Jul 15, 1946, Jul 25, 1946, and Aug 14, 1946, K123.310, AFHRC; ADCR 50–5, "Policy for Training Negro Air Reservists, Mar 7, 1947"; ltr, Beamer to TAC, subj: Active Duty Training of Negro Air Reservists, Aug 26, 1947, w/incl and w/ind—all in MF

Notes

A4002, AFRES.

74. Alan L. Gropman, *The Air Force Integrates, 1945–1964* (Washington, D.C., 1978), pp 108–116.

75. Ltr, Landon to CSAF, subj: Negro Air Force Reservists, Feb 3, 1948, AFRES, A–4002.

76. 1st ind (Landon Ltr), Partridge to ADC, Feb 17, 1948, MF A4002, AFRES.

77. See, for example, ltr, Col R. B. Caants, Actg Asst AG ADC, to CG 2d AF, subj: Training of Negro Air Force Reservists, Mar 24, 1948; 1st ind (Travis ltr, Mar 24), Col E. W. A. Taylor, AG 2d AF, to CG ADC, w/3 incls; 1st ind (Travis ltr), Col L. L. Judge, AG 4th AF, to CG ADC, Apr 8, 1948; 2d ind (Travis ltr), Landon to CG 4th AF, Apr 21, 1948; 1st ind (Travis ltr), Lt Col Herman L. Fogley, Asst AG 11th AF, to CG ADC, Apr 5, 1948; ltr, Col Bonnewitz, AG 11th AF, to CG ADC, subj: Negro Reserve Strengths, Feb 6, 1948, w/incl; 2d ind (Travis ltr), Capt Lee W. Spitler, Actg Asst AG ADC, to CG 11th AF, Apr 21, 1948; 1st ind (Travis ltr), Col Ray A. Dunn, CS 14th AF, to CG ADC, Apr 2, 1948; draft 2d ind (Travis ltr), ADC, comments 6, 7, and 8, HQ ADC IRS, subj: Training of Negro Air Reservists, May 3–6, 1948; comments 9, 10, 11, 12, and 13, HQ ADC IRS, subj: Training of Negro Air Reservists, May 17–20, 1948; 2d ind (Travis ltr), Landon to CG 14th AF, May 21, 1948—all in MF A4002, AFRES.

78. *Women's Armed Services Integration Act of 1948* (Stat 62: 371–75), Jun 12, 1948; ltr, Stone to CG AAF, subj: ADC WAC Air Reserve Plan, Jan 8, 1947, w/incl and w/3 inds, AFRES 14T; *The Air Reservist*, Nov 66.

79. Ltr, Capt Marjorie O. Hunt, ADC WAF Staff Director, to Mrs. Floyd B. Odlum, subj: Air Force Reserve Program for WAF, Aug 16, 1948, MF A4002, AFRES.

80. PL 80–283, *The National Security Act of 1947* (Stat 61: 496–510), Jul 26, 1947.

81. R. Earl McClendon, *Unification of the Armed Forces: Administration and Legislative Developments, 1945–1949* (documentary research paper, Air University).

82. Ibid.; DA Bul No. 1, Nov. 12, 1947, AFRES 34D.

83. DA Cir No. 103/DAF Ltr 35–124, subj: Air Force Reserve and Air Force Honorary Reserve, Apr 14, 1948, MF A4002, AFRES.

84. Joint Army and Air Force Bul No. 12, May 4, 1948, AFRES 34D.

85. Ltr, Whitehead to CSAF, subj: The USAF Reserve Forces, 13 Dec 50, w/3 incl., AFRES 10.

Chapter 4

1. David Rees, *Korea: The Limited War* (New York, 1964), pp 8–12.

2. Steven L. Rearden, *History of the Office of the Secretary of Defense*, vol 1, *The Formative Years, 1947–1950* (Washington, D.C., 1984), pp 465–69; Walter G. Hermes, *Truce Tent and Fighting Front; United States Army in the Korean War* (Washington, D.C., 1966), pp 8–9.

3. Hermes, *Truce Tent and Fighting Front*, pp 8–9.

4. Futrell, *Ideas, Concepts, Doctrine*, pp 128–29; Rearden, vol 1, *The Formative Years*, p 264.

5. Richard F. Haynes, *The Awesome Power: Harry S. Truman as Commander in Chief* (Baton Rouge, La., 1973), p 163.

6. Robert Frank Futrell, *The United States Air Force in Korea, 1950–1953*, (New York, 1961), pp 10–11, 23, 37.

7. Maurice Matloff, *American Military History* (Washington, D.C., 1969), p 549; Futrell, *USAF in Korea*, pp 64–67; remarks, Thomas K. Finletter, SecAF, to Air Reserve Association, Sep 29, 1950, Fort Worth, Tex., Vandenberg Papers, Box 36, LOC.

8. Futrell, *Ideas, Concepts, Doctrine*, pp 159–66.

9. "Special Message to the Congress Reporting on the Situation in Korea," Jul 19, 1950, in Truman, *Public Papers, 1950*,

pp 527-32. The President told the American people about these things in a national radio/television address that night. Ibid., pp 537-42.

10. PL 559, 81st Cong., *Selective Service Extension Act of 1950* (Stat 64: 313); Senate Rpt 80-1784 (Calendar 1789), p 10; Legislative History, 81st Cong., 2d sess. (1950), *Selective Service Extension Act of 1950, U.S. Congressional Service*, p 2669 ff; memo, R. A. Buddke to Felix E. Larkin, subj: Items for the Legislative Program for Use in Connection with Your Proposed Carlisle Speech, Oct 15, 1949, RG 330, Ofc of Legis Progs, Gen Adm File—1949-1953, Box 2, NA; memo, Gen Omar N. Bradley, Ch JCS, to SecDef, subj: Extension of the Selective Service Act, Jan 12, 1950, RG 330, Ofc Adm Sec CD 13-1-30 to CD 13-1-23, NA; S.J.R. 190, "Selective Service Act of 1948—Extension of Period of Effectiveness."

11. Matloff, *American Military History* p 549; Futrell, *USAF in Korea*, pp 64-67.

12. For a detailed account of the Korean mobilization, see Gerald T. Cantwell, *The Evolution and Employment of the Air Force Reserve as a Mobilization Force, 1946-1980* (Robins AFB, Ga., 1981), pp 1-99, copy in AFRES 2. Msg, HQ USAF to CONAC, subj: Ordering of USAFR Units to Active Military Duty and Activation and Reorganization of USAFR units, AFOMA 50193, 281528Z Jul 50.

13. Hist, Spec Asst CSAF/RF, Jul-Dec 1950, pp 5-6; memo, Whitehead for Dep for Ops, subj: Medium Troop Carrier Mobilization, Jul 2, 1950, AFRES 21A.

14. Personal Msg, Whitehead to Upston, subj: Mobilization of 452d LBW, Jul 30, 1950, CG 18969. For a comparable message sent to the Tenth Air Force commander, see AFRES 21A. Hist, 452d LBW, Jul-Dec 1950, pp 1A-11A.

15. 10th AF GO 122, Jul 31, 1950; hist, 437th TCW, Jul-Dec 50, sec 1, p 1.

16. Ltr, Lt Col L. W. Bruhn, Dep for Pers & Adm, 437th TCW, to CG 437th TCW, subj: Critique on Call to EAD and Subsequent Move to Shaw AFB, S.C., Aug 28, 1950, w/atch; hist, 437th TCW, Jul-Dec 50, passim.

17. Ltr, Lt Col Roger E. Lee, mbr 10th AF Deferment Board, to 10th AF, subj: Report of Deferment Board Activity, 2471 AFRTC, O'Hare International Airport, Park Ridge, Ill., Aug 16 1950, as exhibit 6 in hist, 437th TCW, Jul-Dec 50.

18. Ibid.

19. Msg, HQ USAF to HQ CONAC, subj: Ordering of USAFR Units to Active Military Duty, and Reorganization and Inactivation, 3f USAFR Units, AFOMA-A 53424, 141848Z Sep 50; msg, USAF to CONAC, subj: Ordering USAFR & ANG Units to Extended Active Duty, AFOPNM 53008—both in AFRES 21A.

20. Ltr, Col Neal J. O'Brien, Air Adj Gen, CONAC, to NAFs, subj: Recall of Air Reserve Units, Sep 19, 1950, w/5 incls, PPM-R 326; HQ CONAC Staff Memo 45-1, "Unit Call-Ups of Organized Reserve or Air National Guard," Nov 13, 1950—both in AFRES 21A; hist, The Continental Air Command and the Korean War, 1950 (hereafter, CONAC & Korea), pp 72-77.

21. Ltr, AFOOP-00 375, HQ USAF to HQ CONAC, subj: Movement Directive, 375th Troop Carrier Wing, Medium, Oct 13, 1950, AFRES 21A; Maurer Maurer, ed., *Combat Squadrons of the Air Force, World War II* (Washington, D.C., 1969), pp 226-30, 252-58; *Air Reserve Forces Review*, Jun 1951, p 5; hists, 375 TCW, Jul-Dec 50 through Jan-Jun 52.

22. Memo, Maj Gen George G. Finch, ANGUS, Chm, to SecAF subj: Report of the Second Meeting of the Air Staff Committee on National Guard and Reserve Policy, Nov 19, 1950, AFRES VD2; msg, AFPMP 36172, Col C. D. Sonnkalb (AFPMP-1), to AMC et al., subj: Recall of Air Force Reserve and Air National Guard, Oct 24, 1950, Vandenberg Papers, Box 356, LOC.

23. Richard E. Morris, ed., *Encyclopedia of American History*, Bicentennial Edition (New York, 1976), s.v. "The Korean War: Tumultuous Years," pp 292-312.

24. Presidential Proclamation 2914, "Proclaiming the Existence of a National Emergency," Dec 19, 1950; Futrell, *Ideas, Concepts, Doctrine*, pp 160-61.

25. DOD Release, subj: Major Portion of United States Air Forces Organized Reserve and Air National Guard to be Ordered to Active Military Service, Jan 18, 1951; CONAC OPORD 1-51, Jan 30, 1951; ltr, 322 (AFOMO 3q), Col K. E. Thieband, Actg Air Adj Gen, to CONAC, subj: Ordering into the Active Military

Service of Certain USAF Reserve AFRTC Units, Feb 2, 1951; brochure, HQ CONAC Air National Guard and Air Reserve Activation, Jan 1, 1951; ltr, Pers Mob IM-Res 326, O'Brien to Maj Sub Cmds, subj: Ordering of Air Reserve Units to Active Military Services, Jan 23 1951, w/12 incls; ltr, Pers Mob IM-Res 326, Lt Col John C. Hadley, Asst Air Adj Gen to NAFs, subj: Change Number 1 to "Ordering of Air Reserve Units to Active Military Service," Feb 2, 1951; ltr, Pers Mob IM-Res 326, Lt Col W. T. Coleman Asst Air Adj Gen to NAFs, subj: Change Number 2 to "Ordering of Air Reserve Units to Active Military Service," Mar 6, 1951.

26. Hist, 10th AF, Jan–Jun 51, pp 342; 348–69.

27. Ibid., p 369.

28. Hist, CONAC, Jan–Jun 1951, pp 43–46.

29. Chronol, 18th AF, 1951–1953, p 1; CONAC GO 40, Mar 15, 1951; ltr, 322 (AFOMO 3g), HQ USAF to HQ CONAC, subj: Ordering into Active Military Service of Certain USAF Reserve AFRTC Units, Feb 2, 1951; HQ CONAC GO 30, Mar 2, 1951; 10th AF GO 60, Mar 7, 1951.

30. CONAC ANG & AR Activation Brochure, Jan 1, 1951; ltr, 322 (AFOMO 3g), Feb 2, 1951; ltr, Pers Mob IM-Res 210.455, O'Brien to Nays, subj: Reserve Units Designated for Personnel Distribution, Jan 24, 1951—both in AFRES 21A; 14th AF GOs 25–27, Feb 14, 1951; 4th AF GO 15, Feb 9, 1951; 10th AF GO 27, Feb 6, 1951; 1st AF GOs 49 & 50, Feb 21, 1951; 1st AF GO 64, Mar 23, 1951; 4th AF GO 39, Apr 2, 1951; 10th AF GOs 65 & 66, Mar 13, 1951; 10th AF GO 87, Apr 13, 1951; hist, 452d LBW, Jul–Dec 50.

31. Ltr, Finletter to Carl Vinson, Chmn HASC, subj: Recall of 94th Tactical Bomb Wing, Feb 3, 1951, RG–340 60A1055, WNRC. This file contains scores of letters from Reservists and their Congressmen protesting the proposed breakup of mobilized units.

32. IOM, Brig Gen Herbert B. Thatcher, Dep for Ops, to Vice Cmdr et al., subj: Staff Visit to 437th TCW and 452d Lt BW, Sep 1950, AFRES 21A.

33. Ltr, G–370.5, HQ 452d LBW to Gps et al., subj: Movement Order—452d Bombardment Wing, Light, Oct 27, 1950; ltr, PRO 370.5 CONAC to TAC, subj: Movement Directive, 452—both in AFRES 21A; hist, 452d LBW, Oct 1–Dec 31, 1950, sup docs; hist, HQ & Hq Sq, 452d LBW, Oct–Dec 1950, pp 1–3; hist, 452d LBW, Jul–Dec 50 pp 7–22; Futrell, *USAF in Korea*, pp 205–6.

34. Hists, HQ & Hq Sq, 452d LBW, Oct–Dec 1950, pp 1–3; 452d LBW, Oct–Dec 1950, pp 1–2.

35. Hist, 452d LBW, Jan–Jun 51.

36. Ibid.; rpt, "Air Reserve Unit Participation in the Korean Conflict," p 3, K110.7024.2, AFHRC; hist, 5th AF, Jan–Jun 1951, vol 2, p 255; msg, OPO 4133, 5th AF to 452d LBW, subj: Move of 452d, May 12, 1951; ltr, Ag 370 S, 452d CC to Gp Cmdrs, & HQ & Hq Sq, subj: Movement Orders, 452d Bombardment Wing (Light), May 20, 1951; Futrell, *USAF in Korea*, p 303.

37. Draft rpt, HQ FEAF, "FEAF Report on the Korean War," book 1 of 3, Feb 15, 1950, p 99, K720.04D, AFHRC; ltr, 200–3, PERS-MP-1, FEAF to 5th AF et al., subj: Combat Crews, Jun 7, 1951, as atch 8, Pers in FEAF draft rpt cited above.

38. Ltr, Partridge to Brig Gen N. B. Harbold, OOAMA, subj: B–26s in FEAF, Feb 17, 1951, Partridge Papers, Jan–Jul 51, K168.7014–4, AFHRC.

39. Robert Frank Futrell, *United States Air Force Operations in the Korean Conflict, 1 November 1950–30 June 1952* (USAF Hist Study 72, Maxwell, Ala., 1955), pp 84–86; diary, Lt Gen Earle E. Partridge, 1950–51, vol 4, Apr 4, 1951, K168.7014–1, AFHRC; Futrell, *USAF in Korea*, p 369; diary, Lt Gen George Stratemeyer, 1950–51, vol 3, Apr 21, 1951, K168.7018–16, AFHRC.

40. See note 39 above.

41. Draft rpt, FEAF, "Korean War," book 2, tab 4, Light Bomber Operations.

42. Martin R. Goldman, *Morale in the AAF in World War II* (USAF Hist Study 78, Maxwell AFB, Ala., 1953); Craven and Cate, vol 7, *Services around the World*, p 444.

43. Hist, 5th AF, Jul–Dec 51, vol 2, pp 81–82.

44. Diary, Maj Gen Edward J. Timberlake, May 2, 1951, MF 32833, AFHRC.

45. General Sweetser and the Air Force Reserve community have represented it as

443

otherwise, but General Partridge removed General Sweetser for sound operational reasons. For the situation as it evolved through the eyes of the leadership, see the daily diaries of Generals Stratemeyer, Partridge, and Timberlake for the period May 2–10, 1951, in K168.7018–16, K168.7014–1, and MF 32833, AFHRC.

46. Diary, Timberlake, May 29 and Jun 28, 1951.

47. Futrell, *USAF in Korea*, p 418; Futrell, USAF Hist Study 72, pp 65–66; rpt, "Air Reserve Unit Participation in the Korean Conflict."

48. Msg, DAF (AFOMO–A, 59104, a/a 59188), May 23, 1952; 5th AF GO 304, May 24, 1952, AFRES 21A; Maurer, ed., *Combat Squadrons of WWII*, pp 723–26.

49. rpt, "Air Reserve Unit Participation in the Korean Conflict," p 3.

50. Futrell, *USAF in Korea*, p 128. See also diary, Stratemeyer, 1950–51, vol 2, Nov 15, 1950; diary, Partridge, vol 2, Nov 15, 1950.

51. Ltr, Lt Col L. W. Bruhn, Dep for Pers & Admin, 437th TCW, to CG, subj: Critique on Call to EAD and Subsequent Move to Shaw AFB, S.C., Aug 28, 1950, w/atch, AFRES 21A; hist, 437th TCW, Jul–Dec, passim; rpt, "Air Reserve Unit Participation in the Korean Conflict." For a popular history of airlift operations in Korean War, see Annis G. Thompson, *The Greatest Airlift: The Story of Combat Cargo* (Tokyo, 1954), written from the perspective of an information officer with the 315th Air Division and other airlift organizations.

52. Hist, 437th TCW, Aug–Dec 1950, sec 3, p 1; diary, George E. Stratemeyer, Cmdr, Far East Air Forces, 1950–1951, vol 1, Sep 6, 1950.

53. Hist, 437th TCW, Aug–Dec 1950, sec 2, 1.

54. Ibid., sec 2, 2; rpt, "Air Reserve Unit Participation in the Korean Conflict."

55. Hist, 437th TCW, Aug–Dec 1950, CCC Ops, pp 9–10; ltr, Howard T. Markey to author, subj: C–46 Operations in Korea, Nov 30, 1984, AFRES 21A.

56. Hist, 437th TCW, Jan–Feb, 1951, pp 10–11.

57. Ibid., Mar 1951, p 7.

58. Futrell, USAF Hist Study 72, pp 56–57; Futrell, *USAF in Korea*, pp 325–26.

59. See note 58 above; diary, Partridge, vol 3, Mar 23, 24, and 26, 1951; hist, 437th TCW, Mar 1951, p 6.

60. Hists, 437th TCW, Mar 1951, p 7, and Apr 1951, pp 5–6.

61. Futrell, USAF Hist Study 72, pp 80–81.

62. Futrell, *USAF in Korea*, pp 527–28.

63. rpt, "Air Reserve Unit Participation in the Korean Conflict"; msg (AFOMO–A50188), USAF to FEAF & CONAC, subj: Unit Actions, May 24, 1952, AFRES 21A.

64. Hists, 403d TCW, Jan 1–Mar 31, 1951, p 1, Sep 1–Dec 31, 1951, Jan–Mar 1952, and Apr 1952; rpt, "Air Reserve Unit Participation in the Korean Conflict," pp 6–7.

65. DAF Ltr 322 (AFOMO 210h) to CONAC and TAC, subj: Inactivation of All Elements of the 403d Troop Carrier Wing, Medium, Air Force Reserve Combat Training Center Units, Nov 15, 1952; DAF Ltr 322 (AFOMO 234) to CONAC et al., subj: Relief of the 403d Troop Carrier Wing, Medium, from Active Military Service of the United States: Constitution, Redesignation, and Activation of Elements of Replacement Troop Carrier Wing, Nov 15, 1952—both in AFRES 21A.

66. *Air Reserve Forces Review*, Oct 1951, p 7, Mar 1952, p 6, and May 1952, p 4; chronol, TAC Hist Off, "Eighteenth Air Force during the Korean Period" (hereafter, 18th AF Korean Chronol).

67. Maurer, ed., *Combat Squadrons of WWII*, pp 263–73, 276–81; DAF Ltr 322 (AFOMO 206h) to CONAC and TAC, subj: Relief of 514th Troop Carrier Wing, Medium from Active Military Service of the United States; Redesignation and Activation of Replacement Troop Carrier Wing, Nov 26, 1952; DAF Ltr 322 (AFOMO 266h) to CONAC and TAC, subj: Relief of the 434th Troop Carrier Wing, Medium from Active Military Service of the United States; Constitution, Redesignation, and Activation of Elements of Replacement Troop Carrier Wing, Dec 15, 1952—all in AFRES 21A; msg, M&O 00898, CONAC to USAF subj: Unit Actions, Jan 22, 1953.

68. *The Air Reservist*, Jan 1953, p 7; 18th AF Korean Chronol; memo, Maj Gen E. L. Eubanks, Dep IG, to USAF IG, subj: Report on Survey of Recently Federalized

Notes

Air National Guard Units and One Air Force Reserve Wing Recently Ordered to Active Military Service, Mar 16, 1951, 600, Box 26, RG 341, NA; Maurer, ed., *Combat Squadrons of WWII*, pp 226–30, 263–73, 276–81, 375–81.

69. Hist, FEAF, Jan 1–Jun 30, 1951, vol 2, pp 211–12.

70. Diary, Partridge, 1950–51, vol 3, Mar 26, 1951, and vol 4, Apr 10, 1951; diary, Stratemeyer, 1950–51, vol 3, Mar 27, 1951; diary, Timberlake, Mar 26, 1951.

71. Hist, 452d LBW, May 51, p 4, and Jun 51, p 1.

72. Hist, 452d LBW.

73. Russell F. Weigley discusses some of the perplexities the government faced in meeting its manpower needs for the Korean contingency and the overall expansion of its military forces in *History of the United States Army*, 2d ed. (New York, 1977), pp 507–10. Msg, HQ USAF to AMC et al., subj: Voluntary Recalls to Active Duty, AFCPR-2, 072105Z Jul 50; ltr, AFPMP 11, Maj Gen R. E. Nugent, Actg DCS/Pers, HQ USAF to CONAC, subj: Recall of Reserve Officers and Airmen Personnel, Jun 30, 1950, w/l incl, Dec 1950—both in AFRES 21A.

74. Ltr, Nugent to CONAC, subj: Recall of Reserve Officers and Airmen Personnel, Jul 6, 1950, w/atch & ind, Dec 12, AFRES 21A; Ltr, Gen Nathan F. Twining, Actg DCS/Pers, USAF, to CONAC, subj: Recall of Reserve Officer and Airmen Personnel, Jul 20, 1950, w/incl as doc 18 in CONAC & Korea; 1st Ind (ltr, Nugent to CONAC, Jul 6, 1950), CONAC to USAF, Jul 14, 1950.

75. Ltr, PPM-R 210.455, Col Neal J. O'Brien, Air Adj Gen, CONAC, to NAFs, subj: Involuntary Recall of USAF Reserve Personnel, Jul 24, 1950; ltr, O'Brien to NAFs, subj: Individual Recall of USAFR Personnel, Aug 19, 1950, as doc 35 in CONAC & Korea; ltr, PPM–210–455, Lt Col V. E. Murphy, Asst Air AG, to NAFs, subj: Individual Recall of USAFR Personnel, Aug 4, 1950, w/5 incls, as doc 34 in CONAC & Korea; msg, HQ USAF to CONAC, AFPMP 20992, subj: Criteria for Delay in Call to Active Duty, Aug 7, 1951, as doc 29 in CONAC & Korea.

76. CONAC & Korea, pp 60–61.

77. For *Dependency Act*, see msg, AFAFN 26916, HQ USAF to CONAC et al., subj: Dependency Assistance Act, Sep 8, 1950, as doc 52 in CONAC & Korea; PL 771, *Dependency Assistance Act* (Sep 8, 1950). For establishment of the appeal boards, see CONAC & Korea, pp 61–66, and CONAC GO NO 163, Aug 22, 1950.

78. Msg, HQ USAF to CONAC, subj: Recall Instructions, AFPMP 36172, 2422-55Z Oct 1950; memo, Lt Gen Ennis C. Whitehead to Dep/Pers, subj: Recall of Rated Officer Personnel of USAF Reserve, Aug 19, 1950, as doc 36 in CONAC & Korea [policy disseminated to numbered air forces next day]; ltr, PPM-R 210–455, Whitehead to DCS/Pers, HQ USAF, subj: Recall of Deferred Personnel, Aug 17, 1950, AFRES 21A.

79. Memo, Finletter to SecDef, subj: Recall of Reservists, Dec 30, 1950, RG 340, 60A1033, WNRC.

80. Hist, CONAC, Jan–Jun 1951, pp 46–48.

81. Ltr, Pers Mob IM-Res 210.455 O'Brien to NAFs et al., subj: Ordering into Active Military Service of Individual Members of the USAFR, Jan 22, 1951, w/9 incls, AFRES 21A.

82. Hist, CONAC, Jan–Jun 1951, pp 48–52.

83. Msg, AFPMP–4 36222, HQ USAF to FEAF et al., subj: Early Release of Reserve and Air National Guard Airmen from Active Duty; hist, 437th TCW, Dec 1951; msg, USAF to ARDC et al., subj: Release of Reserve Forces Airmen from Active Military Service, AFPDP 33265, 16/2300Z Nov 1951; ltr, Capt S. T. McDonald, Asst Air Adj Gen, CONAC, to NAFs et al., subj: Active Duty for Air Reserve and Air National Guard Airmen, Oct 8, 1951—all in AFRES 21A.

84. Ltr, MP–03–13 326 Air Reserve, O'Brien to NAFs et al., subj: Release of Reserve Forces Officers upon Completion of 17 Months Active Duty, Sep 10, 1951, AFRES 21A.

85. Ltr, MP–03–B 210.455, 210.8, O'Brien to NAFs et al., subj: Release of Reserve Forces Officers upon Completion of 17 Months Active Duty, Dec 29, 1951, AFRES 21A.

86. Ltr, AFPMP–11, Col A. T. Learnard, Ch Pers Rqmts & Anlys Div, Dir/Mil Pers, USAF, to CONAC, subj: Supplementary

445

The Air Force Reserve

Air Force Reserve Officer Recall Program—Fiscal Year 1953, Jan 8, 1953, w/2 incls, AFRES 21A; ltr, Learned to CONAC, subj: Air Force Reserve Officer Recall Program for January 1 to June 30 1953, Jan 19, 1953, w/incl; *United States Air Force Statistical Digest, Fiscal Year 1953*, table 338, "Air Force Reserve Officers Sent to Active Military (AMS) by Grade by Category of Personnel Assignment—FY 1953"; Morris, ed., *Encyclopedia of American History*, pp 479–80; hist rpt, Dir/Res Pers Actions, HQ CONAC, Jun 1953; msg, USAF to CONAC, subj: Curtailment of the AF Reserve Officer Recall and Direct Appointment Program, AFPMP 49602, 06/21532 Jul 1953; msg, ALMAJCOM 670/53, subj: Curtailment of Officer Recall, AFPMP-11, 162323Z Jul 1953—both in AFRES 21A.

87. Hists, ATRC, Jan 1–Jun 30, 1952, pp 105–38, and CTAF, Apr 1–Jun 30, 1952, pp 190–210. These two sources, comprising the second chapters of the two official histories, are excellent detailed, documented accounts of the crisis from the two appropriate perspectives. Also excellent as an official Air Staff discussion of the subject is the package of papers initiated by Maj. Joseph A. Connor, Jr., in March 1952 when he was Acting Chief of the Aviation Medicine Division of the Surgeon General's Office in R&R. Comment No. 1, subj: Fear of Flying and Lack of Motivation to Learn to Fly, Mar 2, 1952, 213, Box 166, RG 341, NA.

88. AFR 35–16, *Flying Status of Military Personnel*, Feb 10, 1950, [9a(3)]; TV release, HQ CTAF, Apr 12, 1952; hist, CTAF, Apr–Jun 1952, p 100.

89. Hist, CTAF, Apr–Jun 1952, p 190; ltr, Col A. M. Minton, CS, ATRC, to FTAF, subj: Suspension from Flying under Air Force Regulation 35–16, Feb 9, 1952, as doc 17 in hist, CTAF, Apr–Jun 1952.

90. AFR 35–16, [9a(6)]; ltr, Col A. M. Minton, C/S ATC [sic], to FTAF, subj: Suspension from Flying under Air Force Regulation 35–16, Feb 9, 1952, as doc 17 in hist, CTAF, Apr–Jun 52.

91. Telephone log, AFCVC, Apr 12, 1952, Twining Papers, Box 1, LOC.

92. Hist, CTAF, Apr–Jun, p 206; ltr, PR 210.49, 5th AF to Wgs, subj: Incapacitating Fear of Flying, May 4, 1952, as App 99, hist, 5th AF, Jan–Jun 1952; AFR 36–70, *Disposition of Certain Rated Officers Evolving Fear of Flying*, Feb 3, 1953.

93. *United States Air Force Statistical Digest, Fiscal Year 1951*, table 304, "USAF Reserve Personnel by Grade Sent to Active Military Service, by Category of Personnel Assignment, Nov 1950 through Jun 1951," [the table is cumulative from July 1, 1950]; ibid., *Fiscal Year 1952*, table 9, "AF Reserve Officers Sent to Active Military Service by Grade and by Category of Personnel Assignment"; ibid., table 10, "AF Reserve Airmen Sent to Active Military Service by Grade and by Category of Personnel Assignment"; ibid., *Fiscal Year 1953*, table 338, "AF Reserve Officers Sent to Active Military Service (AMS) by Grade and Category of Personnel Assignment, FY 1952"; ibid., table 339, "AF Reserve Airmen Sent to Active Military Service (AMS) by Grade and Category of Personnel Assignment, FY 1953." Including Air National Guardsmen, the figure is usually rendered as "about 186,000." The most comprehensive and official Headquarters Continental Air Command source gives the Reserve figure as 146,728 [1st ind (ltr, USAF to CONAC, subj: Disposition of Reservists, Feb 14, 1954), CONAC to USAF, May 5, 1954], a mere 45 difference. Unable to reconcile the figures more closely, I am content to cite the official Air Force statistical digest.

94. IOM, Brig Gen Herbert B. Thatcher, CONAC Dep for Ops, to VCmdr, et al., subj: Staff Visit to 437th TCW and 452d LBW, Sep 1, 1950, AFRES 21A.

95. Ltr, Maj Gen Charles T. Myers, CONAC V/Cmdr, to Cmte, subj: Investigation of Recall Program, Nov 6, 1950; rpt, HQ CONAC, "Proceedings of a Committee Appointed to Investigate the Recall Program," Dec 14, 1950—both in AFRES 21A.

96. Remarks, Gen Thomas D. White, VCSAF, State Convention, Missouri Department, ROA, Apr 30, 1954, St. Louis, Mo.

97. Alfred Goldberg, *A History of the United States Air Force, 1907–1957* (Princeton, N.J.: 1957), pp 156–57; remarks, Finletter, ARA Convention, Sep 29, 1950, Fort Worth, Tex., Vandenberg Papers, Box 36, LOC; ltr, Finletter to Joint

Notes

Secretaries, subj: Air Reserve Forces Situation, Oct 4, 1950, RG 340 60A1055, WNRC.

98. Memo, Finletter to Stuart, subj: Reserve Plans, Mar 27, 1951, RG 340, 60A1055, WNRC; memo, Finletter to John A. McCone, U/SecAF, subj: Reserve Policy, Sep 26, 1950, Vandenberg Papers, Box 36, LOC.

99. Ltr, Finletter to SSgt E. J. Hanyzewski, 437th TCW, subj: Recall of Inactive Reservists, Sep 7, 1951, RG 340 60A1055, WNRC.

100. Memo, Finletter to McCone, Sep 26, 1950; memo, McCone to Stuart, subj: Reserve Programs, Dec 11, 1950, w/atch, Vandenberg Papers, Box 36, LOC.

101. Ltr, Anna M. Rosenberg, Asst SecDef, to Sen Margaret Chase Smith, subj: Reserve Mobilization Problems, Dec 15, 1950, RG 330, Asst SecDef (MPR), Anna Rosenberg, 1951, Box 10, NA.

102. Memo, Rosenberg to John F. Floberg, Asst SecN, subj: Handling of Correspondence, May 21, 1951; ltr, Rosenberg to Elmer H. Bobst, Warner-Hudnut Inc. subj: UMT&SA, Aug 17, 1951—both in RG 330, Asst SecDef (MPR), Anna Rosenberg, 1951, Box 12, NA; ltr, Rosenberg to Eleanor Roosevelt, subj: Recall of World War II veterans, Jan 31, 1951, RG 330, Asst SecDef (MPR), Anna Rosenberg, 1951, Box 10, NA.

Chapter 5

1. Ltr, George C. Marshall, SecDef to Carl Vinson, Chmn, HASC, subj: Draft Legislation Authorizing Universal Military Training and Service, Jan 17, 1951, in *U.S. Code and Administrative Service*, 82d Cong., 1st sess., 1951, vol 2, pp 1505–08.

2. *Universal Military Training and Service Act of 1951*, Hearings before the Preparedness Subcommittee of the Committee on Armed Services, U.S. Senate, 82d Cong., 1st sess., S–1, "A Bill to Provide for the Common Defense and Security of the United States and to Permit the More Effective Utilization of Manpower Resources of the United States by Authorizing Universal Military Service and Training, and for Other Purposes," Jan 10, 1951–Feb 2, 1951 (Washington, D.C., 1951), pp 716–18; PL 82–51, *Universal Military Training and Service Act of 1951*, *U.S. Code Congressional and Administrative Service* (Stat 65: 75), 1951 p 73.

3. Legislative History, 82d Cong., 1st sess. (1951), *Universal Military Training and Service Act of 1951*, *U.S. Code Congressional and Administrative Service*, H.R. Rpt 271, vol 2, pp 1472–86.

4. Hearings, *Universal Military Training and Service Act of 1951*, cited in note 2 above.

5. *Universal Military Training*, in *Sundry Legislation Affecting the Naval and Military Establishments 1952*, Hearings before Committee on Armed Services, 82d Cong., 2d sess. (Washington, D.C., 1952).

6. For opposition to the bill proposed by the National Security Training Commission, see *Universal Military Training*, hearings cited in preceding note, pp 2293–2301, and *Cong. Rec.* vol 98, pts 1–2, 1421–25. Midwestern congressmen opposed the various proposals for universal military training on the basis of their high costs, similarity to peacetime conscription, and introduction to militarism. Southerners were opposed on the ground that no provision was ever made to protect racial segregation.

7. *Cong. Rec.*, pp 1425–1863, passim; ltr, Lt Gen Raymond S. McLain, USA (Ret), to Sen Arthur Vandenberg, subj: Universal Military Training Legislation, Dec 26, 1952—Dwight D. Eisenhower Library (hereafter, DDEL), Official Files, Box 663, 133K—UMTA Draft.

8. *Cong. Rec.*, 82d Cong., 1st sess., vol 97, pts 9–10, p 13156; Senate Committee on Armed Services, *Armed Forces Reserve Act: Hearings on H.R. 5426*, "An Act Relating to the Reserve Components of the Armed Forces of the United States," 82d Cong., 2d sess., May 26–29, 1952 (Washington, D.C.), p 1.

9. Ibid., pp 105–107, 173, 177, 238.

447

The Air Force Reserve

10. PL 476–82, *Armed Forces Reserve Act of 1952* (Jul 9, 1952); Legislative History, PL 82–476, *Armed Forces Reserve Act of 1952, U.S. Code Congressional and Administrative News*, Sen Rpt No. 1795 (Jun 19, 1952), 82d Cong., 2d sess., 1952, vol 2, pp 2005–64; PL 82–476, 82d Cong., 2d sess. (Jul 9, 1952), *Armed Forces Reserve Act of 1952*.

11. Ltr, Dwight D. Eisenhower to Robert Granville Burke, Capt, USNR, Nat Pres, ROA, subj: Eisenhower Position on Reserve Questions, Sep 1, 1952, DDEL, Ann Whitman File, Campaign, Box 6, DOD; John D. Morris, "Eisenhower Scored on '32 Bonus War,'" *New York Times*, Oct 25, 1952, "Campaign Statements of Dwight D. Eisenhower," a Reference Index at DDEL. He told an audience in Baltimore that as long as actual war made the draft necessary, the nation could not simultaneously establish a training program for people without prior service. In Decatur, Illinois, he said the nation could not pile anything else on top of Selective Service until the Korean War was over (Campaign Statements of Dwight D. Eisenhower).

12. Memo, National Security Training Commission (NSTC) to Gen Dwight D. Eisenhower, subj: National Security Training, Dec 31, 1952, AFRES 5 B5; Dwight D. Eisenhower, "Statement by the President on the National Security Training Commission and on Military Manpower Policies, July 23, 1953," *Public Papers of the Presidents of the United States: Dwight D. Eisenhower, 1953* (hereafter, Eisenhower, *Public Papers*) (Washington, D.C., 1953), pp 514–15; ltr, Dwight D. Eisenhower to Arthur S. Flemming, Dir/ODM, subj: National Manpower Needs, Aug 1, 1953; ltr, Flemming to Members of the Committee on Manpower Resources for National Security, Sep 16, 1953—both in AFRES 5 C6.

13. NSTC, *Twentieth Century Minutemen: A Report to the President on a Reserve Forces Training Program*, Dec 1953, AFRES 5 C5.

14. Ltr, NSTC to the President, subj: Summary of Findings and Recommendations in Response to the President's Request of August 1, 1953, Dec 14, 1953, AFRES 5 B13; memo, E. L. Beach for Staff Secretary, subj: National Security Training Commission Report "20th Century Minutemen: A Report to the President on a Reserve Forces Training Program," Dec 1, 1953, Box 662–133G, UMT, Official File, Jan 5, 1954, DDEL.

15. Rpt, Cmte on Manpower Resources for National Security, to the Director of the Office of Defense Mobilization, "Manpower Resources for National Security," Dec 18, 1953, AFRES 5 B12.

16. Memo, Arthur S. Flemming to the President, subj: Manpower Availability Study, Jan 6, 1954, AFRES 5 Bl2.

17. Ltr, Dwight D. Eisenhower to Flemming, subj: Strengthening Reserve Forces, Jan 8, 1954, Official Files, Box 662–133G, UMT 1954, DDEL; "Letter to Julius Ochs Adler, Chairman, National Security Training Commission, Concerning the Reserve Establishment, Jan 12, 1954," Eisenhower, *Public Papers, 1954*, p 46.

18. Memo, Arthur S. Flemming, Dir/ODM, to Gen Cutler, subj: Reserve Mobilization Requirements, May 24, 1954, w/atch, WHO, Ofc Spec Asst NSC Records, NSC 5420/3, Res Mob Rqmts, Box 11, DDEL; atch (Flemming ltr, May 24, 1954), "Reserve Mobilization Requirements," May 14, 1954, DOD.

19. Atch (Harlow memo to Carroll, Jul 26, 1954), memo, for Ex Sec NSC, subj: NSC Action 1161, Jun 17, 1954.

20. Memo, Bryce N. Harlow to General Carroll, [new reserve program], Jul 26, 1954, w/atch, Ann Whitman File, Administration, Reserve Program 1954, Box 30, DDEL; atch (memo, James S. Lay, Jr., Ex Sec NSC, to NSC, subj: Reserve Mobilization Requirements, Jul 28, 1954), memo, Brig Gen Louis H. Renfrow, Dep Dir/SSS, to Ex Sec NSC, subj: Reserve Mobilization Requirements NSC 5420/1, 26 Jul 1954 Comments and Recommendations of the Selective Service System, Jul 28, 1954, WHO Ofc Spec Asst NSC Records, NSC 5420/3, Res Mob Rqmts, Box 11, DDEL.

21. Rpt, NSC, "Reserve Mobilization Requirements," ref NSC 5420/2, Sep 20, 1954, Bryce N. Harlow records, A67–56, Res Legis (1952–55 and 1957) (4), Box 8, DDEL.

22. See, for example, "Address at the American Legion Convention, Aug 30, 1954," Eisenhower, *Public Papers, 1954*, pp 784–85.

23. Memo, Col A. J. Goodpaster, CE, USA, subj: Conference with the President, Dec 6, 1954, 11:30 A.M., Ann Whitman File, Whitman Diaries, Box 3, Dec 54(5), DDEL; L. A. Minnich, Jr., Bipartisan Leadership Meeting, Dec 14, 1954; Notes, Minnich, Legislative Leadership Meeting, Dec 13, 1954, both in Ann Whitman File, DDEL Diaries, Box 4, Staff Notes, Jan–Dec 54, DDEL.

24. Ltr, Fred A. Seaton, SecA, to Speaker of the House, subj: Submission of Draft National Reserve Plan Legislation, Dec 22, 1954; ltr, Lewis B. Hershey, Dir/SSS, to Roger W. Jones, Asst Dir/Legis Ref, Ex Ofc, BOB, subj: Draft National Reserve Plan Legislation, Jan 5, 1955; ltr, H. V. Higley, Adm/VA, to Rowland R. Hughes, Dir/Budg, same subj, Jan 5, 1955; ltr, James P. Mitchell, SecLabor, to Hughes, same subj, Jan 7, 1955—all in Official File, DOD Jan 55, Box 23, DDEL.

25. "Special Message to the Congress on National Security Requirements, January 13, 1955," Eisenhower, *Public Papers, 1955*, pp 72–78.

26. *National Reserve Plan*, Hearings before Subcmte No. 1, HASC, on *Sundry Legislation Affecting the Naval and Military Establishments 1955*, 84th Cong., 1st sess. (Washington, D.C., 1955), pp 1250–5, 1260–75.

27. Ibid., pp 2278–2492; *Cong. Rec.*, 1955, vol 101, pts 3–5, pp 3956, 5250, 6109, 6487, 6541, 6576, 6645, 6657, and 11522, and pt 7, p 9139; memo, Bryce N. Harlow to Mrs. Whitman, subj: Meeting with Generals Adler and Smith, Apr 21, 1955, Ofc of Staff Sec, WH Series, Box 1, DDEL; minutes, President Eisenhower's cabinet meeting, Apr 22, 1955, Ann Whitman File, Cabinet, DDEL.

28. "The President's News Conference of June 8, 1955," Eisenhower, *Public Papers, 1955*, pp 579–80; *Cong. Rec.*, 1955, pts 7–8, pp 9417, 9782, 9834, 10379; ltr, Robert Tripp Ross, Asst SecDef (Legis & PA), to Carl Vinson, subj: HO 7000, Jun 28, 1955, Bryce N. Harlow records, Reserve, May–Dec 55, Box 20, DDEL. For the resolution of conflicting versions, see *Cong. Rec.*, 1955, vol 101, pts 8–10, pp 10508–11, 10727, 11397, 11410–11, 11466, 11939, 13080; ltr, Rep. Overton Brooks, V/Ch HASC, to Dwight D. Eisenhower, subj: Passage of *H.R.* 7000, Jul 26, 1955, Official File, Reserve Forces Jan–Dec 55, Box 109, DDEL.

29. "Statement by the President upon Signing the *Reserve Forces Act of 1955*," Aug 9, 1955, Eisenhower, *Public Papers, 1955*, pp 775–76; PL 305, 84th Cong. (Aug 9, 1955), *Reserve Forces Act of 1955*.

30. Memo, J. F. C. Hyde to Roger W. Jones, subj: H.R. 6573, *Reserve Officers Personnel Act of 1955*, Jul 23, 1954, Official Files, Reserve Forces, Jan 53–Dec 54, Box 109, DDEL.

31. Memo, Bryce N. Harlow, to the President, subj: Reserve Promotion Legislation, Jul 27, 1954; ltr, James Douglas, U/SecAF, to persons, subj: Reserve Promotion Legislation, Jul 27, 1954, Official File, Reserve Forces, Jan 53–Dec 54, Box 109, DDEL.

32. Ltr, Dwight D. Eisenhower to Sen Leverett Saltonstall, subj: Reserve Promotion Legislation, Jul 27, 1954, Official File, Reserve Forces Jan 1953–Dec 1954, Box 109, DDEL.

33. Carlton and Slinkman, *The ROA Story*, pp 418–19.

34. Legislative History, PL 83-773, 83d Cong., 2d sess. (1954), *Reserve Officers Personnel Act of 1954*, U.S. *Code Congressional and Administrative News*, vol 3, p 3930.

35. HQ CONAC Fact Sheet, *Reserve Officers Personnel Act, Sep 1954*, AFRES 13C; PL 83-773 (Sep 3, 1954), *Reserve Officers Personnel Act of 1954*.

36. Ltr, Col L. L. Judge, Air AG, HQ USAF, to CONAC, subj: Designation of Tactical Air Command and Air Defense Command as Major Air Commands, and Reassignment, Establishment, Discontinuance and Redesignation of Certain Other Units and Establishments, Nov 10, 1950, as SD 147-1 in hist, CONAC, Jul–Dec 50; Futrell, *Ideas, Concepts, Doctrine*, p 158; hist, CONAC, Jul–Dec 50, pp 33, 46–48.

37. Legislative History, PL 604, 81st Cong., 2d sess. (1950), *Army and Air Force Authorization Act of 1949*, U.S. *Code Congressional and Administrative Service*, p 2696; PL 604 (Jul 10, 1950), *Army and Air Force Authorization Act of 1949*, U.S. *Code Congressional and Administrative Service*, p 325.

38. Legislative History, 82d Cong., 1st

The Air Force Reserve

sess. (1951), *Air Force Organization Act of 1951, U.S. Code Congressional and Administrative Service*, pp 2192–2202; PL 150–82, 82d Cong., 1st sess. (1951), *Air Force Organization Act of 1951, U.S. Code Congressional and Administrative Service*, pp 472–80.

39. Memo, Maj Gen Robert W. Burns, Asst VCS, to Deputies, Directors, and Chiefs of Comparable Offices, subj: Air Force Position Relative to Composition of the Air Reserve Forces, May 26, 1955, Twining, Box 74, LOC.

40. Hist, Spec Asst CSAF/RF, Jan–Jun 51, pp 1–2.

41. Memo, Gen Nathan F. Twining, VCS, to CSAF, subj: Reorganization of the Office, Special Assistant for Reserve Forces, Sep 7, 1951, Vandenberg Papers, Box 36, LOC; memo, Twining to Spec Asst/RF, subj: Responsibilities of the Office of the Special Assistant for Reserve Forces, Sep 7, 1951, AFRES 5A; memo, Maj Gen William F. McKee, Asst VCS, to Air Staff, subj: The Air Reserve Forces Program, Sep 7, 1951, Vandenberg Papers, Box 36, LOC; USAF HOI 11–203, "Air Staff Responsibilities Pertaining to the Reserve Forces," Nov 13, 1951; memo, Twining to DCS/Compt et al., subj: Air Staff Participation Relative to Air Force Reserve and Air National Guard Matters, Mar 13, 1951, Box 26, RG 341, NA.

42. Pamphlet, *Department of Defense Policies Relating to the Reserve Forces*, Apr 6, 1951, AFRES 11. For Air Force implementation, see AFR 45–1, *Purpose, Composition, and Organization of the United States Air Force Reserve*, Mar 24, 1950; AFR 45–1, *Purpose, Composition, and Organization of the United States Air Force Reserve*, Jul 3, 1950; AFR 45–1, *Mission, Composition, and Organization of the Air Force Reserve*, May 26, 1952; AFR 45–1, *Mission, Composition, and Organization of Reserve Components*, Jan 1, 1953.

43. "Report of the Smith Committee," [appointed to develop the long-range plan for the Reserve Forces of the United States Air Force], Jul 27, 1951; pamphlet, *Department of the Air Force Long Range Plan for the Reserve Forces of the United States Air Force*, Aug 9, 1951—both in AFRES 5B2; memo, Brig Gen Robert J. Smith to Asst SecAF Zuckert, subj: Smith Report, Jul 19, 1951, Box 214, RG 340, NA.

44. "Status and Progress of the Reserve Forces of the Air Force (1 July 1951–31 December 1951)," as atch 4 in hist, Ofc of Spec Asst RF, Jul–Dec 51.

45. Atch [memo, Lt Gen Leon W. Johnson, Ch, Reserve Program Review Board (RPRB), to CSAF, subj: Report of the Reserve Program Review Board, Aug. 24, 1953], "Report of Reserve Program Review Board, Aug 24, 1953," AFRES 5B3. For Air Force progress in implementing the recommendations, see memo, Brig Gen John P. Henebry, Ch, Air Staff Cmte on NG & Res Plcy, to Ch, RPRB, subj: Comments of the Air Staff Committee on National Guard and Reserve Policy on Preliminary Conclusions of the Reserve Program Review Board, Aug 17, 1953, AFRES 5B3; memo, Brig Gen Standford W. Gregory, SecAF ANGUS, et al., subj: Report of the 14th Meeting, Air Staff Committee on National Guard and Reserve Policy, Sep 23, 1953—SAF/MIR; summary, [unsigned], subj: Status of Reserve Program Review Board Recommendations as of 19 February 1954, AFRES 5B3.

46. Hist, Asst CSAF/RF, Jul–Dec 54, pp 9–10.

47. Memo, Gen Nathan F. Twining, CSAF, to Deputies, Directors, and Chiefs of Comparable Offices, subj: Policy Guidance to Meet Air Reserve Forces Objectives, Jan 4, 1955, Twining Papers, Box 74, LOC; ltr, Maj Gen William E. Hall, Asst CSAF/RF, to Lt Gen Leon W. Johnson, subj: Air Force Reserve Program, Jan 6, 1955, w/incl, AFRES 12A.

48. See, for example, remarks by Twining before the National Council Meeting of the ROA, Washington, D.C., Feb 5, 1955, and his statement before the House Armed Services Committee, Feb 9, 1955—both in Twining Papers, Series 4, Box 16, Folder 1, U.S. Air Force Academy Library.

49. Hist, Asst CSAF/RF, Jan–Jun 55, p 6; HQ USAF HOI 45–4, "Policy Guidance to Meet Air Reserve Forces Objectives," Apr 27, 1955, as printed in CONAC Bul No. 20, May 20, 1955, AFRES 5A; hist, CONAC, Jul–Dec 55, p 65.

50. AFM 1–2, *United States Air Force Basic Doctrine*, Apr 1, 1955; Futrell, *Ideas, Concepts, Doctrine*, p 202.

Notes

51. Semiannual Report, Air Reserve Forces Program, "The Air Force Reserve Plans & Programs, for the Period 1 July to 31 December 1955," atch to ASSS, Maj Gen William E. Hall, Asst CSAF/RF, subj: Air Reserve Forces Program, n.d. [ca. Dec 1, 1955], AFRES 21A.

52. Hist, Asst CSAF/RF, Jul–Dec 55, pp 12–13.

Chapter 6

1. ASSS, Maj Gen William E. Hall, Asst CSAF/RF, subj: Reserve Forces Training Program, Dec 1954; ltr, Hall to Lt Gen Leon W. Johnson, subj: Chief of Staff Policy Statement, Jan 6, 1955—both in AFRES 12A; hist, USAF Asst for Programming, Jul–Dec 54, pp 30–31; hist, Asst CSAF/RF, Jul–Dec 55, pp 12–13.

2. DAF Ltr 322 (AFOMO 8589) to CG CONAC, subj: Constitution, Redesignation and Activation of Units of the 94th Tactical Reconnaissance Wing and Other AFRTC Units, Jun 27, 1952, AFRES 12A; CONAC GO 38, Jun 11, 1952; hist, CONAC, Jul–Dec 54, pp 103–109; 1st ind (ltr, CONAC, Aug 5, 1995), HQ USAF, Aug 25, 1955, w/atch, Reserve Flying Wing Program, a/o Sep 19, 1955.

3. Reserve Flying Wing Program, a/o Sep 19, 1955, HQ USAF/DPL, AFRES 12A.

4. Ltr, Brig Gen R. E. Koon, Dep Dir/Ops, USAF, to CG CONAC, subj: Responsibilities for the Training of Units of the Air Reserve Forces, Mar 12, 1954, AFRES 12A; AFR 45–6, *Responsibilities for Training of Air Reserve Forces Units*, Oct 14, 1955; hist, CONAC, Jul–Dec 53, pp 192–93; CONAC Training Objective No. 57–2, Active Duty Training Objective, Calendar Year 1957, AF Reserve Troop Carrier Wings, AFRES 19C; CONAC Training Objective No. 57–1, Active Duty Training Objective, Calendar Year 1957, AF Reserve Fighter Wings, AFRES 19G.

5. MFR, Cantwell, subj: Additional Flying Training Periods, May 20, 1981; msg, USAF to CONAC, subj: Approval of 36 Additional Paid Drills for Rated Personnel, AFODP–PG 45411, 121545Z Apr 56—both in AFRES 14B; hist, Asst CSAF/RF, Jul–Dec 55, p 5; minutes, HQ CONAC, Staff Mtg No. 33, Aug 30, 1955, AFRES 22A1.

6. P. A. Finlayson, CAC staff historian, "Highlights: The Air Force Reserve in Support of the Active Establishment, 1949–1967," Mar 28, 1967, pp 11–12, AFRES 22A1; minutes, CONAC Staff Mtg No. 36, Sep 18, 1956, AFRES 22D1.

7. "Operation SWIFT LIFT," *The Air Reservist*, Sep–Oct 1950, p 5; CONAC OP 151–57, "Operation SWIFT LIFT," Feb 21, 1957; Msgs, USAF AFOOP–OS–T 31878, Nov 30, 1956; ltr, Brig Gen Emmett B. Cassady, Dir/Trnsp, AMC, to CONAC, subj: CONAC Reserve Fleet, Jul 23, 1958, AFRES 21 D2; ltr, Col Harold E. Todd, C/S CONAC, to AMC, subj: CONAC Reserve Fleet, Aug 5, 1958; CONAC Bul No. 25, Jun 19, 1959—both in AFRES 22D2.

8. Memo, Cantwell to Mrs. Mildred Brown, subj: Air Force Reserve Support of Airborne Training at Fort Benning, Georgia, Feb 22, 1971; hist, Asst CSAF/RF, Jul–Dec 1956, pp 4–7.

9. Memo, Cantwell to Brown; Msg, CONAC to 1st AF et al., subj: Air Force Reserve Troop Carrier Wings Performing Aerial Drops Missions, CNNIS 28826, 272140Z Nov 56—both in AFRES 22A1.

10. Hist, CONAC, Jan–Jun 1957, pp 167–73; ibid., Jul–Dec 1956, pp 89–90; memo, Col Harold E. Todd, Dep Asst CSAF/RF, to Dir/Ops, USAF, subj: Utilization of Air Force Reserve Units, Jul 18, 1956, RG 341, 60A1062, WNRC.

11. Hist, Asst CSAF/RF, Jan–Jun 1955, p 7; hist, CONAC, Jul–Dec 1956, p 98; ibid, Jan–Jun 1957, p 182.

12. Hist, Asst CSAF/RF, Jul–Dec 1954, p 8; hist, CONAC, Jan–Jun 1954, pp 133–34; ibid, Jan–Jun 1955, pp 121–22.

13. Hists, CONAC, Jul–Dec 1953, pp 178–83, Jan–Jun 1954, pp 117–120, Jul–Dec 1953, pp 183–184, Jul–Dec 1954, pp 120–22, Jul–Dec 1956, p 99, and Jan–Jun

451

1957, pp 183–84.
   14. Ibid., Jul–Dec 1953, p 245.
   15. Ibid., Jul–Dec 1954, pp 119–21.
   16. Ibid., Jul–Dec 1952, pp 15–17; ltr, Lt Gen Leon W. Johnson, CG CONAC, to CSAF, subj: Use of Non–Prior Service Personnel in Reserve Wings, Sep 29, 1952, w/ind, AFRES 14D.
   17. R&R sheet, Col. Frank A. Hartman, Ex Dir/Pers Plng, USAF, to Dir/Mil Pers, Dir/Tng, subj: Request for Policy, Eligibility for Enlistment in the Air Force Reserve, Sep 19, 1952, Comment No. 1, AFRES 14D.
   18. 1st ind (ltr, Johnson, Sep 29, 1952), Maj Gen Morris J. Lee, Actg Asst DCS/Pers, USAF, to CONAC, Nov 10, 1952, AFRES 14D.
   19. "CONAC Authorized 14,000 Enlistees," *The Air Reservist*, Dec 1953; hist, CONAC, Jul–Dec 1953, p 280, 193; notes, CONAC Commanders, Conference, May 25, 1953, Selfridge AFB, Mich., AFRES 12A; hist, CONAC, Jan–Jun 1953, pp 71–73; CONACR 39–10, *Enlistment of Men without Prior Service as Reserves of the Air Force for Specific Reserve Wing Assignments*, Dec 15, 1953.
   20. Hist, CONAC, Jul–Dec 1954, pp 119–20; memo, Maj Gen William E. Hall, Asst CSAF/RF, to DCS/Pers USAF, subj: Evaluation of Effects of Legislation, Jan 27, 1956, RG 341, 60A1343 AFCRF–F Mil 1–A, WNRC.
   21. Memo, Hall, Jan 27, 1956; Memo, Col R. J. Clizbe for Maj Gen Joe W. Kelly, Dir/LL, USAF, to Asst SecAF (MP&RF), subj: Air Force Position on Certain Reserve Personnel, Feb 27, 1956; memo No. 2, Maj Gen John S. Mills, Asst DCS/Pers USAF, to Asst CSAF/RF, subj: Evaluation of Effects of Legislation, Feb 21, 1956; memo No. 3, Maj Gen William E. Hall, Asst CSAF/RF, to Mills, subj: Evaluation of Effects of Legislation, Feb 29, 1956; ltr, Col W. C. Pratt for Maj Gen John S. Mills to Asst CSAF/RF, subj: Evaluation of Effects of Legislation, Mar 14, 1956—all in 60A1343 AFCRF–F Mil 1–A, RG 341, WNRC.
   22. Bill McDonald, "Reserves to Use 6-Month Trainees in Filling Combat, Support Units," *Air Force Times*, Aug 11, 1956; "The Six-Months Trainee Plan," *Air Force Times*, Aug 18, 1956; hist, CONAC, Jul–Dec 1956, pp 119–22; MFR, Lt Col D. L. Lane, Asst Ch Pers Div, Office Asst CSAF/RF, subj: Asst CSAF/RF Meeting on Six-Month Reserve Training Program, Aug 10, 1956, 60A1343, AFCRF–F Mil 1–A, RG 341, WNRC.
   23. Hist, CONAC, Jan–Jun 1957, pp 189–92; memo, David S. Smith, Asst SecAF, to Asst SecDef (MPR), subj: Reserve Personnel Program, FY 1958, Mar 18, 1957; ltr, Smith to Lt Gen Lewis B. Hershey, Dir/SSS, subj: Draft Eligible Non–Prior Service Personnel, May 1, 1957—both in 61A1674, RG 340, WNRC.
   24. Diary, CONAC, No. 124, Jul 30, 1958, AFRES 14D; hist, Asst CSAF/RF, FY 1954, p 24; AFR 33–4, *USAF Recruiting Service Assistance of Air Reserve Forces Recruiting Programs*, Aug 13, 1955; memo, Maj Gen William E. Hall, Asst CSAF/RF, to CSAF, subj: Status of Reserve Forces, Apr 7, 1955, Twining Papers, Box 74, LOC; hist, CONAC, Jul–Dec 1954, p 75.
   25. Hist, CONAC, Jan–Jun 1953, pp 107–09.
   26. Ibid., Jan–Jun 1955, pp 93–96.
   27. Ibid., Jul–Dec 1954, pp 116–18.
   28. Ibid.; AFR 45–30, *Selective Assignment of Obligated Reservists*, Feb 24, 1956; CONAC Bul No. 51, Dec 23, 1955—both in AFRES 14AG.
   29. Hist, Asst CSAF/RF, Jan–Jun 1955, p 11; hist, CONAC, Jan–Jun 1955, pp 53–55.
   30. Ltr, Lt Gen Leon W. Johnson, Cmdr CONAC, to Maj Gen Roger J. Brown, Cmdr 1st AF, et al., subj: Assignment of Officers Electing Affiliation, Jun 6, 1955, AFRES 14B.
   31. For the background leading to the establishment of the Air Reserve Records Center, see Gerald T. Cantwell, "Evolution of ARPC, 1953–1970," 1978, AFRES 35F.
   32. Ltr, Col Neal J. O'Brien, Air AG CONAC, to 1st AF, subj: Establishment of an AFRES Master Personnel Records Center, Dec 12, 1951, AFRES 35F; hist, CONAC, Jul–Dec 1953, pp 117–26; ltr, Hall to General McCormick subj: Establishment of Records Center, May 21, 1953, as doc 75–4 in hist, CONAC, Jul–Dec 1953; memo, for Commander, Lt Col R. F. Wisniewski, Dir/Res Pers CONAC, subj: Coordination of Staff Study, Sep 16, 1953, as doc 72–1

Notes

in hist, CONAC, Jul–Dec 1953.

33. Ltr, Col John C. Henley, DCS/Pers CONAC, to 1st AF et al., subj: Continental Air Command Air Reserve Records Center, Dec 1, 1953, AFRES 35F; CONAC GO 56, Oct 27, 1953.

34. For a more detailed account of the background and evolution of the air reserve technician program, see the monograph by Gerald T. Cantwell and Victor B. Summers, *The Air Reserve Technician Program: Its Antecedents and Evolution (1948–1978)*, Robins AFB, 1979.

35. AFL 45–11, *Manning of Air Force Reserve Training Centers*, May 9, 1949; AFR 45–22, *Voluntary Call to Extended Active Duty of Enlisted Personnel,* May 9, 1949. For an evaluation of the program's benefits, see Ltr, Maj Gen A. C. Kincaid, CG OAF, to CG CONAC, subj: Category R Program, Jan 11, 1950, AFRES 14C1.

36. Ltr, Maj B. Fidlow, Asst Adj Gen 12th AF, to CONAC, subj: Category R Program, Jan 11, 1950, AFRES 14C1.

37. Ltr, Lt Gen Ennis C. Whitehead, CG CONAC, to CSAF, subj: The USAF Reserve Forces, Dec 13, 1950, AFRES 21A.

38. Ltr, Col L. M. Guyer, CS CONAC, to Dir/Civ Pers USAF, subj: Air Reserve Technician Plan, Aug 18, 1954, w/incl, AFRES 14C2.

39. Disposition Form (DF), DCS/Plans CONAC, to Dir/Civ Pers, subj: DOD Conference on ART Plan, Oct 20, 1955; minutes, HQ CONAC, Staff Mtg 42–1, Nov 1, 1955, as doc 91–3; memo, Jack Pockrass, Ch, Placement & Employee Relations Div, Dir/Civ Pers USAF, to Dir/Civ Pers, subj: The Air Reserve Technician Plan, Jan 17, 1955; memo, John A. Watts, Dir/Civ Pers USAF, to DCS/Pers, subj: The Air Reserve Technician Plan, Jan 25, 1955; memo, Pockrass to Dir/Civ Pers, subj: Air Reserve Technician Plan, Apr 20, 1955; MFR, Pockrass, subj: Follow-up on Status of ART Plan, May 20, 1955; MFR, Pockrass, subj: Status of Air Reserve Technician Plan, Sep 28, 1955—all in RG 341 60A1145, WNRC; hist, CONAC, Jan–Jun 1956, sec 2.

40. Ltr, Carter L. Burgess, Asst SecDef (MPR), to Donald A. Quarles, SecAF, subj: Air Force Implementation of Six-month Reserve Programs, Mar 28, 1956, RG 330 62A1751 Box 7, WNRC.

41. Memo, Quarles, to Asst SecDef (MPR), subj: Manning of Air Force Reserve Units, Aug 14, 1956, Box 7, RG 330 62A1751, WNRC.

42. Memo, Carter L. Burgess to SecDef (MPR), subj: Status of Air Reserve Technician Plan, Apr 18, 1956; memo, Charles E. Wilson, SecDef, to SecAF, subj: The Air Reserve Technician Plan, Jun 21, 1956; "Chronology of Air Reserve Technician Plan," unsigned, n.d. [ca. late 1960]—both in RG 340 60A1283, WNRC.

43. Memo, John A. Watts, Dir/Civ Pers, to Dir/Pers Plng, USAF, subj: The Air Reserve Technician Plan, Jul 6, 1956; MFR, Donald J. Strait, Asst SecAF, subj: Air Reserve Technician Plan, Jul 12, 1956; memo, James P. Goode, Dep for Manpower, Pers & Org, USAF, to Smith, subj: Air Reserve Technician Plan, July 25, 1956; memo, Strait to Smith, subj: Air Technician Plan, Dec 7, 1956—all in RG 340 60A1283, WNRC; ltr, Maj Gen William S. Stone, Actg DCS/Pers, USAF, to CONAC, subj: Unilateral Implementation of the Air Reserve Technician Plan, Dec 3, 1956, w/incl, AFRES 14C2.

44. Stone ltr, Dec 3, 1956; ltr, Col John C. McCurnin, Asst DCS/Pers, CONAC, to CS et al., subj: Air Reserve Technician Plan, Jan 25, 1957, w/incl, AFRES 14C2.

45. ASSS, Watts, subj: Air Reserve Technician Plan, Jan 25, 1957, w/incl; ltr, Smith to Young subj: Air Reserve Technician Plan, Jan 29, 1957—both in AFRES 14C2.

46. Ltr, Ellsworth to Smith subj: Air Reserve Technician Plan, Jun 25, 1957, AFRES 14C2.

47. Msg, AFPDC 47324, USAF to CONAC, subj: Air Reserve Technician Plan, Jul 5, 1957; ltr, Lt Gen William E. Hall, Cmdr, CONAC, to CSAF, subj: Implementation of the Air Reserve Technician Plan, Jul 25, 1957; ltr, Gen Curtis E. LeMay, VCS, to CONAC, subj: Implementation of the Air Reserve Technician Plan, Aug 13, 1957—all in AFRES 14C12; hist, CONAC, Jul–Dec 57, pp 187–90.

48. The status quo phenomenon is discussed extensively in hist, AFRES, FY 1975, p 199, and in Cantwell and Summers, *Air Reserve Technician Program*, pp 25–29.

453

The Air Force Reserve

49. See, for example, rpt, Defense Manpower Commission, *Defense Manpower: The Keystone of National Security* (Washington, D.C., 1976), p 127, and *The Report on Full-Time Training and Administration of the Selected Reserve* (Washington, D.C., 1978), p 4–47. For the rebuttal, see Rand rpt R–1977/1-1-AF, pp 24–25, and Col James C. Wahleithner, "Economic Considerations of the Technician Program," Feb 1979, extracted as app 4 in Cantwell and Summers, *Air Reserve Technician Program.*

50. Ltr, Brig Gen James B. Burwell, CONAC DCS/O, to Col Lloyd E. Arnold, Ofc of Asst CSAF/RF, subj: Reserve Facilities, Oct 7, 1953, hist, CONAC, Jul–Dec 1953; hist, Asst CSAF/RF, FY 1954, pp 28–29.

51. Ltr, Lt Gen Leon W. Johnson, cmdr CONAC, to CSAF, subj: Facilities for Reserve Units, May 14, 1953; hist, CONAC, Jul–Dec 1953.

52. Ltr, CONAC to USAF, subj: CONAC Position on Implementation of Reserve Program Review Board Recommendations 3, 6, 7, 8, 12, and 16, Sep 28, 1953, doc 5–2, hist, CONAC, Jul–Dec 53.

53. Hist, CONAC, Jul–Dec 53, pp 180–81, 187–88; hist, Asst CSAF/RF, FY 1954, pp 28–29; *The Air Reserve Forces Plans and Programs, 1 Jul–31 December 1955*, p 43; memo, Maj Gen William E. Hall, Asst CSAF/RF, to Brig Gen Thomas C. Musgrave, Jr., Ch, Spec Staff Gp, USAF, subj: Preparation for the Symington Investigation, Apr 5, 1956, w/3 incls, RG 341, 60A1343-AFCRF-F Mil 1-A, WNRC.

54. Memo, Gen Nathan F. Twining, CSAF, to Deputies, Directors, and Chiefs of Comparable Office, subj: Policy Guidance Concerning the Provision of Facilities for the Air Reserve, Feb 12, 1957, RG 341, 61 A1367, WNRC.

55. Ltr, Lt Gen Charles B. Stone III, Cmdr CONAC, to Gen Thomas D. White, CSAF, subj: Unit Precedence Categories, Jun 17, 1957, AFRES 12B.

56. Memo, Maj Gen Richard C. Lindsay, Dir/Plans USAF, to DCS/Compt et al., subj: Proposed Reduction of the Ready Reserve Forces, Jul 20, 1956, RG 341, 61A1367, WNRC.

57. Ltr, Lt Gen Charles B. Stone III, Cmdr CONAC, to DO, USAF, subj: Redesignation of Reserve Forces Tactical Bomb Wings, Aug 16, 1956, RG 341, 60A1062, WNRC.

58. ASSS, Maj Gen Kenneth P. Bergquist, Dir/Ops USAF, subj: Revised Reserve Unit Program (Operation ROOF TOP), Oct 23, 1956; ltr, Stone to Lt Gen Frank F. Everest, DCS/O, USAF, subj: Redesignation of Fighter Bomber Units, Oct 31, 1956; msg, ADC to CSAF, subj: Conversion of Reserve Fighter Bomber Units, ADOOP-A 48646, 082204Z Nov 56; memo, Maj Gen Gordon A. Blake, Ass DCS/O, USAF, subj: Revised Reserve Unit Program, Nov 16, 1956, w/3 incls; ltr, Gen Thomas D. White, VCS, to Cmdr CONAC, subj: Revised Reserve Unit Program (Operation ROOF TOP), Nov 19, 1956—all in RG 341, 60A1062, WNRC.

59. Hist, CONAC, Jan–Jun 1957, pp 119–22; ltr, Lt Col N. H. Holbrook, Asst AG TAC, to ADC, subj: Reassignment of Mission of Air Force Reserve Fighter Bomber Wings, Dec 21, 1956, AFRES 19G.

60. Hist, CONAC, Jan–Jun 1957, pp 119–22.

61. Memo, Gen Thomas D. White, CSAF, to DCS/Plans, subj: Air Reserve Forces, Aug 9, 1957, White Collection, LOC.

62. Ltr, Lt Gen William E. Hall, Cmdr CONAC, to Gen Jacob E. Smart, Asst VCS, subj: USAF Manpower Reductions, Sep 9, 1957, AFRES 12B.

63. Ltr, Brig Gen Jack N. Donohew, Dep Dir/Progs, USAF, to CONAC, subj: Air Force Reserve Program, n.d. [ca. Oct 29, 1957], w/3 incls, AFRES 12B.

64. Ltr (AFOMO–641k), DAF to CONAC, subj: Inactivation of the Headquarters, 375th Troop Carrier Wing, Medium, and Inactivation, Activation, and Reorganization of Certain Other Air Force Reserve Units, Dec 13, 1957; msg (AFOMO–M-1 35900), USAF to CONAC, subj: Inactivation of Certain Air Force Reserve Units, Oct 24, 1957; msg (AFOOP–OP–U2 32165), USAF to CONAC, subj: Movement of Air Force Reserve Units, Oct 14, 1957; msg (CNTPL 16184), Col T. L. Mosely, DCS/Plans & Prog, CONAC, to 1st AF et al., subj: Revised Air Force Reserve Program, Oct 3, 1957; msg (CNOMO

16189), Col Donald W. Johnson, Dir/M&O CONAC, to USAF, subj: Air Force Reserve Flying Wing Program, Oct 3, 1957—all in AFRES 12B; hist, Asst CSAF/RF, Jan–Jun 1959, p 32.

As they came back into the program in 1952 and 1953 after the Korean War, the Air Force Reserve units were configured in a wing-group-squadron alignment. In 1958, however, concurrently with implementation of the air reserve technician program, the Tactical Air Command and the Continental Air Command agreed to realign the reserve unit structure in the image of the active force. The reorganization consisted of abolishing the combat and M&S groups and concentrating most maintenance spaces in a consolidated aircraft maintenance squadron (along with the combat squadron, the tactical hospital, and the air group) that directly to wing headquarters. Inactivation of the combat groups was completed on April 14, 1959.

After the Berlin and Cuban crisis mobilizations, the Tactical Air Command decided it required more flexibility in the mobilization of individual elements of its wings. In January and February 1963, therefore, each wing was dismantled into self-supporting reserve groups with the wing headquarters designed as a plans, policy, and command agency. The tactical hospitals, air base and consolidation maintenance groups, air police, civil engineering, operations, support, and transportation squadrons were discontinued while troop carrier groups, combat support squadrons, materiel squadrons, and either tactical hospitals or tactical dispensaries were activated.

In 1974–75, reflecting active force practice, the Air Force Reserve unit structure evolved into a wing-squadron alignment except at the detached squadron locations where combat groups were retained. Gerald T. Cantwell, "Evolution of the Air Force Reserve Unit Structure," Feb 24, 1976, AFRES 19I.

Chapter 7

1. Ltr, Gen Curtis E. LeMay, VCSAF, to CSAF, subj: Plan for the Revised Management of the Air Reserve Forces, May 17, 1960, w/3 atchs, RG 341 63A1790, WNRC.

2. Hist, CONAC, Jul–Dec 59, p 5; memo, Malcolm A. McIntyre, U/SecAF, to CSAF, subj: AF Reserve Manpower Ceiling, Jun 1, 1959, as cited in George F. Lemmer, *The Changing Character of Air Force Manpower* (Washington, D.C., 1961), pp 47–58; intvw, with Maj Gen Robert E. L. Eaton, Oct 17, 1961, K239.0512–765, AFRES; memo, Maj Gen Richard A. Grussendorf, Asst CSAF/RF, to CSAF, subj: AFA ad Hoc Committee (Steve Leo) on Amalgamating Air Reserve Flying Units into a Single Air National Guard Organization, Mar 10, 1958, AFRES 12B; msg, ALMAJCOM 71718, Sep 9, 1959; ltr, USAF to Majcoms, subj: Program Impacts—FY 1961 Minimum Essential USAF Budget, Sep 11, 1959.

3. "Outlook: The Air Force Team," *The Air Reservist*, Oct–Nov 59, p 4; hist, CONAC, Jul–Dec 59, pp 9–10.

4. DAF SO E–2025, Oct 1, 1959; rpt, Reserve Forces Review Group, "The Air Reserve Forces . . . New Roles in a New Era," Nov 1959, pp 6–14, 40–41, 50–52, AFRES 5B7.

5. See note 4 above.

6. Ltr, AFC 13/5a, Gen Curtis E. LeMay, Chm AFC, to CSAF, subj: Concept and Objective Force, Air Reserve Forces, Jan 7, 1960, w/4 atchs, RG 341, 63A1790, WNRC.

7. Memo, Maj Gen Lloyd P. Hopwood, Ch, to SecAF, subj: Recommendations—Special Meeting of the Air Reserve Forces Policy Committee, 25–26–27 January 1960, Feb 1, 1960, AFRES 5D2.

8. Intvw, Arthur K. Marmor with Dudley C. Sharp, May 29, 1961 [Sharp was Secretary of the Air Force, Dec 11, 1959–Jan 20, 1961), K239.0512–790, AFHRC.

9. Memo, Sharp to ARFPC, subj: Reserve Forces Policy Committee: Recommendation 60–1–2 Plan for the Future Development, Employment and Manage-

The Air Force Reserve

ment of the Reserve Forces, Feb 2, 1960, AFRES 5D2; decision (AFC 13/5a), to Asst CSAF/RF, subj: Concept and Objective Force, Air Reserve Forces, Feb 4, 1960, w/3 atchs; ltr, AFC 13/5a, Maj Gen R. M. Montgomery, Asst VCSAF, to Asst CSAF/RF, subj: Concept and Objective Force, Air Reserve Forces, Feb 4, 1960, w/3 atchs—both in RG 341 63A 1790, WNRC.

10. Ltr, LeMay to CSAF, subj: Plan for the Revised Management of the Air Reserve Forces, May 17, 1960, w/3 atchs, RG 341 63A 1790, WNRC; rpt, DAF, "Plan for Revised Management of the Air Reserve Forces," May 20, 1960, AFRES 5C3.

11. AFR 45-6, *Responsibilities for Training Air Reserve Forces Units*, Nov 28, 1960.

12. Sen Thomas D. White, "New Accent on the Air Reserve Forces," *Air Force Magazine*, Jul 1960, p 103.

13. Atch (ltr, Col Alexander Sheridan, Dir/Plans, CONAC, to CONAC staff, subj: Resume of Air Force Objectives, Sep 15, 1961, w/atch) Resume of Air Force Objectives for the Air Reserve Forces, Period 1965–1975, Sep 15, 1961, AFRES 6B.

14. Theodore C. Sorensen, *Kennedy* (New York, 1966), pp 657–58; Morris, ed., *Encyclopedia of American History*, p 493.

15. MFR, Bryce N. Harlow, subj: Berlin Crisis, Mar 26, 1959, Ofc of Staff Sec, WH Series, Box 1, DDEL.

16. For Kennedy's campaign pronouncements, see Ltr, Richard Goodwin to Senator Kennedy, subj: Campaign Promises, Nov 23, 1960, w/atch, President's Ofc Files, Special Correspondence, Richard Goodwin, Nov 11, 1960–Aug 8, 1962, Box 30, John F. Kennedy Library, Dorchester, Mass. (hereafter, JFKL), and campaign speech, John F. Kennedy, Sep 6, 1960, Seattle, Washington; Pre-Presidential Press Secretary's Speech Statement File, Speeches by Date, Sep 6–8, 1960, Box 1057, JFKL. For his defense policy as detailed to Congress, see "Special Message to the Congress on the Defense Budget," Mar 28, 1961, in *Public Papers of the Presidents of the United States: John F. Kennedy, 1961* (hereafter, Kennedy, *Public Papers*), pp 229–40.

17. "Report of Senator Kennedy's National Security Policy Committee," n.d. [ca. Nov 1960], Gilpatric Papers, Box 8, JFKL; intvw, Dennis J. O'Brien with Roswell L. Gilpatric, Dep SecDef, May 5, 27 and Jun 30, 1970, transcript, JFKL; "Record of Actions by NSC at its 475th Meeting," Feb 1, 1961, Mtgs & Memo Series, NSC MTG No. 475, 2/11/61, Box 313, JFKL; memo, Robert S. McNamara, SecDef, to Secs Mil Depts et al., subj: List of Projects for Assignment, Mar 1, 1961, w/atch, Pres Ofc Files, Depts & Agencies, DOD, 1/61–3/61, Box 77, JFKL.

18. "Special Message to the Congress on Urgent National Needs," May 25, 1961, Kennedy, *Public Papers, 1961*, p 401.

19. Arthur M. Schlesinger, *A Thousand Days* (Boston Mass., 1965), pp 372–74. In the memoir papers, translated and edited by Strobe Talbott, Khrushchev said that his blustering was misunderstood by the inexperienced Kennedy, who took him too seriously and overreacted. Strobe Talbott, trans. and ed., *Khrushchev Remembers* (New York, 1966), pp 454–55.

20. Memo, McGeorge Bundy to SecDef, subj: Question of Mobilization for Berlin, Jul 10, 1961, Nat Sec Files, Depts & Agencies, DOD (B), vol 1, General, 1961, Box 276, JFKL; Record of Actions by NSC at its 487th Mtg, Jul 13, 1961, NSC mtgs, 1961, No. 487 7/13/61, Mtgs & Memo Series, Box 313, JFKL; memo, McGeorge Bundy, subj: Discussion in the National Security Council on July 13, 1961, Jul 24, 1961, Nat Sec Files, McBundy, Countries, Germany-Berlin 7/23/61–7/26/61, Box 82, JFKL; memo, Theodore C. Sorensen to Kennedy, subj: The Decision on Berlin, Jul 17, 1961, Pres Ofc Files, Countries, Germany General–7/61, Box 116a, JFKL; "Special Message to the Congress on Urgent National Needs, May 25, 1961, Kennedy, *Public Papers, 1961*, p 401.

21. Suggested comments, mtg with JCS, subj: Seen by Bundy & JJE, Jul 18, 1961, Nat Sec Files, Depts & Agencies, DOD, 6/61–7/61, Box 273, JFKL; memo, Henry A. Kissinger to McGeorge Bundy, subj: Some Observations Regarding the Call-Up of Reserves, Jul 15, 1961, Nat Sec Files, Depts & Agencies, DOD, 6/61–7/61, Box 273, JFKL.

22. Draft Record of Action, NSC Mtg, Jul 19, 1961, Nat Sec Files, NSC Mtgs, 1961, Mtgs & Memo Series, Box 313,

JFKL; memo, Maxwell D. Taylor to President, subj: Military Response to Berlin Crisis, Jul 19, 1961, Nat Sec Files, Staff memo—Maxwell Taylor, 1/61–8/61, Mtgs & Memo Series, Box 326-7, JFKL; National Security Action Memorandum (NSAM) 62, McGeorge Bundy to SecState et al., subj: Berlin, Jul 24, 1961, Nat Sec Files, NSAM 62 Berlin, Mtgs & Memo Series, Box 330, JFKL; intvw, Carl Keysen with Theodore C. Sorensen, Mar 26, Apr 6, 1964, JFKL.

23. Intvw, Chester Clifton with Gen Earle E. Wheeler, Ch, JCS, 1964, pp 8–13, JFKL.

24. "Radio and Television Report to the American People on the Berlin Crisis," Jul 25, 1961, Kennedy, *Public Papers, 1961*, pp 533–40. For the Kennedy administration's strategy of flexible response, see "Annual Message to the Congress on the State of the Union," Jan 11, 1962, Kennedy, *Public Papers, 1962*, pp 5–15, and Thomas D. White, "The McNamara Strategy by William W. Kaufman, New York, Harper & Row, 1964," *Kansas Law Review*, vol 13, 1965.

25. Rpt, "The Defense Department Recommended Program Force Increases and Related Actions," Jul 31, 1961, Nat Sec Files, Germany/Berlin, 7/28/61–7/31/61, Box 82, JFKL; memo, McNamara to President, subj: Actions to Implement Jul 19 Decisions, Aug 9, 1961, Nat Sec Files, Germany/Berlin, 7/28/61–7/31/61, Box 82, JFKL.

26. White House Legislative Notes No. 129, Jul 26, 1961, Pres Ofc Files, Legis Files 7/61, Box 49, JFKL; PL 87–117 (Stat 75: 242).

27. EO 10957, John F. Kennedy, Aug 15, 1961; Sorensen, *Kennedy*, p 668. In the Talbott edition of his memoirs, Khrushchev treated the continuum of pronouncements and related actions on Berlin from 1958 to 1961 as a single crisis, applied the euphemism "border control" to the Wall throughout, and acknowledged the U.S. involvement only once, in connection with the movement of 1,500 troops into Berlin by the autobohn after the Wall went up. Talbott, *Khrushchev Remembers*, pp 454–60. For a journalist's eyewitness account of the appearance of the wall, see Norman Gelb, *Kennedy, Khrushchev, and a Showdown in the Heart of Europe* (New York, 1986).

28. Memo, John F. Kennedy to SecDef, subj: Weekend's Occurrences in Berlin, Aug 14, 1961; memo, Kennedy to SecDef, subj: Call-Up of Reserve Forces, Aug 14, 1961—both in Nat Sec Files, Depts & Agencies, DOD, 8/61, Box 273, JFKL; memo, John F. Kennedy to SecState, subj: Berlin Political Planning, Aug 21, 1961, Nat Sec Files, Bundy, Countries, Germany/Berlin, General 8/21/61, Box 82, JFKL.

29. Memo, McNamara to President, subj: Authority Order to Active Duty Units of Reserve Components of the Army, Navy, and Air Force, Aug 21, 1961, w/atch, approved by John F. Kennedy, Aug 25, 1961, Nat Sec Files, Depts & Agencies, DOD, 8/61, Box 273, JFKL; NSAM 92, Kennedy to McNamara, subj: Questions on European Expansion, Sep 8, 1961, Nat Sec Files, McGeorge Bundy papers, Countries, Germany/Berlin, Box 82, JFKL.

30. Msg, AFPMP 98361, USAF to CONAC et al., subj: Ordering Units to Active Military Service, Aug 25, 1961, AFRES 21C.

31. TAC SO G-34, Sep 1, 1961; historical fact sheet, HQ AFRES, "Air Force Reserve Mobilization Data," Jul 1978. For a detailed treatment of the mobilization of Air Force Reserve units and individuals in 1961, see Cantwell, *Evolution and Employment of the Air Force Reserve as a Mobilization Force*, pp 127–46.

32. For the C-124 conversion and the accelerated preparation of the units for mobilization, see Cantwell, *Evolution and Employment of the Air Force Reserve as a Mobilization Force*.

33. Hist, 442 TCW, 1 Oct 61–27 Oct 62, pp 1–20; hist, 435 TCW, 1 Oct 61–27 Oct 62, pp 1–31.

34. Memo, John F. Kennedy to SecDef, subj: Budgetary Considerations for Army, Jan 22, 1962, Nat Sec Files, Depts & Agencies, DOD, 1/62–3/63, Box 274, JFKL.

35. "The President's News Conference of March 21, 1962," in Kennedy, *Public Papers, 1962*, p 259.

36. "Statement by the President on the Release of National Guard and Reserve Units," Apr 11, 1962, Kennedy, *Public Papers, 1962*, pp 322–23; memo, Benjamin W. Fridge, Spec Asst (MPRF) to Asst

SecDef (M), subj: Post-Berlin Separation, Release, and Retirement Personnel Actions, Jun 5, 1962; memo, Zuckert to CSAF, subj: Recognition of Recalled Reservists, May 23, 1962—both in RG 340 67A5143, WNRC.

37. Ltr, John F. Kennedy to Officers & Airmen, 442 TCW, subj: Return to Civilian Life, Jul 17, 1962, Pres Ofc Files, Depts & Agencies, Air Force, 7/62–12/62, Box 69A, JFKL.

38. Statement, Maj Gen Chester E. McCarty, Asst CSAF RF, before House Armed Services Cmte, n.d. [ca. Apr 16, 1962], AFRES 21C.

39. Hist, CONAC, Jul–Dec 61, 3, p 280; msg, OI 162, Capt John T. Rademacher, Dir/Pub Inf CONAC, to 301 AFRR et al., subj: USAF Answer to Query, Oct 23, 1961; msg, 008–F–10–153, Lt Col Joseph C. Ware, Jr., Dir/Ops CONAC, to 301 ARS et al., Authorization to Recruit Volunteers for Active Duty, Oct 24, 1961; msg, OI 179, Maj Philip J. Mahar, Dir/Inf/Motivation, CONAC, to 3 AFRR et al., subj: Release of Volunteers, Nov 9, 1961; hist, 302 ARS, Jul–Dec 61, pp 57–60.

40. PL 87–117 (Stat 75: 242).

41. Hist, CONAC, Jul–Dec 61, 3, pp 3–4; "Reservist Lawyer . . . Says Recall Illegal," *Air Force Times*, Apr 14, 1962.

42. Hist, CONAC, Jul–Dec 61, vol 3, p 4; "EM Loses 'Illegal' Recall Plea," *Air Force Times*, Apr 28, 1962.

43. Ltr, Benjamin W. Fridge, Spec Asst (MPRF), to Rep Samuel L. Divine, subj: Air Force Procedures for Recall of Reservists, Jan 10, 1962, 340 66A3410, WNRC.

44. Rpt, Subcommittee No. 3 on Military Reserve Posture, "Military Reserve Posture," HASC, H.R., 87th Cong., 21st sess., Aug 17, 1962, p 6660.

45. Ibid.

46. Cantwell, *Evolution and Employment of the Air Force Reserve as a Mobilization Force*, p 146.

47. Sorenson, *Kennedy*, pp 676–77.

48. For general background, see Morris, ed., *Encyclopedia of American History*, pp 489–90; for the perspective of the Eisenhower administration, see Stephen E. Ambrose, *Nixon: The Education of a Politician, 1913–1962*, pp 550, 570, 590–92; and for President Eisenhower's remarks on breaking with Cuba, see "Statement by the President on Terminating Diplomatic Relations with Cuba," Jan 3, 1961, Eisenhower, *Public Papers, 1961*, p 891.

49. Sorenson, *Kennedy*, pp 757–66.

50. "The President's News Conference of September 13, 1962," Kennedy, *Public Papers, 1962*, pp 674–81.

51. "Letter to the President of the Senate and to the Speaker of the House Transmitting Bill Authorizing Mobilization of the Ready Reserve," Sep 7, 1962, Kennedy, *Public Papers, 1962*, p 665; PL 7–736, *Joint Resolution to Authorize the President to Order Units and Members in the Ready Reserve to Active Duty for not More Than Twelve Months, and for Other Purposes* (Stat 76: 710).

52. Legislative History, PL 87–736; White House Legislative Highlights, Sep 19, 1962, Pres Ofc Files, Legis Files 9/19/62, Box 52, JFKL; PL 733, 87th Cong. (Oct 3, 1962), *Expressing the Determination of the United States with Respect to the Situation in Cuba*.

53. NSC Records of Actions, John F. Kennedy, Nos. 505, 506—both in Nat Sec Files, NSC Mtgs, 1962, 10/20/62, Mtgs & Memo Series, Box 313, JFKL; NSM 196, subj: Establishment of an Executive Committee of the National Security Council, Oct 22, 1962, Nat Sec Files, ExCom Mtgs 1–5, 10/23/62–10/25/62, Mtgs & Memo Series, Box 315, JFKL; Robert S. McNamara, "Notes on Oct 21, 1962, Mtg w/the President," Nat Sec Files, NSC Mtgs, 1962, No. 506, 10/21/62, Mtgs & Memo Series, Box 313, JFKL.

54. "Radio and Television Report to the American People on the Soviet Arms Buildup in Cuba," Oct 22, 1962, Kennedy, *Public Papers, 1962*, pp 806–09.

55. Proclamation, John F. Kennedy (No. 3504), subj: Interdiction of the Delivery of Offensive Weapons to Cuba, Oct 25, 1962; EO 11058, John F. Kennedy, "Assigning Authority with Respect to Ordering Persons and Units in the Ready Reserve to Active Duty and with Respect to Extension of Enlistment and Other Periods of Service in the Armed Forces," Oct 25, 1962.

56. Ltr, Maj Wesley C. Brashear, Ch, Ex & Abn Br, CONAC, to Lt Col Spencer, OOP-C, subj: TAC Airlift Request, Nov 7, 1962, AFRES 21D. For detailed treatment of the Air Force Reserve in the Cuban

missile crisis, see Cantwell, *Evolution and Employment of the Air Force Reserve as a Mobilization Force*, pp 147–84.

57. Schlesinger, *Thousand Days*, p 799; atch (memo, McGeorge Bundy to Robert Manning, Asst SecState [PA], subj: Sieverts History of Cuban Missile Crisis, Sep 1, 1963); draft hist, Frank A Sieverts, Spec Asst to SecState for Pub Affairs, "The Cuban Crisis, 1962," Nat Sec Files, McBundy Countries, Cuba Subjects, History of the Cuban Crisis, pp 1–52, Box 49, JFKL.

58. Ltr, Col John O. Hall, CONAC DCS/O, to USAF/OOP–PC, subj: CONAC Activities in Support of Cuban Operations, Feb 1963, AFRES 21D.

59. Msg, OOP–C 10–133, Col John O. Hall, CONAC DCS/O, to TCWs, subj: Requirement to Maintain a Command Post, Oct 23, 1962.

60. Memo, McGeorge Bundy to Robert Manning, Asst SecState (PA), subj: Sieverts History, Sep 1, 1963.

61. Summary Record, NSC ExCom Mtg No. 8, Oct 27, 1962, 4:00 P.M.; Record of Action, NSC ExCom, Mtg No. 9, Oct 27, 1962, 9:00 P.M.—both in Nat Sec Files, Mtgs & Memo Series, ExCom Mtgs 6–10, 110/26/62–10/28/62, Box 316, JFKL; memo, Robert S. McNamara to SecAF, subj: Delegation of Authority, Oct 27, 1962, RG 340 67A5143, WNRC.

62. Robert F. Kennedy, *Thirteen Days* (New York, 1969), p 109.

63. Hist 512 TCW, Jul–Dec 62, p 8.

64. Hist 440 TCW, Jul–Dec 62, p 35.

65. See note 56 above; IOM, Col Louis C. Adams, Jr., Dir/Ops, to Cmdr, subj: Command Participation in Cuban Event, Nov 28, 1962; chronol, HQ CONAC, "The Continental Air Command and the Cuban Crisis, 12 October 1962–30 November 1962," Dec 1962; msg, OOP–CP 331, CONAC to Rgns, subj: Ordering of Reserve Units to Active Duty, Oct 28, 1962—all in AFRES 21D.

66. Msg, AFOOP–CP–ATA 93478, USAF to TAC et al., subj: Order of Units to Active Duty, Oct 28, 1962, AFRES 21; TAC SO G–153, Oct 28 1962.

67. Msg, DPLMO 115047, TAC to 18 APS et al., subj: Additional Aerial Port Detachments Ordered to Active Duty, Nov 3, 1962, AFRES 21D.

68. CONAC Operation Recall Synopsis, Nov 1, 1962, AFRES 21D.

69. Summary Record, Bromley Smith, NSC ExCom Mtg No. 10, Oct 28, 1962, 11:10 A.M.; Record of Actions, McGeorge Bundy, NSC ExCom Mtg No. 11, Oct 29, 1962, 10:00 A.M.; Summary Record, Bromley Smith, NSC ExCom Mtg No. 24, Nov 12, 1962, 11:00 A.M.—all in Nat Sec Files, ExCom Mtgs, 17–24, 11/2/62–11/12/62, Mtgs & Memo Series, Box 316, JFKL.

70. Summary Record, McGeorge Bundy, NSC ExCom Mtg No. 28, Nov 20, 1962, 3:30 P.M., Nat Sec Files, ExCom Mtgs 25–32A, 11/12/62–12/4/62, Mtgs & Memo Series, Box 316, JFKL; "The President's News Conference of November 20, 1962," Kennedy, *Public Papers, 1962*, pp 830–38.

71. Msg, AFOOP, TA PC 97177, USAF to TAC, subj: Separation of Reserve Forces Units and Personnel Ordered to Extended Active Duty under PL 87–736, Oct 3, 1962; msg, AFPMP 97209, USAF to TAC et al., subj: Separation of Reservists Ordered to EAD under PL 87–736, Nov 22, 1962; Ltr (AFOMO–940m), to TAC and CONAC, subj: Reassignment of the Headquarters, 94th Troop Carrier Wing, Medium, and Certain Other Air Force Reserve Units, Dec 3, 1962—all in AFRES 21D; TAC SO G–164, Nov 23, 1962; CONAC SO G–l00, Nov 28, 1962.

72. Msg, DOOP–OA 11 2985, TAC to CONAC, subj: Mission for Extended Duty/ EAD/Personnel of USAF Reserve, Nov 29, 1962; IOM, Lt Col W. L. Spencer, Ch, Current Ops Div, CONAC to Hall, DCS/O, subj: Post–Cuba Airlift Support of TAC, Nov. 30, 1962—both in AFRES 21D.

73. Ltr, Col Downs E. Ingram, Ex Asst CSAF/RF, to Air Staff Agencies, subj: Results of HQ USAF Command-wide Conference of Recent Mobilizations, Jan 18, 1963, w/atch, AFRES 21D.

74. "American Determination Key to Success," *London Times*, Dec 23, 1962.

75. Graham T. Allison, *Essence Decision: Explaining the Cuban Missile Crisis* (Boston, Mass., 1971), pp 643–66. In the Talbott edition of his memoirs, Khrushchev said he put the missiles in Cuba to prevent a second invasion of Cuba by the United States and that he pulled them out to prevent the war the American military would force upon President Kennedy.

Talbott, *Khrushchev Remembers*, pp 492–505.

76. Ltr, Lt Gen Joe W. Kelly, Cmdr MATS, to Lt Gen Edward J. Timberlake, Cmdr CONAC, subj: Active Duty Training of C–124 units, Mar 25, 1963; ltr, CONAC (OOP–C) to MATS and WESTAF, subj: Overwater Transport Training Missions, Dec 13, 1963—both in AFRES 22A; hist, MATS, Jul–Dec 63, pp 102–25; hist, WESTAF, Jul–Dec 63, p 93; hist, CONAC, Jan–Jun 63, p 21.

77. Ltr, CONAC to MATS and WESTAF, subj: Overwater Transport Training Missions, Dec 13, 1963; hist, MATS, Jul–Dec 63, pp 102–25; hist, WESTAF, Jul–Dec 63, p 93.

78. Ltr, Maj Huxley to Asst CS, subj: Flying Activities of Reserve Units, Jul 1, 1964, AFRES 22H; hist, MATS, Jan–Jun. 64, p 245.

79. MFR, Maj Boyce H. Pinson, Current Ops Div, CONAC, subj: C–124 Overwater Flights, Jun 15, 1965; intvw, author with Pinson, Sep 9, 1974; MFR, Pinson, subj: MATS Request for Additional Airlift, Aug 14, 1964; msg, OOP–C, CONAC to USAF, subj: MATS Request for Additional Airlift, Oct 2, 1964—all in AFRES 22H.

80. Pinson MFR, Aug 14, 1964.

81. Rowland Evans and Robert Novak, *Lyndon B. Johnson: The Exercise of Power* (New York, 1966), pp 510–29; MFR, Pinson, subj: Project Power Pack, Jun 1965; intvw, J. J. Lichman with Capt. R. Oliver, Cmd Post, Aug 30, 1965—all in AFRES 22E. For a perspective on the President's decision to intervene in the Dominican Republic see Evans and Novak, *Lyndon B. Johnson: Exercise of Power*, pp 510–29.

82. Rpts, Air Force Reserve Units, "Semiannual CONAC/AFRES Mission or By-product Accomplishments Reports" AFRES 22B; CONAC OPORD 12–65, Dec 1, 1965, AFRES 22A1.

Chapter 8

1. Memo, Clark M. Clifford to John F. Kennedy, subj: Memorandum on Conference between President Eisenhower and President-elect Kennedy and Their Chief Advisers on Jan 19, 1961, Jan 24, 1961; memo, Robert S. McNamara to President, subj: Meeting with President Eisenhower on Jan 19, 1961, Pres Ofc Files, Special Correspondence, Dwight D. Eisenhower, 1/17/61–12/9/61, Box 29a—both in JFKL.

2. *Encyclopedia of Military History*, s.v. "Southeast Asia, 1945–1974."

3. Memo, Lyndon B. Johnson to John F. Kennedy, subj: Mission to Southeast Asia, India and Pakistan, May 23, 1961, Pres Ofc Files, Special Correspondence, Lyndon B. Johnson, Box 30, JFKL.

4. Carl Berger, ed., *The United States Air Force in Southeast Asia, 1961–1973: An Illustrated Account* (Washington, D.C., 1977), pp 5–11. For a comprehensive account of the Air Force's early years in Southeast Asia, see Robert F. Futrell, with Martin Blumenson, *The Advisory Years to 1965* (Washington, D.C., 1981). For a sympathetic view of the Kennedy administration's actions in Vietnam at this point, see Schlesinger, *Thousand Days*, pp 542–45.

5. Defense Manpower Commission, *Defense Manpower: The Keystones of National Security* (Washington, D.C., 1976), p 3.

6. Intvw, Cantwell with Maj Gen William Lyon, Feb 14, 1979, Pentagon, pp 5–6, AFRES 26A.

7. Intvw, Cantwell with Maj Gen Richard Bodycombe, May 28–29, 1985, p 84, AFRES 26A.

8. In a conversation with the author in December 1976 in Macon, Georgia, General Westmoreland related that during a White House meeting with General Wheeler and President Johnson, Johnson had emphasized this reason for not mobilizing.

9. House Armed Services Cmte, *United States–Vietnam Relations, 1945–1967* (hereafter, *U.S.-Vietnam Relations*), book 2, 4B 1 [study prepared by DOD, Washington, D.C., 1971], p 83; Neil Sheehan, Hedrick Smith, E. W. Kenworthy, and Fox Butterfield, *The Pentagon Papers* (New York, 1971), p 97.

Notes

10. *U.S.–Vietnam Relations*, book 3, Summary and Analysis; Lyndon Baines Johnson, *The Vantage Point: Perceptions of the Presidency*, paperback ed. (New York, 1971) pp 66–67; Herbert Y. Schandler, *The Unmaking of a President: Lyndon Johnson and Vietnam* (Princeton, N.J., 1977), pp 4–5.

11. "The President's News Conference of Jun 2, 1964," *Public Papers of the Presidents of the United States: Lyndon B. Johnson, 1964* (hereafter, Johnson, *Public Papers*), vol 1, pp 733–40.

12. "Special Message to the Congress on U.S. Policy in Southeast Asia," Aug 5, 1964, Johnson, *Public Papers, 1963–64*, vol 2, pp 930–31; PL 88–408, *Southeast Asia Policy and Security* (Stat 78: 384), Aug 10, 1964; Legislative History, PL 88–408, 88th Cong., 2d sess. (1964), *United States Code Congressional and Administrative News*, pp 2676–84; "Radio and Television Report to the American People Following Renewed Aggression in the Gulf of Tonkin," Aug 4, 1964, Johnson, *Public Papers, 1964*, pp 927–28. See also David Halberstam, *The Best and the Brightest* (Greenwich, 1969), pp 373–74.

13. Memo, McGeorge Bundy to the President, subj: The History of Recommendations for Increased US Forces in Vietnam, Jul 24, 1965, NSF, Memos to President, McGeorge Bundy Papers, Box 4, Lyndon Baines Johnson Library, Austin, Tex. (hereafter, LBJL); Futrell, *Advisory Years*, p 265.

14. Bundy memo, Jul 24, 1965.

15. Mtg notes, McGeorge Bundy, Jun 5, 1965, McGeorge Bundy Papers, LBJL.

16. Memo, McGeorge Bundy to the President, subj: Meeting Friday Morning on Vietnam, Jul 1, 1965, NSF, Memos to President, McGeorge Bundy, vol 12, Jul 1965, LBJL. See also Larry Berman, *Planning a Tragedy: The Americanization of the War in Vietnam* (New York, 1982), pp 91–92.

17. Memo, Dean Rusk to Dir/CIA, subj: Contingency Plans for Possible Increases in U.S. Forces in Vietnam, Jul 15, 1965; memo, L. Niederlehner, Actg Gen Counsel OSD, to Dep SecDef, subj: Vietnam Buildup—Legislative Situation, Jul 17, 1965, w/4 tabs; Checklist of Actions [Vietnam buildup], William P. Bundy, Jul 17, 1965, NSF, Vietnam, Cables, vol 37, 7/65, Box 19—all in LBJL; Memo, McGeorge Bundy to the President, subj: Vietnam Planning at Close of Business, Monday, Jul 19, 1965, 8:25 P.M., Jul 19, 1965, Nat Sec Files, NSC History, 1965 Deployment of Major U.S. Forces, vol 6, tabs 384–400, LBJL; msg, Vance to McNamara, Saigon, Literally Eyes Only, subj: Actions Associated with 34 Battalion Plan, 172042Z ZFF-1, Jul 17, 1965, David Humphrey files, LBJL.

18. Memo, McNamara to the President, subj: Recommendation of Additional Deployments to Vietnam, Jul 20, 1965, Nat Sec Files, NSC History, Jul 1965, Deployment of Major U.S. Forces, vol 6, tabs 384–400, LBJL; MFR, Bromley Smith, Ex Sec NSC, subj: Deployment of Major Forces to Vietnam, Jul 1965, Nat Sec Files, NSC History, Jul 1965, Deployment of Major U.S. Forces, vol 1, tabs 1–10, LBJL; marginalia on ltr, Cantwell to McNamara, Jun 28, 1988 (marginalia dated Jul 3, 1988), AFRES 11B.1.

19. MFR, Meetings on Vietnam, Jul 21, 1965, Cabinet Room (two meetings), Meeting Notes File, Box 1, LBJL.

20. Mtg notes, NSC, Jul 27, 1965, 5:45 P.M.; mtg notes, Congressional Leadership Meeting, Tuesday, Jul 27, 1965, 6:35 P.M.; mtg notes, McGeorge Bundy, Joint Leadership Meeting, Jul 27, 1965, 6:35 P.M.–8:25 P.M.—Meeting Notes File, Jul 21–27, 1965, Meetings on Vietnam, Box 11, LBJL.

21. Intvw, Dorothy Pierce McSweeny with Gen Earle E. Wheeler, Aug 21, 1969, and May 7, 1970, vol 1, pp 18–21, LBJL.

22. "The President's News Conference of Jul 28, 1965," Johnson, *Public Papers, 1965*, vol 2, p 795. For his earlier remarks on the subject during the month, see "The President's News Conference of Jul 9, 1965," Johnson, *Public Papers, 1965*, vol 2, p 729; "The President's News Conference on Jul 13, 1965," Johnson, *Public Papers, 1965*, vol 2, p 738; and *Department of Defense Annual Report for Fiscal Year 1966* (Washington, D.C., 1967), pp 30–31.

23. "The President's News Conference Held at the Close of the Governors' Conference," Mar 12, 1966, Johnson, *Public Papers, 1966*, vol 1, p 314. For comparable remarks, see "The President's News Conference of Feb 11, 1966," Johnson, *Public Papers, 1966*, vol 1, pp 177–78;

The Air Force Reserve

"The President's News Conference at the LBJ Ranch," Jul 5, 1966, Johnson, *Public Papers 1966*, vol 1, p 704; "Remarks at a Press Briefing Following the Return from Vietnam of Secretary McNamara and Under Secretary Katzenbach," Oct 14, 1966, Johnson, *Public Papers 1966*, vol 2, p 1184.

24. John H. Steadman, Spec Asst, "Draft Summary for Record" [Honolulu Conference], Feb 9, 1966, *U.S.–Vietnam Relations*, book 5, vol 1, pp 29–34.

25. JCSM–130–66, subj: CY 1966 Deployments to Southeast Asia and World Wide Military Posture, Mar 1, 1966, *U.S.–Vietnam Relations*, book 5, vol 1, pp 37–39, 79–81, 105–07, 123–27.

26. Supplemental Foreign Assistance FY 1966, Vietnam, Hearings on S. 2793 to amend further the Foreign Assistance Act of S. 9612, as amended, Jan 28 and Feb 4, 8, 10, 17, 18, Pt 1 (Washington, D.C., 1966); E. W. Kenworthy, "Fulbright Fears Conflict with China over Vietnam," *New York Times*, Feb 8, 1966, p 1; Kenworthy, "Senate Panel Will Conduct Broad Inquiry on Vietnam," *New York. Times*, Feb 4, 1966, pp 1–2.

27. *Cong. Rec.*, 89th Cong., 2d sess., 1966, pt 3, pp 3956–72.

28. Ibid., pt 7, p 8735.

29. "McNamara Inquiry Sought on 'Favoritism' in Reserves," *New York Times*, Dec 10, 1966; B. Drummond Ayres, Jr., "Reserves Told to Enlist Men as Names Come Up: Pentagon Orders Revision—Charge of Favoritism to Athletes Being Studied," *New York Times*, Dec 23, 1966.

30. Legislative History, PL 90–40, 90th Cong., 1st sess. (1967), *United States Code Congressional and Administrative News*, pp 1310–11. Review of the Administration and Operation of the Selective Service System," Hearings before HASC, 89th Cong., 2d sess.; "Draft Panel Calls for a Crackdown: Advisers to Congress Score 6-Month Draft Plan," *New York Times*, Mar 4, 1967.

31. PL 51–82 (Jun 19, 1951), *Universal Military Training and Service Act*; PL 305–84 (Aug 9, 1955), *Reserve Forces Act of 1955*.

32. Table, "Air Reserve Forces NPS Enlistments CAC (PRP–P) & NGB (AF)," Feb 5, 1968, AFRES 14D; Air Force Reserve Manning Summary (Monthly), a/o May 1967, AFRES 14J.

33. See, among other Air Force Reserve unit histories of the period, hist, 445th MAW, Jan–Jun 66, pp 7–8.

34. See note 30.

35. H.R. doc 75, Selective Service, "Message from the President of the United States Transmitting Recommendations for Extending the Draft Authority, Lowering Age for Drafting, Correcting the Deferment Inequities, Developing a Fair and Impartial System of Selection, and Establishing a Task Force to Review Recommendations for a Restructured Selective Service System," Mar 6, 1967, 90th Cong., 1st sess. PL 90–40, *Military Selective Service Act of 1967* (Stat 81: 100), Jun 30, 1967, included the measures the President had requested. For an insight into the developing continuum of Presidential recall powers, see Richard B. Crossland and James T. Currie, *Twice the Citizen: A History of the United States Army Reserve, 1908–1983* (Washington, D.C., 1984), pp 197–98. H.R. doc 75, Selective Service, "Amending and Extending the Draft Law and Related Authorities," hearings before the Senate Armed Services Committee, 90th Cong., 1st sess., on S. 1432 to amend UMT&SA, Apr 12–19, 1967. For the Emergency Presidential Recall Authority, see PL 89–687, *DOD Appropriations Act of 1967* (Stat 80: 980), Oct 15, 1966. The authority was extended to Jun 1969 by PL 90–500, *Military Procurement Act* (Stat 82: 850), Sep 20, 1968, and PL 90–40, *Military Selective Service Act of 1967* (Stat 81: 100), Jun 30, 1967.

36. Memo, William Bundy for U/SecDef Katzenbach, subj: Thoughts on Strategy in Vietnam, May 1, 1961, cited in *U.S.–Vietnam Relations*, book 5, vol 2, pp 85–86. On the growing unpopularity of the war, see Schandler, *Unmaking of a President*, pp 52–56, Halberstam, *Best and Brightest*, p 780, and Dave Richard Palmer, *Summons of the Trumpet: U.S.–Vietnam in Perspective* (San Rafael, Calif., 1978), pp 129–30, 149–50. Charles DeBenedetti, "Lyndon Johnson and the American Opposition," in Robert A. Divine, ed., *The Johnson Years*, vol 2, *Vietnam, the Environment, and Science* (Lawrence, Kans., 1987), pp 24–53; Melvin Small, *Johnson, Nixon, and the*

Doves (New Brunswick, 1988), pp 26–27, 76–77, 94–95, 130–31. See also JCSM 218-67, subj: Force Requirements—Southeast Asia, FY 1968, Apr 19, 20, 1967, encl A to JCS 2339/255-3, cited in *U.S.–Vietnam Relations*, book 5, vol 2, pp 75–77. General Westmoreland also discussed these things with the author during a December 1976 conversation in Macon, Georgia.

37. "Anti-Viet Rally Staged by 10,000," *Macon Telegraph and News*, Nov 21, 1965; Palmer, *Summons of the Trumpet*, pp 129–30; DeBenedetti, "Lyndon Johnson and the American Opposition"; Small, *Johnson, Nixon, and the Doves*, pp 26–27, 76–77, 94–95, 130–31, 165–66; "Antiwar Demonstrations Held Outside Draft Boards across U.S.: 119 Persons Arrested on Coast," *New York Times*, Oct 17, 1967; Wallace Turner, "Police Rout 3,000 at Oakland Protest," *New York Times*, Oct 18, 1967; Sylvan Fox, "Brooklyn Students Battle Police in Peace Protest: 40 Arrested on Campus," *New York Times*, Oct 20, 1967; C. Gerald Fraser, "Boycott at Madison," *New York Times*, Oct 20, 1967; James A. Loftus, "Guards Repulse Protesters at The Pentagon: 6 Break Through Line into Building—Mailer and Dellinger Are Arrested," *New York Times*, Oct 22, 1967; Ben A. Franklin, "War Protesters Defying Deadline Seized in Capital: 208 Refuse to Disperse at Pentagon as Permit for Demonstration Expires," *New York Times*, Oct 23, 1967; Paul Hoffman, "Thousands March Here to Back G.I.'s: Lindsay at Vigil, Qualifies His Support of Its Aims—Gets Mixed Reception," *New York Times*, Oct 23, 1967; Homer Bigart, "Week of Protest Against the Draft Started by Antiwar Groups," *New York Times*, Dec 5, 1967.

38. Memo, Jim Jones for President, subj: Weekly Luncheon with Secretaries Rusk and McNamara, Walt Rostow and George Christian (Gen Harold Johnson Was Also present), Sep 12, 1967, Meeting Notes File, LBJL.

39. Marvin Kalb and Elie Abel, *Roots of Involvement: The U.S. in Asia, 1784–1971*, pp 196, 229; Palmer, *Summons of the Trumpet*, pp 158–59.

40. Msg, Col Hal E. Ercanbrack, Jr., Asst DCS/O, CAC, to USAF, subj: Reserve Troop Carrier Capability to Support Contingency Operations, DCS/O 500, 112230Z May 65, AFRES 21.

41. Address, McConnell, ROA National Convention, Jun 29, 1966, New York.

42. Futrell, *Advisory Years*, pp 253, 255, 265–68.

43. MFR, Maj Boyce H. Pinson, Current Ops Div, CONAC, subj: C–124 Overwater Flights, Jun 15, 1965; intvw, Cantwell with Pinson, Sep 9, 1974—both in AFRES 22H.

44. MFR, Pinson, Jun 15, 1965; msg, WESTAF to MATS, subj: Large Backlog of Cargo in WESTAF Ports, WTODC 753, 222205Z Jun 1965; msg, WESTAF to 1501 ATW et al., subj: Air National Guard and Air Reserve Operations in the Pacific, WCP 2878, 192232Z Mar 65—all in AFRES 22A.

45. Hist, 442 TCW, Jan–Jun 65, p 6; ibid., Jul–Dec 65, p 7; hist, 512 TCW, Jan–Jun 65, p 6; ibid., Jul–Dec 65, p 9.

46. These statistics are extracted from the annual reports "CAC Airlift Accomplishment of Air Force Reserve Units," CY 1966; "CAL Mission Accomplishment of Air Force Reserve Units," CY 1967; "AFRES Mission Accomplishment of Air Force Reserve Units," FY 1968, FY 1969; "AFRES By-product Accomplishment of Air Force Reserve Units," FY 1970, FY 1971; "Annual Report of the Air Force Reserve," FY 1972, 1973—all in AFRES 22H, except for last two which are in AFRES 25C. For a detailed account of the Air Force Reserve's participation in the Air Force's Southeast Asia mission, see Cantwell, *The Air Force Reserve in the Vietnam Decade: 1965–1975* (Robins AFB, Ga., 1979).

47. Atch (ltr, Col C. G. Winn, Jr., DCS/Plans, CONAC, to USAF, subj: Annual Report of the Secretary of the Air Force for Period 1 Jul 1967–30 Jul 19, 1968), Data for Annual Report of the Secretary of the Air Force the Air Force for Period 1 Jul 1967–Jun 1968 (FY 1968), pp 19–20.

48. Ibid.

49. Ltr, Col J. D. White, Asst DCS/O CAC, to Cmdr & CS, subj: Daily Operations Activities, Aug 14, 1968, AFRES 20B1. Additional information was given to the author by Richard P. McFarland at HQ AFRES on September 4, 1979. The background and development of the Air Force

The Air Force Reserve

Reserve Airlift Associate Program are discussed in Chapter 12.

50. See, for example, hists, 903d MAG, Jan–Mar 71, p 11, and Oct–Dec 71, p 13.

51. Berger, *USAF in Southeast Asia, 1961–1973*, p 198.

52. Hist, 349th MAW, Apr–Jun 72, p 5; hist, 903d MAG, Apr–Jun 72, pp 8–10.

53. Ltr, Lt Col Kenneth G. Show, AFRES DCS/Pers, to USAF/REL, subj: USAFR Participation in Project HOMECOMING, n.d. [ca. Jun 30, 1973].

54. Medical Hist, AFRES, FY 1973, p 5.

55. 1127th USAF Fld Activities Gp HO1 200-4, "Debriefing of Returnees," May 26, 1966, AFIS/HO; ltr, Maj Gen George J. Keegan, Cmdr AFIS, to AFMPC, subj: Recommendation for Award of Unit Decoration, Nov 4, 1976, w/9 atchs, AFRES.

56. AFIS-AFIR Plan, May 1973, Annex B, AFRES 22H; Frank W. Barry, Jr., and Hugh R. Farrell, "POW/MIA Family Counseling Program," *Medical Service Digest*, Nov 1973, pp 15–16.

57. Hist, AFIS, FY 1974, pp 234–35, 240; ltr, Lt Gen Richard H. Ellis, VCS, to AFIS, subj: Analysis of Southeast Asia Captivity Experience, Nov 15, 1973, AFIS/HO.

58. Hist, 7602d AIG, Jul 75–Sep 76, p 50; AFIS Reserves Detachment Commanders Conference Report, p 57; Keegan ltr, Nov 4, 1976.

59. Hist, AFRES, FY 1975, pp 142–44; hist, 315th MAW, Apr–Jun 75, p 6; hist, 445th MAW, Apr–Jun 1975, p 7; hist, 446th MAW, Apr–Jun 1975, p 5; hist, 514th MAW Apr–Jun 1975, p 9; Annual Report of the Air Force Reserve, FY 1975, p 38.

60. Hist, AFRES, FY 1975, pp 142–44; Annual Report of the Air Force Reserve, FY 1975, p 25.

61. See note 60 above.

62. Hist, 349th MAW, Apr–Jun 1975, p 116.

63. See note 60 above.

64. Hist, AFRES, FY 1972, pp 186–87. For aircraft ferry missions, see hist, 446th TAW, Jul–Sep 1970, p 4; rpt, AFRES, "Msn Accomp of Air Force Reserve Units, FY 1969," p 7-2; rpt, AFRES, "By-product Accomp of Air Force Reserve Units, FY 1970," p 7-2; rpt, AFRES, "By-product Accomp of Air Force Reserve Units, FY 1971," p 211; and annual report, SecAF, FY 1972, p 29. For aerial port operations at U-Tapao, see ltr, Col Louis J. McKenna, Ch, Pers Div, to Ofc of Info, Ofc of AF Res, subj: Draft Monograph—Air Force Reserve and Southeast Asia, Aug 1, 1979; hists, 514th MAW, Apr–Jun 1974, p 40, Jul–Sep 1974, p 30; and hist, 512th MAW, Oct–Dec 1974, p 4. For JAG activity, see AFRES Activity Input to Project Corona Harvest on the Air Force Reserve in support of the Air War in Southeast Asia, Dec 19, 1969, p 53; ltr, Col Lawrence H. Miller, Res Adv, JAG, USAF, to Cantwell, subj: Draft Monograph—Air Force Reserve and Southeast Asia, Aug 2, 1979; and Historical Summary, DAF, FY 1969, p 62. For chaplain support, see HQ AFRES News Release, 52–68, Capt Joseph J. McDonough, "The AFRES CHAPAR Program," Oct 15, 1968; and Historical Summary, DAF FY 1969, p 59.

65. Among others, Col Lawrence H. Miller, Res Adv to the JAG, USAF, and Lt Col Roger B. Compton, DCS/L&E, USAF, discussed this point in correspondence with the author in August 1979.

66. Johnson, *Vantage Point*, pp 531–32; Townsend Hoopes, *The Limits of Intervention* (New York, 1971), pp 136–37.

67. Memo, George Christian, subj: Minutes Meeting at the State Department on the *Pueblo* incident, Jan 24, 1968, Meeting Notes File, LBJL; memo, L. Niederlehner, Actg Gen Council for Harry C. McPherson, Jr., Spec Counsel to the President, subj: EO 113921, 1100 hrs, Jan 25, 1968, White House Central Files (WHCF), ND 13 Reserve Forces and National Guard (RF & NG), 9/1/67–7/31/68, Box 181, LBJL; memo, Frank M. Wozencraft, Asst Atty Gen, Ofc of Legal Counsel, subj: Proposed Executive Order entitled "Ordering Certain Units of the Ready Reserve of the Naval Reserve, Air Force Reserve, and Air National Guard of the United States to Active Duty," WHCF, ND 13 RF & NG, 9/1/67–7/31/68, Box 131 [sic], LBJL; memo, Harry C. McPherson, Jr., to Marie Fehmer, subj: Executive Order Ordering Reserve and Guard Units to Active Duty, Jan 25, 1968, Appt Files, Jan 25, 1968 [Diary Backup], Box 88, LBJL. Former Secretary Brown expressed his view on the mobilization during an interview conducted by

Thomas G. Belden and others at Pasadena, California. Intvw, Thomas G. Belden, Jacob Van Staaveren, and Hugh N. Ahmann with Harold Brown, Aug 29–30, 1972, K239.0512–619, AFHRC. For a detailed account of the mobilization in January 1968, see Cantwell, *Evolution and Employment of the Air Force Reserve as a Mobilization Force*, pp 185–247.

68. Telephone intvw, author with Col Cecil W. Alford, Mar 3, 1977; chronol, AFCHO, Korean Crisis, 1968, p 9; chronol, AFRES DCS/P, Korean Crisis, 1968; telephone intvw, author with Maj Gen Winston P. Wilson, Dir/ANG, Jan 26, 1986. General Wilson's account conflicts with the other sources cited in this note insofar as he recalled no restrictions placed on the recall, but the others are too consistent on the point to be discredited.

69. For information on the BEEF BROTH program, see msg, OOP–C 1082, Col Robert N. Cyzmoure, Dir/Ops, CAC, to TAC, subj: Recommended Recall Priority Listing for Reserve C–124 and ARRS Units, 061625Z Oct 67; msg, OOP–C 1083, Cyzmoure to TAC, subj: Recommended Recall Priority Listing for Reserve C–119 Units, 061626Z Oct 67; and the Operational Status Report, CAC, "RCS: 1 HAF V21 (STATREP)," Dec 31 1967—all in AFRES 21E; hist, CAC, Jul–Dec 67, pp 88–89.

70. Briefing, Brig Gen Rollin B. Moore, Jr., Cmdr, 349th MAW, at CAC Commanders' Conference, Apr 3, 1968, Robins AFB, Ga., AFRES 21E. General Moore confirmed his memory of the events during a conversation with the author at HQ AFRES in January 1971.

71. Chronol, "The Continental Air Command and the Korean Contingency (Jan 1968–Mar 1968) (1145 EST, 1620 EST, Jan 25, 1968)," Apr 1968, AFRES 21E; Lyndon B. Johnson, EO 11392, Jan 26, 1968; AFCHO Korean Crisis chronol; msg, OFC, J. L. Miles, Ops Analyst, CAC, to USAF/XOP, subj: JOPREP JIFFY Report, RCS: 17-HAF V21 (RELREP), 270333Z Jan 68.

72. MFR, J. J. Lichman, CAC historian, subj: Airlift Missions Flown by Mobilized Groups, Dec 4, 1969, AFRES 21E; msg, OFC, J. L. Miles, Ops Analyst, to HQ USAF/XOP, subj: JOPREP JIFFY Report, RCS: 17–HAF–V21 RELREP, 210333Z Jan 68; congressional testimony, Gen John P. McConnell, Senate Armed Services Cmte, 90th Cong., 2d sess., Feb 21, 1968, p 766; hist, 445th MAW, Jul–Dec 68, pp 46–49.

73. Hist, 349th MAW, Jul–Dec 1968, pp 48–49; hist, 445th MAW, Jan–Jun 1969, pp 41–46.

74. Hist, ARRS, Jan 1967–Jun 1970, pp 1–2.

75. Hists, 305th ARRS, Oct–Dec 1968, pp 4–5, Apr–Jun 1969, pp 6–7.

76. Hist, 305th ARRS, Apr–Jun 1969, p 9.

77. Ibid., Jan–Jun 1968, pp 26–27.

78. Ibid., Jan–Mar 1969, p 10.

79. Hist, 349th MAW, Jan–Jun 1968, p 8; AFCS SO G-45, Apr 26, 1967; hist, 941st MAG, Jan–Jun 1968, p 14; hist, 938th USAF Disp, 26 Jan–15 Aug 1968, p 11; hist, 349th MAW, Jan–Jun 1968, pp 38–39; hist, 445th MAW, Jan–Jun 1968, pp 63–65; hist, 921th MAG, Jan–Jun 1968, p 2.

80. "Fliers Charge Unit's Breakup," *Sunday News*, Jul 7, 1968; "Air Reservists Sue to Prevent Call-Up of Men Individually," *New York Times*, Aug 14, 1968; Harold Gal, "Air Force Defends Shifting Individual Reservists," *New York Times*, Jul 18, 1968; "7 Sue to Stay in Units," *Air Force Times*, Aug 21, 1968.

81. Msg, SAFOIP ALMAJCOM 1207/68, subj: Utilization of Called Up Air Reserve and National Guard Units, 261655Z Jul 1968, AFRES 21E.

82. JCSM 91–689, subj: Emergency Reinforcement of COMUSMACV, Feb 12, 1968, cited in *U.S.-Vietnam Relations*, book 5, 4C6 (c), vol 3, pp 2–12; Schandler, *Unmaking of a President*, pp 99–104, 115–16; Johnson, *Vantage Point*, p 386.

83. Msg, JCS 9926, subj: Deployment of Brigade Task Force of 82d Airborne Division to SVN, 130218Z Feb 68, cited in *U.S.–Vietnam Relations*, book 5, 4C6 (c), vol 3, pp 2–12.

84. Johnson, *Vantage Point*, p 416.

85. News conference, Clark M. Clifford, Thur, Apr 11, 1968, 10:00 EST, Pentagon, Clifford Papers, Reserve Call-Up (7), Releases, Box 4, LBJL; Crossland and Currie, *Twice the Citizen*, pp 201–02; EO 11406, Apr 10, 1968; memo, Clark Clifford

to the President, subj: Reserve Call-Up, Apr 8, 1968; memo, unsigned, no subject, Apr 11, 1968—both in Alfred B. Fitt Papers, Gen Corr, Box 1, LBJL; tele, SAFOI PC to Maj Mary Mackie, CAC OI, subj: Mobilization of Reservists, April 11, 1968, at CAC, 111707Z Apr 68; msg, USAF to MAC et al., subj: Mobilization of Air Reserve Forces Units, AFCCS, 120025Z Apr 68. A second medical service squadron was initially alerted for mobilization, but the Air Force cancelled the requirement. Also, at the last moment, the Air Force avoided some of the January experience by deleting support elements of the tactical airlift group as superfluous to requirements. On these points, see msg, USAF to CONAC subj: Mobilization of Reserve Forces Units, AFOAPD 082023Z May 68, and Msg, PRP-A CAC to IAFRR et al., subj: Mobilization of Air Force Reserve Units, 0914532 May 68—both in AFRES 21F, and memo, Hoopes for SecDef, subj: Selective Recall of Reserve Units in May 1968, 71A2712, Box 12, WNRC.

86. Tele, HQ USAF, SAFOI PC, to CAC OI (Mackie), subj: Mobilization of Reservists, Apr 11, 1968; tele, HQ USAF, SAFOI PC, to Mackie, subj: Identification of Mobilized Units, Apr 11, 1968—both in AFRES 21F.

87. Hist, 433th TAW, Jan–Jun 68, p 3; Annual Report of Air Force Reserve, FY 1969, p 26.

88. Ltr, Col Daniel C. Campbell, Jr., Cmdr USAF Hosp, Scott AFB, to MAC, subj: Recommendation for Award of the Air Force Outstanding Unit Award, n.d.; Annual Report of Air Force Reserve, FY 1969, p 27.

89. Posture Statement, Maj Gen Tom E. Marbanks, Ch AF Res, Aug 4, 1969.

90. TAC SO G–82, Jun 11, 1968; TAC SO G–97, Jul 8, 1968.

91. Hist, 71st SOS, Jul–Dec 1968, pp 5–14; TAC MO 37, 1968; PACAF SO G–295, Dec 13, 1968.

92. Hist, 14th SOW, Apr–Jun 1969, p 3; hist, 1971 SOS, Jan–Mar 1969, p 33.

93. See, for example, hist 349th MAW, Jul–Dec 1968, pp 53–56, and hist, AFRES, Aug–Dec 1968, pp 124–28.

94. Hist, Dir/Aerospace Progs, Jul–Dec 1968, pp 3–4.

95. Ltr, DAF (AFOMO 028p), Col Thomas B. Hoxie, Dep Dir/M&O USAF, to MAC & AFRES, subj: Release from EAD of Units of the Air Force Reserve and Reassignment to Gaining Commands in Reserve Status, Nov 19, 1968, AFRES 21F; MAC SO G–332, Dec 6, 1968; ltr, DAF (AFOMO 048p), Col Thomas B. Hoxie, Dep Dir/M&O, to MAC et al., subj: Release from EAD of Units of the Air Force Reserve and Reassignment to Gaining Commands in Reserve Status, Jan 23, 1969, AFRES 21F; AFRES SO G–9, Mar 18, 1969; AFCS SO G–31, Mar 5, 1969, a/a G–36, Mar 13, 1969; ltr, DAF (AFOMO 049p), Col Thomas B. Hoxie, Dep Dir/M&O, to MAC and AFRES, subj: Release from EAD of Units of the Air Force Reserve and Reassignment to Gaining Commands in Reserve Status, Jan 23, 1969; ltr, DAF (AFOMO 115p), Hoxie to AFRES and TAC, subj: Release from EAD of Units of the Air Force Reserve and Reassignment to Gaining Commands in Reserve Status, Mar 28, 1969—both in AFRES 21F; AFRES SO G–34, May 8, 1969; AFRES SO G–39, May 22, 1969; ltr, Col Lonnie C. Brewer, Asst DCS/Pers, CAC, to Cmdr, subj: Reservists Remaining on Active Duty, Apr 15, 1969, w/3 atchs, AFRES 21F; Msg, AFRPRP, Col John L. Turner, DCS/Pers, to AFMPC et al., subj: Demobilization of Aerial Port Units, 171935Z Oct 68; HQ AFRES Plan 28, *Demobilization Plan,* Nov 15, 1968, AFRES 21F.

96. Atch (ltr, Turner to all AFRRs et al., subj: Personnel Briefing at CAC Commander's Conference, Apr 22, 1968), "Continental Air Command Personnel Management," Apr 1968; MFR, AFRES/IG, subj: TIG Report: Survey of the Effectiveness Procedures for Mobilization of the Air Reserve Forces, 13 Feb–5 Mar 1969, Aug 9, 1968—both in AFRES 21F.

97. Over the years, Air Force and AFRES mobilization guidance became consolidated in AFR 28–5, *USAF Mobilization Planning.* The May 29, 1980, edition provided for great flexibility in mobilization planning.

98. See note 96 above; ltr, Col Russell F. Fisher, CS AFRES, to USAF/TOR, subj: Survey of Effectiveness of Procedures for Mobilization of the Air Reserve Forces, PN

Notes

68–118, Aug 16, 1968, AFRES 21F.

99. See note 98 above; memo, J. William Doolittle, Asst SecAF (MRA), to Asst SecDef (MRA), subj: Lessons Learned from Limited Mobilization, Jan 10, 1969, RG 340 72A6465, WNRC.

100. Atch 2 (Fisher ltr, 5 Dec 68), Personnel; briefing, Brig Gen Rollin B. Moore, Jr., CAC Commanders' Conference, Robins AFB, Ga., Apr 3, 1968; MFR, Rayner, May 9, 1968.

101. Memo, Velma to Dr. Marrs, subj: Problems Encountered by Deploying ARF Units, May 28, 1969, w/atchs, SAF/MIR.

102. Palmer, *Summons of the Trumpet*, p 214; Richard M. Nixon, *RN: The Memoirs of Richard Nixon* (New York, 1978), p 349.

Chapter 9

1. MFR, Gen Curtis E. LeMay, subj: Discussion with Committee, Jan 15, 1963, SAF/MIR.

2. Memo, Maj Gen Charles DuBois, ANGUS, Chmn, to SecAF through CSAF, subj: Recommendations—37th Meeting of the Air Reserve Forces Policy Committee, 12–14 Oct 1963, Oct 25, 1963; remarks, Gen Curtis E. LeMay, CSAF, Executive Session, Special Meeting of ARFPC, Jan 15, 1964—both in SAF/MIR.

3. Memo, Maj Gen Charles DuBois, Chmn, ARFPC, to SecAF, subj: Recommendations and Comments—Special Meeting of the Air Reserve Forces Policy Committee (Executive Session), Jan 20, 1964, AFRES 5B2; memo, Brockway MacMillan, U/SecAF, to CSAF, subj: Recommendations—Special Meeting of the Air Reserve Forces Policy Committee, Jan 15–17, 1964, Feb 11, 1964, AFRES 5B2; ltr, Maj Gen Robert J. Friedman, Asst DCS/Progs and Rqmts, to Air Staff, subj: Management of the Air Reserve Forces, Oct 9, 1964, AFRES 5C4.

4. Memo, Eugene M. Zuckert to Dr. Marrs, subj: McNamara Request for Plan to Merge Reserve into Guard, Oct 28, 1964, RG 340, 68A4994, WNRC; memo, Theodore C. Marrs, AF Dep for Res and ROTC, to VCSAF, subj: Plan to Merge Reserve into Guard, Oct 30, 1964, AFRES 5C5.

5. Atch (memo, Eugene M. Zuckert, SecAF, to SecDef, Nov 21, 1964), United States Air Force Proposed Plan to Merge Units of the Air Force Reserve into the Air National Guard, RG 340, 68A4994, WNRC; MFR, Lt Gen Edward J. Timberlake, Cmdr CAC, subj: Resume of Meeting with Secretary Zuckert on 13 Nov 1964 Concerning Transfer of Air Reserve Units to the Air National Guard, Nov 13, 1964, AFRES 5C4.

6. Ltr, Maj Gen William K. Martin, Asst VCSAF, to Theodore C. Marrs, subj: Outline Plan to Phase Units of the Air Force Reserve into the Air National Guard, Nov 14, 1964; atch (ltr, Maj Gen Benjamin O. Davis, Jr., Nov 4, 1964), "Management of the Air Reserve Forces," Nov 1964—both in AFRES 5C4; ltr, AFC 8/57, Col A. J. Bowley, for Maj Gen William K. Martin, Asst VCSAF, to DCS/Progs and Rqmts et al., subj: Management of Air Reserve Forces, Nov 6, 1964, RG 341 69A6407, WNRC.

7. See note 6 above.

8. Ltr, Gen Curtis E. LeMay, CSAF, to SecAF, subj: Air Reserve Force Management, Nov 27, 1964, w/atch, RG 340, 68A4994, WNRC; hist, Dir/M&O, Jan–Jun 1965, p 63.

9. The Kennedy administration's intention to review national reserve policies can be traced in the memo, Robert H. Johnson to McGeorge Bundy, subj: The FY 1962 Budget—Issues Relating to the U.S. Military Program, Jan 30, 1961, w/atch, Nat Sec Files, Depts & Agencies, DOD, Defense Budget FY 1963, 1/1961–10/1961, Box 275, JFKL; Record of Actions, NSC, Meeting, Feb 1, 1961, Mtgs & Memo Series, Box 313, JFKL; memo, Robert S. McNamara, SecDef, to Secs Mil Depts et al., subj: List of Projects for Assignment, 1 Mar 1961, w/atch, Pres Ofc Files, Depts & Agencies, Defense, 1/1961–3/1961, Box 77, JFKL. For development of the proposal

467

The Air Force Reserve

to reduce the Army Reserve components, see "Annual Report of the Secretary of the Army, Jul 1, 1960, to Jun 30, 1961," *Department of Defense Annual Report for Fiscal Year 1961*, pp 81–82, 122–24; "Annual Report of the Reserve Forces Policy Board," *Department of Defense Annual Report for Fiscal Year 1961*; memo, Maxwell D. Taylor to Dir/BOB, subj: Excesses and Deficiencies on the SecDef Proposed Budget for FY 1963, Nov 21, 1961, Nat Sec Files, Depts & Agencies, DOD, Defense Budget FY 1963, 11/1961–12/1961, Box 275, JFKL; memo, McNamara to President, subj: Reorganization of the Army National Guard and Reserves, Dec 9, 1961, Pres Ofc Files, Depts and Agencies, Defense 9/1961–12/1961, Reorg of NG & Res, Box 77, JFKL.

10. Administration officials were forced to conduct extensive correspondence with governors, congressmen, and other officials on the reserve reorganization issue. See, for example, ltr, Brig Gen Fred C. Weyand, GS, Dep Ch/Legis Liaison Div, USA, to William C. Cramer, H.R., subj: Reorganization of Reserve Components of the Army, Apr 12, 1962; ltr, Ralph A. Dungan, Spec Asst to Pres, to Maj Gen James F. Cantwell, Pres AGA, subj: Resolutions of Adjutants General Association, May 23, 1962—both in ND 13 RF & NG, 3/1/62–4/30/62, Box 631, JFKL; ltr, T. J. Reardon, Jr., Spec Asst to Pres, to Orval E. Faubus, Gov of Arkansas, subj: National Defense, Dec 28, 1961, ND National Security Defense, 8/21/61–12/31/61, Box 593, JFKL.

11. Intvw, Dennis J. O'Brien with Roswell L. Gilpatric, May 5–27 and Jun 30, 1970, JFKL.

12. Crossland and Currie, *Twice the Citizen*, pp 151–61.

13. Minutes, OSD RFPB Special Meeting, Dec 22, 1964; News release, OASD/PA, "Reserve Components Real Signed to Increase Combat Readiness," Dec 12, 1964—both in AFRES 5C4; *Department of Defense Annual Report for Fiscal Year 1965*, pp 28–29. The files of the White House contain many letters opposing the proposed mergers, and Secretary of the Air Force files bulge with protests against any Air Reserve Forces merger. See, for example, WHCF, ND 13 RF & NG, 11/26/63–12/28/64, LBJL; and RG 340, 69A3338 and 68A4994, WNRC.

14. Study, "Management of the Air Reserve Forces," Dir/M&O USAF, Jan 6, 1965, AFRES 5C4.

15. Ltr, Maj Gen Curtis R. Low, Asst CSAF/RF, to CSAF, subj: Reserve Forces Management, Jan 6, 1965, AF5C4.

16. Memo, Lt Gen Edward J. Timberlake, Cmdr CAC, subj: Chronological Events at Puerto Rico on Merger of Reserve and Guard, n.d. [ca. Jan 9, 1965], AFRES 5C4. This is also tab C to Timberlake's briefing to Reserve unit commanders at Robins AFB on Jan 21, 1965.

17. Ibid.
18. Ibid.
19. Ibid.

20. Ltr, Gen John P. McConnell, VCS, to SecAF, subj: Air Reserve Forces Management, Jan 9, 1965; memo, Eugene M. Zuckert, SecAF, to SecDef, subj: Transfer of Air Force Reserve to Air National Guard, Jan 11, 1965—both in AFRES 5C4.

21. Ltr, Brig Gen John D. Lavelle, Dir/Aerospace Progs, to SAF–LL et al., subj: Consolidation of Reserve Forces, Jan 13, 1965; ltr, Lavelle to SAF–LL et al., subj: Plan for Consolidation of the Reserve Forces Units, Feb 10, 1965, w/atch, "National Guard Bureau Initial Planning for the Merger of the Air Reserve Forces," Jan 18, 1965—all in AFRES 5C4; memo, Gerritt W. Wesselink, Gen Counsel, to SecAF, subj: Merger of Reserve Units into the Guard, Mar 2, 1965; memo, Wesselink to SecAF, subj: Merger of Air Force Reserve and Air National Guard, Mar 2, 1965—both in RG 340, 69A3338, WNRC; "Special Message to the Congress on the State of the Nation's Defenses," Jan 18, 1965, Johnson, *Public Papers, 1965*, vol 1, pp 67–68.

22. House Armed Services Committee, *Hearings on Military Posture and H.R. 4016 to Authorize Appropriations during Fiscal Year 1966 for Procurement of Aircraft, Missiles, and Naval Vessels, and Research, Development, Test, and Evaluation, for the Armed Forces, and for Other Purposes*, 89th Cong., 1st sess.

23. Extract from transcript, Hearings before the Committee on Armed Services, H.R., during Military Posture Briefings: Colloquy between Hon. F. Edward Hebert

Notes

and Secretary of Defense Robert S. McNamara, Feb 22, 1965.

24. MFR, Col Jack Reiter, USAF, Ofc of Legis Liaison, subj: Army Reserve/National Guard Realignment, Mar 1, 1965, AFRES 5C4.

25. "Military Procurement Authorizations, Fiscal Year 1966," *Hearings before the Committee on Armed Services and the Subcommitee on Department of Defense of the Committee on Appropriations, United States Senate*, 89th Cong., 1st sess., Department of Defense Programs and Authorization of Appropriations during FY 1966 for Procurement, Research, Development, Test, and Evaluation of Aircraft, Missiles, and Naval Vessels for the Armed Forces, pp 389–405; "Merger of the Army Reserve Components," *Hearings Before Subcommittee No. 2 of the Committee on Armed Services*, H.R., 89th Cong., 1st sess., pp 3555–4190; MFR, Lt Col Rollins C. Swelling, USAF, Ofc of Legis Liaison, subj: Reserve and National Guard Program, Mar 11, 1965; MFR, Snelling, subj: Army Reserve National Guard Realignment, Mar 18, 1965; MFR, Snelling, subj: Army Reserve/National Guard Realignment, Mar 25, 1965—all in AFRES 5C4.

26. Crossland and Currie, *Twice the Citizen*, pp 163–79.

27. MFR, Lt Col Robert J. Dunn, USAF, Ofc Legis Liaison, subj: Army Reserve/National Guard Realignment, Apr 13, 1965; MFR, Snelling, subj: Army Reserve/National Guard Realignment, Apr 12, 1965—both in AFRES 5C4.

28. MFR, Snelling, subj: Army Reserve/National Guard Realignment, Apr 14, 1965; statement, F. Edward Hebert, Chmn HASC, [reviewing the Department of Defense proposal to merge the Army Reserve Components,] Apr 12, 1965—both in AFRES 5C4; ltr, Col George A. Carter, Ch OI CONAC, to staff, subj: Senator Stennis' Statement on Reserve Merger, Jul 29, 1965, AFRES 5C4.

29. Statement, Rep. F. Edward Hebert, Chmn Subcmte No. 2, on H.R. 8243, Aug 2, 1965; statement, Dep SecDef Cyrus R. Vance, before Subcmte No. 2, HASC, Aug 2, 1965—both in AFRES 5C4; MFR, Col Jack Reiter, USAF, Ofc of Legis Liaison, subj: Hearings on H.R. 8243, 89th Congress, Reserve–National Guard Merger, Aug 3, 1965, AFRES 5C4.

30. News release, HASC, "Army Reserve Merger," Aug 12, 1965, AFRES 5C4.

31. *Reserve Bill of Rights*, H.R. Rpt No. 13, 90th Cong., 1st sess., Feb 13, 1967; HASC, *Hearings on H.R. 16435 and H.R. 17195 to Amend Titles 10, 14, 32, and 37, United States Code, to Strengthen the Reserve Components of the Armed Forces, and Clarify the Status of National Guard Technicians, and for Other Purposes*, Subcmte No. 2 & full cmte, 89th Cong., 2d sess.

32. See note 31 above; *Reserve Components of the Armed Forces and National Guard Technicians*, hearings before Senate Arms Services Committee, SASC, 90th Cong., 1st sess.; *Reserve Components of the Armed Services*, S. Rpt No. 732, Nov 7, 1967, SASC, 90th Cong., 1st sess.; Legislative History, PL 90–168, 90th Cong., 1st sess. (1967), *Reserve Forces Bill of Rights and Vitalization Act, U.S. Code Congressional and Administrative News*, vol 2, pp 2033–60.

33. PL 90–168, *Reserve Forces Bill of Rights and Vitalization Act* (Stat 81: 521), Dec 1, 1967.

34. Memo, Theodore C. Marrs, AF Dep for Res, to Chmn ARFPC, subj: H.R. 2 and Requirements for Chief, Office of Air Force Reserve, Apr 5, 1967 (with MFR, Cantwell, Sep 25, 1987), RG 340, 71A6173, WNRC; DAF SO GA 98, Dec 22, 1967; HQ USAF *Daily Staff Digest*, No. 41, Feb 28, 1968; memo, Joe Califano to the President, subj: Nomination of Brig Gen Marchbanks as Chief of Air Force Reserve, Dec 11, 1967, WHCF, ND 13 Guard & Reserve, Box 183, LBJL. On September 25, 1987, Charles F. Bock, Chairman, Senate Office Management Branch, Office of Air Force Reserve, who had been Executive Secretary of AFRPC in 1967, confirmed that the committee nominated five generals, with Marchbanks and Moore in the first and second positions, respectively, for the new Chief's position, but I find no record of the AFRPC's action.

35. MFR, Maj Gen Richard S. Abbey, Asst CSAF/RF, subj: H.R. 2: The Reserve Forces Bill of Rights and Vitalization Act, Nov 30, 1967; MFR, Col C. Wiley Alford, Dep to Ch AF Res, and Maj Gen Tom E. Marchbanks, Jr., Ch AFRES, subj: Briefing

469

for the Chief of Staff, Feb 28, 1968.

36. Memo, Maj Gen Lewis A. Curtis, chmn, to SecAF, subj: Recommendations—Special Meeting of the Air Reserve Forces Policy Committee, Mar 18, 1968, SAF/MIR; memo, Maj Gen Ramsay D. Potts, V/Chmn, to SecAF et al., subj: Special Meeting of the Air Reserve Forces Policy Committee, Mar 18, 1968; memo, Marrs to SecAF, subj: Reorganization of Air Force Reserve, Mar 20, 1968; memo, Harold Brown, SecAF, to CSAF, subj: Organization of Office of Air Force Reserve, Mar 20, 1968—all in 72A5065, RG 340, WNRC; ltr, Maj Gen William B. Campbell, Dir/M&O, to CAC, subj: Organizational Actions Pertaining to Headquarters, Continental Air Command, Jun 21, 1968, as doc 1–27 in hist, CAC, Jan–Jul 68; ltr, Campbell to ARPC, subj: Organizational Actions Pertaining to the Air Force Reserve Personnel Center (ARC), Jun 21, 1968, as doc 1–42 in hist, CNC, Jan–Jul 68.

37. CAC SO G–46, Jul 16, 1968 [discontinued CAC, effective Aug 1, 1968]; AFRES SO G–54, Aug 1, 1968 [constituted, activated, and organized HQ AFRES, effective Aug 1, 1968]; AFRES SO G–55, Aug 1, 1968 [Maj Gen Rollin B. Moore, Jr., assumed command of AFRES]; ARPC SO G–1, Jul 23, 1968 [established ARPC, effective Aug 1, 1968]. Dr. Marrs' observation was included in remarks he made during a CONAC Reserve Policy Committee meeting on Nov 6, 1964 (AFRES 5C4).

38. USAF Biography, Rollin B. Moore, Jr.

39. MFR, Cantwell, subj: The Controversy over Air Reserve Command/Management Prerogatives in FY 1970–1971, 1987.

40. Hist, AFRES, FY 1970, p 46; talking paper, Maj Gen Homer I. Lewis, Ch AF Res, subj: Dual Hat (Chief of Air Force Reserve also Commander of AFRES), n.d. [ca. Jul 1972], AFRES 5C6.

41. AFR 23–1, *HO Air Force Reserve (AFRES)*, Jul 28, 1970; ltr, Marchbanks to AFRES & ARPC, subj: Standard Operating Procedures for CSAF Messages Concerning Air Force Reserve Program Resources, Jul 22, 1970, w/atch, doc 2, hist, AFRES, FY 1971.

42. The author attended several of the briefings for the Program Review Committee as well as General Cragg's debriefing. Remarks, General Moore's HQ AFRES staff meeting, Oct 28, 1970; intvw, with Rollin B. Moore, Sep 7, 1987.

43. Ltr, Maj Gen Rollin B. Moore, Jr., Cmdr AFRES, to Gen John C. Meyer, VCSAF, subj: AFRES Organizational Status, Feb 26, 1971, doc 3, hist, AFRES, FY 1971; talking paper, Lewis, n.d. [ca. Jul 1972]; memo, Col Robert C. Bachtell, Dir/M&O AFRES, to Ex Off et al., subj: Memorandum for the Record on Visit to AFTOR, 15 Jan 1970, Jan 16, 1970, doc 2–23, hist, AFRES, FY 1971.

44. For more extensive treatment of General Marchbanks' tenure as first Chief of Air Force Reserve, see Gerald T. Cantwell, "The Total Force: From Marchbanks to Bodycombe," *Air Force Magazine*, Oct 1981; USAF news release [General Marchbanks' remarks to the Air Section], National Convention of the Reserve Officers' Association, Bal Harbour, Fla.

45. Speech, General Marchbanks, Commanders' Conference, Aug 22, 1968, HQ AFRES.

46. Msg, AFRPRP–C, Col Kenneth G. Shaw, Dir/Ares Pers AFRES, to 446 TAW et al., subj: UPT Quotas, Nov 25, 1969, doc 4–10, hist, AFRES, FY 1970.

47. Hist, AFRES, FY 1970, pp 2–10.

48. Msg, USAF to AAC et al., subj: Nomination of Maj Gen Homer I. Lewis, DPG 081733Z Mar 71, AFRES 5A.

49. MFR, Cantwell, subj: General Moore's Observations at 18 Mar 1971, Staff Meeting, Mar 18, 1971, AFRES 3D.1.

50. Rpt, "Management Inspection of the Air Force Reserve, PN 71–94, 21 Mar–12 Jun 71," app 1 to hist, AFRES, FY 1971.

51. Intvw, Cantwell with Maj Gen Homer I. Lewis, Mar 26, 1975, AFRES 24A.

52. Ltr, Gen John C. Meyer, VCSAF, to CincSAC et al., subj: Reorganization of Intermediate Headquarters, May 17, 1971, doc 8, hist, AFRES, FY 1971.

53. General Lewis confirmed his faith in the dual-hat system during a telephone conversation with the author on November 24, 1986 (MFR, Cantwell, subj: Discussion with Maj Gen Homer I. Lewis on Dual Hat, Nov 24, 1986). ASSS, Lewis, subj: Air Force Reserve Reorganization, May 24,

Notes

1972, AFRES 5C6.

54. Ltr, Maj Gen William W. Berg, Dir/M&O USAF, to AF/RE, subj: Management Structure of the Air Force Reserve, Sep 29, 1971, w/2 atchs, AFRES 5C5; Air Force Reserve Management Study, Option III, Feb 15, 1972; MFR, Col Robert C. Bachtelle, AFRES Dir/M&O, subj: Reorganization of Intermediate Headquarters, Jun 2, 1971; ltr, Brig Gen John R. Kern, Dir/M&O USAF, to Ofc of AF Res, subj: Air Force Reserve Organization, May 16, 1972—all in AFRES 6C.

55. Ltr, Gen John C. Meyer, VCSAF, to AF/RE and AFRES, subj: Dual Function for the Chief of Air Force Reserve, Feb 26, 1972; DAF SO AA-371, Mar 3, 1972—both in AFRES 5A; ltr, Brig Gen Donald J. Campbell, Dep to Ch AF Res, to AFRES, subj: Reorganization of the Office of the Chief of Air Force Reserve, Mar 3, 1972, w/atch, doc 7, hist, AFRES, FY 1972.

56. Cantwell, "Total Force: Marchbanks to Bodycombe."

57. Ltr No. 6, HQ AFRES Commander, Mar 24, 1972; remarks, Gen Lewis, HQ AFRES staff meeting, Mar 16, and upon assuming command, Mar 26—both events being witnessed by the author.

58. Ltr, Maj Gen Homer I. Lewis to HQ AFRES, subj: Delegation of Authority, Mar 16, 1972, doc 7, hist, AFRES, FY 1972.

59. Msg, USAF to TAC et al., subj: Air Force Reserve Management Study Group, PRMMB, 121838Z Jul 72, doc 1, hist, AFRES, FY 1973; ltr, Brig Gen John R. Kern, Jr., Dir/M&O USAF, to ADC et al., subj: Air Force Reserve Management Structure Study—Draft, Sep 13, 1972, w/atch, doc 6, hist, AFRES, FY 1973.

60. Ltr, Maj Gen Homer I. Lewis, Ch AF Res, to USAF/PRM, subj: Air Force Reserve Management Structure Study—Draft, Sep 21, 1972, doc 7, hist, AFRES, FY 1973.

61. Atch 1 (ltr, Col Paul E. Jones, DCS/Plans AFRES, to Ofc of AF Res, subj: Air Force Reserve Management Structure Study—Draft, Sep 28, 1972, w/atch), doc 8, hist, AFRES, FY 1973.

62. Hist, Ofc AF Res, Jan–Jun 72, pp 30–31; MFR, Lt Col Robert H. Schmidt, Asst Ex SecAFC, subj: Study of the Air Force Reserve Management Structure, Oct 17, 1972, w/5 atchs; comments, General Verhulst's HQ AFRES staff meeting, Oct 17, 1972, WNRC; comments, Col Donald L. Peck, C/S AFRES, AFRES joint staff meeting, Jan 5, 1973; ltr, Maj Gen James A. Hill, Asst DCS/Progs & Resources USAF, to AF/RES, subj: Study of Air Force Reserve Management Structure, May 13, 1974, w/atch, case file, Option 5 of Air Force Study, 1972–1974, AFREXR.

63. MFR, Cantwell, subj: Discussion with Maj Gen Homer I. Lewis on Dual Hat, Nov 24, 1986, AFRES 24A.

64. Intvw, Cantwell, with Maj Gen Richard Bodycombe, May 28, 1985, Ann Arbor, Mich., p 143.

65. Intvw, Cantwell, with Maj Gen Homer I. Lewis, Mar 26, 1975, Pentagon, pp 26–28, AFRES 24A.

66. Ltr, Gen John P. McConnell, CSAF, to SecAF, subj: Roles and Missions for Air Reserve Forces, Feb 17, 1968, AFRES 6C.

67. RAND, *The Air Reserve Forces Study*, vol 1, *Summary and Integration* (RM-5326-PR, Santa Monica, Calif., Jul 1967), copy in AFRES 5B15b.

68. Memo, Maj Gen Lewis A. Curtis, ANGUS, chmn ARFPC, to SecAF through CSAF, subj: Recommendations—45th Meeting of the Air Reserve Forces Policy Committee, Sep 25–27, 1967, Sep 27, 1967, AFRES 5B2; memo, Marrs to Lt Col Richard L. Miner, Dep Ex Asst OSAF, subj: Recommendations and Analysis of Rand Study of the Air Reserve Forces, Dec 8, 1967; memo, Townsend Hoopes, U/Sec-AF, to CSAF, subj: Recommendations—45th Meeting of the Air Reserve Forces Policy Committee, Sep 25–27, 1967, Feb 26, 1968; ASSS, Maj Gen Richard S. Abbey, Asst CSAF/RF, subj: Recommendations—45th Meeting of the Air Reserve Forces Policy Committee, 25–27 Sep 67, Oct 9, 1967; memo, Marrs to CSAF, subj: Recommendations and Analysis of Rand Study for the Air Reserve Forces, Jan 19, 1968—all RG 340, 71A6172, WNRC.

69. Ltr, Gen John P. McConnell, CSAF, to SecAF, Feb 17, 1968, AFRES 5C.

70. Ibid.

71. Ltr, Lt Gen Hewitt I. Wheless, Asst VCSAF, to Deputies et al., subj: Air Reserve Forces, Feb 17, 1968, w/atch, AFRES 6C.

72. "Annual Defense Report: National

The Air Force Reserve

Security Strategy of Realistic Deterrence," *Commanders Digest*, May 4, 1972, pp 4–5.

73. Memo, Melvin R. Laird, SecDef, to Secs Mil Depts et al., subj: Support for Guard and Reserve Forces, Aug 21, 1970, AFRES 6C.

74. Air Force Reserve Management Fact Sheet, n.d. [early May 1974], case files, management studies, AFREX. General Lewis also used this same fact sheet to brief the Air Reserve Forces Policy Committee.

75. Ltr, O. C. Fisher, HASC, to William P. Clements, Actg SecDef, subj: Erosion of Authority of Chiefs of Reserve Components, Jun 4, 1973, AFRES 6A.

76. Memo, James R. Schlesinger, SecDef, to Secs Mil Depts et al., subj: Readiness of the Selected Reserve, Aug 23, 1973, AFRES 6C.

77. Ltr, Schlesinger to Hon. O. C. Fisher, subj: Reserve Forces, Aug 23, 1973, case study vol 11, Meyer Studies, book 11, Bennewitz 1973–1974, AFREXR.

78. Memo, Schlesinger to Asst SecDef (MRA), subj: Guard and Reserve in the Total Force, Aug 23, 1973, case study vol 11, Meyer Studies, book 11, Bennewitz 1973–1974, AFREXR.

79. Memo, B. A. Bridgewater, Jr., Assoc Dir, Guard and Reserve in the Total Force Study Group, to Terence E. McClary, Asst SecDef (Compt), subj: Total Force Study, May 21, 1974, AFRES 6C; memo, William K. Brehm, Asst SecDef (MRA), for Secs Mil Depts et al., subj: The Guard and the Reserve in the Total Force, Dec 20, 1974, w/atch, SAF/MIR.

80. Atch 1 (ASSS, Maj Gen George G. Loving, Jr., Dir/Plans, subj: Air Force Response to ASD/MR&A Study, "The Guard and the Reserve in the Total Force," Jan 26, 1975, w/2 atchs); ltr, James W. Plummer, U/SecAF, to Asst SecDef (MRA), Subj: The Guard and the Reserve in the Total Force, Jan 28, 1975, SAF/MIR.

81. Memo, Schlesinger to Secs Mil Depts et al., subj: Total Force Program Guidance, Jun 2, 1975; OSD news release, subj: Study of Guard/Reserve Role in Total Force Completed, Sep 9, 1975—both in AFRES 6C.

82. See note 74 above.

83. Ltr, Brig Gen Donald J. Campbell, Dep to Ch AF Res, to Chief, TAC Forces Div, HQ USAF, subj: Proposed Revision, AFR 45–1 (third draft), Apr 18, 1973, AFRES 6A.

84. Ltr, Maj Gen I. G. Brown, for Maj Gen Francis S. Greenlief, Ch NGB, to CSAF, subj: Proposed Revision AFR 45–1, Oct 24, 1973; Air Force Reserve Management Fact Sheet, Progs & Resources Div Ofc, AFRES, n.d. [early May 1974]—both in AFRES 6A.

85. Ltr, Gen George S. Brown, CSAF, to Maj Gen Jamers L. Murray, Chmn, ARFPC, subj: Air Reserve Forces Policy Committee Consideration of Proposed AFR 45–1, Jun 18, 1974, SAF/MIR; point paper, Progs & Resources Div Ofc, AFRES, subj: Proposed AFR 45–1, Mar 18, 1974, management studies, AFREXR; ltr, Brig Gen Harry J. Huff, Cmdr 433d TAW, to Wing Off, subj: Active Duty Air Force's Rewrite of AFRs 45–1, 45–6, and 45–60, May 14, 1974; ltr, Lt Gen Robert E. Huyser, DCS/Plans & Ops USAF, to CSAF, subj: Letter of Consideration of the NGB/CC and AF RE Nonconcurrences, May 1, 1974—both in AFRES 6A; MFR, Col Bruce H. Berryman, Ex Sec ARFPC, subj: Special Meeting of the Air Reserve Forces Policy Committee, Jun 20–21, 1974, Jun 21, 1974, w/atch, SAF/MIR. In a conversation with the author on April 29, 1987, Brig. Gen. Billy M. Knowles, USAFR (Ret.), an Air Force Reserve activist, remembers with bemusement that for whatever reason the reservists did not involve the Reserve Officers Association but on this occasion went directly to congressmen.

86. Memo, Maj Gen James L. Murray, Chmn ARFPC, to CSAF, subj: Air Reserve Forces Policy Committee Consideration of Proposed AFR 45–1, Jun 21, 1974, SAF/MIR.

87. ASSS, Maj Gen George G. Loving, Jr., Dir/Plans USAF, subj: Revision of AFR 45–1, "Purpose, Policy, and Responsibilities for Air Reserve Forces," Jun 24, 1974; briefing, Col Boris Chaleff, Ch, Progs & Resources Div Ofc, AF Res, at AFRES Commanders' Conference, Jun 20, 1975, San Diego, Calif.—both in AFRES 6A; AFR 45–1, *Purpose, Policy, and Responsibilities for Air Reserve Forces (ARF)*, Mar 3, 1975.

88. Intvw, Cantwell, with Maj Gen

Notes

Homer I. Lewis, Mar 26, 1975, Pentagon, pp 26–28, AFRES 24A.

89. Intvw, Cantwell, with Maj Gen Richard Bodycombe, May 28, 1985, Ann Arbor, Mich., p 143.

Chapter 10

1. Atch (memo, Lt Gen Leon W. Johnson, CH, RPRB, for CSAF, subj: Report of the Reserve Program Review Board, Aug 24, 1953), rpt, Reserve Program Review Board, Aug 24, 1953; summary, unsigned, subj: Status of Reserve Program Review Board Recommendations as of 19 February 1954—both in AFRES 5B3. See also, briefing, Col William L. Kimball, Dir/Res Plng Gp, CONAC, Air Reserve Center Plan, Feb 12, 1954, and memo, Lt Col Robert R. Eaton, Actg Ch Plng Gp, to VCmdr, subj: Minutes of Planning Group Meeting, 3 August 1953, Aug 3, 1953—both in AFRES 16C.

2. Hist, CONAC, Jan–Jun 1954, pp 80–81; AFR 23–25, *Numbered Air Reserve Center,* Apr 13, 1955.

3. Hist, CONAC, Jan–Jun 1955, pp 68–69.

4. Ibid., Jan–Jun 1958, pp 109–10; msg (AFOMO–0–3–30194), USAF to CONAC, Mar 8, 1955, as doc 106 in hist, CONAC, Jan–Jun 1955; hist, CONAC, Jan–Jun 1958, pp 112–14.

5. Ltr, USAF to CONAC, subj: Change in Status of Reserve Personnel Assigned to Program Elements in a Pay Status, Jul 11, 1955, w/3 inds, as doc 37–1 in hist, CONAC, Jul–Dec 1955; hist, Asst CSAF/RF, Jul–Dec 1955, pp 12–14.

6. Hist, Asst CSAF/RF, Jul–Dec 1955, pp 12–14; ltr, Maj Gen John W. Mills, Asst DCS/Pers, USAF, to CONAC, subj: Reserve Mobilization Requirements, Dec 1, 1955 w/atch, AFRES 14U.

7. Hist, CONAC, Jul–Dec 1956, pp 162–70; ibid., Jan–Jun 1957, pp 228–33.

8. For a detailed treatment of the vicissitudes of the Continental Air Command's General Training Program and the experiences of its members, consult the chapters on the individual training program in the histories of the Tenth Air Force, 1956 through 1959. The author was historian of that command and acquired much of his information firsthand during commanders' conferences and visits to the centers.

9. See, for example, hist, CONAC, Jul–Dec 1958, p 155.

10. Rpt, Individual Reserve Training Board, Aug 1956, AFRES 5B4.

11. Ltr, Maj Gen Maurice R. Nelson, VCmdr CONAC, to CSAF, subj: Reserve General Training (Category E), Nov 2, 1956, w/ind, AFRES 16C.

12. Ltr, Brig Gen Cecil E. Combs, Dep Dir/Pers Procurement & Training, USAF, to CONAC, subj: Training for Standby Reservists in the Air Reserve Center System, Jun 20, 1957, AFRES 16C.

13. DAF SO E–2025, Oct 1, 1959; Reserve Forces Review Group, *The Air Reserve Forces . . . New Roles in a New Era* (Washington, D.C., Nov 1959), pp 6–14, 40–41, 50–52; copy in AFRES 5B7; Ltr, Gen Curtis E. LeMay, Chmn AFC, to CSAF, subj: Plan for the Revised Management of the Air Reserve Forces, May 17, 1960, w/3 atchs, RG 341, 63A1790, WNRC; rpt, DAF, "Plan for Revised Management of the Air Reserve Forces," May 20, 1960, AFRES 5C3.

14. Plan, CONAC Reorg No. 3–60, "Plan for Air Force Reserve Base Support Groups," Sep 1, 1960, AFRES 17B; hist, Asst CSAF/RF, Jul–Dec 1961, pp 44–46; rpt, DAF, "Plan for Revised Management of the Air Reserve Forces," app 4 to annex F.

15. Lt Gen William E. Hall, "The Air Force Reserve Mission," *The Air Reservist,* Jun–Jul 1960; speech, Maj Gen Harold R. Maddux, VCmdr CONAC, to Georgia Press Association Convention, Jun 16, 1961, Milledgeville, Ga.

16. Ltr, Maj Gen R. M. Montgomery, Asst VCSAF, to Asst CSAF/RF, et al., subj: Air Reserve Forces–Recovery Unit Program, Apr 13, 1961, w/2 atchs, AFRES 17A; memo, Roswell Gilpatric, Dep SecDef, to SecAF, subj: Air Force Reserve

473

The Air Force Reserve

Recovery Program, Aug 11, 1961; ASSS, Col William F. McNeil, subj: Air Force Reserve Recovery Program, Aug 24, 1961; ltr, Maj Gen Chester E. McCarty, Dep for Air Force Res, to Cmdr CONAC, subj: Air Reserve Forces Recovery Unit Program, Apr 25, 1961, w/atch—all in AFRES 12A.

17. Memo, Joseph V. Charyk, U/SecAF, to Asst SecDef (Manpower), subj: Air Force Reserve Recovery Program, Aug 28, 1961, w/2 incls, AFRES 17A.

18. Memo, Benjamin W. Fridge, Res Dep, to SecAF, subj: Air Force Reserve Recovery Program, Oct 19, 1961; memo, Fridge to CSAF, subj: Air Force Reserve Recovery Program, Dec 13, 1961—both in RG 340, 66A3410, WNRC; hist, Asst CSAF/RF, Jul–Dec 1961, pp 44–46.

19. See note 18 above; memo, Carlisle P. Runge, Dep Asst Sec (M), to Dep SecDef, subj: Air Force Reserve Base Support and Recovery Programs, Nov 30, 1961, RG 330, 65A3212, Box 12, WNRC; hist, CONAC, Jul–Dec 1963, vol 2, pp 1–20.

20. Memo, Roswell L. Gilpatric, Dep SecDef, to SecAF, subj: Air Force Reserve Base Support and Recovery Programs, Jan 5, 1962, RG 340, 67A5143; ltr, Gilpatric to Clarence Cannon, Chmn HAC, subj: Air Force Reserve Recovery Program, Jan 16, 1962, RG 330, 65A3212, Box 12 [the same letter was sent to other committee chairmen]—both WNRC; msg, AFCRF–X 9142 to CONAC, subj: Telecon between Colonels McNeil and Sheridan, 082142Z Jan 62, AFRES 17A. The members of the test units were reduced to twenty-four paid drills per year (ltr, Col Burton H. Rowden, DCS/Pers CONAC, to ARRC et al., subj: Training Category and Pay Group for Recovery and Support Units, May 9, 1962, AFRES 17A).

21. Hist, Ofc of Asst CSAF/RF, Jul–Dec 1962, pp 5–7.

22. MFR, J. J. Lichman, Dir/Hist Svcs, CONAC, subj: Telephone Conversations with Colonel Alford, HQ USAF (AFFRAY), Feb 20, 1964, AFRES 17B.

23. Memo, Eugene M. Zuckert, SecAF, to SecDef, subj: Recovery Groups and Squadrons, Air Force Reserve, Dec 6, 1962, RG 340, 67A5143, WNRC.

24. For an excellent summary of the rise and fall of the test base support units, see the paper by Thomas P. O'Brien, "Resuscitation of Reserve Base Support Groups," Jan 9, 1964, AFRES 17B.

25. Ltr, CG of US to Congress, [transmitting a secret report on ineffective program planning and uneconomical utilization of personnel assigned to the Air Force Reserve Recovery Program (Jan 1964, B–146831)], Feb 1964; ltr, Joseph Campbell, CG of US, to President, subj: Transmittal of Report to Congress, Feb 17, 1964; rpt, Comptroller General to Congress, "Ineffective Program Planning and Uneconomical Utilization of Personnel Assigned to the Air Force Reserve Recovery Program," Jan 1964—all in WHCF, FG 130, DAF, Box 28, LBJL.

26. Memo, Maj Gen Charles DuBois, Ch ANGUS, to SecAF, subj: Recommendations—38th Meeting of the Air Reserve Forces Policy Committee—16–22 Apr 1964, Apr 22, 1964, SAF/MIR; memo, Robert S. McNamara, SecDef, to SecAF, subj: Air Force Reserve Recovery Program, May 16, 1964, AFRES 17A; hist, CONAC, Jan–Jun 1964, pp 61–70.

27. Memo, Eugene M. Zuckert, SecAF, to SecDef, subj: Reclama to Format B, Change Number F–4–110, Air Force Reserve Drill Pay Spaces (F–4–110R), Dec 9, 1964, w/2 atchs, RG 340, 68A4994, WNRC; hist, CONAC, Jul–Dec 1964, pp 48–49; CONAC PCD 65-2, Discontinuance of Recovery Units, Jan 20, 1965, AFRES 17A; CONAC SOs G–60 through G–65, Jun 15, 1964; CONAC SO G–3, Jan 14, 1965.

28. Terminating hists, AFRES recovery units, Jan–Mar 1965. See particularly the foreword to hist, 8574 AFRRG, Feb 1965.

29. The units' training requirements were set out in "CONAC Guide for Air Force Reserve Recovery Units," May 22, 1961, pp 3–4, AFRES 17A. The Air Force Reserve recovery unit histories are replete with accounts of these training exercises. The Military Air Transport Service exercises were described in ltr, Maj Gen Glen R. Birchard, VCmdr MATS, to HQ USAF/XOPC, subj: Air Force Reserve Recovery Program, Sep 26, 1963, AFRES 17A, and the FAA exercise was described in hist, CONAC, Jul–Dec 64, p 58.

30. Intvw excerpt, with Lt Gen William E. Hall, Sep 1961; intvw excerpt, with Maj Gen Robert E. L. Eaton, Oct 17, 1961—

Notes

both in AFRES 26A.

31. Hist, CONAC, Jul–Dec 64, pp 68–71; hist, Ofc of Asst CSAF/RF, Jan–Jun 1961, pp 16–18; hist, Ofc of Asst CSAF/RF, Jul–Dec 1960, pp 15–16; ltr, Maj Hammond, OTR–CE, CONAC, to DCS/Training, subj: Continuation of Reserve Element Training, Sep 13, 1961; ltr, Hammond to DCS/Training, subj: Retention of Det #1, Sep 12, 1961—both in AFRES 16F.

32. Briefing, CONAC, Reserve Element Training, Jul 1962, AFRES 16F.

33. The brief life-span of the specialist training centers may be traced in the following documents: Memo, Col Brian S. Gunderson, Dep Ex Asst/SecAF, to Marrs, subj: Individual Reserve Program, Mar 8, 1965; memo, Eugene M. Zuckert, SecAF, to SecDef, subj: Air Reserve Squadrons, Mar 12, 1965, w/2 atchs; memo of conversation, author with Col William V. McBride, Mar 16, 1965; memo, Theodore C. Marrs, DOD Dep for Res and ROTC Affairs, subj: Revisions in Individual Reserve Programs, Mar 24, 1965; memo, Zuckert to CSAF, subj: Training of Individual Reservists, Mar 26, 1965; memo, Cyrus Vance, U/SecDef, to SecAF, subj: Inactivation of Air Reserve Squadrons, Mar 30, 1965; ASSS, Brig Gen Curtis R. Low, Asst CSAF/RF, subj: Air Reserve Squadrons, Apr 7, 1965, w/2 atchs—all in RG 340, 69A3338, WNRC; CONAC Air Force Specialty Training Squadron Test Implementation Plan, Sep 30, 1965, AFRES 16D; study, Col Cecil W. Alford, Ofc of Asst CSAF/RF, to SecAF, subj: Air Reserve Forces: Air Force Requirements for Individuals, Present Resources and Training Programs, May 19, 1965; ASSS, Maj Gen Curtis R. Low, Asst CSAF/RF, subj: Air Reserve Forces: Air Force Requirements for Individuals, Present Resources and Training Programs, Jul 16, 1965, w/2 atchs; memo, Eugene M. Zuckert, SecAF, for Dep SecDef, subj: Air Force Reserve Individual Training, Jul 29, 1965, w/atch; ltr, Gen William H. Blanchard, VCSAF, to ADC et al., subj: Air Force Reserve Specialty Training Program, Oct 11, 1965—all in RG 341, 67A5358, AFFRA MIL 6–2–3–1, WNRC; CONAC SO G–102, Oct 11, 1965; CONAC Program Control Directive No. 65–20, subj: Air Force Specialty Training Squadron Test Program, Nov 1, 1965; memo, Theodore C. Marrs, Dep for Res Forces, to Eugene T. Ferraro, Dep U/SecAF (Manpower), subj: Specialty Training Program, May 29, 1967, RG 340, 70A5358, WNRC; CONAC SO G–54, Sep 25, 1967; msg, AFFRA 78613, to CONAC, subj: Air Force Reserve Specialty Training Program, 182002Z Jul 67; memo, Eugene T. Ferraro, Dep U/SecAF (Manpower), to Dep SecDef, subj: Air Force Reserve Specialty Training Program, Jun 2, 1967, w/atch; ASSS, Maj Gen Richard S. Abbey, subj: Air Force Reserve Specialty Training Program, Apr 24, 1967; w/2 atchs—both in RG 340, 70A5358, WNRC; MFR, Maj F. C. Aldrich, Ch, Res El Trng Br, CONAC, subj: Staff Visit to Flts B & C, 9301 Specialty Training Squadron, Charlotte, N.C., Jan 11, 1966, AFRES 16D.

34. Ltr, AFRES Cmdr, Oct 2, 1968, as exhibit 3 in hist, AFRES, Aug–Dec 1968; memo, Maj Gen Charles DuBois, Ch ANGUS, to SecAF, subj: Recommendations—36th Meeting of the Air Reserve Forces Policy Committee, 26 Apr through 1 May 1963, May 6, 1963, SAF/MIR; memo Brockway McMillian, U/SecAF, to CSAF, subj: Recommendations—36th Meeting of the Air Reserve Forces Policy Committee, 26 Apr through 1 May 1963, SAF/MIR; AFRES Summary of AF Reserve Element Training (RCS: AFR-T13), a/o Jun 30, 1969, and Jun 30, 1970, as doc 4–268 in hist, AFRES, FY 1970; hist, AFRES, Jan–Jun 1969, pp 41–42; AFRESM 45–3, *Air Force Reserve Element Training*, May 1, 1969, as exhibit 7 in hist, AFRES, Jan–Jun 1969.

35. Hist, AFRES, FY 1970, pp 211–13; ltr, Maj Gen Earl O. Anderson, VCmdr AFRES, to HQ USAF/RE, subj: Air Reserve Squadron, Dec 17, 1973, w/2 atchs, as doc 515 in hist, AFRES, FY 1974; ltr, Maj Gen Homer I. Lewis, Ch AF Res, to AFRES, subj: Reserve Squadrons, Jan 7, 1974, as doc 517 in hist, AFRES, FY 1974.

36. AFRES SO G–35, Jun 4, 1975; ltr, Maj Gen Homer I. Lewis, Ch AF Res, to AFRES, subj: Reserve Element Training, Jul 15, 1975, as doc 559 in hist, AFRES FY 1975; summaries, "AF Reserve Element Training" (RCS: AFR-TSI[SA] 7101), a/o Jun 30 and Sep 5, 1975, as docs 565 and 566, respectively, in hist, AFRES,

The Air Force Reserve

FY 1975.

37. Hist, ARPC, 1981, pp 28–33.

38. Ltr, Lt Gen George E. Stratemeyer, CG, ADC, to NAF Cmdrs, subj: Mobilization Assignments, Apr 8, 1947, AFRES 9A.

39. Ltr, Maj Gen Earle E. Partridge, Asst C/AS–3, to Stratemeyer, subj: Training of Reserve Personnel by Regular AAF Stations and Units, Apr 15, 1947, AFRES 9A.

40. AFL 20–32, "Mobilization Assignments for Air Reserve Personnel at All USAF Bases," Feb 3, 1948; ADCL 35–99, "Administration of United States Air Force Reserve Personnel on Mobilization Assignments," Apr 15, 1948—both in AFRES 14K.

41. AFL 45–5, "Mobilization-Day Assignments for Air Force Reserves Personnel," Jul 19, 1948; AFR 45–3, *Mobilization Assignments and Training Attachments for United States Air Force Reserve Officers*, Oct 8, 1948—both in AFRES 14K.

42. Ltr, McConnell to CG CONAC, subj: Implementation of the Air Force Reserve Training Programs for FY 1950, May 6, 1949, w/3 incls, AFRES 10.

43. Ltr, McConnell to CG CONAC, subj: USAF Reserve Mobilization Assignment Program, Dec 7, 1949, w/ind, AFRES 14K.

44. 1st ind (McConnell ltr, Dec 7, 1949), Lt Gen Dennis C. Whitehead, CG CONAC, to CSAF, Jan 18, 1950, AFRES 14K.

45. AFR 45–3, *Air Force Reserve Mobilization Assignment/Designation Program*, Nov 3, 1954, AFRES 14K; CONACR 45–19, *Training Designations*, Apr 21, 1955, AFRES 16C.

46. Memo, Maj Gen Robert W. Burns, Asst VCSAF, for SecAF, subj: Report of the 15th Meeting of the Air Staff Committee on National Guard and Reserve Policy, Jan 18, 1954, SAF/MIR; hist, Asst CSAF/RF, FY 1954, p 21; memo, Chester D. Seftenberg, AF Dep for Res & ROTC Affairs, to Mr. White, subj: Drill Pay for Mobilization Assignees, Nov 19, 1953, RG 340, 60A1055, WNRC. For the Continental Air Command position, see hist, CONAC, Jan–Jun 1953, pp 138–41.

47. Ltr, Maj Gen William K. Martin, Asst VCSAF, to General Wheless, subj: "M" Day Assignees, Nov 5, 1964; ltr, Maj Gen Benjamin O. Davis, Dir/M&O USAF, to ADC et al., subj: Review of Individual Augmentation Manpower Requirements, Dec 21, 1964, w/atch—both in AFRES 14K.

48. AFR 26–7, *Individual Manpower Augmentation I Procedures*, Apr 21, 1966, AFRES 14K.

49. Intvw, Cantwell with Bodycombe, May 28, 1985, AFRES 26.

50. MFR, Cantwell, subj: Observations on the Perception of MAs among the Active Force, Sep 10, 1986, AFRES 14K. As a staff historian at HQ MATS in 1960 and 1961, the author observed the attitudes of disdain and contempt shown by active force members toward reservists, attitudes often deserved. Generals Lewis and Lyon discussed the phenomenon (intvws, Cantwell with Gen Lewis, Mar 26, 1975, and with Gen Lyon, Nov 10, 1976—both in AFRES 26A).

51. Intvw, Lyon, Nov 10, 1976.

52. Hist, ASD, FY 1973, pp 30–31.

53. Hist, ASD, FY 1979, vol 1, pp 64–65. See also, hists, ASD, 1985, vol 1, pp 61–62, and 1987, vol 1, p 37.

54. Paper, Maj Gen Walter R. Longanecker, "The Air Force Intelligence Reserve Program: A Brief History, 1974–1984," Aug 1985, AFIA, AFRES 16Q.

55. Ltr, Cantwell to HQ USAFR/REX, subj: Background on AFRES Involvement in Civil Defense, Nov 10, 1971, AFRES 3B2c.

56. Memo, Billy M. Knowles, AFRES Dir/Op Plans, to author, subj: Evolution of the MA Program, May 17, 1988, AFRES 11.B1; AFRESR 355–2, *Disaster Preparedness Liaison and Augmentation Officer Programs*, Jan 14, 1974, AFRES 3B2c; point paper, Dir/Op Plans, subj: Mobilization Augmentees, a/o 31 Dec 75, AFRES 14K; ltr, Lt Col Epperson, Dir/Op Plans to HQ USAF, subj: Base Disaster Mobilization Augmentee Program, Sep 29, 1970, AFRES B2a; AFR 355–1, *Disaster Preparedness Planning and Operations*, May 14, 1979, AFRES 3B2a.

57. ASSS, Lyon, subj: Plan for USAFR Mobilization Augmentees in the Total Force, Jun 12, 1975, w/2 atchs, as doc 42 in hist ARPC, FY 1975; ltr, Gen David C. Jones, CSAF, to all Maj Commands, subj: Revitalization of the Mobilization Augmentee Program in the Total Force, Jun 12, 1975, as doc 43 in hist ARPC, FY 1975.

Notes

58. Atch 2 (ASSS, Lyon, Jun 12, 1975), Plan for Revitalization of the Mobilization Augmentee Program in the Total Force.

59. Msg, REW USAF to ADCOM et al., subj: Office of Special Assistant for Mobilization Augmentee (MA) Matters, 141400Z Oct 76, as doc 459 in hist, AFRES, 1976.

60. Intvw, Lewis, Mar 26, 1975.

61. Rpt, "TIG Functional Management Inspection of the Air Force Mobilization Augmentees (MA) Program, PN 78–643, 5 Sep 78–13 Aug 79."

62. Ltr, Bodycombe to Dir/Mil Pers, USAF, subj: Functional Management Inspection (FMI) of Mobilization Augmentee Program, PN 78 643, Nov 27, 1979, w/ atch, as doc 677 in hist, AFRES, FY 1980.

63. ASSS, Maj Gen William R. Usher, Dir/Pers Plan USAF, subj: Functional Management Inspection of the Air Force Mobilization Augmentee (MA) Program, Apr 28, 1980, w/2 atchs, AFRES 24K.

64. ARPCR 27–2, *Programming—ARPC Management Plan, Objective 80–14 (Centralized Manning Administration for Individual Programs)*, Jul 1, 1980, as doc 52 in hist, ARPC 1980; ARPCR 27–2, *Objective 80–12 (Achieve a Base Level Support Operation for May), Quarterly Status Reports*, Aug 22, Oct 6, and Dec 31, 1980, as doc 53 in hist, ARPC, 1980; rpt, ARPC to Ofc of AF Res, "Air Reserve Personnel Center Quarterly Status Report," Feb 12, 1981, as doc 54 in hist, ARPC, 1980.

65. Msg, AFPMC/MPCYC, to ARPC, subj: Base Individual Mobilization Augmentee Administration (BIMAA), Dec 21, 1981, as doc 43 in hist, ARPC, 1981.

66. AFM 30–130, I (c6), *Base Level Military Personnel System Users Manual,* Sep 1, 1988, chap 26, "Base Individual Mobilization Augmentee Administration (BIMAA) (DPMM)," AFRES 24K.

Chapter 11

1. Radio address, Richard M. Nixon, Republican Presidential Nominee, "The All-Volunteer Armed Force," Oct 17, 1968, Republican National Committee release, Oct 18, 1968.

2. Memo, Alfred B. Fitt to Melvin R. Laird, subj: All-Volunteer Force, Jan 30, 1969, Fitt Papers, General correspondence: 10/1/68–1/30/69, LBJL; memo, Peter M. Flanigan, Asst to Pres, to Arthur Burns and John Ehrlichman, subj: Cosmetic Reform of Selective Service System, Apr 26, 1969; memo, Jonathan C. Rose to Flanigan, subj: Interim Reforms of Selective Service System During Approach to an All-Volunteer Armed Force, Apr 26, 1969; memo, Flanigan to President, subj: Interim Reforms of the Selective Service System during Approach to an All-Volunteer Armed Force, Apr 30, 1969; memo, Jonathan Rose to Bud Krogh, Dick Moore, and Martin Anderson, subj: Selective Service Problems, Apr 23, 1969—all in White House Subject Files/White House Central Files (WHSF/WHCF), Subjects Files, Confidential Files, ND 21, Box 43, Nixon Presidential Materials Project (NPMP); "Statement Announcing Appointment of the President's Commission on an All-Volunteer Armed Force," Mar 27, 1969, Richard M. Nixon, *Public Papers of the Presidents of the United States: Richrd M. Nixon, 1969* (hereafter, Nixon, *Public Papers*) (Washington, D.C., 1971) pp 258–59.

3. "Special Message to the Congress on Reforming the Military Draft," May 13, 1969, Nixon, *Public Papers, 1969,* pp 365–69; "Remarks on Signing the Draft Reform Bill," Nov 26, 1969, Nixon, *Public Papers, 1969,* pp 970–71; memo, Patrick J. Buchanan to the President, subj: Legislative Leadership Meeting, Oct 10, 1969, WHCF, Ex FG 31-1, Legislative Leadership Mtgs, Oct–Dec 69, Box 5, NPMP. See also statement, SecDef Laird before the HASC Special Subcmte on the Draft of H.Res. 14001 & H.Res. 14015, Sep 30, 1969, WHCF, Ex 33-3-1, House Cmtes, HASC, Subcmte, 1969, Box 9, NPMP, and ltr, Lewis B. Hershey, Dir/SSS, to Spiro T. Agnew, Pres of Senate, subj: Transmittal of Legislation, Sep 18, 1969.

4. PL 91–124, *Selective Service Amendment Act of 1969* (Stat 83: 220); Leg-

477

islative History, 90th Cong., 1st sess. (1969), *Selective Service Amendment Act of 1969, United States Code Congressional and Administrative News*, pp 1318–1321. For provisions and rationale of the 1967 legislation, see Legislative History, 90th Cong., 1st sess. (1967), *Military Selective Service Act of 1967, United States Code Congressional and Administrative News*, pp 1308–59, and PL 90–40, *Military Selective Service Act of 1967* (Stat 81: 100).

5. "Statement Announcing Appointment of the President's Commission on an All-Volunteer Armed Force," Mar 27, 1969, Nixon, *Public Papers, 1969*, pp 258–59; memo, subj: Meeting between the President and Thomas Gates, former Secretary of Defense, Mar 14, 1969, 4:30 P.M., WHCF, Subject Files, Confidential Files, FG 249, All Volunteer Armed Forces (1969–1970), Box 25, NPMP.

6. *The Report of the President's Commission on an All-Volunteer Armed Force* (New York, 1970); memo, William E. Timmons to the President, subj: Republican Leadership Meeting, Thurs, Apr 23, 1970, 8:30 A.M., The Cabinet Room, Apr 23, 1970, WHCF, Ex FG 31–1, Legislative Leadership Mtgs, Jan–Apr 70, Box 5, NPMP.

7. Memo, H. R. Haldeman to Magruder, subj: The Volunteer Army, Feb 23, 1970; memo, Jeb S. Magruder for H. R. Haldeman, subj: Action Memorandum P290, Mar 19, 1970—both in WHSF/WHCF, Subject Files, Confidential Files, ND 21, Box 43, NPMP; memo, Jeb S. Magruder to Staff Sec, subj: Action Memo P290, Apr 3, 1970, w/atch, WHSF/WHCF, Subject Files, Confidential Files, ND 8 Mil Pers, 1969–1970, Box 41, NPMP; "Special Message to the Congress on Draft Reform," Apr 23, 1970, Nixon, *Public Papers, 1970*, pp 395–98; EO 11527, Apr 24, 1970.

8. Memo, Laird to Secs Mil Depts, JCS, subj: Zero Draft Calls by Jul 1, 1973, Oct 12, 1970, RG 330, 76A068 Box 3, WNRC. For Laird's views on the Gates Commission's report, see memo, Laird to the President, subj: Future of the Draft, May 11, 1970, AFRES 6F.

9. "Special Message to the Congress about Draft Reform," Jan 28, 1971, Nixon, *Public Papers, 1971*, pp 75–78; PL 92–129, *Military Selective Service—Military Pay—Military Active Duty Strengths* (Stat 85: 348), Sep 28, 1971; Legislative History, PL 92–129 (Stat 85: 348), 92d Cong. 1st sess. (1971), *U.S. Code Congressional and Administrative News*, vol 2, pp 139–1511.

10. "Air Force Reserve Manning Strength (Monthly)," AFRES 14J.

11. Intvw, Cantwell with Maj Gen Richard Bodycombe, May 29, 1985, AFRES 26A; intvw, Cantwell with Maj Gen Sidney S. Novaresi, Aug 12, 1982, AFRES 26A.

12. Ltr, Brig Gen Tom E. Marchbanks, Jr., Ch AF Res, to CSAF, subj: Manning of Non-Mobilized Air Force Reserve Units, n.d. [ca. Feb 15, 1968], RG 341, 72A5971; ltr, Gen John P. McConnell, CSAF, to Ofc of AF Res, subj: Manning of Non-Mobilized Air Force Reserve Units, Mar 4, 1968, RG 341, 72A5971—both in WNRC; ltr, Marchbanks to AFRES, subj: Air Force Reserve Unit Manning in Drill Pay Status, Nov 4, 1968, AFRES 14J2.

13. Ltr, Maj Gen Rollin B. Moore, Jr., Cmdr AFRES, to Units, subj: Air Force Reserve Unit Manning in Drill Pay Status, Dec 2, 1968, AFRES 14J2; msg, AFRCR, Moore to Marchbanks, subj: Drill Pay Spaces, Nov 25, 1969; msg, AFRCR, Moore to Marchbanks, subj: Authorizations Lost as Result of Conversions, Dec 12, 1969—both as doc 4–6 in hist, AFRES, FY 1970; hist, AFRES, FY 1970, pp 91–96; ltr, Brig Gen Earl O. Anderson, Dep to Ch AF Res, to AFRES, subj: AF Res Pers Operating Prog. No. 2. for FY 1970, Jan 20, 1970, w/2 atchs, as doc 4–9 in hist, AFRES, FY 1970; AFRES SO G–29, Feb 13, 1970; ltr, Col Donald L. Peck, Ex to Ch AF Res, to AFRES, subj: Establishment of Reserve Recruiting Units, Apr 14, 1970, as doc 4–11 in hist, AFRES, FY 1970.

14. Ltr, Anderson to AFRES, subj: AF Res Drill Pay Strengths for FY 1970, Apr 9, 1970, as doc 4–13 in hist, AFRES FY 1970; "Air Force Reserve Manning Summary (Monthly)," Jun 30, 1970, AFRES 14J1.

15. "Air Force Reserve Manning Summary (Monthly)," a/o Jun 30, 1971, AFRES 14J1; MFR, Walter J. Heckman, AFRES Dir/Pers Plans, subj: FY 1971 Drill Pay, Feb 2, 1971, AFRES 14J2; ltr, Cantwell to Ofc of AF Res [Cooper], subj: Air Force Reserve Program Actions, FY 1959–

74, Jul 11, 1978, AFRES 19Z.

16. Paper, AFRES, "Upheaval in the Air Force Reserve," Apr 1971, as doc 69 in hist, AFRES, FY 1971; ltr, Moore to Ofc of AF Res, subj: Reduction of Reserve Authorizations in MAC and TAC Airlift Units, May 26, 1971, as doc 70 in hist AFRES, FY 1971.

17. Ltr, Maj Gen Homer I. Lewis, Ch AF Res, to AFRES, subj: Retention of Trained Reservists, Jul 2, 1971, w/atch, as doc 71 in hist, AFRES, FY 1971.

18. Msg, ALMAJCOM 1429/70, Ryan, subj: Project Volunteer, Oct 26, 1970, as doc 72 in hist, AFRES, FY 1971; msg, DP ALMAJCOM 478/71, subj: Status Report of Project Volunteer, Feb 17, 1971, as doc 76 in hist, AFRES, FY 1971.

19. HQ AFRES Cmdr's Ltr No. 13, Jun 29, 1973.

20. Hist, AFRES, FY 1972, pp 208–09; ltr, Col Edward C. Murphy, Dir/M&O, HQ USAF, to AFRES and ARPC, subj: Allocation of Numbers for MAJCOM Establishments and Units, Aug 30, 1972; AFRES SO G–94, Sep 8, 1972 [revoked by AFRES SO G–97, Sep 19, 1972]; AFRES SO G–97, Sep 19, 1972; AFRES SO G–19, Mar 20, 1973; intvw, Cantwell with Maj Richard D. Sutton, AFRES Dir/Res Rctrg, Feb 14, 1973; minutes, HQ AFRES staff mtg, Jul 25, 1972, Aug 15, 1972; msg, DPA, Lt Col Arthur Schuler, AFRES Dir/Pers Progs, to AFRES units, subj: Volunteers for Special Tour of Active Duty, 151520Z Aug 72, as doc 280 in hist AFRES, FY 1973; msg, DPAV Col Kenneth G. Shaw, AFRES DCS/Pers, to AFRES units, subj: Active Duty Tours for Reserve Recruiting, 141853Z Aug 72, as doc 281 in hist, AFRES, FY 1973; ltr, Col Joseph C. Deely, Ofc of AF Res, to AFRES, subj: Air Force Reserve Recruiters, Aug 16, 1972, as doc 282 in hist, AFRES, FY 1973; ltr, Deely to AFRES, subj: Air Force Reserve Recruiters, Sep 19, 1972, as doc 283 in hist, AFRES FY 1973; Col William Hughes, AFRES Asst DCS/Pers, to Dir M&O, subj: AFRESM 23–3, Mar 13, 1973, w/atch, as doc 289 in hist, AFRES, FY 1973; AFRESM 23–44, *Headquarters AFRES Organization Functions*, Apr 1, 1973, p 89, as doc 290 in hist, AFRES, FY 1973; msg, AFRES to Units, subj: Reserve Recruiting Structure, RS 301520Z Mar 73, as doc 291 in hist, AFRES, FY 1973.

21. Sutton, intvw, Feb 14, 1973.

22. Ltr, Carl B. Patterson, AFRES Dir/Plans & Prgms, to Ofc of AF Res, subj: Request to Constitute an Air Force Reserve Recruiting Group, May 18, 1973, w/atch, as doc 292 in hist, AFRES, FY 1973: ltr, Shaw to Ofc Of AF Res, subj: Air Force Reserve Recruiters Tours, May 4, 1973, w/atch, as doc 293 in hist, AFRES, FY 1973; briefing, Sutton to AFRES Joint Staff Meeting, Sep 12, 1973, as doc 479 in hist, AFRES, FY 1974.

23. Ltr, Maj Gen Earl O. Anderson, VCmdr, AFRES, to Ofc of AF Res, subj: Accomplishing Reserve Manning Objectives, Jul 30, 1974, w/atch, AFRES 14I.

24. Ibid.

25. Msg, Anderson to Regions, subj: Recruiting Organization [Observations of the author, who attended all sessions of the conference], CV 092120Z Aug 74, as doc 480 in hist, AFRES FY 1975; HQ AFRES, "Personnel Newsletter No. 10," Oct 1974.

26. Msg, Hughes to Regions et al., subj: Active Duty/Reserve Recruiting Test Termination, DP 301700Z Sep 74, as doc 481 in hist, AFRES, FY 1975; memo, Sutton to Dir/Hist Svcs, subj: Historical Data, Dec 17, 1974, as doc 482 in hist, AFRES, FY 1975; msg, Anderson to EAFRR et al., subj: Agreement with USAF Recruiting Service, CV 242038Z Mar 75, as doc 483 in hist, AFRES, FY 1975.

27. Ltr, Hughes to Ofc of AF Res, subj: Transfer of Recruiting Responsibility, Feb 28, 1975, as doc 486 in hist, AFRES, FY 1975; briefing, Hughes, HQ AFRES staff mtg, Mar 20, 1975; msg, Sutton to 459th TAW et al., subj: Two-year Manday Tours, RS 192030Z Mar 75, as doc 487 in hist, AFRES, FY 1975; ltr, Lewis to AFRES, subj: Retention Effectiveness Program, Sep 20, 1974; HQ AFRES, "Personnel Newsletter No. 9," Sep 1975, as doc 518 in hist, AFRES, FY 1975; msg, Hughes to Units, subj: Reassignment of Airmen Moving from Vicinity of Current Unit, DPRC 031742Z Aug 74, as doc 519 in hist, AFRES, FY 1975; AFR 35–16, *United States Air Force Reserve Career Motivation Program*, vol 2, Jun 26, 1974.

28. Ltr, Sutton to Dir/Pers Plans, subj: Annual Report to the Secretary of the Air Force, Jul 15, 1975, as doc 516 in hist,

The Air Force Reserve

AFRES, FY 1975.

29. Hist, AFRES, Jul–Dec 75, pp 81–88; hist, AFRES, 1976, pp 143–46; hist, AFRES, 1977, pp 136–39.

30. Hist, AFRES, FY 1975, pp 198–293; hist, AFRES, 1976, p 198; point paper, Thomas Stonehouse, Ofc AF Res, subj: Draft Legislative Proposal on the Air Reserve Technician (ART) Program, Oct 12, 1976, as doc 440 in hist, AFRES, 1976; talking paper, L. C. Lingelbach, AFRES Dir/Civ Pers, subj: Air Reserve Technician Program Administration, May 7, 1975, as doc 530 in hist, AFRES, FY 1975.

31. Ltr, Richard J. Borda, Asst SecAF, Manpower & Res, to Carl Albert, Speaker of the House, Subj: Legislative Proposal, Jan 12, 1973, w/atch, as doc 531 in hist, AFRES, FY 1975.

32. Ltr, Anderson to Ofc of AF Res, subj: Ad Hoc Study Group Report, Analysis of ART Personnel Structure, Jul 24, 1973, w/atch, as doc 533 in hist, AFRES, FY 1975.

33. ASSS, Lewis, subj: Legislative Proposal—Army and Air Force Reserve Technicians, Nov 14, 1973, w/2 atchs, as doc 535 in hist, AFRES, FY 1975.

34. Talking paper, Lingelbach, subj: Proposed Excepted Service Legislation, May 7, 1975, as doc 536 in hist, AFRES, FY 1975.

35. *Defense Manpower: The Keystone of National Security*, Preface, p 478.

36. PL 93–155, *Department of Defense Appropriations Act, 1974* (Stat 87: 605); ltr, Curtiss W. Tarr, Chmn Defense Manpower Commission, to President, Subj: Defense Manpower Commission Report, Apr 19, 1976, w/atch, WHCF FG 372, Defense Manpower Commission, Box 195, Gerald R. Ford Library (GRFL), Ann Arbor, Mich. For the commission's recommendations on the air reserve technician program, see *Defense Manpower: The Keystone of National Security*, p 127.

37. Hist, AFRES, 1977, pp 8–11; "Report on Full-Time Training and Administration of the Selected Reserve," OASD(RA), Oct 25, 1977, pp i–iv, 1–4, 4–4 to 6–6, as doc 2 in hist, AFRES, 1977; MFR, Cantwell, subj: Briefing, Stonehouse, subj: Gerard Group Staff Mbr at AFRES Civilian Personnel Conference, RAFB, Jan 18, 1978, as doc 1 in hist, AFRES, 1977.

38. Hist, AFRES, 1978, pp 17–18; decision memo, John P. White, Asst SecDef (MRA&L), to Dep SecDef, subj: Report on Training and Administration of the Selected Reserve—DECISION MEMORANDUM, May 24, 1978 [w/Dep SecDef's approval initialed on June 8, 1978], as doc 12 in hist, AFRES, 1978; ltr, Deames C. Siemer, DOD Gen Counsel, to James T. McIntryre, Jr., Dir/OMB, subj: Legislative Proposal DOD 95–91, Jun 28, 1978, as doc 13 in hist, AFRES, 1978.

39. Hist, AFRES, FY 1979, pp 19–23; point paper, Kenneth C. Martin, Ch Empl Rel & Career Mgt Div, AFRES, Subj: Revised ART Agreement—FPM Supplement 930–71, Jan 24, 1979, as doc 33 in hist, AFRES, FY 1979.

40. Ltr, Ramsay, Dep Assoc Dir/Staffing, OPM, to Leonard G. Berman, Dep Dir/Mgt Progs, OPM, subj: Revisions to FPM Supplement 930–71, Jan 24, 1979, w/incl, atchs, as doc 34 in hist, AFRES, FY 1979; ltr, Deely to all AFRES Flying Units et al., subj: Revised ART Agreement—FPM Supplement (Internal) 930–71, Feb 9, 1979, as doc 35 in hist, AFRES, FY 1979.

41. Memo, Harold W. Chase, Dep Asst SecDef (RA), to Dep Asst SecAF (RA), Subj: DOD 96–2, Proposed Draft Legislation, "To Amend Title 10, United States Code, to Authorize, with Respect to Certain Members of the Army Reserve or Air Force Reserve, Their Employment as Army or Air Reserve Technicians, and for Other Purposes," as doc 36 in hist, AFRES, FY 1979.

42. Rpt, House Appropriations Cmte, 95th Cong., 2d sess., "Department of Defense Appropriations Bill, 1979," Jul 27, 1978, as doc 7 in hist, AFRES, 1978; MFR, unsigned [probably Col Edward E. Wooddell, Ch, Compt Div Ofc of AF Res], subj: Congressional Actions Concerning Dual Status Technicians, n.d. [ca. Nov 15, 1978], as doc 8 in hist, AFRES, 1978.

43. MFR, Cantwell, subj: General Lyon's Remarks on Technician Test, Jan 5, 1979, as doc 37 in hist, AFRES, FY 1979.

44. Quoted in msg, Lyon to Unit Cmdrs, subj: ART Militarization Test, CC 0919-30Z Apr 79, as doc 38 in hist, AFRES, FY 1979.

45. MFR, Cantwell, subj: Gen Lew

Allen, CSAF, Remarks 22 Feb 79, at Mid-Winter ROA Convention, Feb 22, 1979, as doc 39 in hist, AFRES, FY 1979.

46. Quoted in OSAF Supplement to the AF Policy Letter for Commanders, Apr 1979, as doc 40 in hist, AFRES, FY 1979.

47. Msg, Lyon, CC 091930Z Sep 79.

48. Statement, Maj Gen Richard Bodycombe, Ch AF Res, before HAC, May 23, 1979, as doc 41 in hist, AFRES, FY 1979.

49. Hist, AFRES, FY 1980, pp 46–56; atch (ltr, Lyon to Staff of Ofc of AF Res et al., subj: Implementation Plan FY 1979 Air Reserve Technician [ART] Militarization Test, Feb 21, 1979), "Air Force Reserve Plan for Testing the Militarization of Air Reserve Technicians (ART) Positions," as doc 61 in hist, AFRES, FY 1979.

50. Point paper, Maj James F. Pauls, Pers Actions Off, Ofc of AF Res, subj: ART Militarization Test, Aug 25, 1980, as doc 81 in hist, AFRES, FY 1980; Eval Rpt, Ofc of AF Res, "Air Reserve Technician Military Conversion Test," Aug 31, 1980, as doc 82 in hist, AFRES, FY 1980.

51. Atch (ASSS, Maj Gen William R. Usher, Dir/Pers Plans USAF, subj: Air Reserve Forces Technician Test Reports, Sep 6, 1980, w/2 tabs); memo, George M. McWilliams, Asst SecAF Res Air, to Dep Asst SecDef (RA), subj: ART Technician Position Conversion Test Results, Sep 12, 1980, w/3 atchs, as doc 85 in hist, AFRES, FY 1980.

52. Atch (ltr, Robert B. Pirie, Jr., Asst SecDef [MRA&L], to Hon. Jamie L. Whitten, chmn, House Appropriations Cmte, subj: DOD Report on Test Conversion of Civilians, Dec 30, 1980, w/atch); rpt, DOD, "Technician Position Conversion Test," as doc 87 in hist, AFRES, FY 1980.

Chapter 12

1. Memo, Robert S. McNamara to SecAF, subj: FY 1968 Air Force Reserve Forces Airlift Units, Jul 1, 1967, as doc 1–5 in hist, MAC, FY 1968; hist, USAF Dir/Aerospace Progs, Jul–Dec 1967, p 133.

2. Hist, MAC, FY 1968, pp 98–58; ltr, Harold Brown, SecAF, to SecDef, subj: Proposed Structure for Military Airlift Command General Reserve Forces, Feb 15, 1967, as doc 1–50 in hist, MAC, FY 1968; hist, CAC, Jan–Jun 1966, pp 20, 36. Secretary McNamara's statement to the Senate Armed Services Committee on FY 1969 budget matters is quoted in hist, CAC, Jan–Jul 1968, p 24. His testimony before a subcommittee of the HAC in 1967 is reprinted as doc 3–58 in hist, CAC, Jan–Jun 1967.

3. The point is discussed in Cantwell, "Total Force: Marchbanks to Bodycombe," pp 60–63. General Lyon also discussed it in an interview with the author (intvw, Cantwell with Lyon, Feb 14, 1979).

4. CAC PPlan 67–67, Nov 30, 1967; MAC PAD 68–5, "Service Test of Associate Air Force Reserve Unit Concept," Jan 1, 1967.

5. "AF Plcy Ltr for Commanders," Mar 1968; ltr, Col J. O. White, Asst DCS/O AFRES, to Cmdr & CS, subj: Daily Operations Activities, Aug 14, 1968. Colonel McFarland provided the author with additional information (intvw, Cantwell with Col Richard P. McFarland, USAF [Ret], Sep 4, 1979, HQ AFRES).

6. MFR, subj: Intvw by Daniel J. Hughes with Richard P. McFarland, May 27, 1983, at HQ AFRES. As Col McFarland frequently observed in later years, "I don't know if we did it right, but we got together and made the thing work."

7. HQ CAC PPlan 68–1, Mar 1, 1968, as exhibit 10 in hist, CAC, Jan–Jul 1968.

8. Hist, AFRES, FY 1970, pp 136–49; msg, Richard George, Dir/Public Info, AFRES, to 4th AFRR et al., subj: AFRES to Convert Two Units to C–130—FY 1970, AFROIP, 291215Z Oct 69, as doc 4–100 in hist, AFRES, FY 1970; msg, Patterson to 4th AFRR et al., subj: C–130 Conversions, AFRXP, 311630Z Oct 69, as doc 4–100 in hist, AFRES, FY 1970; MFR, Cantwell, subj: Intvw, Carl B. Patterson, Dir/Progg, Nov 13, 1970, as doc 4–96 in hist, AFRES, FY 1970.

9. MFR, Cantwell, Nov 13, 1970.

10. AFRES Annual Rpt, FY 1974, as doc 93 in hist, AFRES, FY 1974.

11. AFRES SOs G–119, Nov 8, 1971, G–22, Feb 18, 1972, G–80, Jul 17, 1972, and G–132, Oct 20, 1972.

12. Msg, USAF to AFRES, subj: Program Changes, AFRES, PRP, 031920Z Sep 71, as doc 89 in hist, AFRES, FY 1972; AFRES SOs G–116, Oct 25, 1971, G–29, Mar 6, 1972 [as amended by AFRES SO G–38, Mar 30, 1972], and G–44, Apr 1, 1972.

13. Ltr, Col John J. Shaughnessy, Ofc of Legis Liaison, to interested Congressmen, subj: Air Reserve Forces Program Directive, Mar 18, 1969, as doc 1–50 in hist, AFRES, Jan–Jun 1969; msg, OSAF to 174th TFG et al., subj: Equip Chngs ANG & USAFR Units, SAF/OIP, 032325Z Nov 70; msg, USAF to AFRES et al., subj: Prog Chg: AFRES/ANG, PRPO, 042144Z Nov 70, as doc 34 in hist, AFRES, FY 1971; hist, AFRES, FY 1972, p 69.

14. Hist, AFRES, FY 1970, pp 144–45, 149–53.

15. ASSS, Lt Gen George S. Boylan, Jr., DCS/Progs and Resources, USAF, subj: Air Reserve Forces Equippage, Jan 25, 1972, w/atch; ltr, Gen John D. Ryan, CSAF, to Ch NGB, subj: Air Reserve Forces Equippage, Jan 25, 1972—both in RG 340, 79–5, WNRC.

16. Hist, AFRES, FY 1972, pp 159–72; AFRES PPlan 72–8, "Tinker/Carswell," Mar 3, 1972, as doc 18 in hist, AFRES, FY 1972; msg, USAF to AFRES et al., subj: Program Change, PD 73–4, USAFR, PRPO, 021530Z Feb 72, as doc 87 in hist, AFRES, FY 1972.

17. Minutes, HQ AFRES staff mtgs, Mar 24–Apr 21, 1972, Apr 28, 1972.

18. Msg, 507th TFG to USAF/RE et al., subj: First Air Force Reserve F–105 flight, CC 222020Z Jun 72.

19. Hist, AFRES, FY 1973, pp 116–24; AFRES PPlan 72–12, "Hill/945th," Jul 17, 1972, as doc 126 in hist, AFRES, FY 1973.

20. Memo, Robert C. Seamans, Jr., SecAF, to SecDef, subj: Air Force Reserve Reprogramming, Mar 5, 1971; memo, David Packard, Dep SecDef, to SecAF, subj: Air Force Reserve Reprogramming, Mar 10, 1971—both in RG 340, 73–12, WNRC; msg, USAF to AFRES et al., subj: Program Change, Air Force Reserve, PRPO, 172240Z Mar 71, as doc 36 in hist, AFRES, FY 1971; msg, Daniel F. Doyle, Progg Off AFRES, to Eastern Air Force Reserve Region (EAFRR) et al., subj: Program Change for the 915th MAGP, XPP, 221955Z Jul 71, as doc 86 in hist, AFRES, FY 1972.

21. Ltr, Terence St. Louis, AFRES historian, to DCS/Plans [Simmons], subj: Background on 79th AEW&C Squadron, Oct 29, 1974, AFRES 19Q.

22. AFRES SO G–76, Oct 3, 1973; AFRESR 23–4, *302d Special Operations Squadron (USAFR)*, Oct 31, 1974.

23. Ltr, DAF, USAF to AFRES & TAC, PRM 846p, Feb 25, 1975; AFRES SO G–15, Mar 17, 1975; AFRES PPlan 74–5, "919th TAGp, Eglin AF Aux Fld 3," Sep 6, 1974, as doc 74 in hist, AFRES, Jul–Dec 75.

24. Atch (ltr, Col Justin L. Townsley, Cmdr 302d TAW, to AFRES, subj: Aerial Spray Mission, Feb 13, 1975), rpt, "Aerial Spray Position Report," as doc 313 in hist, AFRES, FY 1975; atch (ltr, Col Clarence E. Horton, Dir/Ops, 302d TAW, to AFRES, subj: Guam Aerial Spray Mission Report, Aug 11, 1975), rpt, "Aerial Spray Report—Guam Marianas Islands, 13 May–30 June 1975," as doc 46 in hist, AFRES, FY 1974.

25. Ltr, Capt Samuel G. Woodrow, Actg Ch, Aer Spr Br, 355th TAS, to 302d TAW et al., subj: 1973 Annual Spray Report, Nov 8, 1973, as doc 46 in hist, AFRES, FY 1974.

26. Intvw, Cantwell with Maj Gen William Lyon, Nov 10, 1976, AFRES 26A.

27. For information on the Goldwater-Stennis Amendment and the follow-on studies, see hist, AFRES, FY 1975, pp 98–100. On the OSD Program Budget Decision and General Lyon's subsequent actions, see Program Budget Decision (PBD) 279, subj: Reserve Component Management, Dec 12, 1975, as doc 2 in hist, AFRES, 1976, and ltr, Lyon, to Lt Col Wilbur D. Peterson, subj: Air Force Reserve Management Implementation Team, Jan 9, 1976, as doc in hist, AFRES, 1976.

28. Program Budget Decision (PBD) 279C, subj: Reserve Component Management, Dec 12, 1975, as doc 3 in hist, AFRES, 1976.

29. Intvw, Cantwell, with Maj Gen

Notes

William Lyon, Nov 10, 1976, AFRES 26A.

30. MFR, Cantwell, subj: Briefing on Proposed Realignment of Regions, Jul 15, 1976, as doc 6 in hist, AFRES, 1976; AFRES, SO G-80, Sep 29, 1976.

31. Hist, AFRES, 1976, pp 14-15.

32. See note 19 above; intvw, Cantwell with Maj Gen Earl O. Anderson, Oct 12, 1976, AFRES 26A.

33. Ltr, Deely to AFRES Units, subj: USAFR General Officer Action, Oct 19, 1976, as doc 36 in hist, AFRES, 1976; intvw, Cantwell with Maj Gen Richard Bodycombe, May 29, 1985, pp 73-74, AFRES 26A.

34. For a resume of the modernization of the AF Res, see ltr, Cantwell to Ofc of AF Res (Cooper), subj: Air Force Reserve Program Actions, FY 1959-74, Jul 11, 1978, AFRES 19Z.

35. Ltr, Brig Gen James B. Currie, Dep Dir/Progs USAF, to Asst VCSAF et al., subj: USAF Decision Letter D75-47, EC-121 Reorganization, Nov 3, 1975, AFRES 19Q; msg, OSAF to Commander-in-Chief, Air Defense Command (CINCAD), et al., subj: Public Information Guidance—EC 121 Reorganization, 082110Z Dec 75, as doc 15 in hist, AFRES, Jul–Dec 1975; msg, USAF to CINCAD et al., subj: EC–121 Program Change, PRP 101551Z, Nov 75, as doc 19 in hist, AFRES, Jul–Dec19 75; msg, 552d Airborne Early Warning & Control Group (AEWCG) to 79th Airborne Early Warning & Control Squadron (AEWCS), subj: Active/Reserve Aircrew Manning of the Iceland TDY Mission, CC, 191745Z Nov 75, as doc 20 in hist, AFRES, Jul–Dec 1975; atch (ltr, Col Walter B. Simmons, AFRES DCS/Plans, to ADCOM, subj: Letter of Agreement, Jan 13, 1976), ltr of agreement, as doc 22 in hist, AFRES, Jul–Dec 1975; ltr, Donald J. Campbell, Actg Ch, Progs & Resources Div, Ofc of AF Res, to Progs Br (Cooper), subj: Review Strategic Air Command and U.S. Forces, Apr 13, 1977, management 9, AFREXR; msg, John J. Morris, AFRES Progg Off, to 10th AF, subj: Planning for Extension of EC–121T Program, XPXP, 171915Z Feb 78, as doc 112 in hist, AFRES, 1978; msg, Personal from Maj Gen Lyon to Col West, subj: Deactivation of the 915th AEWCG, CC, 281315Z Sep 78, as doc 117 in hist, AFRES, 1978; MFR, Col Evan E. Clements, Cmdr 915th AEW-CG, subj: After Action Report, 915th Airborne Early Warning & Control Group 4, Sep 30, 1978, AFRES 19Q.

36. HQ MAC PPlan 75-28, "Transfer of 7 WC-130H Aircraft from MAC to AFRES," Aug 1, 1975, AFRES 19Y; ltr, Directorate of Manpower & Organization, HQ USAF (PRM) 871-p1, USAF, to AFRES & MAC, Sep 30, 1975; AFRES SO G-64, Oct 23, 1975; hist, AFRES, 1976, pp 122-26.

37. Msg, OSAF to SAC et al., subj: Transfer of SAC KC-135 Aircraft to ANG/AFRES, OIP, 242057Z Sep 74, as doc 132 in hist, AFRES, FY 1975.

38. Msg, Col Kenneth E. Klein, Ch OI AFRES, to EAFRR et al., subj: Conversion of 452d and 336th at March AFB, OIP, 021945Z Oct 75, as doc 23 in hist, AFRES, Jul–Dec 1975.

39. Msg, SAC to 452d Air Refueling Wing (AREFW), subj: KC-135 Conversion, CC, 301835Z Sep 76, as doc 90 in hist, AFRES, 1976; msg, 4101 RAS to SAC, subj: Orientation Visits to HQ SAC, CC, 312030Z Aug 76; ltr, Simmons, to AFRES Staff et al., subj: AFRES Programming Plan 76-2, 452d TAW, March AFB, Calif., 1 Apr 1976, as doc 363 in hist, AFRES, 1976.

40. Rpt, "AFRES Unit FORSTAT," a/o Dec 76, as doc 364 in hist, AFRES, 1976.

41. Ltr, Gen. James L. Wade, Cmdr 452d AREFW, to Men and Women of the 452d AREFW, subj: Accomplishments 1 January 76 through 30 June 1977, Jul 1, 1977, as doc 364 in hist, AFRES, 1977; AFRES SO G-69, Sep 22, 1972, a/a G-96, Dec 21, 1977; hist, AFRES, FY 1979, pp 88–89.

42. Wade ltr, as cited in preceding note.

43. AFRES SO G-32, Mar 31, 1981.

44. AFRES SOs G-62, Mar 24, 1971, G-87, Jul 2, 1971, G-22, Feb 18, 1972, G-76, Oct 3, 1973, and G-1, Jan 3, 1974.

45. Ltr, Lt Col Albert E. Tollefsen, Current Ops & A/C Tng Div AFRES, to ARRS/DO, subj: Air Force Reserve Save Data, Dec 16, 1980, AFRES 19B.

46. Point paper, Lt Col Thomas Jones, Cmdr, 304th Aerospace Rescue and Recovery Squadron (ARRSQ), subj: 304th Aerospace Rescue and Recovery Service (ARRS) Disaster Response to Mt St Helens Eruption, Aug 9, 1980, as doc 444 in hist,

The Air Force Reserve

AFRES, FY 1980; MFR, Tollefsen, subj: Mt St Helens Activity, Jun 3, 1980, as doc 495 in hist, AFRES, FY 1980; msg, MAC to Units, PA 131830Z Jun 80, subj: MAC News Service Release, as doc 446 in hist, AFRES, FY 1980.

47. Msg, 302d SOS Deployed, Nellis AFB, Nev., to HQ USAF/RE, subj: Daily Activity Report for 21 Nov 80, Red Flag 81-1, DO, 222350Z Nov 80, as doc 343 in hist, AFRES, FY 1981.

48. Msg, CINCMAC to USAF, subj: Facts and Statistics on Guyanian Airlift, CS, 020050Z Dec 78, as doc 251 in hist, AFRES, 1978; MFR, Lt Col Albert E. Tollefsen, AFRES Current Ops & A/C Tng Div, subj: AFRES Participation in the Guyana Operation, Nov 29, 1978, w/4 atchs, as doc 252 in hist, AFRES, 1978.

49. *Encyclopedia of Military History*, s.v. "The 'October War,' October 6-24, 1973"; *RN: Memoirs*, pp 921-39.

50. Atch 1 (ltr, Col Billy M. Knowles, Dir/Ops AFRES, to EAFRR & WAFRR, subj: Associate Reserve Aircrew Spt for MAC, 15 Oct-15 Nov 73), Summary, Mid-East Participation of Associate Aircrews, 15 Oct-15 Nov 73, AFRES 22I.

51. Talking Paper, Col Hillary Perdue, DCS/O AFRES, Subj: Israeli Airlift (13 Oct 14 Nov 73), n.d. [ca. Nov 30, 1975], AFRES 22I.

52. Richard Nixon, Proclamation No. 3972, "Declaring a National Emergency by the President of the United States," Mar 23, 1970; memo, William H. Rehnquist, Asst Atty Gen, to John D. Ehrlichman, Asst to Pres for Domestic Affairs, n.d. [ca. Mar 23, 1970, A.M.], WHSF, Ehrlichman, Box 33, NPMP; EO 11519, Mar 23, 1970; notes, Dwight L. Chapin, Mar 23, 1970, 1:00 P.M., Cabinet Rm, Dwight L. Chapin Notes 1/1/70-3/31/70, WHSF, NPMP.

53. Msg, USAF to HQC, subj: Mobilization Order, AFXOP, 240636Z Mar 70; msg, HQC to 1 AP&CG et al., subj: Mobilization Order, 241045Z Mar 70; msg, USAF to HQC, subj: Mobilization Order, 252019Z Mar 70; msg, HQC to 1 & 2 AP&CG, subj: Mobilization Order and Release Order EAD of Units of the Air Force Reserve, PRP 261510Z Mar 70; AFRESR 23-14, *Air Postal and Courier Groups and Flights (USAFR)*, Jul 6, 1970; AFRES Fact Sheet, "USAF Postal and Courier Units (Reserve)," a/o Oct 1969.

54. MFR, Theodore C. Marrs, AF Dep for Res Affairs, Mobilization of Air Force Reserve Postal Units, 1430 hrs, Mar 24, 1970; MFR, Marrs, subj: Telephone Conversation with Colonel Kuhn, Mar 24, 1970; MFR, Marrs, Authority for Mobilization of Air Force Reserve Postal Units, 1645 hrs, Mar 24, 1970; msg, USAF to AFRES & ARPC, subj: Pay of Mobilized Reservists, 262003Z Mar 70—all in AFRES 21H.

55. Memo, Col Bruce H. Berryman, Mil Asst Dep for Res Affairs, AF, to Dep Asst SecDef (RA), subj: USAF-ANG/AFRES Relationships, Mar 12, 1971, RG 340, 73-12, WNRC; AFRESR 55-9, *Air Force Reserve Exercise Participation*, Oct 11, 1977, copy in AFRES 23; MFR, Billy M. Knowles, Dir/OP Plans AFRES, subj: Air Force Reserve Exercise Participation, Nov 27, 1984, as doc 395 in hist, AFRES, FY 1981.

56. See, for example, atch (ltr, Lt Col Robert J. Winner, Ch Ex Plans Div, AFRES, to AFRES Staff et al., subj: Updated USAFR Exercise Schedule, Nov 13, 1981), Updated Exercise Schedule, as doc 362 in hist, AFRES, FY 1981.

57. Final rpt, "Coronet Poker/Oksboel—301 Tactical Fighter Wing, 12-27 August 1977," Sep 1977, AFRES 22I.

58. For General Lyon's remarks at his Joint Staff Meeting at Headquarters AFRES on September 13, 1977, see hist, AFRES, 1977, pp 2-3.

59. Cantwell, "Operation REDOUBT: The Evolution of an Idea and Its Implementation," Jan 1982, AFRES 22I; ltr, Bodycombe, to DCS/O, subj: Recall and Mobilization Exercise, Nov 29, 1976, as doc 3 in hist, AFRES, 1977; intvw, Cantwell with Bodycombe, Dec 7, 1977, HQ AFRES; HQ AFRES, *After Action Report for Operation REDOUBT—Phase II* (Robins AFB, Ga., 1978), as doc 255 in hist, AFRES, 1978.

60. HQ AFRES, *After Action Report for Operation REDOUBT—Phase III* (Robins AFB, Ga., 1979), as doc 127 in hist, AFRES, FY 1979.

61. HQ AFRES Exercise Plan 003, *PAID REDOUBT 80*, May 1, 1980, as doc 413 in hist, AFRES, FY 1980; HQ AFRES, *After Action Report for PAID REDOUBT 80* (Robins AFB, Ga., 1980), as doc 40 in hist,

Notes

AFRES, FY 1980; HQ AFRES, *Comptroller Bulletin*, Sep 4, 1980, as doc 422 in hist, AFRES, FY 1980.

62. AFR 28–5, *USAF Mobilization Planning*, May 29, 1980.

63. HQ AFRES Exercise Plan 004, Condor Redoubt 81, as doc 363 in hist, AFRES, FY 1981; HQ AFRES, *After Action Report for* Condor Redoubt 81, as doc 366 in hist, AFRES, FY 1981. See also ltr, Col Jerry G. West, Dir/Insp, USAF, to ALMAJCOM–SOA, subj: FMI of USAF Support of Air Reserve Forces (ARF) during/after Mobilization, PN 81–620, Feb 4, 1982.

64. This assessment was made by Lt Gen Paul W. Meyers, the Air Force Surgeon General (see the Preface to HQ AFRES's, *After Action Report for* Condor Redoubt 81).

65. MFR, Cantwell, subj: General Bodycombe's remarks at Commander's Call, Dec 17, 1981, as doc 8 in hist, AFRES, FY 1981.

66. This view was expressed to the author by Lt Col Charles Srull, 403 RWRW Dir/Ops Plans, during an interview at Selfridge ANGB, Michigan, on December 12, 1981. The author participated as an observer in the exercise at Gulfport and all those in Michigan.

67. ARRS rpt, Maj Gen Ralph S. Saunders, Cmdr, "Visit 53d WRS and 920th WRG and Observe 403d RWRW Forces Participating in SAREX," Apr 4, 1979; After Action Report, 403d RWRW, "Paid CRTE 80," Feb 12, 1981; rpt, Maj Leonard D. Salsbury, Ch, Pen Aids Div, ARRS, "403d RWRW at Alpena, Michigan," Oct 16, 1980; ltr, Maj Michael J. Peters, Dep Air Cmdr, to 403d RWRW, subj: Aggressor Forces After Action Report, Oct 16, 1980, w/2 atch—all in AFRES 23A.

68. After Action Report, 403d RWRW, "Condor CRTE 82," Dec 10, 1982, AFRES 23A.

69. Stanford Smith, "Reserve Readiness: Proving the Total-Force Policy a Success," in Bernie J. Wilson II, ed., *The Guard and the Reserve in the Total Force* (Washington, D.C., 1985), p 117.

70. James W. Browning et al., "The US Reserve System: Attitudes, Perceptions, and Realities," in Wilson, ed., *Guard and Reserve*, pp 67–70.

71. Intvw, Cantwell with Lyon, Feb 14, 1979, pp 11–18.

72. Intvw, Cantwell with Novaresi, Mar 30, 1982, HQ AFRES, pp 63–65, AFRES 26A.

73. 10 USC 262.

74. AFR 45–1, *Purpose, Policy, and Responsibilities for Air Reserve Forces*, Mar 3, 1975.

75. AFRES Ofc PA, "Air Force Reserve Facts and Figures, a/o FY 1985," Jan 1985.

76. Rpt, "Air Force Reserve Command Management Information Digest," Sep 30, 1981, pp 57–58, as doc 149 in hist, AFRES, FY 1981.

77. Hist, AFRES, FY 1981, app 5.

78. Memo, Kenneth R. Cole, Jr., to SecDef Melvin R. Laird, Spec Asst to Pres, subj: PL 90–500, May 20, 1969, WHSF, Erhlichman–475 (Military [General]), Box 32, NPMP.

79. PL 93–365, *Department of Defense Appropriations Act, 1975* (Stat 88: 399); memo, Frank J. Sherlock, Dir/Legis Rep Svc, Ofc of Gen Counsel, OSD, to SecN et al., subj: DOD 93–95, Proposed Legislation, "to Amend Chapter 39 of Title 10, United States Code, to Enable the President to Authorize the Involuntary Order to Active Duty of Selected Reservists, for a Limited Period, Without a Declaration of War or National Emergency," w/atch, May 16, 1974, as doc 13 in hist AFRES, FY 1974; ltr, Brig Gen William J. Crandall, Dep to Ch AF Res, to Dir/Pers Plans USAF, subj: DOD 93–95, Proposed Legislation to Amend Chapter 39 of Title 10, USC, May 16, 1974, as doc 13 in hist AFRES, FY 1974.

80. Memo, Roy L. Ash, Dir/OMB, to President, subj: Reserve Call-Up Authority, Nov 5, 1979, w/atch; memo, Warren Hendricks, Consultant, Secretary to the Cabinet, to Geoff Shepard, Assoc Dir for Gen Govt, Domestic Counsel, subj: Ash Memo (11/5/74) re: Reserve Call-Up Authority; memo, Jan M. Lodal, NSC staff, to Brent Scowcroft, Asst to Pres for National Security Affairs, subj: Reserve Call-Up Authority, Nov 8, 1974; memo, Brent Scowcroft to Ken Cole, Asst for Domestic Affairs, subj: Defense Proposal on Reserve Call-Up Authority, Nov 9, 1974; memo, Jerry H. Jones, Dep Asst to Pres for Sched & Adv Ofc, to Roy L. Ash, subj: Reserve Call-Up

485

The Air Force Reserve

Authority, Nov 18, 1974; memo, Brent Scowcroft to Jerry H. Jones, subj: Reserve Call-Up Authority, Mar 24, 1975; memo, Jan Lodal to Brent Scowcroft, subj: Reserve Call-Up Authority, Mar 20, 1975; memo, James F. C. Hyde, Jr., Actg Asst Dir for Legis Ref, to Jerry H. Jones, subj: Reserve Call-Up Authority, Mar 13, 1975, w/incls—all in WHCF, ND 12 RF & NG, 8/9/74–3/25/75, GRFL.

81. Subcommittee on Manpower and Personnel, Senate Armed Services Committee, *Reserve Call-Up: Hearings on S. 2115*, 94th Cong., 1st sess., Jul 30, 1975 (Washington, D.C., 1975).

82. PL 94–286, *To Amend Chapter 39 of Title 10, USC, to Enable the President to Authorize the Involuntary Order to Active Duty of Selected Reservists, for a Limited Period, Whether or Not a Declaration of War or National Emergency Has Been Declared* (Stat 90: 517).

83. Legislative History, PL 94–286, 94th Cong., 2d sess (1976), *United States Code, Congressional and Administrative News*, vol 3, pp 1034–48.

84. Ltr, Richard A. Wiley, Ofc of Gen Counsel, DOD, to James T. Lynn, Dir/OMB, subj: Enactment of S. 2115, May 7, 1976; memo, Lynn to President, subj: Enrolled Bill S. 2115, *Reserve Call-Up Authority*, May 12, 1976; memo, Richard T. Bovarie, NSC, to Brent Scowcroft, subj: *Reserve Call-Up Authority* (S. 2115), May 12, 1976—all in WHCF, ND 12 RF & NG, 5/2/76–8/31/76, GRFL; memo, Jim Cannon to President, subj: S. 2115, *Reserve Call-Up Authority*, WH Records Ofc, Legis CF, 1979–76, 5/14/76, S. 2115, Box 45, GRFL; "Remarks at Annual Armed Forces Day Dinner in Louisville," May 14, 1976, *Public Papers of the Presidents of the United States: Gerald R. Ford, 1976–77* (hereafter, Ford, *Public Papers*), p 1959; "Remarks upon Signing the Armed Forces Reserve Bill in Louisville," May 14, 1976, Ford, *Public Papers, 1976–77*, pp 1591–92.

85. PL 96–584, *Armed Forces Reserve—Active Duty* (Stat 94: 3377); Legislative History, PL 96–584, 96th Cong., 2d sess. (1980), *United States Code Congressional and Administrative News*, vol 6, pp 7007–16

86. Ltr, Gen Robert C. Mathis, Vice CSAF, to Ofc of Air Force Reserve, subj: Air Force Inspector General Investigation, Jan 16, 1982, w/atch; Formal Report of Investigation, Jan 8, 1982, Maj Gen William R. Usher; MFR, Cantwell, subj: Telephone Conversation with General Usher, Jan 18, 1989; MFR, subj: Telephone Conversation with Gen Robert C. Mathis, Dec 21, 1988; ltr, Gen Lew Allen, Jr., to author, subj: Constitution of the Air Force Management Assistance Group, Nov 7, 1988; intvw, author with Lt Gen Howard W. Leaf, Dec 7, 1988—all in AFRES 11B.1; msg, ALMAJCOM–SOA 36/82, subj: Air Force Reserve Management Assistance Group, CV 292120Z Jan 82, as doc 9 in hist, AFRES, FY 1982; msg, USAF to AFRES, subj: Air Force Reserve Management Assistance Group, w/atch, IG 121930Z Feb 82, as doc 11 in hist, AFRES, FY 1982.

87. Introduction to final rpt, "Air Force Management Assistance Group, Apr 30, 1982," doc 1, hist, AFRES, FY 1982. The author briefed the Management Assistance Group during its first days at Andrews AFB and observed some of its proceedings.

88. Final rpt, "Air Force Management Assistance Group," as cited in preceding note.

89. Ibid.

90. PL 90–168, *Reserve Forces Bill of Rights and Vitalization Act*, Dec 1, 1967.

91. *ROA Air Force Affairs Update*, May 7, 1982, as doc 18 in hist, AFRES, FY 1982.

92. Memo, Tidal W. McCoy, Asst SecAF (MR&A), to Lt Gen Hans H. Driessnack, Asst VCS, subj: Air Force Reserve Management Assistance Group, May 3, 1982, as doc 19 in hist, AFRES, FY 1982.

93. Memo, McCoy to Verne Orr, SecAF, subj: Air Force Reserve Management Assistance Group, May 3, 1982, as doc 20 in hist, AFRES, FY 1982.

94. Ltr, Bodycombe to Orr, subj: Air Force Reserve Views on Air Force Reserve Management Assistance Group Report, Jun 17, 1982, as doc 21 in hist, AFRES, FY 1982.

95. Ltr, Bodycombe to USAF/IG, subj: Status Report on the Air Force Management Assistance Report 30 April 1982, Jun 30, 1982, w/atch, as doc 26 in hist, AFRES, FY 1982.

96. Ltr, Mathis to AFRES et al., subj: Final Report of the Air Force Management Assistance Group, May 10, 1982, as doc 16 in hist, AFRES, FY 1982; remarks, Bodycombe, Aug 26, 1989, Homestead AFB.

97. General Dillon was reassigned by DAF SO AA-703 on April 28, 1982. For the reestablishment of AFRES and ARPC as separate operating agencies, see ltr, DAF/MPM 483q, USAF to AFRES, subj: HQ Air Force Reserve, Apr 6, 1983, a/a ltr, DAF/MPM 483q-1, Apr 28, 1983, docs 1, 2, in hist, AFRES, FY 1983; ltr, DAF/MPM 484q, USAF to ARPC, subj: HQ Air Reserve Personnel Center, Apr 6, 1983, a/a ltr, DAF/MPM 984q-1, Apr 28, 1983, docs 3, 4, in hist, AFRES, FY 1983.

98. MFR, Cantwell, subj: Interview with Maj Gen Sloan R. Gill, Chief of Air Force Reserve, Jan 6, 1984, Jan 9, 1989, AFRES 26A.

Chapter 13

1. Statistical data compiled from hists, AFRES, FYs 1980–89. See also Appendices 2 and 3, this volume.

2. Caspar W. Weinberger, *Fighting for Peace* (New York, 1990), pp 48–51, 68.

3. Ibid., p 79.

4. Caspar W. Weinberger, "U.S. Defense Strategy," *Foreign Affairs*, vol 64, No. 4 (spring 1986), pp 675–697. The "six tests" are summarized and discussed in this article (pp 686–90); the complete text of Secretary Weinberger's November 28, 1984, speech, "The Uses of Military Power," appears as an appendix in *Fighting for Peace* on pp 433–45.

5. Rpt, "AFRES Bases and Units," Oct 1980; rpt, "AFRES Bases and Units," Jan 1990.

6. Testimony, Maj Gen John J. Closner, Ch AF Res, to Comm on Armed Service, US Senate, Apr 1991, excerpted in doc 4–30, hist, AFRES, FY 1991; msg, AFRES to 94 TAW et al., subj: FY 1987/88 Manning Policy, CV 141200Z May 87, doc 285, hist, AFRES, FY 1987.

7. Msg, CV 141200Z May 87, cited in preceding note.

8. For a discussion of the impact the imposition the manpower ceiling had on the command, see Hist, AFRES, FY 1987, chap 3, and Hist, AFRES, FY 1988, chap 5. Most of the turmoil associated with this policy change had subsided by the end of FY 1988.

9. Hearings, DOD Appropriations, FY 1988, SAC, 100th Cong., 1st sess., pt 3, p 666.

10. Ltr, CMSgt Tommie B. Watson, Sp Asst for Career Motivation, DCS Personnel, HQ AFRES, to CC and DP, NAFs, Wgs & Det Gps, subj: Retention Statistics (September 1984), ca. Oct 1984, doc 658, hist, AFRES, FY 1984; point paper, Lt Col Joseph R. Simmons, Jr., Acc Util & Sustnmt Plans, Ofc of AFRES, subj: Retention/Reenlistment (Unit Program), Jan 8, 1987, doc 521, hist, AFRES, FY 1986; AFRNS Release No. 88049, "Retention Losses Get Attention of Leaders," Sep 4, 1988, doc 5–34, hist, AFRES, FY 1988.

11. Ltr, Maj Gen Roger A. Scheer, Ch AFRES, to Maj Gen James C. Wahleithner, Cmdr, 4th AF, et al., subj: Participation/Retention Initiatives, Feb 26, 1988, doc 5–38, hist, AFRES, FY 1988; point paper, CMSgt Henry J. Scott, Dep Dir of Assignments & Career Motivation, DCS Pers, HQ AFRES, subj: Enlisted Reservists Investment Cost Estimate, Apr 16, 1989, doc 6–15, hist, AFRES, FY 1989.

12. AFRES Pamphlet 39–3, *Air Force Reserve Enlisted Incentives*, Feb 3, 1992, as doc 4–47 in hist, AFRES, FY 1992.

13. Point paper, Donnie Powell, ART Officer Placement, DCS Personnel, HQ AFRES, subj: ART Pilot Recruitment/Retention Efforts, Jul 25, 1988, doc 5–68, hist, AFRES, FY 1988.

14. Ibid.

15. This account follows that found in Cantwell and Summers, *Air Reserve Technician Program*, updated by Kenneth C. Kan, Oct 1987, p 50.

16. Point paper, MSgt W. H. Trulove, Ch, Mgmt Info, DCS Personnel, HQ AFRES, subj: Enlisted Force Management Study, Jan 21, 1988, doc 5–60, hist, AFRES, FY 1988; memo, Col D. L. Orme,

The Air Force Reserve

Asst DCS Personnel, HQ AFRES, subj: Enlisted Force Management Study, Jun 13, 1988, doc 5–61, hist, AFRES, FY 1988; memo, Col William P. Carter, DCS, Personnel, HQ AFRES, to Maj Gen Alan G. Sharp, AFRES Vice Commander, subj: Enlisted Force Management Study, Apr 13, 1989, doc 6–24, hist, AFRES, FY 1989.

17. Hists, AFRES, FY 1980, p 159, and FY 1989, pp 181–182.

18. Hist, AFRES, May 1, 1995, p 7; *Air Force Reserve Management Information Digest*, Jun 1995, p B–3; msg, 302d SOS Depolyed, Nellis AFB, Nev., to HQ USAF/RE, subj: Daily Activity Report for 21 November 1980, Red Flag 81–1, DO 222350Z Nov 80, doc 343, hist, AFRES, FY 1981; ltr, Terry L. Biery, Research Entomologist, 907 TAG, to HQ AFRES, subj: Public Health Emergency in Minnesota, Oct 5, 1983, doc 476, hist, AFRES, FY 1983; ltr, Terry L. Biery, Research Entomologist, 907 TAG, to Cmdr 907 TAG, subj: FY 1983 Aerial Spray Activities, Nov 10, 1983, doc 480, hist, AFRES, FY 1983.

19. Details on these and a myriad of other Air Force Reserve operations throughout the decade are provided in the annual command histories prepared by the HQ AFRES Directorate of Historical Services and summarized in the brief annual histories of the United States Air Force Reserve and the semiannual updates to the command's chronological histories that appear in periodic updates of the *Air Force Reserve Management Information Digest*.

20. Point paper, Maj Claire J. Gilstad, Airlift Project Officer, Operations Training Div, Ofc of AF Reserve, subj: Air Force Reserve Participation in Worldwide Contingencies during the Last Week of October 1983, Nov 23, 1983, doc 399 in hist, AFRES, FY 1983.

21. MFR, O'Connell, subj: Air Force Reserve Performance in Air Force Competitions, 1980–1994, Sep 27, 1995, AFRES 23.

22. Winner of the Top Gun Award at Gunsmoke 87 was Maj. Danny Hamilton of the 419th Tactical Fighter Wing, Hill Air Force Base, Utah; Capt. Patrick Shay, 944th Tactical Fighter Group, Luke Air Force Base, Arizona, won the same award at Gunsmoke 89. Hist, AFRES, FY 1988, pp 47–48; ibid., FY 1990, p 56.

23. The 419th Tactical Fighter Wing, Hill Air Force Base, Utah, was the top team at Gunsmoke 85. The 94th Tactical Airlift Wing, Dobbins Air Force Base, Georgia, was the top team at Volant Rodeo 85. The 452d Air Refueling Wing (Heavy) was the best KC–135 team at the SAC Bomb/Nav Comp 85. See O'Connell MFR, Sep 27, 1995.

24. Point paper, Edward L. Kinser, AFRES/DOOM, subj: Hurricane Hugo Support, Oct 20, 1989, AFRES 22.C.1.

25. Hist, AFRES, FY 1989, p 84.

26. Capt Diane M. Lake, "This Was Something Serious," *Citizen Airman*, vol 42, No. 2 (Mar 1990), p 28. Six of the eight members were "traditional" Reservists (that is, part-time personnel), and two were Air Reserve Technicians.

27. Special Study, Patsy R. Stone, AFRES/HO, "Operation JUST CAUSE," ca. Mar 1990, AFRES 22.D.12; Capt Janet G. Tucker, "A Mean Fighting Machine," *Citizen Airman*, vol 42, No. 2 (Mar 1990), pp 20–21. The crew of one of the AFRES AC–130s (55–0046), under the command of Maj Clay T. McCutchan, subsequently received several awards and decorations for their actions on a sortie on December 20, 1990. The crew had been cleared to fire on three enemy armored personnel carriers heading toward an American facility. As they prepared to do so, the Fire Control Officer, Maj James N. Strength, detected on his sensors what he believed were friendly forces in the vicinity of the target. Although the crew received a second and later a third authorization to commence firing, Maj Strength advised Maj McCutchan not to fire. He did not. An investigation later confirmed that American forces had captured the armored vehicles and that the ground forces the crew observed were, in fact, Americans. See "Summary of Accomplishments—919th Special Operations Group, Aircrew of AC–130A #55–0046," n.d., AFRES 22.D.12.

28. Ltr, Col Paul W. Harbison, Asst DCS/Ops, to HQ USAF/REO, subj: Operation JUST CAUSE Recap, Dec 14, 1990, AFRES 22.D.12.

29. Ibid.

30. Stone, "Operation JUST CAUSE," AFRES 22.D.12. The medical units were the

31st Aeromedical Evacuation Squadron, 34th Aeromedical Evacuation Flight, and 32d Aeromedical Evacuation Group, all from Kelly Air Force Base, Texas. The 25th, 34th, 37th, 39th, and 41st Mobile Aerial Port Squadrons and the 35th, 38th, 46th, 47th, 49th, 51st, 81st, 82d, 88th, and 89th Aerial Port Squadrons were involved, as were Security Police volunteers from the 439th Security Police Squadron and the 315th Security Police Flight.

31. Ltr, Col Thomas L. Spruiell, 32d AEG/CC, to HQ 4th AF/SG et al., subj: After Action Report: Operation JUST CAUSE, Jan 12, 1990; ltr, Lt Col Van P. Williams, Jr., Liaison Officer, OL EN, 2400 RRMS, to NGB/XO et al., subj: Operation JUST CAUSE After Action Report, Jan 16, 1990; ltr, Lt Col William R. Tefteller, Dep Cmdr/Ops, 512th MAW (A), to 512th MAW (A)/CC, subj: Lessons Learned in VOLANT EAGLE/Operation JUST CAUSE, Jan 22, 1990; ltr, Lt Col Robert E. Duignan, Dep Comdr/Ops, 459th MAW, to HQ USAF/REO, subj: Operation JUST CAUSE, Jan 24, 1990; ltr, Col Bobby L. Hammond, Jr., Dep Cmdr/Ops, 315th MAW, to HQ USAF/REO, subj: Operation JUST CAUSE Lessons Learned, Jan 25, 1990; ltr, Maj Elmer S. Whittier, Jr., Instructor Pilot, 337th MAS, to HQ USAF/REOO, subj: Lessons Learned from Operation JUST CAUSE, Jan 25, 1990; ltr, Lt Col Lawrence E. Mercker, Asst Dep Cmdr/Ops, 439th MAW, to HQ USAF/REO, subj: Lessons Learned from Operation JUST CAUSE, Jan 25, 1990; msg, 403d TAW to HQ USAF/REO, subj: Lessons Learned from Operation Just Cause, DO 252110Z Jan 90; ltr, Col William D. Peden, Dep Cmdr/Ops, 349th MAW (A), to HQ USAF/REO, subj: Lessons Learned from Operation JUST CAUSE, Jan 25, 1990; ltr, Lt Col Keith G. Lauer, Actg Dir Curr Ops, HQ AFRES, to HQ USAF/REO, subj: Lessons Learned from Operation JUST CAUSE, Jan 25, 1990; ltr, Maj Robert Dodson, Chief, AFRES Command Post, to HQ AFRES/DOO, subj: Lessons Learned from Operation JUST CAUSE, Jan 25, 1990—all in AFRES 22.D.12.

32. All three quotes are from Maj Gen Roger P. Scheer, "When We're Needed, We'll Be There," *Citizen Airman*, vol 42, No. 2 (Mar 1990), p 3.

33. Col David Tretler et al., "Chronology of the Gulf War," in Eliot A. Cohen, ed., *Gulf War Air Power Survey*, 6 vols (Washington, D.C.: Gulf War Air Power Survey Team, 1993) (hereafter, Cohen, ed., *GWAPS*), vol 5, pt 2. The Gulf War narrative that follows is based primarily on the following sources: Hist, AFRES, FY 1990, Annex 1; hist, AFRES, FY 1991, annex 1; Maj Gen John J. Closner, "The Air Force Reserve and the Persian Gulf War," *Airpower History*, vol 39, No. 2 (summer 1992), pp 40–45 (hereafter, Closner, "The AFR and the Persian Gulf War"); rpt, Dept of the Air Force, "Reaching Globally, Reaching Powerfully: The United States Air Force in the Gulf War," Sep 1991. For background on the air war in general, see Richard P. Hallion, *Storm over Iraq: Air Power and the Gulf War* (Washington, D.C., 1992).

34. Rpt, "AFRES Bases and Units," Jan 1990; pamphlet, AFRES Office of Public Affairs, *Air Force Reserve Facts & Figures*, Jun 30, 1990.

35. Ltr, Ronald F. Stuewe, Dir Cost Analysis, HQ AFRES, to Ch AFRES, subj: Air Force Reserve Volunteer Rates to Support Desert Shield, Jan 15, 1991, doc annex 1–1, Hist, AFRES, FY 1990; Closner, "The AFR and the Persian Gulf War," pp 40–41.

36. Closner, "The AFR and the Persian Gulf War," p 41; hist, AFRES, FY 1990, annex 1, pp 2–3.

37. Study, Patsy R. Stone, Dep Dir Hist Svcs, AFRES/HO, "Reservists at Sharjah," Jan 10, 1992.

38. Msg, HQ USAF to AFRES Unit Commanders, subj: Message to the Field from Maj Gen Roger P. Scheer, RE 2830-37Z Aug 90. Reserve crew members who died in the crash were Maj. John M. Gordon, Maj. Richard M. Price, Maj. Richard W. Chase, SMSgt. Carpio Vilarreal, Jr., MSgt. Rosendo Herrera, TSgt. Lonty A. Knutson, TSgt. Daniel G. Perez, SSgt. Edward E. Sheffield, and SSgt. Daniel Garza.

39. Richard A. Gunkel et al., "Support," in Cohen, ed., *GWAPS*, vol 3, pt 2, pp 103–108.

40. Rpt, AFRES Command Post, "AFRES Operation DESERT STORM Duty Status Report" (hereafter, "ODS Duty Status Report"), Mar 15, 1991. The AFRES Com-

mand Post prepared these reports on a weekly basis from early January 1991 through the end of April, when they were replaced by a demobilization report. The March 15 report outlines the mobilization at its peak.

41. Gunkel et al., "Support," in Cohen, ed., *GWAPS*, vol 3, pt 2, pp 109–17.

42. "ODS Duty Status Report," Mar 15, 1991; Col David Tretler et al., "A Statistical Compendium," in Cohen, ed., *GWAPS*, vol 5, pt 1, table 31, pp 98–109.

43. Closner, "The AFR and the Persian Gulf War," table 4, p 44.

44. "ODS Duty Status Report," Mar 15, 1991; rpt, 926th Tactical Fighter Group/706th Tactical Fighter Squadron, "926 TFG/706 TFS Operation DESERT SHIELD/STORM After-Action Report," Aug 17, 1991 (hereafter, "926 TFG AAR"); Maj Rick Dyer, *Westover: The Eye of the Storm* (Westover AFB, Mass., 1993).

45. "ODS Duty Status Report," Feb 3, 1991.

46. Closner, "The AFR and the Persian Gulf War," p 43; "926 TFG AAR."

47. William L. Smallwood, *Warthog: Flying the A–10 in the Gulf War* (Washington, D.C., 1993), pp 167–69; "926 TFG AAR."

48. Closner, "The AFR and the Persian Gulf War," p 43; "926 TFG AAR."

49. "ODS Duty Status Report," Mar 15, 1991.

50. Reserve organizations eventually submitted through the Joint Universal Lessons Learned System (JULLS) more than 700 potential lessons learned. To a great extent these JULLS reports raised most of the same issues brought up during the Gulf War Hotwash, discussed in the paragraphs that follow.

51. Ltr, Col Harvey L Rosenmeier, AFRES Ch of Staff, to HQ USAF/RE, NAFs, and AFRES Staff, subj: DESERT SHIELD/STORM Flying Unit Hotwash, Aug 8, 1991, doc 1–47, hist, AFRES, FY 1992; rpt, HQ AFRES, "Operation DESERT STORM/SHIELD Hotwash 92 Commanders' Report," Jul 20, 1992 (hereafter, "Hotwash Report"), pp 2–3 in doc 1–48, hist, AFRES, FY 1992.

52. "Hotwash Report," p 12.

53. Ibid., pp 15, 80.

54. Ibid., p 31.

55. Ibid., pp 8–52.

56. Ibid., pp 33, 68.

57. Ibid., pp 20, 46, 48.

58. Ibid., pp 9, 13–14, 30, 32, 40, 52; point paper, Ops Div, Ofc of Ch AFRES, subj: Commitment of Reserve Forces, May 29, 1991, doc 1–49, hist, AFRES, FY 1992.

59. Rpt, Recruiting Ops Div, HQ AFRES, "AFR Recruiting Update," Jul 15, 1991, doc 1–52, hist, AFRES, FY 1992.

60. Rpt, Dir Hist Svcs, HQ AFRES, "Reserve Mobilizations and Their Impact on Recruiting and Retention," Oct 25, 1990, doc 1–53, hist, AFRES, FY 1992.

61. Hist, AFRES, FY 1991, annex 1, p 25.

62. *What's Next: A Guide to Family Readiness* (Elkins Park, Pa., 1991), copy in doc 1–54, hist, AFRES, FY 1992.

63. Point paper, Family Readiness Br, HQ AFRES, subj: Reserve Family Support Program, Jun 25, 1992, doc 1–55, hist, AFRES, FY 1992; AFRESR 30–2, *Family Support Program (FSP)*, Jul 15 1992, doc 1–56, hist, AFRES, FY 1992.

64. AFRESR 30–2, Jul 15, 1992, paras 1–1, 1–2.

65. HQ AFRES, "Status Report on Air Force Reserve Employer Concerns and Issues," May 15, 1992, doc 1–57, hist, AFRES, FY 1992.

66. Ibid.

67. Booklet, Air Res Pers Cen Dir PA, *Air Reserve Personnel Center: Guard and Reserve Personnel Fact Sheets*, 1995 ed, pp 16–17, copy in AFRES 14.I.

68. "USAF Leaders Through the Years—USAF Chiefs of Staff," *Air Force Magazine*, vol 78, No. 5 (May 1995), p 58.

69. Press release, Office of Press Sec, The White House, subj: Remarks by the President to the Aspen Institute Symposium, Aug 2, 1990, p 2.

70. Ibid., p 4.

71. Rpt, The White House, "National Security Strategy of the United States," Aug 1991, p 29.

72. Ibid.

73. Lorna S. Jaffe, *The Development of the Base Force, 1989–1992* (Washington, D.C., 1993); United States General Accounting Office GAO/NSIAD–89–27, *Reserve Components: Opportunities to Improve National Guard and Reserve Policies*

Notes

and Programs (Nov 1988); Bernard D. Rostker et al., *Assessing the Structure and Mix of Future Active and Reserve Forces: Final Report to the Secretary of Defense* (Santa Monica, Calif., 1992); William W. Kaufmann and John D. Steinbruner, *Decisions for Defense: Prospects for a New Order* (Washington, D.C.: 1991); press releases, Rep. Les Aspin, Chmn, HASC, subj: New Era Requires Re-Thinking U.S. Military Forces, Jan 6, 1992, subj: Aspin Says Ground-Up Review Needed to Shape U.S. Forces, Jan 24, 1992, and subj: Aspin Recommends '93 Defense Cuts of $12–$15 Billion, Feb 26, 1992; study, Congressional Budget Office, "Structuring U. S. Forces After the Cold War: Costs and Effects of Increased Reliance on the Reserves," Sep 1992.

74. Rpt, Donald B. Rice, SecAF, "The Air Force and U.S. National Security: Global Reach—Global Power," Jun 1990; James W. Canan, "McPeak's Plan," *Air Force Magazine*, vol 74, No. 2; Edward G. Longacre, *Establishment of Air Combat Command, 1 June 1992* (Langley AFB, Va., 1993), pp 2–3.

75. SO G-032, Mar 2, 1992.

76. SO G-304, Jun 8, 1992.

77. AFRES SO G-404, Jul 9, 1992.

78. Congressional (HASC) testimony, Donald B. Rice, "Reshaping for the Future," Feb 20, 1992.

79. PPlan 92–18, AFRES, "AFRES Unit/Base Reorganization, 1 June 1992," May 11, 1992, doc 1–36, hist, AFRES, FY 1992; ltr, AFRES/XPX to Distribution, "Change 1 to AFRES Programming Plan (PPlan) 92–18, AFRES Unit/Base Reorganization," Jun 9, 1992, doc 1–37, hist, AFRES, FY 1992.

80. DAF/MO Ltr 328r, subj: Organization Actions Affecting Certain Air Force Reserve Units, Aug 28, 1992, doc 1–38, hist, AFRES, FY 1992; AFRES SO G-591, Aug 31, 1992; AFRES SO G-647, Sep 24, 1992; AFRES SO G-001, Oct 5, 1992; AFRES SO G-321, Nov 18, 1992; ltr, AFRES/XP to Limited Staff, subj: Redesignation of Certain Air Force Reserve Units, Aug 24, 1992, doc 1–44, hist, AFRES, FY 1992; ltr, AFRES/XP to Limited Staff, subj: Redesignation of Certain Air Force Reserve Units (XP Ltr, 24 Aug 92), Sep 30, 1992, doc 1–45, hist, AFRES, FY 1992; AFRES SO G-323, Nov 18, 1992; AFRES SO GB-0035, Sep 21, 1994.

81. Hists, AFRES, FY 1990, pp 2–3, FY 1992, p 11, FY 1993, p 9, and FY 1994, p 4.

82. Ibid., FY 1990, pp 33–41, FY 1991, pp 32–40, FY 1992, pp 50–59, FY 1993, pp 45–51, and FY 1994, pp 21–26.

83. Ibid., FY 1991, p 9, and FY 1993, pp 10–14; Les Aspin, SecDef, *Report on the Bottom-Up Review* (Washington, D.C., 1993); Andrew F. Krepinevich, *The Bottom-Up Review: An Assessment* (Washington, D.C., 1994).

84. Hists, AFRES, FY 1990, pp 11–16, FY 1991, pp 3, 11–13, FY 1992, pp 3–7, FY 1993, p 7, and FY 1994, p 10.

85. Ibid., FY 1992, p 97, FY 1993, p 70, and FY 1994, pp 58–59.

86. Financial Mgmt & Sys Div, HQ AFRES, *Air Force Reserve Management Digest* (Jun 1995), p B–9. Lt Col Roger A. Disrud, an A–10 pilot assigned to the 442d Tactical Fighter Wing, Richards-Gebaur Air Force Base, Missouri, earned Top Gun honors at the competition.

87. Hists, AFRES, FY 1992, p 97, FY 1993, pp 71–73, and FY 1994, pp 57–61.

88. Ibid., FY 1993, pp 73–75.

89. Ibid., FY 1993, pp 70–73, and FY 1994, pp 57–63.

90. Ibid., FY 1992, pp 98–102, 134–137.

91. Ibid., FY 1992, pp 102–104, FY 1993, p 80, and FY 1994, p 69.

92. Intvws, Charles F. O'Connell, Jr., Dir Hist Svcs, HQ AFRES, with Maj Gen Roger P. Scheer, Ch AFRES, Sep 25, 1990, pp 6–10, with Maj Gen Alan G. Sharp, VCmdr AFRES, Oct 22, 1990, pp 8–11, and with Maj Gen John J. Closner, Ch AFRES, Sep 19, 1994, pp 7–12—all in AFRES 26A.

93. Closner intvw, Sep 19, 1994, pp 7–8.

94. Ltr, Col Ralph L. Francis, Dir PA, HQ AFRES, to HQ USAF/RE et al., subj: Employer Support Survey, Apr 12, 1995, in working files for the FY 1995 AFRES history.

95. Maj Gen Robert A. McIntosh, Ch AFRES, "Quality, Human Resources Top Readiness Issues," *Citizen Airman*, vol 46, No. 6 (Dec 1994), p ii.

96. Maj Gen Robert A. McIntosh, Ch AFRES, "Chief Outlines 1995 Quality of Life Agenda," *Citizen Airman*, vol 47, No.

491

The Air Force Reserve

2 (Apr 1995), p ii.

97. AFRESR 213–1, *The Reserve GI Bill*, Jun 21, 1985, copy in AFRES 14.N.

98. VA Pamphlet 22–90–3, *Summary of Education Benefits under the Montgomery GI Bill—Selected Reserve*, Oct 1994, AFRES 14.N.

99. Timothy N. Miller, "New Jersey Reservist Is One in a Million," *Citizen Airman*, vol 42, No. 5 (Sep 1990), p 7.

100. Ltr, Col Gene A. Miller, DCS/Comptroller, to Flying Units/ACB and Staff Agencies, subj: A Synopsis of Reserve Entitlements, Sep 8 1977; ltr, Sloan R. Gill, Actg Dep Asst SecDef (Guard/Reserve Manpower and Personnel), to Dep Asst SecA (Res Affairs and Mobilization) et al., subj: Incapacitation Pay for Seasonally Employed Reservists, Feb 23, 1988; Office of AF Reserve Personnel Div and Office of Public Affairs, *United States Air Force Reserve Benefits and Entitlements* (ca. Dec 1994); ltr, Col William E. Hughes, AFRES Dir Personnel Plans, to All AFRES Unit Commanders, subj: Military Privileges for Members of the USAFR, Sep 20 1974; fact sheets, AFRES, subj: Reserve Component Survivor Benefit Plan, AFRES VA 190–20, Jun 30, 1987, and Aug 15, 1989; Air Res Pers Cen Dir PA, *Air Reserve Personnel Center: Guard and Reserve Personnel Fact Sheets*, 1995 ed; rpt, IG, AFRES, "Functional Management Inspection of the Management and Utilization of Recreational Services," Sep 24, 1982—all in AFRES 14.N.

101. Ltr, Maj Gen Charles B. Stone III, Dep Cmdr and Ch of Staff, ADC, to Commanding Gen, AAF, subj: ADC WAC Air Reserve Plan, Jan 8, 1947; ltr, Capt Marjorie O. Hunt, WAF Staff Dir, ADC, to Mrs. Floyd B. Odlum [Jacqueline Cochran], subj: [information concerning qualifications for service in the WAF Reserve program], Aug 16, 1948; ltr, Maj Richard A. Toole, Dir, Air Reserve, HQ 4th AF, to Commanding Officers, 4th AF AFRES Training Ctrs, subj: WAF Reservists, Feb 3, 1949; memo, Brig Gen J. P. McConnell, Dep Spec Asst for Reserve Forces, HQ USAF, to Harold C. Stuart, Asst SecAF, subj: [women in the Air Force Reserve], May 9, 1950; AFR 35–30, *Policy, Management, and Administration of Military Women in the Air Force*, Apr 30 1975; intvw, Margaret L. MacMackin, historian, HQ AFRES, with MSgt Dawnn Inge, HQ AFRES/DPXZ, Aug 15, 1995—all in AFRES 14T.

102. Paper, AFRES/HO, subj: Women in the Air Force Reserve, Feb 1987, AFRES 14.T; msg, HQ USAF to ALMAJCOM/CC et al., subj: Removal of Combat Aviation Exclusion, CC 282200Z Apr 93, doc 4–33, hist, AFRES, FY 1993; USAF Biography, Col Betty L. Mullis, May 1995, AFRES 14.H.B.

103. Gropman, *Air Force Integrates*; ADC Reg 50–5, *Policy for Training Negro Air Reservists*, Mar 7, 1947; ltr, Col C. R. Landon, Adj Gen, ADC, to Chief of Staff of the Air Force, subj: Negro Air Force Reservists, Feb 3, 1948; ltr, Maj Gen E. E. Partridge, Dir, Training & Rqmts, HQ USAF, to Commanding Gen, ADC, subj: [training Negro Air Force Reserve personnel], Feb 17, 1948; ltr, Col J. L. Nagley, Adj Gen, HQ 11th AF, to Commanding Gen, ADC, subj: Training of Negro Air Force Reservists, Apr 5, 1948; GO 36, HQ 2d AF, Apr 28, 1948—all in AFRES 14.G; Inge intvw, Aug 15, 1995.

104. Hists, AFRES, FY 1990, pp 16–28, FY 1991, pp 17–30, FY 1992, pp 33–46, FY 1993, pp 15–42, and FY 1994, pp 11–20; USAFR Quality Center, "The United States Air Force Reserve Total Quality Implementation Plan," Jul 9, 1991, doc 1–38, hist, AFRES, FY 1991; *United States Air Force Reserve Long Range Plan, 1993–1999*, Oct 1992, doc 1–71, hist, AFRES, FY 1992; *Application for the 1993 Secretary of the Air Force Unit Quality Award*, Jun 18, 1993, doc 1–95, hist, AFRES, FY 1993; briefing, Brig Gen John F. Harvey, AFRES Dir/Plans, subj: Corporate Planning Initiative," Dec 22, 1992, doc 1–104, hist, AFRES, FY 1993; ltr, Maj Gen Robert A. McIntosh, AFRES VCmdr, to HQ USAF/RE et al., subj: Air Force Reserve Strategic Agenda, May 14, 1993, doc 1–110, hist, AFRES, FY 1992; *United States Air Force Reserve Long Range Plan, 1994–1998*, Oct 1993, doc 1–51, hist, AFRES, FY 1994; *Air Force Reserve Road Map to the Future* (ca. Mar 1991), AFRES HO Library; *The Air Force Reserve Strategic Agenda*, May 1, 1995, AFRES HO Library.

BIBLIOGRAPHIC NOTE

Bibliographic Note

Sources for this work which covers the evolution and operation of the Air Force Reserve over such a lengthy period are necessarily diverse and far-flung. Research began in the historical archives of Headquarters Air Force Reserve (AFRES) at Robins Air Force Base, Georgia, where the author was employed from 1970 through 1989. There, recorded on a combination of paper and microfilm, are to be found eleven categories of valuable records: the histories of the Air Defense Command from March 1946 to November 1948, when it was responsible to administer the civilian components of the Army Air Forces and the United States Air Force; the histories of the Continental Air Command from December 1948, when it took over the responsibility from the Air Defense Command, to July 1968; all the histories of Headquarters AFRES, which acquired the responsibility in August 1968; the histories of Air Force Reserve flying units from July 1958, and some earlier; oral history interviews of Air Force Reserve officials conducted by the author; reports of boards, committees, and study groups which studied the Air Force Reserve; management and reorganization plans pertaining to the Air Force Reserve; significant papers pertaining to the evolution of the Office of the Special Assistant to the Chief of Staff for Reserve Forces, the Assistant Chief of Staff, Reserve Forces, and the Chief of Air Force Reserve; files on legislation and presidential directives pertaining to the Air Force Reserve; files on the Army Air Forces and Air Force service associations; and some old War Department manuals.

Special mention must be made of a mother lode of microfilmed key documents tracing the administration of the Army Air Forces' and Air Force's civilian components and auxiliaries from March 1946 to November 1948. These papers are a collection which the late Thomas A. Sturm, the Air Defense Command historian after the command was relieved of its reserve forces responsibilities, had the perspicacity and managerial acumen to bundle off to the Air Force Historical Archives at Maxwell Air Force Base, Alabama, whence the author retrieved a microfilm copy.

Within Headquarters AFRES, the historian always enjoyed easy access to the files of all agencies. In addition, the successive Staff Judge Advocates, Colonels Merrill Q. Horton, Frank A. Luna, and Edward J. Murphy, threw open their legal libraries to me. There the legislative histories included in the *United States Code, Congressional and Administrative* series provided valuable insight into the mind of Congress as it passed legislation affecting the reserve forces of the nation.

The Air Force Reserve

Air Force Historical Research Agency

The search for information and documentation then branched into two directions. The Air Force Historical Research Agency (AFHRA), formerly the Albert F. Simpson Historical Research Center (AFSHRC), at Maxwell Air Force Base, Alabama, under the successive leadership of Albert F. Simpson, Maurer Maurer, James N. Eastman, Jr., and Lloyd H. Cornett, Jr., was a sociable and fruitful place to do research. Within its vast collections of Air Force holdings, the author made particularly good use of the daily activity reports of AC/AS–3 in 1945 and 1946; the daily diary of the Reserve and National Guard Division of AC/AS–1 in 1946 and 1947, which traced the flow of paper in the Air Staff on Air Reserve matters between July 1946 and October 1947; the papers of Brig. Gen. Aubrey L. Moore, who in 1951 was Deputy Director of Manpower and Organization, U.S. Air Force; and several manuscript collections including the Korean War diaries of Lt. Gen. George E. Stratemeyer, Lt. Gen. Earle E. Partridge, and Maj. Gen. Edward J. Timberlake, Jr., which offered valuable insight into the role and performance of the mobilized Air Force Reserve units in the Korean War.

The National Archives

The other trail led to the National Archives of the United States in Washington, D.C., administered by the National Archives and Records Administration, formerly the National Archives and Records Service. Records pertaining to the planning of a post–World War II Air Reserve, insofar as such planning was done in the years preceding 1949, were integrated with those of the War Department, Headquarters Army Air Forces, and Headquarters United States Air Force (USAF). The most fruitful collections of such records were found in Record Groups 18, Headquarters Army Air Forces; 165, the War Department General and Special Staffs; 340, the Office of the Secretary of the Air Force; and 341, Headquarters USAF. The record number for some of these files is preceded by a decimal and a box number.

Beginning in 1949, records of Headquarters USAF and the Office of the Secretary of Defense that pertained to the planning and administration of the Air Force Reserve became elusive. Either the Office of the Special Assistant for Reserve Forces did not retire many records or the National Archives misplaced them, because they were not found. The situation improved after 1953 and the establishment of the Office of the Assistant Chief of Staff, Reserve Forces, and it improved immeasurably with the creation of the Office of the Air Force Reserve in 1968.

Bibliography

The Washington National Records Center

The records of the Office of the Secretary of Defense and the Air Force after some point in 1955 are housed in the Washington National Records Center in Suitland, Maryland. It is a rather tedious process to recover this material. The researcher must first ascertain the administrative documents by which the records were retired to the center and then cross-reference this information to the center's file accession numbers. The Washington National Records Center does not pretend to be an archive; it is merely a record storage area, and recovering documents from the center can be very difficult, especially if the records were retired as classified documents. Nevertheless, the researcher who wants to look into Record Groups 330, 340, and 341 after 1955 must go to Suitland.

Library of Congress

The Library of Congress in Washington, D.C., was helpful in providing two classes of information: papers of the Chiefs of Staff of the United States Air Forces and congressional documents not available elsewhere. Among the former, the papers of Lt. Gen. Curtis E. LeMay, which seemed incomplete as a collection, were of no use; Lt. Gen. Nathan F. Twining's documents were of some help, but the collection of his papers held by the United States Air Force Academy was superior; and the material obtained from the records Lt. Gen. Ira C. Eaker provided some help on the state of the Army Air Corps Reserve in the late 1930s. The papers of H. H. Arnold, Carl A. Spaatz, Hoyt S. Vandenberg, Muir S. Fairchild, and Thomas D. White, on the other hand, contained significant information pertaining to the Air Corps Reserve and Air Force Reserve. Of greatest help among the Manuscript Division's pertinent holdings were the papers of John McAuley Palmer, consultant and adviser to General George C. Marshall on civilian component matters during and after World War II.

Harry S. Truman Library

Since this book was written in terms of national policy, it was essential that the author conduct research in the presidential libraries administered by the National Archives and Records Administration. Within the huge collections of executive branch papers documenting the character, policies, practices, and activities of each administration, the Harry S. Truman Library in Independence, Missouri, offered superb records. Of particular interest and help to the author was documentation of the relationship between President Harry S. Truman's

The Air Force Reserve

efforts to balance the budget after World War II and the state of national defense; the political motivations behind his issue of Executive Order 10007 in October 1948, the Secretary of Defense's vigorous objections to it, and the circumstances of its publication; and the decision to mobilize reserves to both build up the active forces and fight the Korean War.

Dwight D. Eisenhower Library

The Dwight D. Eisenhower Library in Abilene, Kansas, contains excellent documentation of the Eisenhower administration's development of the National Reserve Plan which Congress incorporated into the Reserve Forces Act of 1955, the third of the landmark laws that reshaped the nation's reserve programs subsequent to the Korean War.

John F. Kennedy Library

The holdings of the John F. Kennedy Library in Dorchester, Massachusetts, include extensive files pertaining to the Kennedy administration's effort to establish a new defense policy of selective response; the mobilization of the Air Reserve Forces in the Berlin and Cuba missile crises; and Secretary of Defense Robert S. McNamara's reorganization of the Army Reserve Components and subsequent effort to merge the Army Reserve into the Army National Guard.

Lyndon B. Johnson Library

The Lyndon B. Johnson Library, on the campus of the University of Texas in Austin includes many files of papers relative to President Johnson's disinclination to mobilize the reserves as the central Air Force Reserve issue with respect to the war in Southeast Asia. Also found are the details of two minor mobilizations in 1968.

Gerald R. Ford Library

The passage of Public Law 96–584 gave the President more flexibility to mobilize reserve forces, and the files of the Gerald R. Ford Library on the campus of the University of Michigan in Ann Arbor contain excellent documentation of the development of the Ford administration's policy on this issue.

Bibliography

Richard M. Nixon's Presidential Materials Project

While not a presidential library, the Nixon Presidential Materials Project located in Fairfax, Virginia, makes certain of President Richard M. Nixon's presidential papers available to researchers. Among the open collections were several that provided good documentation on the President's position on ending the draft and calling for an all-volunteer force.

Office of Air Force History

Other agencies which provided rich source material were the Office of Air Force History, the Office of Air Force Reserve, and the U.S. Army Library, all in Washington, D.C. The Office of Air Force History at Bolling Air Force Base provided copies of the Air Service and Air Corps newsletters, the three editions of the Pentagon Papers, Air Staff agency histories, and the *USAF Statistical Digest*. The U.S. Army Library housed in the Pentagon provided complete sets of the annual reports of the War Department, the Air Service, and the Army Air Corps, all valuable source documents for the development and implementation of reserve policies between the two World Wars. The Office of Air Force Reserve opened on January 1, 1968, and studies to reorganize it and the Air Force Reserve program followed immediately and continue. Files of the Programs and Resources Division under Col. Walker M. Williams III contain much material that complements the management studies located in the Air Force Reserve historical archives.

Local Resources

Macon, Georgia, is not the worst place in the country to write a government-oriented history. The city's cultural assets include a university, a college, a junior college, and a law school as well as its own well-stocked city library. The resources of the Stetson Library on the main campus of Mercer University, the library of the university's Walter F. George School of Law, and the city's Washington Memorial Library were so rich that the author never had recourse to the facilities of Wesleyan College or Macon Junior College. The History Department of Mercer University is supported by an outstanding collection of books on all aspects of early American history. The law library is a repository of U.S. government documents which made the *Congressional Record* and many other congressional documents available along with the bound series of *Public Papers of the Presidents of the United States*. The real research asset in Macon, however, is the personable and efficient Thomas Jones who happily held the positions of research assistant at both the Washington Memorial

The Air Force Reserve

Library during the day and the law library in the evening. From that dual perspective, Thomas seemed to know the location of every book and collection in Macon and to know what books were not there, and he shared his knowledge. He also provided access to the interlibrary loan system, unfortunately sabotaged by the terribly inefficient policies and procedures of the State of Georgia which exercised sort of a first refusal on all requests, even for one-of-a-kind documents that could exist only in a single out-of-state location, such as the Dwight D. Eisenhower Library.

Governmental Sources

Presidential Papers

Public Papers of the Presidents of the United States: Harry S. Truman, 1945. Washington: Office of the Federal Register, National Archives and Records Service, 1961.

Public Papers of the Presidents of the United States: Harry S. Truman, 1950. Washington: Office of the Federal Register, National Archives and Records Service, 1965.

Public Papers of the Presidents of the United States: Dwight D. Eisenhower, 1953. Washington: Office of the Federal Register, National Archives and Records Service, 1960.

Public Papers of the Presidents of the United States: Dwight D. Eisenhower, 1954. Washington: Office of the Federal Register, National Archives and Records Service, 1960.

Public Papers of the Presidents of the United States: Dwight D. Eisenhower, 1955. Washington: Office of the Federal Register, National Archives and Records Service, 1959.

Public Papers of the Presidents of the United States: John F. Kennedy, 1961. Washington: Office of the Federal Register, National Archives and Records Service, 1962.

Public Papers of the Presidents of the United States John F. Kennedy, 1962. Washington: Office of the Federal Register, National Archives and Records Service, 1963.

Public Papers of the Presidents of the United States: Lyndon B. Johnson, 1965, vol 1. Washington: Office of the Federal Register, National Archive and Records Service, 1966.

Public Papers of the Presidents of the United States: Lyndon B. Johnson, 1968–1969, vol 1. Washington: Office of the Federal Register, National Archives and Records Service, 1970.

Bibliography

Public Papers of the Presidents of the United States Lyndon B. Johnson, 1968–1969, vol 2. Washington: Office of the Federal Register, National Archives and Records Service, 1970.

Public Papers of the Presidents of the United States: Richard M. Nixon, 1969. Washington: Office of Federal Register, National Archives and Records Service, 1971.

Public Papers of the Presidents of the Unites States: Richard M. Nixon, 1970. Washington: Office of Federal Register, National Archives and Records Service, 1971.

Public Papers of the Presidents of the United States: Richard M. Nixon, 1971. Washington: Office of the Federal Register, National Archives and Records Service, 1972.

Public Papers of the Presidents of the United States: Richard M. Nixon, 1972. Washington: Office of Federal Register, National Archives and Records Service, 1974.

Public Papers of the Presidents of the United States: Gerald R. Ford, 1976–1977. Washington: Office of the Federal Register, National Archives and Records Service, 1979.

Executive Orders

Executive Order 10007. *Organization of the Reserve Units of the Armed Forces.* Oct 15, 1948. Harry S. Truman.

Executive Order 10957. *Assigning Authority with Respect to Ordering Persons and Units in the Ready Reserve to Active Duty and with Respect to the Extension of Enlistments and Other Periods of Service in the Armed Forces.* Aug 15, 1961. John F. Kennedy.

Executive Order 11058. *Assigning Authority with Respect to Ordering Persons and Units in the Ready Reserve to Active Duty and with Respect to Extension of Enlistment and Other Periods of Service in the Armed Forces.* Oct 15, 1962. John F. Kennedy.

Executive Order 11392. *Ordering Certain Units of the Ready Reserve of the Naval Reserve, Air Force Reserve, and Air National Guard of the United States to Active Duty.* Jan 26, 1968. Lyndon B. Johnson.

Executive Order 11406. *Assigning Authority with Respect to Ordering Units in the Ready Reserve to Active Duty.* Apr 10, 1968. Lyndon B. Johnson.

Executive Order 11519, *Calling into Service Members and Units of the National Guard,* Mar 23, 1970. Richard M. Nixon.

Executive Order 11527, *Amending the Selective Service Regulations.* Apr 24, 1970. Richard M. Nixon.

The Air Force Reserve

Presidential Proclamations

Presidential Proclamation 2914, *Proclaiming the Existence of a National Emergency.* Dec 19, 1950. Harry S. Truman.

Presidential Proclamation 3504, *Interdiction of the Delivery of Offensive Weapons to Cuba.* Oct 25, 1962. John F. Kennedy.

Presidential Proclamation 3972, *Declaring a National Emergency by the President of the United States.* Mar 23, 1970. Richard M. Nixon.

Congressional Hearings, Records, and Reports

House. Hearings before the Committee on Military Affairs. *Universal Military Training.* Hearings on H.R. 515, "An Act to Provide Military or Naval Training for All Male Citizens Who Attain the Age of 18 Years, and for Other Purposes." 69th Cong, 1st sess. Washington, D.C.: GPO, 1945.

House. Hearings before the Select Committee on Postwar Policy. *Universal Military Training.* 79th Cong, 1st sess. Washington, D.C.: GPO, Jun 16, 1945.

House. Hearings before the Committee on Armed Services. *Hearings on the Bill to Authorize the Compositions of the Army of the United States and for Other Reasons.* 81st Cong, 1st sess. Washington, D.C.: GPO, Jun 1950.

House. House Armed Services Committee. Sundry Legislation Affecting the Naval and Military Establishments, 1951. *Hearings on Universal Military Training.* 82d Cong, 1st sess. Washington, D.C.: GPO, 1951.

House. Committee on Armed Services. Statement of Maj. Gen. Charles E. McCarty. 87th Cong, 2d sess. Washington, D.C.: GPO, Apr 16, 1962.

House. Subcommittee No. 3 of the Committee on Armed Services. *Military Reserve Posture.* 87th Cong, 2d sess. Washington, D.C.: GPO, Apr 16, 1962.

House. Committee on Armed Services. News Release, "Army Reserve Merger." 89th Cong, 1st sess. Washington, D.C.: GPO, Aug 12, 1965.

House. Committee on Armed Services. Statement of Secretary of Defense Robert S. McNamara on FY 1966–1970 Defense Program and 1966 Defense Budget. 89th Cong, 1st sess. Washington, D.C.: GPO, Feb 18, 1965.

House. Hearings before the Committee on Armed Services. *Reserve Components.* Hearings on H.R. 4860, "A Bill Relating to the Reserve Components of the Armed Forces." 82d Cong, 1st sess. Washington, D.C.: GPO, Jan 8–Aug 22, 1951.

House. Eilene Galloway. *United States Defense Policies Since World War II, House.* 84th Cong, 1st sess., H. Doc. 100. Washington, D.C.: GPO, 1955.

House. Hearings before Subcommittee No. 1., Committee on Armed Services.

Bibliography

National Reserve Plan in Sundry Legislation Affecting the Naval and Military Establishments 1955. 84th Cong, 1st sess. Washington, D.C.: GPO, Feb 8–Mar 25, 1955.

House. Eilene Galloway for Subcommittee No. 1, Committee on Armed Services. *United States Military Policy on Reserve Forces, 1775–1957.* 85th Cong, 1st sess, H. Report 17. Washington D.C.: GPO, 1957.

House. Committee on Armed Services. *Hearings on Military Posture and HR 4016 to Authorize Appropriations During Fiscal Year 1966 for Procurement of Aircraft, Missiles, and Naval Vessels, and Research, Development, Test, and Evaluation, for the Armed Forces, and for Other Purposes.* 89th Cong, 1st sess. Washington, D.C.: GPO, Feb 2–Mar 22, 1965.

House. Subcommittee No. 2, Committee on Armed Services. *Hearings on HR 16435 and HR 17195 to Amend Titles 10, 14, 32, and 37, United States Code, to Strengthen the Reserve Components of the Armed Forces, and Clarify the Status of National Guard Technicians, and for Other Purposes.* 89th Cong, 2d sess. Washington, D.C.: GPO, Aug 4–29, 1966.

House. Hearings before Subcommittee No. 2, Committee on Armed Services. *Merger of the Army Reserve Components.* 89th Cong, 1st sess. Washington, D.C.: GPO, Mar 25–Sep 30, 1965.

House. Hearings before the House Armed Services Committee. *Hearings on Review of the Administration and Operation of the Selective Service System.* 89th Cong, 2d sess. Washington, D.C.: GPO, Jun 22–30, 1966.

House. *Reserve Bill of Rights.* 90th Cong, 1st sess, H. Report 13, Washington, D.C.: GPO, Feb 13, 1967.

House. *Selective Service.* "Message from the President of the United States Transmitting Recommendations for Extending the Draft Authority, Lowering Age for Drafting, Correcting the Deferment Inequities, Developing a Fair and Impartial System of Selection, and Establishing a Task Force to Review Recommendations for a Restructured Selective Service System." 90th Cong, 1st sess, H. Doc. 75, Washington, D.C.: GPO, Mar 6, 1967.

House. Report of the Committee on Appropriations. *Department of Defense Appropriations Bill, 1979.* 95th Cong, 2d sess. Washington, D.C.: GPO, Jul 27, 1978.

Senate. Hearings before the Committee on Military Affairs. *Preparedness for National Defense.* Hearings on Bills for the Reorganization of the Army and for Creation of a Reserve Army. 64th Cong, 1st sess. Washington, D.C.: GPO, 1916.

Senate. *Selective Service Act of 1948: Extension of Period of Effectiveness.* 80th Cong, 2d sess, S. J. Res 190. Washington, D.C.: GPO, 1948.

Senate. National Aviation Policy. *Report of the Congressional Aviation Policy Board.* 80th Cong, 2d sess. Washington, D.C.: GPO, Mar 1, 1948.

Senate. Hearings before the Committee on Armed Services. *Universal Military*

The Air Force Reserve

Training and Service Act of 1951. Hearings on "A Bill to Provide for the Common Defense and Security of the United States and to Permit the More Effective Utilization of Manpower Resources of the United States by Authorizing Universal Military Service and Training, and for Other Purposes. 82d Cong, 1st sess. Washington, D.C.: GPO, Jan 10, 1951.

Senate. Hearings before a Subcommittee of the Committee on Armed Services. *Armed Forces Reserve Act*. Hearings on H.R. 5426, "An Act Relating to the Reserve Components of the Armed Forces of the United States." 82d Cong, 2d sess. Washington, D.C.: GPO, 1952.

Senate. Hearings before the Committees on Armed Services and Appropriations. *Military Procurement Authorizations, Fiscal Year 1966*. 89th Cong, 1st sess. Washington, D.C.: GPO, Mar 15, 1965.

Senate. Hearings before the Preparedness Investigation Subcommittee, Committee on Armed Services. *U.S. Army Combat Readiness*. 89th Cong, 2d sess. Washington, D.C.: GPO, May 3–4, 1966.

Senate. Hearings before the Senate Armed Service Committee. *Amending and Extending the Draft Law and Related Authorities*. Hearings on S. 1432, "To Amend the Universal Military Training and Service Act." 90th Cong, 1st sess. Washington, D.C.: GPO, Apr 12–19, 1967.

Senate. *Reserve Components of the Armed Services*. 90th Cong, 1st sess, S. Report 732, Washington, D.C.: GPO, Nov 7, 1967.

Senate. Testimony of General John P. McConnell. Senate Armed Services Committee. 90th Cong, 2d sess. Washington, D.C.: GPO, Feb 21, 1968.

Senate. Senate Armed Services Committee. *Posture Statement of Maj. Gen. Tom E. Marbanks, Jr.* 90th Cong, 1st sess. Aug 4, 1969.

Senate. Statement of Roger T. Kelley, Asst Secretary of Defense (MRA). Special Subcommittee of the Senate Armed Services Committee on Volunteer Armed Forces and Selective Service. 91st Cong, 2d sess. Washington, D.C.: GPO, Mar 13, 1972.

Senate. Hearings before the Subcommittee on Manpower and Personnel of the Committee on Armed Services. *Reserve Call-up*. Hearings on S. 2115, "To Amend Chapter 39 of Title 10, United States Code, to Enable the President to Authorize the Involuntary Order to Active Duty of Selected Reservists, for a Limited Period, Whether or Not a Declaration of War or National Emergency Had Been Declared." 94th Cong, 1st sess. Washington, D.C.: GPO, Jul 30, 1975.

Congressional Record, vol 53. 64th Cong, 1st sess. Washington, D.C.: GPO, May 5, 1916.

Congressional Record, vols 97, 98. 82d Cong, 1st sess. Washington, D.C.: GPO, Feb 26, 1952.

Congressional Record, vol 101. 84th Cong, 1st sess. Washington, D.C.: GPO, 1955.

Bibliography

Acts

Air Corps Act of 1926. 44 Stat 780 (Jul 2, 1926).
Armed Forces—Reserve Components: Disability or Death Benefits Act. 63 Stat 201 (Jun 20, 1949).
Army and Air Force Authorization Act of 1949. Jul 10, 1950.
Army and Air Forces Vitalization and Retirement Equalization Act of 1948. 62 Stat 1087 (Jun 29, 1948).
The Army-Navy Nurses Act of 1947. 61 Stat 46 (Apr 16, 1947).
Army Reorganization Act of 1920. 41 Stat 759 (Jun 4, 1920).
Career Compensation Act of 1949. 23 Stat 802 (Oct 12, 1949).
The Dick Act of 1903. 32 Stat 755 (Jan 21, 1903).
The Militia Act of 1792. 1 Stat 271 (May 8, 1792).
National Defense Act of 1916. 39 Stat 166 (Jun 3, 1916).
Naval Reserve Act of 1938. 52 Stat 1184 (Jun 25, 1938).
Women Armed Services Integration Act of 1948. 62 Stat 371–5 (Jun 12, 1948).

Public Laws

Public Law 80–283, *The National Security Act of 1947.* 61 Stat 495 (Jul 26, 1947).
Public Law 80–460, *Organized Reserve Corps—Inactive Duty Training Pay.* 62 Stat 87 (Mar 25, 1948).
Public Law 759, *The Selective Service Act of 1948.* 62 Stat 606 (Jun 24, 1948).
Public Law 599, *Selective Service Extension Act of 1950.* 64 Stat 313 (Jun 30, 1950).
Public Law 150–82, *Air Force Organization Act of 1951.* 65 Stat 407 (Jan 19, 1951).
Public Law 51–82, *Universal Military Training and Service Act.* 65 Stat 144 (Jun 19, 1951).
Public Law 476, *Armed Forces Reserve Act of 1952.* 66 Stat 608 (Jul 9, 1952).
Public Law 773, *Reserve Officers Personnel Act of 1954.* 68 Stat 1257 (Sep 3, 1954).
Public Law 305–84, *Reserve Forces Act of 1955 . . ..* 69 Stat 598 (Aug 9, 1955).
Public Law 87–117, *Joint Resolution to Authorize the President to Order Units and Members in the Ready Reserve to Active Duty for Not More Than Twelve Months, and for Other Purposes.* 75 Stat 242 (Aug 1, 1961).
Public Law 87–736, *Joint Resolution to Authorize the President to Order Units and Members in the Ready Reserve to Active Duty for Not More Than Twelve Months, and for Other Purposes.* 76 Stat 710 (Oct 3, 1962).
Public Law 89–687, *Department of Defense Appropriations Act of 1967.* 80

The Air Force Reserve

Stat 980 (Oct 15, 1966).
Public Law 90–8, *Supplemental Defense Appropriation Act, 1967.* 87 Stat 8 (Apr 4, 1967).
Public Law 90–40, *Military Selective Service Act of 1967.* 81 Stat 100 (Jun 30, 1967).
Public Law 90–168, *Reserve Forces Bill of Rights and Vitalization Act.* 81 Stat 521 (Dec 1, 1967).
Public Law 90–500 *The Military Procurement Act.* 82 Stat 850 (Sep 20, 1968).
Public Law 91–124, *Selective Service Amendment Act of 1969.* 83 Stat 220 (Nov 26, 1969).
Public Law 92–129, *Military Selective Service—Military Pay—Military Active Duty Strengths.* 85 Stat 348 (Sep 28, 1971).
Public Law 93–155, *Department of Defense Appropriations Act, 1974.* 87 Stat 605 (Nov 16, 1973).
Public Law 93–365, *Department of Defense Appropriations Act, 1975.* 88 Stat 399 (Feb 9, 1976).
Public Law 96–584, *Armed Forces Reserve—Active Duty.* 94 Stat 3377 (Dec 23, 1980).
Public Law 94–286, *To Amend Chapter 39 of Title 10, USC, to Enable the President to Authorize the Involuntary Order to Active Duty of Selected Reservists for a Limited Period, Whether or Not a Declaration of War or National Emergency Has Been Declared.* 90 Stat 517 (May 14, 1986).

Legislative Histories

Legislative History. Public Law 80–460, *United States Code, Congressional and Adminisrative Service.* 80th Cong, 2d sess. Washington, D.C.: GPO, 1948.
Legislative History. *The Selective Service Act of 1948*, in *United States Code, Congressional and Administrative Service.* 80th Cong, 2d sess. Washington, D.C.: GPO, 1948.
Legislative History. *Selective Service Extension Act of 1950*, in *United States Code, Congressional and Administrative News.* 81st Cong, 2d sess. Washington, D.C.: GPO, 1950.
Legislative History. *Army and Air Force Authorization Act of 1949*, in *United States Code, Congressional and Administrative News.* 81st Cong, 2d sess. Washington, D.C.: GPO, 1950.
Legislative History. *Air Force Organization Act of 1951*, in *United States Code, Congressional and Administrative News.* 82d Cong, 1st sess. Washington, D.C.: GPO, 1951.
Legislative History. *Universal Military Training and Service Act*, in *United States Code, Congressional and Administrative News*, vol 1. 82d Cong, 1st

Bibliography

sess. Washington, D.C.: GPO, 1951.

Legislative History. *Armed Forces Reserve Act of 1952*, in *United States Code, Congressional and Administrative News*, vol 2. 82d Cong, 2d sess. Washington, D.C.: GPO, 1952.

Legislative History. *Reserve Officers Personnel Act of 1954*, in *United States Code, Congressional and Administrative News*, vol 3. 83d Cong, 2d sess. Washington, D.C.: GPO, 1954.

Legislative History. Public Law 87–117. *United States Code, Congressional and Administrative News*. 87th Cong, 1st sess. Washington, D.C.: GPO, 1961.

Legislative History. Public Law 87–736. *United States Code, Congressional and Administrative News*. 87th Cong, 2d sess. Washington, D.C.: GPO, 1962.

Legislative History. Public Law 90–40. *United States Code, Congressional and Administrative News*. 90th Cong, 1st sess. Washington, D.C.: GPO, 1967.

Legislative History. *Reserve Forces Bill of Rights and Vitalization Act*, in *United States Code, Congressional and Administrative News*. 90th Cong, 1st sess. Washington, D.C.: GPO, 1967.

Legislative History. *Selective Service Amendment Act of 1969*, in *United States Code, Congressional and Administrative News*. 90th Cong, 1st sess. Washington, D.C.: GPO, 1967.

Legislative History. Public Law 92–129. *United States Code, Congressional and Administrative News*, vol 2. 92d Cong, 1st sess. Washington, D.C.: GPO, 1971.

Legislative History. Public Law 94–286. *United States Code, Congressional and Administrative News*, vol 3. 94th Cong, 2d sess. Washington, D.C.: GPO, 1976.

Legislative History. *Armed Forces Reserve—Active Duty Act*, in *United States Code, Congressional and Administrative News*, vol 6. 96th Cong, 2d sess. Washington, D.C.: GPO, 1980.

Other

Constitution of the United States. Sep 17, 1787.
Congressional and Administrative News. 80th Cong, 2d sess. Washington, D.C.: GPO, 1948.

Air Force Histories and Chronologies

History. AFRES, Dec 1948–Dec 1949 through Jan 1968–Jul 1968.
History. AFRES, Fiscal Year 1990

The Air Force Reserve

History. Headquarters AFRES. Aug–Dec 1948 through Fiscal Year 1982.
History. Headquarters USAF. Jun 1949–Jun 1950.
History. Air Force Reserve Forces Special Assistant to the Chief of Staff. Jul–Dec 1950.
History. Air Force Reserve Forces Assistant Chief of Staff. 1954, Jul–Dec 1955, Jul–Dec 1961.
History. USAF Assistant for Programming. Jul–Dec 1950.
History. Air Training Command. Jan–Jun 1952.
History. Crew Training Air Force. Apr–Jun 1952.
History. Far East Air Forces. Jan–Jun 1951; Jul–Dec 1951.
History. Fifth Air Force. Jan–Jun 1951.
History. Tenth Air Force. Jan–Jun 1951, Jan–Jun 1956 through Jul–Dec 1959.
History. Military Airlift Command. Fiscal Year 1968.
History. Air Force Reserve Recovery Groups. Jan–Mar 65.
History. Aeronautical Systems Division. Fiscal Years 1973, 1979, 1985, 1987.
History. Air Reserve Personnel Center. 1980, 1981.
History. Office of Air Force Reserve. Jan–Jun 68 through Jan–Jun 82.
Chronology. The Continental Air Command and the Korean Contingency, Jan 1968–Mar 1968 (CAC, Apr 1968).
Chronology. Chronology of the Korean Crisis, 1968 (Office of Air Force History, 1968).

Monographs and Special Papers

Cantwell, Gerald T. *The Air Force Reserve in the Vietnam Decade: 1965–1975.* Robins AFB, Georgia: Headquarters Air Force Reserve, 1979.
———. *The Evolution and Employment of the Air Force Reserve as a Mobilization Force, 1946–1980.* Robins AFB, Georgia: Headquarters Air Force Reserve, 1981.
———. *Operation REDOUBT: The Evolution of an Idea and Its Implementation.* Robins AFB, Georgia: Headquarters Air Force Reserve, 1982.
Cantwell, Gerald T., and Victor B. Summers. *The Air Reserve Technician Program: Its Antecedents and Evolution, 1948–1978.* Robins AFB, Georgia: Headquarters Air Force Reserve, 1979.
Futrell, Robert Frank. *United States Air Force Operations in the Korean Conflict, 25 Jun–1 Nov 1950.* USAF Historical Study No. 71. Maxwell AFB, Alabama: USAF History Division, 1952.
———. *United States Air Force Operations the Korean Conflict, 1 Nov 1950–30 Jun 1952.* USAF Historical Study No. 72. Maxwell AFB, Alabama: USAF History Division, 1953.
Greer, Thomas H. *The Development of Air Doctrine in the Army, Air Arm, 1917–1941.* USAF Historical Study No. 89. Maxwell AFB, Alabama:

Bibliography

USAF History Division, 1955.

Hennessey, Juliette A. *The United States Army Air Arm, Apr 1861 to Apr 1917.* USAF Historical Study No. 98. Maxwell AFB, Alabama: USAF History Division, 1958.

Layman, Martha E. *Legislation Relating to the Air Corps Personnel and Training Programs, 1907–1939.* AAF Historical Study No. 39. Washington D.C.: AAF History Division, 1945.

Longanecker, Maj. Gen. Walter R. *The Air Force Intelligence Reserve Program: A Brief History, 1974–1984.* Fort Belvoir, Virginia: Headquarters Air Force Intelligence Agency, 1985.

Mooney, Chase C., and Martha E. Layman. *Organization of Military Aeronautics, 1907–1935.* AAF Historical Study No. 25. Washington, D.C.: AAF History Division, 1944.

Saunders, Chauncey E. *Demobilization Planning for the United States Air Force.* Maxwell AFB, Alabama: USAF History Division, 1954.

Williams, Edwin L., Jr. *Legislative History of the AAF and USAF, 1949–1951.* USAF Historical Study No. 84. Maxwell AFB, Alabama: USAF History Division Maxwell AFB, 1955.

Studies and Reports

AFRES By-Product Accomplishment of Air Force Reserve Units. Robins AFB, Georgia: Headquarters Air Force Reserve, Fiscal Years 1970 and 1971.

AFRES Mission Accomplishment of Air Force Reserve Units. Robins AFB, Georgia: Headquarters Air Force Reserve, Fiscal Years 1968 and 1969.

AFRES Unit FORSTAT Report, as of Dec 1976. Robins AFB, Georgia: Headquarters Air Force Reserve, Jan 1977.

After Action Report: CONDOR REDOUBT 81. Robins AFB, Georgia: Headquarters Air Force Reserve, Sep 1981.

After Action Report for Operation REDOUBT, Phase II. Robins AFB, Georgia: Headquarters Air Force Reserve, Jun 30, 1978.

After Action Report for Operation REDOUBT, Phase III. Robins AFB, Georgia: Headquarters Air Force Reserve, Aug 15, 1979.

After Action Report for PAID REDOUBT 80. Robins AFB, Georgia: Headquarters Air Force Reserve, Aug 1, 1980.

Air Force Management Assistance Group. Final Report. Headquarters United States Air Force, Apr 1982.

Air Force Reserve Air Staff. Draft Management Structure Study. Headquarters United States Air Force: Washington, D.C.: Sep 13, 1972.

Air Force Reserve Annual Reports. Washington, D.C.: Office of Air Force Reserve, Headquarters United States Air Force, Fiscal Years 1969 through 1975.

The Air Force Reserve

Air Force Reserve Management Study. Washington, D.C.: Headquarters United States Air Force, Feb 15, 1972.
Air Force Reserve, Office of. *Air Force Reserve Organization Study.* Washington, D.C.: Headquarters United States Air Force, Oct 1969.
Air Reserve Forces Plan and Programs, 1 Jul–31 Dec 1955. Washington, D.C.: Headquarters United States Air Force, 1956.
Air Staff. *Management of the Air Reserve Forces.* Washington, D.C.: Headquarters United States Air Force, Nov 14, 1964.
———. *Management of the Air Reserve Forces.* Washington, D.C.: Headquarters United States Air Force, Jan 6, 1965.
Assistant Chief of Staff, Reserve Forces. *Air Reserve Forces: Air Force Requirements for Individuals, Present Resources and Training Programs.* Washington, D.C.: Headquarters United States Air Force, May 19, 1965.
Bruhn, Lt. Col. L. W. *Critique on Call to EAD [extended active duty] and Subsequent Move to Shaw AFB, S.C.* Shaw AFB, South Carolina: 437th Troop Carrier Wing, Aug 25, 1950.
CAC Airlift Accomplishment of Air Force Reserve Units. Robins AFB, Georgia: Headquarters Continental Air Command, 1966.
CAC Mission Accomplishment of Air Force Reserve Units. Robins AFB, Georgia: Headquarters Continental Air Command, 1967.
Chief of the Air Corps Annual Reports. Washington, D.C.: Fiscal Years, 1927, 1931–1933, 1937, 1939.
Chief of the Air Service Annual Reports. Washington, D.C.: Fiscal Years 1919; 1921–1925.
Clements, Col. Evan E. "915th Airborne Early Warning & Control Group After Action Report." Sep 30, 1978.
Committee on Civilian Components. *Reserve Forces for National Security.* Report to the Secretary of Defense. Washington, D.C.: 1948.
The Committee on Manpower Resources for National Security. *Manpower Resources for National Security.* A Report to the Director of the Office of Defense Mobilization. Washington, D.C.: GPO, 1953.
Comptroller General. *Ineffective Program Planning and Uneconomical Utilization of Personnel Assigned to the Air Force Reserve Recovery Program.* Report B–146831. Washington, D.C.: Jan 1964.
Coronet Poker/Oksboel Final Report, 12–27 Aug 77: Deployment Report of 301st Tactical Fighter Wing. Carswell AFB, Texas: Sep 1972.
Coronet Roundup Mission Report: Detachment A, 94th Tactical Airlift Wing. Dobbins AFB, Georgia: Jun 1975.
Defense Manpower Commission. *Defense Manpower: The Keystone of National Security.* Report to the President and Congress. Washington, D.C.: GPO, 1976.
Department of Defense Annual Reports. Washington, D.C.: Fiscal Years 1961–1965.

Bibliography

FEAF Report on the Korean War. Tokyo: Headquarters Far East Air Forces, 1954.

Guam Aerial Spray Mission Report. Rickenbacker ANGB, Ohio: 302d Tactical Airlift Wing, Aug 11, 1975.

Guard and the Reserve in the Total Force. Washington D.C.: Office of the Secretary of Defense, Sep 1975.

The Inspector General. *Functional Management Inspection of the Air Force Mobilization Augmentees (MA) Program, PN 78–643, 5 Sep 78–13 Aug 79.* Washington, D.C.: Headquarters United States Air Force, Aug 1979.

Laird, Melvin R., Secretary of Defense. *Report to the President and the Chairman of the Armed Services Committees of the Senate and the House of Representatives (PL 92–129): Progress in Ending the Draft and Achieving the All-Volunteer Force.* Washington, D.C.: Aug 1972.

Lee, Lt. Col. Roger E. *Report of Deferment Board Activity, 2471 AFRTC.* O'Hare International Airport, Chicago, Illinois: Tenth Air Force Deferment Board, Aug 16, 1950.

Monthly Report of Personnel Statistics in United States Air Force Reserve Units of the Continental Air Command, as of Jul 25, 1950. Mitchel AFB, New York: Headquarters Continental Air Command, 1950.

Personnel Activities in Support of Operations in Southeast Asia, 1 Jan 1965–31 Mar 1968. Project CORONA HARVEST Final Report. Maxwell AFB, Alabama, 1973.

Report of Management Inspection of the Air Force Reserve, PN 71–94. Washington, D.C.: Headquarters United States Air Force, Jun 1971.

Report of Proceedings of a Committee Appointed to Investigate the Recall Program. Mitchel AFB, New York: Headquarters Continental Air Command, Dec 14, 1950.

Report of Senator [John F.] *Kennedy's National Security Policy Committee.* Hyannisport, Mass.: [Nov 1960].

Report of the Advisory Committee on Universal Training. Washington, D.C.: 1947.

Report of the Air Force Individual Reserve Training Board. Washington, D.C.: Headquarters United States Air Force, Aug 1956.

Report of the Air Staff Committee on National Guard and Reserve Policy. Washington, D.C.: Headquarters United States Air Force, Aug 4, 1950.

Report of the Reserve Program Review Board. Washington, D.C.: Headquarters United States Air Force, Aug 24, 1953.

Report of the Second Meeting of the Air Staff Committee on National Guard and Reserve Policy. Washington D.C.: Headquarters United States Air Force, Nov 10, 1950.

Report of the Smith Committee (Appointed to develop the Long Range Plan for the Reserve Forces of the United States Air Force). Washington, D.C.: Headquarters United States Air Force, Jul 27, 1951.

The Air Force Reserve

Report on Full-Time Training and Administration of the Selected Reserve. Washington, D.C.: Office of the Secretary of Defense, 1978.
Reserve Forces Review Group. *Air Reserve Forces . . . New Roles in a New Era.* Washington, D.C.: Headquarters United States Air Force, Nov 1959.
Secretary of the Air Force Annual Report, Fiscal Year 1972.
Studies Prepared for the President's Commission on an All-Volunteer Armed Force. 2 vols. Washington, D.C.: GPO, 1970.
Twentieth Century Minutemen: A Report to the President on a Reserve Forces Training Program. Washington, D.C.: National Security Training Commission, 1953.
The United States Army in the World War, 1917–1919: Reports of the Commander-in-Chief, A.E.F.: Staff Sections and Services, part 1. Washington, D.C.: 1948.
War Department Annual Reports. Washington, D.C.: Fiscal Years 1912, 1915–1916, 1918–1919, GPO, 1921–1929, 1930–1934.

Plans and Programs

ADC Plan to Activate the Air Reserve Program. Mitchel Field, New York: Headquarters Air Defense Command, May 15, 1946.
AFIS AFIR Plan. Air Force Reserve Intelligence Forces. Fort Belvoir, Virginia: Headquarters Air Force Intelligence Service, May 1973.
AFRES Exercise Plan 003, PAID REDOUBT 80. Robins AFB, Georgia: May 1, 1980.
AFRES Exercise Plan 004, CONDOR REDOUBT 81. Robins AFB, Georgia: Headquarters Air Force Reserve, Mar 20, 1981.
AFRES Plan 28, *Demobilization Plan.* Robins AFB, Georgia: Headquarters Air Force Reserve, Nov 15, 1968.
AFRES Programming Plan 72–8, *Tinker/Carswell.* Robins AFB, Georgia: Headquarters Air Force Reserve, Mar 3, 1972.
AFRES Programming Plan 72–12, *Hill/945th.* Robins AFB, Georgia: Headquarters Air Force Reserve, Jul 17, 1972.
AFRES Programming Plan 74–5, *919th TAGp, Eglin AF Aux Fld 3.* Robins AFB, Georgia: Headquarters Air Force Reserve, Sep 6, 1974.
Air Defense Command Mobilization Plan (ADC MP–47). Mitchel AFB, New York: Headquarters Air Defense Command, Jan 30, 1947.
Air Force Reserve Specialist Training Center Plan. Mitchel AFB, New York: Headquarters Continental Air Command, Mar 13, 1953.
Air Force Specialty Training Squadron Test Implementation Plan. Robins AFB, Georgia: Headquarters Continental Air Command, Sep 30, 1965.
Army Air Forces Plan for the Air Reserve. Assistant Chief of the Air Staff–3. Washington, D.C.: Headquarters Army Air Forces, Jul 12, 1946.

Bibliography

CAC Operations Plan 151–57, *Operation SWIFT LIFT*. Mitchel AFB, New York: Headquarters Continental Air Command, Feb 21, 1957.

CAC Programming Plan 67–67 (directing the test of the Associate Air Force Reserve unit concept). Robins AFB, Georgia: Headquarters Continental Air Command, Nov 30, 1967.

CAC Programming Plan 68–1. Robins AFB, Georgia: Headquarters Continental Air Command, Mar 1, 1968.

CAC Reorganization Plan 3–60, *Plan for Air Force Reserve Base Support Groups*. Mitchel AFB, New York: Headquarters Continental Air Command, Sep 1, 1960.

MAC Programming Plan 75–28, *Transfer of 7 WC–130H Aircraft from MAC to AFRES*. Scott AFB, Illinois: Headquarters Military Airlift Command, Aug 1, 1975.

Plan for Revised Management of the Air Reserve Forces. Washington, D.C.: Headquarters United States Air Force, May 20, 1960.

Plan for the Air Reserve. 2d rev. Washington, D.C.: Headquarters Army Air Forces, Jun 3, 1946.

The United States Air Force Reserve Program for Fiscal Year 1950. Washington, D.C.: Headquarters United States Air Force, Jun 1949.

U.S. Air Force Reserve Program for Fiscal Year 1949. Washington, D. C.: Headquarters United States Air Force, Oct 6, 1948.

War Department Affiliation Program. War Department. Washington, D.C.: Headquarters Air Defense Command, May 26, 1947.

War Department Basic Plan for the Post-War Military Establishment. Washington, D.C.: War Department, Mar 13, 1945.

Books

Berger, Carl, ed. *The United States Air Force in Southeast Asia, 1961–1973*. Washington, D.C.: Office of Air Force History, 1977.

Crossland, Richard B., and James T. Currie. *Twice the Citizen: A History of the United States Army Reserve, 1908–1983*. Washington, D.C.: Office of the Chief, Army Reserve, 1984.

Department of Defense. *United States–Vietnam Relations, 1945–1967*. 12 vols. Washington, D.C.: GPO, 1971.

Futrell, Robert Frank. *The Advisory Years to 1965* [The United States Air Force in Southeast Asia]. Washington, D.C.: Office of Air Force History, 1981.

———. *Ideas, Concepts, Doctrine: A History of Basic Thinking in the United States Air Force*. 2d Printing. Maxwell AFB, Alabama: Air University, 1974.

Gropman, Alan L. *The Air Force Integrates, 1945–1964*. Washington, D.C.: Office of Air Force History, 1978.

The Air Force Reserve

Gross, Charles Joseph. *Prelude to the Total Force: The Air National Guard, 1943–1969*. Washington, D.C.: Office of Air Force History, 1985.

Hermes, Walter G. *Truce Tent and Fighting Front*. Washington, D.C.: Office of Chief of Military History, 1966.

Hewes, James E., Jr. *From Root to McNamara: Army Reorganization and Administration, 1900–1963*. Washington, D.C.: Center of Military History, 1975.

Kreidberg, Marvin A., and Merton G. Henry. *History of Military Mobilization in the United States Army, 1775–1945*. Washington, D.C.: GPO, 1955.

Matloff, Maurice, ed. *American Military History*. Washington, D.C.: GPO, 1969.

Maurer, Maurer. *Aviation in the U.S. Army, 1919–1939*. Washington, D.C.: Office of Air Force History, 1987.

Maurer, Maurer, ed. *Combat Squadrons of the Air Force: World War II*. Maxwell AFB: USAF Historical Division, 1969.

Rearden, Steven L. *The Formative Years, 1947–1950* [History of the Office of the Secretary of Defense, Office of the Secretary of Defense]. Washington. D.C.: Office of the Secretary of Defense, 1984.

Watson, Mark Skinner. *The War Department, Chief of Staff: Prewar Plans & Preparedness* [United States Army in World War II, Office of the Chief of Military History]. Washington: GPO, 1950.

Wilson, Bernie J., ed. *The Guard and the Reserve in the Total Force*. Washington, D.C.: National Defense University, 1985.

Wolk, Herman S. *Planning and Organizing the Postwar Air Force, 1943–1947*. Washington, D.C.: Office of Air Force History, 1984.

Periodical Articles

"Annual Defense Report: National Security Strategy of Realistic Deterrence." *Commanders Digest*, May 4, 1972.

Closner, Maj. Gen. John J. "Air Power in DESERT SHIELD/DESERT STORM: Part III. The Air Force Reserve and the Persian Gulf War." *Air Power History*, summer 1992.

Coyne, James P. "TOTAL STORM: The Air Guard and Reserve Were Involved from the First Hour on the First Day." *Air Force Magazine*, Jun 1992.

Hall, Lt. Gen. William E. "The Air Force Reserve Mission." *The Air Reservist*, Jun–Jul 1960.

"Outlook: The Air Force Team." *The Air Reservist*, Oct–Nov 1959.

"Retention: The Military Selective Service Act." *Commanders Digest*, Nov 18, 1971.

Bibliography

Newsletters

Air Corps Newsletter. Jan 15, 1931; Jul 19, 1932; Dec 30, 1932; May 1, 1938; Oct 15, 1938; Feb 15, 1939; May 1, 1939; Nov 1, 1939; Jun 1, 1941.

Weekly Newsletter [Air Service, Director of Military Aeronautics]. Dec 14, 1918.

Interviews

By the Author:

Anderson, Maj. Gen. Earl O., USAFR. Robins AFB, Georgia: May 1976. AFRES 26.

Bodycombe, Maj. Gen. Richard, USAFR. Ann Arbor, Michigan: May 1985. AFRES 26.

Brown, Harold. Telephone, Jul 1988.

Bundy, McGeorge. Telephone, Oct 1988.

Knowles, Brig. Gen. Billy M., USAFR. Robins AFB, Georgia: Aug 1986, Dec 1988. AFRES 26.

Leaf, Lt. Gen. Howard W., USAF. Washington, D.C.: Dec 7, 1988. AFRES 2B.1.

Lewis, Maj. Gen. Homer I., USAFR. Washington, D.C.: Nov 1986, Mar 1975. AFRES 26.

Lyon, Maj. Gen. William., USAFR. Washington, D.C.: Nov 1976, Feb 1979, Apr 1979. AFRES. 26.

Mathis, General Robert C., USAF. Telephone, Dec 1988. AFRES 21B.1.

Moore, Maj. Gen. Rollin B. Jr., USAFR. Robins AFB, Georgia: Jan 1982. AFRES 26.

Norvaresi, Maj. Gen. Sydney S., USAFR. Robins AFB, Georgia: Aug 1982. AFRES 26.

Sutton, Maj. Richard D., USAFR. Robins AFB, Georgia: Feb 1973. AFRES, 14 A1.

Timberlake, Lt. Gen. Edward J., USAF. Hilton Head, South Carolina: Sep 1983. AFRES 26.

Usher, Maj. Gen. William R., USAF. Telephone. Jan 1989. AFRES 2B.

Wilson, Lt. Gen. Winston P., ANGUS. Telephone. Jan 1984. AFRES 26.

By Others:

Ball, George W. 1971. Lyndon B. Johnson Library.

Brown, Harold, by Thomas Belden, Jacob Van Staaveren, and Hugh Ahmann, Office of Air Force History. Pasadena, California: Aug 29–30, 1972. AFHRC K239.0512–619.

Burgess, Carter. 1967. Columbia Oral History Project.
Clifford, Clark M. 1979. Lyndon B. Johnson Library.
Cooper, Chester L. 1969. Lyndon B. Johnson Library.
Eaton, Maj. Gen. Robert E. L. October 17, 1961. AFHRC K239.0512–765.
Eisenhower, Dwight D. 1967. Herbert Hoover Presidential Library Project.
Fitt, Alfred B., by Dorothy Pierce. 1968. Lyndon B. Johnson Library.
Gates, Thomas S., Jr. 1967. Columbia Oral History Project.
Gilpatric, Roswell L., by Dennis J. O'Brien. 1970. John F. Kennedy Library.
Gray, Gordon. 1973, 1975. Harry S. Truman Library.
Hall, Lt. Gen. William E., by Joseph Angell, Jr., and George Lemmer, Office of Air Force History. Sep 8, 1961. AFHRC K239.0512–614.
McFarland, Richard P., by Daniel J. Hughes. Headquarters Air Force Reserve: May 27, 1983.
Lawton, Frederick J. Jun 17 and Jul 9, 1963. Harry S. Truman Library.
McConnell, General John P. 1963. Lyndon B. Johnson Library.
McNamara, Robert S., by Roger Trask and Maurice Matloff, Office of the Secretary of Defense History Office. 1986.
Pace, Frank, Jr. 1963. Harry S. Truman Library.
Quesada, Lt. Gen. Elwood R., by Steve Long and Ralph Stephenson. May 1975. AFHRC K239.0512–838.
Rusk, Dean. 1969. Lyndon B. Johnson Library.
Sharp, Dudley C., by Arthur K. Marmor, Office of Air Force History. May 29, 1961. AFHRC K239.0512–790.
Wheeler, General Earle E. 1964. John F. Kennedy Library.
Wheeler, General Earle E., by Dorothy Pierce McSweeny. 1970. Lyndon B. Johnson Library.

Non-Governmental Sources

Books

Allison, Graham T. *Essence of Decision: Explaining the Cuban Missile Crisis*. Boston: Little Brown & Co., 1961.
Ambrose, Stephen E. *Eisenhower*. Vol 2, *The President*. New York: Simon & Schuster, 1984.
———. *Nixon: The Education of a Politician, 1913–1962*. New York: Simon & Schuster, 1987.
Baker, Ray Standard. *Woodrow Wilson Life and Letters: Facing the War 1915–1917*. New York: Doubleday Doran & Co., Inc., 1937.
Baker, Ray Stannard, and William E. Dodd, eds. *The Public Papers of Woodrow Wilson*. Authorized ed. Vol. 1, *The New Democracy: Presiden-*

tial Messages, Addresses, and Other Papers (1913–1917). New York: Harper & Bros., 1926.

Berman, Larry. *Planning a Tragedy: The Americanization of the War in Vietnam*. New York: W. W. Norton & Co., 1982.

Carlton, John T., and John F. Slinkman. *The ROA Story Chronicle of the First 60 Years of the Reserve Officers Association of the United States*. Washington: Reserve Officers Association, 1982.

Chomsky, Noam. *American Power and the New Mandarins*. New York: Pantheon Books, 1969.

Cole, Wayne S. *Roosevelt and the Isolationists, 1932–45*. Lincoln: University of Nebraska Press, 1983.

Cooper, Chester. *The Lost Crusade: America in Vietnam*. New York: Dodd, Mead, 1970.

Craven, Wesley Frank, and James L. Cate. eds. *The Army Air Forces in World War II*. 7 vols. Chicago: University of Chicago Press, 1948–1958.

De Weerd, Harvey A. *President Wilson Fights His War*. New York: Macmillan, 1968.

——, ed. *Selected Speeches & Statements of General of the Army George C. Marshall, Chief of Staff United States Army*. Washington: The Infantry Journal Inc., 1945.

Divine, Robert A. *Roosevelt and World War II*. Baltimore: The Johns Hopkins Press, 1969.

——, ed. *The Johnson Years*. Vol 2, *Vietnam, the Environment, and Science*. Lawrence: University Press of Kansas, 1987.

Donovan, Robert J. *Conflict and Crisis: The Presidency of Harry S. Truman, 1945–1948*. New York: W. W. Norton, Inc., 1977.

——. *Tumultuous Years: The Presidency of Harry S. Truman, 1949–1953*. New York: W. W. Norton, Inc., 1982.

Eisenhower, Dwight David. *The White House Years: Mandate for Change, 1953–1956*. Garden City: Doubleday & Co., 1963.

Evans, Rowland, and Robert Novak. *Lyndon B. Johnson: The Exercise of Power*. New York: The New American Library, Inc., 1966.

Futrell, Robert Frank. *The United States Air Force in Korea, 1950–1953*. New York: Duell, Sloan & Pearce, 1961

Galambos, Louis. *The Papers of Dwight David Eisenhower*. 9 vols. Baltimore: John Hopkins University Press, 1970–1978.

Gallup, George H. *The Gallup Poll: Public Opinion, 1935–1971*, Vol 1. New York: Random House, 1972.

Goldberg, Alfred, ed. *A History of the United States Air Force, 1907–1957*. Princeton: Nostrand Co., 1957.

Goldman, Eric F. *The Tragedy of Lyndon Johnson*. Paperback ed. New York: Dell Publishing Co., 1974.

Goulding, Phil G. *Confirm or Deny: Informing the People on National*

Security. New York: Harper and Row, 1970.
Gravel, Mike, ed. *The Senator Gravel Edition: The Pentagon Papers: The Defense Department History of United States Decisionmaking on Vietnam.* 5 vols. Boston: Beacon Press, 1971.
Halberstam, David. *The Best and the Brightest.* Paperback ed. Greenwich: Fawcett Crest, 1968.
Hayes, Richard F. *The Awesome Power: Harry S. Truman as Commander-in-Chief.* Baton Rouge: Louisiana State University, 1973.
Hill, Jim Dan. *The Minute Man in Peace and War: A History of the National Guard.* Harrisburg: The Stackpole Company, 1964.
Holley, I. B., Jr. *General John M. Palmer, Citizen Soldiers, and the Army of a Democracy.* Westport: Greenwood Press, 1982.
Hoopes, Townsend. *The Limits of Intervention.* New York: David McKay Co., Inc., 1971.
Hoxie, Gordon. *Command Decision and the Presidency: A Study in National Security Policy and Organizations.* New York: Thomas Y., Crowell Co., 1977.
Huntington, Samuel P. *The Common Defense: Strategic Programs in National Politics.* New York: Columbia University Press, 1961.
———. *The Soldier and the State: The Theory and Practice of Civil-Military Relations.* Cambridge: Harvard University Press, 1959.
Isaacson, Walter, and Evan Thomas. *The Wise Men: Six Friends and the World They Made.* New York: Simon and Schuster, 1986.
Johnson, Lyndon Baines. *The Vantage Point: Perceptions of the Presidency.* Paperback ed. New York: Popular Library, 1971.
Kalb, Marvin, and Ellie Abel. *Roots of Involvement: The U.S. in Asia, 1784–1971.* New York: W. W. Norton Co., 1971.
Kearns, Doris. *Lyndon Johnson and the American Dream.* New York: Harper & Row, 1976.
Kennedy, Robert F. *Thirteen Days.* New York: Signet Books, 1969.
Lewy, Guenther. *America in Vietnam.* New York: Oxford Press, 1978.
Link, Arthur S. *Wilson: The Struggle for Neutrality 1914–1915.* Princeton: Princeton University Press, 1960.
———. *Wilson: Confusion and Crisis 1915–1916.* Princeton: Princeton University Press, 1964.
Mahon, John K. *History of the Militia and the National Guard.* New York: Macmillan Publishing Co., 1983.
Marshall, George C. *Biennial Report of the Chief of Staff of the United States Army, Jul 1, 1943 to Jun 30, 1945 to the Secretary of War.* Philadelphia: J. B. Lippincott Company, 1947.
McNamara, Robert S. *The Essence of Security: Reflections in Office.* New York: Harper and Row, 1968.
Miller, John C. *Origins of the American Revolution.* Boston: Atlantic Monthly

Bibliography

Press. Little, Brown and Co., 1943.

Millett, Allan R., and Peter Maslowski. *For the Common Defense: A Military History of the United States of America.* New York: The Free Press, 1984.

Millis, Walter, ed. *The Forrestal Diaries.* New York: Viking Press, 1951.

———. *Arms and Men: A Study of American Military.* Paperback ed. New York: The New American Library, 1963.

———, ed. *American Military Thought.* Indianapolis: Bobbs-Merrill Co, Inc., 1966.

Nixon, Richard M. *RN: The Memoirs of Richard Nixon.* New York: Grosset and Dunlap, 1978.

———. *The Real War.* New York: Warner Books, 1980.

Palmer, David Richard. *Summons of the Trumpet: U. S.—Vietnam in Perspective.* San Rafael: Presidio Press, 1978.

Palmer, Frederick. *Newton D. Baker: America at War.* New York: Dodd, Mead and Co., 1931.

Palmer, John McAuley. *America in Arms: The Experience of the United States with Military Organization.* New Haven: Yale University Press, 1941.

Podhoretz, Norman. *Why We Were in Vietnam.* New York: Simon and Schuster, 1982.

Pogue, Forrest C. *George C. Marshall: Education of a General, 1880–1939.* New York: The Viking Press, Inc., 1963.

———. *George C. Marshall: Ordeal and Hope.* New York: The Viking Press, 1966.

———. *George C. Marshall: Organizer of Victory, 1943–1945.* New York: The Viking Press, Inc., 1973.

Rauch, Basil, ed. *The Roosevelt Reader: Selected Speeches, Messages, Press Conferences, and Letters of Franklin D. Roosevelt.* New York: Rinehart & Co., Inc., 1957.

Rees, David. *Korea: The Limited War.* New York: St. Martin's Press, 1964.

Rostow, Walt W. *The Diffusion of Power: An Essay in Recent History.* New York: The Macmillan Co., 1972.

Schandler, Herbert Y. *The Unmaking of a President: Lyndon Johnson and Vietnam.* Princeton: Princeton University Press, 1977.

Schlesinger, Arthur C. *A Thousand Days.* Boston: Houghton Mifflin Co., 1965.

Shaw, Albert, ed. *The Messages & Papers of Woodrow Wilson.* 3d ed. New York: The Review of Reviews Corp., 1924.

Sidey, Hugh. *A Very Personal Presidency: Lyndon Johnson in the White House.* New York: Atheneum, 1968.

Small, Melvin. *Johnson, Nixon, and the Doves.* New Brunswick: Rutgers University Press, 1988.

Sorensen, Theodore. *Kennedy.* Paperback ed. New York: Bantam Books, 1966.

Stimson, Henry L., and McGeorge Bundy. *On Active Duty in Peace and War.* New York: Harper and Brothers, 1947.

Straubel, James H. *Crusade for Airpower: The Story of the Air Force Association*. Washington: Aerospace Education Foundation, 1982.
Taylor, Maxwell D. *Swords and Plowshares*. New York: W. W. Norton and Company, 1972.
Thompson, Annis G. *The Greatest Airlift: the Story of Combat Cargo*. Tokyo: Dai-Nippon Printing Co., 1954.
Truman, Harry S. *Memoirs by Harry S. Truman*. 2 vols., Vol. 2. *Years of Trial and Hope*. Garden City: Doubleday and Company, 1956.
Washington, H. A., ed. *The Writings of Thomas Jefferson*. 9 vols. Washington: Taylor and Maury, 1853–54.
Weigley, Russell F. *Towards An American Army: Military Thought from Washington to Marshall*. 2d ed. Westport: Greenwood Press, 1974.
———. *History of the United States Army*. 2d ed. New York: Macmillan Publishing Co., 1977.
White, Theodore, H. *The Making of the President, 1968*. Pocketbook ed. New York: Atheneum Pocket Books, 1969.
Williams, T. Harry. *Americans At War: The Development of the American Military System*. Baton Rouge: Louisiana State University Press, 1960.
Yergin, Daniel. *Shattered Peace: Origins of the Cold War and the National Security State*. Boston: Houghton Mifflin Co., 1977.

Studies and Reports

RAND Study RM–5326–PR, The Air Reserve Forces Study, The RAND Corporation: Santa Monica, California, Jul 1967.
The Report of the President's Commission on an All-Volunteer Armed Force, The Macmillan Company: New York, 1970.

Encyclopedias

Encyclopedia of American History. Bicentennial ed. Richard B. Morris, ed. New York: Harper & Row, 1976.
The Encylopedia of Military History: from 3500 BC. to the Present. Dupuy, R. Ernest, and N. Trevor, ed., 2d rev. ed. New York: Harper and Row, 1986.

Periodical Articles

"7 Sue to Stay in Units." *Air Force Times*, Aug 21, 1968.
"Air Force Reservists Appeal for Release." *Macon News*, [Georgia] Jul 25, 1968.

Bibliography

"Air Reservists Sue to Prevent Call-up of Men Individually." *New York Times*, Aug 14, 1968.

"American Determination Key to Success." *London Times*, Dec 23, 1962.

"American Legion Post 2 Opposes Viet Protests." *Macon Telegraph*, Oct 28, 1965.

"Anti-Viet Rally Staged by 10,000." *Macon Telegraph and News*, Nov 21, 1965.

Ayres, Drummond B. Jr. "Reserve Told to Enlist Men as Names Come Up. Pentagon Orders Revision—Charge of Favoritism to Athletes Being Studied." *New York Times, Dec* 23, 1966.

Baldwin, Hanson W. "To Strengthen the Reserves." *New York Times, Oct* 18, 1948.

———. "Gesture of Reserves." *New York Times, Oct* 18, 1948.

Barry, Frank W., Jr. and Hugh R. Farrell. "POW/MIA Family Counseling Program." *Medical Setrvice Digest*, Nov 1973.

Bigart, Homer. "Week of Protest Against the Draft Started by Antiwar Groups." *New York Times,* Dec 5, 1967.

Brown, Harold. "Planning Our Military Forces." *Foreign Affairs*, Jan 1967.

Cantwell, Gerald T. "The Total Force: From Marbanks to Bodycombe." *Air Force Magazine,* Oct 4, 1981.

Clifford, Clark M. "A Vietnam Appraisal—The Personal History of One Man's View and How it Evolved." *Foreign Affairs*, Oct 1970.

"Draft Panel Calls For A Crackdown: Advisers to Congress Score 6-Month Draft Plan." *New York Times*, Mar 4, 1967.

"EM Loses 'Illegal' Recall Plea." *Air Force Times*, Apr 28, 1962.

"Fliers Charge Unit's Breakup." *Sunday News*, Jul 7, 1968.

Fox, Sylvan. "Brooklyn Students Battle Police in Peace Protest: 40 Arrested on Campus." *New York Times,* Oct 20, 1967.

Franklin, Ben A. "War Protesters Defying Deadline Seized in Capital: 208 Refuse to Disperse at Pentagon as Permit for Demonstration Expires." *New York Times,* Oct 4, 23, 1967.

Fraser, C. Gerald. "Boycott at Madison." *New York Times,* Oct 20, 1967.

Gal, Harold. "Air Force Defends Shifting Individual Reservists." *New York Times,* Jul 18, 1968.

Hoffman, Paul. "Thousands Mar Here to Back G.I.'s; Lindsay at Vigil, Qualifies His Support of its Aims—Gets Mixed Reception." *New York Times,* Oct 23, 1967.

Kenworthy, E. W. "Fulbright Fears Conflict With China Over Vietnam." *New York Times,* Feb 8, 1966.

———. "Rusk Says Peace of World Is Issue In Vietnam War." *New York Times,* Feb 19, 1966.

———. "Senate Panel Will Conduct Broad Inquiry on Vietnam." *New York Times,* Feb 4, 1966.

The Air Force Reserve

———. "Taylor Asserts A 'Limited' War Is Intent of U.S." *New York Times*, Feb 18, 1966.
"Legion Panel Backs U.S.'s Viet Policy." *Macon Telegraph*, [Georgia] Oct 26, 1965.
Loftus, James A. "Guards Repulse Protesters at the Pentagon: 6 Break Through Line into Building—Mailer and Dellinger Are Arrested." *New York Times*, Oct 22, 1967.
———. "Mail Service Here is Paralyzed by Postal System's First Strike; Business Beginning to Feel Pinch." *New York Times*, Mar 19, 1970.
"McNamara Inquiry Sought On 'Favoritism' in Reserves." *New York Times*, Dec 10, 1966.
"Mercer Supports Nixon, War Cut." *Macon Telegraph*, [Georgia] May 14, 1968.
"Mercer Votes to Support War Protest." *Macon Telegraph*, [Georgia] Oct 3, 1969.
"Mercerians Cast Vote on Vietnam." *Macon Telegraph*, [Georgia] Oct 8, 1969.
Morton, Louis. "The Origins of American Military Policy." *Military Affairs*, Summer, 1958.
Republican National Committee Release. "Radio Address by Richard M. Nixon, Republican Presidential Nominee, Thursday Oct 17, 1968, 'The All-Volunteer Armed Force.'" Oct 18, 1968.
"Reservist Lawyer . . . Says Recall Illegal." *Air Force Times,* Apr 14, 1962.
Semple, Robert E., Jr. "Nixon Sends Troops to City to Move Mail; Calls 27,500 Guardsmen and Reservists; Strike Firm Here; Some Return in Nation." *New York Times*, Mar 24, 1970.
Stetson, Daman. "Postal Walkout is Ending Across the Nation; Some Returning Here." *New York Times*, Mar 25, 1970.
Stuckey, John D. and Joseph H. Pistorous. "Mobilization for the Vietnam War: A Political and Military Catastrophe." *Parameters*, 15, no. 1 (Spring 1985).
Turner, Wallace. "Antiwar Demonstrations Held Outside Draft Boards Across U.S.; 119 Persons Arrested on Coast." *New York Times*, Oct 17, 1967.
Turner, Wallace. "Police Rout 3,000 at Oakland Protest." *New York Times*, Oct 18, 1967.
Waggoner, Walter. "Truman Orders Reserve Strengthened and Trained, But His Peace Hopes Gain." *New York Times*, Oct 17, 1948.
Welles, Benjamin. "Again the Question—Why Not Reserves?" *New York Times,* Aug 21, 1966.
White, Thomas D. "New Accent on the Air Reserve Forces." *Air Force Magazine*, Jul 1960.
———. "The McNamara Strategy by William W. Kaufman, New York, Harper and Row, 1964." *Kansas Law Review*, 13 (1965).
Wright, Jim. "Call Reserves by Units." *Dallas Daily News*, Aug 20, 1966.

Bibliography

Correspondence with Author

Allen, General Lew, Nov 7, 1988.
Bodycombe, Maj. Gen. Richard.
Bundy, McGeorge, Oct 5, 1988.
Colwell, Brig. Gen. James L. Jan 14, 1986.
Ginsburgh, Maj. Gen. Robert Neville, Jan 23, 1984.
Hoopes, Townsend, Jul 11, 1988.
Knowles, Brig. Gen. Billy M. May 17, 1988.
Lewis, Maj. Gen. Homer I. May 17, 1988.
Lichman, J. J. Jan 15, 1986.
Markey, Maj. Gen. Howard T. Nov 30, 1984.
McNamara, Robert S. Jul 3, 1988.
Rusk, Dean, Jul 13, 1988.
Timberlake, Lt. Gen. E. J. Sep 3, 1983.

INDEX

Names of operations and exercises appear as individual entries under their specific names. All legislation entries are grouped under the heading Legislation, congressional *in addition to appearing in their normal alphabetical sequence according to the title of the specific legislation.*

Acheson, Dean: 89
Active Reserve: 28, 29, 36–37
Adjutant Generals Association: 61
Adler, Julius Ochs: 126, 128
Aerial port operations: 221, 358
Aero Club of Cincinnati: 9
Aero Clubs of America: 2, 7
Aeronautical Division: 2
Aeronautical Systems Division: 276
African-American (black) reservists: 82–83, 133, 384–385
Air Active Reserve class units: 36–37
Air Combat Command: 377
Air Corps Reserve: 13, 14–16, 17, 18, 20, 21
Aircraft and equipment: v, 10, 75–76, 290, 349–353
    A–37 (Tweetie Bird): 313
    in the Air Corps Reserve: 13, 14, 16, 17
    in the Air Defense Command: 38
    in the Air National Guard: 35
    in the Air Reserve: 35, 40–41
    C–5: 312, 349
    C–9: 350
    C–119: 352
    C–123: 352
    C–124: 353
    C–141: 312, 349
    in Class A units: 46
    EC–121: 314–315, 322–323
    in emergency relief missions: 357–360
    F–4: 351
    F–105: 313–314
    in the Flying Wing program: 147
    in humanitarian missions: 380
    KC–10: 325, 350
    KC–135: 351, 380
    in the Korean War: 99, 101–102
    modernization and conversion of: 317–321, 334–335
    in rescue missions: 326–327
    in special operations: 367–368
    UC–123K: 315
Air Defense Command: 45–46, 72
    aircraft and equipment in: 38
    base units development: 38, 39, 42
    composite units formation: 46–47
    in the Cuban missile crisis: 187
    establishment of: 37, 38
    management changes, 1950: 136
    training in: 42, 43–45, 54–55, 148
Airdromes system establishment: 8
Air Force Association: 51, 52, 238, 267, 342
Air Force Intelligence Service: 276, 278
Air Force Logistics Command: 377
Air Force Management Assistance Group review of 1982: 347
Air Force Materiel Command: 377
Air Force Regulations:
    AFR 23–1: 242, 243
    AFR 28–5: 330–331
    AFR 35–16: 113, 114
    AFR 36–70: 114–115
    AFR 45–1: 138, 254–256
Air Force Reserve unit program: 146
Air forces, U.S. (numbered)
    Eighteenth Air Force: 97, 106–107, 108
    Fifteenth Air Force: 318, 319
    Fifth Air Force: 99, 105
    Fourteenth Air Force: 318, 319, 364
    Fourth Air Force: 92, 318, 319, 364
    Ninth Air Force: 318, 319
    Tenth Air Force: 92, 96, 318, 319, 364
    Twelfth Air Force: 318, 319
    Twenty-first Air Force: 318, 319
    Twenty-second Air Force: 318, 319
Air Force Sergeants Association: 342
Air Force Systems Command: 377
Airlift operations: vi, viii, 149–150, 192–194, 193–196, 335, 356
    and the associate airlift program: 210
Airline pilots: 15, 19
Air mail program: 17
Air Material Command: 47, 77
Air Mobility Command: 377
Air National Guard: 1–2, 29, 33, 75
    aircraft and equipment of: 35, 41

The Air Force Reserve

and air refueling: 323
D-Day requirements for: 146
definition of: 136
and the fighter program: 168
in the Korean War: 112, 115
and the merger proposal: 35–36, 70–72, 173, 174, 227–237
mission of: 33–34, 35
in the *Pueblo* incident: 214
training in: 39
and the Twining memo: 142
Air power, definition of: 142–143
Air Power League: 51
Air Reserve: 29, 33
  aircraft and equipment in: 35, 40–41
  and the budget issue: 41–42, 51, 52
  management structure and organization of: 37–38
  McConnell evaluation, 1948: 53–55
  and the merger proposal: 35–36
  mission of: 34
Air Reserve Association: 22, 51, 61
Air Reserve Center Program: 260–261
Air Reserve Forces Policy Committee: 174–175, 228, 238, 344
Air Reserve Personnel Center: x, 239, 279, 281, 282, 284, 342
Air Reserve Records Center: 146, 158, 180, 283–284
Air Service: 10, 11–12
Air Staff Committee on National Guard and Reserve Policy: 149
Air Staff Committee on Reserve Policy: 74
Air Training Command: 79, 151
Air Transport Command: 47
Alexander, MSgt. James: 325
Alford Col. Cecil W.: 214
Allen, Gen. Lew, Jr.: 303, 305, 337
Allison, Graham T.: 192
All-Volunteer Force: 252
Anderson, Maj. Gen. Earle O.: 294, 295, 299, 319, 320
Anderson, Maj. Gen. Frederick L.: 29
Anderson, Maj. Rudolph: 187
Appley, Lawrence A.: 128
Arab-Israeli War: 309, 327–328, 357–358
ARC WIND (Operation): 379
Armenia relief: 358–359
Army, U.S. *See* United States Army
Army Air Forces Reserve Plan: 39
Arnold, Gen. Henry H.: 28, 29, 30, 32
Associate airlift program: 210

Associate units: 378
Astafan, Maj. Gen. Alice: 384
Auxiliary Reserve: 128–129

BABY LIFT (Operation): 212–213
Bagby, Brig. Gen. John S.: 172
Baker, Newton D.: 6
Balch, Col. Donald H.: 297
Ball, George: 201
Banton, Col. William C., II: 385
Base closures and unit reorganization: 378–379
Base Disaster Preparedness Augmentation program: 278–279
Base individual mobilization augmentee administrators: 282
Baumler, Brig. Gen. Dale R.: 356
Baumler panel review: 356
Bay of Pigs invasion: 184
Bear Bombers interception: 359
Beef Broth units: 214–215
Bergquist, Maj. Gen. Kenneth P.: 235
Berkely, Lt. Col. William R.: vii
Berlin crisis: v, viii, 172, 177–184, 231, 361
Berlin Wall: 179
Berry, Col. William F.: 259, 270
Beyl, Col. Donald F.: 296
Bird, Capt. Ron: 325
Black (African-American) reservists: 82–83, 133, 384–385
Blalack, Maj. Ronald D.: 311
Bodycombe, Maj. Gen. Richard: 1, 198, 249, 305, 321, 322, 336, 337
  impact of his management and organizational style: 257, 279, 339, 342, 343
  and mobilization assignees: 275
  and mobilization augmentees: 281
  and mobilization exercises: 329, 331
Boettcher, Brig. Gen. Byron K.: 276
Bolling, Lt. Col. Raynal C.: 2, 3, 7
Bosnia relief operations: v, 379–380
Boston airdrome: 14, 16
Bott, Capt. Francis: 325
Boylan, Lt. Gen. George S.: 247, 254, 255
Brashear, Maj. Wesley C.: 186
Bray, William, G.: 132–133
Brewer, Col. Zane C.: 246
Brooks, Overton: 124, 133
Brown, George S.: 255
Brown, Harold: 220, 239, 303

Index

Brown, Maj. Gen. I.G.: 255
Bundy, William: 201
Burgess, Carter L.: 131, 161, 162
Burwell, Brig. Gen. James B.: 165
Bush, George H.: 364, 365, 376

C–119 units: 195–196, 208, 244–245, 357
C–124 units: 192–194, 209, 214, 216, 222, 223, 313–314, 357
Campbell, Brig. Gen. Donald J.: 245–246, 254–255
Carlton, John T.: 236
Carroll, Capt. Philip A.: 7
Carter, Jimmy: viii, 338–339
Castro, Fidel: 184
Category A unit: 193
Category R reservists: 85–86, 93, 95, 101, 108, 139, 159–160
Catlin, Benjamin S.: 303, 304
Catlin, Lt. Benjamin S.: 10
Chanute Field: 13
Chaplains, reserve: 213
Charyk, Joseph V.: 266
Chayes, Antonia Handler: 303–304
Checkered Flag program: 229
Cheney, Richard B.: 366, 376
Circular 347: 26–27
Citizen army concept: 26, 27
Civilian components: 59–61
Civilian Components Group: 63
Civil Service Commission: 160–161, 162, 163
Clark, TSgt. James W.: 163
Clark, Gen. Mark W. (Ret.): 205–206
Clark Air Base evacuation: 379
Clay, Gen. Lucius D.: 180
Clements, William P., Jr.: 252
Clifford, Clark: 220, 221
Closner, Maj. Gen. John J.: 320, 381
Clover Field: 10, 11
Colange, Capt. Anthony: 311
Coleman, Col. Charles B.: 319
College undergraduate deferments: 289
Combat Cargo Command: 105
Commonwealth of Independent States relief: 379
Composite units formation: 46–47
CONDOR CRTE (Exercise): 333
CONDOR/REDOUBT (Exercise): 329, 331
Congress, U.S. *See also* Legislation, congressional
 and the Air Corps Reserve establishment: 13
 and Korean War requirements: 90–92
 and presidential recall authority: 337–339
 and reserve policy: 232, 236–237, 252–253, 290, 291, 348
 and reservist services policy: 383
 and the technician program: 302–303
 Total Force concept and policy: 252–253
 and universal training: 68–69, 121–126
CONTAC (Operation): 240
Continental Air Command: 72
 and the Air Force Reserve unit program: 146
 and the Air Reserve Personnel Center: 239
 and the Air Reserve Records Center: 146, 158
 budget of: 168–169
 and the corollary units: 79
 in the Cuban missile crisis: 186–187, 189
 and the Detached Squadron concept: 156
 and the field management structure reorganization: 239–240
 in the Korean War: 92, 94–96, 110–112, 115, 117
 management changes, 1950: 136
 manning and personnel development of: 145–146
 non–prior service personnel in: 152–154
 and option letters: 157
 and the Reserve Airlift Associate program: 310
 and the reserve program, 1950: 72–79
 and reserve recovery units: 265–266
 and reserve regions: 278
 and the Selective Assignment program: 156–157
 training in: 148, 151
 in Vietnam and Southeast Asia: 208
 and the Volunteer Air Reserve: 76–78
Continental Air Forces disestablishment: 37
Corcilius, Col. Charles R.: 297
Corollary units: 73, 74, 78, 79, 85
CORONET OAK (Operation): 362
CORONET POKER/OKSBOEL (Exercise): 329
Counseling programs: 211, 358
Cragg, Maj. Gen. Ernest T.: 242–243

529

The Air Force Reserve

Crissy Field: 9–10, 17
Crosby, 1st Lt. Leslie DeAnn: 384
Cuban missile crisis: viii, 172, 184–192, 267, 361
Curtis, Gen. Gilbert L.: 311
Curtiss schools: 6

Davison, Col. F. Trubee: 14, 28–29
D-Day
 defined: 36
 requirements of: 146
Defense Finance and Accounting Service: 371
Defense Manpower Commission: 198, 300–301
Deferments: 93–94, 110–111, 289
DENY FLIGHT (Operation): 380
DESERT STORM/SHIELD Hotwash: 369–370
DESERT STORM/SHIELD (Operation): 364–370
Detached squadron concept: 156
Devereux, James P.S.: 132
Diest, Col. Leonard F.: 297
Dillon, Maj. Gen. Edward: 339, 340
Directorate of Reserve Recruiting: 293
Disaster relief: 380–381
Divinity students exemption: 289
Divisions (numbered, U.S.)
 82d Airborne Division: 150, 210, 220
 91st Division, Organized Reserve: 9–10
 316th Division, Organized Reserve: 9–10
Dixon, Lt. Gen. Robert J.: 293
Dominican Republic crisis: viii, 195–196, 357
Donaldson AFB: 95
Donovan, Maj. Gen. Stanley J.: 186
Draft. *See* Selective Service system
Driessnack, Lt. Gen. Hans H.: 341
Dual Hat option: x, 241, 246–247, 248–249
Dual reserve system policy: 26
Dunn, Col. Ronald C.: 297
Dutton, SMSgt. Rudel: 298

Eaker, Lt. Gen. Ira C.: 29, 31, 32
Early warning and control: 314–315
Eaton, Maj. Gen. Robert E.L.: 174, 175, 263, 264, 271
Eaton Board: 263
EC-121: 314–315, 322–323
Education benefits: 383

Eisenhower, Dwight D.: vii, 50, 126–128, 132, 133, 134, 177, 184, 197, 361
Ellsworth, Harris: 145, 162–163
Employers' responsibilities and job rights: 374
Enlisted Reserve Corps: 5, 8, 28, 80, 85
Estes, Gen. Howell M.: 235, 310, 311
European Recovery Program: 58
European Tanker Task Force: 325
Evans, Gen.: 125
Everest, Lt. Gen. Frank F.: 141, 168
Executive Committee of the National Security Council (ExCom): 185, 187
Exemptions: 289

Fail, Capt. Woodrow T.: 311
Fairchild, Gen. Muir S.: 79
Family Support Centers: 372
Fear of Flying incident: 113–115, 117
Federal Preparation Liaison Officer program: 278–279
FIERY VIGIL (Operation): 379
Finletter, Thomas K.: 87, 88, 98, 117–119
First in, first out policy: 371
First Line Reserve: 128–129
Fisher, O.C.: 252–253
Flemming, Arthur S.: 127, 128, 129
Flying Wing program: 146–148, 150, 169
Ford, Gerald R.: 337
Forrestal, James V.: 59, 60, 61, 64, 65, 66, 67, 68, 69, 70–71, 84
Foulois, Maj. Gen. Benjamin D.: 16
Frank, Capt. Tom: 325
Fridge, Benjamin W.: 182, 266, 267
Fulbright, J. William: 204

Gabriel, Gen. Charles A.: 344
Garrison, Lindley M.: 3
Gates, Thomas S., Jr.: 288
Gates Commission: 288–289
Gerard, Maj. Gen. Francis R.: 301
Gerard Group: 301
Gerhart, Gen. John K.: 235
Germany. *See* Berlin crisis
Gill, Maj. Gen. Sloan R.: 306, 343
Gilpatrick, Roswell: 232, 267
Global air power concept: 37
Global Reach—Global Power, paper: 377
Graff, Col. T.G.: 50
Gray, Gordon: 59, 61
Gray Committee on Civilian Components: 159
Gray Committee report: 59–61, 64, 68

530

Index

Greenville AFB: 95
Grenada invasion: v, 359
Groups (numbered, U.S.)
   1st Air Postal and Courier Group: 328
   2d Air Postal and Courier Group: 328
   32d Aeromedical Evacuation Group: 379
   331st Air Refueling Group: 325
   506th Tactical Fighter Group: 314
   507th Tactical Fighter Group: 314, 324
   508th Tactical Fighter Group: 314
   904th Military Airlift Group: 215, 217, 220
   906th Tactical Airlift Group: 212, 312, 315
   907th Tactical Airlift Group: 360
   914th Tactical Airlift Group: 368
   915th Airborne Early Warning and Control Group: 315
   915th Tactical Fighter Group: 305–306
   916th Air Refueling Group (Associate): 381
   918th Military Airlift Group: 215
   919th Special Operations Group: 316, 362, 363
   919th Tactical Airlift Group: 315
   920th Tactical Airlift Group: 323
   921st Military Airlift Group: 215
   924th Tactical Airlift Group: 310, 330
   925th Tactical Airlift Group: 310
   926th Tactical Fighter Group: 366
   927th Tactical Airlift Group: 368
   930th Special Operations Group: 223, 312
   930th Tactical Airlift Group: 221
   931st Air Refueling Group: 305–306, 378
   931st Special Operations Group: 313
   935th Troop Carrier Group: 209
   937th Military Airlift group: 314
   938th Military Airlift Group: 215
   938th Military Airlift Group (Associate): 211
   939th Military Airlift Group (Associate): 211
   940th Air Refueling Group: 324–325
   941st Military Airlift Group: 215
   944th Military Airlift Group (Associate): 311
   944th Military Airlift Group (Provisional): 311
   944th Tactical Airlift Group: 310
   944th Tactical Fighter Group: 379
   2600th Reserve Recruiting Group: 343
Gruening, Ernest: 205
Gulf of Tonkin incident: 200
Gulf War. *See* Persian Gulf War
Gunsmoke series of competitions: 359, 379
Guyana, Jonestown operation: 326

Haiti relief operations: 380
Hall, Col. Richard L.: 333
Hall, Maj. Gen. William E.: 11, 141–142, 154, 155, 157, 162, 163, 169, 270
Handy, Gen. Thomas T.: 32
Hannah, John: 134
Harding, Warren G.: 9
Harsh, Col. Forest: 180
Hartridge, Gen.: 35
Hathaway, Brig. Gen. William G.: 296
Hay, James: 4
Health insurance benefits: 382–383
Hébert, F. Edward: 232, 236, 238
Henebry, Brig. Gen. John P.: 104
Herndon, Col. Theron B.: 51
Herold, Capt. Armin F.: 10
Hoag, Maj. Gen. Earl S.: 79, 137
Hoff, Maj. Gen. John T.: 295, 319, 320
HOMECOMING (Operation): 211
Huff, Brig. Gen. Harry J.: 297
Humanitarian missions: 380
   Armenia relief: 358–359
   Bosnia relief operations: v
   after the California earthquake: 359
   and civilian rescue: 326–327
   and counseling: 211–212, 358
   Haiti relief: 380
   after Hurricane Andrew: 380
   after Hurricane Hugo: 359–360
   after Hurricane Janet: 149
   Indochina refugee evacuation: 212–213
   in Jonestown, Guyana: 326–327
   and Kurdish refugees: 379, 380
   medical evacuations: 212–213, 221, 362, 363, 368
   in Mexico: 7, 149
   the MGM Grand Hotel rescue: 326, 358
   Mongolia relief: 379
   after the Mount Saint Helens eruption: 326, 358
   in Russia and the Commonwealth of Independent States relief: 379
   Rwanda relief: 380
   Somalia relief: 380
   after the typhoid fever outbreak in New

531

England: 149
Yugoslavia relief: 379–380
Hunt, Capt. Marjorie O.: 83
Hurricane Andrew: 380
Hurricane Hugo: 359–360
Hurricane Janet: 149

Iceland: 217, 322–323, 359
Ignatius, Paul: 232
Inactive Reserve: 28, 32, 36–37, 111
Indications and Warning Center: 210
Indochina Refugee Airlift: 212–213
Ingraham, Lt. Col. R.E.: 219
Insect spray missions: 315, 336, 358, 360
Intelligence specialists: 211–212
Iraq: v, 380. *See also* Persian Gulf War
Isaacs, Brig. Gen. James D.: 295
Israel. *See* Arab-Israeli War

Japan: 88
Jenkins, Brig. Gen. Cecil T.: 297
Job rights and employer responsibility: 374–375
Johnson, Louis: 72
Johnson, Lt. Gen. Leon W.: 43, 140–141, 152, 153, 157, 158, 165, 166, 260, 321
Johnson, Lyndon B.: viii, 180, 232, 236, 357, 361
    and Vietnam and Southeast Asia involvement: 198, 199–200, 204, 207–208
Johnson Board: 140–141, 148, 154, 156
Joint Mid-Range War Plan: 141, 142, 146
Joint Strategic Objectives Plan: 167, 168
Jones, General David C.: ix, 279, 322, 337
Jones, Maj. Gen. Junius W.: 61–62
Jonestown rescue mission: 326–327
JUST CAUSE (Operation): 362–364

Kaine, Maj. Gen. J.W.: 237
KC–10 associate units: 325
KC–135 associate mission: 378
Keegan, Maj. Gen. George J., Jr.: 278
Kelly, Lt. Gen. Joe W.: 192, 193
Kelly Field: 14, 18
Kennedy, John Fitzgerald: viii, 171–172, 176, 360
    and the Berlin crisis: 177–184, 361
    and the Cuban missile crisis: 184–192
    and Vietnam and Southeast Asia involvement: 197–198, 200

Kennedy, Robert F.: 188
Kern, Brig. Gen. John R., Jr.: 233, 234, 247
Khrushchev, Nikita: 177, 184, 187, 191, 361
Kim Il-Sung: 88
Kissinger, Henry A.: 178
Kittell, Capt. Charles J.: 221
Koje-do Island POW riot: 107
Korea. *See* Korean War; *Pueblo* incident
Korean War: v, vii, 88–90, 95
    403d Troop Carrier Wing: 97, 106–107
    437th Troop Carrier Wing: 95, 104–106
    452d Bombardment Wing (Light): 92, 93, 98–103
    731st Bombardment Squadron: 92, 99, 103
    and the Air National Guard: 112, 115
    and Category R reservists: 101, 108
    congressional support for: 90–92
    deferments during: 93–94, 110–111
    and the Fear of Flying incident: 113–115, 117
    filler unit mobilization: 97–98
    individual reservist recalls: 109–113, 117
    and the Koje-do Island POW riot: 107
    and the length of service issue: 108–109
    the mobilization program assessment: 115–118
    mobilization for: 87, 90–98, 360
    and morale: 102–103
    national emergency proclamation: 95
    and the National Guard: 94
    and officers' early release eligibility: 112–113
    Public Law 599: 98
    and the recall program investigation: 115–116
    and reservists' records: 93, 96, 115, 116
    and rotation: 100–101, 109
    and the Tactical Air Command: 101–102
    United Nations role in: 90
    and voluntary recall: 110
    and the Volunteer Air Reserve: 92–93, 95, 110–111, 115
Kurdish refugees relief: 379, 380

Laird, Melvin R.: 249, 251, 288, 289
Landry, Brig. Gen. Robert B.: 69–70
Lawhon, Col. Brooks A.: 103

Index

Lawton, Frederick J.: 162
Lawyers, reserve: 213
Lebanon evacuation: 359
Lee, Maj. Gen. Morris J.: 152–153
Legislation, congressional
  Air Corps Act: 18
  Air Corps Act of 1926: 15
  Air Force Authorization Act of 1949: 72
  Air Force Organization Act of 1951: 136
  Armed Forces Reserve Act of 1952: 124–126, 128, 132
  Army and Air Force Authorization Act of 1949: 136
  Army Reorganization Act of 1920: 8
  Dependency Assistance Act of 1950: 111
  Dependents Assistance Act: 289
  Dick Act of 1903: 2
  First Supplemental Appropriation Act of 1951: 90
  Military Selective Service Act of 1967: 207
  Montgomery GI Bill: 383
  Morrill Act of 1862: 15
  Mutual Defense Assistance Act of 1949: 89
  National Defense Act of 1916: 1, 2, 4–5, 6, 15, 27, 80, 94
  National Defense Act of 1920: 8–9, 21, 27
  National Security Act of 1947: 84
  Officer Personnel Act of 1947: 134
  Public Law 51–82: 112, 133, 182–183, 206
  Public Law 80–460: 80
  Public Law 80–759 (Selective Service Act): 57–59, 122
  Public Law 87–117: 171, 182
  Public Law 87–736: 185
  Public Law 88–773: 133–135
  Public Law 90–168: viii, 158, 164, 227, 232, 238, 248, 249, 252, 254, 256–257, 287, 341, 344, 346, 347
  Public Law 92–129: 289
  Public Law 96–584: 339
  Public Law 99–661: 339
  Public Law 253–80: 84
  Public Law 599: 98
  Public Law 810–80: 82
  Reserve Forces Act of 1955: 132–133, 135, 153, 154, 161, 206
  Reserve Forces Bill of Rights and Vitalization Act (PL 90–168): viii, 158, 164, 227, 232, 238, 248, 249, 252, 254, 256–257, 287, 341, 344, 346, 347
  Reserve Officer Personnel Act of 1954: 233
  Reserve Officers Personnel Act: 133–135
  Russell Amendment of 1967: 337
  Selective Service Act of 1948 (PL 80–759): 57–59
  Selective Service Amendment Act of 1969: 288
  Selective Service and Training Act: 58
  Selective Service Extension Act of 1948: 91
  Selective Service Extension Act of 1950: 91
  Thomason Act: 18
  Unification Act of September 1947: 136
  Uniformed Services and Reemployment Rights Act of 1994: 375
  Universal Military Training and Service Act of 1951: 122–124
  Universal Military Training and Service Act (PL 51–82): 112, 133, 182–183, 206
  Veterans Preference Act of 1944: 163
  Veterans Reemployment Rights Act: 370, 375
LeMay, Gen. Curtis E.: 173, 174, 227, 228, 230–231, 235
Lewis, Maj. Gen. Homer I.: 245, 275, 276, 277, 279, 280, 292, 293, 294, 295, 314
  impact of his management and organizational style: 246, 247, 249, 255, 257, 284, 291
Lingelbach, L.C.: 160, 161, 162, 300
Lingle, Col. Joseph J.: 188, 189
LONG HORN (Exercise): 108
Long-Range Plan: 139–140, 146–151, 170, 385
Lottery system: 288
Low, Maj. Gen. Curtis R.: 233, 234
Lusitania sinking: 3
Lyon, Maj. Gen. William: 198, 249, 275–276, 280, 297, 298, 300, 303, 304–305, 317, 318, 319, 320, 322

MacArthur, Gen. Douglas: 90

533

The Air Force Reserve

MacCloskey, Col. Monro: 40
Management Assistance Group: 339–343
Management structure and organization: ix–x. *See also* Manning and personnel development
   of the Active Air Reserve: 36–37
   in the active force–reserve force conflict: 254–257
   AFR 45–1: 138, 254–256
   in the AFRES/Office of Air Force Reserve conflict: 241–249
   African-American participation in: 384–385
   Air Force Management Assistance Group review, 1982: 347
   Air Force Reserve Chief's role in: 342, 343
   of the Air Reserve: 37–38
   and the Air Reserve Forces Policy Committee: 174–175
   of Air Reserve technicians in leadership positions: 321
   of the Army Air Force: 345–346
   of associate units: 378
   in base closure and unit reorganization: 378
   of base individual mobilization augmentee administrators: 282
   and the Baumler panel review: 356
   and the Campbell report: 245–246
   changes, 1950: 135–138
   changes, 1960s: 172–176
   and the command status issue: 242–244, 246
   and the Comptroller General's report, 1964: 269
   and Cuban missile crisis problems: 191–192
   in the defense buildup, 1980s: 348
   and DESERT STORM/SHIELD Hotwash: 369–370
   and the Dual Hat option: x, 241, 246–247, 248–249
   and the Eaton Board: 263
   of the flying program, 1958: 346
   the Inspector General report on: 279, 281
   and the Kern study: 247–248
   and the Lyon program: 317–321
   and the Management Assistance Group: 339–344
   and the Match-Merge process: 262–265
   the merger proposal: 227–237
   and Mobilization augmentee programs: 273–276, 278–279, 281–284
   and the objective wing structure: 378
   and the Office of Air Force Reserve establishment: 346–347
   Organization and Equipment table, 1950: 75–76
   post–Cold War changes in: 377–379
   and promotion progression: 244
   Public Law 90–168: viii, 158, 164, 227, 232, 238, 248, 249, 252, 254, 256–257, 287, 341, 344, 346, 347
   and the quality initiative: 385
   RAND Corporation study of: 249–250
   and the records issues: 43, 51, 93, 96, 115, 116, 148, 158, 225, 239
   and the reserve facilities problem: 165–167
   and the Reserve Forces Program Review Group: 172–174
   of the reserve leadership: 257, 344
   of the Reserve Recovery Program: 265–271
   of reserve regions: 317–319
   and the Sharp policy: 175
   and the status quo problem: 355
   of tactical units: 346
   and the Total Force concept and policy: 249–257, 347
   and the Total Force study group report: 253–254
   and unit type code tailoring: 370
   women's participation in: 383
Manning and personnel development: ix, 132–133, 134–135, 151–152, 244, 355. *See also* Recruitment; Selective Service system
   absences policy: 354–355
   in the Air Corps Reserve: 14–16, 18–21
   of the Air Reserve Records Center: 158
   in the All-Volunteer Force: 287–298
   in the Army Air Corps, 1938: 19–20
   of Category R reservists: 85–86, 93, 95, 101, 108, 139, 159–160
   and congressional policy, 1987: 348
   and the Defense Manpower Commission report: 198, 300–301
   of the detached squadron program: 146, 156
   and the excepted service controversy: 298–302
   and the Gates Commission report: 288–289

Index

and the Gerard Group report: 301
and the Gray Committee on Civilian Components: 159
militarization test for reserve technicians: 302–306
of non–prior service personnel: 146, 152–154, 161–162
and option letters: 157
and the Palace Acquire program: 355
and Personnel Support for Contingency Operations (PERSCO): 371
of pilots, technician: 355
and reserve personnel administration specialists: 294
in retention: 152, 292, 297–298, 354, 355, 372
in the selective assignment program: 146, 156–157
and the status quo problem: 163–164, 298–299, 355
in the stop-loss program: 294, 372
in the technician program: 146, 159–164, 169–170, 298–307
Universal Military Training and Service Act (PL 51–82): 112, 133, 182–183, 206
and Vietnam and Southeast Asia enlistments: 205–207
Marchbanks, Maj. Gen. Tom E., Jr.: 214, 215, 238–239, 240, 242, 243, 244, 245, 290, 310, 311
Marderosian, Rafael L.: 276
Markarian, Col. Ronald H.: 278
Marrs, Theodore C.: 220, 229, 240, 328
Marshall, Brig. Gen. Roy M.: 296, 320, 321
Marshall, Gen. George C.: 24–26, 27, 33
Match-Merge process: 262–265
Mather Field: 13
Mathis, Gen. Robert C.: 339
Maxey, Capt. William: 210, 311
Maxwell, Lt. W.A.: 10
McAdoo, Col. James E.: 296
McCarty, Gen. Chester E.: 106–107
McConnell, Brig. Gen. John P.: 70, 74, 197, 208–209, 223, 241, 273–274
impact of his management and organizational style: 53–55, 59, 62, 63, 233–234, 235, 239, 249, 250–251
McCormick, MSgt. Samuel C.: 163
McCoy, Tidal W.: 341
McFarland, Col. Richard P.: 210, 296, 311

McGann, Brig. Gen. Donald A.: 276
McIntosh, Maj. Gen. Robert A.: 382, 385
McIntyre, Malcolm A.: 173
McLucas, John L.: 279
McMullen, Col. A.B.: 125
McNamara, Robert S.: 176, 177, 178, 179, 180, 185, 187, 191, 310
and the merger issue: 229, 231, 232, 233, 234, 235, 236, 237
in the reserve recovery program: 267, 268, 269
during the Vietnam and Southeast Asia era: 199, 201, 202, 203, 204, 220
McNeil, Brig. Gen. Joseph A.: 385
McPartlin, Col. James E.: 180
McPeak, Gen. Merrill A.: 375, 377
McWilliams, George M.: 306
M-Day (mobilization day): 36, 78
Medical and evacuation operations: 212–213, 221, 362, 363
Menoher, Maj. Gen. G.T.: 9, 11, 12
Merger proposal: 60, 61, 70–72, 173, 174, 227–237
Mexico: 7, 149
Meyer, John C.: 242, 243, 245, 248
Meyers, Maj. Gen. Charles T.: 115
MGM Grand Hotel rescue: 258, 326
Middle East: viii, 358
Militarization test for reserve technicians: 302–306
Military Airlift Command: 310, 356, 377
Military Air Transport Service: 79, 176, 192–194
navigator shortage in: 210–211
offshore missions of: 195–196
in Vietnam and Southeast Asia operations: 209–211
Mission: v–vi, 34, 36, 335, 357. *See also* Humanitarian missions
of the aerial port function: 221, 336
of the Air Force Reserve: 34, 36
of airlift operations: vi, viii, 149–150, 192–194, 193–196, 335, 357
of the Air National Guard: 33–34, 35
of the Air Reserve: 34
and bomber assignment: 378
of C–119s offshore: 195–196
in domestic emergencies: 149
and early warning and control: 314–315
of the European Tanker Task Force: 325
forces furnished, 1981: 335–336
insect control spray: 315, 336, 358, 360

535

The Air Force Reserve

intelligence: 211–212, 358
KC–135 associate: 378
medical and evacuation: 212–213, 221, 335, 362, 363, 368
in the Pacific: 193–194
and paratroops: 150
in peacetime: 171, 176
in the post–Cold War era: 375–376, 378
and POW debriefing: 211–212
refueling: 323–325
rescue and recovery: 150, 216–217, 218, 219, 265–266, 336
runway alerts: 150
satellite operation: 378
special operations: 315
surveillance: 322–323
in Vietnam and Southeast Asia: 196, 357–358
weather surveillance: vi, 323, 336, 378
Mitchel Field: 38, 49
Mitchell, Brig. Gen. Clyde H.: 115
Mobilization: 87–88
  of the Air Corps Reserve: 13
  and Air Defense Command policy: 45–46
  of augmentees: 78, 347
  of Beef Broth units: 214–215
  in the Berlin crisis: 179–184, 361
  of Category R reservists: 85–86, 93, 95, 101, 108, 139
  of corollary units: 78
  in the Cuban missile crisis: 73, 74, 79, 85, 186–191, 361
  D-Day requirement for: 146
  Defense Manpower Commission report: 198
  and deferment boards: 93–94
  and the Fear of Flying incident: 113–115, 117
  global air power concept: 37
  of individual reservists, Korean War: 109–113, 117
  Joint Mid-Range War Plan: 141, 142, 146
  Joint Strategic Objectives Plan: 167, 168
  in the Korean War: 87, 90–98, 97–98, 115–118, 360
  Match-Merge process: 262–265
  assignee program: 73, 74, 78
  mobilization day (M-Day) definition: 36
  requirement for, establishment: 128–130
  in the Persian Gulf War: 364–367
  in the postal strike: 328
  presidential authority for: 18, 20, 91–92, 98, 171, 182, 185, 337–339
  Public Law 87–117: 171, 182
  Public Law 87–736: 185
  Public Law 599: 98
  in the *Pueblo* incident: 214–216
  Reserve Mobilization Recall Requirements: 143
  and reservists release, 1968: 222–223
  Stratemeyer principles for: 63
  in Vietnam and Southeast Asia: 198–210, 220–223, 225
  Whitehead evaluation of: 85
Mobilization assignee program: 73, 74, 78
Mobilization augmentees: 78, 275–276, 278–279, 281–284
Mobilization day (M-Day) definition: 36
Modernization and conversion: 317–321, 334–335
Modernization and equipment conversion: 309–313, 323–325, 348
Mongolian relief: 379
Montgomery, G.V. "Sonny": 383
Montgomery GI Bill: 383
Moore, Brig. Gen. Rollin B., Jr.: 215, 240, 241, 243, 246, 290, 291, 295, 319
Moore, Gen. William G., Jr.: 381
Morse, Wayne: 204
Mosely, Lt. C.C.: 10
Moser, Brig. Gen. Alvin A.: 297
Mosquito and insect control spraying: 315, 336, 358, 360
Mossman, Col. Frances: 384
Mount Pinatubo eruption: 379
Mount Saint Helens eruption: 326, 358
Mullis, Col. Betty L.: 384

National Advisory Committee on Selective Service: 207
National defense policy: 89
  during the Eisenhower administration: 346, 361
  and the global air power concept: 37
  Global Reach—Global Power, paper: 377
  during the Kennedy administration: 360
  North Atlantic Treaty: 89
  Quality Air Force Concept: 377
  during the Reagan administration: 347–

Index

348
during the Truman administration: 24–27, 64–68, 360
National Defense University: 333–334
National Guard: 2, 13, 25, 85, 91
  defined: 33, 36
  during the Eisenhower administration: 132, 133
  federalization of: 4–5, 8
  in the Korean War: 94
  and the Truman reserve initiative: 65, 66
National Guard Association: 61, 124, 125, 342
National Guard Bureau: 255
National Military Establishment: 84
National Military Intelligence Center: 211
National Reserve Plan: 130–132
National reserve policy
  and the Air National Guard: 136
  air power, defined: 142–143
  Air Staff Committee on Reserve Policy: 74
  Air Staff role in: 137–138, 139
  Armed Forces Reserve Act of 1952: 124–126, 128, 132
  Army and Air Force Authorization Act of 1949: 136
  and the Army deactivation proposal: 231–233, 236
  and black reservists: 133
  and the Category R program: 139
  Circular 347: 26–27
  and the citizen army concept: 26, 27
  and civilian components: 59–61
  dual reserve system policy: 26
  during the Eisenhower administration: vii–viii, 126–135
  and flexible response: 176, 177
  during the Ford administration: 338
  and the Gray committee report: 59–61, 64, 68
  and the Johnson Board: 140–141
  and the Joint Mid-Range War Plan: 141, 142
  and Jones recommendations: 61–62
  during the Kennedy administration: 171, 176, 231–233
  and the Long-Range Plan: 139–140
  and mobilization requirement: 128–130
  and the National Reserve Plan: 130–132
  during the Nixon administration: 251–254, 287–289, 290

promotion with legislation: 132–133, 134–135
  and the Ready Reserve: 131, 133, 138
  Reserve Forces Act of 1955: 132–133, 135, 153, 154, 161, 206
  Reserve Mobilization Recall Requirements: 143
  Reserve Officers Personnel Act: 133–135
  and the Reserve Program Review Board: 140–141
  and the Retired Reserve: 138
  segregation issues: 133
  and the Selectively Callable Reserve: 129, 130, 131
  and the Service Callable Reserve: 128–129, 129, 130, 131, 143
  and the Standby Reserve: 125, 131, 133, 138, 264
National Security Action Memorandum 288: 199–200
National Security Training Commission: 123, 127–128, 129–130, 131
National Security Training Corps: 123, 124, 129
Naval Reserve: 60, 68
Navigators: 150–151
Navy League: 3
Neblett, William H.: 64, 69
Nelson, Maj. Gen. Maurice R.: 263–264
NEW LIFE (Operation): 212–213
Nicaragua: 315
NIMROD DANCER (Operation): 362
Nixon, Richard M.: viii, 225, 251, 252, 287–288, 327, 328
Non–prior service personnel: 146, 152–154, 161–162
Norstad, Maj. Gen. Lauris: 30, 63
North Atlantic Treaty: 89
North Korea. *See* Korean War
North Pole weather station airlift: 108
North Vietnam. *See* Vietnam and Southeast Asia, war in
Novaresi, Brig. Gen. Sidney S.: 296, 319, 334–335

Objective wing structure: 378
Office of Air Force Reserve establishment: 346–347
Officers' Reserve Corps: 5, 8, 28, 80, 85
Option letters: 157
Organization. *See* Management structure and organization

537

The Air Force Reserve

Organization and Equipment table, 1950: 75–76
Organization of American States: 186
Organized Air Reserve: 8, 9–10, 13, 21, 27–28, 80, 112, 115, 273
Organized Reserve Corps: 5, 6, 7, 21–22, 28, 29, 32, 33, 41
Orr, Verne: 341
Otto, Lt. Stephan K.: 368
Overmanning: 348, 353

Pace, Frank, Jr.: 66–67, 72
Packard, David: 314
PAID REDOUBT (Exercise): 330
Palace Acquire program: 355
Palmer, Brig. Gen. John M.: 26, 27
Panama invasion: v, 359, 362–364
Paratroop operations: 150
Partridge, Maj. Gen. Earle E.: 23, 24, 44, 51–52, 83, 101, 102–103, 273
Patrick, Maj. Gen. Mason M.: 11, 12
Pay related issues: 2, 18, 73, 131, 225
  and the Defense Finance and Accounting Service: 371
  and drill strength: 290–291
  and inactive duty status: 69, 80–81
  of the mobilization augmentees: 260, 273, 274
  Personnel Support For Contingency Operations (PERSCO): 371
  Public Law 80–460: 80
  and unassigned reservists: 263
Pershing, Gen. John J.: 26
Persian Gulf War: v, 1, 364–370
Personnel. See Manning and personnel development
Personnel Support For Contingency Operations (PERSCO): 371
PHIBRIGLEX 62 (Exercise): 186–187
Philbin, Edward: 342
Philippines: 379
Pilots, air reserve technician: 355
PINE CONE (Operation): 150
Pinson, Maj. Boyce N.: 209, 213
Pleiku: 200
POSITIVE LEAP (Exercise): 330
Postal strike mobilization: 328
Postwar Planning Board: 26
Powell, Adam Clayton: 133
Powell, Gen. Colin L.: 376
Power, Lt. Gen. Thomas S.: 114
POWER PACK (Operation): 240, 195–196
POWs debriefing: 211–212

Preparedness Movement: 3, 5, 7
Prisoner of War Experience and Analysis Program: 212
Prisoner of War/Missing in Action Program: 211
Promotions: 132–133, 134–135, 244, 356
PROVIDE COMFORT (Operation): 379
PROVIDE COMFORT II (Operation): 380
PROVIDE HOPE (Operation): 379
Public laws. See Legislation, congressional
Pueblo incident: 210, 214–216, 220

Quality Air Force Concept: 377
Quality initiative: 385
Quarles, Donald A.: 161–162
Quesada, Maj. Gen. Elwood R.: 44, 70, 71, 73, 136–137

Rambo, 2d Lt. Kathleen A.: 384
RAND Corporation study: 249–250
Randolph Field: 18
Ready Reserve: 125, 126, 131, 133, 138, 183, 238, 262
READY SWAP (Operation): 240, 149–150, 356
Records. See Management structure and organization
Recovery units program: 265–271
Recruitment: 151–152, 153, 289–298, 342–343
  manning ceiling: 348, 353–354
  and overmanning: 348, 353
  Palace Acquire program: 355
  during the Persian Gulf War: 372
  recruitment system test, 1973: 293–296
  and stop-loss management: 294, 372
REDOUBT series of exercises: 329–332
Refueling operations, air: 323–325
Rescue and recovery operations: 216–217, 218, 219
Reserve Airlift Associate program: 310–312
Reserve Element Training program: 271–272
Reserve Enlistment Program: 206
Reserve facilities problem: 165–167
Reserve Family Support Program: 373–374
Reserve Forces Policy Board: 134, 137, 138, 233
Reserve Forces Program Review Group: 172–174

Index

Reserve Forces Review Group: 265
Reserve Mobilization Recall Requirements: 143
Reserve Officers Association: 22, 51, 61, 68, 71, 124, 233, 236, 238, 267, 342
Reserve Officers Training Corps: 5, 15, 29, 85
Reserve Policy Council: 238
Reserve Program Review Board: 140–141
Reserve Recovery Program: 265–271
Reserve regions: 317–319
Reserve Road Map to the Future: 385
Reserve technician program, Air Force: 159–164, 169–170, 298–307, 346, 355, 384
Reservist relations and related issues. *See also* Pay related issues
  deferments: 93–94, 110–111, 289
  educations benefits: 383
  family support: 372–374, 382
  Fear of Flying incident: 113–115, 117
  first in, first out policy: 371
  health insurance benefits: 382–383
  inactive duty training pay: 80–81
  individual reservists, recall of: 110, 117
  information and communications failures: 48–52
  information and public relations: 141, 154, 156
  job rights and employer responsibilities: 374–375
  Johnson Board recommendations: 140–141
  JUST CAUSE concerns: 363–364
  during the Korean War: 98, 102–103, 108–109
  the mobilization augmentees: 276
  obsolete weapons and equipment complaints: 225
  personnel records and pay: 225
  quality of life concerns: 382–383
  a reassignment suit: 217, 220
  Reserve Family Support Program: 373
  retention incentives: 292, 297
  retirement benefits: 82
  rotation policy, Korean War: 100–101
  secure placement: 383
  unit type code tailoring: 370
  Veterans Preference Act of 1944: 163
  Veterans Reemployment Rights Act: 370
  Vietnam and Southeast Asia–era complaints: 222

volunteerism: 381–382
RESTORE HOPE (Operation): 380
Retention: 152, 292, 297–298, 354, 355, 372
Retired Reserve: 125, 138
Retirement: 82, 264
Rice, Donald B.: 377
Riley, Lt. Col. John C.: 216
Rivers, L. Mendel: 205, 236
Robinson, Maj. Gen. Gwynn H.: 318
Rodeo series of competitions: 359, 381
Roosevelt, Franklin D.: 17, 19
Rosenberg, Anna M.: 117, 119, 125
Rotation: 100–101, 109
Runge, Carlisle P.: 183, 266, 267
Runway alerts: 150
Rush, Col. Stanley: 188
Rusk, Dean: 201, 202
Russell Amendment of 1967: 337
Russia and the Commonwealth of Independent States relief: 379–380
Rwanda relief: v, 380
Ryan, Gen. John D.: 245, 292, 314

Saltonstall, Leveret: 134
Saudi Arabia. *See* Persian Gulf War
Scheer, Maj. Gen. Roger P.: 353, 354, 363
Schlesinger, James R.: 253–254, 338
Scriven, Brig. Gen. George P.: 2
Secure placement issue: 383
Segregation: 133
Selected Reserve: 238, 252
Selective Assignment program: 156–157
Selectively Callable Reserve: 129, 130, 131
Selective Service and Training Act: 58
Selective Service system: 122–124, 127, 131
  deferments: 93–94, 110–111, 289
  the draft: viii, 152, 287–288
  exemptions: 289
  lottery system: 288
  Military Selective Service Act of 1967: 207
  National Advisory Committee on Selective Service: 207
  Selective Service Amendment Act of 1969: 288
  Selective Service and Training Act: 58
  Selective Service Extension Act of 1948: 91

The Air Force Reserve

Selective Service Extension Act of 1950: 91
during the Vietnam and Southeast Asia period: 203, 205–207
Selff, Lt. Robert E.: 10
Selfridge Field: 12, 14
Service Callable Reserve: 128–129, 129, 130, 131, 143, 262
Sharp, Maj. Gen. Alan G.: 354
Sharp, Dudley C.: 175
Shotts, Lt. Gen. Bryan M.: 229, 334
Signal Corps, Aviation Section: 2, 5–7
Signal Enlisted Reserve Corps: 5–6
Sikes, Bob L.F.: 205, 314
SIXTEEN TON (Operation): 148, 149, 356
Smith, David S.: 154, 155, 161, 162
Smith, Brig. Gen. Robert J.: 74
Smith, Maj. Gen. Sory: 172, 265, 266
Smith, W. Sandford: 309
Smolinski, Sgt. William C.: 217, 219
SNOWFALL (Operation): 108
Somalia relief: v, 380
Sorensen, Theodore: 184
Southeast Asia. *See* Vietnam and Southeast Asia, war in
SOUTHERN WATCH (Operation): 380
South Vietnam. *See* Vietnam and Southeast Asia, war in
Soviet Union. *See* Union of Soviet Socialist Republics
Spaatz, Gen. Carl A.: 32–33, 43, 44, 48, 49, 51, 61, 63, 84
Special operations missions: 315
Spencer, Lt. Col. W.L.: 186
Spray, insect control mission: 315, 336, 358, 360
Squadrons (numbered, U.S.)
  1st Reserve Aero Squadron: 3, 7
  2d Reserve Aero Squadron: 7
  7th Space Operations Squadron: 378
  26th Aero Squadron: 7
  31st Aeromedical Evacuation Squadron: 327
  33d Aerospace Rescue and Recovery Squadron: 216
  34th Aeromedical Evacuation Squadron: 221, 223
  40th Aeromedical Evacuation Squadron: 211, 213
  45th Aero Squadron: 7
  52d Medical Service Squadron: 221, 223
  52d Military Airlift Squadron: 216
  58th Aerospace Rescue and Recovery Squadron: 216
  65th Aeromedical Evacuation Squadron: 213
  68th Aeromedical Evacuation Squadron: 211, 213
  68th Military Airlift Squadron: 365
  71st Air Commando Squadron: 221–222
  71st Special Operations Squadron: 221–222, 223, 224, 313
  71st Tactical Airlift Squadron: 221–222
  73d Aeromedical Airlift Squadron: 211
  74th Aeromedical Evacuation Squadron: 379
  78th Air Refueling Squadron (Heavy) (Associate): 325
  78th Troop Carrier Squadron: 169
  79th Airborne Early Warning and Control Squadron: 323
  79th Air Refueling Squadron: 381
  79th Early Warning and Control Squadron: 315
  82d Aerial Port Squadron: 221, 223
  83d Aerial Port Squadron: 223
  86th Aerial Port Squadron: 221, 223
  88th Aerial Port Squadron: 221
  91st Observation Squadron: 10
  93d Bombardment Squadron: 378
  301st Air Rescue Squadron: 150
  301st Rescue Squadron: 380–381
  302d Aerospace Rescue and Recovery Squadron: 315
  302d Special Operations Squadron: 326, 358
  304th Aerospace Rescue and Recovery Squadron: 326, 358
  305th Aerospace Rescue and Recovery Squadron: 215, 216–217, 218, 219, 223, 326, 327, 332–333
  315th Airlift Squadron (Associate): 378
  317th Airlift Squadron: 378
  320d Special Operations Squadron: 316
  336th Air Refueling Squadron: 384
  355th Tactical Airlift Squadron: 212
  430th Pursuit Squadron: 16–17
  711th Tactical Airlift Squadron: 315
  731st Bombardment Squadron: 92, 99, 103, 109
  815th Weather Reconnaissance Squadron: 358, 359
  1648th Provisional Squadron (Alpha

540

Index

Rotational): 216
9223d Air Force Recovery Squadron: 268
9342d Air Reserve Squadron: 272
9633d Recovery Squadron: 313
VMF–513 Marine Squadron: 103
Squier, Brig. Gen George O.: 6
Srull, Capt. Charles M.: 217
Standby Reserve: 125, 131, 133, 138, 264
Stappler, TSgt. John P.: 311
State Preparation Augmentation program: 278–279
Status quo problem: 163–164, 298–299, 355
Steelman, John R.: 65, 66, 67
Stennis, John C.: 236
Stetson, James C.: 303
Stewart, Lt. Gen. James T.: 276
Stimson, Henry L.: 2, 27
Stone, Maj. Gen. Charles B., III: 46, 165, 166, 167, 168, 263
Stone, Maj. Gen. William E.: 162
Stop-loss management: 294, 372
Strategic Air Command: 37, 96, 334–335, 377
Strategic Reserve: 203, 214
Stratemeyer, Lt. Gen. George E.: 34–35, 38, 43, 44, 45, 46–47, 49, 50, 62, 63, 159, 273, 284
  and the Korean War: 90, 92, 102, 103, 109
Streett, Maj. Gen. St. Clair: 35–36, 44
Structure. *See* Management structure and organization
Surveillance operations: 322–323
Swain, Capt. Bob: 368
Sweeney, Gen. Walter C., Jr.: 172
Sweetser, Brig. Gen. Luther W.: 29, 98–99, 100
SWIFT LIFT (Operation): 240, 149, 356
Symington, W. Stuart: 43, 49, 69, 71, 73, 84
Syngman Rhee: 88, 89, 90

Table of Organization and Equipment, 1950: 75–76
Tactical Air Command: 72, 377
  in the Berlin crisis: 180
  in the Cuban missile crisis: 189–190, 191, 192
  establishment of: 37
  in the Korean War: 96–97, 101–102
  management changes, 1950: 136

training objectives of: 148
training policy and programs: 47
Taft, William H.: 2–3
Talbott, Harold E.: 91, 122, 155
Taylor, Col. John E.: 296
Taylor, Gen. Maxwell D.: 199, 200
Teams, combat (numbered, U.S.)
  137th Regimental Combat Team: 107
  187th Airborne Regimental Combat Team: 92, 105, 107
Technician program, Air Force Reserve: 159–164, 169–170, 298–307, 346, 355, 384
Tet offensive: 220
Thatcher, Lt. Gen. Herbert B.: 115, 116, 235
Thomas, Brig. Gen. Joe A.: 320, 321
Thompson, Lewis S.: 266
Thompson, Llewellyn: 178
Thurmond, Strom: 134
Timberlake, Maj. Gen. Edward J.: 103, 192–193, 229, 231, 234, 236
Total Quality Implementation Plan: 385
Total Force concept and policy: ix, viii, 164, 249–257, 344, 347
  Air reserve role in: 309–310
  National Defense University report: 333–334
  in the post–Cold War era: 376
Total Force study group report: 253–254
Townsley, Col. Justin L.: 297
Training: 14, 16–17, 42, 44
  in 1916: 6
  of the Active Air Reserve: 37
  active duty tours: 48
  in the Aeronautical Systems Division: 276
  of the Air Corps Reserve: 13–14
  in the Air Defense Command: 38–39, 42, 43–45, 47, 54–55
  in the Air Force Intelligence Service: 276, 278
  of the Air National Guard: 39
  of the Air Reserve: 40–41
  in the Air Reserve Center Program: 260–261
  in the Air Training Command: 151
  base units role in: 38
  of black reservists: 82–83
  at the Boston airdrome: 14, 16
  in the Continental Air Command: 148, 151
  in the corollary units: 73, 74, 79

541

decentralization to the commands, 1960: 346
and the Fear of Flying incident: 113–115, 117
the fifteen-day tour issue: 12
flying field facilities, designation of: 39–40, 42
and flying hours: 13–14, 16, 37, 55
for gunnery and bombing: 17
inactive duty training pay issue: 80–81
of individuals, programs for: 259–260
Johnson Board recommendations for: 140
and the Long-Range Plan: 139
and medical field exercises: 331
of mobilization augmentees: 273–276, 278–279, 281–284
National Security Training Corps: 123, 124
of navigators: 150–151
and night flying: 16
and the reserve facilities problem: 165–167
in the Reserve Officers Training Corps: 15
of specialists: 271
in summer camps: 37
in the Tactical Air Command: 47
universal training program: 58–59
of the Volunteer Air Reserve: 73–74, 77–78, 260
and the Woodrum Committee hearings: 33
after World War I: 8, 10–11
after World War II: 32–33, 53
before World War II: 18–21
Transfer Order 1: 84
Transfer Order 10: 84
Troop carrier program: 168
Truman, Harry S.: 13, 41, 57, 125
and the Korean War: vii, 87, 89, 90, 91, 94, 95, 360
national defense policy: 24, 25, 58
national reserve policy: 130, 131
and the Reserve Element Training program: 271–272
the reserve revitalization initiative: 64–68
and universal military training: 122, 123
Tuchman, Barbara W.: ix
Turkey: 187
Tweetie Bird (A–37): 313

Twentieth Century Minutemen: 127–128
Twining, Gen. Nathan F.: 91, 121, 122, 137, 139, 140, 142, 166, 260
Twining memo: 141–142, 170
Typhoid fever, New England mission: 149

Union of Soviet Socialist Republics: 88
the Bear bomber interception: 359
in the Berlin crisis: v, viii, 172, 177–184, 231, 361
in the Cuban missile crisis: viii, 172, 184–192, 267, 361
United Nations: v, 88, 90
United States Air Force Basic Doctrine: 142–143
United States Army
468th Army Air Forces Unit (Reserve training): 39
Aeronautical Division: 2
Army Air Forces Reserve Plan: 39
Army Reorganization Act of 1920: 8
and the militarization test: 302
post–World War II reserve policy: 28
REDOUBT (Exercise): 332
Reserve Enlistment Program: 206
reserve policy: 23, 28–29, 32–37, 231–233, 236
Signal Corps, Aviation Section: 2, 4
United States Congress. *See* Congress, U.S.
Units, military (numbered). *See* Divisions; Groups; Squadrons; Teams, combat; Wings
Unit type code tailoring: 370
Universal military training: 29, 121–126
URGENT FURY (Operation): 359
Usher, Maj. Gen. William R.: 281, 339
USS *Pueblo*: 210, 214–216, 220

Vance, Cyrus R.: 201, 232, 237, 238
Vandenberg, Lt. Gen. Hoyt S.: 29, 31, 70, 71, 90, 91, 103, 114
Van Zandt, James E.: 132
Vaughan, Maj. Gen. Harry H.: 64, 65, 67, 69
Verhulst, Maj. Gen. Alfred: 247, 295, 319
Viccellio, Lt. Gen. Henry: 239–240, 241
Vietnam and Southeast Asia, war in: v, viii, 357–358
305th Aerospace Rescue and Recovery Squadron: 215, 216–217, 218, 219, 223

Index

1968 mobilizations: 220–221
  associate airlift program during: 210
  congressional support for: 204–205
  counseling as a result of: 358
  enlistments during: 205–207
  Gulf of Tonkin incident: 200
  intelligence operations in: 358
  mobilization for: 198–210
  National Security Action Memorandum 288: 199–200
  Pleiku, attack on: 200
  Prisoner of War/Missing in Action Program: 211
  refugee evacuation: 212–213
  Tet offensive: 220
Villa, Pancho: 7
Vinson, Carl: 71, 123
VOLANT OAK (Operation): 362
Volant Rodeo competition: 359
Volunteer Air Reserve: 73–74, 76–78, 85, 260
  in the Korean War: 92–93, 95, 110–111, 115

Wade, Lt. Gen. Horace M.: 238, 247, 248, 254
Wade, Brig. Gen. James L.: 296, 324
Wahleithner, Col. James C.: 319, 333
Walsh, Maj. Gen. Ellard A.: 33, 124–125
Watts, John A.: 162
Weather surveillance: vi, 323, 326, 378
Webster, Maj. Gen. Robert E.: 50
Weinberger, Caspar: 348
Westmoreland, Gen. William C.: 201, 202, 220
Westover, Lt. Gen. Charles B.: 235
Westover, Brig. Gen. Oscar: 15–16
What's Next; A Guide to Family Readiness: 373
Wheeler, Gen. Earle G.: 203, 220
Wheless, Lt. Gen. Hewitt T.: 230, 251
White, Gen. Thomas D.: 91, 117, 143, 166, 168, 172–173, 175–176
Whitehead, Lt. Gen. Ennis C.: 76–77, 78, 79, 85–86, 92–93, 160, 274
Whitehead, MSgt. Faye: 384
Whitney, Brig. Gen. Lafeton: 159
Whitney board report: 62–63
Whitney, Cornelius V.: 59, 62, 63
Wilson, Charles E.: 132, 161, 162
Wilson, Lt. Col. Greg: 368
Wilson, Capt. Joseph A.: 16
Wilson, Maj. Gen. Winston P.: 214

Wilson, Woodrow: 3, 4, 7, 8
Wings (numbered, U.S.)
  3d Bombardment Wing (Light): 99, 101, 103
  94th Tactical Airlift Wing: 364
  301st Tactical Fighter Wing: 359
  302d Tactical Airlift Wing: 315, 379
  310st Tactical Fighter Wing: 329
  311th Troop Carrier Wing: 105
  314th Troop Carrier Wing: 97, 240
  315th Military Airlift Wing (Associate): 359, 360
  319th Fighter Bomber Wing: 150
  336th Tactical Airlift Wing: 323
  349th Military Airlift Wing: 215
  375th Troop Carrier Wing: 94–95, 97, 108
  403d Rescue and Recovery Wing: 333
  403d Tactical Airlift Wing: 358, 362
  403d Troop Carrier Wing: 97, 106–107
  433d Tactical Airlift Wing: 365
  433d Troop Carrier Wing: 94–95, 97
  434d Troop Carrier Wing: 96, 97, 108, 188
  435th Troop Carrier Wing: 97, 108, 180, 181
  437th Military Airlift Wing: 360
  437th Troop Carrier Wing: 95, 104–106, 108, 109
  437th Troop Carrier Wing (Medium): 92, 93
  439th Military Airlift Wing:
  440th Airlift Wing: 381
  440th Tactical Airlift Wing: 365
  440th Troop Carrier Wing: 188
  442d Troop Carrier Wing: 97, 107, 181, 182, 194
  443d Troop Carrier Wing: 97, 107
  445th Military Airlift Wing (Associate): 379
  446th Airlift Wing: 379, 381
  446th Military Airlift Wing (Associate): 362
  452d Air Mobility Wing: 384
  452d Air Refueling Wing: 323
  452d Bombardment Wing (Light): 92, 93, 95, 98–103, 108, 109, 116–117
  452d Tactical Airlift Wing: 323
  482d Fighter Wing: 380
  512th Troop Carrier Wing: 188, 191
  514th Troop Carrier Wing: 97, 108, 150
  516th Troop Carrier Wing: 97, 108

The Air Force Reserve

940th Air Refueling Wing: 364
1650th Tactical Airlift Wing (Provisional): 368
Women reservists: 83, 383–384
Wood, Capt. John F.: 217
Wood, Maj. Gen. Leonard: 2
Woodrum Committee hearings: 33
World War I: 2–7, 7
World War II preparations: 17–21

Wright, Orville: 2

Yakovlev fighters: 99
Yom Kippur War. *See* Arab-Israeli War
Young, Philip: 162
Yugoslavia relief: 379–380

Zuckert, Eugene M.: 139, 229, 231, 235, 268, 269, 274